Signposts and Settlers

The history of place names in the middle Atlantic states

Robert I. Alotta

Bonus Books, Inc., Chicago

© **Robert I. Alotta, 1992**
All rights reserved

Except for appropriate use in critical reviews or works of
scholarship, the reproduction or use of this work in any form or
by any electronic, mechanical or other means now known or
hereafter invented, including photocopying and recording, and in
any information storage and retrieval system is forbidden without
the written permission of the publisher.

96 95 94 93 92   5 4 3 2 1

Library of Congress Catalog Card Number 91-77011

International Standard Book Number: 0-929387-44-9

Bonus Books, Inc.
160 East Illinois Street
Chicago, Illinois 60611

Printed in the United States of America

To the dreams that became memories.

Contents

Preface

I was sitting in the doctor's office waiting for The Word. I was not alone. I had undergone a series of tests and the results were in. The minutes ticked by, as my apprehension grew. *Did I notice the nurse avoiding my eye, or was that just imagination?*

After what seemed an eternity, the door to the inner sanctum opened, and my heart dropped. It was the doctor. *It's got to be the worst possible scenario,* I thought.

"Bob," he began, "I was thinking about you last night." *God, my mind whirled, it's worse than I thought.* "I came across this little place in New York State. It's got a real strange name, and you should include it in one of your books." *He's letting me down easy. Oh, my God. I'm too young to die.*

His voice droned on and on about this particular town—until I interrupted him: What about the tests?

"Oh, they all came back negative. Nothing to worry about. Nothing at all. Now, about this town. . . ."

He was wrong. There was something wrong. The healer had been infected with the place-name virus. No matter where he goes, no matter what he sees, he will always wonder about the derivation of a name. And he is not alone. I've been carrying this virus since the late fifties and I haven't been able to shake it. In fact, I've even infected other people!

Let me tell you about this disease. It attacks the imagination and makes you think. It tickles your fancy, causing uncontrollable spasms of laughter and/or tears. Without warning, you shout out: "Wow!" "Why?" "Damn!" "How could they?" and "Gee!"

The only known therapy for this chronic disease, as far as my case is concerned, is to write books about street- or place-names. This particular book marks the fourth I've produced and my symptoms have not improved. In fact, they have intensified. I still wax eloquent as I drive through the countryside. "Do you know why blankety-blank is named blankety-blank?" My family's toleration has improved over the years. No one throws things at me in the car. No one yells at me to shut up. But then, my children have grown up and left home.

My daughter, Amy, found out the hard way that this disease is contagious. Amy has acquired it. She's written a book on the street names of Washington, D.C. I now tolerate her when she asks "Dad, do you know why blankety-blank is called blankety-blank?"—and doesn't give me a chance to answer. I don't throw things at her; perhaps because she won't let me sit in the back seat of her car.

While you read this book, I'm trying another cure: I'm researching and writing another book in the *Signposts and Settlers* series, this time about the West Coast. Maybe by the early twenty-first century, I'll have the disease under control. By the way, by buying this book, you too are infected. Welcome to the club!

Signposts and Settlers: The History of Place Names in the Middle Atlantic States was not created in a vacuum. There were many people to whom I turned for help. Some still speak to me.

- The American Automobile Association office in Richmond, Virginia, was extremely helpful in providing me with maps. Ah! The benefits of being a member. Years ago, I relied on Rand McNally for my maps. Unfortunately, they have ceased to publish the definitive state maps that were so helpful.
- Aloha South, from the National Archives, was a great traffic cop when I needed to go through postal records.
- Dr. Carol Kefalas assisted me in cutting my research time in half by loaning me her lap-top computer. Sadly for my budget, I got hooked on it and bought one of my own. Now I can read my notes!
- Joe Kornik and Sharon Lovering, staff writers for James Madison University's *The Breeze*. They heard of my research and wrote a fantastic full-page article on my progress and helped spur on other newspapers.
- Sharon M. Browne, of the Harrisonburg *Daily News-Record*, followed up on the student journalists' story and almost got me killed crossing an interstate to get "the right picture."
- Julie Henry, a former student and good friend, comes from Riva, Maryland, and saved my fat when I could not locate several books on Maryland's history. Julie stole time from her lunch hours in Annapolis, trekked over to the Archives and dug up the material so that I could just pop in and do my work. It was nothing, she said. How wrong she was!
- Aaron Cohodes, publisher of Bonus Books, believed in the *Signposts and Settlers* series and gave me the moral support I needed.
- Larry Razbadouski, editor and jack-of-all-trades at Bonus, has listened to my sad stories, jokes, and delaying tactics with stoic perseverance. As an editor, he gets what he wants—even if he didn't know that's what he wanted.
- Sharon Turner Mulvihill, my editor, has now edited two of my books. There will be more. I would trust her with my publishing life. As it is, I've passed on to her my only begotten daughter. I would do the same thing with my son Peter but, as they say, "like father like son."

- While writing *Signposts and Settlers,* I used four different word-processing programs. The first laptop used WordPerfect 5.0, and my laptop uses Write for Windows and Works. All have their benefits, but I finished up with MultiMate 4.0, the same program with which I've written four other books. I really don't know if this is the best program, but I've grown quite comfortable using it. My comfort level would rise considerably if they'd just arrange to include mouse capabilities in future releases. By the way, the programs, though not completely compatible, do download to Smart ASCII and can be read in that manner, even if hard returns must be manually removed. (Rereading this paragraph, I realize how unintelligible we become when we become comfortable with computers.)

While on the subject of computers and word-processing, I did not see "hard copy" of this book until Bonus Books made up galley sheets. In fact, Larry Razbadouski received six 5¼-inch, high-density floppy disks of manuscript. It didn't cost that much to send out by UPS. Just imagine the cost for six to seven pounds of paper manuscript . . . and the number of trees that would have died for that final draft!

All my research and writing was done on the computer. I constantly tell my students that they should think on the machine and not waste precious time copying hand-written text. At my age, this new way of using technology was a strange procedure. Raised in the newspaper business, I was used to editing on paper—this was a complete departure. Poor Sharon, a much younger person than I, needed the printed version on which to work. I can joke about it, but I understand. More than once, I was ready to press the print key to see what I was doing.

Perhaps I should have from time to time. At the eleventh hour, I could not find my bibliography. Since I kept so many backup copies, sometimes I lost sight of where one item was. Dumb me! I forgot I had labeled the disk "Bib-1" so I would not forget.

There are no footnotes in the book, primarily because I think that footnotes interfere with a reader's progress. With so many reasons to stop reading, why add others? Copies of my notes are available at the state archives in each state . . . for those who would like to see them. I hope this does not inconvenience anyone.

A number of individuals from businesses and historical attractions throughout the six-state area were helpful, including Jerry Post, Free Library of Philadelphia; M. M. Pernot, administrator, Burlington County Historical Society, Burlington, N.J.; Robert K. Sweet, president, Old Bedford Village, Bedford, Pennsylvania; Margaret Perry, Thomas Shepherd Inn, Shepherdstown, West Virginia; Hugh B. Miller, vice president/sales manager, The Daniel Weaver Company, Lebanon, Pennsylvania; Richard L. Tritt, photo curator, Cumberland County Historical Society, Carlisle, Pennsylvania; Doug Tarr, Edison National Historic Site, West Orange, New Jersey; Kathleen Bierly, Rebersburg, Pennsylvania; Christopher

Lee, director of the Boal Mansion Museum, Boalsburg, Pennsylvania; Gigi McNamara, Greater Pittsburgh Convention & Visitors Bureau, Pittsburgh, Pennsylvania; Rodney Fisher, The General Lewis Inn, Lewisburg, West Virginia; Hester Waterfield, Department of Convention & Visitor Development, Virginia Beach, Virginia; Susan Cummings, Maryland State Archives, Annapolis, Maryland—who saved me countless hours by getting me copies of some of the reference material I needed; and the countless others who have helped me along.

Finally, I have to thank my wife, Alice Danley Alotta. She has stood beside me for more than thirty years—even when some of my schemes were off-the-wall. She was there while I spent ten years trying to restore Old Fort Mifflin, Philadelphia. She got me up in the mornings to play "Colonel Bob, the Revolutionary War Soldier" on the "Captain Noah and His Magical Ark" television show. She didn't balk when I decided to leave my job at The Philadelphia Housing Authority and commence a teaching career.

As the years go by, we have grown closer to each other. She's encouraged me, told me off, nursed me through real and imagined ills, warded off slings and arrows that came my way, defended me, ignored my shortcomings, and kicked my butt on more than one occasion. I only wish the vows we took back in 1960 did not all come true. I would have liked to rewrite them to delete two phrases: "in sickness," and "or worse." She deserved better, but she picked me.

Introduction

Once upon a time, long before recorded history, the First Americans traveled eastward across this continent. It is said they came from the northwest. Perhaps they moved from the Bering Strait area that separates Alaska from Siberia—though neither state existed then, and neither did the body of water.

As the people moved from freezing weather to cold to chilling weather to warm and then to hot, groups dropped off and decided that this particular climate, this particular site was ideal for them.

When the bands of men, women, and children reached the Father of All Rivers, their number was greatly diminished. Some did not have the energy to cross. Those who did, as the legend tells us, traveled northward, northeast, southeast, and south until they found a home. And they named their habitations in what modern Americans might consider a strange manner.

Where do you live? a First American might be asked.

"I live at the place where the weeping willow sits." Or ". . . at the echoing rocks."

Their place-names, though strange sounding—and long—to us today, made sense at the time. Their place-names were purely descriptive of the areas in which they lived. To be sure, there were many weeping willow trees and many canyons where the least little sound ricocheted off the rocky walls. But the names were only for their locale. It did not matter if there were forests of willows, there was one known to this particular group.

The First Americans did not name their village or their camps for their leaders, their families, or themselves. They might use a tribal name to signify that this particular area belonged to them and no other group, but they avoided the use of personal names. They were not interested in personal aggrandizement. They were more concerned with getting from one place to another. The land, they also believed, belonged to everyone—not to one person alone—and so the given name was merely descriptive or directional . . . nothing more.

After the period of European exploration, the names those First Americans placed on the land were in jeopardy, as were their very lives, their culture, and their way of life. As the Europeans—the Spanish, the Dutch, the Swedes, and the English—arrived on the Atlantic coast, they brought a lust for the natural resources the First Americans took for granted. They also brought with them a craving for freedom from the constraints of despotic rulers and rigid thinking. This hunger for freedom abridged the freedom of the First Americans, who were systematically befriended, alienated, exploited, abused, and ousted from their homes.

The names the First Americans placed on their villages were bastardized by the European pioneers. Since the tongues of the many tribes were not written down, the Europeans tried to translate the sounds of these words into their own languages. The names of these places might sound like that which the First Americans called them, but the meanings were often lost in the translations.

When they tired of First-American names, many of the European settlers tried using the tribal method of naming, e.g., for a key landmark, but that practice paled in the face of ego.

New towns took on the names of the first European settler, or someone from whom they could curry favor. And they named their new towns for themselves and their sponsors, and their children and their sponsor's children.

As the wilderness receded into provinces, then into colonies, homesick settlers wistfully thought they saw elements of similarity between this brand-new home carved from the forest and ancient cities of their homeland. These names too were adopted.

Following the War for Independence, Americans (really, they were—and are—United Staters) sought to commemorate the decisive battles of that war, and its major leaders and heroes. With independence, the nation needed strong lines of communication among the various states. The population shifted from the "old" New World to previously untouched areas. The traders who accompanied the hunters and trappers set up their posts at crossroads, often nothing more than the junction of two footpaths through the wilderness, near streams, or wherever numbers of people (excluding, of course, the First Americans) might pass.

The pioneering men and women would leave messages for those who followed or for each other at these mercantile establishments. It was not too long before the fledgling federal government allowed these shopkeepers to turn a corner of their place of business into a post office. Of course, these storekeepers—not the federal postal authorities—realized their importance, and named that location after themselves. Local historians, seemingly afraid to offend, would often cite the family, rather than the individual, as the name-source.

When settlers tired of depleting the forest of flora and fauna, and discovered natural resources they had not previously exploited, such as fossil fuels, they raised coal, oil, and their by-products to godlike status. The coal mine and oil-field owners praised the black gods of anthracite and bituminous, the viscous deity of petroleum in the place-names. And, when those names became pedestrian, they, their financial backers, and boards of directors shared the spotlight by bestowing their names on company towns.

With all these new towns growing hither and yon—and in dire need of names, one would expect that politicians would follow close behind. And they did. Elected leaders from the state houses and Capitol Hill saw the opportunity of gaining the public attention due them or, perish the thought, eternal recognition for their vaunted deeds.

The United States matured as a nation. The dusty paths and rutted roadways gave rise to a national highway system and today's interstates. But through our growing-up process, our naming process remained the same. We still named places after battles of the Mexican, Spanish-American, and Civil wars, World Wars I and II. We continued to memorialize those who fell in those encounters. And we continued to name places after ourselves, even if some of the namers attempted to hide it. Reston, Virginia, for example, was named for Robert E. Simon, the town's architect. By taking his initials and adding -ton to the end, he gave himself a never-ending memory. Unfortunately for Reston's idea of immortality, not too many people know that fact. That is the reason behind this book: to shed light on who we are and how we got there. The place-names of America, every other nation in this world, and, if there are other worlds out there in the ether, elsewhere reflect the times when they were named. The names reflect the culture and the mentality of the people. The names reflect the image, the credibility that the namers wanted to convey to future generations.

Just as parents ponder over the name of a newborn, so too did the place-namers. And, just as parents, they wanted their hamlet, their village, their town to have just the right name to attract greater populations and more business operations. Were these namers successful? Not always. Do the names continue to represent the thoughts behind them at the time of their baptism? Not always. Do the names continue to intrigue and vex the reader? Almost always.

The study of the history behind place names is exciting, but it also can be very frustrating. It can be some of the most boring research ever conducted, yet there are days when it is nothing but great fun.

There is the excitement when the researcher locates a name that has escaped the eye of others, such as Vadis, West Virginia. Stuffy professonial types, showing their ignorance, supply references to the Latin word, etc. But, Senator Henry Gassaway Davis ran out of names, such as Henry, Gassaway, Davis, and others to use on places in his state. He reverted to playing with the letters and, in an almost pig-Latin approach, created an anagram of his name! There were many moments like that.

There were also the days and weeks of research at the National Archives looking at hand-written records. The records start in 1832 and stop in 1971, when Congress voted to reduce paperwork and ordered the Archives to destroy the rest of the material. We wonder if the destruction of the records was done to save some red-faced representatives who might have been gravely embarrassed by an investigation into the naming process.

The records themselves were fascinating to view, but at times almost as impossible to read as my own handwriting. Anyone who works with a computer knows that the longer you write—or, heaven help us, "word process"—on a machine, the worse your handwriting becomes. College students often come to me after I've returned their paper with comments and ask, "What did you write?" But my handwriting is not nearly as bad as some I've encountered at the Archives.

Anyone who has conducted research gets to know the handwriting of a source. After a few hours, you begin to feel the rhythm of the text. Letters that were impossible to read suddenly make sense in a new context. With the postal records, this was not always the case. Different hands, different people maintained these records and, we are certain, few of them were trained in the Palmer Method.

There were also days and nights going over the traditional works on place-naming, written by such experts as George Stewart and Henry Gannett, only to find they sometimes took the easy way out and guessed at the derivation. Postal records, in many cases, proved them wrong. There was no joy in these discoveries, because this author respected those individuals and relied on their research. They were not always wrong, but they presented an erroneous interpretation too often to be accepted in any situation without a double check. This is not to say that this book is flawless.

In 1984, when I sat before my doctoral committee and defended my dissertation, I was asked if my work was complete. It was not, and it took me another five years of added research to shape that material into a book. Before I sat down to write this introduction, I received a letter from England—including photocopies of pages from a book—that added heretofore unknown to me information on two military executions, the subject of my dissertation! A long time ago, I learned that there is no "last word."

Throughout the research process, we relished the quaint folklore and tradition that adheres to place-naming. Harrisonburg, Virginia, is just one example.

As the story goes, Thomas Harrison and George Keezel ran a horse race to see whose name would be on the Rockingham County Court House. As the story goes, Harrison saw that Keezel rested for the night and made it to Richmond without changing horses. Even in a race, Harrison did not abuse his horse. Currently, forces are afoot to lose Harrison's name and return the town to its origin: Rocktown. The sponsor of this move thinks that Rocktown has more sex appeal; he also operates the Rocktown Tavern. Civic pride, we find, has not died.

We also loved the legends that last to this day about hometowns. A good example is Perth Amboy, New Jersey. There are people who still today believe the story that their town was named from a reply to an Indian exclamation at seeing the town's patron: "Perth am girl!" The retort was "No! Perth am boy!" Though the story has no basis in reality, it sounds so much better than the true derivation.

The place-naming of American places, we have found, is organic. It grows from year to year, century to century. Never is the development of a place-name static or dull. People have fought over their town's name. In one case, a tavern-keeper announced he would refuse to serve anyone who voted to change the town's name. After all, the old name was his! In other cases, we find one man putting out a big spread for the population, then announcing his name as a candidate for the town's name!

During the course of our study, we came across an old friend—unintentionally, of course. That discovery proved to this author that my research will probably continue until the day I die.

Back in the mid-seventies, while researching and writing *Street Names of Philadelphia*, I uncovered the delightful story behind Wingohocking Street. James Logan, William Penn's secretary, was asked to swap names, an Indian tradition, by Chief Wingohocking. Logan, a shrewd operator, talked the Indian into giving his name to a local creek. The stream was ultimately replaced by a roadway which bears Wingohocking's name. Fifteen years later, I learned that the chief took on the Quaker's name. That is why Logan, West Virginia, is not called Wingohocking!

This introduction could continue for countless pages, but you picked up this book to read details about the name of your favorite place. Don't let me stop you.

New Jersey

New Jersey's historical and cultural life has always been closely tied to the surrounding areas.

North Jersey historically has close ties to New York. New Jersey residents commute regularly from local bedroom communities to the business and financial mecca of New York City, and New Yorkers enjoy playtime on the Atlantic coast. South Jersey has, in a similar way, acted as a suburb of Philadelphia, and the Jersey shore has been Philadelphia's summer playground.

These relationships go back to the state's founding. New Jersey's earliest colonial history links it to New Netherlands (New York) of which it was part. The Dutch surrendered to the English in 1664, and just one year later the English established New Jersey as a colony under Governor Philip Carteret.

By the late seventeenth century, New Jersey was divided between Carteret and Pennsylvania's William Penn. Later, the province was administered by New York's royal governor. Not until 1738 was New Jersey completely separated from New York, and given its own royal governor, Lewis Morris.

New Jersey, because it lay between Philadelphia and New York, saw a great deal of action during the American Revolution. The names of battles such as Princeton, Monmouth Court House, Red Bank, and others recall the sacrifice made by New Jersey in the fight for freedom.

The place names of New Jersey reflect its past. The names of the original movers-and-shakers stand out, from Carteret and Penn to Morris and Mercer. Place-names also exhibit evidence of elements of a strong feminist movement in the state, with the founding of such places as Elizabeth, Haddonfield, and Gould. The Atlantic Ocean affected the naming of places on the eastern coast of the state, including the world-famous Atlantic City, as did tourist promotion. And New Jersey place-names provide a strong reminder that English-speaking people were not the first ones to place names on the land.

ABSECON

As a settlement, Absecon, Atlantic County, dates back to before the end of the eighteenth century. The Dr. Pitney House—he was called the "Father of Atlantic City" because it was his vision for that city to become a bathing spot—was built prior to 1800.

The name is a variant of the Indian *agsegami,* Algonquian for "small water."

ALLAMUCHY

The name for Allamuchy, Warren County, is possibly a corruption of the Algonquian *Allamachtey,* "place within the hills" or "inward," a reference to a pond isolated among hills.

In his *Indian Place-Names in Alabama,* William Read reported a tributary of the Sucanochee Creek called Alamuchee. From the Choctaw, the name translates loosely as "a little hiding place." How the name moved from Alabama to New Jersey, if that suggestion is valid, is a mystery.

ALLENDALE. William Allen, of Philadelphia, served as Pennsylvania's chief justice from 1750–1774. His name and memory appear in Allendale and Allentown, New Jersey, and Allentown, Pennsylvania. (Print and Picture Department, Free Library of Philadelphia)

ALLENDALE

The town of Allendale, Bergen County, was named for Colonel William C. Allen, an Erie Railroad surveyor.

ALLENTOWN

This Monmouth County village was named for Pennsylvania Chief Justice William Allen. (See Allentown, Pennsylvania.)

ALLOWAY

This Salem County community takes its name from the name of an Indian chief who once lived here.

ALPHA

Though alpha is the first letter in the Greek alphabet, Alpha, Warren County, did not derive its name from that source. Its name comes from the Alpha Portland Cement Works located here.

A. B. Bonneville discovered a large supply of excellent-grade limestone and began a cement company. Fire later destroyed the Bonneville plant, and it was taken over by Thomas Whitaker. Bonneville was not easily discouraged; he started another plant, the Vulcanite Cement Company, on the east side of town.

ANDOVER

The town site in Sussex County was part of the 11,000-acre Penn brothers' tract. The town takes its name from the nearby Andover Furnace and Forge that dates back to the eighteenth century.

ASBURY (— Park)

The notion of Asbury Park in Monmouth County, probably the best-known resort in northern New Jersey, dates back to 1870 when James A. Bradley, a New York brush manufacturer, visited a nearby Ocean Grove camp meeting. Bradley saw the potential for a large summer resort and purchased 500 acres of wilderness. He developed his site primarily as a summer place for temperance advocates. Bradley banned liquor and gambling, vices he felt corrupted the nearby seaside resort of Long Branch.

Bradley had no opinion of rock 'n' roll, but in the late sixties and early seventies, Bruce Springsteen and his E Street Band helped revive the ailing Asbury Park by drawing attention to it with their album, "Greetings from Asbury Park."

Asbury and Asbury Park derive their names from Francis Asbury, the first American Methodist bishop.

ASHLAND

This Camden County community was named for the estate of Henry Clay. The name of Clay's abode is a fairly popular one.

ATCO

There is some confusion over the name of this Camden County community.

On one hand, some try to pin the name on an Indian heritage. These people believe the name refers to the Atco Swamp, with the word Atco deriving from the Lenape term for "many deer." Others, still using the Indian connection, suggest the word translates to "pure water."

Another group believes that the name has a more commercial, and more recent, origin. They theorize that there was a transportation company located in the community, and the contraction of that company's name—either Atsion Transport Company or Atlantic Transport (or Transportation) Company—produces the name Atco. As a matter of record, as late as 1959 "rusty streaks" of a primitive railway that went ten miles east to Atsion were still visible. The rail's right-of-way, it is said, is currently used as a road.

Atco was laid out in 1866 by George W. Hancock.

ATLANTIC CITY (Atlantic Highlands)

Atlantic City, Atlantic County, began as a small fishing village at the north end of Absecon Island. It would remain a sleepy fishing village until someone noticed that the coastal configuration protected the island from heavy storms, and the nearby Gulf Stream tempered the climate. The area was ideal for a vacation spot.

The Camden & Atlantic Railroad pounced on the idea and, while railroad track was still being laid, promoted Atlantic City as a tourist mecca. The first train arrived in 1854, and Atlantic City was incorporated.

The most famous attraction at Atlantic City is the Boardwalk. Its fame began in 1870 when the first eight-foot wide lane of planks was laid directly on the sand. The present-day Boardwalk is five miles long—ten, including adjacent town footage—and sixty feet wide. Though surfaced with a herringbone pattern of boards, the walk itself is constructed of steel and concrete.

Many people first become aware of Atlantic City through the popular board game Monopoly, developed by Philadelphian Charles Darrow and marketed by Parker Brothers in 1935. An interesting footnote is that Marvin Gardens is the only non-Atlantic City address in the game. In fact, the property name was borrowed from nearby Margate where it is spelled correctly as Marven Gardens. Others know of Atlantic City as the home of the Miss America Pageant. Today the city is the East Coast mecca for gambling.

The name derivation is quite obvious: it was considered "the city on the Atlantic Ocean." The ocean's name comes from the Greek, and means "the sea beyond Mount Atlas."

Atlantic Highlands was founded by Richard Hartshorne, a London Quaker, in 1671 as Portland Point. By 1881, the town was called Bay View and served as a Methodist camp meeting site.

AUBURN

Auburn was the name of a Yorkshire, England village. It is possible this Salem County town took its name from the British Isles, or may have borrowed it from Goldsmith's 1770 "Deserted Village," a very popular poem at the time of the city's founding. It was the source for a New York state community which, in 1805, quoted the poem at the town meeting in which it adopted the name.

AUDUBON

This community, located in Camden County, was named for the famous naturalist and ornithologist, John James Audubon, born Jean Rabine (1785–1851). Audubon studied birds in this section of

4

New Jersey in 1829. He devoted the bulk of his life to painting illustrations of American wildlife. His 1827–38 *The Birds of America* continues to stand as a masterpiece.

AUGUSTA

The name of Augusta, Sussex County, has appeared in a number of states in honor of the Princess of Wales, daughter-in-law of George II. The originals were in Georgia and Virginia, and it is possible this location borrowed the name from the South.

AVALON

This resort community was formerly known as Seven Mile Beach, Leaming, and Piermont. It was founded in 1887 by a Philadelphia land development company, the Seven Mile Beach Company.

The name comes from the island of Welsh mythology, immortalized in Tennyson's 1893 *Idylls of the King*.

AVON BY THE SEA

Avon by the Sea, Monmouth County, is an old community whose name is a Shakespearean reference.

AVONDALE

Essex County's Avondale is another local name with Shakespearean overtones.

AWOSTING

According to the Brinton-Anthony *Lenape-English Dictionary*, the name is derived from *awossagame*, translated as "heaven," "the place beyond or out of sight." At the same time, the book defines *awossin* as "to warm one's self."

Both words are equally likely place-name sources, but whichever the case, this Passaic County community has a name with an Indian origin.

BAPTISTOWN

Early settlers located in this Hunterdon County area as early as 1714. The first Baptist church in this town was organized about 1720, though available records date it as late as 1742. At the time of naming, there were two Baptist churches in town.

BARGAINTOWN

A developer apparently named this Atlantic County location to entice buyers—at bargain prices.

BARNEGAT (— Beach, — Light, — Pines)

Barnegat Light, Ocean County, was settled by Scandinavian fishermen. The name first appeared on a 1656 map as Barndegat, for *barende gat*, "breaker's inlet," an indication that there was a break in the barrier islands. This name was given by Henry Hudson.

The village of Barnegat Light takes its name from the famous lighthouse nearby. The lighthouse, sometimes called "Old Barney," was built in 1858 under the supervision of George Gordon Meade. Meade later commanded Union forces at Gettysburg.

Meade's efforts replaced the original structure, built in 1834, that collapsed in 1856. Barnegat Light was known as Barnegat City until 1948.

During the American Revolution, Barnegat Light figured in the "Long Beach Massacre." In 1782, Revolutionary Captain Andrew Steele and a band of men, tired from carrying cargo ashore from a grounded British vessel, fell asleep on the beach. Loyalist sympathizer John Bacon and a group of his men stole up on the sleeping men and murdered all twenty-one of them.

BASKING RIDGE

The earliest record of this Somerset County name appeared in 1733 on the Basking Ridge Presbyterian Church.

A local legend suggests that in the eighteenth century, settlers saw wild animals come up from the marshes to "bask" in the sun on the ridge. Others feel the community name came from a family name.

BATESVILLE

Batesville has been described as the "natural overflow of the borough of Haddonfield." In other words, a suburb.

It was named for William Bates, who owned considerable property in the area, laid out the town lots and built the first houses at the junction of the Milford and Berlin roads.

BATSTO

The land for Batsto was purchased in 1758 by John Munrow from the Council of West Jersey Proprietors. Eight years later, Joseph Wharton purchased the big Batsto plantation in Burlington County. Charles Read built the Batsto iron works the same year.

During the American Revolution, the furnace, supervised by Colonel John Cox, produced cannon and cannon balls for Washington's army.

Atsion and Batsto (also known as Batstow, Batso, Batstowe, Battstoe, Barthstow, Five Forks, Batsto Furnace, Batstoo, Badston, Badstove, Badstowe, and Batstoo) served as arsenals for the Continental Army during the Revolution.

The name Batsto comes from the river, called Swimming River until 1752. The word is possibly Lenni-Lenape for "bathing place" or "bath house," though it might also originate from the Dutch *een badstoof,* "a hot bath" or *baatstoo,* "steam bath." It is possible that the Scandinavian name was corrupted by the Indians.

BAYONNE

Until 1861, Bayonne was a part of the city of Bergen. Many think it was named for the city in France. Others suggest that the use of "bay on" by real estate promoters might be the real source.

BEACH GLEN

In 1751, John Johnston bought a tract of land at the Falls from the Proprietaries of East Jersey. On his land, he built a forge, and the area around his place of business became known as Johnston's Iron Works or Horse Pound Forge.

Sometime between 1753 and 1765, Johnston sold the forge to Job Allen. On 30 December 1771, Allen sold it to Benjamin Beach and Henry Tuttle. Beach bought out his partner and installed his son, Benjamin, Jr., in his place. The area became known thereafter as Beach Glen, Morris County. Beach Glen is one of those rare communities in New Jersey bearing the name "beach" that has no relation to the "beach" at the shore.

BEACH HAVEN (— Crest, — Gardens, North —, — Park, — Terrace)

Beach Haven, Ocean County, dates back to at least the mid-nineteenth century. In 1851, Captain Thomas Bond, a leader in the lifesaving movement, built Bond's Hotel at Beach Haven. Bond so named his town because its beach was a "safety haven."

BEACHWOOD

Located in the pine forest below Toms River, Beachwood, Ocean County, was the late-nineteenth-century terminus for a mule-powered wooden railway. The railway ran between the charcoal-burning pits at Lakehurst to Toms River.

BEATTYSTOWN
Beattystown, Warren County, was originally called Beatty's Mills, for the local mill owner. General John Burgoyne's redcoats marched through here on the way to Virginia after their defeat at Saratoga.

BEDMINSTER
Bedminster, named for a town in England, dates back to the mid-eighteenth century. The First Dutch Reformed Church, located here, was built in 1759 by Jacob Vanderveer.

Near the site of the church, which is no longer standing, is the grave of General Henry Knox's daughter, who died here in 1779. Legend has it that Vanderveer had an insane daughter who the church refused burial, so he buried her on his own property— next to the church's graveyard. The remains of Knox's infant daughter were also refused, because the general was not Dutch Reformed, but a Congregationalist. Vanderveer allowed Knox to bury the girl next to his daughter. Later the church annexed Vanderveer's property.

BEEMERVILLE
As far as we know, the name of this Sussex County town has nothing to do with the nickname for a Bavarian Motor Works vehicle. It is more likely that the name commemorates an early family . . . probably not Yuppies.

BELCOVILLE
This Atlantic County town took its name from its local industry: the Bethlehem Company.

BELLEPLAIN
Prior to 1890 this Cape May County community was in Cumberland County. The first post office was established in that year by Postmaster Albert T. Peacock. The name was changed to Belle Plain in 1921, and comes from the French "beautiful and plain."

BELLEVILLE
Originally called the Second River Section of Newark, Belleville was the site of an early Dutch settlement. Evidence indicates that it had a large population by 1682.

This Essex County locale was the site of a Revolutionary War battle on 27 September 1778, and became a separate community in 1839. The name comes from the French for "beautiful city."

The first low-pressure steam engine made in America was manufactured here. John Stevens installed the engine in a boat and steamed down the Passaic to New York. This was in 1798, nine years before Fulton operated his *Clermont*, but eight years after John Fitch ran his steamboat on the Delaware River.

BELLMAWR

This Camden County site acquired its name from Ernest C. Bell, a local horse breeder. Mawr is Welsh for "hill," so the name would translate to Bell's Hill. (See Bryn Mawr, Pennsylvania.)

BELMAR

This Monmouth County community appears to have the same name as the one in Camden County, with a variant spelling to avoid confusion.

BELVIDERE

The county seat of Warren County, Belvidere was known before 1775 as Greenwich-on-the-Delaware. The present name was first used by Major Robert Hoops, who purchased land from the first settler, Robert Patterson.

Belvidere was incorporated in 1845, though as early as 1828 a manufacturing company used the name as its address. In 1830, the Belvidere Bank was chartered under that name. The name is from the Italian, meaning "beautiful to see."

In the mid-nineteenth century, the park before the Court House was used for "invitation affairs," public hangings. The last took place in 1892.

BERGENFIELD

Bergenfield took its name from its county, and the county, from the Dutch city of Bergen-op-zoom.

BERKLEY HEIGHTS

This land in Union County, between the Hudson and Delaware Rivers, was given to John, Lord Berkeley, in June 1664. Berkeley was one of the Duke of York's favorites. The other recipient of local land was Sir George Carteret.

BERLIN (East —, West —)

Berlin is the site of the oldest village in Camden County. Until 1872, it was known as Long-a-Coming. There are several versions of how the name Long-a-Coming came to be.

According to one legend, a group of sailors were traveling from the Atlantic coast to Philadelphia in the late seventeenth century. Tired and thirsty, they expected to find drinking water. Finally they came upon a stream, and exclaimed: "Here you are at last, though long-a-coming." Unfortunately for the credibility of those tale-tellers, the lands located here, owned by Peter Rich and Richard Moss, were already called Long-a-Coming in 1714.

Another source suggests that the passengers on the stage-coach from the Atlantic coast to the Delaware River ferry usually got hungry about here. The stage, due at 3 a.m., was always late, or so tradition tells us, hence the name Long-a-Coming. Whatever the reason, the village name was changed to Magnolia in February 1867.

The town became Berlin three months later with the opening of a post office. Joseph Shreve was the first postmaster. The source of the current name is Berlin, Germany.

BERNARDSVILLE

Bernardsville, Somerset County, was originally known as Vealtown Tavern. It received its present name from Roderick Mitchell, who settled here in 1840. For whom Mitchell named it is a mystery!

The original tavern, a log cabin, was replaced by a frame building, which later became the town's public library building.

BEVERLY

Beverly was known as Ferry Point as early as 1712. Originally, the area was called Marachonsicka, and it was divided into two divisions: Churchville, east of Cooper Street, where all the churches stood, and Dunk's Ferry, west of Cooper Street, named for Dunken Williams or "Dunk" Williamson, who operated the ferry as early as 1749. The ferry was abandoned in 1795.

The city was incorporated in 1857, and derives its current name from Beverly Township, which commemorated Beverly, England. A post office was established in 1849. The town's name is supposed to have been suggested by *Burlington Gazette* editor Edmund Morrs.

Another "authority" contends the name came from the fact that the area was overrun with beavers. How one gets "beverly" from "beaver" escapes this author.

BIVALVE

Bivalve derived its name from its chief industry. Oyster beds were recognized as an important natural resource as early as 1719.

A "bivalve," by the way, describes any mollusk with two shells hinged together.

BLACKWOOD

This Camden County community was first settled in 1701. Forty years later, 95 acres were sold to Colonel John Blackwood. Less than a week later, he puchased 100 more. For many years it was known as Blackwoodtown.

BLAIRSTOWN

In the 1830s, this town was known as Gravel Hill. John I. Blair, the Lackawanna Railroad tycoon, took an interest in the area and, in 1848, founded the Blair Academy. The town's name honors him.

BLOOMFIELD

Bloomfield, Essex County, was founded by members of the colony of New Englanders who founded Newark. At first, it was called Wassessing, Watsessing, or Wardsesson. That name may come from the Indian word to indicate a "crooked place"; probably a reference to the bend, or crook, in the Third River. Other suggestions for the source of the name include a derivation of *watschu*, "hill," and *assan*, "stone." In other words, a hill of stone. T. Sherwin Reider points out in his *The Viking and the Red Man* that the name is close in sound to an Algonquian word that means "the sun is brilliant." In this case, "the crooked place" translation makes more sense.

By 1796, the valley community was named Bloomfield in honor of General Joseph Bloomfield, a Revolutionary War officer and later governor of New Jersey (1801–12). In 1812, Bloomfield Township was organized.

BLOOOMINGDALE

The Bloomingdale Bloomery, or Furnace, was built in 1765 by John and Uzal Ogden. This Passaic County community takes its name from their enterprise—not from an upscale department store.

BLOOMSBURY

This Hunterdon County community was named for the Bloomsbury Forge, located here. The town is built on both sides of the Musconetcong River. When originally constructed, the town boasted houses of uniform design, which gave the town a prosperous appearance. Unfortunately, many of the houses were empty.

BLUE ANCHOR

Blue Anchor, in Camden County, takes its name from the old Blue Anchor Tavern, which was built here in 1737 by Abraham Bickley.

BOGOTA

Though it seems to have a South American flavor, Bogata, Bergen County, was named for the Bogert family, early settlers.

BOONTON

Boonton, Morris County, was known as Old Forge before 1759. The name was later changed to Boonetown, for Thomas Boone, an early colonial governor (1760–61). The name was spelled Booneton in 1772, Boonton in 1778, and Boun Town in 1794.

Old Boone Town, an iron-making community, was flooded in 1902 to provide a supply of water for Jersey City. It is now below the Parsippany Reservoir.

BORDENTOWN

Bordentown was immortalized in Francis Hopkinson's famous poem of the American Revolution, "The Battle of the Kegs."

The Burlington County town, also Hopkinson's residence, dumped gunpowder-filled barrels into the shipping lanes of the Delaware River in aid of the war effort. Only one barrel exploded, but the British command ordered sailors and soldiers to fire at any keg in the river, which caused a great deal of confusion.

The kegs were built in the cooperage of Hopkinson's father-in-law, Colonel Joseph Borden. Bordentown derives its name from him.

Colonel Borden, in addition to being a cooper, operated in 1734 a stage line and packet service. The town was first settled in 1682 by Thomas Farnsworth and called Farnsworth's Landing.

A post office was established under the name of Bordentown in 1801. The town was incorporated as a borough in 1825, reincorporated in 1849, and became a city in 1867.

BOUND BROOK (South —)

These Somerset County communities lie along the Raritan River, which was used as a "pathway" by settlers before 1664.

It is said that on 2 April 1777, Philip Van Horn, a Tory who later became neutral in the struggle, entertained Lord Cornwallis at breakfast in his home here. Later the same day, he entertained the Continental Army's General Benjamin Lincoln at dinner. The next day, the troops of the breakfast guest surprised the troops of the dinner guest with great losses to the Americans, who fled into the Watchung hills.

The name Bound Brook came from the nearby creek, which empties into the Raritan. At the time of the naming of the waterway, the creek was the northern limit of a land grant to Governor Carteret. The name signifies a "boundary."

BRADLEY BEACH

This Monmouth County community was the first resort in the United States to charge admission to its fenced-in "public" beaches.

Bradley Beach was founded by James A. Bradley, who also founded Asbury Park.

BRASS CASTLE

Brass Castle, Warren County, is not descriptive of a grandiose structure made of shiny metal. It has a more mundane origin; it was named for Jacob Brass, an early settler.

Brass operated a sawmill and a papermill in this location near the Morris Canal.

BRETON WOODS

A Breton is a person from Brittany, but Breton Woods, Ocean County, was named for the English seat of the earls of Stratford.

BRICKSBORO

Bricksboro, Cumberland County, was founded by John Brick and developed by Joshua Brick.

The original John Brick House, constructed of guess-what, is located here on the Maurice River.

BRIDGEBORO

The name of Bridgeboro is of simple origin. The town is located at the west end of a bridge built in 1838 by a T. Baker.

Originally called Ancocas Ferry or Lower Ferry in 1748 when the Burlington Pike was laid out, the city later became Toll Bridge. By 1828, it was called Draw Bridge, and a post office bearing that name first appeared in 1849. Before that, the community was called Bridgeborough. As with all good things, the name returned for those who waited.

BRIDGETON

The original name for this Cumberland County community was Cohansey, after Indian Chief Cohanzick. Quakers settled the town in 1686, though there is evidence other white settlers were here before them.

By 1716, they built a bridge over the Cohansey Creek and named the village Cohansey Bridge. The construction of a bridge in those days was quite an accomplishment. This particular bridge was a collection of logs nesting on pilings set into the river. Later, the name was shortened to Bridge Town.

In 1816, with the establishment of the Cumberland Bank, the name became Bridgeton. The City of Bridgeton was incorporated in 1864.

Inside the cupola of the Cumberland County Courthouse there once hung a bell that was cast in 1763 and sent to the community from Bridgewater, Massachusetts. This particular bell was the area's "Liberty Bell," rung to celebrate the signing of the Declaration of Independence.

BROADWAY

Once owned by Colonel William McCulough, who founded the town of Washington and also helped to develop Asbury, this Warren County town was named for its wide main street.

The most famous citizen of Broadway was Peggy Warne, sister of Continental Army General Garret Vliet, ancestor of former New York Governor John Vliet Lindsay. Warne left her ten children to attend sick Revolutionary War soldiers. She was not a physician, but an experienced midwife and nurse.

BROWNS MILLS

Browns Mills, Burlington County, commemorates Abraham Brown, who operated a gristmill near the town site and owned most of the real estate. The Brown's Mills post office dates to 1850, though the town was in existence before 1766. In 1798, the name was changed to Biddle's Mills to reflect the change in ownership of the mills. The Browns Mills name was restored in 1805.

Browns Mills was once a health resort for tuberculosis patients, back when doctors recommended the pine forest air for such an affliction.

BUDDTOWN

A 1719 survey of the Buddtown, Burlington County, area by Daniel Leeds indicated the town was "near a saw-mil on 'Stop the Jade,' owned by Thomas Budd." The name "Stop the Jade" came from a folktale telling of persons chasing a horse down the stream. "Jade" was an ancient word for horse. Budd's mill operated from 1718–75.

A post office, giving status to the town—called Budd Town—went into operation in 1868.

BUENA

The Midway Tavern, a stagecoach station, was located here. Legend has it that George Washington had his horse shoed in this Atlantic County village.

Buena is the feminine form of the Spanish "good."

BURLEIGH

Formerly Gravelly Run, this community received its more sophisticated name from a Pennsylvania Railroad official.

Burleigh is one of many New Jersey locations where townspeople contend that they have seen the "Leeds Devil." According to local tradition, in 1887 a child was born to a Mrs. Leeds who, in an angry moment, asked Satan to take the child. That devil was blamed for all sorts of crimes and capers. A Philadelphia newspaper even offered a $10,000 reward—never collected—for the devil's capture. (See Estellville.)

BURLINGTON

Burlington was known by that name as early as 1675. Captain William Toms (see Toms River) received a letter from Governor Lovelace recommending "a good work about Matinicunk house on Burlington Island which, strengthened with a considerable guard, would make an admirable frontier."

Prior to the English involvement giving the English name to the community, three Dutchmen were recognized as the area's owners. Peter Jegou operated a tavern here as early as 1668.

Thomas Holme, Penn's surveyor-general, called the town Bridlington—an old form of the name Burlington—in his 1682 map.

Two companies of Quakers, one from London, the other from Yorkshire, settled the town in 1677. As the first capital of West Jersey, Burlington was laid out in 1678 (a map by Dunkers and Shuyter in the same year calls it Borlingtowne) and incorporated in 1693. Reincorporated by letters of patent from George III in 1734, Burling Town established its post office in 1798.

The Indians called the area Techichohock, the "oldest planted land." The town has also been known as New Beverly, Bridlington, and Burlington, for towns in England where the settlers had prior ties. The name Bridlington is so old that it is recorded in the Doomsday Book (1086) as Brelington and in the charter of 1147 as Berlinton.

C

CALDWELL (North —, West —)

Caldwell, in Essex County, lies on land purchased in 1740. It was named for the Reverend James Caldwell, the "fighting parson" of the American Revolution.

One of Caldwell's famous sons was President Grover Cleveland, who was born here in 1837.

CALIFON

In this Hunterdon County community, rumor has it that a number of "volunteers" offered to paint the railroad's California station sign. After a mite too much imbibing they ran out of space after painting as far as C A L I F O N.

CAMDEN

Camden, Camden County, grew up around the ferryboat operation of William Cooper, and was originally known as Cooper's Ferry, then later Coopersville.

The first settlement was founded by Richard Arnold and Cooper, who emigrated to America in 1679. They arrived at Burlington and, on 12 June 1682, obtained 300 acres at the junction of the Delaware and the Aroches (now Cooper) River.

William Cooper built a house below the river and called it Pyne Point. The rest of the land was taken over by John Kaighn. His area became known as Kaighnton. In 1773, Jacob Cooper, grandson of the first settler, followed his dream of establishing a village on his lands—one hundred acres given to him by his father. When it came time to name his village, Cooper had two preferences: Prime Minister William Pitt, Earl of Chatham, and Lord High Chancellor Charles Pratt, Earl of Camden. Since Pitt's name was already in use for Fort Pitt (see Pittsburgh), he decided on Pratt. The Earl of Camden was staunchly in favor of the American colonists, saying before the House of Lords:

> I am convinced that the British Parliament never had a right to tax the Americans. Taxation and representation are inseparable; this position is founded on the laws of nature. For whatever is a man's own is absolutely his own; and no man has a right to take from him without his consent or that of his representative.

16

CAMDEN. The house where Walt Whitman spent his last days. The famed poet's remains are located in Camden's Harleigh Cemetery. [CREDIT: New Jersey State Park Service, Walt Whitman House]

In 1828, the City of Camden incorporated. At that time, five independent villages—Camden Village, Cooper's Point Ferry Village, Kaighnton, Pinchtown, and Dogwood—were brought together to make the city.

Camden really began to grow in 1834 when the Camden & Amboy Railroad established its terminus at Camden. In 1844, it became the seat of Camden County. Walt Whitman lived the last years of his life in the city, and is buried in Harleigh Cemetery on Camden's Haddon Avenue.

CANTON

The origin of this Salem County name is obscure. Frank D. Andrews, one-time secretary of the Vineland Historical and Antiquarian Society, suggested this explanation:

"Since the early settlers came from . . . New England and as there is a Canton about forty miles from New Haven and one in Massachusetts, it was called 'New' Canton, by men who came from Canton in either Massachusetts or Connecticut, or from both."

CAPE MAY (— Court House, — Point, North —, West —)

Cape May, Cape May County, is one of the oldest seashore resorts on the Atlantic coast; perhaps it is America's first resort. Philadelphian John Drinker wrote a poem in 1760 about "the fam'd Amusements of Capt May." A 1766 advertisement indicated the spot "where a number resort for Health and Bathing in the water."

During the first half of the nineteenth century, it rivaled Newport, Rhode Island, as a favorite summer retreat for affluent Philadelphians and New Yorkers. In 1801, Ellis Hughes built the first hotel, Atlantic Hall, between Perry and Jackson Streets, and advertised in the Philadelphia *Daily Aurora* that "The subscriber has prepared himself for entertaining company who use sea bathing, and he is accommodated with extensive house room, with fish, oysters and crabs and good liquor."

Cape May's first post office opened in 1804, as Cape Island, with Ellis Hughes as postmaster. The name was changed in 1869 to honor Captain Cornelius Jacobsen (Jacobse) Mey, a navigator for the Dutch West India Company, who explored the area in the early seventeenth century. In fact, Mey sailed past the cape in 1623, fourteen years after Henry Hudson. Mey named the bay (now Delaware) New Port Mey, and the Jersey cape, Cape Mey. The opposite side of the bay, the Delaware side, he called Cape Cornelius. A marker in Cape May indicates that "New England and Long Island whitemen first settled Cape May on the Delaware Bay shore about 1685. . . ." (See Mays Landing.)

Cape May was known as Cape May Town, and before 1700, as Portsmouth. Cape May was slated to be the home of the first Ford plant in the U.S., but town leaders rejected Henry Ford's offer.

Cape May Court House, seat of Cape May County, first appeared in history when, in 1705, the county grand jury decided to build a small jail "upon the Queen's Highway, eastwardly of Gravelly run." Before that, county affairs were conducted at Cape Town or Town Bank, which had been swept away by the waves of the Atlantic Ocean. Subsequently, the "court house" was known as Middletown.

Cape May Court House has been known as Shamgar Hand Plantation, Rumly Moch, and Romney Marsh.

CARLSTADT

Carlstadt, Bergen County, was named for Dr. Carl Klein, the leader of the German settlers. The land was purchased from the original landholders by a group of "German liberals and freethinkers" who left Germany for political freedom. For a time, the village was known as Tailor Town, because a large number of the inhabitants worked for tailor shops in New York.

CARMEL

This Cumberland County town was first settled in the 1880s. Along with Norma, Alliance, Rosenhayn, and Brotmanville, Carmel was an experiment in social service.

An influx of penniless Jewish immigrants from Russia and Poland prompted the Hebrew Immigrant Society to establish agricultural communities for the new arrivals. Alliance was the first, followed by the others. To supplement their farming income, the settlers began doing garment work and handicrafts. Only Carmel, Norma, and Rosenhayn remain. The name apparently is a reference to the mountain in Biblical Palestine.

CEDARVILLE

Cedarville was first settled about 1700 as part of New England Town. It was also known as Cedar Creek and Williamsburg.

Because it is located on Cedar Creek, the reason for the name is obvious. The creek's name apparently was drawn from the presence of buried cedar logs.

CENTERTON

Situated on land once owned by the Deacon family, Centerton was first known as Five Points; it was at the intersection of roads which formed five points. The name was changed to Centerton in 1832 when a bridge was built. As the legend goes, it was called Centerton because it was midway between Bridgeon and Elmer.

Around 1910, the name was changed again, this time to Bougher, in honor of Reading H. Bougher, a prominent resident. The Centerton name returned a few years later.

CHANGEWATER

Changewater, Hunterdon County, takes its name from the Change Water Forge that was erected by Jonathan Robeson after 1742.

CHATHAM

This Morris County town was once called Bonnel or Bonnell Town, for a Mr. Bonnell who operated a gristmill on the Passaic. The name was changed to Chatham to honor William Pitt, Earl of Chatham, who was friendly to the colonists during the Revolution. The name Pitt had already been used (see Pittsburgh, Pennsylvania), so the New Jerseyites took as their name his earldom.

CHEESEQUAKE

This Middlesex County name was created by folklore, probably from the Algonquian *-che*, meaning "big." The name appeared in Virginia as Cheesecake Church, and arose from the tribal name Chiskiak. At least that is what one authority says.

A more logical explanation for the name of this community is that it originated in the "quaking bogs" along the creek.

CHESTER

Like many "new" names given to American land, this Morris County community was named to recall Chestershire, England. Chester was first settled in 1713.

Pioneering families were attracted to the industrial possibilities of the waters of the Black River and built sawmills, gristmills, and distilleries. The Chester House, the first brick house in town, was built by Zephaniah Drake in 1810. The building is still standing.

CHEWS LANDING

The name for Chews Landing, Camden County, is derived from Colonel Jeremiah Chew, a Revolutionary War officer and descendent of Thomas Chew of Upton. Jeremiah built a wharf, or landing, for the flatboats that traveled between here and Philadelphia. The town has been known at different times in its history as Abraham Roe's Landing and Hodgson's Landing.

CINNAMINSON

The Burlington County town which grew around the Friends Meeting House in this area was originally called Westfield, because the 1801 meetinghouse was built on Thomas Lippincott's "west field." Prior to that it was called Lower Chester.

The name Cinnaminson appears in 1836, when the town's post office was opened. The derivation of the name is uncertain. Translated from the Indian, it could mean "tangled roots," "stone island" or "stone tree," such as the sugar maple.

Another possibility, and the more likely, is that the name comes from Sinamensmick or Cimissimck, Indian names for the Pennsauken Creek. To rose growers, Cinnaminson is known, sadly, as the first point of entry of the Japanese beetle. The first beetle arrived in America in 1916.

CLEMENTON

In about 1736, this Camden County community was known as Newman's Mills. The land was purchased before 1825 by Samuel Clements, who operated mills and a glass factory here. The name changed to reflect the new ownership.

A later industry was Rowan's Charcoal Pit. John R. Rowan started the business in 1879, when he discovered a new technique to develop the charcoal needed by metalsmiths in America and Europe to melt precious metals. It was once said that the fires in Rowan's original pits never went out.

CLINTON

Formerly Hunt's Mills, this Hunterdon County community was renamed for De Witt Clinton (1769–1828), governor of New York, who was responsible for the promotion of the Erie Canal.

Clinton House, once a stop for the Easton stagecoaches, was built in the eighteenth century. Not far from the inn or tavern is the Old Red Mill, built in 1763, which now houses the Clinton Historical Museum.

COLLINGSWOOD

When settled by Quakers in 1682, the village was called Newton Colony. The oldest house in Collingswood, however, dates to the mid-eighteenth century. It was built in 1754 by Isaac and Mary Thackara.

The current name began in 1888 when the town was incorporated. The name commemorates John Collings and his family.

Collings was a pioneer whose farm appears on maps of the area in 1700. Richard T. Collings was the keeper of the Sunday school. Another source suggests the name came from the mother of Edward Collings Knight. Collingswood's Knight Park was donated to the town on the provision that no liquor license be given within the park's limits.

COLTS NECK

A reasonable explanation for this Monmouth County town's naming can be found on any map. A "neck" of land is formed between Yellow Brook and Mine Brook which resembles a horse's neck.

This name was used as early as 1675. In fact, a 1676 bill of sale was registered with the Board of Proprietors conveying a certain neck of land, called Colt's Neck, from two Indians.

Another source suggests that the original name was "Caul's Neck," for an early settler. This cannot be authenticated, however.

COLUMBIA

Dutch settlers, led by mining prospectors, built a dam at this site. A ferry crossed the Delaware River here to Portland, Pennsylvania, around the turn of the nineteenth century. Columbia's name is derived from the poetic name for the United States.

COLUMBUS

When Thomas and Elizabeth Scattergood arrived from England in about 1676, they established their home in a cave on Craft Creek in this Burlington County locale.

The town originally was known as Encroaching Corners, because, as one tale has it, residents of the area allegedly "encroached" on the highway with their fences. Another story contends that the building that housed the post office and the state police barracks projected into the highway.

The name was changed to Black Horse for the tavern by that name. A tavern apparently was open as early as 1745, and known by the Sign of the Black Horse by 1761.

The name was changed to Columbus by a vote of the residents in 1827. Columbus became popular as a place name in the 1820s, following a period of anti-Columbus, pro-Cabot school of American discovery. One loud dissident voice at the town meeting in New Jersey was that of the tavern keeper, who threatened never to sell to any man who refused to call the town Black Horse.

CONVENT STATION

The first Roman Catholic college in New Jersey, the College of St. Elizabeth, began in this Morris County location as the Academy of St. Elizabeth. The academy dates back to 1859; the college, 1899.

The name derivation is quite obvious.

COOKSTOWN

Cookstown was named for William Cook, who operated a grist- and sawmill on the North Run at this location from 1776 to 1801.

Cookstown first appears in 1785 road returns. Cook's mill was built by Richard Kirby in 1732, but Kirby's name never appeared on town records. The Cookstown post office was established in 1851.

CRAGMERE

The name for Cragmere, Bergen County, is descriptive of a lake, or "mere," found in a craggy spot.

CRESSKILL

This Bergen County town was so named because a local stream, or kill, was full of cresses (watercress). The name comes from the Dutch *kers-kil.*

CROSS KEYS

This Gloucester County village name came from a local tavern sign.

CROSSWICKS

The town of Crosswicks, labelled Crosswicke on old maps, derived its name from the Indian *crossweeksung,* a "separation" or the "house of separation." The name was originally applied to the creek which separates into two branches about two miles east of the village.

According to Indian lore, the separation referred to the tribal custom of sending Indian maidens who reached maturity away from the village during certain times of the year to live in a hut for a fixed number of days, after which they were allowed to return to the tribe. This would equate to the ovulation stage of the women's menstrual cycle. It is possible that the land on the other side of the stream was the location of the maidens' separation huts.

This Burlington County land was settled by the Quakers in 1681, but a post office was not established until 1823. Crosswicks is the only community in the United States to bear that name.

CROTON

Apparently, Croton was named for a river in New York. The Croton River was named for an Indian chief whose name was Kenoten, Knoten, or Noten. The name translates to "the wind."

DEERFIELD

The post office established in this Cumberland County community was first called Deerfield Street. Settlers, the tale goes, protested that the high price of land here made their fields too "dear."

Another possibility is that some of the settlers came from Deerfield, Massachusetts.

DELANCO

In 1848, the Delanco Land Company laid out the streets of this Burlington County town. The name was originally spelled Delranco: located on the Delaware River and Rancocas Creek, the town derives its name from a contraction of the names of those two bodies of water. When the railroad was built in 1849, the town was renamed Rancocas Station. A post office was established in 1857, discontinued in 1860, and re-established a year later.

DELAWANNA

This Passaic County town's name comes from a combination of Delaware and Lackawanna.

DELAWARE

Originally called Delaware Station, this Warren County locale is located on the banks of the Delaware River.

The Delaware Station name originated because this town was the scene, in July 1856, of the first passenger-train run of the Delaware, Lackawanna & Western Railroad.

DELRAN

This Burlington County town name comes from the Delaware River and Rancocas Creek. (See Delanco.)

DENNISVILLE

Located on the Dennis Creek, this Cape May County town had the first Methodist Church in the county, completed in 1803.

The town itself was initially called Dennis Creek when the post office opened in 1802, with Jeremiah Johnson as postmaster. The name was changed to Dennisville fifty years later.

Buried below the surface of Dennisville are remains of prehistoric white cedars. Hand-split cedar shakes (shingles) made from these logs were one of Dennisville's major industries during the early nineteenth century. Shingles from Dennisville were used to replace the roof on Independence Hall. Mining for the white cedar logs died out by the 1930s.

DIAS CREEK

Formerly known as Dyer's (or Dyars) Creek, the name of this Cape May County community was changed when phonetic spelling was used in the application for a post office.

The first post office, as Dyer's Creek, was opened in 1854.

At one time, Dias Creek was the local center for horseshoe crabs. The cooked meat from these relics of some past geologic era were sold for chicken feed, and the remainder of the crustacean was ground up and used as fertilizer.

DOUBLE TROUBLE

A preacher and his wife lived near the dam that forms Cedar Creek Lake in the 1870s. They were not alone, though—their neighbors included a colony of muskrats. Once a week, over a lengthy period of time, the muskrats burrowed through the dam. One week they burrowed through twice, and, as the legend goes, the preacher shouted, "Here's double trouble."

Another story agrees that the name came from aquatic animals, but in a different way. This version suggests a beaver crew built one dam after another on a mill run, cutting off the flow of water. No matter which story you prefer, this Ocean County village became Double Trouble.

DOVER

Sometime between 1790 and 1796, this town became Dover. Prior to that it was called Old Tye, and before that, Beamans. In 1792, this Morris County location only boasted four dwellings and a forge. It was incorporated in 1826 as Dover.

At one time, Dover was an important port on the Morris Canal and was called the "Pittsburgh of New Jersey." The town name reportedly was borrowed from Dover, New Hampshire, even though the first Dover was located in Delaware.

DUMONT

This Bergen County village was named for its first mayor, Dumont Clarke.

DUNELLEN

This community was not named for the divorce settlement of a liberated woman. It was named by the president of the Central Railroad of New Jersey, when the town was incorporated in 1887.

According to his daughter, Mrs. Emily de Forest, her father took the first name of a friend, Ellen Betts, and added the "dun" because he liked the phonics of the combination.

DUTCH NECK

In 1736, two Dutch families settled on a section of Mercer County land that could be described as a neck.

The Bergens and the Voorhees families came from New Amsterdam (now New York City) and bestowed their name on a number of sites in the New Jersey area.

EATONTOWN

Prior to 1685, Thomas Eaton emigrated from Rhode Island to this Monmouth County location. He built a gristmill here that operated until 1920.

Eaton befriended, or at least the legend says he did, Indian Will, a renegade who did not move away when his tribe's land was sold. The tribe sent messengers to either convince Will to return to the tribe—or kill him. Apparently, Will wanted to remain, and so he killed the messengers. He also found time to drown his wife.

In exchange for a red coat and a cocked hat, Indian Will gave the Eaton family a large collection of silverware. Shortly after this gift, the Eatons became quite affluent. No one knew where Indian Will got the silver or whose it was.

EDISON

This Middlesex County community was named for Thomas Alva Edison (1847–1931), the "Wizard of Menlo Park."

During his lifetime, Edison invented more than 1,300 items, including the stock ticker and the electric light bulb, and supplied ideas and innovations that paved the way for motion pictures, the modern world of electronics, telephones, and electrical generation systems. At the time of his death, Edison's inventions were valued at twenty-five billion dollars!

EGG HARBOR CITY

Egg Harbor City's main occupation has nothing to do with chickens. Eggs did, however, have a role in the naming.

When sailors from the Dutch ship *Fortuyn* came up the Mullica River in 1614, they combed the countryside looking for berries and fruits. All they could find were birds' eggs. They named the land they explored *Eyren Haven*, "harbor of eggs."

Egg Harbor City, Atlantic County, is nowhere near Egg Harbor. It was named in anticipation of a canal that was to connect it with Gloucester Furnace and the Millica River. The canal was never dug, and the only seafaring thing about the town is its name.

In 1858, John F. Wild discovered that the soil in the area was conducive to growing wine grapes. Entrepreneurs brought in German vintners and, after the Civil War, the Italians arrived. Some Egg Harbor City vineyards are still operated by the same families.

Some of the Germans who came to Egg Harbor City were escaping the Native American or Know-Nothing party, a group that was torturing Catholics and immigrants in Philadelphia and elsewhere.

EDISON. Thomas Alva Edison sitting outside Glenmount, 30 June 1917. Both Edison, New Jersey, and Edison, Pennsylvania, bear his name. (National Park Service, Edison National Historic Site, West Orange, N. J.)

ELIZABETH

The origins of the city of Elizabeth, Union County, date back to 1649. A group of men including John Baily, Daniel Denton, and Luke Watson, formerly of a New Haven, Connecticut, colony but living in Jamaica on Long Island, were permitted by Richard Nicholls to purchase from the Indians a tract of land stretching from the Raritan River to Newark Bay. That action was subsequently known as the "Elizabeth-Town Purchase."

By 1664, the Elizabethtown Associates had built four huts in the area, making Elizabeth the first English settlement (third settlement overall) in New Jersey. The name was given by Philip Carteret, a relative of the proprietor, in 1665. It honored Sir George Carteret's wife, Elizabeth. In 1740, George II gave the city a charter as the Free Borough and town of Elizabeth; a second charter was given by the state legislature in 1789. A city charter was issued in 1855 and amended in 1863.

An alternative origin suggests the town was named for Castle Elizabeth on the island of Jersey.

Elizabeth was home to Alexander Hamilton and Aaron Burr. Both attended the old academy that stood where the First Presbyterian Church's parish house now stands. The school, later to become Princeton University, was founded there in 1746 as the College of New Jersey. (See Princeton.)

ELIZABETHPORT

Elizabethport, also in Union County, lies on Staten Island sound. It is the port for Elizabeth.

ELMER

The Borough of Elmer, Salem County, was named after Judge Lucius Q.C. Elmer of Bridgeton. Previously known as Pittstown, it was named in honor of William Pitt, Earl of Chatham.

There was another Pittstown in the northern part of the state, and when the town fathers decided upon a name, to avoid any confusion over the delivery of mail, they decided to honor the judge.

EMERSON

This community was named for author Ralph Waldo Emerson.

ENGLEWOOD

Englewood is a either a made-up or mispronounced name. In its early days this Bergen County spot was called "the English neighborhood." Later it was known as Liberty Pole, because of the pole that stood near the former Liberty Pole Tavern on the Common. The name Englewood was bestowed in 1859 by a real estate developer. Some think that the "engle" prefix indicates "English."

Another authority insists the name comes from the English "wood ingle," "a woody nook or corner."

ENGLISHTOWN

Englishtown, Monmouth County, was named, contrary to popular thought, for James English, a landowner.

George Washington made his headquarters here on 27 June 1778, the day before the Battle of Monmouth. He stayed at Hulse House, the home of Moses Laird.

ESSEX FALLS

This is a unique naming. It probably took "Essex" from Essex County, and "Falls" from John Fells, an area resident.

ESTELLVILLE

Estellville has a place in New Jersey folklore because it is the place where, in the early eighteenth century (perhaps 1735), the famous

Leeds Devil was first seen. A devil was said to have been born to a Mrs. Leeds in this town. While pregnant, Mrs. Leeds cried: "Not another child! I hope this one's a devil." When her labor was over, she had delivered "a grotesque, horned, winged creature with the face of a horse and the tail of a devil." Mrs. Leeds' devil, better known as The Jersey Devil, has been blamed for any unsolved crime in the Pine Barrens area for years.

Some say that it was not Mrs. Leeds who put a curse on her child. They say the "devil" was punishment to the woman for a hot and heavy affair with a British Army officer. (See Burleigh.)

EVESBORO

The town of Evesboro probably adopted the name of its township, which was drawn from early settlers, the Eaves family.

The road returns for 1801 call it Evesham Meeting House. An 1839 map refers to it as Bodines, after Bodine's Tavern. Other references call it Green Tree.

EWANSVILLE

Ewansville, Burlington County, was named for Chris Ewan, Jr., whose mills burned down in 1849. Ewan rebuilt and the mills stayed in operation until 1925. Ewansville was mentioned in the 1864 road returns, but called Ewansville Station around 1910 when the Mount Holly-Pemberton Railroad was in operation.

FAIR—

The prefix "fair" usually translates to "pleasant," as in the names Fairfield, Fair Haven, Fair Lawn (though the name was taken from that of the Ackerson estate), Fairmount, Fairton, and the Fairviews in Bergen, Burlington and Camden counties.

FAIRFIELD

Fairfield, Essex County, was so named because it is rich bottom-land. The town dates back to the early eighteenth century, when the Dutch Reformed Church was organized there in 1720. The Fairfield Reformed Church, built in 1804, is still standing.

The church has a humorous past. It was built by Aaron Vanderhoof, who agreed to build it as long as he and his family had first choice of pews. When his work was almost completed, he learned the pews had been assigned and he would only be given second choice.

Construction stopped at that point, and the church opened its doors without a steeple. In a rage, Vanderhoof walked off the job, leaving this message: "Beautiful Fairfield, Proud people: Elegant church, No steeple!"

FAIRVIEW

The view across the Hackensack Valley in Bergen County was, in the eyes of the namers, "a pretty fair view."

The Fairview in Burlington County was originally called Cross Keys, after a tavern sign. (Crossed keys are the symbol of treasure.) There was an old gristmill on Swede's Run which was built about 1750 and was known until 1800 as Borton's Mill, but this name did not seem to take hold. The town is listed as Cross Keys in an 1849 map, but Fairview in an 1859 one.

Fairview, Camden County, was formerly Yorkship Village and Yorkship.

FANWOOD

A cidermill was built by Simeon Lambert on the site of present-day Fanwood as early as 1740.

Fanwood actually dates to 1878, when portions of Westfield and Plainfield were combined. The town was named for Fannie Wood, a writer and daughter of a Jersey Central Railroad official.

FAR HILLS

Far Hills, Somerset County, was originally developed to be a center of "rolling regions of grand estates where the wealthy engaged in farming and fox hunting." Far Hill's twin, Bedminster, is located on the other side of the North Branch of the Raritan River.

FARMINGDALE

Farmingdale, Monmouth County, was earlier known as Upper Squankum and Marsh's Bog. In the early nineteenth century, Farmingdale became important as a source for marl, used in fertilizer and in the stiffening sand in the manufacture of glass.

The name Farmingdale, however, is descriptive of a farming community established in a "dale." (See Marlton.)

FELLOWSHIP

The post office for this town was established in 1849 on what was once known as the Robert's Tract. The name Fellowship is Quaker in origin. The village on the Tract was settled prior to 1800.

FAR HILLS. Visitors to the Golf House, Far Hills, New Jersey, can view a complete club-maker's bench from the time when golfing equipment was made to order for each individual player. (New Jersey Division of Travel and Tourism)

FIELDSBORO

Fieldsboro was incorporated as a borough in 1850. Two years later it became part of Bordentown Township, Burlington County. It separated again in 1894.

The community was first called White Hill in 1693, when Marmanduke Horseman operated a plantation on the site. The present name is derived from the Field family, who took up land in the area. Benjamin Field is mentioned in a 1694 survey. Another Benjamin Field acquired land as late as 1762, while Robert Field, "of White Hill" is mentioned in a 1777 will.

A post office was established as Fieldsborough in 1889, and the name was modernized in the late nineteenth century.

FLANDERS

This Morris County community takes its name from the World War I Flanders Field, or Flanders, Ontario.

FLEMINGTON

Though John Philip Kase was the first settler in this area, this town was named for Samuel Fleming, who built an inn in 1756.

The first public hanging in the county took place here in 1794. In 1932, the famous Lindbergh kidnapping trial was held here in the county courthouse.

Flemington is the twentieth-century home of pottery and cut glass, and the seat of Hunterdon County.

FLORENCE

In 1849, this Burlington County site was known as High Bank. That year, the Florence City Company purchased two farms—about 600 acres—and laid out a town, naming it Florence City. At another time, it was known as Florence Heights.

The developers most likely acquired the name from an already-established business—the Jones brothers from Hanover Furnace organized the Florence Iron Works there in 1853.

A post office was established in 1854, under the name of Florence.

FLORHAM PARK

Florham Park, Morris County, was named for the estate of Florence and Hamilton Twombly.

The one hundred-room mansion, modeled after the palace of Hampton Court on the Thames, near London, is now part of Farleigh-Dickinson University.

FORT DIX

The first stages of this military installation began on the Samuel Davis farm. Established originally as Camp Dix in 1917, it was named for John Adams Dix, Civil War general, U. S. senator, New York governor, secretary of the treasury, and minister to France.

In 1939, Dix became a permanent military station and became Fort Dix. It is located in both Burlington and Ocean counties.

FORT LEE

Fort Lee, Bergen County, began as a Revolutionary War fort named for Major General Charles Lee.

Located on a plateau at the crest of the Palisades, it was an ideal location for a fort. Fort Lee was built to prevent the British from sailing up the Hudson to West Point. Washington watched the surrender of his troops at Fort Washington, directly across the river, in November 1776. A few days later, General Nathanael Greene abandoned Fort Lee as the British crossed the river in force.

From 1907 until the mid-1920s, Fort Lee was the capital of the American filmmaking industry. Early moving-picture audiences watched cowboys and Indians fight their way across the New Jersey "frontier." Before World War I, seven studios and twenty-one film companies produced silent films there.

FOUR MILE

On an 1849 map, this community is called Four Mile Hollow, apparently because the town is four miles from Butler Place. In 1868, however, another map names the place Flour Mill Hollow. Still another source suggests it was named after a tavern.

FRANKLIN (Lakes, Park, —ville)

Franklin Lakes, Bergen County, was named for William Franklin, son of Benjamin and the last royal governor of New Jersey. The railroad's name for the station, however, was Campgaw.

Franklin Park, Somerset County, and Franklinville, Gloucester County, both were named for members of the Franklin family.

FREDON

Fredon, Sussex County, is a shortening of Fredonia, a word coined by Dr. Samuel Latham Mitchill. In the years following 1800, he proposed that the English "freedom" with a Latin ending would convey the image of "place of freedom" and could be used as the name of the American nation.

FREEHOLD

Freehold, seat of Monmouth County, was settled about 1650, but a permanent village was not established until 1715. The Scottish settlers came from New Aberdeen (now Matawan). They left England because of the persecution by Charles II, and named their village after Monmouthshire, England, which was a "freehold," a place where real estate was held for life.

In 1714, a year after the assembly named Freehold Township as the site of the county courthouse, John Reid purchased an extensive tract of land. He sold part of his land to county officials for the courthouse. He charged them a trifling thirty shillings, but that small investment increased the value of the rest of his property.

In 1758, Monmouth Court House witnessed part of the Revolutionary War Battle of Monmouth.

The courthouse's name was shortened to Monmouth in 1795, when a post office opened. Six years later, Monmouth (nee Monmouth Court House) became Freehold. Postal officials changed the name to avoid confusion with other Monmouths in the county.

FRENCHTOWN

This village began in 1785, when Thomas Lowrey arrived from Flemington and built a grist- and sawmill near the Delaware River. In 1794, he deeded 893 acres of the land, along the river, to Paul Henri Mallet-Prevost (1756–1833), a fugitive from the French Revolution. His name was on the list of those to be guillotined.

Mallet-Prevost called the settlement Alexandria, after the township. A 1749 map of the area indicates the area was then called Sunbeam. Frenchtown was originally part of both Alexandria and Kingwood Townships, but was incorporated as a borough in 1867.

GARFIELD

The memory of President James A. Garfield (1831–81) is recalled with this Bergen County community's name.

Garfield was in office only four months when he was shot by a mentally disturbed job-seeker. He lingered for a short time at his home in Long Beach before dying. (See Long Beach.)

GEORGETOWN

Before a post office was established in 1847, this town was known as Fool- or Foolstown. The reason for the name was simple: a local man spent more to build a brick house than he could afford.

When the post office was opened here, it honored George Sykes, a Quaker surveyor and congressman (1843–48).

GIBBSTOWN

This Gloucester County community was developed as a response to the need for housing for the workmen at the DuPont Company, or Hercules, Incorporated, plants north of town.

GILLETTE

Gillette, Morris County, probably was named for King Camp Gillette (1855–1932), inventor of the safety razor and blade. He founded the Gillette Company in 1901.

GLADSTONE

This community bears the name of William E. Gladstone (1809–98). Gladstone was the British prime minister who promoted Irish Home Rule, despite the policy's unpopularity, attempted to expand suffrage, and reorganized the British court system.

GLASSBORO

In 1775, Catherine Stanger, a German widow, and her seven sons emigrated to this Gloucester County locale. Two of her sons apprenticed with the Wistar glassworks in Alloway. A few years later, the two started their own glassworks in an area rich in green sand and silica. That area became modern-day Glassboro.

The glass industry reached its peak during the 1840 presidential campaign. A bottle made in Glassboro, shaped like a log cabin, was used by William Henry Harrison as a symbol of his rural roots. The bottles were filled by a Philadelphia distiller, who put his name on the bottles. The rest is history! No one remembers that E. C.

Booz and his "Booz bottles" popularized the noun which, as early as 1812, had been a stinging part of the vocabulary of Parson Weems, the "manufacturer" of the George Washington myths.

Glassboro returned to the spotlight in 1967 when President Lyndon B. Johnson selected the campus of Glassboro State College for a summit meeting with Alexsai B. Kosygin, premier of the Soviet Union. They met in Hollybush, the 1849 house that became the college president's home.

GLENDORA

Some sources suggest that the name of this Camden County village is a combination of Glen and the woman's name Dora. This cannot be confirmed.

GLEN GARDNER

Glen Gardner was at one time known as Clarksville, but even earlier as Sodom. According to some sources, it was called Sodom up to about 1850, but maps show it as Clarksville in 1834.

The town, also called Spruce Run for the nearby stream, was named Glen Gardner for the Gardner brothers, who arrived in the 1860–70s and set up factories to manufacture chairs and picture frames.

GLEN RIDGE

Located in Essex County, Glen Ridge is actually a ridge in a glen, formed by Toney's Brook.

Its history goes back to the seventeenth century, but Glen Ridge did not become a borough until 1895. Glen Ridge gained notoriety in 1976 when the town tried to evict five nuns from their ten-room residence. Town law stated that no more than two unrelated people could live under the same roof. The nuns countered the ruling by claiming that they were related by their religious vows. Townspeople agreed, and the nuns were allowed to remain—but the ordinance was not amended.

GLEN ROCK

This Bergen County community ostensibly was named for a large glacial boulder that rested in the middle of a field.

GLOUCESTER CITY

Gloucester City, Camden County, was the site of the first white settlement on the east bank of the Delaware River. In 1623, Captain Cornelius Jacobsen Mey (see Cape May) built Fort Nassau at the mouth of Big Timber Creek. Ten years later, the settlement of two dozen men and women had vanished.

A permanent settlement began with the arrival of the Irish Quakers. The first pioneers in 1682 were Mathew Medcalf, Samuel Harrison, John Reading, William Harrison, and Thomas and Richard Bull. They laid out the town four years later. The Gloucester vicinity was labeled the Irish Tenth when West Jersey was divided by the Proprietors.

The name is borrowed from a cathedral town on the banks of the Severn in the west of England.

GOSHEN

A post office was established in this Cape May community in 1818. The name alludes to the Biblical "Land of Goshen" where the Israelites lived in Egypt.

GOULDTOWN

This Cumberland County community was founded by four mulatto families: Gould, Pierce, Murray, and Cuff.

The Goulds were alleged to be descendents of John Fenwick, the Quaker proprietor of the "Salem Tenth" in West Jersey, who first colonized the region. Elizabeth Adams, Fenwick's granddaughter, inherited 500 acres of land, married a West Indian named Gould, and settled there.

About 1750, as the legend goes, Richard and Anthony Pierce, both from the West Indies, joined them. The Pierce brothers paid passage for two white sisters to sail from Holland, and married them on their arrival.

With only a few exceptions, it is said, all Gouldtown residents are descended from the four families.

GREAT MEADOWS

The land that is now Great Meadows, Warren County, was once pure bog. The land was reclaimed by Dr. J. Marshall Paul of Belvidere when the town entered the onion-celery-lettuce business in 1850 . . . and thus the name!

Before 1850, the town was called Denville, with its chief industry the Kishpaugh iron mine.

GREAT NOTCH

Great Notch, Passaic County, is so named because of its location in an opening in the Watchung Mountains.

GREEN (— Bank, — Brook, — Pond, — Village, —ville)

Swedes from the Delaware River settlement, led by Eric Molica (Mullica) arrived in this Burlington County area in 1697, making Green Bank one of the oldest settlements in South Jersey. Mullica lived here for a number of years, but eventually returned to Mullica Hill.

By 1832, it was the home of Paul Sooy, a postmaster who operated out of Sooy's Inn. A post office was formally established in 1840 and named Green Bank. A year later, it was renamed Sooy's Inn. In 1856, the official name returned to Green Bank. Though the post-office name was official, Green Bank did suffer from multiple personalities. On 1849 maps, it was called Upper Bank, to distinguish it from Lower Bank. In 1873, another map called it Upper Green Bank.

Green Brook, Somerset County, takes its name from the waterway.

Green Pond, Morris County, takes its name from that body of water.

Green Village, Morris County, was named to commemorate Dr. Ashabel Green, the president of Princeton.

GREENWICH

Founded by Major John Fenwick, the first manor tract was sold to Mark Reeve, an English Quaker, in 1684, and called Manor Town.

The name apparently migrated south from Greenwich, Connecticut, where many of the settlers arrived before settling on the banks of the Cohansey in Cumberland County.

On 22 November 1774, the townspeople protested the British tax on tea. Disguising themselves as Indians (does that sound familiar?), they burned a shipload of the East India Company's tea, taken from the English brig *Greyhound*.

GREENWICH. The building on the left side of Greate Street is the Friends Meeting House, built in 1857. Meetings were conducted on the first floor, while the second floor was used as a school.

A group of young men, disguised as Indians, "borrowed" the cargo of British tea that had been brought here by the brig *Greyhound* on the night of 22 December 1774— and burned it. There were only a handful of tea-party towns in America. [CREDIT: Gary F. Cooper, Cumberland County Historical Society, Greenwich, New Jersey]

GROVERS MILLS

Before the American Revolution, a small settlement existed at this Mercer County location. Jacob Bergen built and operated the earliest gristmill in East Windsor Township. During the war, his son George carried on the operation. Bergen's Mill seemed like a logical name for the site.

In 1859, Joseph H. Grover bought the mill—and gave his name to the town. Grovers Mill, Mercer County, is quite famous to science-fiction fans. The space creatures brought to life by Orson Welles and his Mercury Theatre "came" to Grovers Mill and caused a small national panic on 30 October 1938. Welles and his radio troop broadcast a dramatization of H. G. Wells' *The War of the Worlds*, which, while clearly prefaced as a fictional account, still managed to provoke widespread hysteria.

GUTTENBERG

This Hudson County community took its name from Johannes Gutenberg, the early printer—with a misspelling.

HACKENSACK (North —, South —)

Hackensack, Bergen County, began in 1647 when a small group of Dutch settlers from Manhattan started a trading post on Chief Oratam's land. The Indian influence is commemorated in this name, though the name is of fairly recent origin.

Officially known as New Barbadoes until 1921, when a city charter was issued, the name is derived from the Hackensack River. All reliable sources translate the name to include some mention of water: *hacquan-sauk,* "hook mouth," *hocquan sakuwit,* "mouth of a river," and *hackink saquik,* "a stream that unites with another on low ground," and "land of the big snake." Additionally, the area was once inhabited by a Lenni-Lenape clan, the Achensachys or Ackinsachys.

One wag jokingly suggested that the name was obtained from the sign of an old tavern, the "Hock and Sack." Hock and sack, by the way, are both wines.

Different spellings of the name, from Achkinchesacky to Hockumdachgue, have appeared in various documents. George Washington, in a military communique, rendered it Hackensac.

HACKETTSTOWN

The original name for this Warren County municipality was Helm's Mills or Musconetcong.

The name was changed in the mid-eighteenth century to

honor Samuel Hackett, the largest landowner in the district. Hackett, it must be noted, greatly increased his popularity by setting up plenty of free drinks at the opening of a new hotel.

HADDONFIELD

In 1701, twenty-year-old Elizabeth Haddon was sent to the colonies by her Quaker father. Since he had no sons, it was up to Elizabeth to develop his vast acreage of land southeast of Camden in what is now Camden County, and acquired by him in 1698.

In less than a year, Elizabeth Haddon built a house, established a colony and proposed marriage to missionary John Estaugh. Their romance is the theme of "The Theologian's Tale" in Longfellow's *Tales of a Wayside Inn*. Until her death in 1762, Elizabeth Haddon Estaugh was known locally as the maker of a highly regarded medicinal whiskey.

HADDON HEIGHTS

This community also owes its name to the Haddon family. It was formerly known as Baker's Corner and Borton's Hill.

The first house in Haddon Heights was built by John Glover in 1705. Glover arrived in the colonies two years earlier after being released from his impressment in the British Navy. Glover married Hannah Thorne in 1704. She and her father had arrived earlier, but settled in Pennsylvania. (See Haddonfield.)

HAINES (—burg, —port, —ville)

"Hainesburg was known more than a century ago," Henry Charlton Beck wrote in 1939, "as Sodom, for what specific sins the historians do not relate." "Sodom" generally was a name that itinerant preachers bestowed on any town that was not open to their preaching.

The name Hainesburg, however, appears as early as 1842. As a Warren County town, it actually dates to 1843, when the Beck brothers acquired the site which Andrew Smith had owned and cut into town lots. The name was given to honor Joseph Haines, who donated the land on which the first school was built.

The first pioneer to the Hainesport area was John Cook. He also built the first tavern, around 1844. Allen Haines arrived and built a foundry in 1872—apparently on the land of a relative, Barclay Haines, who had purchased acreage in 1850. Haines' buildings blew away in 1877.

In its early days, Hainesport, Burlington County, was known as Long Bridge, Herring Hall (or Haul) for a tavern or inn. A post office was established in 1853 only to be closed, then opened again. The Hainesport post office was firmly established in 1876.

HALEDON (North —)

During the 1913 Paterson Silk Strike, Haledon's socialist mayor allowed strikers to meet in the home of co-worker Pietro Botto. Speakers included William "Big Bill" Haywood, writers Upton Sinclair and John Reed (memorialized by Warren Beaty in "Reds").

The name for Haledon, Passaic County, is supposedly borrowed from Haledon, England.

HAMILTON SQUARE

This Mercer County community was originally called Crossroads in Nottingham Township. The name was later shortened to Nottingham Square. In 1842, the name was changed to its present form, in honor of Alexander Hamilton (1755–1804).

Hamilton was the first secretary of the treasury and coauthor, with James Madison, of *The Federalist Papers*. He died following a duel with Aaron Burr.

HAMMONTON

Hammonton, a center for fruit-farming in Atlantic County, was named for John Hammond Coffin. Coffin owned the glassworks that operated here in the 1870s.

HAMPTON

Clayton Earl sold this Hunterdon County land to William Lane and John W. Godfrey, both of Philadelphia, in 1879. The town, however, was named in honor of Jonathan Hampton, who donated the land for the local church.

HANOVER (East —) (— Neck)

The Hanover Furnace converted "bog ore" into iron and gave its name to this town. The business was abandoned in 1850, but the name in Morris County remained.

HARLINGEN

Harlingen, Somerset County, is part of 9,000 acres of rich farmland granted Dutch settlers in the early eighteenth century.

The town takes its name from the Van Harlingen family. Johannis Van Harlingen was a founder of Rutgers University.

HARMONY

Harmony, Monmouth County, bears a name that describes an idealistic place. The name may have been borrowed from the Harmony Society of Pennsylvania. (See Harmony, Pennsylvania.)

HARRISON (—ville)

Harrison, Hudson County, is an outgrowth of Newark.

Harrisonville, Gloucester County, was founded by Quakers after 1673. During the Civil War, it was the site of a popular tavern. The tavern, the Pig's Eye, gave its name to the town and the area around it. Later, the name was changed to a more conventional one to commemorate a town father.

HARTFORD

Hartford, Burlington County, grew around the old Talman tract, then owned by the Joseph Davis estate. The tract was purchased by Enoch Hollinshead in 1845 or 1846. A blacksmith had operated in the vicinity as early as 1838.

The name Hartford first appears in 1860 road returns. It may have been borrowed from the Connecticut town of the same name, or from the English village.

HARVEY CEDARS

Harvey Cedars is the oldest settlement on Long Beach Island. The resort was a haven for whalers following the War of 1812. Very few of the cedar trees that gave the town its name are alive today—neither is the Harvey of the first part of the name, but many skeletons of the trees remain to brace themselves against the seas.

The town was originally called Harvey's Whaling Quarters, and legend suggests the name came from Daniel Harvey, a cave-dwelling early resident.

HAWTHORNE

Hawthorne takes its name from novelist Nathaniel Hawthorne.

HAZEN

Hazen, Warren County, may have been named for the Revolutionary War's Moses Hazen (1733–1803).

Hazen, a former British officer, was looked upon with suspicion by both sides when hostilities broke out. He conveyed news to both sides in the early days of conflict, and was imprisoned for his actions. In 1776, he was commissioned colonel of the 2nd Canadian Regiment, "Congress's Own." Most of his recruits came from Canada and fought bravely at Long Island, Brandywine, and Germantown.

Throughout his military career, Hazen was court-martialed—and acquitted—for numerous offenses. He retired from the military in 1783 and settled on land he owned in Vermont.

HEDDING

The history of Hedding's name swings from a bar to a church.

Between 1793 and 1813, this Burlington County village was known as Bryant's Tavern, after William Bryant or Brian. In 1817, the tavern underwent a change of ownership—and name. It was then known as Three Tuns, depicted on the tavern sign as three wine casks or "tuns."

Thirty years later, the Methodist Episcopal Church arrived and built there, calling the place of worship Hedding Methodist Episcopal Church, for Elijah Hedding, a bishop of that denomination.

The town retained the Three Tuns name until 1920, when it was changed to reflect the church's name.

HELMETTA

Helmetta, Middlesex County, was named for Etta Helme, the daughter of a local factory owner.

George W. Helme built his snuff factory here about 1825.

HEWITT

Abram S. Hewitt and Peter Cooper owned Ringwood, a legendary mine in Passaic County. The mine produced about two-and-a-half million tons of iron ore during its lifetime. It was founded in 1765.

Besides being an ironmaster, Hewitt was mayor of New York.

HIBERNIA

Hibernia, Morris County, gets its name from the Hibernia Furnace which was in operation from 1763–64 as "The Adventure." The Furnace, carrying the Latin and romantic name for Ireland, was used from 1767–82 by William Alexander, son of New Jersey's surveyor general.

The young Alexander served under George Washington in the Revolution and called himself Lord Stirling, a title the British would not accept.

Accompanying the Furnace was Hibernia Mine, which was closed down in 1912. (See Stirling.)

HIGH BRIDGE

High Bridge, Hunterdon County, was named for the home of Robert Taylor, who operated the confiscated Union Iron Works during the American Revolution. Later, he purchased part of the land and operated it as Taylor Iron Works, predecessor to the Taylor-Wharton Iron & Steel Company.

Taylor built Lake Solitude on his property, and John Penn, the last royal governor of Pennsylvania, was held prisoner in this house for six months during 1776.

Another authority suggests that the name came from a remarkable railroad bridge erected here.

HIGHLANDS (— Beach)

Highlands, Monmouth County, gains its name from the hills that rise abruptly from the shore. It was formerly known as Parkertown.

The name is drawn from the Dutch *hoeland*, or *hoogland*, meaning "highland." In 1668, Richard Hartshorne obtained use-rights for Sandy Hook from the Indians for thirteen shillings. He then purchased the Highlands area from the original English settlers who had arrived about five years earlier.

James Fenimore Cooper was a frequent visitor here in the 1820s. Though *The Water Witch* was written in Paris, Cooper's novel was set here.

HI-NELLA

This Camden County community takes its name from an earlier Indian village. The name translates to "high rolling knoll."

HOBOCKEN

The name of this city, founded by Dutch settlers, is also the name of a village in Belgium, close to the Dutch border. Some sources suggest the name has some Indian roots, such as *hobocan hackingh*, the Algonquian term for "land of the tobacco pipe." The site once served as a quarry for the stone from which pipes were made.

The Dutch settled in this Hudson County locale in 1640 and quickly antagonized the Indians. The Indians drove them out and burned down all the Dutch buildings—except the brewery. The Indians evidently had a sense of history: the brewery, built in 1642 by Aert T. van Putten, was the first in America.

The Hudson County land for Hobocken was mapped out by Colonel John Stevens, who called it "The New City of Hobocken" and auctioned off lots in New York. Stevens introduced the first regular steam ferry, the *Juliana*, in 1811. A creative inventor, Stevens had operated the steam-powered *Phoenix* on the Hudson as early as

1808. He was forced to stop his service after Robert Fulton, who had secured sole rights to the invention, protested.

Hetty Green, the "Witch of Wall Street," was a shrewd money manager and the richest woman in the world in the 1870s. She lived in a $20-a-month apartment on Washington Street. While she earned $5,000 a day, she shared a bathtub with other tenants. Anything to save a buck!

HO-HO-KUS

In colonial times, Ho-Ho-Kus was called Hoppertown, after an early settler. Later it was named for the Chilohokies, a sub-tribe of the Lenapes who had a major camp on the site.

The name has various interpretations. It has been translated to mean "running water," "cleft in the rock," "under the rock," "hollow rock," and "the wind whistling through the bark of a tree"; even "a shout," just to name a few. The name for this Bergen County city actually comes from the Lenape *mehohoku*, "red cedar."

Ho-Ho-Kus was settled in the late eighteenth century. The spelling of its name is varied. The hyphenated version is on the municipal building, but the unhyphenated version of this Bergen County community is preferred by the post office, the U. S. Census Bureau, and the telephone company.

HOLMDEL

Holmdel takes its name from the Holmes family. The family home, built about 1754, is still standing and open to the public.

HOPATCONG

This Sussex County community received its name from the local lake. Hopatcong (earlier called Huppakong) Lake was named by the Lenni-Lenape. The name, it has been suggested, means "honey waters from many streams."

It is more likely that the name comes from another word meaning "stone over water." The Indians built an artificial stone walkway from the shore to an island in the lake.

HOPE

Hope, Warren County, was settled somewhere between 1769 and 1806—sources vary—by Moravians from Bethlehem, Pennsylvania. They purchased 1,000 acres and, using native bluestone, constructed substantial homes.

During the Revolution, the Moravians were dubbed Tories because of their pacifistic beliefs, but their devoted care for sick and wounded soldiers disproved that charge. A smallpox epidemic in the early nineteenth century nearly decimated the population of this community. In 1808, many of the colonists returned to Bethlehem, leaving the town to others.

The name is drawn from *Hope of Immortality* by Count Zinzendorf, the spiritual leader of the Moravians.

HOPEWELL

Hopewell, located in Mercer County, was the town from which the Lindbergh baby was kidnapped (see Flemington).

The town dates back to the early eighteenth century. In fact, the Old School Baptist Meeting House, built in 1748, replaced one built thirty-three years earlier. The building was used as a hospital during the Revolution.

John Hart, a local resident who, though not a Baptist, donated the land on which the church sits, signed the Declaration of Independence. A plain granite shaft, erected in 1856 by the New Jersey legislature, commemorates Hart.

Some authorities suggest the name comes from the Puritan manner of speaking. The same source indicates the first settlers were Puritans from Connecticut, via Long Island.

HOWELL

Situated in Monmouth County, Howell was most probably named for Richard Howell, an early governor of New Jersey.

HURDTOWN

In 1804–05, Joseph and Daniel Hurd built a forge on the Weldon Brook, a branch of Beaver Creek, in Morris County. The original name for their land was "Two Partners Tract," and the village that sprung up around their tract was called Two Partners. The name was later changed to Hurdtown in honor of its founders.

IRONIA

Using the Latin ending, the name of this village translates to the "place of iron," a fitting name for an iron-mining area.

IRVINGTON

Irvington, Essex County, was first called Camptown. William Campe was one of the original settlers of Newark, and his children farmed this area. After a while, the Camptown area became known as a "rendezvous of the fast and wicked young men of Newark and

Orange, the goal of straw-rides and the Gretna Green of dance, frolic and fun," or so a contemporary thought.

The Irvington name was put in place in 1852 and honors author and historian Washington Irving, who was at the peak of his fame at that time.

ISLAND HEIGHTS

This Ocean County community is a survivor of the Methodist meeting settlements founded in New Jersey after the Civil War.

In 1903, department store tycoon John Wanamaker established a summer camp here for his employees. The Wanamaker camp has since become a Presbyterian summer camp. Island Heights is the only "dry" resort in the county.

JACKSON (—burg, —ville)

The Jacksons, located in Camden and Ocean counties; Jacksonburg, Warren County; and Jacksonville, Burlington County, were named in honor of President Andrew Jackson (1767–1845).

Jackson, hero of the War of 1812 and celebrated for his victory at New Orleans (a victory that took place after the war was over), was the first president elected by the popular vote. He thanked his supporters by providing them with patronage appointments to government.

Prior to 1750, Jacksonville was called Slabtown, named for the "slabs" of wood produced at the local sawmill. Early nineteenth-century settlers included Abel Gaskill, Daniel S. Zelly, Solomon Thomas, and Stacy Haines.

Prior to 1800, an old tannery operated on the Thomas property.

When a tavern was opened in 1829, the name was changed to Jackson to honor the president. A few months later it became Jacksonville.

JACOBSTOWN

Jacobstown existed as a village in Burlington County perhaps as early as 1777. A tavern was located here in 1807.

The post office was established in 1849 as Jacobstown. The name may have come from Jacob Platt (see Plattsburgh). In 1862, Daniel L. Platt was postmaster.

JEFFERSON

Jefferson, Gloucester County, was named in honor of President Thomas Jefferson (1743–1826).

Jefferson was the author of the Declaration of Independence and a great supporter of freedom of the press—as long as that freedom did not interfere with him.

JENKINS

The village of Jenkins, Burlington County, was named for the Jenkins family, a well-respected Quaker family. In fact, in the Sarah Jenkins' 1808 will, she notes "Daughter Nancy to have four cows now in care of William Pen, until of age."

JERICHO

It is suggested that this Gloucester County town's name came from Jericho, where Joshua "fit the battle" in Biblical times.

JERSEY CITY (—ville)

Under an agreement with the Dutch West India Company, Michael Pauw was required to settle fifty individuals on a certain tract of land in order to retain possession of it. Pauw sent Cornelius Van Vorst to establish his plantation, to be called Pavonia. Van Vorst built a house here in 1633.

JERSEY CITY. The State of New Jersey contends that the Statue of Liberty is actually located in that state. Pictured here is Liberty State Park, Jersey City, New Jersey. (New Jersey Division of Travel and Tourism)

Not satisfied with the progress of their system, the company bought out Pauw's interest in 1634, and built two more houses on the land. Frequent trouble and bloody conflict with the Indians ended in 1645, with everything destroyed except the Van Vorst house. Ten years later, the Indians raided the settlement again in reprisal of a hostile act by the settlers.

Peter Stuyvesant would not permit any re-settlement until a fortified village could be developed. This occurred in 1660 when the village of Bergen was laid out as an 800-foot square surrounded by a log wall. The settlement grew rapidly and, within a year, ferry service to New Amsterdam was needed.

The British took control in 1664 in a smooth transition.

Jersey City, Hudson County, according to some sources, was named as a counterpart to New York City. Others say the name came from one of the channel islands of England.

JOBSTOWN

Job Lippincott owned a major part of the land in the area and built a tavern there about 1798. The Burlington County locale was known variously as Liplincoats, Lippingwell, or Lippinwatts.

The post office was established as Jobstown in 1817.

JOHNSONBURG

From 1753 to 1765, this town was the seat of Sussex County. It is now part of Warren County. Because of the town's log houses, including a log jail, the town was known as Log (Logg) Gaol or Log Jail. The town was renamed to honor an early postmaster.

Joseph Thomas, the "White Pilgrim," was a well-known itinerant preacher who died in Johnsonburg in 1835. He arrived in town wearing whitewashed boots, astride a white horse, and died after giving one sermon. Leaders of the more orthodox church did not want to bury him in their cemetery, so they buried him in a small plot behind the Dark Moon Inn reserved for the losers of arguments over cards or cockfights. Eleven years later, the Christian Church voted to move his remains to the church cemetery.

The town's name comes from the Johnson family.

KEANSBURG (East —)

Keansburg was named in 1884 for Senator John Kean.

KEARNEY

Kearney, Hudson County, was named for Major General Philip Kearny (1814–62), who lived in town when he was not off fighting

48

wars. He lost his left arm during the Mexican War, fought with the French against Austria in 1859, and led the first New Jersey troops into the Civil War. He was killed at Chantilly in 1862.

KENILWORTH

Kenilworth, Union County, was named for Kenilworth Castle, England, or for the Sir Walter Scott novel of that name.

KENVIL

This Morris County community was formerly known as McCain-ville. Kenvil seems to be a contraction of of McCain to "Ken—," and —ville to "vil." It once advertised itself as the "Home of the Oldest Continuously Operating Dynamite Plant," which was the Hercules Powder Company, founded in 1871.

KEYPORT

Indian deeds of 1665 indicate that Keyport is one of New Jersey's oldest white settlements. At that time, it was called Chinagora. Chinagora oysters are considered a delicacy and, by 1714, oysters were being planted and farmed in the Chinagora Creek.

The name, however, suggests the influence of a chamber of commerce, as Keyport has welcomed an array of celebrities. A ten-year-old Fred Astaire began his theatrical career here in Keyport's Old Palace Hotel in 1910. And the legendary Phineas T. Barnum once owned property in town.

KINGSTON

Kingston was settled about 1700 and was once the preferred dining place for George Washington and the provincial governors.

Washington eluded the British here in January 1777 following the Battle of Princeton. Cornwallis thought the Continental Army would forge ahead to New Brunswick, but Washington recognized the condition of his men as he approached Kingston, and decided to let them rest at Rocky Hill before marching to Morristown.

KINKORA

The name of this Burlington County town is of Indian origin. It is a corruption of *quinkoringh,* the name of the area before William Biddle purchased Biddle's Island.

The post office was established as Kinkora in 1873, even though the name appears as Kinkora Station in 1886. Another source suggests that the name refers to the stronghold of Irish King Brian, but that seems to be a mite far-fetched.

KINNELON

Kinnelon, Morris County, sits upon a portion of the estate of Francis Kinney, of the Sweet Caporal tobacco fortune. The name is a modification of the family name.

The original owner named the community Smoke Rise, after the name given it by the Pequannock Indians meaning "vapors that drifted up from the lakes."

KIRKWOOD

This Camden County village was named in honor of Joel P. Kirkbride, an influential farmer who lived in Waterford.

L

LAFAYETTE

Marie Joseph Paul Ives Roch Gilbert du Motier de Lafayette, the Marquis de Lafayette (1757–1834), is recalled in the name of this Sussex County community.

The marquis, a very young man at the time of the Revolution, fought valiantly at Brandywine and wintered with Washington's troops at Valley Forge. He helped negotiate aid from France which assured victory for the colonists.

LAKEWOOD

A smelter was established in this Ocean County location in 1814 to take advantage of large bog-iron deposits. The name of the community that grew up around the smelter was Washington Furnace. Later, the town became known as Bergen Works, then Bricksburg, for James W. Brick, the ironmaster.

In 1879, two Wall Street brokers purchased 19,000 acres of pine land and built the Laurel House, which entertained such luminaries as Mark Twain, Rudyard Kipling, Oliver Wendell Holmes, and others. By the turn of the twentieth century, there were more than one hundred hotels catering to visitors from New York City.

The name was changed to describe the area.

LAMBERTVILLE

Samuel Coryel started a ferry service in this Hunterdon County locale in 1732. His ferry came into great use during the American

Revolution: it was the point where George Washington crossed the Delaware. Washington stayed in the John Holcombe House before the battles of Germantown and of Monmouth. His son, George Coryel, served as a pall bearer at Washington's funeral.

Until 1812, the town was called Coryel's Ferry or Georgetown. In that year, John Lambert opened a hotel, built a bridge, set up the post office, and renamed the town. The townspeople called it "Lambert's villainy." Lambert was a member of the United States Senate from 1809–15.

LAMINGTON

The Lamington name was first applied to the river in the seventeenth century. The name of this Somerset County community translates from the Algonquian *allametuck*, "within hills at."

LANOKA HARBOR

Originally, this Ocean County harbor community was called Good Luck, then Cedar Creek. It was later called Lanes Oaks, a name which honored—in part—an old resident, George Oakes.

In order to gather some publicity for the port, which was hidden from the highway, the word "Harbor" was attached. Finally, Lanes Oaks Harbor became Lanoka Harbor, a phrase that is much less of a mouthful.

LAUREL SPRINGS

Laurel Springs, Camden County, was founded in 1893, the year after the death of Walt Whitman. Residents thought the town would become popular because the poet used to visit the medicinal springs in a nearby laurel grove for his health. During the spring of 1875, Whitman stayed with friends at the Stafford House.

LAUREL SPRINGS. In his later days, poet Walt Whitman would visit the medicinal springs at this Camden County location in an effort to improve his health. Because of his notoriety, the springs were promoted to the general public the year after his death. [CREDIT: New Jersey State Park Service, Walt Whitman House]

LAVALLETTE

Lavallette was founded in 1887 and was named for Admiral Lavallette. Other sources claim the name came from a local family.

LAWNSIDE

Lawnside was the first black-owned and -governed borough in New Jersey. Purchased in 1840 by abolitionist Quakers, it was named Free Haven because the land was so inexpensive. The original owners arranged for long-term mortgage payments.

After the Emancipation Proclamation, many freed slaves arrived in Free Haven from Snow Hill, Maryland, and renamed their New Jersey home Snow Hill.

When the Philadelphia & Reading Railroad built a station here, it became Lawnside, because the station was located next to a lawn.

LAWRENCEVILLE

Lawrenceville, Mercer County, was originally opened as a post office village in 1798 with the name Maidenhead. The name was changed in 1816 to honor Captain James Lawrence (1781–1813), the naval hero of the War of 1812. Lawrence is noted for his dying cry of "Don't give up the ship!"

LEBANON

This community was founded in 1731 by German immigrants. As more Germans moved down from New York, the entire valley lying northward was called the German Valley.

The name itself comes from the Biblical mountain in Palestine.

LEONARDO

This Monmouth County town was not named for Leonardo da Vinci. The name is an adaptation of Leonard, the name of a prominent local family.

Located not far from Leonardo, the former home of Oscar Hammerstein, Sr., was taken over during Prohibition by the "mob." During the late 1920s, the house concealed a powerful radio transceiver that allowed the liquor smugglers to contact ships and planes from Maine to Florida. In 1929, federal agents raided the place, but everyone arrested was later acquitted of all charges.

The mob boss, Al Lillien, was found dead many years later. He was shot dead after apparently having coffee with his murderer. His killer was never identified or apprehended.

LEONIA

Leonia is most likely a name coined from that of Fort Lee.

LINCOLN PARK

Once a canal port, Lincoln Park, Middlesex County, was named for President Abraham Lincoln.

LINWOOD

Linwood, Atlantic County, dates back at least to the end of the eighteenth century, when the customhouse was located there to accommodate traffic from Somers Point, then the county port-of-entry. Some sources claim the name refers to the local abundance of linden trees.

LITTLE FERRY

Little Ferry, Bergen County, was named for the colonial ferry that crossed Overpeck Creek.

LITTLE YORK

Legend has it that this Hunterdon County village was so named because it was on the road to New York.

LIVINGSTON

This Essex County community was named for William Livingston, governor of New Jersey (1776–90) and signer of the Declaration of Independence.

LODI

Robert Rennie, a French dyer, named this Bergen County town in 1825 in celebration of Napoleon's 1796 victory over the Austrians at the Bridge of Lodi, Italy.

LONG BEACH

The Dutch were the first to notice this area. But it was New England whalers who realized its importance for its proximity to the migration routes of whales. Whaling was this Ocean County community's first industry. The industry died in the early nineteenth century. By the middle of that century, a stagecoach route was established between Philadelphia and the shore, which created the tourism industry that revived the area.

The name is descriptive. Long Beach is located on a barrier island that sits four miles off the coast of Ocean County.

LONG BRANCH (West —)

Long Branch, Monmouth County, was one of America's first

seashore resorts and rivaled Saratoga, New York, in popularity. In fact, Long Branch and Cape May still dispute which is the oldest.

Though miles away from Philadelphia, the high-minded moral codes of the nineteenth-century City of Brotherly Love prevailed in Long Branch. A white flag was flown to signal the ladies' turn on the beach; a red flag, the mens'. Women were required to have male escorts to the edge of the water. This "escort service" became a lucrative business for attractive—and available—young men until the Gay Nineties.

Long Branch was the birthplace of Bruce Springsteen, though most people do not associate him with this town. The town was also the preferred summer home for Presidents Ulysses S. Grant, Rutherford B. Hayes, James A. Garfield, Chester A. Arthur, Benjamin Harrison, William McKinley, and Woodrow Wilson. In 1869, Grant decided to make Long Branch the summer capital of the United States. His successors followed suit. After Wilson, presidents looked elsewhere for a summer White House.

President Garfield died in Long Branch, less than two weeks after being shot by a disgruntled office-seeker in 1881.

Long Branch takes its name from its location on the longest branch (or arm) of the Shrewsbury River.

LONG VALLEY

This Morris County town was settled by Germans around 1740. It was known as German Valley until the beginning of the World War, when it was renamed Long Valley. Such a designation still makes sense, as the valley is ten miles long.

LOVELADIES

We are confident that there are many people at this seashore resort who "love ladies," but that is not the source of its name.

Loveladies, once known as Loveladies Harbor, was named for its original owner, Thomas Lovelady, a well-to-do Englishman of the early eighteenth century who came here to hunt duck.

LOWER BANK

Eric Mullica settled here in 1698. "Mullacker's Plantation" was on land that is occupied by the present community. It is the oldest settlement in the old Randolph Township, and was the first white settlement in the area.

It received its name to differentiate it from Upper Bank, now Green Bank. The post office at this site was established in 1854.

LUMBERTON

This Burlington County community took its name from the colonial lumber industry.

The pioneer landowner of Lumberton was physician Robert Dimsdale, who purchased the land from William Penn in 1683–84 and built a sawmill. Dimsdale Run or Bobby's Run, which flows into the Rancocas, was named for him.

The Lumberton Hotel operated in town beginning in 1790. In 1784 road returns, the town was called Old Long Bridge. The name was changed prior to 1793, and the post office was established as Lumberton in 1848.

LYNDHURST

First called New Barbadoes—an early settler came from the island—the name of this town was changed to Lyndhurst to honor Lord Lyndhurst, a frequent visitor and friend of the landowner.

William R. Travers, a wealthy New York entrepreneur, built many of the houses near the Passaic about 1880. He had a summer house here, complete with a race course. "Boss" Tweed, the leader of Tammany Hall, was also a frequent visitor.

MACOPIN (Upper —), New Jersey

Most translations of the Lenape tongue attribute Macopin's name to a "wild, white potato," or agree with Daniel Brinton's translation in his *The Lenape and Their Legends,* as "where pumpkins are cultivated" or "pumpkin place." Neither explanation really makes any sense for this Passaic County location.

MADISON

Originally settled about 1685, Madison was known as Bottle Hill, after a local tavern that existed from colonial times. Some local historians contend, however, that the name was really Battle Hill, to commemorate two Indian skirmishes fought here. No proof can be brought to support that claim, however, and so Madisonians must be content with their "wet" past.

The tavern opened in 1804 as the Waverly and was the scene of an 1825 fete for Lafayette. This Morris County town was renamed in honor of President James Madison in 1834.

Madison (1751–1836) was a strong supporter of the Constitution and coauthor of *The Federalist Papers.* He also sponsored the first ten amendments to the Constitution, or The Bill of Rights.

MAGNOLIA

This community was originally two separate villages: Turkeytown, to the east, and Scrapetown, to the west. Turkeytown is first mentioned in road returns of 1825, the "road from Turkeytown to Buddtown Cedar Bridge Road." Scrapetown appears on an 1849 map. Magnolia, on the other hand, is first mentioned in 1886.

The Camden County locale was known during the Civil War as Greenland, because of the greenish tinge of the soil. It was renamed to commemorate the trees in the area.

MAHWAH (West —)

This Bergen County locale derives its name from the Mahwah River. The river's name comes from the Algonquian *mawewi*, "meeting place" or "beautiful."

The difficulty in interpreting Indian names to determine place-name origins is the wide choice of definitions. This makes it easy, however, to choose whichever interpretation seems most appropriate.

MALAGA

Malaga, Gloucester County, was founded as a window-glass works in 1780. The factory closed in 1840.

The town probably was named by early glassmakers for the Spanish city of Malaga, though another valid suggestion is that the name came from the Malaga grapes grown in the area.

MANAHAWKIN

This Ocean County community dates back to the mid-eighteenth century. The old Baptist Church here was built in 1758.

The town's name comes from the name of the waterway, which, in translation from the Algonquian, means "small island." Others suggest the name means "good corn land," a reference to the fertility of the soil.

MANALAPAN

Manalapan was founded in the early eighteenth century.

The Presbyterian congregation here was chartered by George II in 1749, making it one of the oldest of the Scotch Presbyterian groups in the area.

A church was built in 1731, but replaced with a larger structure twenty years later. Originally called Old Scots Meeting House, and then Old Freehold Church, the name was subsequently changed to Old Tennent Church to honor its original ministers, the Reverends William and John Tennent, strong supporters of the colonial cause. The name comes from that of the Manalapan River and is derived from the Indian for "good bread" or "good country."

MANASQUAN

Manasquan, Monmouth County, takes its name from the Manasquan River. The name translates from the Indian as "an enclosure with a house." Apparently the braves left their women here when they went off hunting.

Another authority suggests the name comes from *wanasquan*, a "point" or "top."

MANSFIELD

Road returns for 1775 mention a road from Mansfield Meeting House to Foster's Lane, a reference to the Friends meeting house erected at an earlier date.

Some sources indicate this Burlington County name was drawn from the township formed in 1688, which adopted the name of Mansfield, England.

MANTOLOKING (South —)

Mantoloking was founded in 1878 by real estate developers. The name comes from the Indian, and means "sand at."

MANTUA

Though most United States locations with this name derive it from the Italian city, this Gloucester County town does not. The name is derived from the Algonquian tribal name Mana, meaning "sand at," the same root as Mantoloking. (See Mantoloking.)

MANUNKA

The name for Manuka, Warren County, is from the Algonquian "mountain," with the same root as Mauch, as found in Mauch Chunk (see Jim Thorpe, Pennsylvania).

MARGATE. Lucy the Elephant has served many different functions over the years. Today, she is restored and a National Landmark in Margate. (New Jersey Division of Travel and Tourism)

MARGATE CITY

When it was no more than a stretch of sand dunes, this Atlantic County resort area was known as South Atlantic City. Philadelphia real estate broker James V. Lafferty invested in the dunes of South Atlantic City and came up with a unique marketing approach. He advertised buildings in the shape of animals.

Lucy the Margate Elephant was built in 1881, and drew a great deal of attention. Unfortunately, Lafferty was unable to realize a profit on his investment. In 1887, he sold Lucy to John Gertzen, a local resident, who exploited it for tourist purposes. Lucy has been a bazaar, a real estate office, a residence, and a tavern. The author remembers Lucy from his childhood. My grandfather always made it a point to stop there so we could eat our sandwiches—and visit "Mrs. Murphy"—before heading into Atlantic City.

Margate (local residents drop off the "city") was incorporated in 1885. In 1909, it became a city. The name is borrowed from Margate, England.

MARKSBORO

Colonel Mark Thompson, a Revolutionary War soldier, built a gristmill on this site in 1783. This settlement bears his name.

The graves of Thompson's two sons are located in the cemetery adjoining the Marksboro Presbyterian Church.

MARLBORO

Just as with Marlton, the Cumberland County village of Marlboro received its name from the rich local deposits of marl. The neighborhood has several "marl beds," and deep excavations bear evidence to where marl was dug.

Other sources, less willing to dig for the truth, suggest the name comes from the Duke of Marlboro or the English town.

MARLTON

This land was once owned by Joseph Eves and Abraham Lippincott. In 1787, the town was called Evesham; 1800, Swain's; and, in 1812, Rising Sun. Swain's and Rising Sun were both taverns.

Abraham Inskeep, while digging post holes, discovered "marl." Marl is a natural deposit, composed of clay and calcium carbonate, used as a fertilizer for lime-deficient soils. It is also used to soften water and to mix with sand for molding steel. A village was laid out in 1814. In 1841, the Marlton Inn Tavern was opened.

In 1845, the post office's name was changed to Marlton to reflect the area's money crop.

MASONVILLE

There was no settlement in this Burlington County area until 1794, when the highway from the county seat to Cooper Ferries was laid out. In 1849, the intersection was called Five Points. By 1868, when the post office was established, the name was changed to Masonville, for tavern-keeper Solomon Mason.

MATAWAN

Matawan, Monmouth County, was inhabited by at least 1697, when the Hawkins House was built. The house is sometimes known as Minisink Hall, and during the Revolution, the Liberty Boys held meetings in the house.

The name Matawan is taken from the lake. The waterway's name is derived from the name of a tribe, the Matovancons, and was first recorded in 1656.

MAURICETOWN

Settled originally as a port on the Maurice River by the Petersons and Mattocks, this Cumberland County community was originally called Mattock's (or Mattox) Landing.

The name was changed to Mauricetown about 1812. The name is drawn from the river. The river was named for a ship, the *Prince Maurice*, which was captured and burned by Indians at a bend in the stream known as No Man's Friend. The Indians called the river Assveticons. To be honest, Maurice is just so much easier to say.

One authority credits the name origin to Maurice, Count of Nassau and Prince of Orange, the stadtholder of the United Dutch provinces.

MAYS LANDING

Mays Landing, Atlantic County, was founded in 1760 by Philadelphian George May. May traded bog iron and timber for salt, rice, and indigo from the Carolinas. Others suggest the name came from that of Cornelius Jacobson Mey, Dutch navigator for the West Indian Company. (See Cape May.)

In 1937, Mays Landing received a dubious honor when it was named the nudist capital of the nation.

McKEE CITY

McKee City, Atlantic County, was named for Colonel John McKee, a black leader who purchased thousands of acres of land in New Jersey, Pennsylvania, and several southern states. His idea was to develop strong tenant farming in those areas and to establish an integrated military college in Pennsylvania. McKee died before his dreams could come true.

MEDFORD

Medford, Burlington County, was orginally an Indian gathering spot. The first name given to the area by English settlers was Belly Bridge or Bella Bridge, about 1748. There was no real community here until 1767, but by 1772 the town was known as Upper Evesham. Later it became known as Shinntown (even though the 1802 road returns indicate that Ballinger's Saw Mill and Shinntown were one and the same) and Nebo.

The name of Medford was suggested by Mark Reeve, the town eccentric and its first storekeeper, who visited Medford in Massachusetts—and liked the name. Medford was adopted at a town meeting, and became official in 1828 when the post office was established. It means "middle ford."

MEDFORD LAKES

Great confusion exists between Medford and Medford Lakes. Both are in Burlington County. Originally, Medford Lakes was Etna, then Etna Mills. Other sources call it Ballinger's Mills, later Cotoxen. Ballinger's Mills became known as Medford Lakes in 1825, several years after the name Medford became official, and so it would seem logical that the lakes adopted the name. (See Medford.)

MENDHAM

The original name for this Morris County town was the Indian name of Roxiticus. The Black Horse Tavern was established here in either 1735 or 1743 by E. Byram. When told of the quality of neighbors he would be serving, he remarked: "I'll mend 'em." The difference in the dates of origin comes from the owner's idea of when the place was built (1735) and the local sign painter's (1743).

Spoilsports from the 1939 Federal Writers Project state the name comes from Myndham (Mendham), England.

MENLO PARK

Thomas Alva Edison, the "Wizard of Menlo Park," moved to this Middlesex County location in 1874, and spent the next decade inventing. The first Menlo Park was in California, founded in 1854 by two brothers from Menlough, Ireland. (See Edison.)

MERCERVILLE

Mercerville, Mercer County, took its name from the county, which was named for General Hugh Mercer. The town was also known as Sandtown and Five Roads.

Mercer (1725–77) was a physician, trained at the University of Aberdeen in Scotland, who came to the colonies in 1746–47. He settled in what is now Mercersburg, Pennsylvania.

Mercer joined a Pennsylvania regiment and fought during the French-Indian War. He met George Washington during that period. Following the war, he opened an apothecary shop in Fredericksburg, Virginia and practiced his profession. When hostilities with the British broke out, Mercer became a colonel of the 3rd Virginia Regiment. He died of wounds suffered at the battle of Princeton.

METUCHEN

Metuchen, Middlesex County, was named for an Indian chief by the name of Metochshaning (Matochshoning). It was founded by Dutch and English settlers in the late seventeenth century.

MIDDLETOWN

Middletown has a name descriptive of its location. The same is true for Middle Valley, Middleville, Midland Park, and Midvale.

MILFORD (West —)

Originally known as Burnt Mills, because mills located here had been destroyed by fire, this Hunterdon County town was called Lowreytown until 1810.

A ford over the river at this point was later replaced by a bridge, and the mills and the ford blend to give us the name. West Milford was originally called New Milford, to differentiate it from Milford. The town dates back at least to the turn of the nineteenth century.

The existence of a mill at a location often eased the naming process, so we have Millbrook, Millburn, Millhurst, Millington, Milltown, and Milton.

MILLBROOK

The stream, or brook, that runs through this Warren County town supplied power to the gristmill. (See Milford.)

MILLBURN

This community was formerly known as Rum Brook, Riverhead, Vauxhall, Croton, and Millville. It was originally settled in the 1720s by farmers from Elizabeth and Dutchmen from Upper Montclair.

Around 1800, Scotsman Samuel Campbell bought a papermill here. The Scottish word for a stream or brook that produces power for paper- and other types of mills is a "burn," ergo, Millburn. The Diamond Mill produced paper until shortly after World War I. The local name for the community was the "mill-on-the-burn." The mill later became a theater. (See Milford.)

MILLHURST

Some suggest that the name of this Monmouth County community comes from the combination of a mill at the location and the Old English hurst, or "wooded area."

MILLSTONE (East —)

Millstone, Somerset County, began its existence in 1693 when a Dutch smithy settled here with his own tools and anvil. After a few generations, Ed Wycoff took over the operation and continued until 1959, when he retired at age seventy-two.

Millstone was the site of the 1779 raid by Major John Graves Simcoe and his Queens Rangers. They burned down the courthouse.

The local stone was found suitable for use in milling grain.

MILLVILLE

Millville came into being as a river port and in 1755, a settlement there was called Shingle Landing. Forty years later, Colonel Joseph Buck envisioned a town of mills along the Maurice River and laid out town lots. With the discovery of silica sand, the key ingredient in glass-making, the town became a glass-making center. James Lee, an Irishman from Belfast, opened a glass factory in 1806. The Wheaton Glass Company began producing pharmaceutical and chemical glassware in Millville in the 1880s.

In 1884, Dr. T. C. Wheaton opened his pharmacy, later became a licenced physician, and finally entered into the lucrative glass-making business that is known today as Wheaton Industries.

Millville has also been known as Maurice River Bridge.

MINE HILL

The Scrub Oak Mine, founded in 1856, was the main industry of this Morris County town. Residents built their town along the slope of the steep hill that led to the mine.

MIRAMAR

The name of Miramar, Cape May County, first appeared in San Diego County, California. The name translates from the Spanish to mean "behold the sea."

MILLVILLE. "Holly" frequently appears in the names of cities and towns. Here, at Hollyland, U.S.A., in Millville, New Jersey, visitors can see a wide variety of holly plants, with berries of red, yellow, black, or white. (New Jersey Division of Travel and Tourism)

MONROE (—ville)

Monroe, Morris County, and Monroeville, Salem County, were named in honor of President James Monroe.

Monroe (1785–1831) is remembered for his "Monroe Doctrine," in which he warned European powers not to interfere in the Western Hemisphere and promised the U.S. would stay out of European affairs. The doctrine became one-way after his death.

MONTCLAIR (Upper —)

In 1868, West Bloomfield wanted a rail link to New York City; Bloomfield did not. The towns underwent a "divorce," West Bloomfield became Montclair, Essex County, and built the railroad.

The original purchase price for the town, paid to the region's Indians, was "2 guns, 3 coats and 13 cans of rum." Montclair is French for "bright, or clear, mountain."

MOONACHIE

One of the more traditional sources for the name of this community claims that it comes from the name of an Iroquois who invaded the area from New York and collected tribute. This was, of course, long before white politicians took over the practice.

Another source suggests the name is derived from the Lenape language and translates to "groundhog" or "badger."

MOORESTOWN

The early town was laid out in 1682. The eastern portion of town was Chestertown, after Chester Township; the western part, Rodmantown, owned by Clark Rodman in 1722.

By the mid-eighteenth century, both names were discarded and the town was called Chester. Road returns for 1762 mention Moorestown; the 1777 Faden map calls it Moorefields.

The donor of this Burlington County town's name was, without question, Thomas Moore (not the poet, as the Federal Writers Project suggested), the first tavern-keeper. He died in 1760. Moorestown became the official name when a post office was established in 1802.

MORRIS

If Morris were located in Morris County, most likely the name would have come from that earlier naming. But because it appears in Camden County, it seems more likely the name commemorates Revolutionary War financier Robert Morris.

MORRIS PLAINS

Unlike Morris, Camden County, this Morris County community does take its name from its county. The county, in turn, was named to honor Lewis Morris, first governor of New Jersey (1738–46).

MORRISTOWN

About 1710, settlers in Newark learned there was abundant iron ore to be had beyond the Watchung Mountains. A small group of pioneers set out to begin a new industry. They settled in what is now Morristown, but which they called West Hanover.

In 1739, a new county was laid out and named in honor of Lewis Morris. Morristown is the seat of that county.

In 1799, the Aquaduct Company came into being; in 1812, the State Bank; 1836, the Morris County Bank; and, in 1862, the Morristown Bank. Morristown was incorporated in 1865. (See Morris Plains.)

MOUNT—

For a state as flat as New Jersey, it has a large number of towns, villages, and cities using the name "mount." Some of these names are Biblical in reference; others belie description. These include: Mount Pleasant, Mount Rose, Mount Royal, and Mount Tabor.

MOUNT ARLINGTON

Mount Arlington, Morris County, was named in honor of Henry Bennet, Earl of Arlington.

MOUNT BETHEL

This community takes its name from the Bethel of Biblical Palestine.

MOUNT EPHRAIM

Formerly known as Ephraim's Mount or Crossroads in the Town of Gloucester, Mount Ephraim, Camden County, took its name from Ephraim Albertson, a farmer and tavern-keeper.

Albertson's tavern was used as a station on the stage between Philadelphia, Camden, and the coast.

MOUNT FREEDOM

Though the Federal Writers Project considers the name of this community as having come from the Quakers' desire to be free from persecution, the town was called Walnut Grove as early as 1877—a long time after the Quaker influence had waned.

MOUNT HOLLY

This old Quaker town dates back to 1676, as described in a deed conveyed by Edward Byllynge and trustees to Thomas Rudyard and John Ridges. The nucleus of the town originated around 1723–37 with the erection of a tavern and mills.

Originally called Bridgeton (1730–50) for several bridges over the Rancocas Creek, it was known later as Crip[p]s Mount, for John and Nathaniel Cripps, who owned land in this Burlington County locale in 1681.

It became Mount Holly when a post office was established in 1801, though in 1748 it is listed as "Mountholli." The name came from a 183-feet above sea level hill where grew "a store of holley."

The oldest firefighting company in America, the Britannia Fire Company of Bridgetown was organized here in 1752. In 1784, the name was changed to the Mount Holly Fire Company; in 1804, the Relief Fire Company of Mount Holly. The legislature transferred the Burlington County seat from Burlington to Mount Holly in 1779. For two months in that same year, it served as New Jersey's state capital.

MOUNT HOPE

The name of this Morris County town comes from the Mount Hope Furnace that was built here by John Jacob Faesch in 1772.

MOUNT OLIVE

The reference in this Morris County community name is Biblical.

MULLICA HILL

Eric Molica (Mullica) settled his Swedish colony on the shores of the river in 1697. This community bears his name.

MYSTIC ISLAND

The name of this Ocean County town has Algonquian roots. *Mystic* or *mistic* means "big [tidal] river." The name obviously migrated to New Jersey from New London County, Connecticut.

An unusual historical "artifact" rests at this site, the concrete base—three large blocks—of a radio tower built by the Germans in 1912. Some believe the signal to sink the *Lusitania* was broadcast from here. When the United States entered World War I, it took over the tower. It was also used by the military during World War II. It was dismantled in 1949.

NATIONAL PARK

This small Gloucester County community takes its name from the park, set aside by the federal government in 1870 to commemorate the Revolutionary War Battle of Red Bank (Fort Mercer).

During the fall of 1777, Fort Mercer and its sister fort across the Delaware River, Fort Mifflin, held off the navy of Sir Richard Howe, allowing Washington sufficient time to escape to Valley Forge.

NAVESINK

The name for this Monmouth County village comes from the Algonquian, meaning "point at." Sometimes it is transformed into "never sink."

Other authorities imply the name translates to "high land between waters."

NEPTUNE (— City)

This Monmouth County residential area was established in 1881, when it broke away from Neptune Township. The reference is obvious: King Neptune. In the late nineteenth century, Neptune was famous for its clambakes and shore dinners.

NESCO

Nesco, Atlantic County, is a shortening of the Algonquian *Nescochague*. (See Nescopeck, Pennsylvania.)

NESHANIC STATION

Neshanic Station, Somerset County, is from the Algonquian name meaning "double stream at." It is also the name of a tribe. (See Neshaminy, Pennsylvania.)

NETCONG

The source of the name for Netcong, Morris County, appears to be a corruption of the Algonquian *hannek*, "stream," and *onk*, "place of." The town was first settled by workers from nearby iron works and mines.

NEWARK (East —)

The largest city in New Jersey, Newark, Essex County, had its first two streets laid out in 1666 by Captain Robert Treat and thirty families from New Haven, Connecticut and the surrounding environs.

The group had spent five years searching for a site where they could obtain self-government and religious freedom. The Essex County city was founded as a theocracy with the Puritan Congregational Church. Newark was granted a charter in 1713, and the first savings bank established in the state of New Jersey, the Newark Savings Fund Association, was chartered here in 1828.

There have been several suggestions as to the derivation of the name. Some suggest Newark-on-Trent, England, claiming that city was the home of the Reverend Abraham Pierson, pastor of the first church. This has been disproved. The possibilities that remain include: New Ark, with its obvious biblical connotation, or New Work, meaning a new project. The latter seems more logical when one considers that in early documents, Newark was spelled "Nieworke."

East Newark was created in 1895 as a wedge between Harrison and Kearny. The Passaic River separates it from Newark.

NEW BRIDGE

Townspeople used the building of a new bridge over the Hackensack River as sufficient inspiration for naming their town.

NEW BRUNSWICK

Settlers arrived in this area in 1681, when John Inian and ten of his friends from Long Island purchased 10,000 acres here.

New Brunswick began in 1686 when Inian started a ferry crossing in the settlement of Prigmore's Swamp.

Chartered as New Brunswick in 1720, the town was named in honor of George I, also Duke of Brunswick. New Brunswick received a royal charter for a college in 1766. A second charter in 1770 resulted in the establishment of Queen's College. In a manner fitting for a college environment, the institution was opened in a New Brunswick tavern. The college did not have a permanent location until 1809 when it finally took shape. The college was renamed Rutgers in 1825.

NEW DURHAM

This Hudson County community was founded by settlers from Durham. That much is sure, but did they come from Durham Maine, North Carolina, or England?

NEW EGYPT

The tavern in New Egypt, Ocean County, dates back to 1825. One source suggests the name came from Egypt, and was given because of the extensive corn fields in the area.

NEWFOUNDLAND

According to the Federal Writers Project, the name for Passaic County's Newfoundland came from a pioneer's report calling it "The only land we found." Newfoundland, by the way, also resides in Morris County.

Locals contend that Lincoln's secretary of state, William H. Seward, was born here. Historians disagree. They say he was born in Florida, New York.

NEW GRETNA

This Burlington County community was first called Bass River. The name New Gretna appeared when the post office opened in 1850. Between 1849–73, the settlement at the north end of town was called Harmony, and west of the village was called Allentown, as it was settled by Robert Allen in 1716. Both were absorbed into New Gretna. The name comes from Gretna Green, Scotland. Some have suggested that the first attempt at naming leaned toward calling the town New Gretna Green, but cooler minds prevailed.

NEW MARKET

Baptist members of this Middlesex County could not agree on which day to celebrate the Sabbath, Saturday or Sunday. The argument began in 1707 and apparently lasted a century, thereby giving the town its unofficial name of Quibbletown, or, as Revolutionary War soldiers wrote it, Squabbletown.

New Market refers either to a "new" market, or to the English town. (See New Market, Virginia.)

NEW MONMOUTH

New Monmouth, Monmouth County, at the time of its founding was the "new" town in its county.

NEW PROVIDENCE

Falling beams endangered workmen's lives while they were building a new church. When they walked away unscathed, they decided to name their community New Providence.

NEWTON (—ville)

The connotation in the name of Newton, Sussex County, is that it is a "new town." On the other hand, the name of Newtonville, Atlantic County, honors the Newton family.

NEW VILLAGE

New Village, Warren County, was created by the construction of the Morris Canal and settled in 1899 to house workers at the then-projected Edison Cement Plant.

NORMA

Salem County. (See Carmel.)

NORTH—

The directional "north" appears on several New Jersey places, including North Beach, Ocean County, located at the north end of Long Beach; North Branch, Somerset County, laid out in 1884 and located on the north branch of the Raritan River; North Dennis, Cape May County, at the northern end of Dennisville; Northfield, Atlantic County, established on a landowner's "north" field; and Northvale, Bergen County, located in the northern end of the county and situated in a valley.

NORWOOD

Because of its location in the north woods of the county, Norwood, Bergen County, received its name.

NUTLEY

Nutley, Essex County, was named for a resident's estate. It was once called Franklintown, for William Franklin, New Jersey's last royal governor.

O

OAK—

Many New Jersey towns and villages carry the prefix "oak." It signifies the location of oak trees at the town site at the time of naming. These include Oakhurst, Monmouth County; Oakland, Bergen County; Oaklyn, Camden County; Oak Ridge, Passaic County; Oak Tree, Middlesex County; and Oakwood Beach, Salem County.

OAKLYN

This Camden County community was settled by Quakers a few months before the founding of Philadelphia in 1682. (See Oak—.)

OCEAN (— Beach, — City, — Gate, — Grove, — View, —port, —ville)

Ocean, Ocean Beach, Ocean Gate, Oceanport, Oceanville, and all the rest have names that refer to the Atlantic Ocean.

Ocean City, Cape May County, was established by the three Lake brothers (Samuel, James and Ezra Lake)—all Methodist ministers—in 1879 as a "proper" Christian resort. Simon Lake, Jr., a little-known inventor, is the "father of the American submarine."

As a basis for their community, the Lakes decreed that alcohol would not be sold in the town. That restriction is still in effect, though youngsters—and oldsters—can get as much booze as they want from nearby communities.

The first post office to carry the name Ocean City was established in 1881, with William H. Burrell as postmaster. Previously, the area had been known as Peck's Beach, Peter's Beach, Pet's Beach, and New Brighton. Its current name comes from its location on the Atlantic.

Ocean Grove, Monmouth County, was created as a family-oriented Methodist seaside resort. Ocean Grove was founded by the Camp Meeting Association in 1869, making it the first of its kind in New Jersey. Meetings were held under tents or outdoors until 1894, when the Great Auditorium was constructed. Still in use today, the Great Auditorium was once the stage for William Jennings Bryan, Stephen Crane, Enrico Caruso, W.E.B. Dubois, and Will Rogers. In 1970, President Richard Nixon used the stage to present his plans to stop the Vietnam War.

OLD BRIDGE

This Middlesex County town commemorates a bridge that once was located here. Old Bridge was once a stop on the Camden & Amboy division of the Pennsylvania Railroad.

OLD TAPPAN

Old Tappan, Bergen County, was named for a "peaceable" Indian sub-tribe, the Tappans.

Old Tappan was once called Taphaune, "cold stream," for the Sparkhill Creek. Edward Ruttenber, in *Footprints of the Red Men*, states otherwise. He contends that the "name was conferred by the Dutch via old possessions: Tap-Pan-Ooli on the west coast of

Sumatra . . ." Tappan-Huaconga is presumably from a Dutch dialect and means "lowlands," applied to a Dutch possession in Brazil.

OLDWICK

In Anglo-Saxon, the name of this Hunterdon County village translates to "old town." Originally known as Smithfield in colonial times, and then New Germantown, the new name came into vogue during World War I, when anything German was unpopular.

ORADELL

It has been suggested that this Bergen County community's name is a combination of the Latin word *ora*, "mouth" and dell.

ORANGE (East —, West —, South —)

Orange, Essex County, was settled in 1678 as Mountain Plantations. It was not until about 1720 that the Mountain Society erected its first meetinghouse. It was renamed in honor of William, Prince of Orange, later William III. The Orange farmers were anti-colonial rule and, in 1776, came down from the mountains to fight the British.

There was conjecture at one time that the name had Indian overtones. Ruttenber hints that the chiefs of the Raritans called themselves "Oringkes from Orange." Oringkes, he contends, might be a word meaning "original, pure." It makes sense that the Indians might use the latter name to describe themselves and from whence they came. East and West Orange were essentially part of the city of Orange, which was chartered in 1860.

East Orange was the largest of "The Oranges." People from Newark first "went over" in 1678. The town remained part of Orange until the Civil War. It was incorporated as a city in 1899.

South Orange was originally called the Orange Dale section of Orange. It was established as a village in 1869.

West Orange separated from Orange in 1862.

ORTLEY BEACH

Ortley Beach, Ocean County, was settled in 1818 by Mitchell Ortley. He saw the possibility of earning big dollars by building an inlet here, so that ships could avoid the trip south to Barnegat Inlet.

Ortley and his crew dug for four years. When the work was completed, they celebrated. By the next morning, the canal to the inlet had vanished. Instead of deepening it, the running tide had filled it in.

OXFORD

Oxford Furnace, started by Jonathan Robeson before 1747, was located at what was called the Town of Greenwich and operated until 1884. It was the first in the nation to use the Scottish hot-blast process.

Greenwich had been settled about 1730 by John Axford and his partner, a man called Green. Axford's name was apparently mispronounced and misspelled in the naming of the furnace.

In 1824, Tacey Robeson, widow of one of the Robesons, petitioned for the Warren County seat to rest at Oxford. She offered the county two acres of land on the road from Bethlehem to Oxford, plus $5,000 payable thirty days after the completion of the public buildings, and "water for use of same, without expense forever; except of logs—or other means of conveying the water." Belvidere got the nod in 1825.

PACKANACK LAKE

The name for this Passaic County location is a variation of *pequannock*, Algonquian for "small farm." The name was given because of the community's location.

PALISADE

Palisade, Bergen County, received its name because of its location on the Palisades of the Hudson River. (See Palisades Park.)

PALISADES PARK

This Bergen County community was named for the Palisades of the Hudson River, first appearing in print in the early nineteenth century. The name probably was used because the rock formations in the area give the impression of stakes driven into the ground, resembling military pallisades.

PALMYRA

Palmyra, Burlington County, came into existence prior to 1848. In 1849, Isaiah Toy sold 352 acres to the east of his site to Elias Morgan. In 1850, Joseph W. Saunders purchased about 100 acres of Dilworth Buckman's land west of the village and laid out town lots.

A post office was established as Palmyra in 1851.

Palmyra Borough was incorporated in 1823, with its name coming from Palmyra, Syria, made famous by the story of Zenobia.

PARAMUS

The Saddle River was known to the Indians as *Peram-sepus*, the "good, fine and pleasant stream." On the other hand, it has been suggested that the name actually has different roots and means "place of wild turkeys."

Jacob Ephe Banta, a Dutchman who patented land in 1686 in the east section of what is now Bergen County, was one of the earliest recorded pioneers. He was known as "Peremus Kirk."

PARSIPPANY

Parsippany is located near Lake Parsippany, the source of the name. The lake takes its name from an Indian sub-tribe, Parsippanong. In 1844, the name of the town was spelled Parcipany.

Parsippany's history goes back to at least 1718. In that year, local schoolmaster John Richards donated land for the building of the Presbyterian Church. In 1828, the current church replaced the earlier one. Not far from Parsippany is a marker that indicates that the village and forge of Old Boone Town "lies [sic] submerged 60 feet in the valley inundated by metropolitan drinking water."

The name translates as something like, "the place where the river winds and creeps through the valley."

PASSAIC

Hartman Michielsen purchased Menehenicke Island (now Pulaski Park) from the Lenni-Lenape in 1678 and established a fur trading post there. Seven years later, Michielsen and others from Communipaw (Jersey City) obtained the extensive Acquackanonk Patent. During the American Revolution, this Passaic County community was known as Acquackanonk Bridge. The name was changed to Passaic in 1854, for the river. Passaic was chartered as a city in 1873.

The most obvious source for the city's name is the Passaic River. But what does Passaic mean? Depending on the historian, the Indian words *passaic* or *passajeek* can mean "valley or peace," "valley," or "black, silty earth." John G. E. Heckewelder, while saying the name means "valley," believed it came from *pach*, "to split or divide," which makes more sense: the river would split or divide the land.

PATERSON (West —)

Paterson, Passaic County, was named for William Paterson (1745–1806), governor of New Jersey at the turn of the nineteenth century. In 1678–79, Dutch settlers obtained the first tract of land within the present bounds of the town.

Secretary of the Treasury Alexander Hamilton was inspired by the potential power of the Great Falls of the Passaic River and organized the Society for the Establishing of Used Manufactures. He planned Paterson as America's first industrial city. Pierre L'Enfant, the Washington, D.C., planner, designed Paterson's three-tiered raceway that harnessed the falls and supplied water power to the neighboring mills. At the time Hamilton picked the name Paterson, it had "no more than ten houses." Governor Paterson, it must be explained, signed the act incorporating Hamilton's society. The incorporation of his name was "an essential provision of the statute."

Samuel Colt manufactured the first successful repeating revolver in the Old Gun Mill at Van Hunter and Mill Streets in Paterson. Washington Irving memorialized the city in the 1807 poem, "The Falls of the Passaic."

In 1828, Paterson was the site of America's first factory strike.

PAULSBORO

Paulsboro began in 1681, when 250 settlers arrived in this Gloucester County area. Philip Paul, for whom the town is named, arrived four years later. His family Bible is still in the borough hall.

PEAPACK

The name of Peapack, Somerset County, seems to be a corruption of the Algonquian *paupock*, "quail."

PEMBERTON

Pemberton, Burlington County, was settled by Quakers before 1690. It was first called Hampton Hanover, because it was situated in both Northampton and Hanover Townships. Later it became New Mills, and in 1856 took the current name in honor of Philadelphian James Pemberton, a shipping merchant.

PENNINGTON

Johannes Lawrenson purchased the land in this Mercer County area in 1697. The town was originally called Queenstown, for Queen Anne. Because of its insignificance, it was renamed Penny Town. In 1714 it assumed its current name, which retains some of the insignificance—with a touch of sophistication.

PENNSAUKEN

In 1633, 155 English colonists arrived and built Fort Eriwoman, on the eastern shore of what is now called the Pennsauken Creek. The fort, abandoned four years later, was named for a local Indian chief. The Swedes took over, and controlled the abandoned fort until 1664.

Pennsauken was a stagecoach stop between Philadelphia and New York until 1830, when it was put out of business by the Camden & Amboy Railroad, and later the Camden & Atlantic.

The name is apparently a combination of Penn, for William Penn, and *sauk, sakuwit,* or *sacunk,* meaning the "outlet of a small stream into a larger one."

Over the years, the name has appeared in countless forms, including Pensaukin, Pennsawken, Pensoakin, Pemisoakin, Pemsokin, Pimsauquim, Pimsawquim, Pennysoaking, Pensokin, Pennsoakin, Pansawkin, and Pemisawkin.

PENNS GROVE (— Neck, —ville)

Towns using Penn in their names were frequently named for the Penn family, as is the case in these towns.

Penns Grove, Salem County, began in about 1732, when Andrew Helm built his tavern here. The first community, because of the tavern-keeper, was called Helm's Cove.

Helm's tavern, still standing, received a cannonball in its wall from a British ship in 1776. The shot was in retaliation for the town's celebration over the Crown vessel being grounded.

PEQUANNOCK

In *The Indians of New Jersey,* William Nelson suggests the name is derived from the Algonquian *paau qu'un auke,* "land made clear for cultivation." This is also the name of the stream that flows across the Highlands from Hamburg, New Jersey. It was spelled Pachquakonck by Van Der Donck in 1656. *The Origin of New Jersey Place Names* suggests the name originated with a sub-tribe, Pequannuc.

It is likely the name of this Morris County village was derived from that of the lake.

PERTH AMBOY

In 1687, the Proprietors of East Jersey called this place New Perth. The settlers had begun turning the wilderness into home as early as 1651. Augustine Herrmann, a Dutchman from Staten Island, was one of the first. When the British took possession, the charter to Woodbridge in 1669 stated "that Ambo Point be reserved . . . to be disposed of by the lord proprietors."

In 1685, the Earl of Perth permitted 200 Scots to migrate here. Many of them were dissenters who came from English prisons. The town was renamed New Perth in the earl's honor. Although that was its official name, the locals still refered to it as Ambo and then Ambo Point.

The name of Amboy was the result of a lengthy transformation through the Indian tongue. From the original *ompage,* a "point or elbow of land," came *emboyle, amoyle,* and finally Amboy. Why this name eventually merged with Perth is unknown. A local legend, however, jokingly suggests an answer:

When the Earl of Perth visited this area, in full Scottish regalia—including kilt, an Indian said: "Perth am girl." Not so, the earl responded; "Perth am boy." What a waste of a great story! He never visited the American continent.

PETERSBURG

Formerly known as Littleworth, this Cape May County town was called Petersburgh until 1893, when they took the "h" out of the name, changing the sense from German to English. The name recalls the first name of one of its early settlers.

PINE—

Pine Beach, Ocean County, takes its name from the appearance of pine trees near the beach during the early stages of development.

Pine Brook, Monmouth County, and Pine Brook, Morris County, take their names from the waterway.

In German, wald is a forest, so Pinewald, in Ocean County, was once a "pine forest."

PISCATAWAY (— Town)

The name of Piscataway, Middlesex County, is derived from the Algonquian *piscataqua,* "fork of the river at," or "divided tidal river." It is also probably the name of a tribe.

PITMAN

Pitman was known as the Camp Meeting Town. It is one of the survivors of the summer religious camps that came into being after the Civil War. Its name comes from the Pitman family.

At Pitman Grove, where the Pitman Grove Camp Meetings are held, stands the Tabernacle. From the Tabernacle, twelve streets radiate out like spokes on a wheel. This arrangement follows the plan of the Holy City found in the Book of Revelation. Famous fire-and-brimstone minister Billy Sunday preached here.

PLAINFIELD (North —, South —)

By the seventeenth century, fur traders from Scotland and Holland were settling in this Union County locale. Along with these traders, the Quakers arrived. By 1788, they were so well emplaced that they had to build a larger meetinghouse to accommodate their flock.

Plainfield is geographically located in an area of extensive plains, though one source suggests it was named after a resident's estate; another, because it is located on a "beautiful plain."

PLEASANT MILLS (— Plains)

Pleasant Mills was originally called Sweetwater. The name was changed in 1821, when Philadelphian William Lippincott built a cotton textile factory here, operated by water power, called Pleasant Mills. Lippincott later also opened a paper mill here.

PLEASANTVILLE

This "pleasant" town in Atlantic County is noted as the home of the Lake family, whose members founded Ocean City. (See Ocean City.)

PLUCKEMIN

Pluckemin, Somerset County, began its life before 1735. In that year, a small log church atop First Mountain became home to the Church of the Raritan, or the Church in the Hills. This marked the first meeting of the Lutheran synod in America. The meeting, or "consistorium" as the founders called it, was arranged to protest the high fees the Reverend Johann Wolf was charging for sermons, baptisms, and funerals—twice the going rate in Hackensack. The meeting did not make him repent his flawed way, and he was re-placed. What would have happened if he were selling indulgences?

Some sources list this name as of Indian origin. Others note that there is a Pluckemin in Scotland.

POMONA

Pomona was named for the Roman goddess of fruit trees.

POMPTON LAKES (— Plains)

The name originates with a sub-tribe of the Lenape, the Pomptons (even though through Anglification it sounds English). Pompton's first homes were built about 1682. The area, settled largely by the Dutch, was noted for its early iron furnaces.

Not far from town is the Terhune Memorial Park, Sunnybank, where Albert Payson Terhune (1872–1942) lived. Terhune, a dog fancier and author, wrote *Lad, A Dog* and other books about collies. "Sunnybank," his home, was razed before dog fanciers could raise sufficient funds to restore it. It has since become a memorial park, with a statue of a collie by the lakeside.

The name of Pompton Lakes, Passaic County, also refers to the tribe.

Pompton Plains, Morris County, was once the home of Dan Voorhees, a leader of Tammany Hall for many years. He was active in politics well past his hundredth birthday.

PORT COLDEN

Cadwalader B. Colden was president of the Morris Canal, and this was named in his honor. Port Colden, Warren County, was once a port on the canal.

PORT ELIZABETH

The Swedes built a church in this Cumberland County port of entry as early as 1637, but in 1790, Elizabeth Bodeley, a widow from Salem County, purchased the land and laid out a village. The town carries her name.

Abolitionists gathered freed New Jersey slaves here and sent them off to Haiti as farmers; most of them returned discouraged. Because of the fine sand in the area, James Lee opened Eagle Glass Works here in 1799. Seven years later, he moved on to Millville.

PORT MONMOUTH

As the name implies, Port Monmouth is "the port" for Monmouth County. It is an old community. The Whitlock-Seabrook House (the Spy House) located here was built in 1663, the first house constructed on the Jersey Shore.

During the Revolution, Colonel John Stilwell sent messages concerning British ship movements to patriots staying at the house, which was an inn at the time. Using this information, the seafaring rebels attempted to sink or damage the enemy's fleet.

PORT MURRAY

Port Murray, Warren County, came into existence when the Morris Canal opened in 1834. And, like Port Colden, it was named for an official of the canal company.

PORT NORRIS

This Cumberland County locale was formerly Dallas Ferry, named for William Dallas who, in 1738, operated the ferry service across the Maurice River. The name was changed in 1810 to that of the oldest son of Joseph Jones, a prominent citizen.

PREAKNESS

The name "Preakness," we are sorry to note, has nothing to do with horse racing. It does, however, have something to do with another equine: the deer. *The Origin of New Jersey Place Names* suggested that Preakness comes from *parekuis*, or "young buck." On the other hand, it has also been suggested the root word is Dutch. In Dutch, *preeken* means to preach. Preakness is located in Passaic County.

PRINCETON (— Junction)

The Quaker settlement of Stony Brook was established in the 1690s near the plantation of Captain Henry Greenland. Greenland had arrived fifteen years earlier.

The Mercer County town's name was changed in 1724 to Princeton ("prince town," because of its proximity to Kingston or "king's town"). In 1756, the College of New Jersey, founded in Elizabeth by royal charter in 1746, moved here. The name of the college did not change until 1896.

When New Jersey changed from a colony to a state, legislators met in Nassau Hall and adopted the state's constitution and the great seal. They also inducted their first governor.

Following his success at Trenton in January 1777, George Washington decided to launch a surprise attack on British forces at Princeton. Unfortunately, the British surprised the colonials. Pennsylvania troops, under Brigadier General Hugh Mercer, were caught by the British at the bridge at Stony Brook. The Continental troops were able to fire off three musket volleys before falling under a British bayonet attack.

Washington rushed up with reinforcements, but it was too late to save Mercer. He was knocked off his horse and bayonetted to death. The British retreated to Nassau Hall where, after a fierce battle, they surrendered.

PROSPECT PARK

According to the Federal Writers Project, Prospect Park, Mercer County, borrowed its name from a section of Brooklyn.

QUAKERTOWN

Quakertown, as the name implies, was named for its Quaker settlers. The Quakers built a stone meetinghouse in this Hunterdon County area in 1720. The meetinghouse is still in use.

Q

RAHWAY

Originally settled by descendents of settlers from Elizabethtown, the first house in this Union County city was built about 1720.

R

During the American Revolution, this city was called Spanktown, because of a well-known local physician who habitually spanked his wife, regardless of what people thought. That name appears in Washington's military maps of the area.

Rahway is allegedly a variation of Rockaway, but local legend prefers to advance the notion that the town was named for an Indian chief by the name of Rahwack who lived where the town now stands. Another source contends the name comes from the Lenni-Lenape *na-wak-way*, "in the middle of a forest."

RANCOCAS (— Woods)

The land for Rancocas, Burlington County, was located by Dr. Daniel Wills in 1681 and sold by his descendents as town lots. A Friends Meeting House was built in 1772. Early colonists lived in caves along the Rancocas Creek before they built their village.

The first post office was established in 1836 as Ancocas. Early settlers did not think the Indians used the "R," though the local waterway was called Rancocas, or the Northampton River. In 1838, the post office was reestablished as Rancocas.

The creek is the probable donor of the town's name, and is derived from the Ancocus, a sub-tribe of the Lenape.

RARITAN

Raritan, Somerset County, takes its name from the Raritan River. The river's name was derived from the Indian *lalatan*, "forked river" or from a variation that translates to "stream overflows."

RAVEN ROCK

This town was called Bool's Island in 1841. It was renamed to commemorate Edgar Allan Poe's masterpiece, "The Raven."

RED LION

In 1787, this town was known as Corless Tavern, because William

Corless established his drinking spot there. The name was changed when the tavern changed hands. Err Joyce renamed the tavern "Red Lion" about 1810. Another source suggests the name was Red Lion from about 1710, but it seems more likely that the earlier date is a typographic error.

The Red Lion post office was opened in 1877.

REPAUPO

Repaupo was colonized in the early seventeenth century by Scandinavians who were later replaced by the Swedes.

The name is probably a word in the Algonquian tongue.

RIDGEWOOD

Ridgewood, Bergen County, was settled by rich Dutch farmers in the seventeenth century. The name, we are told, was selected to describe its location.

Nearby is the Old Paramus Reformed Church, which was built about 1800. In an earlier edifice at the site, Aaron Burr and Theodosia Prevost were married in 1782, and General Charles Lee was court-martialed for his behavior at the Battle of Monmouth and dismissed from the Continental Army.

RINGOES

Named for Ringo's Old Tavern, established in 1720 by John Ringo, this Hunterdon County community is the only post office in the world with that name.

John Ringo was forced into the tavern business out of necessity: he was frequently visited by relatives and friends who expected food and lodging. The original tavern was destroyed by fire in 1840, but it was replaced. The first settlers were Germans who developed a trading center in the Amwell Valley area. A 1721 survey called it "the palatin's land."

RINGWOOD

Ringwood, Passaic County, was an iron mining and forging center. The Ringwood Furnace was located on the northern branch of the Pequannock River, also called the Ringwood River, and occupied the site of a small forge built by Cornelius Board in 1739. The Ringwood Company was formed in 1740 by the Ogden family: Colonel Josiah, David, Sr., David, Jr., John, Jr., and Judge Uzal Ogden. Two years later they erected the furnace.

A German entrepreneur, the self-styled "Baron" Peter Hasenclever, tried to exploit the resources of Ringwood when he purchased the furnace in 1764. He formed the American Iron Company in London, but after he had spent 54,000£—without turning a profit—he was replaced. His successor was Robert Erskine, who arrived in the colonies in 1771 to manage the operation.

When the colonies declared their independence, Erskine joined them and became Washington's surveyor general and chief mapmaker. Ringwood's forges worked hard during the Revolution, producing cannon, munitions, and much of the iron chain that was used across the Hudson at West Point to prevent the passage of British ships. The mine produced iron steadily until it closed in 1931.

The Ringwood name derives from the town in England.

RIO GRANDE

This Cape May County community dates back to colonial times, but under the name Hildreths.

A post office was established in 1849, with Jeremiah Hand as postmaster. The name of the town allegedly comes from a popular song of the Mexican War.

RIVERSIDE

Prior to 1852, this town was an ordinary farm. In that year, Samuel Bechtel, Jr., had his farm surveyed and laid out into town lots. It was settled by the second wave of German settlers.

Before a post office was established, the section along the railroad tracks was known locally as Goat Town. In 1854, the post office opened in the name of Progress. Legend has it that Bechtel himself provided the name.

Because the town is located at the confluence of the Rancocas and Delaware Rivers, Riverside seemed a much more appropriate name. The name of the post office was changed in 1867. Riverside became a township in 1890.

RIVERTON

Riverton, Burlington County, was laid out as a village in 1851–52 on Caleb Atkinson's land, which had been purchased by Joseph Lippincott. It is a "town on the river"; the Rancocas, that is.

ROADSTOWN

Roadstown is a crossroads village in Cumberland County.

The Cohansey Baptist Church was founded in Roadstown about 1737. First known as Kingston, a name discarded when kings became unpopular, it was later called Sayre's Cross Roads, for Ananias Sayres, sheriff of the county on two different occasions. It has also been known as Cross Roads and Roads Town. Its present name notes the fact that four roads intersect here.

ROCKAWAY

The city of Rockaway is located on both sides of the Rockaway River. The river probably derives its name from Rechouwakie, "place of sands," from l'eckwa, "sand," and auk, "place." The *Historical Collection of the State of New Jersey* indicates there was a sub-tribe in the area, the Rockawack, that also might have given its name to the waterway.

Another authority indicates the name is drawn from *reckawackes* or *achewek*, meaning "bushy" or "difficult to cross."

ROCKLEIGH

Rockleigh, Bergen County, was named, it is said, for the Virginia estate of Robert L. Tait, its first mayor.

ROEBLING

Roebling was a company town established by John A. Roebling (1806–69), the Prussian founder of a steel-cable factory. Roebling was the first person to recognize the strength of steel wire and to weave wire into cable. He and his company were known to engineers nationwide for building the Brooklyn Bridge, George Washington Bridge, and Golden Gate Bridge, among others.

The town came into existence when Jacob D. Hoffner put together two tracts of land, one of which he sold to Roebling for the mill. The town was owned by the Roebling family until 1946, when the utilities were sold to the township and homes were sold to private individuals.

The John A. Roebling Sons & Company operated the plant from 1900–55.

ROOSEVELT

Originally an experimental project of Franklin D. Roosevelt's Resettlement Administration, Roosevelt, Monmouth County, came into existence in 1935 as Jersey Homesteads.

Two hundred houses were built here for garment workers from the tenements of Philadelphia and New York. The houses were equipped with all the modern conveniences, including air conditioning. Each family contributed $500 to a general equipment fund, and agreed to buy the home on a long-term mortgage. A 414-acre farm and a women's clothing factory were part of the experiment. Profits were to be equally divided among all residents.

One purpose of the experiment was to prove that sweatshop industries concentrated in one area could be decentralized, and their workers improve their living conditions. After considerable federal investment, the farm was declared unworkable; the clothing factory, unsuccessful. The only way out was for the government to open housing to anyone who wanted to live there. When President Roosevelt died in 1945, the residents changed the name of their town to honor him.

ROSELLE (— Park)

Thomas Edison once had a laboratory in this Union County locale, where he installed the world's first electric lighting plant. Roselle was the first community in the world to have its streets lit by incandescent bulbs.

Abraham Clark (1725–94), who signed the Declaration of Independence, was born here.

Roselle and Roselle Park are separated by the tracks of the old Central Railroad of New Jersey.

ROSENHAYN

Cumberland County. (See Carmel.)

RUMSON

The name for Rumson, Monmouth County, is a shortened version of the Algonquian *navaarumsuck*. (See Navesink.)

RUNNEMEDE

Settled in 1683, the Quakers called this city New Hope. Later, the name was changed to Marlboro. Finally, the name was changed in 1844 to Runnemede, in memory of Runnymede, England. Imitation of the name honors the signing of the Magna Carta.

RUTHERFORD (East —)

Rutherford, Bergen County, was laid out in 1862 on the land of John Rutherford, son of a retired British officer but an active patriot and personal friend of George Washington.

Rutherford is the home of Farleigh Dickinson University. The university was inspired by several academics involved in experimental studies at the former New College of Columbia University. One thought that his father-in-law's Rutherford home would make an ideal location.

With the assistance of banker and surgical-instrument maker Farleigh S. Dickinson, the seat of higher learning was incorporated. It opened in 1942 as a two-year junior college and moved to four-year status six years later. It became a university in 1956.

East Rutherford—formerly known as Boiling Springs Township, for a spring that bubbled on the surface—is separated from Rutherford by the tracks of the former Erie Lackawanna Railroad.

SADDLE BROOK
This Bergen County village derived its name in the same way as did Saddle River. (See Saddle River.)

SADDLE RIVER (Upper —)
This community, "previous to the formation of Passaic co., comprised within its limits what is now Machester of that co. It was then shaped like a saddle, from which it derived its name."

Local tradition has it that the Scottish land speculators, Captain Nichols and Richard Stillwell, who bought these several thousand acres from the Indians, saw in the land a strong resemblance to Saddle Burn in Argyleshire, Scotland.

SALEM
This Salem County area was settled in 1675 by Quakers, led by John Fenwick. They called their settlement New Salem, a name used by the Puritans in Massachusetts in 1629. The town was the first permanent English-speaking settlement on the Delaware River. The word is an abbreviation of Jerusalem, and roughly means "peace," from "shalom."

SCOTCH PLAINS
Scotch Plains, in Union County, was settled by Scottish Quaker and Presbyterian immigrants about 1684. The town's name combines the first settlers and the type of land on which they settled.

SEA ISLE CITY
Sea Isle City, in Cape May County, was developed by Charles K.

Landis, who also developed the towns of Hammonton and Vineland. His vision for this town was to clone Venice, Italy, but it didn't work out. Sea Isle City more closely resembles Ocean City, except you can buy liquor in Sea Isle.

Formerly known as Ludlam's Beach and Strathmere, Landis changed the name in 1880. A post office under the name of Sea Isle City opened in 1882.

The name describes its location near the seashore.

SEAVILLE (South —)

Seaville is an old village settled by English Quakers. The Old Cedar Meeting House was built in 1716, to replace a circa-1700 log building.

A post office opened as Seaville at this locale in 1849.

SECAUCUS

The name for this Hudson County city comes from the Algonquian for "salt sedge marsh."

Another authority, however, compares the word to *sekakes*, used by the Indians to refer to snakes.

SERGEANTSVILLE

Prior to 1827, this Hunterdon County community was known as Skunktown. When the post office was opened in that year, a poll was taken and Skunktown was history. But then a crucial decision had to be made. Should the town be named after the Thatchers or the Sergeants? A count of family members tipped the scale, and the Sergeant family won.

SHARPTOWN

Until the time of the American Revolution, Sharptown was called Blessington, the name of the Sharp family's plantation. Prior to the Civil War, it served as a station on the Underground Railroad.

SHILOH

There are some who say the town of Shiloh, Cumberland County, was named by a Union army veteran to commemorate the Civil War Battle of Shiloh. Stronger evidence exists for another name source.

Cohansey Corners, the original name, was a large settlement on the Cohansey Creek founded by the Seventh Day Baptists who fled persecution in England in 1705.

This denomination was composed of those individuals who worked on Sundays, but observed the seventh day (Saturday) according to the Bible. When they were moving their frame church to a new location in 1771, they reached Six Corners at sundown on Friday. All work stopped because, as their pastor, Jonathan Davis, said: "The Ark of the Lord resteth [on the Sabbath] at Shiloh." The name change from Cohansey was achieved by agreement of the townspeople.

SHIP BOTTOM

There are a number of legends attached to the name of this Ocean County town. One has it that during an 1817 storm, Captain Stephen Willits came upon a ship run aground—bottom up, a victim of the deadly Barnegat Shoals. His men heard a tapping sound, and cut through the hull. From the gaping hole emerged a beautiful young woman, speaking a strange language that some suggest was Spanish. She sank to her knees and traced the sign of the cross in the sand. Someone thought she said New York, and they shipped her off there—never to hear from her again.

Another tale, dating back to 1846, is basically the same, except the young lady remained in town and married a sailor.

The truth of the matter is that in 1854, the *Powhattan* sank near here with a loss of 354 crew members. Dr. William A. Newell, known as the father of the U. S. Life Saving Service, later to become the U. S. Coast Guard, established a lifesaving station at this location.

As usual, the truth is not half the fun of the legend.

SHREWSBURY

Shrewsbury, Monmouth County, was founded in 1664 by members of the Congregationalist Church.

By the end of the seventeenth century, bog iron was being mined at this location, and Shrewsbury became the first ironworks in the Province of New Jersey. By 1674, James and Henry Leonard had their works operating here. Two years later, Colonel Lewis Morris and his associates opened another iron mine. The name comes from the nearby Shrewsbury River. The river takes its name from the English city.

SMITHVILLE

Smithville, Burlington County, occupies one of the first settled areas of New Jersey. The first name was Parker's Mills, because Jacob Parker built a dam and established a grist- and sawmill around 1780. Later on, it was called French's Mills. In 1828, Jonathan L. and Samuel Shreve, pioneers in the calico trade, came from Springfield Township, built a fabric factory, and called the town Shreveville (or Shreeville or Shreveport). The name was changed to Smithville to honor Hezekiah B. Smith, who operated the H. B. Smith Machine Plant there. The post office, as Smithville, was established in 1866.

Smith manufactured high-wheel Star bicycles. He built a locally famous bicycle railway—a monorail, known as the Hotchkill Bicycle Railroad—from Smithville to Mount Holly. Smith also served in Congress. He provided for his own burial in an iron casket imbedded in cement set between iron slabs. His remains are buried in St. Andrew's Cemetery, Mount Holly.

SOMERDALE

Somerdale, Camden County, once had a Noah's Ark House. An old sea captain, who believed the world would end with a flood, built his home in the shape of an inverted ark. He figured that the flood would upend his house and he would be able to sail away, with the roof serving as the hull.

SOMERS POINT

John Somers, a Quaker, established his plantation in 1693 in this Atlantic County locale. In 1726, his son, Richard Somers, built the Somers Mansion, which is still standing with bricks transported from Leyden, Holland. The roof is the house's most unusual feature; allegedly built by a shipwright, it resembles a ship's hull. Old-time residents contend that if the house tipped over in a flood, it would float safely away. (See Somerdale.)

John Somers' grandson, Richard, was born in the house in 1778, and grew up to be a brilliant naval officer. By the time he was twenty-six, he held the rank of commander, in charge of the schooner *Nautilus* during the war with Tripoli.

Somers was quickly given command of the *Intrepid* and charged with destroying the enemy fleet and liberating the captain and crew of the *Philadelphia*. An hour after the valiant Somers set out, his ship, laden with explosives, was blown up by the Turks.

SOMERVILLE

Originally called Raritan, Somerville is the seat of Somerset County. Though settled in the late seventeenth century by Dutch traders, the town only took form with the railroad's arrival in the nineteenth century.

SOMERVILLE. The Dutch Parsonage in Somerville was built in 1751, and stands in memory of the contribution made by the Dutch in New Jersey. (New Jersey Division of Travel and Tourism)

In 1842, Somerville became the western terminus of the Elizabethtown & Somerville Railroad (later the Central Railroad of New Jersey). Four years later, the first telegraph line between New York and Philadelphia followed the railroad line.

Though the name might appear to be a combination of Somerset and village, some authorities contend it was named for an English nobleman.

SPOTSWOOD

Before the Revolution, there were two forges operating at Spotswood, Middlesex County; one opened as early as 1763. Unlike many others, the owners of the Spotswood forges remained loyal to the crown.

The forges were destroyed by 1780.

SPRAY BEACH

At one time there must have been a contest to come up with unique, tourist-attracting names for resort communities on the Jersey shore. This Ocean County community's name, developed by some chamber of commerce, is descriptive of that soft, slightly salty mist that wafts up from the beach on sultry summer nights.

SPRINGDALE

Springdale, Sussex County, was the site of some interesting Revolutionary War activities.

James (Bonnell) Moody, a "plain, contented farmer," launched several raids on the unsuspecting countryside and was rewarded with a lieutenancy in the British Army. He released several Tory prisoners from Newton, staged mock "Indian" raids, and intercepted General Washington's dispatches. He also tried to capture Governor Livingston and rob congressional archives.

In 1783, while a guest of Sir Henry Clinton in London, Moody wrote an account of his exploits in which he described his hideout, a rock ledge that juts out twenty-five feet from the face of a cliff. That ledge is now called Moody's Rock.

Springdale's name comes from the local natural springs.

SPRINGFIELD

The earliest accurate record of settlement of this community dates to 1717, when the Briant family arrived from Hackensack.

During the American Revolution, British and Hessian troops torched the town on 23 June 1780, burning all four buildings to the ground. When the colonial defenders ran short of wadding, or powder patches, the Reverend James Caldwell, a minister from Elizabeth and chaplain to Dayton's New Jersey regiment, broke into the First Presbyterian Church and gathered an armful of Watts' hymns. "Give 'em Watts, boys," he shouted. "Give 'em Watts."

Loyalists called Caldwell the "high priest of the Revolution," but to the patriots he was the "fighting parson." Just one more reason to rejoice that history is written by the victors!

It is possible the name was brought here from Springfield, England.

SPRING LAKE (— Heights)

Both Spring Lake and Spring Lake Heights, Monmouth County, are located on the Atlantic Ocean. Spring Lake has been called "The Irish Riviera," because of the large number of Irish men and women who vacation here. Both places take their names from Spring Lake.

SPRINGSIDE

Springside, Burlington County, has gone by this name since 1920. Before that it was known as Fountain Woods Station.

The first pure water for Burlington was piped from this area in 1804 when the Burlington Aqueduct Company was organized. The water came from nearby Sylvan Lakes.

STAFFORDVILLE

Staffordville takes its name from the old Stafford Forge. The forge was built in 1797 and was located about two miles from town.

Stafford Forge was originally called Westecunk Forge and owned by John Lippincott. The forge proved unprofitable and closed by 1839.

STANHOPE

During the American Revolution, Stanhope was known as Sussex Iron Works. In 1821, Sussex boasted the first American iron furnace fired by anthracite.

The Sussex County town grew up around the furnace. In fact, the workers' houses were styled after French peasant cottages.

Stanhope is the name of one of the residents.

STANTON

Stanton, Hunterdon County, was named for Edwin M. Stanton, Lincoln's secretary of war.

Stanton (1814–69) administered the Union army during the Civil War, only to be ousted by President Andrew Johnson for demanding stronger Reconstruction measures than the president proposed.

STELTON (North —)

In the summer of 1912, the New York *Call* ran advertisements urging weary city dwellers to "get back to the land."

By the fall, a small group of German socialists and a few others raised enough money to buy a farm. The group, known as the Fellowship Farm Cooperative Association, created a socialist experiment: acreage in this Middlesex County locale was parceled out based on the amount of investment.

They purchased the Letson Farm and set to work. The farming was unsuccessful, but their poultry experiment thrived. Some of the "colonists," however, continued to commute to their jobs in New York and elsewhere. Though the group saw some scattered successes, the program as a whole failed.

The town's name, by the way, is an anagram of Letson, the farm's name.

The nearby Francisco Ferrar Colony was another experiment, built around a "progressive" school presenting an anarchistic philosophy. Teachers included Manuel Komroff, Will Durant, and Rockwell Kent.

STIRLING

The Morris County town of Stirling commemorates William Alexander, a general on Washington's staff and the self-styled Lord Stirling.

Alexander (1726–83) was the son of a prominent lawyer and patriot, James Alexander, who was disbarred for a year for defending John Peter Zenger in the classic First Amendment case.

He served in the French and Indian War and, in 1756, accompanied his commander, Massachusetts Governor Shirley. The next year, Alexander defended the governor against charges of mismanaging military operations. While in England, Alexander attempted to claim the earldom of Stirling but was unable to make it official. Nonetheless, he affected the title of Lord Stirling.

William Alexander married the sister of New Jersey's Governor Livingston and became prominent in state affairs. "For some reason," George Washington's biographer wrote, "a field operation entrusted to Stirling was apt to get snarled. Neither he nor his Chief would know exactly why plans went astray, but they did."

STOCKTON

This Hunterdon County town was named for the Stockton family, the most illustrious of which was Richard Stockton, who signed the Declaration of Independence.

The principal attraction in Stockton was the Stockton Inn, built in 1832 by Asher Johnson. It served as a stop on the stagecoach route. Legend has it that the hotel was the inspiration for the song, "There's A Small Hotel." A small waterfall graces the outdoor terrace of the Stockton Inn.

Richard Stockton (1730–81) was considered one of the most eloquent lawyers in the middle colonies within ten years of his admission to the bar in 1754.

His credentials were impeccable. He was married to Elias Boudinot's sister; his own sister was married to Boudinot; his eldest daughter was married to Benjamin Rush, making his family one of the rarest in America: three members signed the Declaration.

Stockton served as a member of Congress. Shortly after the proclamation of the Declaration of Independence, he was captured by the British and imprisoned in the infamous Provost Jail in New York City. His imprisonment shattered his health, and he died at age fifty-one.

STONE HARBOR

Stone Harbor was built on seven manmade lagoons.

Originally known as Stoneharbor when the post office was

opened in 1894, the town was incorporated in 1914. The name was changed to its present form in 1931. It refers to Captain Stone, who opened the harbor.

A noted resting place for herons, the Stone Harbor Bird Sanctuary is the only heronry in the nation situated within a town.

STRATFORD

The old White Horse Hotel, which served as the stagecoach stop, post office, and town hall, was located in Stratford. The hotel gave its name to the White Horse Pike (now U.S. 30). The eighteenth-century White Horse had a simple sign: a white horse on a plain wooden board.

Because of its location and date of founding, it appears likely that this Camden County community was named after the Stratford-on-Avon, England.

SUCCASUNNA

Most historians believe that the name for Succasunna is derived from the Algonquian name for some sort of black stone. *Sukit* is "black," and *assan* is stone. On the other hand, others contend the name was intended to mean the location of iron ore.

SUMMIT

Summit, Union County, is so named because of its location on the crest of First Watchung Mountain. The ridge was used during the Revolution as a barrier to the British incursion into the hill country of western New Jersey. A small cannon, called "Old Sow," was used to alert Washington to raiding parties.

SURF CITY

Surf City, Ocean County, was settled in 1690 by whalers. Back in those days, the beach sported a fifteen-foot high pole with a railed platform. From the platform, a sentinel alerted the whalers to the approach of a whale. The men set out to sea, and the beached whales were stripped and their blubber rendered on the beach.

It became an early resort with the construction of the Mansion of Health, a hotel built in 1873. Surf City was built on the Great Swamp, but that was considered an inappropriate name. The first official name was Long Beach City, but the final choice was Surf City. The name is another attempt by a chamber of commerce to draw attention to this location and away from other beaches along the coast.

SUSSEX

Sussex was originally called Deckertown, for Peter Decker, a Dutchman who built himself a log cabin here in 1734. No one is quite sure where the original site is, so two possible sites are marked in town.

The town takes its name from the county, which was named for the English county.

SWAINTON

Known as Townsend's Inlet when the first post office opened here in 1849, this Cape May County town undertook a name change to avoid confusion with the other Townsend's Inlet.

Postmaster Luther M. Swain circulated a petition to change the name to Swainton shortly after he became postmaster. The change was effective April 1896.

SWEDESBORO

Swedesboro, Gloucester County, is one of the oldest Swedish settlements in New Jersey. When first settled in the seventeenth century, it was called Raccoon, because of its location on the Raccoon Creek.

The name has an obvious derivation.

SYKESVILLE

Sykesville, Burlington County, was orginally called Plattsburgh. A post office by that name was established in 1857, but was changed to Syketown, then to Sykesville to honor surveyor George Sykes, a member of Congress from 1843–45. The Sykesville post office was established in 1874.

TABERNACLE

This Burlington County community was first settled by Quakers. A small log church existed there in 1778, and the name Tabernacle appeared on an 1828 map. The official Tabernacle post office was established in 1877.

It is believed that David and John Brainerd lived here while bringing their missionary work to the Indians in the pines.

TANSBORO

A settlement was made at this Camden County location soon after 1800. Its first industry was a tannery.

TAUNTON LAKE

This community surrounds the lake of the same name. The town began as early as 1766 as Read's Mill. The name Taunton (also spelled Tanton, Tintern) appears to come from the Tanton Forge, or Furnace, which was advertising in Philadelphia in 1773.

Later, Joseph Hinchman operated a cranberry bog in the area from 1855–1910. In 1920, Edward P. Moore, Sr., purchased the property and built houses.

The source of the name is debatable. The most logical source would be Tanton Earl, who owned an interest in the property called the Tanton Tract. There is also a Taunton, Massachusetts, where another furnace once operated.

TEANECK

Teaneck, in Bergen County, derives its name from the Dutch for "on a neck" of land, or for a local Dutch family by the name of Teneyck.

TENAFLY

The name of Tenafly, Bergen County, can be translated from the Dutch as "on a meadow" or "garden meadow." *Thyne* (or *tuin*) *vly* can also be translated as "garden valley." The name can also be interpreted in an entirely different manner.

The Erskine map of 1776, the earliest map to show this area, shows the name as Tienevly. In the Dutch language that can be translated to Ten Swamp, and there were a number of swamps in the vicinity. In 1898, the spelling became Tienevlie.

Elizabeth Cady Stanton, an early suffragette, lived at Grindenwald house. Hetty Green also established residence here to avoid New York taxes.

THREE BRIDGES

Located in Hunterdon County, Three Bridges was named for the three bridges that once spanned the Raritan River in the area.

TINTON FALLS

This Monmouth County location's name is a corruption of Tintern, Monmouthshire, England.

TOMS RIVER (South —)

Toms River, the seat of Ocean County, was the haven from which colonial privateers wreaked havoc against British shipping in the early days of the American Revolution. It was also the 1782 scene of a historic event of local interest.

Captain Joshua Huddy and his men were attacked by British regulars who tried to capture the Toms River Blockhouse and salt stores. Huddy fended off the redcoats until he and his men ran out of gunpowder and escaped. Huddy was later captured and hanged at Highlands for a murder most believe he did not commit.

Until the early 1960s, the Ocean Hotel, built in 1787, stood in the center of town. The hotel was the main stop on the Freehold to Tuckerton stage route.

A group of Mormons settled at the South Toms River, just below Toms River, in 1837. They constructed their church without using nails or any other metal. The church later served as the first Ocean County courthouse. Joseph Smith, founder of the Church of Jesus Christ of the Latter-day Saints, visited the Toms River colony in 1840. Twelve years later, the Toms River Mormons joined their fellow Mormons in Salt Lake City, Utah.

TOTOWA

Based on etymology, it would appear that the first use of this name depicted the Totowa Falls. According to Heckewelder, the name means "to sink or be forced down under water by weight," "or to dive and disappear." Brinton, on the other hand, believes the word is "certainly the Delaware *tetauwi*, "it is between" the river and the mountains. The reference here is to the neutral ground between the Hackensack and Pompton tribes.

Another source suggests the name *totowa*, or *totua* as it was spelled originally, is Dutch and means "where you begin," indicating the end of the settlement and the beginning of the frontier.

Another authority considers the name of this Passaic County community as coming from *tosawei*, which translates as "to sink," "dive," or "go under water." The word is used to visualize logs going over a waterfall.

TOWACO

A sub-tribe known as the Towakan apparently provided this town's name. Various historians translate the name to mean "snake." In fact, Brinton recounts the eastward migration of the Lenape and refers to *towako*, "Father Snake" several times. Each of his references suggests that snake means "enemy."

TOWN BANK

Formerly known as Portsmouth, Cape May Town, New England

Village, and Falmouth, Town Bank is named for a sand bank. It is situated in Cape May County.

TRENTON (West —)

Trenton was settled about 1680 with the building of a mill on the falls of the Delaware River in Mercer County. Philadelphia merchant William Trent bought the mill in 1714. Five years later the town changed its name from The Falls to Trenton in his honor, and Trenton became the state capital in 1790.

Trenton is well-remembered for the events of 26 December 1776, when General George Washington crossed the Delaware and surprised a Hessian detachment in Trenton, capturing more than a thousand prisoners and giving a much-needed morale boost to both the Continental army and Congress.

TUCKAHOE

Depending on the Lenape language expert, Tuckahoe, Cape May County, can be translated in several ways.

Heckewelder found an 1844 spelling of the town as Tuchahowe, or "where deer are shy [few]—difficult to come at." On the other hand, if one were to use *tawho-tuckah*, the word would mean "turnip." Several others have come up with the same basic idea: Ruttenber lists the word *ptuckweoo*, "it is round," or the name of a bulbous root the Indians used to make bread, or *tockawhough*, the Indian turnip or jack-in-the-pulpit.

Tuckahoe, once an important seaport on the Tuckahoe River, was settled by Quakers before 1700. The earliest post office for this Cape May County town, located on the Tuckahoe River, was opened in 1828. It was known earlier as Head of the River and Williamsburg.

TUCKERTON

Tuckerton is located on the Tuckerton Creek. The creek itself has gone by numerous names in its history. The Indians called it Pohatcong; the English named it Mill Stream, Andrew's Mill Creek, Jacob Andrew's Mill Creek, and Shourd's Mill Creek. The town that grew up around the stream was called Fishtown, and later, Clamtown.

The area was first settled by whites about 1699 when Edward, Mordacai, and Jacob Andrews and David Gaunt from Long Island settled here. By 1702, the Quakers had built a meetinghouse. That building was replaced by the present one in 1872.

Around 1765, Reuben Tucker came down from New York and purchased the beach from Little Egg Harbor to Brigantine inlet. His son Ebenezer, in 1778, located himself in a settlement he called Middle of the Shore, then owned by the Shourds family.

At the close of the Revolution, Ebenezer Tucker purchased the farm of John and Joseph Gaunt. The main section of Tuckerton is built on that farmland. In 1786, the village people resolved that the name should be Tuckerton.

Legend, which is usually more fun than factual research, has it that Judge Ebenezer Tucker, member of Congress, feted his neighbors—provided they name the town after him. The party day was set sometime after 1800 . . . fourteen years after the fact!

UNION

Union is located in Union County. Because the earliest settlers came from Connecticut in 1749, this Essex County village was called Connecticut Farms. Before that, it was known as Wade's Farm, for settlers of that name.

Two weeks before the battle of Springfield, the village of Connecticut Farms was annihilated by the British. The town that rose from the ashes came from a "union" of several neighboring communities. Another source suggests the name was given during the Civil War to show the patriotism of this section of New Jersey.

UNIONVILLE

This Burlington County community was long known as Turpentine, from its pre-Revolution industry. In 1820, Samuel Parker operated a tavern in the town. In 1856, the Union Sunday School was built here for non-denominational services.

VENTNOR CITY

Ventnor City, Atlantic County, was once called a "piece of Philadelphia moved to New Jersey," because the long lines of row houses made it look like a clone of the City of Brotherly Love. The first house was built here in 1888.

In 1929, Ventnor rejected a proposal to be annexed by Atlantic City, even though it is considered a suburb of that city today.

VERONA

About 1730, Verona was known as Buttertown—not because of the dairy product, but because some of the first inhabitants were members of the Butters family.

This Essex County area was once owned by Caleb Hetfield, a Tory. He sold his property before patriotic colonists had a chance to confiscate it. Later it became the property of Christian Bone, a Hessian deserter.

The town was called Vernon, but because of conflict with another Vernon, the postal department requested another name. They selected Verona, which is close. Others seem to think Verona was named for the location in Italy.

VIENNA

This village takes its name from the Vienna Foundry, which produced double-bottom corn plows for Simon Cummins. It was in existence from 1860 to the end of the nineteenth century.

VILLAS

Formerly Fisher's Creek, with a post office established under that name in 1818, the town became known under its present name with the establishment of the Villas post office in 1931.

The name appears to be suggestive of the type of dwellings expected to be built in the town.

VINCENTOWN

Vincentown, Burlington County, was called Weepink when the Indians had a village here.

There are early English references to the town as Quakytown, for the quivering of the ground near a millpond; Quakertown, for the number of members of the Society of Friends who lived there; and Brimstone Neck, for the "sulphorous exhalation of the old pioneers."

The town was named for Vincent Leeds, who purchased a half-interest in the Batsto tracts in 1758–59. Following his purchase, it was called Vincent's Town. One source suggests that the name donor was actually Vincent Ledds, a traveling Quaker minister, but this explanation seems unlikely.

VINELAND (East —)

Just as we learned that eggs have little to do with present-day Egg Harbor City, vines no longer have much to do with Vineland.

Vineland, Cumberland County, is one of the nation's largest poultry-producing centers. It was originally intended as a wine-grape growing area. In 1861, Philadelphia lawyer and promoter Charles K. Landis bought about 32,000 acres of flat, swampy, and fire-swept real estate. He set up vineyards and attracted farmers from the mid-Atlantic region and Italian immigrants to the area. For a quarter of a century, the area flourished, but disease attacked the vines and virtually destroyed the wine business.

Vineland is noted for some fantastic discoveries. In the 1850s, a local tinsmith, John L. Mason, invented the first fruit jar with a screw-top tight enough to preserve food for months. In 1869, an enterprising young dentist developed a way of preserving grape juice without going through the fermentation process. His name will forever be attached to the drink: the dentist was Thomas Welch.

WADING RIVER

A 1760 land survey mentions a tract of land "15 rods above the old Wading Place." A settlement existed there as early as 1761.

Wading River is first mentioned in a 1713–14 survey as Leaks Wharf, after Captain James Leak. According to an 1828 map, the name became Bridgeport. In 1900, it became Wading River, taking its name from the nearby waterway. The suggestion is that one could cross this river by walking or "wading" across.

WALDWICK

The name for Waldwick, Bergen County, is derived from the early Anglo-Saxon for a "village in a grove."

WALLINGTON

This Bergen county community was named for Walling Van Winkle, the former town owner.

WALPACK CENTER

This Sussex County community has not given birth to a competitor for WalMart. The name comes from the Algonquian and means "hole pond." In other words, a pond with a deep hole in it.

Another authority suggests a more long-winded version of the Indian word. He maintains the word translates to "sudden bend of a stream around the base of a rock."

WANAQUE

Sources agree that the name for this Passaic County town comes from the river and valley.

Wanaque is derived from an Indian word which means "place where the sassafras tree grows."

WARETOWN

The Rogerenes, a religious sect founded by John Rogers, settled this area in 1737, after being thrown out of Connecticut. They had the annoying habit of heckling preachers in their pulpits, because the sect opposed any observance of the Sabbath.

This Ocean County town was named for Abraham Waeir, who succeeded John Colver as the local leader of the Rogerenes. The sect disbanded during the Revolution, but reappeared later in Morris County.

WARREN (— Glen, — Grove, — Point, —ville)

Many authorities suggest that Warren, Warren Glen, Warren Grove, Warren Point, and Warrenville were named in honor of General Joseph Warren of Revolutionary War fame.

Warren (1741–75) sent Paul Revere and William Dawes on their famous ride. He was killed at Bunker (Breed's) Hill. Because of his apparent martyrdom, his name became a popular one in place-naming.

WASHINGTON

Obviously, Washington, Warren County, was named in honor of George Washington, Revolutionary War general and first president of the United States. Or was it?

The site was once called Mansfield Woodhouse, after the local Presbyterian church. The present name came from a tavern of the same name. The Washington Tavern was built in 1811 by Colonel William McCullough, founder of the borough.

In 1867, the townspeople established a Vigilante Society to combat horse thieves. Much later, they expanded their scope to car thieves.

WASHINGTON CROSSING

Washington Crossing, Mercer County, is where George Washington and his troops crossed the Delaware River to surprise sleeping Hessians in Trenton on Christmas night 1776. (See Trenton.)

WASHINGTON TOWNSHIP

Like Washington Crossing, Washington Township, Bergen County, was named for George Washington.

WATCHUNG

Watchung, Somerset County, appears to derive its name from *watschu*, Indian for "hill," or *watchaug*, *watchic*, or *watchoog* for "mountain country" or "mountain at."

WATERFORD WORKS

Three brothers, Sebastian, Ignatius, and Xavier Woos, fled their native Germany in 1760 to escape military service. They built a tight little log cabin in Camden County that people traveled to view. The Woos brothers called it *schoen*, German for "beautiful." The neighbors referred to the area as Shane's Castle. That was the beginning of Waterford.

Religious intolerance forced Catholic workers to attend masses secretly held at the Castle and led by traveling priests.

The present name came from the establishment of the Waterford Glass-Works in 1822–24 by Jonathan Haines. He named it after another glass-producing town, Waterford in Ireland.

WATSESSING

Watsessing, Essex County, apparently draws its name from two Indian words: *watschu*, "hill," and *assan*, "stone."

WAYNE

Wayne, Passaic County, is the setting for Albert Payson Terhune's *Lad, A Dog*. Terhune raised collies—and wrote about them—until his death in 1942. (See Pompton.)

The place-name commemorates the Wayne family name, most probably that of General "Mad" Anthony Wayne, of Revolutionary War fame.

WEEHAWKEN

The Dutch settlers apparently took an Indian word and proceeded to render it almost indefinable. One authority says the word translates to "maize land."

Weehawken, Hudson County, was also the site of the famous Burr-Hamilton duel. On the morning of 11 July 1804, Alexander Hamilton, secretary of the treasury, and Aaron Burr, vice president of the United States, faced each other and "resolved" a fifteen-year enmity. After each man had fired, Hamilton fell with a bullet in his breast. "I am a dead man!" Hamilton cried. "He may thank me," Burr responded. "I made him a great man." Burr was forced to flee to the South, where he stayed until Congress reconvened. Some historians contend that Thomas Jefferson used this incident to push through legislation that precluded the runner-up in a presidential election from becoming vice president.

Hamilton's son, Philip, had been killed at the same spot three years earlier.

WENONAH

The name for this Gloucester County town is a variation of Winona. In *Hiawatha*, however, Longfellow spelled the name "Wenonah," the town's way.

Longfellow drew the name he used from the Iroquois, meaning "first-born daughter."

WESTMONT

Originally called Rowandtown, after the Rowand family that farmed the area in 1786, this Camden County town's name was changed to Glenwood when the Camden & Atlantic Railroad came to town. Later, it was changed to Westmont.

WEST NEW YORK

West New York, Hudson County, is located across the Hudson River from Manhattan—to the west, of course.

WEST PORTAL

This Hunterdon County town was so named because it was the western end of the tunnel of the former Lehigh Valley Railroad. Neighboring communities called it Little Switzerland because of its mountainous setting.

WEYMOUTH

Weymouth, Atlantic County, was named for the Weymouth Furnace, which was founded in 1800. In the town's graveyard, one can find some grave markers made of iron from the furnace.

WHARTON

Wharton derives its name from the Wharton Steel Company.

WHIPPANY

The Indians who populated this Morris County area before European settlers used the abundance of willow trees along the nearby waterway to make strong arrows. The Lenape *wipit* means "tooth" or arrow. The final syllable could come from *onk*, "place," *hanne*, "stream," or *ani*, "path."

The town's name, once spelled Whipponong, takes its name from the river.

WHITE HORSE
This Mercer County village was named for the White Horse Tavern. The tavern's name is said to be the result of George Washington passing by here riding a white horse.

WHITEHOUSE (— Station)
Whitehouse, Hunterdon County, was named for the White House Tavern, a white-washed stucco building that is no longer standing.

WHITESBORO
Whitesboro, Cape May County, was founded by Henry C. White, a former African-American congressman from North Carolina.

A post office was first established as White in 1903, and the name was changed to Whitesboro in 1909.

WICKATUNK
This Monmouth County site was named from the Algonquian word for "end of stream."

WILDWOOD (— Crest, East —, North —, West —)
Formerly known as Holly Beach and Five Mile Beach, a post office was established in the name of Wildwood, Cape May County, in 1889.

A post office for Wildwood Crest was opened in 1909.

North Wildwood was formerly called Anglesea.

The name for all the Wildwoods apparently comes from the abundance of flowers that once suffused the area.

WILLIAMSTOWN
Williamstown, once known as Squankum, used to be known for its glassmaking industry. Squankum (an Indian name that translates to "place of the evil god") was moved here in 1772 from Squankum, Monmouth County, by Deacon Israel Williams. In 1842, the name was changed to honor Williams.

WILLINGBORO

Thomas Olive, an early settler and one-time governor of the province, gave this Burlington County community its original name. Olive came from Wellingborough, England. The spelling of the name on early documents varies from Wellingborow to Wellingborough to Willingborough. It was one of the first New Jersey townships, incorporated in 1688.

The borough was incorporated in 1798 and maintained a peaceful existence for more than a century. In 1958–59, Levitt & Sons built houses there and changed the name to Levittown. On 12 November 1963, the people got their way and Willingboro returned as the official name. (See Levittown, Pennsylvania.)

WINFIELD

Some sources suggest this Union County community was named for General Winfield Scott (1786–1866).

"Old Fuss and Feathers," as he was called, was a hero of the War of 1812, defeating the British at Chippewa. He led American forces during the Mexican War, and was general-in-chief of the U.S. Army from 1841–61. The "Anaconda Plan," his plan to defeat the Confederates during the Civil War was rejected when Scott proposed it, but later became the Union's strategy.

Scott was the presidential candidate of the Whig Party in 1852.

WOODBINE

A post office opened in the name of Woodbine in this Cape May County area in 1891.

Milton referred to a "well-attired woodbine," and there was a popular mid-nineteenth century song, "Gone where the woodbine twineth," but no one is sure what a woodbine is; is it ivy? Is it honeysuckle? Whatever it is, it is the name source for this town.

WOODBRIDGE

Woodbridge was settled by Puritans from Massachusetts Bay and New Hampshire in 1665. By 1682, it had become a town.

The first press in New Jersey was operated here in 1751 by James Parker. Parker's *American Magazine* was published seven years later, but stayed in distribution for only two years. Parker was fined and jailed for voicing his opinions.

One source suggests Woodbridge's name came from a wooded ridge rising above the Hackensack meadows. Another indicates it came from the town in Suffolk, England. The first suggestion fits more aptly to Wood Ridge.

WOODBURY (— Heights)

Woodbury, seat of Gloucester County, was settled as early as 1681. Richard Wood and his brother were the original settlers and came from Bury, England. The town suffered from slow growth until the 1860s.

The name came from the English town.

WOODS TAVERN

A tavern, operated by the Wood family, gave its name to this Somerset County village.

WOODSTOWN

Jackanias Wood built the first house in Woodstown, Salem County, early in the eighteenth century. The Quaker Meeting House was erected in 1784. The town was named for the early settler.

WRIGHTSTOWN

In 1742, John (or Jonathan) Wright owned part of the land on which this Burlington County town rests.

The original name was Penny Hill, named in honor of a woman finding a penny on a mound in this place sometime before the Revolution. The name changed to Wrightstown in 1834 with the opening of the post office.

WYCKOFF

This Bergen County community claims to take its name from an Indian name. An early spelling of the name, Wikoff, translates to "house on a hill"; though *wik* is an acceptable contraction of the Lenape *wikwam*, "house," *off* does not translate easily as "on a hill."

Another possibility comes from the Dutch. Wyckoff, some sources contend, derives from the Dutch compound *Wijk-hoff*, "town official." To add further uncertainty, the name may originate with Wicaugh, in Malpas, England. To add even more confusion, Wycoff is also a family name.

YARDVILLE

Yardville was formerly known as Sand Hill. Passengers left the Camden & Amboy Railroad here to change for the stage ride to Trenton. The town was named for the railroad yards.

Pennsylvania

The Dutch, English, and Swedes fought over Pennsylvania in the early seventeenth century. With the capture of New York in 1664, England acquired the area. And, in 1681, Charles II granted the province to William Penn . . . to help repay debts the Crown owed to Penn's father.

Penn's idea for his "new province" was to create a land where religious freedom would be available to members of his religious sect: the Society of Friends, more frequently referred to as the "Quakers."

Penn's plan was well-intentioned, but it did not extend to all religions. Religious persecution continued toward certain groups, such as Roman Catholics, under Penn's subordinates, even though Pennsylvania's founder continued to buy fish from a Jesuit in Philadelphia.

Philadelphia, Penn's "City of Brotherly Love," was the center of Pennsylvania's and the United States' history for more than a century. It was in Philadelphia that the Declaration of Independence was signed; the Liberty Bell "proclaimed Liberty throughout the land" from the clock tower of the State House (now Independence Hall); the U.S. Constitution was drafted here; and in Philadelphia, major league sports teams can have the worst seasons of their franchises and still beat the No. 1 teams in the land.

Pennsylvania was ravaged by two wars. Historians of the Revolutionary War recall the battles of Brandywine and Germantown, the siege of Forts Mercer and Mifflin, the encampments at Whitemarsh and Valley Forge. Historians of the Civil War will recall the turning point of that great conflagration: Gettysburg. The names of those battles and the leaders are recalled in many Pennsylvania place names.

Pennsylvania was rich in natural resources. It was in Pennsylvania that the first American oil well spewed forth "black gold" and spawned the petroleum industry. It was in Pennsylvania that coal mining was raised to a multi-million dollar business. The same was true for steel. But times changed. The oil industry moved to the southwest United States, then to the Middle East. Coal was dirty and polluted the air. The steel industry followed the way of oil and coal. And the railroads that grew fat from those other industries also suffered and declined.

Regardless of the demise of its historic industries, Pennsylvania diversified and created new businesses to replace the old. Each old industry and each new industry is recalled by the names on signposts throughout the state. The same is true of the local taverns and inns, such as Blue Ball, Bird in Hand, and Paoli. Pennsylvania retains rich cultural traditions, from those of the Lenni-Lenape and other Indian tribes to the German-American traditions of the Amish. The religious beliefs that William Penn fostered appear on the land, but not to the exclusion of those of many other religions, including the Roman Catholics, who were spurned in the beginning.

Though long considered a major section of the "Rust Belt," Pennsylvania has the largest rural population in the nation, and that comes through clearly in its place names.

AARONSBURG

Aaronsburg was named for Aaron Levy, who laid out the town in 1786. He sold all his land in 1804 to other Jewish merchants, Simon and Hyman Gratz. Levy founded the community as a place where people of differing religious beliefs could live in harmony.

ACADEMY CORNERS

This Tioga County community took its name from the old Union Academy that once was located here.

ACME

Located in Westmoreland County, Acme's name is taken from the Greek for "summit."

ADAMS (—burg, —town, —ville)

Adamstown, Berks County, was patented in 1739 by ironmaster William Bird. Bird obtained a patent to 356 acres, including Adam's Mill. A lack of ore caused the mill eventually to be abandoned.

ADDISON

Addison was named for Joseph Addison, an English writer.

Addison was on the route of the Washington-Braddock Road that was "supplanted" by the National Road (U.S. 40). The toll-booth there was built in 1835.

AKRON

Akron, Lancaster County, was originally settled by German settlers, and incorporated as a borough in 1884. The name comes from the Greek word for "summit" or "peak."

ALBANY

Though some sources like to suggest that this Berks County village took its name from a city in New York, the name really was drawn from James Stuart, Duke of York. The duke, who later became James II, held the Scottish title of Duke of Albany.

ALBION

This Erie County town bearing the ancient name for England was settled in 1815. Its growth was taken for granted when it became a station on the Erie Extension Canal.

ALCOA CENTER

This Alleghany County community was named for the Aluminum Company of America.

ALFARATA

This Mifflin County town was named for Marie Dix Sullivan's nineteenth-century poem, "Alfarata, the Maid of Juniata."

ALIQUIPPA

Aliquippa, Beaver County, was named for Queen Aliquippa, an Iroquois Indian who lived on the site of McKeesport. Though Aliquippa has been cited as the "Queen of the Delawares," she was probably of the Mohawk tribe.

The queen took her "royalty" seriously. When George Washington passed through her territory in 1753, he failed to pay his respects to her. On a return visit, he stopped and "I made her a present of a watch-coat and a bottle of rum, which latter was thought much the better present of the two." Queen Aliquippa died in 1754.

ALLEMANS

The name for Allemans, Clearfield County, is a possible corruption of Allemands, the French designation for Germans.

ALLENTOWN

Originally incorporated as Northamptontown in 1762, the community later adopted the name of its founder, Pennsylvania Chief Justice William Allen. In 1735, Allen acquired a large tract of land from Joseph Turner, who obtained it from Thomas Penn in 1732. In the mid-eighteenth century, he built a hunting and fishing lodge, but did not lay out a town until 1762, when the area became known as Northampton or Northamptontown. In 1803, Northampton had its own post office; eight years later it was incorporated. By 1838, the name was changed to Allentown.

Allen served as chief justice from 1750 to 1774. His daughter Anne was married to John Penn, grandson of William Penn.

After the Battle of Brandywine, George Washington was certain that Philadelphia could not be saved and so informed Congress. They sent the Liberty Bell and the bells of Christ Church to Allentown for safekeeping in Zion's Church.

Allendale, Allenport, Allens Mills, Allensville and Allenwood are also named for Chief Justice Allen.

ALTOONA

Altoona, Blair County, was founded in 1849 by the Pennsylvania Railroad when it built the first railroad over the Alleghany Mountains. According to Robert Steele, the engineer who drove the first train into Altoona in 1851, the town was named by Colonel Beverly Mayer, a civil engineer for the Pennsylvania Central Railway from Columbia, Pennsylvania, who laid out the tracks here. Steele said the name came from Altona, Schleswig-Holstein, which became part of Germany in 1862.

A more popular explanation gives the name a Cherokee Indian origin. John Archibald Wright, who laid out the town, is supposed to have so named the town thinking it was a Cherokee word meaning "the high lands of great worth." Unfortunately, the Cherokee roots are so different from this name that it makes this origin unlikely.

Another suggestion is that the name came from the Latin word altus, because of the town's high position in the Alleghany Mountains.

Before the American Revolution, this site was the location of Delaware, Shawnee, and Tuscarora Indian camps. Early settlers in the Sinking Spring Valley were protected by Fort Roberdau. The first trace of a city began in 1849, when Wright purchased farmland here. Soon area settlers included the German, Scottish, and Irish. With the arrival of the railroad and its shops, the population grew. Wright sold a piece of his land to the company for a depot, shops, and offices. The governors of the Northern states met at Altoona in September of 1862 and pledged to support Lincoln in the Civil War.

AMARANTH

Amaranth is named for that imaginary flower that never fades.

AMBLER

Ambler, Montgomery County, was named for the Ambler family, even though others had settled here at least eight years before Joseph Ambler arrived in 1723.

Ambler was the site of the worst train crash of its time in American history. On 17 July 1856, sixty people were killed and more than one hundred were injured. The Ambler home was used as an emergency hospital.

AMBRIDGE

In 1901, the American Bridge Company purchased the land in this area from the Harmony Society and began to build a town. When the Pennsylvania Railroad opened a station opposite the main plant—the amount of business at the nearby Economy village was too much and required an additional rail station—it became Ambridge, a combination of elements of the company's name.

Ambridge was incorporated in 1905, and includes the old village of Economy and Ambridge itself.

AMITY (— Hall)

This Washington County town was laid out in 1797. It grew up around the old Amity Presbyterian Church. The church's name was selected to signify "the religious and social amity which the people desired to foster."

The Reverend Solomon Spaulding is reputed to have written the first draft of the *Book of Mormon* shortly before he died in 1816. Spaulding had in fact written a romance that he claimed was translated from inscriptions on tablets found in one of the area's Indian burial mounds. The book, titled *The Manuscript Found*, was submitted to a Pittsburgh publisher who never published it. A few years later, one of his printers made a copy of it and showed it to

Joseph Smith. Smith made some revisions, and eventually, Spaulding's findings were said to have come from the "Golden Bible, or Book of Mormon."

Smith declared that an angel appeared to him in a vision and sent him to the Hill Cumorah where he found gold plates bearing hieroglyphics. When translated, the words became the *Book of Mormon*.

Amity Hall takes its name from an 1810 inn located here.

ANALOMINK

This Monroe County community was originally called Spragueville, because spragues were manufactured here.

A "sprague" was a round piece of lumber, about three inches wide and sharpened at both ends. Miners would throw them into the spokes of the wheels of ore carts to stop them.

The name was changed to Analomink, which translates to "rapid water," a reference to the Brodheads Creek that flows through town.

ANNVILLE

Abraham Miller, who laid out this Lebanon County town in about 1762, named it for his wife Ann. The town was more popularly called Millersville until old Annville Township—now Annville and North and South Annville Townships—was formed in 1799.

Local tradition has it that Miller requested the town change its name to honor his wife.

ANSONIA

Ansonia carries a Latinized version of the personal name Anson.

ANTES FORT

This Lycoming County village takes its name from a famous late-eighteenth-century fortification, built by settlers to fend off Indian attacks. The first commander of the installation was Lieutenant Colonel John Henry Antes.

Settlers from the surrounding area raced to the fort for safety during Indian attacks. Antes was born in Pottstown, Montgomery County, in 1736, and held a commission in the Continental Army.

ANTRIM

Duncan S. Magee founded this Tioga County town and named it for his home in County Antrim, Ireland.

In 1868, together with a number of real-estate promoters, Magee formally toasted the new site and christened it with spring water.

APOLLO

Apollo was originally named Warren, for Edward Warren, an Indian trader who often stopped at this Armstrong County settlement. It was sometimes called "Warren's Sleeping Place."

The name was changed in 1827 when the first post office was established by Dr. Robert McKisson, physician, poet and student of the classics. McKisson later edited Apollo's first newspaper and became its first burgess.

AQUASHICOLA

This Carbon County community is named for the stream that flows through the valley to the Lehigh River at Lehigh Gap. The name is a variation of the Delaware Indian *achquoanschicola*, and means "where we fish with the bush net."

ARCHBALD

Archbald, Lackawanna County, was known as White Oak Run until 1846, when the Delaware & Hudson Canal Company began to exploit the coal deposits here. The town was renamed to honor James Archbald, a civil and mining engineer with the company.

A native of Scotland, Archbald came to Carbondale in 1828 and was charged with achieving some of the most difficult railroad construction across Moosic Mountain.

ARDMORE

This Montgomery County community was called the Welsh Baronry by settlers who arrived here two months before William Penn. Later, the town became known as Athensville. When the Pennsylvania Railroad opened a new station at Humphreysville and dubbed it Bryn Mawr, Welsh for "high place," the Athensvillers changed their name to Ardmore. Ardmore is "high hill" in Irish.

ARMAGH

Irish immigrants came to the area in 1792 and named it Armagh, which translates in their native tongue, Erse, to "field on a hill." They founded the town in an area that was nothing more than a bare field, save for a few scrubby oaks. At one time, one source contends, Armagh had as many taverns as it has homes today.

ASHLAND

Ashland, Schuylkill County, was laid out in 1847 by Samuel Lewis, and named for Henry Clay's estate near Lexington, Kentucky.

Land was first purchased here in 1845. Two years later, when the town was laid out, coal mining began in earnest.

ASHLEY

Ashley was established as a coal town in 1851. Over the next twenty years, the town changed names nine times, going from Skunktown, Peestown, Hightown, Newton, Scrabbletown, Coalville, Hendricksburg, Nanticoke Junction, and Alberts to Ashley.

Ashley became the permanent name when the town was incorporated in 1870. It honored Herbert Henry Ashley, of Wilkes-Barre, a member of a family of prominent coal operators.

ATGLEN

The residents of Atglen adopted that name in 1875, because the town was located near Glen Run.

ATHENS

This Bradford County village took its name from the name of its old township, which was formed in 1786. The township was named for the Greek capital. Some sources suggest that the ring of hills around this town resembles the area of the same name in Greece.

Athens had great notoriety under its former name: Tioga Point. *Tioga* is Indian and means "meeting of the waters." In 1778, Colonel Thomas Hartley and a 400-man force attacked at Tioga Point and burned the palace of "that Indian fury," Queen Esther, a granddaughter of Madame Montour, in retaliation for the Wyoming Massacre.

The next year, General John Sullivan erected Fort Sullivan at Tioga Point and made it the base of his operations against the Iroquois.

Tioga Point became Athens about 1803. The borough was incorporated under that name in 1831.

ATHOL

Athol, Berks County, was named for James Murray, second Duke of Athol. A town by the same name exists in Massachusetts.

ATLAS

Located in Northumberland County, Atlas commemorates the mythological figure.

AUBURN (— Center, West —)

The name of a Yorkshire village was used in Goldsmith's 1770 *Deserted Village*. It is commemorated in this Schuylkill County village.

AUDUBON

AUDUBON. John James Audubon, naturalist and painter, lived in Pennsylvania but roamed the Delaware Valley in pursuit of examples of flora and fauna which he duly registered with his art. His name is remembered by the towns of Audubon, located in both New Jersey and Pennsylvania. (Print and Picture Department, Free Library of Philadelphia)

During his young manhood, John James Audubon, the famous ornithologist, lived on the Perkiomen Creek. This village, located on land owned by Audubon's father, bears his name.

Audubon (1785–1851), born Jean Rabine in Haiti and educated in Paris, came to this area in 1804. While here, he wandered through the woods collecting flora and fauna and capturing them on paper and canvas. He also captured the affections of Lucy Bakewell, daughter of William Bakewell, who lived across the Perkiomen at Fatland, properly called Vaux Hall. The artist was considered strange until 1838, when the folio edition of *Birds of America* was sold by subscription for $1,000 a set—to eighty-two subscribers in America and seventy-nine in Europe.

AUSTIN (—burg, —ville)

Within six months of the founding of Austin, Potter County, as a lumber town in 1886, it had more than 700 residents.

The town was named for F. P. Austin, a local historian. It was more likely named for his position on the first borough council than for his historical prowess.

AVALON

When first settled in the late eighteenth century by John Taylor, an Irish trader, this Allegheny County community was called West Bellevue. When the railroad opened its station, it was named Birmingham, for a Captain John Birmingham who bought land there from the Taylor family. In 1874, the settlement incorporated as West Bellevue. When the post office opened, it was called Myler.

These three names caused confusion so, at an 1893 town meeting, the residents voted to name the entire area Avalon. Some seem to think the name was given for the Isle of Avalon, "Abode of the Blessed" in the tales of King Arthur. More likely, it came from the Celtic definition of "avalon," which is "orchard, or land of apples." That translation is fairly descriptive of what the town looked like when Captain Birmingham built his log cabin there in 1803.

AVOCA

Avoca was originally named Pleasant Valley. The name was changed, it has been suggested, in deference to Thomas Moore's poem "Sweet Vale of Avoca."

AVON (—dale, —more)

Avondale takes its name from the Avondale Mine. The mine was the scene of a major disaster in 1869 when fire and smoke filled the only outlet to the mine and caused the death of 108 miners.

AXEMANN

The traditional occupation of the Mann family was making axes. Thomas Mann came to America from Ireland in 1750, and made axes and other edged tools at a shop in Braintree, Massachusetts, and later in New York. His son and grandsons followed the trade.

In 1828, Mann's grandsons William, Jr., and Harvey came to Centre County and opened the Mann Axe Factory, not far from Bellefonte. The family later opened factories in Mill Hall, Tyrone, and Yeagertown, Pennsylvania. Mann axes were shipped all over the world, and those in the know contend that the Manns were the greatest ax makers in the history of the world.

BAINBRIDGE

This Lancaster County town commemorates Commodore William Bainbridge (1774–1833), a hero of the undeclared war with Great Britain in the 1790s, and the war with Barbary pirates.

Bainbridge also organized the first school of naval officers in the United States.

BALDWIN

Baldwin was named for Matthias W. Baldwin (1795–1866).

Baldwin began his career as a jewelry maker, but by 1827 he was manufacturing steam engines. In 1832, he constructed *Old Ironsides* for the Philadelphia & Germantown Railroad. This began his rise to fame in the manufacture of steam engines and locomotives. The M.W. Baldwin Company became the world-famous Baldwin Locomotive Works (the site of the Works is now occupied by offices for *The Philadelphia Inquirer,* among others.)

Baldwin was quite active in civic affairs, including the founding of the Franklin Institute. His abolitionist views and his concern for the welfare of Negroes caused him to be boycotted by Southern railroads in the years before the Civil War.

BALLY

Bally, Berks County, was laid out in 1742, on land owned by the Jesuits. It was named for the Reverend Augustin Bally, S.J., who was a missionary to the territory from 1837–82.

A year after the town was laid out, the Reverend Theodore Schneider, S. J., built the Chapel of St. Paul, the third Roman Catholic church in Pennsylvania. The chapel was replaced in 1827 by the Church of the Blessed Sacrament.

BANGOR (East —, North —)

R.M. Jones, an expert in matters relating to slate, came to this area in about 1866. There had been a settlement here as early as 1773. Jones, a Welshman, followed the slate strata westward from the Delaware River, and when he arrived at the site of Bangor, thought he had found an inexhaustible supply of high-grade slate.

Jones opened the quarries, and started a town. The name comes from Bangor, Caernavonshire, Wales, which was the center of the slate quarries of Wales. The name Bangor translates from the Welsh to "the white choir."

BARBOURS

Barbours, Lycoming County, takes its name from Philip Pendleton Barbour (1783–1841).

Barbour served on the Supreme Court. Together with Chief Justice Roger B. Taney, he fought for states' rights, and sought to reverse the nationalistic decision-making of John Marshall.

BARD

Some sources indicate this Bedford County village was named as a reference to Shakespeare. That may be so, because one of the town fathers was a voracious reader of the Bard's works.

BARNESBORO (—ville)

Cambria County's Barnesboro was named for Thomas Barnes.

Barnes, a coal operator, laid out the town in 1891, shortly after the discovery of bituminous coal in the area.

BART

Bart, Lancaster County, takes its name from its township. The township was named for an abbreviation: Sir William Keith, Pennsylvania's provincial governor from 1717–26, added his title to his name; "Bart" was an abbreviation for baronet.

BAUMSTON

Baumston, Berks County, was the birthplace of Daniel Boone (1734–1820), even though many biographical directories list him as being born "near present-day Reading."

Boone was a legendary hunter and trapper. He spent most of his adult life fighting Indians, trapping, and hunting. He settled in Kentucky at what is now Boonesboro, and is greatly credited with expanding the new nation beyond the Allegheny Mountains.

BEAUMONT

This Wyoming County village takes its name from the French for "beautiful mountain."

BEAVER (— Center, —dale, — Falls, — Meadows, — Springs, —town)

Beaver Falls, Beaver County, was opened to settlement in 1793, but angry Indians delayed any permanent occupation. The town was finally laid out in 1806 by the Constable brothers, who called it Brighton for their native home of Brighton, England.

The Harmony Society, in 1866, enlarged on the town plan by including land the society had purchased adjacent to Brighton. The town grew along the Beaver River. After the establishment of New Brighton, the name was changed to Beaver Falls, for the proximity of the falls to the town. Townspeople and others were tired of referring to "old" Brighton and "new" Brighton.

Beaver Falls was incorporated as a borough in 1868, and chartered as a city in 1930.

Beaver, the major city of Beaver County, takes its name from the county formed in 1800 and named for the Big Beaver River or Creek. Beaver, the county seat, was located on the site of Fort McIntosh. The fort had been built in 1778 by General Lachlan McIntosh. Twenty-one years later, Governor Thomas Mifflin approved the act laying out the town. Within the next year, Daniel Lee surveyed the land and laid out "Beaver-town." Ten years later, the town was incorporated as Beaver.

Beaver was the home of Matthew S. Quay (1833–1904). At the turn of the twentieth century, Quay controlled the then-powerful Pennsylvania Republican machine.

Beaver Meadows, Carbon County, also takes its name from the waterway. It was founded in 1787, and was an established settlement when nearby Hazelton was merely a trading post.

Beaver Springs was laid out as a town in 1806.

Beavertown took its name, not from the Beaver Creek, but from the beaver colonies once numerous near here.

BEDFORD (— Springs)

Bedford was first settled before 1752 by John Wray. For a number of years it was called Raystown. Wray operated an important trading post at this Bedford County location.

A stockade fort was built here six or seven years later, and the town took on the name of Camp Raystown. In 1759, when General John Stanwix took over the fortification, he renamed it to honor the Duke of Bedford, and called it Fort Bedford. At the time of the naming, John Russell, fourth Duke of Bedford, was Lord Lieutenant of Ireland. For naming the fort after him, the duke gave the commander a "beautiful silken English flag." Alas, and some people wonder why the colonists revolted against the Crown.

In 1761, the Penns set aside the Manor of Bedford, about 2,800 acres. Five years later, the provincial government ordered John Lukens, the surveyor general, to lay out the town. Bedford took its name from the fort.

BEDFORD. A contemporary view of Old Bedford Village. (Old Bedford Village, Bedford, Pennsylvania)

Captain James Smith, commanding the Sideling Hill Volunteers, learned in 1769 that the British had imprisoned several pioneers at the fort. The settlers stood accused of destroying weapons and other goods destined for the Indian trade.

Smith announced loudly that he would free the prisoners, and marched up to Fort Bedford with a force of eighteen men—making sure that the British garrison watched his every move. He ostensibly camped at Juniata Crossing, but under cover of night marched his men to within 100 yards of the fort. At daybreak, when the gates were opened, Smith and his men charged the gate, overpowered the guards, and freed the prisoners. In his memoirs, Smith wrote: "This was the first British fort in America that was taken by what they called 'American rebels.'"

Bedford Springs has been a resort since 1795 when people discovered the healing qualities of its waters. In the early days, legend has it, a nearby cave was the hiding place of Davy Lewis, a well-known bandit.

Lewis was supposed to have robbed the rich and given to the poor. He was jailed for counterfeiting in 1815, but escaped by digging his way under a wall. Before he left the prison, he freed all the prisoners, except "a common fellow who had robbed a poor widow."

BEECH CREEK (— Glen, —wood)

Beech Creek, Clinton County, takes its name from the nearby waterway. The name is a translation from the Indian *schauweminsch-hanna*.

BELKNAP

Belknap, Armstrong County, was named in honor of William Worth Belknap (1829–90), Grant's secretary of war.

In 1876, Belknap was accused of accepting bribes for the sale of trading posts in Indian Territory. After the House of Representatives passed a resolution of impeachment, he resigned to avoid trial in the Senate. The day after he resigned, the Senate voted him not guilty.

BELLEFONTE

Built on seven hills at the base of Bald Eagle Mountain in Centre County, Bellefonte was named for its "beautiful fountain," the spring that supplies the town with water. Legend has it that the name is Talleyrand's exclamation of pleasure when he saw the spring here during his exile from France, 1794–95.

According to local tradition, Charles Maurice, Duke of Talleyrand-Perigord, a political exile in the United States during the 1790s, visited Willow Bank, the home of James Harris and his wife. The family contends the duke suggested the name, though the family did not speak French.

The town was surveyed in 1769 and settled shortly thereafter. It was laid out in 1795 by Colonel James Dunlop, father-in-law to James Harris.

Noted sculptor George Grey Barnard (1863–1938) was born here. Barnard was accepted in Paris art circles at a time when American artists were not considered on a par with the Europeans. Barnard's most famous work, *The Apotheosis of Labor*, decorates the entrance to the state capitol in Harrisburg.

BELLEVUE

Bellevue, Allegheny County, was named simply because the town, on the north bank of the Ohio River, provided a "beautiful view."

Before the start of white settlement in 1802, this area was the hunting ground of the Delaware tribe under Chief Killbuck. Bellevue was incorporated as a borough in 1867.

BEN AVON

Ben Avon, a suburb of Pittsburgh, was incorporated as a borough in 1891. Its name is Scottish for "hill by the waters."

BENEZETTE

This Elk County community most probably honors Anthony Benezet (1713–84), who, in 1765, helped French Huguenots fleeing religious oppression in Canada. The Acadians, as they became known, are recalled in Henry Wadsworth Longfellow's famous poem "Evangeline."

Many of the Acadians migrated south into Louisiana. Today they are known as Cajuns.

BENFER

The name of Benfer, Union County, appears to take the Hebrew *ben* and add to it the Latin *fer*, to come up with "son of iron."

BENSALEM

The original name for this Bucks County town was Salem, but in the early eighteenth century the name was changed to Bensalem. Apparently the name change hinted at the "son of Salem."

BENTON, Pennsylvania

Benton, Columbia County, was named for its township. The township, organized in 1850, was named for Thomas Hart Benton (1782–1858), a U.S. senator from Missouri who, at the time of organization, was at the peak of his popularity.

Benton became prominent as editor of the *Missouri Enquirer*, in St. Louis. Taking advantage of this notice, he ran for the Senate in 1820 and served for the next thirty years. He was a strong supporter of a separate U.S. treasury and the gold standard, and an opponent of the extension of slavery into the Territories.

BERLIN (East —)

Berlin was settled about 1769 by the members of the German religious sect, the Dunkard Brethren. The Somerset County community was named Berlin, for the former and present capital of Germany. The surrounding area became known as Brothers' Valley.

East Berlin, located in Adams County, was laid out in 1764 by John Frankenburger, a German immigrant. He originally named it Berlin.

BERWICK (East —)

Berwick, Cumberland County, was founded as a religious refuge in 1786 by Quaker Evan Owen. Owen named the site after Berwick-upon-Tweed, his former hometown in England on the Scottish border. The name Berwick is a corruption of Aberwick, "river-mouth town."

When first established, Berwick was located in Northumberland County. The town was incorporated in 1818.

BERWYN

This Chester County community took the name of the railroad station, which was named by a railroader of Welsh ancestry.

BESSEMER

Bessemer was named for Sir Henry Bessemer (1813–98).

Bessemer discovered the "blast furnace" approach to making steel from cast iron. His process blew air onto the molten iron, causing the carbon impurities to burn off. This reduced the price of steel ten times, making modern steel construction economical.

BETHANY

Bethany, Wayne County, was founded in 1801 by Philadelphian Henry Drinker. Four years later, Jason Torrey laid out town lots and named it for the village in ancient Palestine. The name translates from the Hebrew as "the house of dates."

From its founding to 1842, Bethany was the county seat. Honesdale is the current seat. David Wilmot (1814–68), author of the famous "Wilmot Proviso" which started the "Free Soil" movement in American politics, was born in Bethany.

BETHLEHEM (South —)

BETHLEHEM. Count Nicholas Louis Zinzendorf was the founder of the Moravian Church in America. He and his church's influence is remembered in both Bethlehem and Lititz, Pennsylvania. (Print and Picture Department, Free Library of Philadelphia)

In 1741, a group of Moravian missionaries from Europe established a communal church-village at this site. The leader of the group, and its bishop, Count Nicholas Ludwig von Zinzendorf, helped christen the settlement during one of the group's Vigils on Christmas Eve. "Because of the day," one Moravian diarist wrote, ". . . we went into the stable and sang with feeling. . . ." The hymn they sang, a Christmas carol, provided them with a name.

The Moravian (or Unitas Fratrum) Church originated in Bohemia and Moravia in the mid-fifteenth century. During the years that followed, the sect came under strong persecution that lasted until 1722. In that year, von Zinzendorf opened his estate in Saxony as a refuge for the refugees. He joined the church and financed the immigration of several groups to America.

Bethlehem, which in Hebrew means "the house of bread," was incorporated in 1845. In 1910, Bethlehem became a city.

BIG BEAVER

Beaver County. See Beaver.

BIGLER

Bigler, Clearfield County, was named for William Bigler (1814–80), governor of Pennsylvania from 1852–55.

Bigler began his career as a newspaperman with the *Clearfield Democrat*, "an eight by ten Jackson paper intended to counteract the effect of the seven by nine Whig [sic] paper." He was not reelected to a second term as governor because of the activities of the Native American Party, the Know-Nothings.

BINGHAM CENTER (North Bingham, West Bingham)

Those towns, all located in Potter County, bear the Bingham name to honor William Bingham (1752–1804), of Philadelphia.

Bingham was a prominent merchant and land speculator. He was married to Anne Willing, who commissioned Gilbert Stuart to paint a full-length portrait of George Washington. She later presented the painting to Lord Lansdowne, and it has been known since then as the "Lansdowne portrait."

BINGHAM CENTER. William Bingham, a Philadelphia banker and legislator, was the first president of the Philadelphia & Lancaster Turnpike Corporation. (Scharf and Wescott's *History of Philadelphia, 1609–1884*)

BIRD-IN-HAND

This Lancaster County town took its name from a tavern sign of a bird resting in a hand. It was located on the main road between Lancaster and Philadelphia. No one is sure when the tavern was established, but it was in use in 1734, when the first surveyors in the area made it their headquarters.

The tavern name comes from an old piece of advice: "A bird in the hand is worth two in the bush."

BIRDSBORO

This Berks County borough was named for ironmaster William Bird, who opened a furnace here in 1740. The town grew up around the iron works on both sides of the Hay Creek.

James Wilson, who signed the Declaration of Independence, was married in Bird's home.

BIRMINGHAM

Located in Huntingdon County, Birmingham was laid out in 1797 by John Cadwallader. Cadwallader wanted to establish the site as a manufacturing center at the head of the Juniata River.

Iron was Birmingham's earliest industry, and Cadwallader named it for the manufacturing town in England.

John Cadwallader (1742–86) was a brigadier general in the Pennsylvania militia. During the summer of 1778, he dueled with General Thomas Conway and wounded him. Conway led what has become known as the "Conway Cabal," an attempt to oust Washington as commanding general of the Continental forces.

BLAIRS CORNERS (— Mills, —ville)

These several Blairs take their name from the county, which was named for Captain John Blair, of Blair's Gap.

The captain was one of the first promoters of the state's

turnpike and canal-portage system. Blairsville was settled in 1792. The western section of the canal reached Blairsville in 1828, bringing with it prosperity from turnpike traffic. With the completion of the eastern portion, business declined. The profits anticipated by area businessmen sailed past them on the Conemaugh River.

BLAKELY

Blakely, Lackawanna County, takes its name from the old township of the same name which was organized in 1818.

It was named for Captain Johnston Blakely, commander of the *Wasp* during the War of 1812. Blakely was lost at sea in 1814.

BLAWNOX

Blawnox took its name from that of a local steel company. The town was settled by a land development company in 1867.

Prior to white settlement, the area was peopled by the Allegewi Indians, and later the Shawnee and Iroquois.

BLOOMSBURG

BLOOMSBURG. Major General George Cadwalader led the troops sent to quell the "Fishing Creek Confederacy" in this Columbia County village. An ancestor founded Birmingham, Pennsylvania. (War Library, Military Order, Loyal Legion of the United States, Philadelphia)

Bloomsburg was laid out by Ludwig Eyer in 1802. For a long time, the Columbia County location was called Eyersburg or Eyertown.

When the townspeople decided on a name for their first post office, they turned down Eyer's name and instead chose the name of the township in which they were located.

Bloom Township was named for Samuel Bloom, a commissioner of Northumberland County. In 1870, Bloom Township and Bloomsburg were merged into "the town of Bloomsburg." Bloomsburg was the only Pennsylvania place incorporated as a town, the rest were cities or boroughs.

The area surrounding Bloomsburg was the scene of the famous Fishing Creek Confederacy during the Civil War. The "Confederacy" was a semi-organized protest against the government's draft during the last days of the war. At one point, federal officials were told that a large number of draft dodgers had fortified a position along the Fishing Creek. Mustering a thousand federal troops, the government sent them against the Confederacy.

A member of the federal force recalled: "Well do we remember the heroic charge . . . on the supposed battlements after a fortnight's preparation . . . as [the troops] reached the summit of the mount where we were taught to believe the Fishing Creek army was massed . . . and found not a man, nor . . . evidence that a man had ever been there. In a word . . . such a thing as a confederacy to resist the U. S. Government never existed in Columbia county."

BLOSSBURG

Blossburg was named for Aaron Bloss, who settled here in 1806. Bloss bought the local watering hole, Gaylord's Tavern. At the time he made his purchase, the town was called Peters' Camp.

BLUE BALL

Blue Ball took the name of the Blue Ball Inn, established here in 1766. The tavern sign was a single ball, painted blue.

BLUE BELL

The original name for this Montgomery County town was Pigeon-town, for the abundance of wild passenger pigeons that nested here in the early nineteenth century.

The town takes its name from the Blue Bell Inn, established about 1743. The tavern sign was a bell, similar to the Liberty Bell, painted blue.

BLUE (— Knob, — Mountain, — Ridge Summit)

From a distance, the mountains have a blue, hazy look. That holds true for Blue Knob, Blair County; Blue Mountain, Franklin County; and Blue Ridge Summit, Franklin County.

BOALSBURG

Boalsburg, Centre County, was settled in 1799 by Scotch-Irish pioneers. They named their settlement in honor of Captain David Boal, a native of County Antrim, Ireland, who arrived here in 1798. Others suggest the naming was for his son David.

Boalsburg was an early stagecoach stop, opened in 1808. Two years later, Andrew Stroup laid out an addition to the town, and attempted to change the name to Springfield, for the large springs in the area. He was unsuccessful.

It is said that the nation's first Memorial Day celebration was held in 1864 in the village cemetery.

BOILING SPRINGS

In the eighteenth century, Boiling Springs, Cumberland County, was a bustling iron-manufacturing village. It takes its name from Boiling Springs Lake, a seven-acre, man-made lake that goes back to the mid-eighteenth century. The lake is fed by approximately thirty underwater springs. The springs bubble to the surface and present the appearance of boiling water.

BOLIVAR

Bolivar was named for General Simon Bolivar (1783–1830).

Bolivar, known as "The Liberator," was a popular figure in the years after 1820 because of his success in the revolutionary wars in South America. He led in the liberation of northern South America from Spanish domination. He was, at various times, president of Colombia and Peru.

BONNEAUVILLE

The name for Bonneauville, Adams County, translates to the "village of good water."

BOONEVILLE

The name of this Clinton County community honors Daniel Boone (1735–1820), frontiersman. (See Baumstown.)

BOALSBURG. The historic Boal Mansion was built in 1789 by members of the founding family. The town is also the site of the Columbus Chapel, once part of the Columbus family castle in Spain. The chapel contains artifacts that date back to the fifteenth century. (Boal Mansion Museum, Boalsburg, Pennsylvania)

BOSTON

Boston's name may have come indirectly from Booston, England. More likely, the name was transported from Massachusetts.

BOWLDER

The name for this Adams County village is really the archaic spelling of "boulder."

BOYERTOWN

Boyertown, Berks County, grew up around the tavern and store owned by Henry Boyer. Boyertown began its existence when the Colebrookdale Furnace was opened in 1720 by Thomas Rutter. Rutter's operation was the first iron furnace in Pennsylvania.

In 1893, the nation's second-largest coffin company, the Boyertown Burial Casket Company, opened here. As a young Boy Scout, the author camped in the shadow of that plant. Ghost stories told there seemed to have greater effect than those told elsewhere.

BRACKENRIDGE

Brackenridge, Allegheny County, was built upon the estate of Judge Henry Marie Brackenridge. Local historians suggest the name was derived from his grandson, Henry Morgan Brackenridge, who was instrumental in developing industry in the area.

Brackenridge was incorporated as a borough in 1901.

BRADDOCK (— Hills)

Braddock, Allegheny County, takes its name from Braddock Township, which was named for Major General Edward Braddock, who died in 1755. Braddock's defeat at Fort Duquesne during the French and Indian War was brought about by his total ignorance of the ways of Indian warfare. The largest number of troops were slaughtered near what is now Jones and Bell Avenues.

Braddock became a borough in 1867.

BRADFORD (—woods)

Bradford, McKean County, began its existence as Littleton. That name came from Colonel Levitt C. Little, of Boston, agent for the United States Land Company, which had purchased thousands of acres in this area in 1836. The next year, Little built a log cabin, the first structure in the town.

In 1850, the land company sold the Littleton site to Daniel Kingsbury, who named it Bradford. Kingsbury's ancestors came from Bradford, England. Another source suggests that the name came from that of the county, formed in 1812 and named for William Bradford, then U. S. attorney general.

Bradford was a very small community on the Tunungwant Creek before oil was discovered in 1875. With the discovery of "black gold," land that had sold for six-and-a-half cents an acre in 1836 began to sell for one thousand dollars or more. Residents sunk oil wells in every available piece of land.

Bradford was incorporated as a city in 1879.

BRADYS BEND

Bradys Bend, Clarion County, is located at a "bend" in the Allegheny River. The town was named for a Captain Brady, the same man who settled East Brady. Brady originally owned the land, but sold it to Judge James Ross. When in private practice, the judge had represented the captain and won him acquittal on charges of murdering an Indian.

Brady's father and brother were killed by Indians and he swore vengeance. For many years, he led "hunting" parties against the Indians. Bradys Bend began to prosper in 1839, with the opening of the Great Western Iron Works. The boom lasted forty years.

BRANDYWINE MANOR

The congregation of Manor Presbyterian Church was organized here in 1735. The current church was built here in 1875. In naming the community, the townspeople of this Chester County community merged the church's name with that of the Brandywine Creek.

BRICKCHURCH

This Armstrong County town was named for a brick church.

BRICKERVILLE

The early houses in Brickerville, Lancaster County, were usually made of brick.

"Baron" Heinich Wilhelm Stiegel (1729–85), whose title described his wealth and his lifestyle, spent his last days in the Lutheran parsonage here—in relative poverty.

The most successful glass and iron manufacturer in this area in the mid-eighteenth century, the baron went bankrupt. He did, however, leave a legacy. Manheim is named for his glassworks.

BRIER HILL

There was a tavern operating in Brier Hill, Fayette County, as early as 1796. The Colley Tavern was operated by Abel and Peter Colley. The town's name is taken from a description of the original site, a hill covered with briars (or briers).

BRISTOL

This Bucks County town, an early river port of call, was first laid out in 1697 and named Buckingham. Around the turn of the eighteenth century, the name was changed to New Bristol, after Bristol, the chief seaport in the west of England. William Penn's second wife, Hannah Callowhill, came from Bristol.

BROAD AXE

The name was taken from a tavern sign.

BROADFORD

Broadford (Broad Ford, until the post office got hold of the name) was known to the Indians as the "crossing place" on the Youghiogheny. At the turn of the nineteenth century, Henry Overholt, a Mennonite from Bucks County, moved into the Fayette County area and built a cabin at the crossing. His son, Abraham, while pursuing the weaver's trade, tended the family still.

Abraham recognized the marketing potential of "firewater" and built a distillery that produced 200 gallons a day. In 1834, a grainmill was erected near the distillery. "Old Overholt" became a very popular brand of whiskey thereafter.

BROWNBACKS

Brownbacks is how the settlers pronounced the surname of eighteenth-century settler Gerhart Brumbaugh.

BROWNSDALE (—town, —ville)

Brownsville, Fayette County, was an early boat-building center. The *Comet*, the first steamer to navigate the Monongahela, Ohio, and Mississippi Rivers, was built here in 1813.

Brownsville was built on the site of Redstone Old Fort, an early Indian outpost selected by Colonel James Burd in 1758. The town was founded in 1785 by Thomas and Basil Brown, who lent their name to the development.

The famous Whiskey Rebellion (1791–94), the organized protest against a four-pence per gallon tax on whiskey, took place here. Farmers had realized that their corn was worth six times less than whiskey of comparable bulk, and they found it easier to convert their excess crop into liquor and transport the end result to the East. The government then realized there was tax money to be made.

The rebellion ended when General Daniel Morgan arrived at Uniontown with a federal force of 13,000 men—with orders to collect the tax and end all resistance.

Brownstown and Brownsdale both recall the names of their founding fathers.

BRUIN

Bruin, Butler County, takes its name from Bear Creek, which runs through the village. The stream was named for the great abundance of bears once found here. Because townspeople thought the name "Bear" was overused, they decided to use a synonym.

BRYN ATHYN

The history of Bryn Athyn, Montgomery County, is the latter-day history of the Church of the New Jersusalem, a system of theology developed by Emanuel Swedenborg, a Swedish scientist and philosopher.

The Swedeborgian religion started in London in 1787; the first American branch was established at Baltimore in 1792. Over a century later, a chapel was built at this location. In 1908, John Pitcairn, a multi-millionaire who made his money from railroad, oil, and plate-glass interests, donated money for a cathedral. The cornerstone was laid in 1914, and the church dedicated five years later.

Bryn Athyn is Welsh for "hill of cohesiveness" or "hill-clinging." The town was named when Welsh derivations were considered quite prestigious.

BRYN MAWR

Rowland Ellis named his Main Line estate Bryn Mawr, Welsh for "high ground," after his birthplace in Wales.

In 1869, Joseph Lesley, secretary of the Pennsylvania Railroad, named the new station at Humphreysville, Montgomery County, for the Ellis estate. The town assumed the same name. At about the same time, the residents of nearby Athensville changed their community's name to Ardmore, Irish for "high hill."

BUCK (— Hill Falls, —horn, — Run, —stown, —town)

The names of these communities refer to the appearance of a male deer.

BUCKINGHAM

Buckingham, Bucks County, was founded in 1702. The General Green Inn is located here, a building that once served as headquarters to that Revolutionary War general. Local legend says that Continental sharpshooters hid themselves in the chimney and took pot shots at the British.

It has been suggested that the name was borrowed from Buckinghamshire, England.

BUFFALO (— Mills, — Run)

Buffalo and Buffalo Run were named for the buffalo, also known as the wild ox or bison, that frequented the area.

Buffalo Mills on the other hand, was named for the industry.

BULLION

"Bullion" was the name given in the nineteenth century to un-coined precious metal. The name was a common one for mining camps. The town of Bullion is located in Venango County.

BUNKER HILL

Bunker Hill, Lebanon County, was named for the 17 June 1775 battle of the American Revolution.

BURGETTSTOWN

During the American Revolution, Sebastian Burgett, a German native, established Fort Burgett on this site. His son, George, laid out the town in 1795.

BURNHAM

First known as Freedom Forge, for the Freedom Forge opened here in 1795, the Mifflin County town was later called Logan. The current name was bestowed in 1911, to honor William Burnham, a steel-mill official.

BURNSIDE

This Clearfield County village was named in honor of Ambrose Everett Burnside (1824–81).

At the outbreak of the Civil War, Burnside recruited a Rhode Island regiment and commanded it as a colonel. Following the battle of Bull Run, he was commissioned brigadier general.

His victories on the North Carolina Coast in January 1862 brought him to the attention of the Lincoln administration. Promoted to major general, Burnside joined the Army of the Potomac and took part in the battles of South Mountain and Antietam. Lincoln chose Burnside to replace General George B. McClellan as commander of the Army of the Potomac. His first action after taking command was the disastrous defeat at Fredericksburg in December 1863. He was replaced the next month.

Following his demotion, he was transferred to the Department of the Ohio. Following the mine explosion at the seige of Petersburg, Virginia, Burnside was called before a military court of inquiry and found responsible for the failed attempt. He resigned from the Union army, and became an officer of several railroad companies, governor of Rhode Island, and, from 1874 to the time of his death, served as senator from his home state.

Burnside is best remembered, however, for the style of sidewhiskers he wore. The word has been switched around to become "sideburns."

BURNT CABINS

This village received its name from a strange incident in 1750. The cabins of early settlers—squatters—were burned down by order of the provincial government . . . after the Indians complained about the whites illegally taking over their land.

BUSHKILL

This Pike County village was settled in 1812. It is situated at the confluence of the Little Bushkill and Big Bushkill Creeks, and takes its name from those waterways. The name is Dutch and translates to "little river."

BUTLER (East —)

Butler, seat of Butler County, was laid out in 1803 on land donated by John and Samuel Cunningham. The land was originally owned by Robert Morris, financier of the Revolution. Settlement of this locale, however, began at least ten years earlier.

The borough of Butler was incorporated in 1817. It takes its name from its county. Butler County was named for Richard Butler, a native of Dublin, Ireland, and a lieutenant colonel with Morgan's Rifles in 1777. He spent most of his life practicing law in Carlisle.

Butler, a major general by 1791, died in that year in the bloody battle of Miami, in which Arthur St. Clair was so badly defeated.

CALEDONIA

This was the Roman name for the northern parts of Great Britain, especially Scotland. The name was carried over by Scottish immigrants.

CALIFORNIA

This Washington County town was established shortly after news of the discovery of gold in California reached Pennsylvania.

California, the town, was laid out in 1849. The word "California" appears to be a contrived word. It first appeared in a sixteenth-century poem, "Las Sergas de Esplandan" by Garci Ordez de Montalvo. Most sources suggest the name was influenced by the word "caliph."

CAMBRIDGE SPRINGS

While prospecting for oil in 1884, Dr. John H. Gray located a mineral springs at this location. He advertised the medicinal qualities of the water found on his property to great advantage at a time when people believed that the iron in the water would cure just about everything.

CAMERON (East —)

Cameron was named for Cameron County. The county was named for Simon Cameron (1799–1889), the czar of Pennsylvania politics. Cameron was Lincoln's first secretary of war.

CAMERON. Simon Cameron was Lincoln's first secretary of war. In Pennsylvania, however, he is better known as the "Czar of Pennsylvania Politics." He influenced the state's political life well into the twentieth century. (Print and Picture Department, Free Library of Philadelphia)

CANADENSIS

The name for this community comes from the giant hemlocks, *Tsuga canadensis*. Hemlocks played a major role in nineteenth-century America, since the bark, heavily laden with tannic acid, was widely used for tanning leather.

CANONSBURG

Canonsburg, Washington County, was settled about 1773 and laid out in 1787 by Colonel John Cannon (Canon), from Virginia.

Cannon was an officer in the colonial militia, a member of the Pennsylvania Assembly, and an Indian fighter. He donated the land for Jefferson College, which became part of Washington and Jefferson College.

CANTON

Canton was founded in 1800. The town was once a center for stage celebrities, who congregated here to enjoy the local mineral springs and stay at the Crockett Lodge, the home of Frank Mayo (1839–96), an actor who specialized in playing Davy Crockett.

The source of the name is uncertain. Suggestions include canton, a French word for "district, subdivision"; the Chinese seaport; or the town by that name in Massachusetts, named in 1797.

CARBONDALE

William and Maurice Wurts, from Philadelphia, opened coal mines in this Lackawanna County area in 1814, and created a settlement.

The name, obviously a reference to a valley or dale where coal can be found, was supposedly named by Washington Irving. Chances are the namer was an unnamed officer of the Delaware & Hudson Company. Tools and supplies were addressed to the "dale where carbon was found."

In 1843, Carbondale was mentioned as a "prosperous borough, which has sprung up within a few years by the magic power of anthracite coal." The greater part of Carbondale burned down on 15 December 1850.

CARLISLE (— Springs)

Carlisle, Cumberland County, was founded in 1751 and takes its name from Carlisle, England.

The town began its existence when James Le Tort, a French Protestant trader, built his cabin here in 1735. The settlement that grew up around the cabin became known as Le Tort's Springs. Nicholas Scull, Penn's surveyor general, laid out the town in 1751 and named it Carlisle. The name translates to "city of the tower, or fort, at the end of the wall."

Carlisle was home to two signers of the Declaration of Independence: James Wilson and George Ross. It was also the home of Mary Ludwig Hays, better known as Molly Pitcher. A life-size monument in the cemetery on East South Street marks her grave.

Dickinson College, the oldest college in Pennsylvania, was chartered here in 1783. The Carlisle Indian School, the first school for Indians not located on a reservation, was opened in 1879 at

Carlisle Barracks. Olympian Jim Thorpe was once a student there (see Jim Thorpe).

Carlisle Springs was a popular spa in the mid-nineteenth century until its principal hotel burned down in 1867.

CARNEGIE

Before 1894, two distinct boroughs, Chartiers and Mansfield, co-existed on both sides of the Chartiers Creek, in Allegheny County. In that year, the townspeople consolidated the two towns into one and named it Carnegie.

Carnegie was named for Andrew Carnegie. Prior to the naming, Carnegie had no interest in this locale. But after it incorporated with his name, he endowed the library with $200,000.

Woodville, located at Carnegie, was the home of General John Neville (1731–1803), a veteran of the French and Indian War and the Revolution.

Neville achieved his footnote in history as the inspector of survey for the collection of the whiskey tax that culminated in the Whiskey Rebellion.

CARROLL

See Carrolltown.

CARROLLTOWN

Carrolltown, Cambria County, was named by Father Demetrius Augustine Gallitzin for his close friend, John Carroll. In 1788, Carroll became the first Roman Catholic bishop in the United States. Twenty years later, he became Archbishop of Baltimore. His cousin was "Charles Carroll of Carrollton," the only signer of the Declaration of Independence to give his home address.

Gallitzin was also instrumental in the naming of Loretto and Gallitzin.

CASHTOWN

A major landmark in this town is the Cashtown Tavern, dating back to 1797. It is said the town received its name for an early tavern-keeper who would only accept cash as payment.

CASSVILLE

Located in Huntindon County, Cassville was named in 1843 for the distinguished statesman General Lewis Cass (1782–1866), from

Michigan. The naming took place shortly after Cass returned, to great public acclaim, from service as U. S. minister to France.

CATASAQUA (West —)

Previously named Calisuk and Caladqua, Catasaqua takes its name from the Catasaqua Creek, which empties into the Lehigh River south of the town.

The first settlement in this Lehigh County community was in 1839, called Cranesville. The name came from George Crane, the ironmaster for the Lehigh Crane Iron Company. Five years later, the name was changed to Sideropolis, Greek for "iron city," a reference to the town's major industry.

In 1853, the town dropped the Greek name and was incorporated as Catasaqua. The name, some say, comes from the Delaware tongue and translates to "big rock." Another source suggests the name is a corruption of *gotto-shacki*, "the earth thirsts for rain," "dry land," or "burnt ground." The Indians made a practice of burning out undergrowth to make hunting easier.

CATAWISSA

This Columbia County town was named for the branch of the Susquehanna River. The name is a corruption of the Indian word *gottawisi*, "growing fat" or, as some others contend, "clear water." The latter seems more logical.

Catawissa was laid out in 1787 by William Hughes, a Quaker from Berks County.

CECIL

Cecil was named for Cecil Calvert, second Lord Baltimore.

CENTRALIA

Centralia was founded in 1826, and named for its commercial location.

CENTRE HALL

Centre Hall, Centre County, was settled by John Lion, a Scotch-Irish ironmaster. The town was built on his farmland. In 1847, Henry Whitmer named the locale Centre Hall, probably because it was in Centre County. Others contend the name came from the village's location. It stands at the midpoint between the eastern and western ends of Penn's Valley.

The Hall in the name, it appears, comes from the English custom of calling a manor-house located amidst a hamlet a "hall."

CESSNA

The man responsible for having the railroad stop in this Bedford County village was John A. Cessna. The appreciative townspeople named their location in his honor.

CHADDS FORD

This Chester County village was named for Francis Chadds or Chadsey, a landowner.

Chadds arrived from Wiltshire in 1689, and settled a tract that became the present Chadds Ford. As immigration moved westward, travel increased. Because the Brandywine flooded under heavy rains, Chadds was asked to establish a ferry at this site. The authorities in Chester County felt that Chadds' efforts were for the public good, and gave him thirty dollars to help meet the expenses in building a "flat or schowe." His ferry was in operation by 1737. Chadds also ran a tavern for about ten years, though he operated the ferry until his death in 1760.

Chadds Ford was made famous by the 11 September 1777 battle of Brandywine. At the battle, George Washington hurled 12,000 ragtag troops against 18,000 British and Hessian regulars under Generals Howe and Knyphausen. The troops maneuvered in the fog for hours, until the British crossed the Brandywine and flanked Washington's men. This defeat, coupled with the loss at Germantown, allowed the British to capture Philadelphia. The young Marquis de la Fayette was wounded here.

CHALFONT

Chalfont, Bucks County, was originally the name of the Philadelphia & Reading Railroad's station on the Doylestown branch. The town, Butler's Mill, later made the railroad name its own.

Some sources suggest the name was given in honor of Chalfont St. Giles in Buckinghamshire, England, where William Penn is buried. Chalfont St. Giles is also where Milton wrote the latter part of *Paradise Lost*.

According to local tradition, the famous Delaware Chief Tamenend (Tammany) is buried here along the Neshaminy Creek. (William Penn purchased land from Tamenend in 1683.) The Sons of King Tammany was formed in Philadelphia in 1772; the Tammany Society of New York—better known as the Democratic Party machine—in 1786.

CHAMBERSBURG (—ville)

Chambersburg served as the base of operations for John Brown before his foray into Harpers Ferry. He lived here during the summer of 1859, posing as a "prospector."

During the Civil War, Chambersburg was occupied three times by the Confederates, and pillaged and burned by them on 30 July 1864 in retaliation for the Union raid on the Shenandoah Valley.

The community was named for its founder, Benjamin Chambers, who came to Falling Springs in 1730. Four years later, he obtained a grant for 400 acres, and built a sawmill and gristmill here. A born mediator, Chambers settled many differences between his rowdy Scotch-Irish neighbors. He even was sent to England to help settle the ongoing boundary controversy between Lord Baltimore and the Penn family. He laid out his town in 1764.

CHARLEROI (North —)

Charleroi, Washington County, was laid out in 1890 and named for the Belgian town of Charleroi. The Belgian community was renowned for its glass manufacture, and the first important industry of Pennsylvania's Charleroi was a plate glass plant. Charleroi translates to "Charles the King."

CHATHAM

Chatham, Chester County, honors William Pitt, Earl of Chatham.

CHESTER (— Heights, — Hill, — Springs, West —)

Chester, settled by the Swedes and Finns in 1644 on land granted to Joran Kyn, a bodyguard to Governor Printz, is one of the oldest settlements in Pennsylvania. It was the seat of provincial government until 1683.

Chester, originally named Upland, was allegedly renamed by George Pearson, a friend of William Penn, for the Penn's home in England.

When Penn arrived at Upland, he turned to Pearson and said: "Providence has brought us here safely. Thou hast been the companion of my perils. What wilt thou I should call this place?" Pearson answered: "Chester, in remembrance of the city from whence I came." Penn also promised to name a county Chester.

A. Howry Espenshade could not locate anyone by the name of Pearson arriving on the *Welcome* with Penn. He concluded the name was given because, when the townspeople petitioned in 1704 to have the Church of England established here, the majority of people were from Cheshire, England. It seems likely the name change was made to accommodate the people's wishes.

CHRISTIANA

Christiana, Lancaster County, was not named for Sweden's Queen Christina, as some contend.

William Nobel built the first house here in 1833, and started a machine shop. He named the town for his wife.

Christiana was the site of an 1851 gunfight between a slave-owner and the "stationmaster" of a stop along the Underground Railroad. Edward Gorsuch, a slave-owner from Maryland, and a federal marshall approached the cabin of William Parker. They had a warrant for the return of several escaped slaves, as stipulated by the Fugitive Slave Law. After the marshal read the warrants, Gorsuch said he was going to get "his property, or breakfast in hell." A short time later, shots were exchanged and Gorsuch fell dead; his son was wounded. Parker and thirty-seven of his neighbors were tried for treason, but their attorney, U. S. Representative Thaddeus Stevens, a strong abolitionist, pleaded their case so well that the whole group was declared "not guilty."

CHURCHILL

This town was not named for Sir Winston. It was named because the main house of prayer was located on a hill.

CLAIRTON

There are a number of possibilities for the name source of Clairton. One school of thought suggests the name was descriptive, a "clear, bright, or illustrious town." Others suggest the name comes from Arthur St. Clair. A more likely source would be Samuel Sinclair, who owned the land on which Clairton was built.

Clairton was almost entirely residential until 1892, when a brickyard and a glass plant opened. It was incorporated as a borough in 1903, and received its city charter in 1922.

CLARENDON

Like Clairton, the town of Clarendon, Warren County, has supporters who contend their town was named for Edward, Earl of Clarendon. The truth of the matter is Clarendon was laid out in about 1872 and named for Thomas Clarendon, who was part-owner of a tannery and sawmill located here.

Oil was discovered along Dutchman's Run here in 1868, precipitating great growth and prosperity . . . that did continue.

CLARION

Both Clarion County and this town owe their names to the Clarion River. Some suggest the waterway's name was derived from the sound of the river. Surveyors thought the "silvery mellowness" of the river sounded "like the distant note of the clarion." The name is also French, meaning "clear."

Clarion was laid out in 1839 by John Sloan, after it had been named the county seat. Clarion was incorporated as a borough in 1841.

CLARK (—sburg, — Ferry, — Green, — Mills, — Summit, —town, — Valley, —ville)

Clarks Ferry is located opposite the mouth of the Juniata River. In 1788, the Clark family began operating a ferry across the Susquehanna River, at a spot the Indians called Queenashawkee. The ferry was replaced by a state bridge in 1829.

Clarks Green is a small borough, named for Deacon William Clark. Clark cleared the "green" in 1799, and built a home here in 1811.

Clarks Summit was also named for William Clark. The "summit" was the high point of the grade.

CLAYLICK

Wild animals came here to lick salt from the clay deposits.

CLAYSBURG (—ville)

Claysburg once relied on a brickyard for the town's major employment. The town was founded by John Ulrich Zeth in 1804.

CLEARFIELD (— Spring, —ville)

These communities and Clearfield County adopted the name of the Clearfield Creek. The creek was so named by pioneers for all the clearings along its banks. Another source, however, contends the name is a translation from the Delaware Indian language.

Clearfield, the seat of its county, was once the site of Chingleclamouch's (Chinklacamoose, "no one tarries here willingly") Old Town. During the early eighteenth century, it was the largest Indian settlement on the West Branch of the Susquehanna. The chief's name, or at least the last syllable, is recalled in the name of

Moose Creek. The chief, or so the legend goes, would dress up in frightening costumes and terrify unsuspecting hunters who would drop the game and pelts and run away. The chief would then gather up the goodies for his people.

Abraham Witmer laid out Clearfield in 1805 on the site of Old Town, and named it for the county. Witmer donated land for the county courthouse, jail, market house, and an academy. However, he is remembered more for the stone bridge he built in 1799 that spans the Conestoga Creek at Lancaster.

CLYMER

In 1905, the Dixon Run Land Company laid out Clymer, Indiana County, and named it for George Clymer. Clymer signed the Declaration of Independence and helped frame the Constitution.

COAL CENTER (—dale, — Glen, — Hill, —mont)

Coaldale, Schuylkill County, was incorporated in 1906 and named for its rich deposits of anthracite coal. The other towns beginning with Coal were also named for their major industry.

COCALICO

Cocalico, Lancaster County, takes its name from the creek. Cocalico Creek is a corruption of the Delaware Indian *achgookwalico,* "where snakes gather in holes" or "snake den."

COGAN HOUSE (— Station)

In about 1825, David Cogan built a log house at this site. His house rapidly fell into disrepair; even the hunters noticed and began to call the settlement Cogan's House. The township in which this town rests is Cogan House Township, organized in 1843.

COLEBROOK (—grove, —sburg)

Colebrook takes its name from the name of the man who began Coleman's Furnace here in 1781.

COLLEGEVILLE

Collegeville, Montgomery County, is home to Ursinus College, and takes its name from that institution.

The town was originally called Perkiomen Bridge, and later Freeland. Todd's School was founded here in 1832, and in 1848, Freeland Seminary was opened nearby. The seminary was purchased by a group of Philadelphians twenty years later. After the seminary became Ursinus, the town's name was changed to Collegeville.

Ursinus was named for Zacharias Ursinus, a distinguished German scholar of the Reformation. When the Pennsylvania Female College closed in 1881, Ursinus opened its doors to women, making it one of the earliest coeducational colleges.

COLUMBIA (— Cross Roads)

Samuel Wright laid out Columbia in 1788. Wright was grandson to John Wright, a Quaker who was one of the first settlers in the area. John Wright came to the area in 1726 to preach to the Indians. He stayed and began a ferry. For a time, the town was called Wright's· Ferry, but the ferry was replaced by a bridge in 1812.

No one is sure why the town is named Columbia because it was named before the name became popular through Joseph Hopkinson's famous song, "Hail Columbia," first sung in Philadelphia in 1798. The first time the name was used in print was in Philip Freneau's 1775 poem, "American Liberty." Another source seems to think the name came about when this location was being considered as a possible site for the nation's capital.

COLUMBUS

Both the borough and township in Warren County were named for Christopher Columbus, long touted as the discoverer of America.

COMPASS

Compass, Chester County, took its name from an old tavern on the Lancaster Road. The signboard was a "Mariner's Compass."

CONCORDVILLE

The Quakers who settled here in the seventeenth century named it for their central desire. They were settled for only a short time when they began petitioning the Proprietors to punish the Indians for "ye Rapine and destruction of Hoggs."

CONESTOGA

Conestoga was once called Conestoga Center, because it was the

144

principal village in Conestoga County. It was known by that name until World War II.

The village was platted in 1805 by John Kendig. It takes its name from the township, which takes its name from the Conestoga Creek, named for the Conestogoe Indians, who lived in the area.

The highway marker indicates this town was home to the famous Conestoga wagon. It is more likely that the big, wide-wheeled wagons that forged the frontiers were built throughout the Conestoga Valley. Conestoga, which translates to "crooked stream," is in Lancaster County.

CONFLUENCE

Confluence, Somerset County, is located where its name implies: at the confluence of three waterways, the Laurel and Casselman Creeks and the Youghiogheny River.

CONNEAUT LAKE (— Lake Park, —ville)

The name of Conneaut Lake and Conneautville was corrupted from the Indian language. *Gunniate,* in the Delaware tongue, translates to "it is a long time since they are gone."

Another source seems to think the name comes from the Seneca, meaning "many fish." Still another contends the name translates to "snow place," because snow remained frozen on the lake longer than it did on the land.

CONNELLSVILLE (South —)

Connellsville, Fayette County, was visited by Zachariah Connell in 1770. He and several other pioneers came when coal was first discovered. Twenty-three years later, Connell laid out the town.

George Washington visited the site in October of 1770, while visiting with Captain William Crawford, who had a cabin across the river. "We went to visit a coal mine," Washington wrote, "on the banks of the Youghiogheny River. The coal seemed to be of the very best kind, buring freely, and abundance of it."

Connellsville was incorporated as a borough in 1806, and chartered in 1811 as a city.

CONNOQUENESSING

Settled in 1792 as Petersville, for settler Peter McKinney, the name of this Butler County locale was changed to the Indian *gunachquene' sink,* which translates to "a long way straight" or "long reach."

CONSHOHOCKEN (West —)

Almost 300 years ago, the Lenni-Lenapes called their valley Conshohocken. It means "beautiful or pleasant valley." Another source suggests the name is Algonquian for "roar-land-at," an allusion to an incident that might have taken place here.

The Montgomery County community, founded in the nineteenth century after the construction of the Schuylkill Canal, was incorporated as a borough in 1850.

CONYNGHAM

Conyngham was named for Gustavus Conyngham, a seafaring man of the Revolutionary War times. After being captured by the British and confined to the Tower of London, he escaped by digging his way out with a spoon. He always told people he had committed treason through the earth.

COPLAY

This Lehigh County community's name has nothing to do with the Pennsylvania Lottery, or Blue Cross/Blue Shield payments.

It takes its name, instead, from the Coplay Creek. The waterway's name is drawn from the name of an Indian, *Kolapechki*, and means "that which runs evenly" or "fine-running—or smooth-running—stream."

CORAOPOLIS

There are two schools of thought concerning this town's name. The snobbish ones like to say it comes from the Greek Koreopolis, the "Maiden City." The more realistic ones contend it was named for Cora Watson (Mrs. William T. Tredway), daughter of an influential townsman.

The site of this town was acquired in 1769 by Andrew (sometimes called Henry) Montour, son of Madame Catherine Montour, for whom Montour County was named. During the Revolution, Robert Vance settled near Montour's land, and the first post office honored him with the name Vance Fort. Before 1886, however, the town was known as Middletown because it was the midpoint between Pittsburgh and Beaver. But there was an older Middletown, so the village was incorporated as Corapolis.

CORNWALL

The Cornwall Ore Banks contain the most valuable iron ore deposits in the East. The mines operated from 1735–1972.

The Cornwall Iron Furnace was built in 1742 by Peter Grubb and produced cannon for the Revolution, operating until 1883. This Lebanon County community takes its name from the Furnace.

CORRY

This Erie County community was named for an early landowner. Two railroads intersected on Hiram Corry's farm in 1861.

The town grew because of the oil discovered by Drake in Titusville, only twenty-five miles away. The year after the railroads arrived, the town boasted two hotels, an oil works, and several mills. Development was so swift that it was known as "the city of stumps," for the remains of trees in the building lot clearings.

Corry was chartered as a city by 1866.

COUDERSPORT

Coudersport, the seat of Potter County, was founded by John Keating, an Irish mercenary who managed the Ceres Land Company, the principal landholder in the area. Keating gave fifty acres each to the first fifty settlers and named the community after a Dutch banker, Jean Samuel Couderc. Couderc, senior member of Couderc, Brants & Changuion in Amsterdam, handled the finances for some of the French exiles who located here.

When they established the town as county seat, they dropped the "c" from Couderc's name "for the sake of euphony."

COUPON

First settled in the late nineteenth century, this town was called DeLaney for the founding family.

In 1893, a coal company moved in and virtually took over the town. The company issued coupons, or scrip, for its workers to redeem at the company store. The postmaster, who also owned the general store, was quite upset, and when it came time in 1894 to choose a name for the post office, the name was changed to Coupon.

COVINGTON

Settled in 1801, Covington was known for about thirty years as The Corners. It was renamed when land speculators rushed in to take advantage of the coal and iron boom. But, early in the 1840s, the bubble burst.

The town was ostensibly named for General Leonard Covington, hero of Fort Recovery, 1794.

COVODE

Covode honors the memory of "Honest John" Covode, a member of the U. S. House of Representatives from this county, 1854–70.

Covode's grandfather was Garret Covode, a Dutchman who was kidnapped from the streets of Amsterdam and sold as a "bond-servant," or "redemptioner," in Philadelphia. The congressman liked to suggest that granddad had been a servant in George Washington's household.

COWANESQUE

Cowanesque, Tioga County, takes its name from the creek. The name is an Indian word meaning "overrun with briars."

CRAFTON

Crafton was laid out about 1873 by Charles C. Craft, and named for his father, James S. Craft, from whom he had inherited the land. The town site was located on the former Indian village of Killiman.

Where Crafton now stands, General Edward Hand, commander of Fort Pitt, built a hospital in 1777 to care for sick and wounded soldiers. A suburb of Pittsburgh, Crafton was incorporated in 1890.

CRAMER

Cramer takes its name from Kramer's Mill, a sawmill erected along Stump Creek sometime before 1885.

CRESCO

Cresco's name is taken from the Latin for "I grow," a hopeful thought for the town's future.

CRESSON

Located in Cambria County, Cresson was once a fashionable health resort. It was named for Elliott Cresson, a Philadelphia merchant and philanthropist. The name was suggested by Dr. Robert Montgomery Smith Jackson, a local physician.

Cresson was the "Summer Capital of the United States" when President Harrison summered here during his administration.

CRESSONA

This community was laid out by John Chapman Cresson. Cresson, of Philadelphia, was a civil engineer and manager of the Schuylkill Navigation Company, president of the Mine Hill & Schuylkill Haven Railroad, and chief engineer of Philadelphia's Fairmount Park. The name was modified to avoid confusion with Cresson.

CUMBOLA

Cumbola's name seems to have been derived from a combination of railroads: Cumberland Valley, Baltimore & Ohio, and Lehigh, with the "a" attached for euphony.

CURWENSVILLE

Curwensville, Clearfield County, was named for John Curwen, of Montgomery County. Though Curwen gained title to the land on which the town was built in 1798, he never lived here. The town, located at the junction of Anderson Creek and the West Branch, was laid out in 1812.

CUSTER. George Armstrong Custer was one of the youngest generals in the Civil War. Though destined for greatness during the war, he was reduced to lieutenant colonel and sent out West to fight Indians. He met his doom at the Little Big Horn in Montana. (Photograph by Matthew Brady, National Archives)

CUSTER CITY

This McKean County location was named in honor of George Armstrong Custer, who was killed by an overwhelming Sioux force at Little Big Horn in 1876.

To entertain themselves, townspeople in 1879 staged a bull-and-bear fight. The state S.P.C.A. demanded the fight be halted, but they refused the promoter's offer to "go ahead and stop it yourselves!" While the humans were arguing, the bear escaped the ring and wounded several spectators. He was finally roped and returned to the ring, but he was too tired to fight the bull.

DAGUSCAHONDA

Founded in 1860, the name of this Elk County community is drawn from the Indian and means either "wildcat run" or "pure water," two pretty widely separated sources.

Daguscahonda was founded in 1860 as housing for labor in the local lumber industry.

DALLAS (—town)

Dallastown, York County, was founded in 1842. Two years later it was named for George Mifflin Dallas, who served as a U. S. senator from Pennsylvania, then as Polk's vice president (1845–49). He was the only Pennsylvanian ever to serve as vice president.

DANVILLE

Danville, Montour County, was laid out by General Daniel Montgomery in 1792. He was the son of General William Montgomery, who settled here during the Revolution. His home, Montgomery House, was built in 1777.

The father opened a gristmill; the son, a store. The town that grew up around the mill and store was first called Dan's Town, which was altered into Danville.

The first iron rail for railroad track was rolled in Danville on 8 October 1845. English and Welsh craftsmen produced the rail for the Montour Iron Works, established in 1840.

Danville became the county seat in 1850. Previously it had been the seat of Columbia County, from 1813–45.

DARBY

Darby has a transplanted English name. The Delaware County community, settled in 1682, was called Derbytown as early as 1698. The English were not consistent in their spellings, and the name Derby/Darby appears interchangeable. The English town is located on the Derwent River, but the name is more likely a modification of *deor*, meaning "wild beast, or deer," and by, "a town."

John Bartram, the world-famous botanist, was born in Darby in 1699.

DAUPHIN

Dauphin was settled around a gristmill established here as early as 1770. The name is taken from the county, formed in 1785 and named for the Dauphin of France, the son of Louis XVI.

DEFIANCE

This Bedford County community takes its name from Fort Defiance, a frontier defense during the Indian wars.

DELANO

Delano commemorates Columbus Delano, Grant's secretary of the interior.

DELMONT

Delmont's name translates to "mountain on the Delaware."

DERRICK CITY
Derrick City takes its name from the early petroleum industry.

DICKSON CITY
This Lackawanna County community was named for Thomas Dickson, president of the Delaware & Hudson Canal Company, from 1869 until his death in 1884. At one time, he held large coal interests in the Dickson City area. Coal drifts were opened here in 1859 by William H. Richmond, of Scranton.

Dickson City was incorporated in 1875.

DINGMANS FERRY
Dingmans Ferry, founded in 1735, was named for the ferry operated by first settler Andrew Dingman. The ferry, opened in 1750, crossed from Pennsylvania to New Jersey. It was replaced by a bridge.

DIVIDE
Divide's name comes from the definition of a "divide," a height of land marking the division between two important drainage systems.

DONORA
Donora was laid out by the Union Improvement Company on the west bank of the Monongahela River in 1900.

The president of the company was William H. Donner, and Andrew W. Mellon, of Pittsburgh, was a major stockholder. The name for this company town was made from the first syllable of Donner's name and the given name of Mellon's wife, Nora. Mrs. Mellon's maiden name, by the way, was Donner.

DORMONT
Dormont, Allegheny County, was incorporated in 1909 and named by its first mayor. Gilbert M. Brown picked the French *d'or mont*, "mountain of gold," because of the beauty of the location and the unlimited opportunities available to its residents.

DORRANCE
Dorrance, Luzerne County, takes its name from Dorrance Township, formed in 1840 and named for Colonel George Dorrance. At one time it was known as Dorranceton.

DOWNINGTOWN

Originally settled by English immigrants from Birmingham, this Chester County city was originally known as Milltown.

In 1739, Thomas Moore sold his mill and farm of 561 acres to Thomas Downing. Forty years later, though the mill had changed hands, the town was still called Milltown.

Downing vigorously resisted making his town the seat of Chester County in 1786, saying "not a lot could be obtained on which to erect the county buildings." Downingtown was incorporated as a borough in 1859.

One of the early American portrait painters to gain national recognition, Jacob Eichholtz (1776–1842), was born here.

DOYLESTOWN

In 1778, this Bucks County community was called Doyle's-town, named for William Doyle, who settled here about 1735. He maintained a tavern at the crossroads as early as 1742. In those days, Doylestown was the overnight stop on the stage between Philadelphia and Easton.

DRUMS

One might conjure up images of Indians beating tom-toms, alerting other tribes to the passage of bands of white men. Wrong!

Drums, Luzerne County, first known as East Sugarloaf Township, then as Butler Township, was named for George Drums, who operated a tavern here.

DRY RUN

Dry Run's name did not come from a rehearsal. Rather, it was named for the stream that would periodically dry up.

DRY TAVERN

Dry Tavern is one of the best oxymorons we have seen in a long time.

DU BOIS

Located in Clearfield County, this city was settled in 1865. It was originally called Rumberger, for John Rumberger, who laid out the town and sold building lots in 1872.

That same year, the famous lumberman John DuBois arrived on the scene. DuBois had exhausted his supply of white pine in forests elsewhere in Clearfield County, and moved here to begin extensive lumber operations.

The post office established here took on the name of DuBois and, in 1880, the town was incorporated under that name. DuBoistown, a village in Lycoming County and the site of his first lumbering operations, also bears his name.

DUNBAR

This Fayette County community was named for Colonel John Dunbar, who commanded British troops here and was defeated by the French and Indians.

DUNCANSVILLE

There is an interesting story attached to Duncansville. The town was founded by Samuel Duncan. At the same time, Jacob Walter owned another site east of here, which he called Walterstown. Because the two towns were closely allied, the two town fathers, at about the turn of the nineteenth century, met on a bridge across Blair Creek and flipped a penny to see which name would survive. Samuel Duncan won. Before the name was finalized, the town was nicknamed Irontown—for the operations of Old Forge.

DUNKARD

Dunkard, Greene County, takes its name from the Dunkards, or German Baptists, who migrated here from eastern Pennsylvania.

DUNMORE

This community takes its name from Charles Augustus Murray, second son of George Murray, fifth Earl of Dunmore.

The young Murray vacationed in this area in 1838, enjoying hunting and fishing in the Moosic Mountain and the Lackawanna Valley. Three Pennsylvania entrepreneurs, Henry W. Drinker, William Henry and Edward Armstrong, interested the wealthy Englishman in their project to build a railroad to connect this area with the Morris Canal in New Jersey.

Upon his return home, Murray was expected to raise $1.5 million. To compliment the Englishman, they changed the name of this town from Buckstown to Dunmore. Sadly, Murray lost interest in the project and failed to raise any money.

The community was settled in 1783 by William Allsworth. Until 1840, it was known as Buckstown.

DUPONT

Dupont was founded in 1917 and named for the duPont family, which operated a nearby powder plant.

DUQUESNE

The city of Duquesne, Allegheny County, was named for old Fort Duquesne, which was built at the forks of the Ohio River in 1754. It was named for a distinguished French officer, the Marquis Duquesne de Menneville, then governor of New France.

Prior to 1885, the town was a collection of small farms. In that year, the Duquesne Steel Company opened a plant here.

DURHAM

In 1727, an iron works was opened here and called Durham Furnace. One of the principal owners was James Logan, William Penn's secretary. The furnace ceased operations in 1789.

Durham produced something other than iron. To facilitate transport of iron across the rapids and falls in the Delaware River, the "Durham" boat was designed in about 1750. These flat-bottomed boats were capable of carrying fifteen to twenty tons of metal. George Washington used Durham boats to transport his men across the Delaware before the battle of Trenton.

DURYEA

The original name for Duryea was Babylon, "because it was a Babel of tongues and nationalities." The mines drew a wide variety of immigrant labor, all of whom spoke a different language. It takes its current name from New Yorker Abram Duryea, who bought coal lands near here in 1845 and opened mines. The town that grew around the mines became Duryea.

Duryea was a colonel of the 5th New York Infantry at the beginning of the Civil War. At war's end, he was brevetted major general "for gallant and meritorious services."

DUSHORE

Dushore, Sullivan County, is named for its founder: Aristide Aubert Dupetit-Thouars, a French naval captain—and a refugee from the French Revolution—who liked being called "Admiral." The name was modified and corrupted into Dushore. That was the name accepted in 1859, when Dushore was incorporated.

Dupteti-Thouars cleared the ground for the settlement in 1794.

154

EAGLES MERE

Eagles Mere, or "eagle's lake," in Sullivan County, was originally known as Lewis' Lake, for an Englishman who opened extensive glass works here in about 1810. His enterprise was a failure, but the area continues to thrive as a popular summer resort. The current, rather fanciful name was given in about 1875.

EASTON

Easton, Northampton County, is not a directional name. It was named for the estate of Lord Pomphret. Thomas Penn wrote to Governor James Hamilton in 1751 and instructed him to lay out some ground for a town here. "I desire it may be called Easton," Penn wrote, "from my Lord Pomfret's house; and whenever there is a new county, it is to be called Northampton."

Easton's original name, however, was the Delaware Indian *Lechauwitank*, "place at the forks" of the Delaware. This designation included both the city and the triangular tract of land between the Lehigh and Delaware Rivers.

The first public reading of the Declaration of Independence took place on the steps of the Northampton County Court House in Centre Square—on 8 July 1776. Local tradition contends that a flag of "stars and stripes" flew above Easton's courthouse that day, a year before the Flag Resolution was adopted by the Continental Congress.

As early as 1752, Easton was the county seat.

EAU CLAIRE

Eau Claire is French for "clear water."

EBENSBURG

Ebensburg, Cambria County, received its name in 1805, when the town was designated the county seat. The town was laid out by the Reverend Rees Lloyd, a religious dissenter from Wales. He named it for his son, Eben Lloyd, who died at birth.

There was a Welsh settlement here as early as 1796. Lloyd was the religious leader of the group.

Ebensburg was selected as county seat when legislators recognized it as the geographic center of Cambria County.

ECHO (— Lake)

Echo, Armstrong County, takes its name from three ravines located here. Almost any sound made in the area ricochets through the space and creates echoes.

ECONOMY

Economy was founded in 1825 by a Harmonist society, and named for the tenets of their governance and style of living.

EDGEWORTH

It would seem logical that this town would be at the "edge of a worth." In some respects it is; it was located at the edge of the Worth property.

Edgeworth was the first Pennsylvania municipality to adopt the borough-manager form of government. It was also the birthplace of Ethelbert Nevin (1862–1901), who composed many well-known piano pieces of his day, including "The Rosary" and "Narcissus."

EDISON

Edison was named for Thomas Alva Edison, inventor. (See Edison, New Jersey.)

EDWARDSVILLE

The borough of Edwardsville, Luzerne County, was created in 1884 by the merger of parts of old Plymouth and Kingston Townships.

It was named for Daniel Edwards, the Welsh superintendent of the Kingston Coal Company. The company's operation was totally within the limits of the new borough. Edwards was in charge of the company from 1868 until his death in 1901.

EFFORT

An apocryphal tale has it that the townfolk met to select a name for their new post office. They met on more than one occasion . . . without success. Finally, one man stood up and applauded the group for the effort they had made. Then he moved that the town be named Effort. The townspeople, frustrated and tired, agreed.

EIGHTY FOUR

In the late nineteenth century, this Washington County town was called Smithville, but, because there was another community of the same name in the state, the residents had to select a new name.

In 1884, the townspeople met and decided to name their town Eighty Four, for the year. Grover Cleveland won a hard-fought battle that year for the presidency.

ELIZABETH (—town, —ville, West —)

Elizabeth, Allegheny County, was laid out by Stephen Bayard in 1787, and named for his bride, Elizabeth Mackey, daughter of Colonel Aeneas Mackay, who once commanded Fort Pitt.

In 1732, Captain Thomas Harris, whose brother founded Harrisburg, operated the trading post at what would become Elizabethtown, Lancaster County. Three years later, the captain opened a tavern which he called The Black Bear.

The town lots in Elizabethtown were sold in about 1795 by Michael Reeby. Some sources claim the name honors his wife Elizabeth. On the other hand, other sources contend the name came from the wife of Captain Barnabas Hughes, who purchased Harris' tavern and his land in 1750.

Dauphin County's Elizabethville has a similar history. Tavern-keeper John Bender laid out the town in 1817 and named it for his wife.

ELK CITY (— Grove, — Lake, —land, — River)

Elkland, Carbon County, took its name from Elkland Township, organized in 1814 but no longer in existence. Elkland is located in a narrow valley which drew elk down to drink.

ELLWOOD CITY

This Beaver County town was laid out in 1880 by the Pittsburgh Company, and named for Colonel I.L. Elwood, of DeKalb, Indiana, one of the major stockholders of the wire-fence company.

ELMO

Elmo, some authorities contend, was named for the 1867 novel by A. J. Evans, *St. Elmo.*

ELMORA

See Elmo.

ELVERSON

Elverson was founded in 1790, and called Blue Rocks, for the formation of blue rocks on the outskirts of town.

The town was renamed in honor of James Elverson, publisher of *The Philadelphia Inquirer* from 1889–1911.

EMERALD

The jury is still out on Emerald. Some suggest the name was descriptive of the landscape; others say it came from settlers from Ireland, or the "Emerald Isle."

EMMAUS

This Lehigh County community was first settled by Moravians about 1745, and named by them for the little village in ancient Palestine. It remained a "close denominational town" until 1835.

The Indians called the place Maguntchi, "place of the bears," but the new settlers named it Salzburg. In 1761, Bishop August Spangenberg, founder of the American Moravian Church, conducted a feast here and renamed the town Emmaus. Over the years, one "m" was dropped, but the earlier spelling was returned in 1939.

EMPORIUM (— Junction)

Emporium takes its name from the Latin for "center of trade."

The original name of the town was Shippen, because it was located in Shippen Township, named for Edward Shippen, who settled in the vicinity in 1810. Emporium was the name in 1864 when the town was incorporated. But the name was in use as early as 1785.

According to tradition, in that year an agent for the Holland Land Company camped here with others of his company at the confluence of the Driftwood branch of the Sinnemahoning Creek and Portage Creek. As the story goes, the man shaved the bark off a tree and carved into it the word "Emporium."

If Pennsylvania could have one "emporium," Virginians had to go them one better. (See Emporia, Virginia.)

EMSWORTH

Prior to 1872, this community was known as Courtneyville, for James and William Courtney, who settled the area in 1805. The town was renamed for a British duke who held an early land patent.

ENDEAVOR

In the early part of the twentieth century, the Reverend J.V. McAnich organized a Christian Endeavor Society here. The society grew into a Presbyterian church. The town was originally called Christian Endeavor, and later shortened to Endeavor.

ENERGY

Asking for the reason behind the naming of Energy produces a disagreement among the authorities. Some think it descriptive of the ethos of the settling people; another, expectations for future growth; and another, business interests.

ENHAUT

Enhaut translates from the French for "on high."

ENOLA (West —)

One of the more popular tales about the naming of Enola, Cumberland County, was from a telegraph operator who performed his lonely task in a tower across the river from Harrisburg. Someone suggested the word "alone" was reversed "enola."

Another tale, slightly more plausible, deals with a novel by the name of *The Dangers of Darkness*. In 1861, Mrs. Amanda Gingrich Underwood, of Mechanicsburg, Pennsylvania, read the novel and was attracted to one of the characters, a woman called Enola. When Mrs. Underwood had a daughter, she named her Enola Underwood. A cousin of Mrs. Underwood, Fannie Longsdorf Miller, also named her first daughter Enola.

When the Pennsylvania Railroad came into this area, the company purchased a tract of land from the Millers. He proposed his wife's maiden name—the land had been Mrs. Miller's parental homestead—for the station but that name was already in use elsewhere. So he suggested the name of his four-year-old daughter, which was accepted.

ENON VALLEY

Enon is a simplified version of Aenon, a place mentioned in the New Testament as "there was much water there." There is no truth to the story that the namers spelled "none" backwards.

EPHRATA

The Ephrata Kloster or Cloister was one of America's earliest communal societies. In 1735, Johann Conrad Beissel, leader of a little (about thirty-five member) German religious sect of Seventh Day Baptist Brethren, founded the community along the Cocalico Creek. Three years later, the community became Ephrata.

The Cloister was an early center for publishing and printing, and printed the first American edition, in German, of Bunyan's *Pilgrim's Progress*.

Located in Lancaster County, Ephrata takes its name from the old designation for the Palestinian town of Bethlehem.

EQUINUNK

The name for Equinunk, Wayne County, translates from the Indian to mean "place where clothing was distributed." The town takes its name from the Equinunk Creek, which joins with the Delaware here.

The town was settled prior to the Revolution by Josiah Parks, an intelligence officer for Washington's army.

ERCILDOUN

Named for Thomas of Ercildoun, known from his association with the ballad "Thomas the Rhymer."

ERIE

Erie is Pennsylvania's only port on the Great Lakes. The first known inhabitants of the area were the Eriez Indians, known as the "Cat Nation." They gave their name to the lake; the lake gave it to the county; and the town borrowed it. The tribe was exterminated by the Seneca in 1654.

The French built Fort de la Presqu'isle on the site of present-day Erie in 1749. In 1795, the British ordered the establishment of four new towns: these became Erie, Waterford, Franklin, and Warren. These new towns were created mainly to prevent greater French expansion. In 1805, Erie became the seat of its county.

Erie was laid out by Major Andrew Ellicott and General William Irvine on a modification of L'Enfant's plan of Washington, D.C. It was incorporated as a borough in 1805, then incorporated as a city in 1851.

ETNA

This Allegheny County town was originally owned by General William Wilkins. Wilkins sold the land to David Anderson, who laid out the town and named it Stewartstown for David Stewart, a prominent resident. Later it was called Centerville.

About 1832, H.S. Spang and his son came to the area from Catharine Township, Blair County, where they operated the Etna Furnace. The Spang family opened furnaces and mills here, and the town was incorporated as Etna in 1868.

The name comes from the Sicilian volcano of the same name. In Greek, *aith*, means "to smoke or burn."

EUCLID

Contrary to whatever image the name Euclid creates in one's mind, the real source of the name for this Butler County community is Euclid Avenue, Cleveland, Ohio. The town's first postmaster, Thomas McCall, named it in 1880.

EVANS CITY (— Falls)

In 1796, George Boggs swapped a mare for 400 acres of land in this area. He built a cabin and started a mill. Forty years later, he sold half the land and the mill to Thomas B. Evans. Evans laid out a village, and called it Evansburg. Evansburg was the corporate title for the town, but Evans City was the name of its post office.

EVERETT

Everett, Bedford County, was laid out by Michael Barndollar in 1795 and named Waynesboro. When the railroad arrived in 1862, the name was changed to Everett. Some sources suggest the name came from Edward Everett, of Massachusetts. A more plausible source would be a railroad official.

EXCELSIOR

Excelsior takes its name from the Latin word for "higher" or "ever upward." The namer usually found the word in Longfellow's poem.

EXCHANGE

Exchange was located on an old mail route . . . at a point where it was necessary to change or "exchange" horses.

EXETER

Exeter, Luzerne County, takes its name from the old Exeter Township, which was founded in 1790 by settlers from Exeter, Rhode Island. That town took its name from Exeter, England.

The town was the site of Fort Wintermute. The fort was surrendered to the British by its garrison of Loyalists during the early part of the Battle of Wyoming. (See Wyoming.)

EXPORT

Incorporated in 1911, this town was the first in the area to mine coal for more than local markets, ergo, Export.

EXTON

Exton is a play on words. The community is a little too far from Philadelphia to be considered a suburb, and is therefore "out of town." The term used today is "exurbia."

FACTORYVILLE

In the 1840s, there was a woolen mill located at this site. The mill (or factory) was established to accommodate the settlers from New England who brought their wool here to be woven into cloth.

Some sources suggest the mill was for cotton, but it does not seem likely that the local residents raised cotton in this clime.

FAIRHOPE

When the town was laid out after the Civil War, the townspeople selected this unusual name because they thought they had a "fair hope" of getting a railroad built through town.

FALLEN TIMBER

A legend in this area has it that the name comes from the results of a major storm that blew a path through the forested area.

FALLS (— Creek)

Falls, founded in 1824, takes its name from its location on both sides of the Susquehanna River.

FALMOUTH

Falmouth takes its name from the seaport town in Cornwall, one authority swears. Another contends it came from the town in Virginia. (See Falmouth, Virginia.)

FARRELL

The borough of South Sharon, Mercer County, decided to change its name in 1911, just ten years after it had been incorporated.

They selected Farrell for James A. Farrell, president of the United Steel Corporation. Steel played an important part in the town's life.

FASSETT

Fassett was originally called State Line, because of its location. It was renamed to honor Philo Fassett, an early settler.

FAYETTEVILLE

The name comes from Fayette County, which was named for Marquis de la Fayette.

FILLMORE

Fillmore was named for President Millard Fillmore.

FISHERS FERRY

Fishers Ferry takes its name from the ferry operated by Mr. Fisher early in the town's life.

In Fishers Ferry stands the Penn House, or Stone Tavern, built in 1756 and the site of a tragic legend. The story unfolds as William Penn's grandson John married Mary Cox, the daughter of a London silversmith. This did not please the Penns, so they spirited John away to Switzerland. The pair conspired successfully to meet in America. But, after only a year together, Mary disappeared. After weeks of searching for his wife, John gave her up for dead and returned to England.

He returned to America in 1763 as lieutenant governor of the province, and married the daughter of Pennsylvania's chief justice. Six years later, on one of his inspection trips, he stopped at Stone Tavern.

While there, he heard a woman coughing convulsively. He walked to the woman and discovered his long-lost wife. Close to death, Mary told the tale of being kidnapped and kept by Indians in Canada. Penn buried her, the legend goes, on the slope of a hill overlooking the river.

Though old-time local residents swear by the tale, historians can find no proof of these events.

FLOURTOWN

Flourtown, founded in the 1740s, was noted for a flourishing flour business.

FORD CITY

This Armstrong County site was named for Captain John B. Ford, "the father of the plate-glass industry in America." Ford opened his factory here in 1887 and turned the city into a manufacturing center.

Ford's enterprise became Pittsburgh Plate Glass.

FOREST CITY (— Hill, — Hills, — Inn, — Lake, —ville)

Forest City, Susquehanna County, was a lumber camp called Pentecost in 1885. This Pentecost has no religious significance; it was the name of one of the camp's owners, William Pentecost.

As time passed, the place was nicknamed Forest City and the name took hold. When the lumbering town was incorporated in 1888, it officially became Forest City.

The emphasis from lumber was changed in 1873, when coal was discovered on a nearby farm.

FORT LITTLETON

The town of Fort Littleton grew around the frontier stronghold of the same name.

The fortification was built in 1756 by Governor Robert Hunter Morris and named for an English statesman, Sir George Littleton. The town began the same year.

FORT LOUDON

This Franklin County community took the name of old Fort Loudon, built in 1756 by Colonel John Armstrong.

The fort was named for John Campbell, Earl of Loudon, who very briefly commanded the British forces in the colonies. The earl was very unpopular in the colonies because he was incompetent.

The village was founded in 1795.

In 1765, an event at Fort Loudon presaged the growing dissatisfaction Americans felt with British rule. Settlers took the law into their own hands when a convoy of supply wagons moving under a military permit of the "King's goods" arrived. The settlers were still smarting from a Delaware Indian massacre of nine children and their schoolmaster the year before. When they found that the supplies were actually an attempt by a Philadelphia entrepreneur to reestablish trade with the Indians, the settlers tried to change the British minds. Unsuccessful, they empowered James Smith to resolve the situation.

Smith disguised himself and a small band of volunteers as Indians and attacked the wagon train, destroying almost the entire shipment. A platoon of English troops came to the rescue and eight "Indians" were captured and confined in the fort. Smith arranged a swap for those men after he captured an equal number of British troopers. But the British attempts to renew the Indian trade continued. Smith and 300 volunteers finally stormed the fort and forced the British to withdraw. He performed a similar feat four years later at Fort Bedford.

FORT WASHINGTON

Fort Washington, Montgomery County, was named for Washington's camp which was located here before the retreat to Valley Forge.

FORTY FORT

This town is named for the fort built in 1770 by a group of settlers—forty in number, who arrived a year earlier in the valley.

FRANKLIN (— Center, —dale, — Forks, — Park, —town, —ville, West —)

Franklin began when the French built Fort Machault, at what is now the intersection of 6th and Elk Streets, in 1753. Fort Machault was replaced in 1760 when the British constructed Fort Venango at the current intersection of 8th and Elk Streets.

Venango was lost to a successful ruse during Pontiac's Rebellion in 1763. The Indians often played ball near the fort. Whenever their ball accidently came over the walls, the British would open the gates and let them retrieve it. On this particular occasion, there was a larger number of ballplayers than usual. When the ball came over the wall, the gate opened and the Indians entered—and captured the fort, killing the garrison and burning the stockade.

In 1787, the Americans built Fort Franklin on that spot to protect frontier settlements. The state commissioners laid out a town on the fort's site in 1795. In 1860, oil was discovered. Franklin became the seat of Venango County in 1805.

Franklinville, also named for Benjamin Franklin, was an early iron manufacturing center. It was also the home of David Rittenhouse Porter (1788–1867), the first Pennsylvania governor under the constitution of 1838.

Benjamin Franklin's name is the second most popular source of place names in America; George Washington is number one.

FRANKSTOWN

Located in Blair County, Frankstown takes its name from Frankstown Township. The township was named for Frank Stevens, though some sources say the man's name was Stephen Franks.

Stevens was an important Indian trader who operated in central and western Pennsylvania as early as 1734.

Frank's Town was the name given the location by the Indian traders who visited here. The town grew between 1830 and 1840 with the completion of the first unified transportation system across the state, the Portage Railroad being the major link between Johnstown and Hollidaysburg.

FREDERICKSBURG

Fredericksburg, Lebanon County, was laid out in about 1755 by Frederick Stump, and named for him. He is not, one source demands, to be confused with Frederick Stump, who, after the French and Indian War, murdered ten peaceable Indians near Selinsgrove, Pennsylvania.

FREDERICKTOWN

This Washington County town was laid out in 1790 by Frederick Wise, and named in his honor.

FREDONIA

Dr. Samuel Latham Mitchill coined the word from the English "freedom" given a Latin ending. The combined name was supposed to mean "place of freedom." It was the name he proposed for the United States. It never received serious consideration.

FREEDOM (East —, West —)

Freedom was founded in 1832, the year Stephen Phillips and Johnathan Betz moved their boatyard there. They had moved from what is now Monaca, after selling their land to Bernhart Mueller (Count de Leon) and a group of his followers from the Harmony Society.

FREEHOLD

See Freehold, New Jersey.

FREELAND

Freeland, Luzerne County, was built on the farmland of Joseph Birkbeck. Birkbeck's land was different from most in this area of Pennsylvania—its soil was not underlaid with coal!

In 1868, A. Donop purchased the Birkbeck farm, laid out

streets and divided the land into town lots. The Donop tract was "free land," land that was not controlled by the coal companies and "free" to be sold. The coal companies, when selling lands for development, usually transferred only the surface rights to land, keeping for themselves all mineral rights.

Donop preferred the name Freehold for his town, but postal authorities in 1874 requested a new name—there was a more important town by that name in New Jersey. The town took on its nickname.

FREEPORT

William and David Todd laid out this Armstrong County town in 1796, establishing it as a "free port" for all river craft. The town is located at the confluence of the Allegheny and Kiskiminetas Rivers and Buffalo Creek. Though the Todds wanted to call it Freeport, it was known for years as Toddstown.

Freeport became the official name in 1833 upon incorporation.

FRENCHVILLE

Frenchville received its name because the area was primarily established by French settlers from Normandy and Picardy.

FRIEDENS (—burg)

Located in Lehigh County, Friedens takes its name from the old German and means "peace."

FRIENDSVILLE

Dr. R.H. Rose, for whom Montrose was named, laid out this Susquehanna County village in 1819. The Quaker physician named it Friendsville because he influenced members of the Society of Friends to settle here.

GALLITZIN

This town was founded by Prince Demetrius Augustine Gallitzin, son of a Russian diplomat. He arrived in Baltimore in 1792 as part of a world tour. While in America, he decided to enter the Roman Catholic priesthood. He was ordained three years later.

By 1800, Gallitzin and members of his group purchased 20,000 acres in Cambria County and established a settlement. For forty years, the priest labored in the area, leaving his name on this location, as well as helping to name Carrolltown and Loretto.

G

GENESSEE

The name for this Potter County community is drawn from an Indian word which means "shining or beautiful valley." The area once produced a most delicious beer.

GEORGETOWN

Georgetown is one of the oldest settlements in Beaver County. It was settled in 1793 by Benoni Dawson, and named by him for his son, George.

GERMANIA (— Station)

Germania, Potter County, was originally settled as a German colony in 1854 and named with a Latinized version of the name of their home country. The pioneers intended that the language and customs of Germany be perpetuated here.

GETTYSBURG

This Adams County seat was originally settled about 1780 and called the Marsh Creek Settlement. About ten years later, General James Gettys, anticipating the creation of a new county, laid out a town at this location and called it Gettys-town.

When the state authorized funds for the Adams County courthouse to be built here in 1800, the name was officially changed to Gettysburg. Gettysburg was incorporated in 1806. It was the scene of one of the bloodiest battles of the Civil War. On 3 July 1863, the ground trembled under the heaviest artillery battle ever fought on the American continent. Abraham Lincoln came to Gettysburg to offer "a few appropriate remarks" for the men who had died here. He began, "Four score and seven years ago. . . ." Gettysburg was also the retirement home of one of this nation's greatest military and political leaders, Dwight D. Eisenhower.

Gettysburg was incorporated as a borough in 1806. In 1895, Congress created the Gettysburg National Military Park.

GILBERT (—ton, —sville)

Gilberton, Schuylkill County, is the result of the consolidation of a number of smaller settlements. The "merger" took place in 1873, and was named for John Gilbert, a wealthy coal operator.

GIRARD (—ville)

Girard, Erie County, and Girardville, Schuylkill County, were both named for Stephen Girard (1750–1831).

Girard was settled before the turn of the nineteenth century and incorporated as a borough in 1846.

Girard was a wealthy Philadelphian—at one time the richest man in the world. He owned the large tracts of land in both locations and, prior to his death, planned to develop them.

GIRDLAND

Girdland took its name from the procedure foresters used to kill trees.

GIRTY

This community was named for the famous renegade Simon Girty (1741–1818).

GLADE MILLS

Glade Mills, located on Glade Run, was the site of an early gristmill and sawmill. Both were built here early in the nineteenth century by John Woodcock.

The Glade Run oil fields opened in 1886, and the town prospered—until the wells petered out.

GLASSPORT

The name for this Allegheny County city, located on the Monongahela River, came from the United States Glass Company. In 1888, the company opened a plant here. The town was literally a place where glass was made and shipped from a new port on the river.

GOOD INTENT

No one is sure how this Washington County location really got its name, but local residents have a story to tell. It seems that Peter Wolf built a gristmill at this location in the early nineteenth century. Shortly after he finished construction, the mill pond filled with silt and he was forced to build another mill downstream.

Over the years, two gristmills, two blacksmith shops, a tannery, a stage company, a harness-and-saddle shop, a post office, and a Baptist church all came to town and, after a short time, moved on. This town might well have proven Samuel Johnson's quotation true: "Hell is paved with good intentions."

GOOD YEAR

The name of this town shows the hope the settlers had for the growth of their community.

GORDON

The land on which Gordon, Schuylkill County, was built was once owned by David and James McKnight. Their descendents laid out the town and named it for Judge David F. Gordon, of Reading. The McKnights had given him a building lot.

GRAMPIAN

When Dr. Samuel Coleman looked at the area in which Grampian, Clearfield County, is located, he thought it looked like Scotland's Grampian Hills, where his family originated.

GRANGE

The name of this community comes from the nineteenth-century farmers' organization, The National Grange of the Patrons of Husbandry.

GRANVILLE (— Center, — Summit)

Granville, Mifflin County, takes its name from old Fort Granville, built near the site of Lewistown about 1756.

The fort was named for John Carteret, the Earl of Granville and a member of the English cabinet. (See Carteret, New Jersey.)

GRATZ. This Pennsylvania locale was named for the Gratz family of Philadelphia. None of the family members were as attractive as Rebecca Gratz, said to be the model for Sir Walter Scott's character of the same name in *Ivanhoe*. (Print and Picture Department, Free Library of Philadelphia)

GRATZ

Gratz is named for the Philadelphia Gratz family. The most famous of the Gratz clan was Rebecca Gratz, the supposed model for Sir Walter Scott's heroine of the same name in *Ivanhoe*.

The Gratz family had strong Pennsylvania roots. In fact, Edward Gratz was active in the construction of the Pennsylvania Railroad.

GREAT BEND

Great Bend, Susquehanna County, was founded in 1787 on the site of a Tuscarora tribe village and named for its location. It is near a deep curve in the North Branch of the Susquehanna River.

GREELEY

At this location in 1842, the publisher of the *New York Tribune*, Horace Greeley (1811–72), founded a settlement based on the utopian socialist ideas of Francois Marie Charles Fourier (1772–

1837). Fourier advocated establishing small, self-sufficient communities of 1,600 members, called phalanxes, and each community inhabiting a phalanstery.

Greeley's colony, first called Sylvania, was organized on the principle of "common ownership of property and equal division of labor." The place, Greeley later announced, was capable of growing only snakes and rocks. The colony did not survive the crop failure of 1845. In that year, the last frost came on July 4th!

GREENSBURG (South —)

Greensburg was laid out in 1784–85 on land owned by Christopher Truby and named for General Nathanael Greene (1742–86).

The town was organized in 1787. Arthur St. Clair, another general on Washington's staff, spent his last days in a log hut on nearby Chestnut Ridge, penniless and in poor health and spirit. He and his wife are buried in St. Clair Park.

The inn at Greensburg was where Pennsylvania officials met to settle the "Whiskey Rebellion." The tavern sign was a full-length portrait of General Greene.

GREENVILLE (East —)

Greenville, located at the confluence of the Shenango and Little Shenango Rivers in Mercer County, was named for Revolutionary War General Nathanael Greene, as was Greensburg.

The town was settled in 1796 by German families. It was laid out by Thomas Bean and William Scott in 1819. Later, however, the principal part of the town grew up on the east side. For a long time, the town was called West Greenville.

West Greenville was incorporated in 1837, and the West was dropped from the corporate title in 1865.

GRINDSTONE

The stones used by the mills to grind grain were a valuable commodity in the early days of settlement. This location was named for the availability of such stones.

GROVE CITY

When first settled in 1798, this Mercer County community was called Pine Grove for the clump of pine trees on the west side of town. Unfortunately, another Pine Grove already existed, and so, when the town was incorporated in 1883, the name was shortened to Grove City.

GWYNEDD

Gynedd is the Welsh name of North Wales. The town was named by Welsh settlers in the late seventeenth century.

HALIFAX

About half a mile from the present-day location of Halifax, Dauphin County, a fort was built in 1756 by Colonel William Clapham. Clapham called the fortification Fort Halifax. The name was suggested by Robert H. Morris, the deputy governor, who wanted to honor George Montague, Earl of Halifax. For a time, Halifax was called "father of the colonies," because as head of the British Board of Trade, he helped to increase commerce in America.

Near Halifax is the Clemson Mount, on the southwest tip of Clemson's Island, where excavations have uncovered remains of an ancient Algonquian culture. The burial mound is eight feet high, forty feet in diameter, and cone shaped.

HALLSTEAD

This community was named for William Felton Hallstead, general manager of the Delaware, Lackawanna & Western Railroad.

HAMILTON

Alexander Hamilton (1757–1804), was the leader of the Federalist Party. Along with James Madison, he coauthored *The Federalist Papers*, which helped "sell" the Constitution to its critics.

Hamilton served as first secretary of the treasury, and in that role created the Bank of the United States. He was killed by Vice President Aaron Burr in a duel.

HAMLIN

Hannibal Hamlin (1809–1891), Lincoln's first vice president, was an antislavery Democrat who left his party over the issue. During his vice presidency, Hamlin was bored silly and joined a Maine regiment as a private, serving his country in that manner during the Civil War. Lincoln replaced him in 1864 with Andrew Johnson. Hamlin returned to the capital in 1869 as a senator—and radical reconstructionist.

HANNASTOWN

Hannastown was western Pennsylvania's "capital" in the pre-Revolutionary War period. An early settlement grew up around a fortification there, built in 1774 by General Arthur St. Clair.

The name comes from the Hanna family. Marcus Alonzo Hanna (1837–1904) was a political kingmaker, and played a key role in getting William McKinley elected president. He was not happy, however, with the party's choice for vice president: Theodore Roosevelt. Roosevelt assumed the Oval Office following McKinley's death in 1900.

HANOVER (East —)

Founded by Colonel Richard McAllister, Hanover, York County, was known in its infancy as McAllister's Town, originally as Hickory-town, and later as Rogue's Nest. Sometimes the word "Folly" was added to McAllister's name when describing the settlement. McAllister kept a tavern here in the middle of a hickory forest. The first name is quite obvious, but the latter name is not.

Rogue's Nest was given because the town was a haven for renegades and outlaws, who took advantage of the lack of law enforcement resulting from the Pennsylvania-Maryland boundary dispute.

In the mid-eighteenth century, Michael Danner (Tanner), an influential German settler, became one of the Crown's justices of the peace. He was the one to suggest, in 1755, the renaming of McAllister's Town to honor his native German home. Hanover was incorporated in 1815.

The first Civil War battle, north of the Mason-Dixon Line, took place here 30 June 1863 with Confederate cavalry, led by General J.E.B. Stuart, facing a Union cavalry division led by Generals Kilpatrick and Custer. This engagement kept Stuart from reaching Gettysburg on time, and he arrived a day after the major battle began. Lee was deprived, as he wrote, of the "eyes of his army."

HARDING

Warren Gamaliel Harding (1865–1823) was the twenty-ninth president of the United States. He campaigned with a promise of "a return to normalcy." He might have lived up to his promise, even if American citizens disagreed with his methods. Harding's administration was plagued by scandals and corruption.

HARMONY

George Rapp and his Harmony (or Rappite) Society established their first communal settlement on Connoquenessing Creek, in Butler County, in 1804. Rapp purchased about 5,000 acres in the Conoquenessing valley from the eccentric Dettmar W. F. Basse.

During the first year of settlement, the Harmonites cleared 150 acres, and built fifty log houses, a church, a barn, and several shops. There is a throne-like rock formation on a hill overlooking the town which is known as Father Rapp's Seat.

The basic tenets of Rapp's religious sect were that all members owned all things in common; they wore distinctive clothing; and most practiced celibacy. Since the second coming was near at hand, or so Rapp preached, his followers wished to remain pure. Lord Byron referred to Rapp's approval of celibacy in the fifteenth canto of *Don Juan*.

The Rappites were a quite productive—if not reproductive—community, because they worked as if the end of the world was at hand. Ten years later, they were enticed to leave Pennsylvania and take up residence in the Posey Valley of Indiana. They sold off their Butler County property in 1814 for $100,000, and bought 25,000 acres in Indiana, and founded New Harmony, their "Second Terrestrial Home."

The Indiana climate was not to their liking, and they were plagued by malaria. They sold off that land for $150,000 to Robert Owen, a British socialist who wanted to start a commune of his own. The Harmony Society members returned to Pennsylvania in 1825, bought 3,000 acres in Beaver County, and founded the town of Economy. Rapp died in 1847, and his followers began to suspect that the end was not as near as they thought. The religion died a natural death.

One of the first charcoal blast furnaces to operate in Western Pennsylvania is still standing in Harmony.

HARRISBURG

John Harris, a native of Yorkshire, England, opened a trading post in this area in 1710. Twenty-three years later, Harris received a grant of land from the Penns at Paxtang, now Harrisburg. Parson John Elder, minister of the old Paxtang Presbyterian Church, remarked "John Harris was as honest a man as ever broke bread."

By 1753, his son, John Harris, Jr., was operating a ferry across the Susquehanna River. The town became known as Harris's Ferry. When his father died in 1748, the son took title to the land.

He and his son-in-law, William Maclay, laid out the town at the ferry in 1785 and called it Harrisburg. State legislators were not quite happy with Harrisburg. They reasoned that since the county was named Dauphin, it would follow to name the county seat Louisburg, for Louis XVI. Harris, Jr., would hear nothing of this. "The members of the Council," he said, "may Louisburg as much as they please, but I will never execute a title for a lot in any other name than Harrisburg." As later generations know, Harris won!

Harrisburg was named capital of Pennsylvania in 1810, and two years later assumed that role. After John Harris' death in 1791, his son-in-law gave additional land "for public use." Maclay was the first U.S. senator from Pennsylvania and, with Thomas Jefferson, a founder of the Democratic Party.

Harrisburg was incorporated as a city in 1860.

HARRISON CITY (— Valley, —ville)

Harrisonville, Fulton County, was named in 1840 for William Henry Harrison. He was campaigning for president at the time.

HARTLETON

Hartleton was incorporated in 1858 and named for Colonel Thomas Hartley. Hartley had received the neighboring lands for his service during the Revolutionary War.

HASTINGS

This Cambria County community was named in 1894 for Daniel Hartman Hastings.

Hastings, of Bellefonte, was initially interested in coal-mining interests in the area, but he just happened to be at Johnstown at the time of the flood. As Pennsylvania's adjutant general, he assumed command of the rescue operations. His performance gained great public attention and, five years later, he was elected governor. He served from 1895–99.

HATBORO

This Montgomery County town was named for its onetime main industry: the manufacture of hats.

Londoner John Dawson, who cut a clearing here and built a cabin in 1701, practiced the hatting trade in the 1740s at this site in an old stone house, which later became the Crooked Billet Tavern. That name was taken from the Philadelphia inn where Benjamin Franklin dined when he first arrived in Philadelphia. The earliest spelling of the town's name was Hatborough, which appeared as early as 1749.

HAVERFORD

Haverford, Montgomery County, was named by early Welsh settlers who came from Haverford-West, Pembrokeshire, in the 1680s.

Haverford Township, in existence as early as 1722, is presently located in Delaware County.

HAZLETON

Hazleton, Luzerne County, takes its name from Hazel Township, which in turn takes its name from the Hazel Creek—noted for an abundance of hazel trees. Hazleton was founded in 1836 and laid out the next year, but, as one can see, its name is the result of a typographical error.

In 1856, when the town was incorporated, the lawyer who drew up the legal papers misspelled the name, and so it continues to this day.

A local legend tells that a deer pawed the ground and unearthed veins of anthracite on nearby Spring Mountain in 1818.

West Hazleton was named for its geographic location a few miles west of Hazleton.

HELEN FURNACE

Local tradition contends this village was named for the wife or daughter of the local furnace owner. That is not the case.

The name of Helen Furnace appears to be a corruption of Hieland (Highland) Furnace. The furnace was named in honor of Alexander McNaughton, who prided himself on his Highlander heritage. A Highland Township in the county drew its name from the same source.

HELVETIA

This Clearfield County community carries the Latin name for Switzerland.

HERMITAGE

The popularity of President Andrew Jackson prompted many small towns and villages to name their communities for Jackson's home in Nashville, Tennessee.

HERNDON

Officials of the U. S. Post Office Department suggested that the townspeople in this Northumberland County village name their new post office for Commander William Lewis Herndon. Herndon lost his life in 1857 while attempting to rescue passengers from his sinking steamer, the *Central America*.

One of Herndon's daughters became the bride of Chester Alan Arthur, who later became president of the United States.

HERSHEY

Derry Church, one of the oldest Presbyterian churches in Pennsylvania, was organized in 1725 by the Reverend Robert Evans. The church took its name from the town, established five years earlier by Scotch-Irish from Derry, now called Londonderry, Ireland.

Hershey was founded in 1903 by Milton S. Hershey, who planned and built an industrial community here. His new town was built on the site of Derry.

Hershey Foods in Hershey is one of the largest chocolate and cocoa plants in the world. The main street of Hershey is appropriately named "Chocolate Avenue."

HICKORY (— Corner, — Grove, — Hill, East —, West —)

Hickory was named for Hickory Tavern. The name was given by early road builders to a hickory tree located in one of their camp sites.

HIGHSPIRE

An old church spire was used by boatmen on the Susquehanna River as a beacon. The town, settled in 1775 and laid out in 1814, took that landmark as its name.

HOLLIDAYSBURG

Adam and William Holliday, immigrant Irish brothers, founded this Blair County settlement in 1768.

When Adam drove his first surveying stake into the ground, he remarked: "Whoever is alive 100 years from now will find a considerable town here." Adam was not too far off the mark.

Hollidaysburg was laid out in about 1790, then incorporated in 1834. The town showed great growth between 1830 and 1840, when the first unified transportation system was completed across Pennsylvania. The Portage Railroad was the key link between Johnstown and Hollidaysburg.

HOLLSOPPLE

The strange name for this Somerset County town was actually the surname of the man on whose farm the town was developed.

HOME (—stead, —town, —ville)

Homestead was laid out by the Homestead Bank & Life Insurance Company of Pittsburgh in 1871. The company's name became that of the town, which originally was called Amity Homestead.

One of the farms purchased by the firm was "the McClure homestead," and local tradition has it that the town's name came from that farm. Members of that family denied it back in the 1940s. The company's name was in existence—and in use—before it acquired this land.

Homestead was the site of a violent steel strike in 1892. The strike at the Homestead Works grew volatile when, on 5 July, a tugboat came up the Monangahela River towing two barges of Pinkerton men. A raging gunfight resulted. Pennsylvania's Governor Robert E. Pattison then ordered in 8,000 National Guard troops to quell the disturbance. The plant was reopened after that—on the company's terms.

A senate investigation later declared that the use of the Pinkerton men was an "assumption of State authority" and that there was "no evidence of damage done . . . to property . . . by strikers."

HOMER CITY

Homer City was founded in 1854. Most sources suspect that the name was borrowed from the Greek poet.

HONEOYE

The name of this community is Iroquoian for "finger-lying." The name is probably transported from New York, where it was used to describe an incident in which an Indian cut off his finger after being bitten by a snake.

HONESDALE

Honesdale was established in 1827 as a terminal for canal barges from the Delaware & Hudson Canal Company carrying coal to New York. The location was called "the forks of the Dyberry."

It was also the site of the first trip made by a steam locomotive in the United States. The Stourbridge Lion made its debut 8 August 1829 on the "little railroad at Hone's Dale." The second test proved that the light rails made such an operation too dangerous. It was cheaper to return to horses and mules than replace the rails, so the experiment was scrapped. The locomotive was cannibalized, its boiler used to heat the company's shop. A replica of the engine is currently on display near West Park Street. The remains of the Lion were sent to the Smithsonian Institution in 1889.

Honesdale was named for Philip Hone, a major stockholder and the first president of the canal company, and later mayor of New York. Hone arrived at the settlement in 1826 and pushed for the construction of a canal that would divert the flow of coal to his city.

HONEY BROOK

Honey Brook, Lancaster County, is named for the stream. Who said our forefathers lacked a sense of humor? The next town north of Honey Brook is Beartown.

HOUSTON

General Sam Houston (1793–1863) was president of the Texas Republic, and later served as the U.S. senator from Texas.

Born in Virginia, Houston became politically active in Tennessee, then moved on to Oklahoma and finally Texas. In Texas he commanded troops of the provincial Texas government against the Mexican army. He defeated Santa Ana at San Jacinto in a brilliant battle. When Texas became a republic, Houston was its first president. When Texas was admitted to the Union, Houston served as an antisecessionist Union Democrat in the senate. He returned to Texas in 1859 to become that state's governor.

HOWARD

Howard, located in Centre County, took the name of John Howard (1726–90), an English philanthropist who devoted his life to bettering the living conditions of all prisoners and captives.

HUBLERSBURG

Hublersburg, Centre County, was known as Logan when it was located in Lycoming County in 1829. Ten years later, when it became part of Centre, the name was changed to Hublersburgh.

Three years went by and the name became Heckla; another three years, Hublersburgh. The "h" was dropped in 1893. The name commemorates a local family.

HUMBOLDT

Freidrich Wilhelm Heinrich Alexander, Freiherr von Humboldt (1769–1859), was a German traveler and writer who enjoyed great popularity during the mid-nineteenth century.

It was the Baron von Humboldt who first suggested building of the Panama Canal. He made the first isothermic and isobaric maps, and wrote *Kosmos*, a five-volume review of astronomy and the earth sciences. The baron contributed his entire fortune to the advancement of science.

HUMMELSTOWN

Hummelstown, Dauphin County, was first called Frederickstown. It had been laid out as a town in about 1762 by Frederick Hummel, the town's founder.

The name was changed to its present form about 1780. During the Revolution, Hummelstown was an important storage location for arms and munitions.

HUNTERS—

The places where hunters congregated sometimes were called by that generic title of "hunter." In that vein, we find such places as Hunters Run (which took its name from the stream), Hunterstown, and Huntersville.

HUNTINGDON (— Valley, North —)

The Reverend William Smith, D.D., the first provost of the College of Philadelphia (now the University of Pennsylvania), purchased a piece of land on the Standing Stone tract in 1766. The next year he laid out a town and named it Huntingdon, for Selena, Countess of Huntingdon. The countess had been quite generous in her donations to the small college.

Early residents called the place Standing Stone. The Oneida Indians—Oneida means "standing stone"—camped here before the white settlers arrived. Their wigwams were arranged around a fourteen-foot high, six-inch square stone pillar etched with petroglyphs. The Indians left following the Albany Congress treaty of 1754, which took the entire Juniata Valley from the Indians and gave it to the Penns, and took their stone with them.

The settlers created a stone of their own, which was replaced in 1869 by the Standing Stone Monument, at Penn and 3rd Streets.

HYNDMAN

First called Bridgeport, this Bedford County community changed its name to Hyndman at the time of its incorporation in 1877. The name honored E.K. Hyndman, president of the Pittsburgh & Western Railroad.

ICKESBURG

Ickesburg, Perry County, was named for H.L. Ickes, Roosevelt's secretary of the interior (1933–46).

Harold LeClair Ickes (1874–1952) was a native-born Pennsylvanian who moved to Chicago, attended school, and became a newspaperman. While working for a number of newspapers, he studied law and received his degree in 1907. Though a Republican, Ickes followed progressive candidates and organizations, such as Teddy Roosevelt's Bull Moose party.

During the 1932 presidential race, Ickes supported Franklin D. Roosevelt. When FDR was elected, he appointed Ickes to head up the Department of the Interior. The appointment was mainly an effort to gain support for his cabinet by appointing a Republican. Once in office, Ickes became a strong protector of the nation's natural resources.

Ickes left his cabinet post after an argument with President Harry Truman, who assumed the presidency upon Roosevelt's death.

IMPERIAL

This Allegheny county village was laid out in 1879 by the Imperial Coal Company, and allegedly named for its Imperial Mine. More likely, the town was named for the company.

INDEPENDENCE

The name of this town, according to several authorities, commemorates the Declaration of Independence.

INDIANA

Indiana was founded in 1805 when Philadelphian George Clymer, a signer of the Declaration of Independence, donated 250 acres of his lands for county buildings. Before the Civil War, Indiana was an important station on the Underground Railroad. The town's name comes from the Territory of Indiana, which Congress carved from the Northwest Territory in 1800. Or it may have been named for the Pennsylvania county, which commemorated Indians in general.

Indiana was incorporated as a borough as early as 1816.

Actor Jimmy Stewart was born here. A bronze statue of the movie star stands on the lawn of the Indiana County Courthouse.

INDIAN HEAD

Indian Head, Fayette County, was named by the post office for its location at the head of Indian Creek. (For a more gruesome description of a town with that name, see Indian Head, Maryland.)

INDIANOLA
This name is a word coined from Indiana and a Latin-like ending. There was a time when people suggested that all town names end in an "a."

INDUSTRY
Industry, named for the many early businesses that employed the town's people, was laid out in 1836. In its earliest days, Industry was home to lumbering, coal mining, and the building of keelboats.

INGLESMITH
"Ingle" is Scottish for "nook" or "corner." This town's name is a play on words: Smith's Corner.

INTERCOURSE
Named Cross Keys, when it was founded in 1754, after a local tavern, Intercourse was renamed in 1813–14. There are several theories about the source of the name, including that the town was located near the entrance to an old racecourse, the "Enter Course," or that it was near the joining, or "intercourse" (interchange), of the old Kings Highway and the Washington-Erie Road.

One thing is sure; the early settlers did not play to the prurient interests of modern-day travelers.

IRVINE
This town was laid out in the 1840s by Dr. William A. Irvine, on land inherited from his grandfather, General William Irvine. The lands were given to the general for his Revolutionary War service.

IRVONA
Irvona was named for its founder, Colonel E. A. Irvin, of Curwensville. It is apparent that he could not name it Irvine, since one such town already existed, so they Latinized his name.

IRWIN (North —)
This Westmoreland County village, once a bustling coal town, was

named for John Irwin, on whose land the town was built. Irwin laid out the town on Brush Run in 1853.

John Scull, father-in-law of the town's founder, started the *Pittsburgh Gazette* here in 1786, the first newspaper in the area.

JACKSON (— Center, — Crossing, — Summit, —ville)

Jackson Center was settled in 1835, and named for President Andrew Jackson (1767–1845). References to Jackson can also be found in towns named Hermitage and Hickory.

JAMESTOWN

John Keck laid out this Mercer County community in 1832. It was named for James Campbell, the first white settler in the area, who founded the town in 1798.

JEANNETTE

Jeannette, Westmoreland County, was named for Jeannette McKee. Her husband, H. Sellers McKee, opened his glassworks here in 1889. The manufacture of glass was responsible for turning the one-farmhouse town of 1888 into an industrial community. Jeannette has been called "The Glass City," because of its early industry.

JEFFERSON (— City)

Jefferson, Jefferson County, takes its name from the county. The county was named for President Thomas Jefferson (1743–1826).

JERMYN

This town was originally called Gibsonburg, for John Gibson of Philadelphia, who sold some of his land to the Delaware & Hudson Canal Company. In 1874, when the railroad station, post office, and town were named by the canal company, it was in honor of John Jermyn, a wealthy Englishman who helped create business opportunities in this Lackawanna County area.

JERSEY SHORE

The first settlers to this site in 1785 were Reuben Mannin and his nephew, Thomas Forster, from New Jersey. The town was called Jersey Shore in their honor. About 1805, the name was changed to Waynesburg, one of the many place names to honor Anthony

Wayne, but, the settlement continued to be called Jersey Shore. The name was originally a joke, but in the end the name took hold.

When the community was incorporated in 1826, the act directed "the place shall be called and styled Jersey Shore."

JIM THORPE

James Francis "Jim" Thorpe (1888–1953) was an outstanding Native American athlete. A native of Oklahoma, he attended the Indian School at Carlisle. In the 1912 Olympics at Stockholm, Thorpe won two gold medals in the decathalon and the gold medal in every pentathalon event except the javelin. Later stripped of his honors because of "professional" sports activities—he earned sixty dollars a month playing semi-pro baseball, Thorpe died penniless . . . but not forgotten. His professional sporting career included playing baseball for the New York Giants and the Cincinnati Reds, and at the same time playing professional football for several teams—"Bo" Jackson was not the first! He also served as the first president of the National Football League.

In the mid-1950s, the towns of Mauch Chunk and East Mauch Chunk merged and incorporated as Jim Thorpe. The naming of the town was instigated by Thorpe's widow, who wanted a fitting monument for her husband and his memory. Through her efforts, his Olympic records were reinstated in 1982 and his medals returned to the family. Thorpe's remains are buried here.

JOHNSONBURG

The usual source given for the name of this Elk County community is John Johnson, who settled here in the 1830s. He built a cabin at the junction of the east and west branches of the Clarion River.

Johnsonburg was laid out in 1888, and its main industry became paper-making.

JOHNSTOWN

Johnstown suffered four major floods, in 1862, 1869, 1936, and 1977. Some of the older buildings still show high-water marks from the 1889 flood. During the course of its history, the town has been flooded at least eighteen times—since 1808!

The town was named for an early settler from Switzerland, Joseph Johns (Jahns or Yahns). Johns arrived in this country in 1769. After settling for a brief time in Berks County and then Somerset County, he purchased 249 acres of "the Campbell tract."

The town was named Connemaugh, for the Connemaugh River, when Johns laid out the town. It was still Connemaugh when the town was incorporated in 1831. Five years later, however, the Pennsylvania legislature changed the name to Johnstown.

JOLLYTOWN

No matter how happy the people are in this locale, their state of mind is not the source of its name. Jollytown was named for Titus Jolly, who once owned the land upon which the town was built.

JULIAN

This town's name came from the Julia Ann Furnace company, named for Julia Ann Irvin, wife of one of the owners.

JUNIATAVILLE

The name of Juniataville comes from the Indian word for the river, which translates to "they stay long" or "beyond the great bend."

KANE (—ville, East —)

General Thomas Leiper Kane of Philadelphia led an explorer team into this McKean County area in 1859.

Kane was the brother of noted arctic explorer Dr. Elisha Kent Kane. Thomas Kane was quite impressed with the promise of the area and purchased an extensive tract of land. He began building a home there in 1860, but the Civil War interrupted construction. Kane dropped everything and organized the legendary "Bucktails," a Pennsylvania regiment made up of hunters and woodsmen. During the war, Kane participated in thirty-five battles and was wounded in five. Following the war, he was brevetted major general for his "gallant services at the battle of Gettysburg."

With the advent of peace, General Kane returned to McKean County and resumed work on his house. His town grew slowly until the Philadelphia & Erie Railroad was completed; then it blossomed.

Another famous Kane raised here was Dr. Evan O'Neill Kane, the first surgeon to perform a self-operation.

KAOLIN

Kaolin, Chester County, was named for the discovery of large deposits of kaolin, or porcelain clay.

KARTHAUS

Karthaus, Clearfield County, takes its name from Karthaus Township. The township was named for Peter A. Karthaus of Baltimore, who built an iron furnace here in about 1820.

KEARSARGE

The word *kearsarge* is Indian for "peaked mountain." But this town probably was named for the sinking of the Confederate *Alabama* by the Union's *Kearsage*.

KEEWAYDIN

The name of this town comes from that of the northwest wind in Longfellow's *Hiawatha*.

KELAYRES

Kelayres made headlines at the height of the 1934 Pennsylvania's governor's race. Campaigners marching through the streets of town during a Democratic parade were shot down by crossfire from the darkened windows of two houses. Five were killed, fourteen injured.

Joseph J. Bruno, a former county official, and five of his relatives were arrested for the crime. Bruno was convicted and sentenced to three life terms. He engineered a "walk-away escape" from the Schuylkill County jail in Pottsville in 1936, but was apprehended eight months later in New York City.

KENNETT SQUARE

This Chester County community was named for the village of Kennett, in Wiltshire, England. The name was suggested by Francis Smith, who came from the English village in 1686 and settled at the mouth of the Pocopson Creek.

The name, Kennet Township appears in court records as early as 1705. Kennett Square has a strong economy in mushrooms.

KERRMOOR

The founders of this Clearfield County town were James Kerr, and Milton and Robert Moore. The surnames of the two founding families combine to create Kerrmoor.

KEYSTONE

Pennsylvania has always been called the "Keystone State." This town assumed that nickname as its own.

KING

Vice President William Rufus de Vane King (1786–1853) was a "close" personal associate of President James Buchanan. During their Washington days, there was a great deal of gossip about their relationship.

King served in the North Carolina legislature, the House of Representatives, as the U.S. Senator from Alabama, and minister to France, where he wrote to Buchanan about the depth of his feelings and how much he missed his friend.

When he returned home, he returned to the Senate. When Millard Fillmore succeeded to the presidency following the death of Zachary Taylor, King became president of the Senate. In 1852, he supported Buchanan for the Democratic nomination. Though Buchanan lost to Franklin Pierce, King was given the consolation prize: the vice presidential candidacy.

Pierce was elected, but King never served as his second in command. In fact, he received special permission to take the oath of office in Cuba. He died the day after he reached King's Bend, his home near Cahaba, Alabama, on 18 April 1853.

KING OF PRUSSIA

The first proprietor of the tavern in this Montgomery County area was a native of Prussia. In 1709, he named his establishment the King of Prussia Inn, for Frederick I, the Brandenburg prince who forged the duchy into a kingdom in 1701.

KINGSTON

When a band of pioneers arrived here from Kingston, Rhode Island, they were known as the "first forty." That name was transferred to the township which became Forty Township—Forty Fort was situated there.

In 1771, Forty Township became Kingstown Township. Three years later the name appeared in its current form.

Located in Luzerne County, the town took its name from the hometown of some of the "first forty."

KISHACOQUILLAS

This Mifflin County locale was named for the waterway of the same name. The Kishacoquillas Creek was named for a Delaware Indian chief.

His name translates to "the snakes have gone into their dens" or "already-snakes-in-dens"—a pretty obscure statement.

KITTANNING (West —)

Kittanning is the seat of Armstrong County. The town is located on the site of an Indian village that Colonel John Armstrong had destroyed on 8 September 1756. Armstrong killed Chief Jacob and thirty-two of his braves, and released eleven captives.

The town was settled as early as 1791, but a major settlement did not appear until six years later. The town was formally laid out in 1803 by Judge George Ross and incorporated in 1821. From this location, a famous Indian trail called the Kittanning Path led across the mountains to Standing Stone (now Huntingdon).

The town's name is a corruption of the Delaware *kit-hannink*, "the town on the great river, or *kit-hanne*, "great river." Both refer to the Allegheny River.

KNOX (— Dale, —ville)

Knoxville, Allegheny County, is located on land that once was the Reverend Jeremiah Knox's fruit farm. For years, the reverend's strawberries, blackberries, and grapes were much in demand in the Pittsburgh market. In 1873, the Knox heirs laid out the town and named it Knoxville in honor of the reverend.

KOSSUTH

Lajos (Louis) Kossuth (1802–94), the Hungarian patriot, was a political exile in the United States in 1852. He traveled widely and was greeted everywhere with great public attention.

Kossuth led his country's revolution in 1848 and became president of the independent Republic of Hungary. He was forced to leave Hungary the next year when the rebellion was quelled.

KREAMER

Kreamer is located near the site of Hendrich's Fort, a safe haven for pioneers during the Indian raids between 1770 and 1783. The name comes from one of those early families.

KUSHEQUA

Kushequa is an Iroquian word for "spear."

LACEYVILLE

Laceyville is the twin to Skinners Eddy. In fact, Ebenezer Skinner, founder of both towns, built a story-and-a-half log cabin here in 1790.

LACKAWAXEN

This Pike County community, located at the confluence of the Delaware River and Lackawaxen Creek, takes its name from the creek. The waterway's name is derived from an Indian word that translates to "at the river fork" or "swift waters."

Zane Grey described the creek as "a little river hidden away . . . dashing white sheeted over ferny cliffs, wine-brown where the whirling pools suck the stain from the hemlock roots . . . [and] harbor the speckled trout."

The town was founded in 1770.

LAFAYETTE

The Marquis de Lafayette was honored by many during his lifetime for his role in the American Revolution. His memory stays alive in a number of place names across the United States. In Pennyslvania, Fayette County and others bear his name.

Marie Joseph Paul Yves Roch Gilbert du Motier, the Marquis de Lafayette (1757–1834), served without pay—or a permanent command—as a major general in the Continental army. At the time of his commissioning, the marquis was all of twenty years old! Regardless of his age, he fought valiantly for American independence and became an icon, as Thomas Jefferson wrote, "of the soldiers of liberty of the world."

LAFLIN

This town in Luzerne County was named for a partner in the powder manufacturing firm of Laflin & Rand.

LAHASKA

The village at Lahaska, founded in 1725, is from the Indian and means "great mountain."

Another source suggests the word translates to "writing-much," with the suggestion that a treaty might have been signed here. However, the village sits on a mountain.

LAKE—

Most of the towns that bear the prefix "lake" were named for a body of water near the townsite. These include such places as Lake Ariel, Lake Carey, Lake Harmony, Lake Como, and Lake Winola. Others take their names from their location, such as in the case of Lake City, Lakemont, Lakeside, Lakeville, and Lakewood.

LAMAR

Lamar, Clinton County, was named for Lamar Township. The township was named in honor of Major Marion Lamar, a member of the Fourth Pennsylvania Line, who was killed in 1777 at the battle of Paoli. An alternative suggestion for the name donation was Major James Lamar, an early landowner.

Lamar was originally called Yankeetown.

LAMARTINE

Several sources suggest that Lamartine was named for Alphonse de Lamartine (1790–1869), French poet, novelist, and statesman.

Lamartine is credited with helping to instigate the February Revolution of 1848. He headed the provincial government until being supplanted by Napoleon III.

LAMONT

Lamont is the French word for "the mountain."

LANCASTER

Lancaster, Lancaster County, was laid out in 1730 by James Hamilton, later two-time governor of Pennsylvania (1748–52, 1759–63). Though he arranged the site in town lots, he did not put any up for sale until five years later.

In 1735, the governor approved the site, calling it "the town-stead of Lancaster." Lancaster was incorporated as a borough in 1742. The town, seat of Lancaster County, took its name from the county, which had its name transported from the country town of Lancastershire, England. Lancaster was Pennsylvania's capital from 1799–1812, and capital of the United States for a single day: 27 September 1777.

LANGHORNE (— Manor)

Both locales in Bucks County are named for Jeremiah Langhorne, an early settler who became prominent in Pennsylvania politics. Langhorne was chief justice of the province, from 1739–43.

LANSDALE

Lansdale was incorporated in 1872 from Gwynedd and Hatfield townships. It carries the name of Philip Lansdale Fox, a railroad surveyor.

LANSDOWNE (East —)

Most sources believe this Delaware County community takes its name from Lord Lansdowne.

LANSE

This town's name is a corruption of the French *l'anse,* "the bay."

LANSFORD

Lansford, Carbon County, was once two separate communities. One was called Ashton, the surname of an early settler; the other, Storm Hill. Storm Hill recalled the day a storm overturned the house of Peter Fisher.

In 1877, the two settlements were consolidated and incorporated under the name Lansford, the middle name of a prominent citizen, Asa Lansford Foster. Foster, a native of Massachusetts, helped organize the Buck Mountain Coal Company in 1837.

LA PLUME

La Plume is French for "the feather."

LAPORTE

Laporte is the seat of Sullivan County, and was named for a French family with large landholdings. The name translates to "gateway, gate."

The town was founded in 1847, and laid out in 1850 by Michael Meylert. It was named for Laporte Township. The township was named for Meylert's friend, John Laporte, who was speaker of the Pennsylvania General Assembly in 1832. He was a member of Congress from 1832–36, and was also the last surveyor general of the state, 1845–51.

LARKSVILLE

The first name of Larksville, Luzerne County, was Blindtown. Most sources indicate that name was given because a blind person lived in the town.

In 1895, the name was changed to Larksville, for Peggy Lark, who owned the township, and lived to the ripe old age of 106!

LATROBE

Latrobe, Westmoreland County, was laid out in 1851 by Oliver J. Barnes, a civil engineer for the Pennsylvania Railroad.

LEBANON. Lebanon is known today not for its religious beginnings, but for its present product: Lebanon Bologna! The Daniel Weaver Company is the oldest commercial manufacturer of this all-beef smoked sausage. (The Daniel Weaver Company, Lebanon, Pennsylvania)

Barnes bought the land for himself, and named the town for his friend Benjamin Henry Latrobe, Jr., an engineer and architect. The senior Latrobe has been called "the father of architecture in the United States." The town was incorporated in 1854.

LAUREL—

Mountain laurel is the state flower for the Commonwealth of Pennsylvania. Its name is recalled in several communities, including Laureldale, Laurel Lake and Laurel Run (which take their names from a body of water), Laurelton, and Laurelville.

LEBANON (West —)

Lebanon was named for Lebanon Township, and also known as Steitztown, for John Steitz, who had laid out the town lots in 1756. Lebanon County was also named for the township.

The township, organized in 1729, appears to carry a Biblical name. It is probable that the abundance of cedar trees in the region sparked notice of a similarity to the "White Mountain" of the Bible.

Lebanon was incorporated as a borough in 1821, and chartered as a city in 1868. Lebanon is known worldwide for its chief product:

Lebanon Bologna, a distinctive deli meat that is still smoked over hardwood, the same way it was prepared in the eighteenth century.

LEHIGH TANNERY
This community takes its name from the tannery that was located on the nearby Lehigh River.

LEHIGHTON
Lehighton, Carbon County, was laid out in 1794 by Colonel Jacob Weiss and William Henry. The town takes its name from the Lehigh River, with the addition of the English "-ton," for town.

An old Moravian settlement was located here as early as 1745. The Moravians called their village Gnadenhutten. It was destroyed by one of the Indian raids precipitated by Braddock's defeat in 1755.

Lehighton was incorporated as a borough in 1866, and its name is a corruption of the Delaware *lechauwekink,* "where there are forks."

LEIDY
Joseph Leidy (1823–91), anatomist and paleontologist, was born in Philadelphia, but donated his name to this town. Leidy's research helped him discover *Trichinella spiralis,* a pork parasite, in 1846. Two years later, the publication of *Researches into the Comparative Anatomy of the Liver* established him as the nation's outstanding anatomist.

Leidy was not only a superior researcher but also an excellent teacher, who held down appointments at both the University of Pennsylvania and Swarthmore College.

LEMONT (— Furnace)
Lemont, laid out in 1870, is located on Spring Creek, in Penn's Valley at the western end of Nittany Mountain. The name is a modification of *le mont,* French for "the mountain."

LEMOYNE
The site of Fort Washington, 8th and Ohio Streets, marks the northernmost point the Confederates reached during the Civil War. On 29 June 1863, Confederate cavalry under Colonel A.G. Jenkins exchanged shots with Union troops defending the state capital.

This Cumberland County community was named for Dr. Francis LeMoyne, an ardent anti-slavery advocate. His home, built in 1812, was a stop on the Underground Railroad of the pre-Civil War era. The home still exists as the LeMoyne House Historical Museum, 49 E. Maiden St.

LENAPE

Lenape, Chester County, was named for the Lenni-Lenape Indians, the "original or first people." One source suggests the tribal name means "Indians of the same nation."

LENOX (—ville)

Lenox was settled in the late eighteenth century. Its name may refer to the family name of the Duke of Richmond.

LE RAYSVILLE

This Bradford County community was named for Vincent le Ray de Chaumont, the son of a large landowner. The elder Chaumont had purchased the land from Robert Morris.

LE ROY

This town's name is a modification of *le roi*, French for "the king."

LEVITTOWN

Levittown was named for the building company that constructed this planned community. (See Willingboro, New Jersey.)

LEWISBURG (East —)

In about 1772, Lewis Derr (Ludwig Doerr) purchased 320 acres of land in this area, built a mill, and opened a trading post.

Six months before he died in 1785, he laid out the town. For a number of years, it was alternately called Lewisburg or Derrstown. Lewisburg finally emerged as the official name.

This town is the home to Bucknell University, founded in 1846 as the University of Lewisburg. The university was renamed in 1886 for William Bucknell, a long-time trustee and donor.

LEWISTOWN

Mifflintown was selected as the county seat for Mifflin County, but people living in the county soon found it an inconvenient location.

In 1790–91, Samuel Edminston, who owned 300 acres of land, laid out town lots and named the new village for his friend, William Lewis. Lewis, an ironmaster, owned and operated the Hope Furnace, a few miles west of town. In the 1730s, James LeTort and Jonah Davenport reported seeing the Shawnee village of Ohesson at this site.

After the forest had been cleared for homesites, the town fathers punished public drunks by setting them the task of pulling out tree stumps and throwing them into a ravine in the center of town.

LIBERTY (— Corners, North —, West —)

Liberty began as the site for a blockhouse. The Liberty Blockhouse was built in 1792 as a provision station and haven during the construction of the Blockhouse (or Williamson) Road that linked Northumberland with Canoe Camp. The road reduced travel-time between Pennsylvania and New York, and opened a wide territory for settlement.

The blockhouse construction began soon after the adoption of the Constitution and the Bill of Rights, which might have triggered the name.

LICK—

Licks were places where wild animals went to find salt. The towns that grew up around these places usually added the "lick" to their name, such as in the case of Lickdale, Lickingville, and Lick Run (which took its name from a nearby stream).

LIGHTSTREET

When the Reverend Marmaduke Pearce came to this Columbia County area in 1844, he decided the walk from his mill to the post office was too long.

The Methodist minister applied for his own post office. When he got it, he named it for a street on which he had lived in Baltimore, Maryland.

LIGONIER

Ligonier, Westmoreland County, was laid out in 1816, and named for Fort Ligonier which was 1758.

The fort had been named for Sir John Louis Ligonier, Lord Viscount of Enniskillen.

LIME (—port, — Ridge, — Stone, — stoneville)

Lime was an important product mined in the state, and settlers often added the name to their towns. The port from whence lime was shipped would be called Limeport; a ridge where one found lime could be called Lime Ridge; a simple name would be Limestone; and the town where limestone was mined would be called Limestoneville.

LINCOLN

Lincoln, Lancaster County, was laid out as a town by John Reist in 1813 and called New Ephrata. During the Lincoln administration the name was changed.

Abraham Lincoln is also remembered in Lincoln Falls, Lincoln Hill, and Lincolnville.

LINESVILLE

Linesville, Crawford County, carries the name of Amos Line, a surveyor for the Pennsylvania Population Company, who laid out the town in about 1825.

LIONVILLE

Lionville, Chester County, got its name from the old Red Lion tavern around which the community grew.

LITIZ

Settled in 1754 by Moravians, this Lancaster County community was named for the baronry of Bohemia where the Moravian Church was founded in 1443. The town had previously been called Warwick by the smattering of English settlers who lived there. Count von Zinzendorf changed the name to Lititz in 1756. Warwick remained as the name of the township in which Lititz resides.

In 1757, John Reuter and the Reverend Nathaniel Seidel laid out the town. For many years, the town was owned by the Moravian Brotherhood.

In 1861, the first hard-pretzel bakeries in the United States were opened here, and for years, Litiz was called the "Bretzel" town.

LITTLE—

The use of the prefix "little" is usually descriptive of a smaller-sized community, as is the case with Little Britain, Little Cooley, Little Gap, Little Marsh, and Little Meadows. Sometimes the name describes the settlers' feelings, as in Little Hope.

LITTLESTOWN

This Adams County village was founded in 1765 by Peter Klein. It was alternately called Petersburg and Kleine-staedtel until the latter name was translated from the German to Littlestown.

LOCK HAVEN

This Clinton County town was laid out on the site of Fort Read. The fort was evacuated—very rapidly—during an Indian attack in 1778. The evacuation has become known as "the great runaway."

Jeremiah Church bought a large cornfield along the Pennsylvania Canal and the West Branch of the Susquehanna in 1833. The next year, he laid out the town he called Lock Haven, because it is located near two locks and a safe harbor.

Church was a genuine "character," and prided himself on his eccentricities. For six years, he lobbied for a new county to be carved out of Lycoming and Centre. He met with obstacles that might have stopped a lesser man, but succeeded in 1839. Lock Haven became the county seat for the new county, and the town began to grow. It became a borough in 1840 and, in 1870, received a city charter.

LOGANVILLE

Loganville was laid out in about 1820, and named for Colonel Henry Logan, a congressman from York County.

LONDON (— Grove)

London Grove was named for the London Company, which owned about 17,000 acres of Chester County land, from which were formed the old townships of New London, London Grove, and London Britain.

LOGANVILLE. The name of James Logan, Penn's colonial secretary, appears on several locations in the mid-Atlantic states. Unfortunately, they were not named for him, but instead for Chief Wingohocking with whom he exchanged names. (Scharf and Wescott's *History of Philadelphia, 1609–1884*)

LONGWOOD

Longwood was the name of Napoleon's residence in St. Helena, the place of his death.

LOOKOUT

Lookout's location was once used as an observation spot.

LORETTO

Loretto, Cambria County, was founded and named by Father

Gallitzin (Prince Demetrius Augustine Gallitzin), who lived here for many years. He named it for Loreto, Italy, home of the famous shrine of "Our Lady of Loreto." He was also instrumental in the naming of Carrolltown and Gallitzin.

Gallitzin's grave and a monument honoring him stand in front of St. Michael's Roman Catholic Church.

LOYALSOCK

This Lycoming County community's name comes from the branch of the Susquehanna River, and is a corruption of the Delaware *lawi-saquik*, "middle creek."

LUCINDA

Lucinda was originally known as Vogelbacher. Herr Vogelbacher was a native of the German Black Forest who settled here in 1820 when the area was still an Indian hunting ground. Because ammunition was scarce, the German hunter only shot when his prey was in front of a tree. That way, he could pull his shot from the tree after killing the animal.

The town was named after the Lucinda Furnace, which was built here in 1833.

LUNDYS LANE

The name of Lundys Lane commemorates the War of 1812 battle of Lundy's Lane, near Niagara Falls. The battle, which took place 25 July 1814, was the most hotly contested of the war. It was declared a draw, even though the Americans left the field in British possession.

LUZERNE

This town in Luzerne County takes its name from the county, which honors the Chevalier de la Luzerne, former minister of France to the United States.

The town was formerly known as Hartseph for Zachariah Hartseph, an early settler.

LYKENS

Lykens was founded in 1826, the year after anthracite coal was discovered at the lower end of Short Mountain.

The town was named for Andrew Lykens (or Lycan), who settled here in 1732. The site was originally purchased for $19.90.

MACUNGIE

Macungie, Lehigh County, takes its name from the Indian word meaning "the feeding place of bears."

MADERA

Rather than call their town "lumber"-something, settlers of this area opted for madera, Spanish for "lumber."

MADISON (—burg, --ville)

Madison was incorporated in 1876, and named for James Madison (1751–1836), fourth president of the United States.

Madisonville takes its name from Madison Township. The township was also named in honor of President Madison.

Madison was most influential in the adoption of the U.S. Constitution, through his co-authoring of *The Federalist Papers*, and his strong activity in support of the Bill of Rights.

MAHANOY CITY

The name of Mahanoy City, Schuylkill County, is derived from the Mahanoy Creek which flows through town. The stream's name comes from the Indian *mahoni*, a "lick," signifying the presence of saline deposits to which animals flocked.

MAINVILLE

Mainville's name is descriptive of what the original townspeople felt the town would be: a "main" village.

MAMONT

Mamont, translated from the French *ma mont*, means "my mountain."

MANHEIM

Manheim was founded by "Baron" Heinrich Wilhelm Stiegel, originator of the famous Stiegel glass. Enameling on glass was first successfully attempted here. Stiegel came from Philadelphia in 1761, purchased 600 acres of land, and laid out this Lancaster County town, naming it for his hometown in Germany.

Stiegel built himself a "grand castle, very singular in its structure" where he entertained in a grand manner. He also donated land to the Lutheran Church—provided the church pay the annual rent of one red rose.

MANNS CHOICE

Job Mann, a Pennsylvania congressman, petitioned for a post office in 1890 for Foot of the Ridge, as this community was known then. When Mann went to the postal authorities in Washington to fill out the paperwork, he hesitated when asked for a name.

The clerk, as legend has it, merely shrugged and wrote in Mann's Choice.

MAPLETON

When the Pennsylvania Railroad was completed to this Huntingdon County community, it was called Mapleton Depot, probably because the area surrounding the station was filled with maple trees. The town did not begin to flourish until about 1860.

MARCUS HOOK

The name of Marcus Hook, Delaware County, dates back to the early Dutch settlers. In the patent to the "Marcus Hook Tract," dated 1675, the name appears as Marreties Hoeck. The first word is a person's name. That individual remains anonymous, but the name has been corrupted to Marcus.

Some sources claim that Marretie or Maarte is the name of an Indian chief who lived near here, but no one is certain. Another suggestion, dating back to 1660, cites the word *marikes*, derived by the Swedes from an Algonquian word for "witchcraft," as signifying ceremonies held here. Hoek is from the Dutch, and means a "corner, point, or spit of land." In 1682, the English changed the name to Chichester, but the older name had great staying power and the legislation did not take effect. Still another legend has it that Marcus Hook was one of the many haunts of Blackbeard the Pirate and others who flew the "Jolly Roger."

MARIETTA

Marietta was originally two separate communities: New Haven, laid out in 1803 by David Cook, and Waterford (originally called Anderson's Ferry), established by James Anderson in 1804.

The two villages were incorporated in 1812 under one charter as Marietta, named for the wives of the two landowners. Mrs. Cook and Mrs. Anderson were named respectively Mary and Etta.

The town was settled by Scotch-Irish pioneers. Travelers could identify the Scotch-Irish cabins from those of the Germans by a simple test: the Scotch-Irish had two chimneys, one at each end; the Germans, only one—central to the dwelling.

MARTHA FURNACE

Martha Furnace, Centre County, was named for Martha Curtin. Her father, Roland Curtin, was one of the cofounders of the furnace started here about 1830.

MATAMORAS

Matamoras, Pike County, has a name of Spanish origin that means "Moor slayer." What that has to do with a town settled by the Dutch in the early eighteenth century misses this author completely. One source suggests it was named for the city captured by Americans during the Mexican War.

MATTAWANA

This community in Mifflin County takes its name from an Indian word which means "river of shallows."

MAXATAWNEY

The name of this Berks County town was taken from the stream. In the Delaware language, *machsit-hanna* means "bear path creek," the stream where bears have beaten a path.

MAYTOWN

Maytown, Lancaster County, was so named because the town was laid out on the first day of May 1762.

MAZEPPA

It is possible that this town bears a literary name. "Mazeppa" was a poem by Lord Byron honoring the Cossack leader (1644–1709).

McADOO

This town was founded in 1880, but received its name later from postal authorities. They named it for William Gibbs McAdoo (1863–1941), son-in-law to Woodrow Wilson, who served as his father-in-law's secretary of the treasury. He also floated eighteen billion dollars worth of loans to finance the efforts of the Allies in World War I.

McALEVYS FORT

The first settler in this Huntingdon County area was Captain

William McAlevy. The town took its name from the fort the captain built here in 1778.

McCLURE

McClure was founded in 1867, and carries the name of Alexander Kelley McClure (1828–1909). McClure was a prominent journalist, politician, and author.

McCONNELLSBURG

McConnellsburg, seat of Fulton County, was laid out by Daniel and William McConnell in 1786, and named for them. Before the creation of the town, Daniel McConnell operated a tavern "in the Big Cove." McConnellsburg was incorporated in 1814.

McDONALD

This locale was laid out in 1781, and took its name from Fort McDonald, built here during the Revolution on land owned by John McDonald. He was in no way related to Ronald McDonald.

McKEAN. Thomas Mc-Kean, a former Pennsylvania governor, was the only signer of the Declaration of Independence to sit in the Continental Congress from the beginning to the end of the American Revolution. Along with John Dickinson, he served in Washington's army. McKean and Dickinson were the only two congressmen who put their money where their mouths were. (Philadelphia Municipal Archives)

McKEAN

McKean took its name from the county. McKean County honored Thomas McKean (1734–1817), a signer of the Declaration of Independence and an early governor of Pennsylvania.

McKean was also the politician who introduced the "spoils" system to Pennsylvania. He acknowledged that he preferred to hire his political friends rather than his enemies.

McKEANSBURG

See McKean.

McKEE

See McKees Half Falls.

McKEES HALF FALLS

This Snyder County locale was named for Thomas McKee who, in 1752, settled here on the Susquehanna River on a large tract above and below the "half falls."

McKEESPORT (East —)

McKeesport, Allegheny County, was named for David McKee, who arrived in the area shortly after the French and Indian War. In 1769, the colonial authorities granted him the exclusive right to operate a ferry over the Monongahela and Youghiogheny Rivers.

In the same year, he and his sons gained title to 844 acres on which the present-day McKeesport resides. It was not until 1795 that the city was laid out by David's son, John, who named it for his father.

The town was the center of conflict during the 1794 Whiskey Rebellion.

McKeesport was a quiet country village until 1830, when John Harrison opened coal mines. The mining and shipping of coal changed the future of the town.

East McKeesport, located to the east of McKeesport, was incorporated about 1895.

McKEES ROCKS

This Allegheny County community, settled in 1764, was named for Alexander McKee, an early settler, and for the massive rock formation along the Ohio River nearby.

Because of his close friendship and association with Dr. John Connolly, Alexander McKee was suspected of treason. Connolly, a Tory, was an active agent for Virginia's Lord Dunsmore. When McKee heard of his impending arrest, he and the infamous Simon Girty fled Pittsburgh and aided the British and their Indian allies against the unprotected frontier settlements.

McKees Rocks was originally called Chartiers, because it was situated on the Ohio River at the mouth of Chartiers Creek. It was incorporated as a borough in 1892.

McMICHAELS

Morton McMichaels (1807–79) published the *North American* newspaper in Philadelphia, served as mayor of that city, and was the first president of Philadelphia's Fairmount Park Commission.

McVILLE

This town was rather whimsically named for the large number of Irish residents, whose last names began in "Mc."

MEADVILLE

Meadville, Crawford County, is the seat of Crawford County, and was named for General David Mead. Mead established the first permanent white settlement in northwestern Pennsylvania.

In 1787, Mead read a copy of a report George Washington made to Governor Dinwiddie, and decided to seek adventure and fortune in the wilderness. He and his brother forged westward and traversed the present-day counties of Clearfield, Jefferson, Clarion, Venango, and Crawford, cutting their way through on what became known as "Mead's Path."

The men returned in 1789 with their families and founded Mead's Settlement. Six years later, Mead laid out a town which he called Cussewago, Indian for "the snake with a big belly." When the town became county seat in 1800, the name was officially changed to Meadville. The town was incorporated in 1823.

Meadville was the home of the first successful slide fastener (zipper) factory.

MECHANICSBURG

This town was named for the large number of mechanics who lived and worked here in the foundries and factories.

It was known as Drytown when it was first settled around 1790. The name had nothing to do with an abhorence of alcoholic spirits, but referred to the scarcity of water. The name was changed when Mechanicsburg was incorporated as a borough in 1828.

MECHANICS GROVE

See Mechanicsburg.

MECHANICSVILLE

See Mechanicsburg.

MEDIA

Media, laid out in 1848 as the Delaware County seat, occupied the site of the county's old Poor Farm.

The first name suggested was Providence, because the town was located in the township of that name, but Minshall Painter suggested Media because of the town's location: it is midway between Philadelphia and Wilmington and basically in the center of its county.

There was some dissent to this simple name. One member of the opposition, who favored Pennrith (Welsh for "red hill"), stated: "To say that it was called after the ancient country of Media would place us in a purely ridiculous position. To derive it from the Latin adjective, converting it into a noun as the name of a place, would give it, if it were etymologically defensible, an origin so feeble as to ally it very closely to contempt." No one today looks with contempt at Media.

MELROSE

Melrose is a borough in Scotland, but the name most probably comes from the nineteenth-century writings of Sir Walter Scott.

MENDENHALL

T. C. Mendenhall was the superintendent of the U.S. Coast and Geodetic Survey (1889–94).

MERCER (—burg)

Located on the banks of the Neshannock Creek, Mercer, Franklin County, was laid out eight years after it was settled. It was named for Hugh Mercer (ca. 1725–77), Scottish physician and Revolutionary War general, who was killed at the battle of Princeton.

The county seat, Mercer was laid out in 1803 by John Findley, William Mortimer, and "Little Billy" McMillan on land donated to the county by John Hoge. Mercer was made a borough in 1814.

Mercersburg, settled in 1729–39, was also named for the general. Mercerburg's location near the Mason-Dixon Line made it a haven for abolitionist activity in the 1840s and 1850s. Hunters of fugitive slaves contended that the ground around here "swallowed up" their prey. Another said "there must be an underground road somewhere." That expression took hold and became part of ante-bellum lore. (See Princeton, New Jersey.)

MERIDIAN

The term "meridian" was used by surveyors to indicate a place on or near a meridian.

MERION

Merion takes its name from the old Merion Township. The township, formed before 1714 by settlers from Merioneth, a county in Wales, is now divided into Upper and Lower Merion.

MESHOPPEN

Settled in 1742 as a stagecoach stop, Meshoppen, Wyoming

County, takes its name from the stream. The name of Meshoppen Creek is Delaware Indian for "place of beads" or just "glass beads." Indians once bartered with wampum on the banks of the stream.

Another source, however, contends the name is Algonquian for "big potato." Take that, New York City, the "Big Apple" indeed!

METAL
This name arose from the location of metal ores.

MEXICO
Mexico was a popular name for towns and villages in the early nineteenth century, fostered by increased sympathy for the Mexican independence movement.

MIDDLEBURG
Laid out in 1800 on the land of John Swineford, this Snyder County town was long called Swinefordstown.

About 1825, the name was changed to reflect the town's location on Middle Creek, in the heart of Middle Creek Valley, and near the center of the old Centre Township. Middleburg is the county seat.

MIDDLEPORT
Middleport, situated midway between Pottsville and Tamaqua on the Schuylkill Canal, was founded in 1821.

MIDDLETOWN (— Center, West —)
Middletown, the first town laid out in Dauphin County, was named for its geographic location: it is located midway between Lancaster and Carlisle. It was a halfway station for wagoneers and stagecoach drivers.

The town was laid out in 1755 by Philadelphian George Fisher on land given him by his father.

Stubbs Furnace, formerly located in the southwestern part of town, was one of the first steel producers in the United States.

MIDLAND
Midland, Beaver County, was laid out and incorporated in 1905 by the newly-formed Midland Steel Company . . . though white settlers had occupied this early Indian camping ground in the 1820s.

MIFFLIN. Thomas Mifflin, a general in Washington's army and later governor of the Commonwealth of Pennsylvania, contributed greatly to the state's progress and donated his name along the way, to such places as Mifflin County, Mifflin, Mifflinburg, Mifflintown, and Mifflinville. (The Copley painting of Major-General and Mrs. Mifflin, The Historical Society of Pennsylvania)

The name for the town—and the company—was suggested by a company vice president, J. Ramsey Speer. He contended that the location was midway between Pittsburgh and the Shenango Valley.

MIDWAY

Midway, Washington County, is roughly "midway" between Pittsburgh and the West Virginia state line.

MIFFLIN (—burg, —town, —ville, West —)

When Mifflin County was formed, "John Harris' plantation" competed with Lewistown for county seat. When Harris' location was not selected, he laid out a new town in 1791 and named it in honor of Thomas Mifflin, who was then governor of the state. The early residents were "bitterly disappointed" when Lewistown was named county seat of Mifflin County, but their disappointment was appeased when their town was named the seat of the newly-formed Juniata County in 1831.

There was another Mifflin on a post office in the state, so this town added the "town" to its name.

Mifflinburg also honors Thomas Mifflin.

MILESBURG

Milesburg, Centre County, was laid out in 1793 by General Samuel Miles of Philadelphia. General Miles was a veteran of the Revolution and had just finished a term as mayor of Philadelphia when he settled this spot.

Milesburg was built on the site of an old Indian village, "the Bald Eagle's Nest," where Chief Wapalanne, or Bald Eagle, lived. Captain Samuel Brady killed the chief here, and put the Indian's body in a canoe, stuck a piece of "johnnycake" in his mouth—as a sign of disrespect—and let the canoe drift downstream. Bald Eagle was buried where the craft landed.

MILFORD

Milford, seat of Pike County, was laid out about 1796 by John Biddis, a Welshman from Philadelphia. The first settler to the area was Thom Quick, who arrived in 1733. Twenty-two years later he was killed by Indians who had, up to that point, been friendly. Quick's son witnessed his father's death and spent the next forty years of his life killing Indians. At the time of his death, he had killed ninety-nine, and begged friends to drag one more to his bedside so that he could even the score at one hundred.

Though some sources suggest the name was drawn from the town of Milford Haven, Pembrokeshire, Wales, or Milford, Connecticut, the reason is not that remote. In the 1770s, the Wells brothers from Connecticut settled here, establishing a sawmill, gristmill, and a ferry across the Delaware River. Near where the brothers established their mills on the Saw Creek, there was a ford. It would seem more likely that the naming came about in this way.

Mills were very important in early communities, and a number of locations have commemorated the industry in their name, such as Mill City, Millgrove, Millmont, Millport, Mill Run, Mills, Millsboro, Milltown, Millview, Mill Village, Millville, and Millwood.

MILL CREEK

Documentation exists to show that Mill Creek takes its name from the Mill Creek Furnace, built here in 1838, even though a small settlement of grist- and sawmills existed here from before the Revolution.

The furnace assumed the name of Mill Creek, from which it was supplied with waterpower. The creek, we must assume, was named from the mills that dotted its banks.

MILLERSTOWN

Millerstown, Perry County, was named for its founder, David Miller. The town was settled in 1790 and was the site of seventeen inns during the time the Pennsylvania Canal was being built.

Millerstown, Clarion County, was settled in 1793 as a lumber village. The trees were replaced in 1873 with oil derricks. The Millerstown Oil Exchange, organized in 1882, was an influence in the world oil market. In fact, it had as much influence then as OPEC does today.

Another Millerstown is in Allegheny County.

MILLHEIM

Philip Gunkel laid out this Centre County locale in 1797. It was so named because there was little else in town besides the mills. Millheim translates from the German to mean "home of mills." There is also a Mülheim in Württemberg.

MILLVALE

In 1844, the city of Allegheny purchased almost 200 acres from John Sample to establish a place for the poor. The Directors of the Poor decided in 1867 that they needed land farther away from the city, and so they divided up the Poor Farm into building lots.

The people who lived close to the Poor Farm, notably those in Bennett, feared the lots would be "gobbled up" by people living in Duquesne. In 1868, several residents rushed to the state capital in Harrisburg and obtained the incorporation of the Poor Farm lots into the "borough of Millvale."

The name for this Allegheny County community was decided, we are told, on the spur of the moment. H. P. Lyons is supposed to have come up with the name based on the iron mills of Graf Bennett & Company, that were located in the valley that had overnight become an incorporated borough.

MILROY

Until the mid-nineteenth century, this Mifflin County community was known as Perryville. In 1847, the name was changed to honor Captain (later General) Robert Huston Milroy, who had distinguished himself in the Mexican War.

MILTON (West —)

Andrew Straub was a miller and millwright who arrived in this Northumberland County area in 1780. Twelve years later he planned a mill at the site. Because of a fluke of nature—a spring freshet diverted the Limestone Run—he had to build his mill "near where the present stone bridge is." He built his log mill there in 1792, "with a wheel outside and one run of stones." Some sources, however, try to suggest poet John Milton's name for this site.

Straub's location was first called Mill-town. A village grew around the mill and the name shortened to Milton. The post office was opened in 1800, and the town incorporated in 1817.

MILWAUKEE

This town may have been named for the city in Wisconsin. The word, however, is Algonquian for "good-land."

MINERSVILLE

This Schuylkill County town was started in 1830 by Titus Bennett and was incorporated the next year. Minersville was named in the same way as Mechanicsville—it takes its name from the fact that many of its residents were coal miners.

The town was first settled in 1793 by Thomas Reed, who built a tavern, sawmill, and distillery here.

MINGOVILLE

The Mingo tribe name is a possibility for the name-source of this town. Some suggest the name came from James Fenimore Cooper's novels, but the author wrote disparagingly of the Mingoes.

MODENA

Alexander Mode ran a sawmill on the Brandywine about 1739. W. A. Mode, in about 1850, opened a papermill here and called the location Modeville. The town maintained that name until 1873, when the Wilmington & Reading Railroad came through. Officials of the railroad named the station there Modena, and the post office that followed took the same name. Some suggest the name-change was made because Modena sounded better, or because telegraphers found it an easier name to handle.

MOHNTON

Benjamin Mohn bought a farm in this Berks County location in 1846. He built a mill, while his cousin, Samuel Mohn, opened a store. The first post office in the town was opened in the store eleven years later, and was called Mohn's Store. When the town was incorporated in 1907, the name became Mohnton.

MONACA

Monaca was first settled in 1831 by Francis Helvedi, an exiled Polish nobleman, who raised merino sheep.

The next year, Bernhart Mueller (the Count de Leon) and 250 dissenters from the Harmony Society bought the land and established their own community. While the Rappites endorsed celibacy, Mueller and his followers advocated marriage. The split in the religion was settled when Father Rapp arranged for the dissidents to leave Economy and settle elsewhere. Mueller's group also received $150,000 in payment for claims against the society. His followers did not stay together too long; some migrated to Louisiana and Missouri, while others stayed here and went into business.

MONESSEN

The National Tin Plate Company of Pennsylvania opened up the iron and steel industry in this Westmoreland County city in 1897. Two years later, Monessen was incorporated.

The name is a hybrid: "mon" comes from the Monongahela River, and "essen" from the German home of the famous Krupp Works.

MONOCACY

Monocacy takes its name from the Monocacy Creek. The name is from the Delaware Indian for "stream containing many large bends." There is also a Moncacy River in Maryland.

Another source suggests the name is Algonquian for "fortified" or "enclosed," as in a fort or a cultivated field.

MONONGAHELA

In 1796, Joseph Parkinson laid out this Washington County town and named it Williamsport, for his son. When the post office opened, it took the name of Parkinson's Ferry, because there was another Williamsport in the state. The name Monongahela City was given in 1837; the post office took on the same name but dropped the "city."

Monongahela takes its name from the river, which is a corruption of *menaun-gehilla* or *menaunge-hilla*, "river with the sliding banks."

MONROE (—ton, —ville)

Monroeton was settled in 1796, thus, it does not seem possible it was named for President James Monroe.

On the other hand, Monroeville was named for the president.

MONT—

The French *mont* translates to "mountain," and is found in such places as Mont Alto, "high mountain," and Montdale, "a valley in the mountain."

MONTGOMERY (— Ferry, —ville)

Montgomery was named for Robert Montgomery who, in the mid-nineteenth century, donated a portion of his land for the railroad station and yards. It was then known as Montgomery Station.

In the 1890s, at the time of incorporation, the name was shortened to Montgomery.

MONTOURSVILLE

Montoursville takes its name from its early residents, not from the county, as some sources contend.

The site of the town was once an Indian village named Otzinachson. The land was given to Andrew Montour, a half-caste Indian interpreter. With his mother, Madame Montour (ca. 1682–1752), also a person of mixed blood, he lived here for twenty-seven years before taking legal possession. White pioneers settled here in 1807.

MONTROSE (South —)

At the turn of the nineteenth century, Captain Bartlett Hinds and his family established a settlement at this location.

Dr. Robert H. Rose, from Chester County, bought about 100,000 acres of land in the area, which included the Hinds settlement. In 1812, when surveyors laid out the town, Rose fashioned the name to include the French *mont*, for mountain, and his family name. Some sources suggest the town was named for Montrose, Scotland, or Sir Walter Scott's legend of "Montrose." It seems more likely that Dr. Rose's surname influenced the name-choice.

Montrose is the county seat of Susquehanna County.

MOOSIC

As strange as it may seem, Moosic, Lackawanna County, takes its name from the large herds of moose that once roamed the valley. It is, however, also an Indian word. (See Moshannon.)

MORAVIA

Moravia, Lawrence County, was originally settled by David Zeisberger, a Moravian missionary.

MORRIS (—dale, — Run, —ville)

Morrisville, Bucks County, was the former home of Robert Morris (1734–1806), financier of the American Revolution. When it seemed that the fledgling government would fall to bankruptcy, Morris used his personal fortune to prevent it. He also signed the Declaration of Independence. Regardless of his financial backing of the new government, when Morris found himself bankrupt, he was held in Philadelphia's debtor's prison from 1789–1801.

The town was first called Falls of the Delaware. In 1783, when Congress was arguing over where to locate "the Federal town," Morrisville was a strong candidate. In fact, it lost out by only two votes!

The area was orginally settled by the Dutch West India Company sometime in the 1620s, and a ferry crossed the Delaware here more than half-a-century before William Penn's arrival.

MORTON

The memory of John Morton, who is said to have cast the deciding vote of the Pennsylvania delegation in favor of the Declaration of Independence, is recalled in this Delaware County town. Morton also signed the document he supported.

MOSELEM SPRINGS

Moselem Springs has nothing to do with misspelled Semitic religions. The word "moselem" is Algonquian for "trout."

MOSHANNON

Moshannon, Centre County, takes its name from the creek. The name of the waterway is a corruption of the Delaware Indian *moos-hanne*, "moose stream" or "elk-creek-at."

MOUNT— and MOUNTAIN—

The nearness to a mountain, or even a slight elevation of land, caused many settlers to attach "mount" or "mountain" to their settlement's name. We find this to be true for Mountdale, Mountainhome, Mountain Top, Mount Summit, and Mount Top.

Some of these references are Biblical, such as Mount Bethel, Mount Lebanon, Mount Nebo, and Mount Zion. Others commemorate a family or reflect similarities to some historic person or place. This is the case with Mount Alton, Mount Braddock, Mount Chestnut, Mount Cobb, Mount Gretna, Mount Jackson, Mount Royal, and Mount Wolf. Mount Aetna and Mount Carbon remind us of furnaces and coal.

MOUNT CARMEL

Felix Lerch, of Northampton County, leased a two-story log tavern in 1832, "on the northern side of the turnpike (Pottsville-Danville Turnpike)" in this area. The tavern was marked with a sign: "Mt. Carmel Inn, 1824." However, the area had been settled before the Revolution.

The owner of the old Mt. Carmel Inn property laid out the town and named it after the inn. The earliest dating for the town by that name is 1848. Five years later, Mount Carmel received its post office. No one knows why the tavern carried that Biblical name, unless we really dig deep and discover that the Mount Carmel in Syria was named for the altar to Karm-el, "the vineyard god."

MOUNT JOY

This town was named for one of the Penn family's manor houses.

Mount Joy was formed from the merger of Rohrerstown, Richland, and Walleckstown, all settled in the 1760s and 1770s by Scotch-Irish immigrants.

A local historian, Israel Rupp, intent upon focusing attention on his town in the mid-nineteenth century, mistakenly identified this town as the place where Anthony Wayne spent the winter of 1777–78. Wayne probably would have preferred this place to where he was: Mount Joy at Valley Forge.

MOUNT OLIVER

Mount Oliver, Allegheny County, is built upon a hill. The hill and the land that now make up the center of this town was owned in 1840 by Oliver Ormsby.

Before 1872, there was a small borough called Ormsby that was absorbed into the city of Pittsburgh.

Mount Oliver was incorporated in 1892.

MOUNT PLEASANT (— Mills)

The Redstone Presbytery organized a church in this Westmoreland County locale in 1774 and called it Mount Pleasant Church. The village, located about two miles from the church, was incorporated in 1828 and adopted the church's name as its own.

In the early days, Mount Pleasant was called Helltown, because of the wild goings-on there when it was a relay station on the Baltimore and Pittsburgh Pike.

MOUNT UNION

In 1849, the lumber firm of Dougherty & Speer laid out the town of Mount Union, Huntingdon County, on land the company owned. The partners had no role in the naming, however.

The first postmaster, Colonel William Pollock, named it Mount Union "in consequence of such a number of mountains coming together at or near this place."

MOUNTVILLE

When laid out as a town in 1814, this town was named Mount Pleasant by its founder, Isaac Rohrer, who owned iron mines in the area. The name change was made by postal authorities.

MUIR

John Muir (1838–1914) was a famed nature-lover and writer. He was the driving force behind the first land-conservation laws in the United States and the establishment of Yosemite and Sequoia National Parks.

MUNCY (— Valley)

Muncy, Lycoming County, was originally named Pennsborough, in 1826, because it was built on John Penn's Manor of Muncy. A year later, the name was changed to Muncy.

Muncy is a corruption of the name of a sub-tribe of the Delaware Indians which formerly inhabited central Indiana. Minsi translates to "the great stone." The Minsis or Monseys were known as the "people of the stony country."

It is more likely the town's name came from the Muncy Creek, which passes nearby.

MUNSON

The source of this name is clouded. Some suggest it was transported from Munson, Massachusetts; others, that the name is a corruption of an Indian tribal name. (See Muncy.)

MURRYSVILLE

The first gas well in this area was bored in 1878. Following that discovery, wild speculation over land leases erupted into what became known as the "Haymaker Riots." This town was named for one of the men killed in the riot.

NANTICOKE (West —)

Though settled in the early nineteenth century, Nanticoke, Luzerne County, was a sleepy little village until 1825, when the first coal was mined here. The town's original settlement took advantage of the waterpower available from the Nanticoke Falls.

The name is from the Nanticoke tribe, the "seashore settlers" or "the tidewater people," from the eastern shore of Maryland.

NANTY GLO

Nanty Glo was settled by settlers from Wales. Founded in 1888, the name comes from the Welsh *nant-y-glo*, "the coal brook."

NAPIER

The town of Napier derives its name from a family name. The most prominent Napiers have been John Napier, Laird of Merchiston (1550–1617), the Scottish mathematician who discovered the value of exponential notations, and Robert C. Napier, the first Baron Napier of Magdala (1810–1890), the British field marshall who fought against the Sikhs and led expeditions to Abyssinia and China.

NATRONA HEIGHTS

This Allegheny County community takes its name from the Spanish *natron*, "native carbonate of soda." The town was founded in 1850. As early as 1853, salt was being manufactured in the area.

NAUVOO

The first city to bear this name was established by Mormons in Illinois. It was "named in obedience to a 'revelation' made to Joseph

Smith," one of the founders of the Church of Jesus Christ of Latter Day Saints, the Mormons. Several other towns have adopted this name, most times without the Mormon connection.

NAZARETH

In 1740, evangelist and orator George Whitefield purchased a 5,000 acre tract in Northampton, at the "Forks of the Delaware." He employed Peter Boehler and a small group of Moravians from Georgia to open a school for blacks. Boehler later became a Moravian bishop, but at the time of settlement he was working as mason on Whitefield's house.

After a dispute with Whitefield, the Moravians bought a nearby tract of land and set up the town of Bethlehem. A year later, they acquired Whitefield's property.

In 1755, the Moravians completed Whitefield House, or Ephrata, as it was then called.

Nazareth was exclusively Moravian for more than a century. The name comes from the home of Christ in Galilee.

NEEDFUL

Apparently the early residents of this community were dissatisfied with the rigors of their existence and felt they were "needful" of some help.

NEEDMORE

The name Needmore is usually attached to a town that needs all the amenties of life. There are eight different Needmores in the United States.

NESCOPECK

Nescopeck, Luzerne County, was named after the nearby creek. The name is from Delaware Indian and means "dark, deep, and still water" or "black spring."

NESQUEHONING

The earliest name for this Carbon County town, settled in 1824 by the Lehigh Navigation & Coal Company, was Hell's Kitchen. The current name translates from the Indian as "at the black lick" or "narrow valley."

NEW—

In naming villages, towns, and cities, many times the early settlers looked at their surroundings and decided that (1) the area resembled another, more famous, place; (2) it looked like home; (3) it would be a place where the mistakes made elsewhere would not be made again; (4) some of the glory or richness of the other place would rub off; or (5) the name already existed, they were too infatuated with it to give it up, and so just added a "new." In the following list of "new" towns, one of those concepts will almost always apply.

New Albany, New Alexandria, New Ashtola, New Baltimore, New Beaver, New Bloomfield, New Boston, New Bridgeville, New Britain, New Buena Vista, New Buffalo, New Centerville, New Chester, New Columbia, New Columbus, New Danville, New Derry, New Eagle, New Enterprise, New Era, New Florence, Newfoundland, New Franklin, New Freeport, New Galilee, New Germantown, New Grenada, New Hanover, New Holland, New Jerusalem, New Kingstown, New Lebanon, New Lexington, New Mahoning, New Milford, New Millport, New Paris, New Park, New Philadelphia, New Salem, New Texas, Newville, New Washington, New Wilmington.

NEW BERLIN (—ville)

When Union County was formed out of Northumberland County in 1813, the legislature decided that the most logical location for the county seat was at Longstown. The name was then changed to New Berlin, because the majority of settlers in the area were German.

Longstown was laid out in 1792 by George Long. In 1855, when Union County was divided, the seat moved to Lewisburg.

NEW BETHLEHEM

New Bethlehem, located on Red Bank Creek, was originally called Gumtown, for an early resident. The town, incorporated in 1853, was renamed for the steel capital of Pennsylvania.

NEW BRIGHTON

New Brighton, Beaver County, began in 1830 on David Townsend's land. It was named "new" because it was across the Beaver River from Brighton. "Old" Brighton, which took its name from the resort fifty miles south of London, is now Beaver Falls.

New Brighton, incorporated in 1838, began with the Big Beaver Blockhouse, built in 1789.

NEW CASTLE

About 1798, John Carlysle Stewart, a civil engineer, was resurveying the "donated lands"—those lands granted Revolutionary War soldiers for their service—when he discovered something strange. The original surveyor, it seemed, missed a tract of about fifty acres at the confluence of the Neshannock Creek and the Shenango.

Stewart took up the land in his own name. In 1802, he laid out the town and called it New Castle. The traditional story is that Stewart was originally from New Castle, Delaware. That is not the case.

From the beginning, Stewart dreamed of turning his town into a manufacturing town. It would seem likely that he drew the name from Newcastle upon Tyne, England.

New Castle, seat of Lawrence County, became a city in 1859.

NEW CUMBERLAND

New Cumberland, Cumberland County, takes its name from the county. The county took its name from the county of Cumberland, England. To support that notion even further, the county seats of both counties are named Carlisle.

New Cumberland was laid out in 1810 by John Haldeman and, for a time, was called Haldeman's-town. Located at the junction of Yellow Breeches Creek and the Susquehanna River, New Cumberland was a Shawnee Indian village until about 1738.

NEW FREEDOM

This York County town was not named for the liberty experienced after the Revolution.

New Freedom was first named Freedom, for the Free family, whose members were among the town's first settlers. E.K. Free was a member of the first borough council in 1879. The name was changed from Freedom because there was an older town and post office by that name in Beaver County.

NEW GENEVA

Albert Gallatin purchased a plantation in this Fayette County area in 1785. With his brother-in-law, James W. Nicholson, and the Kramer brothers, Gallatin became a pioneer in the manufacture of glass. He was born in Geneva, Switzerland.

NEW HOPE

New Hope, originally Coryell's Ferry, takes its name from the old

New Hope Mills. The mills were built by Benjamin Parry after his earlier mill was destroyed by fire in 1790.

William Lathrop established an art colony here in 1900. The artists and writers who came included Edward W. Redfield, Daniel Garber, John F. Folinsbee, Pearl S. Buck, Dorothy Parker, and George S. Kaufman.

NEW KENSINGTON

This Westmoreland County community was named "New" because there was another Kensington in Pennsylvania. That Kensington took its name directly from the London district.

NEW LONDON

New London was named directly for the London Company, which owned about 17,000 acres of land in Chester County. London Grove also received its name from the company.

NEWPORT

This Perry County community was originally known as Reider's Ferry and Reidersville. Settled in 1789 by Daniel Reider and laid out by him in 1814, the town bore his name.

Six years later, when the Pennsylvania Canal opened, the town lobbied strongly to become the county seat, and changed its name to Newport to show it had become a "new port" on the canal.

NEWRY

Newry was founded by Patrick Cassidy in about 1793. Cassidy, an Irishman, had come to America as the servant of a British officer. After the war, he purchased 300 acres of land and named his town after his hometown of Newry, County Down, Ireland.

NEWTOWN

In 1724, the county seat for Bucks County was moved from Bristol to a more central location, called Newtown.

Newtown began as Newtown Township, and the name appeared on records as early as 1683. Legend has it the name came directly from William Penn. While riding through this area with his surveyor general, Thomas Holme, Penn said: "Here I will lay out my new town."

Bucks County's county seat moved from Newtown to Doylestown after almost a century.

NEW TRIPOLI

This Lehigh County community was named in 1816 to recall the U.S. Navy's success against the Tripolitan pirates. Only time will tell if the Persian Gulf War, "Operation Desert Storm," will create names of its own.

NIAGRA

This is the Iroquoian word for "across the neck" or "at the neck." The name apparently migrated from New York.

NICHOLSON

Nicholson, Wyoming County, was named for John Nicholson, comptroller of Pennsylvania from 1782-94.

Nicholson speculated in Pennsylvania lands, at one time holding title to 3.7 million acres in thirty-nine counties. In 1797, the state laid claim to his unsettled land warrants and accounts, and the land reverted to the state. Nicholson died in 1800—in prison. He lost everything but his name on this town.

NICKLEVILE

The name for this village comes from the presence of that hard silver-white metal used in alloys.

NICKTOWN

This Cambria County village grew up around the Roman Catholic Church of St. Nicholas, and took its name from the parish.

NINEVEH

Nineveh was the capital of Assyria, and was strongly denounced in the Bible as a place of wickedness. Heck of a name to stick on a town!

NORDMONT

Nord is German for "north," and *mont* is French for "mountain." Therefore, this community's name means "north mountain."

NORMAL (—ville)

Normalville, Fayette County, was originally named Springfield, but changed its name to honor a local school for teachers. These teaching academies were called normal schools.

NORRISTOWN

Norristown is the county seat of Montgomery County, and named for Isaac Norris.

In 1704, William Penn gave his son, William Penn, Jr., 7,482 acres: the Manor of Williamstadt. Three days later, the younger Penn sold the land to William Trent and Isaac Norris. About 1712, Trent sold his share to Norris and moved to New Jersey.

After Isaac Norris' death, his son Charles inherited the land. Charles' widow sold most of the land to Colonel John Bull in 1766. Ten years later, the patriotic John Bull sold the land to Dr. William Smith, the first provost of what is now the University of Pennsylvania. The "town of Norris" was laid out in 1784 by his son, William Moore Smith. Locally, however, it was known as the Norriston Plantation and Mill Tract. Norristown was incorporated in 1812.

NORTH—

The prefix "north" before a name usually points out direction. In many instances, the place is north of something else of a similar name, such as: North Fork, North Mountain, and North Point.

NORTH BEND

North Bend was once known as Young Woman's Town. The name was not given for a local resident, but was derived from the nearby Young Woman's Creek.

Tradition says the creek received its name from an early incident. An Indian killed a young woman captive near here, and then avoided the spot for fear her ghost would revenge the murder.

NORTH EAST

North East, Erie County, takes its name from North East Township. The township was formed in 1800, and so named because it was located in the northeast part of the county.

NORTHUMBERLAND

Northumberland was laid out in 1772 on a wedge of land formed by the meeting of two branches of the Susquehanna River.

Joseph Priestley (1733–1804), who discovered oxygen, lived in Northumberland from 1794 until his death.

Northumberland takes its name from the county, which drew its name from the English county.

NORVELT

The name of this town was made by combining the final syllables of Eleanor Roosevelt's first and last names.

Norvelt was the site of Westmoreland Homesteads, an attempt to offset the effects of the decline in coal and coke operations in Westmoreland County.

The concept of the Homesteads was to combine industrial employment with part-time farming. Each individual homestead averaged two-and-a-half acres. The experiment did not succeed.

NUANGOLA

This may be a play on words. Could this be "New Angola"? (See Numidia.)

NUMIDIA

Numidia was originally named New Media. The new name is a slurred version of the original. Some sources suggest the name came from that of an ancient country in Africa.

NU MINE

Rather than call this community "New Mine" and fall into the category of all those other nouveaux, the town namers decided to be cute and call it "nu."

OBERLIN

Oberlin, Dauphin County, was named for Jean Frederick Oberlin, preacher, teacher, and philanthropist who tended his flock at Steinthal, on the borders of Alsace and Lorraine.

ODIN

The name of Odin is usually found on villages and towns founded by Scandinavians, and named for the Norse supreme being.

OGONTZ

This Montgomery County community was named for Chief Ogontz, a missionary among his own people.

OHIOPYLE

This Fayette County community takes its name from the Ohiopyle Falls on the Youghiogheny River. The Indians called the falls *Ohio-pehhle*, for the "white frothy water." This was the area where Delaware, Shawnee, and Iroquois tribes hunted.

OIL CITY

Oil City, Venango County, is located on both banks of the Oil Creek and both banks of the Allegheny River. At one time it was the site of a Seneca Indian village. It became an instant town in 1860 when oil was discovered.

The first settlement, Oil City, was laid out on the west side of the creek by the Michigan Rock Oil Company. It was incorporated two years later. On the south bank of the river, in 1863, William L. Lay started a town of his own, calling it Laytonia. Shortly after that, Vandergrift, Forman & Company laid out a town adjacent and called it Imperial City. By 1866, Laytonia and Imperial City had merged—and became incorporated—under the name of Venango City. Five years later, Venango City and Oil City became one.

OLD—

Just as with "new," early namers sometimes looked at a new place, thought of what had been there before, and thus added "old" to the name. We find this in Old Concord, Old Forge, and Old Fort.

OLD FORGE

Dr. William Hooker Smith emigrated from New York to the Wyoming Valley in 1772. A pioneer physician, Smith built a forge at this locale in 1789. The forge, built near the mouth of the Ascension Brook on the edge of the Lackawanna River, was soon abandoned because of the poor grade—and scant supply—of iron ore.

When the current village was started in the early twentieth century, it took on the name of its landmark.

The author recalls, as a young boy, his "Uncle Boss" (Phillip) Avisato taking him to see the ruins of the forge.

Some of the best days of his life were spent here.

OLEANA

Oleana, Potter County, was colonized by Norwegian violinist Ole Bornemann Bull (1810–80). The town took its name from the first part of his name.

Bull wanted "to found a new Norway, consecrated to liberty,

baptized with independence, and protected by the Union's mighty flag." In 1852, he purchased 11,144 acres of land from John F. Cowan. A contemporary wrote that he would "as soon as pick the bait from a steel trap as have any dealing with [Cowan]." Bull learned the hard way.

The violinist began to gain support and brought to the area about 800 colonists who laid out the towns of Oleana, New Norway, New Bergen, and Walhalia. Henry Clay supported the plan by donating horses. Others gave Bull equipment and materials. But Bull soon learned that Cowan was not the rightful owner of the property. It was really the land of a Quaker named Stewardson. Stewardson was willing to sell the land to Bull at a very low price, but Bull could not afford it. Most of Bull's colonists moved to Wisconsin and settled there.

Bull went back to Europe, and visited America three times. On his last visit, he lived in Cambridge, Massachusetts, a neighbor to Longfellow. He died in his native Norway.

OLEY

Oley, a community in Berks County, takes its name from an Indian word: *olink* translates to mean "a hollow."

OLYPHANT

Olyphant, Lackawanna County, was originally settled in 1798 by James Ferris, who erected a cabin in a clearing. The town was eventually named for George Talbot Olyphant.

In 1858, Olyphant was president of the Delaware & Hudson Canal Company. During that year, his company extended its railroad six miles down the valley from Archbald to open unexploited coal fields. The town began on this extension.

Olyphant was incorporated in 1876. The name was suggested by Thomas Dickson, Olyphant's successor as president of the company.

ONEIDA

One of the tribes of the Six Nations, this name means "granite people" or "people of stone."

ONO

The legend attached to this town relates that when the townsfolk were attempting to find a name, every suggestion was received with an "Oh, no!" Finally, someone suggested "Oh, no" for the name, and it was accepted.

Other places in the United States bear this name, and some sources suggest the name is drawn from the Bible (I Chron. 8:12), where it is mentioned once—without identification.

OREFIELD

The presence of iron ore, coal, or any other commodity prompted early settlers to name their town for the find. Other examples include Ore Hill and Oreland.

ORWIGSBURG

Orwigsburg, Schuylkill County, was named for founder Peter Orwig and his wife Gloria, who settled here in 1747. Peter Orwig, one of the Orwigs' four children, laid out the town in 1796.

Orwigsburg was the county seat from 1811–51 when it was removed to Pottsville.

OSCEOLA (— Mills)

Osceola, Tioga County, was named for the Seminole chief, or for the medicinal drink used by the Seminoles in certain rites.

OSWAYO

Oswayo, Potter County, was named for the neighboring creek. The name comes from the Delaware Indian language and means "place of flies" or "pine forest."

PACKERTON

Packerton, Carbon County, was named for Asa Packer, president and onetime owner of the Lehigh Valley Railroad. Packer also was a member of Congress and founder of Lehigh University.

PALMERTON

Palmerton, Carbon County, was planned and laid out by the New Jersey Zinc Company in 1898.

The first president of the company was Stephen Searles Palmer. Palmerton was incorporated as a borough in 1913.

PALMYRA

Palmyra was founded in the mid-eighteenth century by John Palm. Palm arrived from Germany in 1749 and called his settlement Palmstown. Much later, the name was romanticized to Palmyra.

PALO ALTO
Palo Alto was named for the famous battle of the Mexican War. In Castillian Spanish, the name translates to "tall tree."

PAOLI
There once was a popular inn at this location, called the General Paoli Tavern. The tavern, destroyed by fire in 1905, honored General Pasquale Paoli, who liberated Corsica from the Genoese in 1755–68, before the American Revolution. Colonists felt a strong kinship to the general and his efforts.

On the night of 20 September 1777, General "Mad Anthony" Wayne's unit was the victim of a surprise attack here. The army was so badly defeated that the encounter became known as the Paoli Massacre.

PARADISE (— Valley)
Paradise was settled by Dunkards and Mennonites. The choice of the name, we are told, was given to Abraham Witmer, who built a mill at this site. When the post office opened in 1804, Witmer said he thought that the place was "paradise." The name stuck.

PATTON
Patton, located in Cambria County, was named for Colonel John Patton of Curwensville.

PAUPACK
This Pike County location takes its name from the Wallenpaupack Creek. The translation of the waterway's name indicates it contains "deep, stagnant water."

PAXINOS
Paxinos, Northumberland County, adopted the name of the Shawnee Indian chief who befriended the white settlers during the French and Indian War.

PAXTON (—ia, —ville)
Paxton takes its name from the creek of the same name. Paxton Creek could be named for the Delaware Indian for "pool at," or for the town in England.

PEACH BOTTOM

Peach Bottom, Lancaster County, takes its name from John Kirk's peach orchard, a well-known landmark in the 1840s.

PEN ARGYL

Pen Argyl was founded in 1868 by Welsh slate workers. The town was incorporated as a borough in 1882.

PENN (— Cave, —del, — Hills, —line, — Run, —sburg, —s Creek, —sdale, —sville)

Pennsbury was named for William Penn's country estate, Pennsbury Manor, built in 1683. The original cost for construction of the manor house was $7,000. In 1938–40, the house was reconstructed. The expense this time was $200,000!

Other "Penn" names are related in some way to William Penn, the state's founder.

PERKASIE

The Manor of Perkasie, a land grant during William Penn's day, gave its name to this Montgomery County town.

The name is derived from the Delaware Indian and translates as "hickory-nuts-cracked-at."

PERKIOMENVILLE

This Montgomery County town is located on the Perkiomen Creek, a branch of the Schuylkill River. Perkiomen is a corruption of *pakihmomink*, "where there are cranberries."

PERRYOPOLIS

Perryopolis was named for Oliver Hazard Perry (1785–1819) when it was laid out in 1814. Perry, a navy captain, won the decisive battle of Lake Erie during the War of 1812.

At one time, George Washington owned over 1,600 acres of land here. He leased the property in 1789, and later sold it for $4,000.

Perrysville and Perryville were also named for Perry.

PHILADELPHIA. This head of William Penn, founder of Pennsylvania, is now in its proper place. This photo, however, was taken before the head was placed atop the body of the statue which graces Philadelphia's City Hall. (Philadelphia City Planning Commission)

PETERSBURG (East—)

Petersburg, Huntingdon County, was laid out in 1795 by Peter Shoenberger. The town acquired his name.

PETROLIA

The obvious is true; Petrolia took its name from the oil industry.

A part of the Bear Creek wilderness until the "Fannie Jane" well was drilled here in 1872, Petrolia became a boom town, then fizzled as the oil business moved west.

PHILADELPHIA

On 12 August 1684, William Penn sent forth an address to the Quaker meetings in Pennsylvania. In it he said: "And thou, Philadelphia, virgin settlement of this province, named before thou wert born, what care, what service, what travail has there been to bring thee forth, and preserve thee from such as would abuse and defile thee."

229

Penn had the idea for the name of his city long before it became reality. He combined the Greek words *philos*, "brotherly love," and *delphia*, "city of." As a point of fact, there was a Biblical city of Philadelphia, Lydia, one of the locations of the early Christian churches.

Philadelphia is a hallowed spot in American history. It was in Philadelphia that the Continental Congress met and voted for independence. It was here that Thomas Jefferson penned the Declaration of Independence. It was here that the U. S. Constitution was drafted and ratified. It is in Philadelphia that the Liberty Bell rests.

PHILIPSBURG (South —)

Philipsburg, located in Centre County, took its name from Henry and James Philips. The Englishmen laid out the town in 1797.

The first factory in the United States to manufacture screws was located in Philipsburg, built about 1820 by Hardman Philips. It was closed in 1836, when the Cold Steam Forge, which supplied it with raw material, burned to the ground.

PHOENIXVILLE

Phoenixville, Chester County, is located on the site of the Manavin Tract, a 1,000-acre tract owned by David Lloyd. He named it Manavin for his home in Wales. In 1720, more than half of the land was sold off to the Reverend Francis Buckwalter, a German immigrant. Buckwalter and his followers settled the area.

About 1785, Benjamin Longstreth started the iron business here. A few houses cropped up, but in 1800 Longstreth's property was sold by the sheriff.

By 1812, three other ironmasters attempted to carry on the business—without success. Twice the buildings were severely damaged by floods, and three times the dam that supplied power was washed away. In 1813, Lewis Wernwag, a German of indomitable courage, tried again, and named his operation the Phoenix Iron Works. The name comes from the mythical bird that rose from its own ashes. The town took on the name of the works, but Wernwag followed the path of his predecessors; the Phoenix Iron Works, like all the others, failed.

PICTURE ROCKS

About a quarter of a mile from this village, there once were Indian drawings on a craggy section of rocks overlooking Muncy Creek. Over the years, rock slides and weather have removed the "murals."

PITTSBURGH. Once a national disgrace because of pollution and disrepair, the city of Pittsburgh grew into a renaissance model for all American cities during the administration of Mayor David Lawrence.

The historic incline provides visitors with a spectacular view of the Golden Triangle. (Andrew A. Wagner, courtesy of the Greater Pittsburgh Convention & Visitors Bureau, Inc.)

PIGEON

"The great pigeon roost" of 1868–71 took place in this Forest County locale, when millions of passenger pigeons flocked here to roost.

PITTSBURGH (East —, West —)

Pittsburgh began during the eighteenth century dispute between the French and English over the Ohio Valley.

After the French built an outpost on the Allegheny River, the English did the same. The English built a fort at the junction of the Monongahela, Allegheny, and Ohio Rivers. The site was selected by a young British officer, Major George Washington.

In 1758, the settlement that grew around the safety of the fort was named Pittsborough or, as General John Forbes reported, "Pitts-Bourg." Sometimes the fortification was called Fort Pitt, but inconsistently. The town was named in honor of Sir William Pitt, Earl of Chatham, a British statesman. The Penn family set aside the "Manor of Pittsburg" in 1769, but town lots were not sold off until 1784. After the Revolution, Pittsborough grew and the name became Pittsburgh.

PITTSFIELD
See Pittsburgh.

PITTSTON (West —)
Pittston, Luzerne County, grew out of Fort Pittston. First settled by Connecticut settlers in 1770, it was named, as was Pittsburgh, for Sir William Pitt. The town was incorporated in 1855.

West Pittston was incorporated four years later. Before then it was called Fort Jenkins, a pioneer stockade named for Revolutionary War Colonel John Jenkins.

PITTSVILLE
See Pittsburgh.

PLEASANT—
Early town-namers apparently thought that "pleasant" was a great name for a town. We find it in Pleasant Corners, Pleasant Gap, Pleasant Hall, Pleasant Hill Church, Pleasant Mills, Pleasant Mount, Pleasant Unity, Pleasant Valley, and Pleasantville.

PLYMOUTH (— Meeting, — Valley)
Plymouth, Luzerne County, takes its name from Plymouth Township, one of the five townships formed by the Susquehanna Company in 1768. It took its name from Plymouth, Lithfield County, Connecticut.

Originally, Plymouth was known as Shawneetown, because of its proximity to an old Shawnee village.

Plymouth Meeting was founded about 1685–86, by Francis Rawle and his family. The Rawles had arrived on the *Desire*, which sailed from Plymouth, England.

The Quakers built their first meetinghouse here in 1710–12. It was destroyed by fire, but rebuilt in 1867. The town was originally called Plymouth, but because of possible confusion with another Plymouth in central Pennsylvania, the name was changed in 1832.

POCOHONTAS

Pocohontas was named for the Indian princess, born Matoaka (ca. 1595–1617). As a young woman, Pocohontas is supposed to have saved the life of Captain John Smith and helped keep the peace between the English colonists at Yorktown and her tribe. She married John Rolfe and converted to Christianity. She took the baptismal name of Rebecca.

POCONO (— Lake, — Manor, — Pines, — Summit)

Pocono Lake, Pocono Manor, and Pocono Pines are all located in Monroe County, and named from an Indian word.

The name is, according to one source, a corruption of *pocohanne*, "a stream between two mountains." Others suggest that the word is a modification of Pahackqualong or Pahaqualing, the Indian name for the Delaware Water Gap, meaning "a mountain with a hole (or gap) in it."

POINT MARION

This community, located at the confluence of the Cheat and Monongahela Rivers, was laid out in 1842 and named for General Francis Marion (ca. 1732–95), the "Swamp Fox" of the American Revolution.

POLK

Polk was settled about 1798, but took shape in 1839 when Aaron McKissick acquired the land and laid out the village.

When Polk was incorporated in 1886, it was named for President James K. Polk (1795–1849). Polk was the first "dark horse" candidate to capture the top job at the White House.

PORTAGE

This community was named for the old Portage Railroad. The railroad, extending from Hollidaysburg to Johnstown and completed in 1832, was a series of canals and horses and cable cars. The town is named for the "portage" across the mountain at this point.

When the Pennsylvania Railroad extended to Pittsburgh in 1852, it spelled the end of the Portage Railroad.

PORT—

When a town was established on a body of water and could be used as a port, it sometimes was called Port something-or-other. This is the case with Port Alleghany, Port Carbon, Port Clinton, Port Matilda, Port Royal, Port Trevorton, and Port Vue.

The site of Port Alleghany was known to the Indians as Canoe Place. They would stop here to construct canoes after overland treks. After the Fort Stanwyx Treaty of 1784, the land was opened to private buyers who flocked into the area.

Samuel Stanton was one of those buyers. Stanton's son Daniel arrived in 1824 and built a sawmill, and the town grew around his mill.

The name comes from the town's function and location on the Allegheny River.

Port Carbon was just what its name describes. It was a port on the Schuylkill where, in the 1830s, large cargoes of coal were shipped on the Schuylkill Canal.

Port Clinton was founded in 1829, and was an important point in canal-boating days. It takes its name from a combination of De Witt Clinton and its function as a port.

PORTERSVILLE

This Butler County village was originally named Stewartsville, for the man who founded the town: Robert Stewart.

At the time of incorporation in 1844, the town was renamed in honor of David Rittenhouse Porter (1788–1867), then governor of Pennsylvania.

Porter was a partner in the Sligo Iron Works in Huntingdon County. When that venture failed, he looked for other ways to make money . . . and became a politician. During his two terms as governor of Pennsylvania, he helped suppress the anti-Catholic riots, upheld the state's credit, and stirred up his political enemies enough to almost get impeached.

POTTERS MILLS

Potters Mills was named for General James Potter, who served under George Washington. Potter settled here after the Revolution and built several mills.

POTTSTOWN

An iron forge was established by Thomas Rutter at what is now the north end of Pottstown between 1714 and 1716.

Ironmaster John Potts founded this Montgomery County city

in the 1750s, which has been known alternately as Pottsylvania and Pottsgrove. In 1815, the town was incorporated as Pottstown, a name that appeared on records as early as 1770.

POTTSVILLE

John Pott, a German pioneer, settled in this Schuylkill County location in about 1816. By 1822, he was the owner of the White Horse Tavern, a popular stopping spot for stages on the Sunbury road. He also built a small coal furnace and a mill, and laid out the town. He quite appropriately called it Pottsville.

Pott's family arrived in America in 1734 with the Schwenkenfelders, though they were not members of that religious sect. The first settlers in this area were Henry Neyman and his family. They were massacred by Indians in 1780.

PRINCETON

Princeton takes its name from the New Jersey site of the death of General Hugh Mercer. (See Princeton, New Jersey.)

PROSPERITY

The name for this Washington County community was given by postal authorities who thought the name reflected the glowing comments of the residents who petitioned for a post office.

PULASKI

Pulaski honors the memory of Count Casimir Pulaski (ca. 1718–1779), a Polish hero of the Revolutionary War.

PUNXSUTAWNEY

Since 1887, believers have trekked here on 2 February to see Punxsutawney Phil, the official groundhog of Groundhog Day. Phil is roused from his sleep and brought to the surface. Onlookers check to see if his shadow shows. If it does, the country is in for six more weeks of winter.

The superstition has its roots in German folklore, where people watch for the groundhog on Candlemas Day. It also has its place in the lore of the Lenni-Lenape tribe.

The Lenni-Lenape believed that man was descended from animals and began life in the mother earth. After eons underground, the wolf, turkey, and turtle—three clans of the tribe—emerged. The earliest residents of this particular area were the

Alligewi. The Alligewi's "grandfather" was the groundhog, who remained under ground when they moved northeast.

Punxsutawney, Jefferson County, was first settled by Jacob Hoover in 1814, following the evacuation of the Indians in accordance with the treaty of Fort Stanwix.

Punxsutawney gained its name from the "punkies" or gnats that pestered early settlers. In a July 1772 entry in the journal of the Reverend John Ettwein, a Moravian missionary, we learn that ". . . we could hold no service because the ponkies were so excessively annoying that the cattle pressed into the camp to escape their persecuters in the smoke of the fire." According to Ettwein, the Indians called the area *ponsetunik*, "the town of the ponkies." The Moravians called the town Ashtown, and nicknamed it Gnattown.

Q QUAKAKE

The name of this Schuylkill County village is a corruption of *cuwenkee*, Delaware Indian for "pine lands."

QUAKERTOWN

This Bucks County community was founded in 1715 by members of the Society of Friends, the Quakers. At first the town was called Flatland; later, Richland, for the township.

It was the site of the little-known Fries' or "Hot Water" Rebellion. When war with France seemed inevitable in 1798, the federal government attempted to raise two million dollars by taxing land, houses, and slaves. The house tax was based on the number and size of a dwelling's windows. The Pennsylvania German housewives quickly tired of the assessors measuring their windows, greeted them with buckets of hot water.

The leader of the "rebellion" was John Fries. When his supporters "armed" themselves against the opposition, Fries became a wanted man. He was caught when his dog, Whisky, gave him away. Though he was convicted of treason, he was later pardoned. The main result of the rebellion was the shift of the German population from Federalist sympathies to Jefferson's new views.

QUARRYVILLE

Quarryville takes its name from the development of limestone quarries here about 1820. It was the birthplace of Robert Fulton (1765–1815), artist, inventor, and engineer. Fulton was the first to develop a profitable, practical steamship, the *Clermont*, in 1807.

QUINCY

Quincy is located in Quincy Township. It takes its name from the township which was named for President John Quincy Adams.

RACCOON

Raccoon takes its name from the creek of the same name. The name is a corruption of the Indian *arrath-kune* or *arathcone*.

R

RAILROAD

This name, simple and to the point, tells the main interest of this town.

RALSTON

Ralston, Lycoming County, was founded in 1831 by Matthew C. Ralston, a wealthy Philadelphian.

Ralston dreamed that this area would be an iron-producing center, and he built a blast furnace. Then he constructed a road and later a railroad to the site. The expenses, especially for the railroad, drained him of his resources and his venture failed . . . leaving him almost penniless.

RAYMILTON

In 1844, A.W. Raymond built a furnace and gristmill at this site. By taking the first syllable of his last name and the fact that this was a mill-town, he created a town to honor him and his business.

READING

Reading, Berks County, was named in 1748 by William Penn's sons, Thomas and Richard, for their ancestral home in England.

The land was surveyed by Nicholas Scull, surveyor general of the province. In 1752, when Berks became a county, Reading was made the county seat.

Though settled and named by the English, Reading's main population became German. The town is sometimes referred to as the capital of "Pennsylvania German-land."

REAMSTOWN

The land on which Reamstown stands was originally owned by John Lesher. Town founder Everhard Ream pitched a tent there in 1723, and began the settlement.

RED LION

This York County community took its name from the signboard of the Red Lion Tavern located here. Another Red Lion Tavern was the source of the name for Lionville.

RENO

Reno began as a dream of entrepreneur C.V. Culver. Culver sent out a prospectus in 1866, encouraging investment in the area, which he saw as a new oil center. In fact, he wrote, "there is not a particle of doubt of the success of the plan." The bank Culver founded floundered, and Reno never had its day in the sun.

The town was named for Union General Jesse L. Reno, who was killed at South Mountain in 1862.

RENOVO (South —)

The Philadelphia & Erie Railroad established this town in 1862 as the site of its newest shop to repair and renovate the railroad cars. Renovo is Latin for "renew," which is basically what went on in the shops. The town was incorporated in 1866.

RESSACA

Ressaca bears a name from the Mexican War. It celebrates the American victory at Resaca de la Palma.

REVERE

Revere was named for Paul Revere (1735–1818), the American patriot and silversmith. An organizer of the Boston Tea Party, Revere is best remembered for his famous 1775 ride to warn of the British march on Concord.

REYNOLDSVILLE

Reynoldsville, Jefferson County, was settled in 1838 by Woodward Reynolds and his bride. The bridal couple came from Kittaning and occupied a 300-acre wedding gift from his father. The town, laid out in 1861 by his sons David and Albert, was named for him.

At one time, the Soldier Run Mine located here was the most productive bituminous coal mine in the world.

RIDGWAY

Jacob Ridgway, one of the richest men in the world at the time, bought thousands of acres of land in McKean County and what later became Elk County. A town was laid out in 1833 by Ridgway's agents and named in his honor.

Some sources suggest the name came from John Jacob Ridgway, Ridgway's son. The son spent most of his life in Paris, however, and seems to have had nothing to do with this area of the country.

RIEGELSVILLE

Riegelsville, Bucks County, was founded in 1800 and named for John C. Riegel, a prominent citizen. The Riegel family was responsible for establishing paper mills across the river in New Jersey.

RIMER

See Rimersburg.

RIMERSBURG

Rimersburg, Clarion County, was named for John Rimer, the first settler in the area. Rimer arrived in the area in 1829, and later opened a tavern.

When Rimer opened his tavern, the southern part of town was known as Pinksville, for James Pinks. In 1853, when the town was incorporated, a three-way fight ensued. Which name should the town bear? That of Rimer, Pinks, or Colonial Levi Sloan, who wanted to name the town Sloansville, after himself. The tavern-keeper won!

RINGGOLD (New—)

Ringgold, Jefferson County, established its first post office in 1847. It adopted the name of Major Samuel Ringgold, the first American officer to die in the Mexican War.

New Ringgold, Schuylkill County, also remembers him.

ROCHESTER (— Mills)

In 1834, this Beaver County community was a village called East Bridgewater, because it was located at the confluence of the Beaver and Ohio Rivers, opposite Bridgewater. This was also the site of Logan Town, named for James Logan (nee Wingohocking), the Mingo Indian chief. A year later, another village was developed, and called Fairport.

About 1838, the name Rochester was used for the adjoining communities. Ovid Pinney, who laid out a large addition to the town, is supposed to have come from Rochester, New York. Another source suggests Rochester, England.

The first white settler was the Reverend Francis Reno, who built a house here in 1799.

ROCK (— Glen, —hill, —land, —ledge, —port, — Springs, —ton, —wood)

Rockville is at the eastern end of the Rockville Bridge, the longest stone-arch bridge in America. The 3,798-foot span is supported by thirty-eight stone arches. The other "Rock" towns all have a relationship with a geologic element.

ROSECRANS

This town was named for William Starke Rosecrans (1819–1898), a Civil War general noted for routing the Confederate troops from Tennessee and his defeat at the battle of Chicamauga in 1863.

ROULETTE

This town is not in competition with Las Vegas, Reno, or Atlantic City—its name has nothing to do with gambling. It was settled in 1816 and named for Jean Roulette of the Ceres Land Company.

ROUSEVILLE

Until 1861, this town was known as Buchanan Farm. It was renamed in that year for Henry Rouse, who drilled an oil well that produced 150 barrels a day.

RUTAN

Rutan spelled backwards is "natur," a play on words.

S

SABULA

It has been suggested that Sabula takes its name from the Latin *sabulum*, "sand, gravel."

SAGAMORE

Sagamore takes its name from the Algonquian for "chief."

ST. MARYS. One of the neatest things about St. Marys is the Straub Brewery. Making beer the way it used to be made is one of Straub's strongest selling points. But, don't run out to your nearest convenience store; Straub Beer can only be purchased within a limited area near the brewery. [CREDIT: Perry Straub, Straub Brewery, Inc., St. Marys, Pennsylvania]

SAINT CLAIR (—sville, Upper —)

The borough of Saint Clair, Schuylkill County, was separated in 1904 from Lower Saint Clair Township. Lower Saint Clair was once part of Saint Clair Township, formed in 1788 and named to honor General Arthur St. Clair (1737–1818). St. Clair served as a general in the Continental army, and was the officer who surrendered Fort Ticonderoga in 1777.

St. Clair was a member of the Continental Congress, served as its president in 1787, and was governor of the Northwest Territory from 1787–1802.

St. Clairsville was also named for Arthur St. Clair.

SAINT MARYS

St. Marys, Elk County, was founded in 1842 by the "German Catholic Brotherhood of Philadelphia and Baltimore." The groups, fleeing the "Know-Nothing" or anti-Catholic riots, traveled separately until they reached Columbia, then they traveled together by canal and then over land.

They arrived here on 8 December, the feast of the Immaculate Conception of the Virgin Mary. They named their town for Mary. The first white woman to set foot on the town site was also named Mary. The town was incorporated in 1848.

St. Marys is also the home of Straub Brewery, one of the smallest independent breweries in the United States.

SAINT PETERSBURG

St. Petersburg, Clarion County, was first called simply Petersburg, for Judge Richard Peters of Philadelphia. When the post office was established in 1862, the "saint" was added to differentiate this town from the Petersburg in Huntingdon County.

SAINT THOMAS

Saint Thomas was originally settled in 1736. It was first named Campbellstown, for Captain Thomas Campbell, a Revolutionary War veteran who laid out the town in 1790. Later, the town adopted Campbell's first name and tacked on the holy-sounding prefix.

SALEM (East —)

The first church in Pennsylvania west of the Alleghenies was a log building, erected in 1780 by the congregation of the Salem Lutheran and Reformed Church. The name is a Hebrew word for "peace," and possibly came from the town of the same name in Massachusetts.

SALINA

Salina was named for the salt deposits found nearby.

SALONA

In about 1840, the residents of this Clinton County community met to decide on a name for their settlement. They were not quite happy with Mudtown, McGheestown, or Mechanicsburg—as the town had been known.

Mrs. Samuel (Betsy) Wilson, a very pious Methodist, suggested Salonica for the town in Turkey. She had just read an article about the mission there in her copy of the *Christian Advocate*. The town liked the idea, and shortened the name slightly.

SALTILLO

Saltillo, Huntingdon County, was named for the town in Mexico which was occupied by American troops during the Mexican War. The name translates from the Spanish and means "leaping."

SALTSBURG

For many years, this part of Indiana County was one of the major locations for the manufacture of salt. Tradition has it that a Mrs. Deemer discovered the salt deposits when she noticed that the food she cooked in local water was pre-salted. Previously, hunters only "watched the lick" to locate deer and other game. Now the town discovered that salt-mining could be profitable. The industry began here in 1813. It petered out by 1876, but the salt-mining technique—a stone chisel attachment to a drill—was later exploited by Drake in his oil-drilling enterprise.

Saltsburg was laid out in 1817, and presumably took its name from the many salt mines in the area.

The earliest spelling of the name is Saltzburg. This might suggest early German settlers who combined the main operation of the area with their hometown in Germany.

SALUNGA

Salunga, Lancaster County, takes its name from the Delaware Indian *chickiswalunga*, "place of crawfish." The name of Chickies, Lancaster County, is derived from the same source.

SAULSBURG

This Huntingdon County village was founded by Henry Widersall, who was known casually as Sall. The nickname was modified to Saul and used as the town's name.

SAXONBURG

In 1831, Karl and Johann (John) A. Roebling, of Muhlhausen, Saxony, purchased land in this Butler County locality. A year later, 300 families left Bremen for America, but because of difficulties caused by colonizing agents in Philadelphia and Baltimore, only a few families arrived at this site. The name was taken from their former home.

John A. Roebling, one of the founders, became a famous engineer and suspension-bridge builder. (See Roebling, New Jersey.)

SAYLORSBURG

Saylorsburg, located on Saylors Lake, was laid out about 1825 by Charles and Samuel Saylor. The Indians called the lake Paupaunoming.

SAYRE

Sayre was known in 1870 as the "Ithaca and Athens and Southern Central Junction." The Lehigh Valley Railroad built a roundhouse here and began a locomotive works.

A town quickly grew around this activity, and was named for Robert H. Sayre, chief engineer of the Lehigh. Sayre's youngest son, Francis B. Sayre, was Woodrow Wilson's son-in-law.

SCALP LEVEL

The area on which Scalp Level is located was patented in 1787 to Luke Morris. Seven years later, Jacob Eash, Jr., erected his grist- and sawmills there, along Paint Creek.

In order to provide some lumber for his mill, or so the legend goes, Eash got a number of townsmen together and, as they began to clear the underbrush, he shouted: "Scap 'em level," or cut them close to the ground. A more logical suggestion would be that the area had been "scalped" of trees.

SCANDIA

The name comes from the Scandanavian agricultural society. It is also the Latin name for a Scandinavian island.

SCENERY HILL

Scenery Hill received its designation from the magnificent view which can be seen from here . . . but not when it was first founded.

When this Washington County site was originally settled in 1785, it was called Hillsborough. Nine years later, Stephen Hill opened a tavern. He laid out the town in 1819. His tavern, Century Inn, is still in operation.

It was not until the early twentieth century that a local physician, Dr. Byron Clark, suggested the name change to Scenery Hill. The name also appears to play on Hill's name.

SCHAEFFERSTOWN

Schaefferstown, Lebanon County, was once known as Heidleberg, for the numerous Germans who arrived here from that German city. Before the Germans came here, the area had been settled to some degree by descendents of Brazilian and West Indian Jews.

The town was named for Alexander Schaeffer, who founded and laid out the town after fleeing the Palatinate in 1744. About two miles from town, the celebrated "castle"—a wooden structure, seventy-five feet high and shaped like a truncated pyramid—of "Baron" von Stiegel once stood.

SCHUYLKILL HAVEN

This site was named for its location at the head of the Schuylkill Canal, and because it was a "haven" for anthrancite coal.

The river was named by the Dutch because they considered it *schuilplaats*, a "hidden stream." The Lenni-Lenape called the river *ganshowe-hanne*, "waving stream."

Schuylkill Haven was settled in 1748 by John Fincher, a Quaker from Chester.

SCHWENKSVILLE

Schwenksville, located on the banks of the Perkiomen, dates back to the Revolution. In fact, the Pennypacker Mills ground flour for Washington's troops quartered in town.

The town was home to Samuel W. Pennypacker (1843–1916), a governor of Pennsylvania.

SCIOTA

Sciota takes is name from the Indian word *seeyotah*, which translates to "great legs." Not a sexist term, the word refers to a river with many branches. Another source suggests that the name, when appearing in Ohio, came from the Iroquoian for "deer."

SCOTCH HILLS

This hilly community was settled by pioneers from Scotland.

SCOTTDALE

Scottdale, Westmoreland County, was laid out by Julius Shipley in 1872 on land owned by Peter and Jacob Loucks. The next year, the southwest branch of the Pennsylvania Railroad was completed as far as the Loucks brothers' farm.

Congressman George F. Huff suggested calling the new town Scottdale, in honor of Colonel Thomas Alexander Scott, president of the Pennsylvania Railroad. Scott served as an assistant secretary of war during the Lincoln administration.

Before the railroad arrived and the town was laid out, the place was known as Fountain Mills, for an old mill located there. Scottdale was incorporated as a borough in 1874.

SCRANTON

On this site there once stood the Indian village of Capouse, named for the chieftain of the Monseys. Following the Wyoming Massacre, the area was deserted and became known as Deep Hollow, then later Slocum Hollow. The Slocum family tried to change the name to Unionville, but it appears they were unsuccessful.

In 1840, George W. and Selden T. Scranton, along with their partners, William Henry, Sanford Grant, and Philip Mattes, came to the area to build a forge. Operating under the name of Scranton, Grant & Company, the men tried to manufacture iron using anthracite coal as fuel.

Though they conquered the procedure, they had to wait until the Delaware, Lackawanna & Western Railroad was built to achieve business success.

The Scrantons named their town Harrison, for President William Henry Harrison, in 1845. They next named it Lackawanna Iron Works. When the firm ran short of funds, they solicited a loan from their cousin, Joseph Hand Scranton, of Georgia. Joseph Scranton bought out Sanford Grant in 1847 and assumed control of the company. When the post office was established in 1850, it was called Scrantonia. A year later the name was shortened to Scranton.

The first Scranton in this country, John Scranton, who arrived in 1637, founded the Connecticut settlement at Guilford, and named it for his home in England.

SELINSGROVE

Selinsgrove was laid out in 1790 by Anthony Selin. Selin, a Swiss soldier of fortune, accompanied Lafayette to America.

Simon Snyder (1759–1819), governor of Pennsylvania from 1808 to 1817, lived here in a mansion built in 1816.

SELLERSVILLE

Founded in 1738, this Bucks County town was named for the Old Sellers Tavern (Washington House). In fact, the earliest name for the post office was Sellers' Tavern.

Samuel Sellers—his name was anglicized from Zoellers—was an early settler and the tavern-keeper.

SENECA

This was the name of a nation in the Indian Territory. The Dutch called them Sinnekaas, which was corrupted to Seneca.

SEVEN STARS

The innkeeper's seven daughters at an early tavern would entertain guests by singing and playing the organ. One legend tells us that an overnight guest applauded the young ladies and told their father that he had "seven stars" in his family. He liked the compliment so much, or so they say, that he named his inn the Seven Stars. The community that grew around it adopted the name.

SEVEN VALLEYS

This village was named for the Siebenthal, or Seven Valleys, within the view of the village.

SEWARD

This community bears the name of William H. Seward (1801–72), secretary of state during the Lincoln, Johnson, and Grant administrations. During his tenure, he kept European nations out of the Civil War and acquired Alaska from Russia. That deed has been called "Seward's Folly." Seward was seriously wounded in an assassination attempt that was part of the Lincoln conspiracy.

SEWICKLEY

Sewickley, Allegheny County, takes its name from an Indian tribe. The name itself comes from the Indian for "sweet water."

Sewickley had been known as Fifetown, Dogtown, Contention, and Devil's Race Track.

SHAMOKIN (— Dam)

In 1830, Jacob Graeff acquired an interest in this Northumberland County area and attempted—unsuccessfully—to establish a settlement. Five years later, John C. Boyd laid out the town of Coal.

The name was changed to Shamokin in 1840, ostensibly for the Shamokin Creek, which flows through town. The waterway received its name from an Indian village that once existed at the stream's mouth, the present town of Sunbury.

The Delaware Indians, some sources contend, called the village *schahamoki*, "eel stream" or "place of eels." A more likely source would be *sachem-okhe*, "the place where the chief lived." Chief Shikellamy, father of Logan (born Wingohocking), ruled the Indian town of Shamokin from 1728 to 1749.

SHARON (— Center, — Hill)

Sharon started with a mill built on the Shenango River in 1802. William Budd laid out the village in 1815, and four years later a post office in the name of Sharon was opened.

Sharon was incorporated in 1841, and was named for Sharon, in Palestine. In Hebrew, the name translates to "a plain."

SHARPSBURG

Sharpsburg, located in Allegheny County, was named for James Sharp, who owned the land and settled it in 1826. With the opening of the canal, the town grew and was incorporated in 1841. Sharp operated a temperance hotel in town until his death in 1861.

It was in Sharpsburg that eight-year-old Howard J. Heinz began his multi-billion-dollar empire by selling produce from his mother's garden patch.

SHAWNEE ON DELAWARE

When first settled, this town was known as Shawnee. But, because of possible confusion with the town of Shawneese, postal authorities requested, around the turn of the twentieth century that the name be changed. C. C. Worthington, a large landowner who came from Irvington-on-Hudson, New York, suggested the compound name, and it was accepted.

Shawnee, a nation in Indian Territory, has been translated as "southerners" in the Indian tongue.

SHENANDOAH

Before the Civil War, this community was wilderness, even though settlers had begun to establish sites in 1835.

In 1862, the Philadelphia Land Company instructed P.M. Schaeffer to lay out a town—in anticipation of the opening of extensive coal-mining operations. Schaeffer named the town Shenandoah, from the creek of the same name that flows through town.

Shenandoah is an Iroquois word that means "sprucy stream."

The first Greek Catholic parish in the United States, St. Michael's, began here in 1884.

SHESEQUIN

Shesequin, Bradford County, takes its name from an Indian word which means either "mysterious rattle" or "place of a rattle." The reference seems to allude to a snake.

Captain Simon Spalding, who viewed the site while he was with the Sullivan Expedition, settled here in 1783.

SHICKSHINNY

This town takes its name from a flat above the Susquehanna River.

The spot is ringed by Newport, Lee's, Rocky, Knob, and River mountains, and thus the Choctaw name. *Shickshinny* translates from the Indian to mean "five mountains."

Shickshinny was laid out in 1857, and incorporated four years later.

SHINGLEHOUSE

A Frenchman by the name of Jaundrie built a house here in 1806. He used shingles instead of clapboard to cover the exterior, and thus gave rise to the name of this Potter County village.

SHINGLETOWN

Many of the houses in this town were shingled when the town's name was selected.

SHIPPENSBURG

As early as 1730, families were living in this area. Edward Shippen took title to a great deal of the land in 1730 and laid out the town bearing his name. Shippensburg is the second oldest town in Pennsylvania west of the Susquehanna River.

Shippen was the grandson of Philadelphia's first mayor, who carried the same name. This Edward Shippen was later mayor himself. By 1837, Shippen was described as having "the biggest person, the biggest house, and the biggest coach" in Philadelphia. His granddaughter, Peggy Shippen, married Benedict Arnold.

SHIRLEYSBURG

Fort Shirley, built in 1755, once stood within the town limits of this Huntingdon County community.

The fort was named for General William Shirley, an early governor of Massachusetts who commanded the post. The town also absorbed the old Indian village of Aughwick, or Old Town.

The town was founded in 1757.

SHOHOLA (— Falls)

Shohola and Shohola Falls, Pike County, take their names from the stream. Shohola Creek translates from the Indian, *schauwihilla*, as "weak, faint or depressed." The name probably refers to an incident when someone took ill in the area.

SHUNK

Shunk was named for Francis R. Shunk, governor of Pennsylvania from 1845 to 1848.

SINKING SPRING

Sinking Spring, Berks County, takes its name from "a singular spring, which here rises out of the ground with considerable volume of water, and almost immediately sinks again. . . ."

The town was founded in 1793. The spring was located at what is now 402 Penn Avenue.

SINNEMAHONING

This town's name comes from the Indian for "stony lick." A nineteenth-century poem reflected life in this community and ended with the lines:

> So well indeed its fame is known
> That people think they should begin
> To drop the useless word Mahone,
> and call the country simply Sin.

SKINNERS EDDY

Ebenezer Skinner built a tavern here in 1792, and the name of the town commemorates him and the "eddy" in the nearby Susquehanna River.

The location made this a particularly popular stopping place for boatmen.

SKIPPACK

This Montgomery County community takes its name from Skippack Creek. The name comes from the Lenni-Lenape *schki-peek,* "a pool of stagnant water."

SLABTOWN

The town takes its name from the "slabs," pieces of wood that came from the sawmill and were used as firewood.

SLATEDALE

See Slateford.

SLATEFORD

Slateford, Northampton County, was so named because it was the center for the manufacture of school slates.

During the first half of the nineteenth century, slate deposits were uncovered, and hundreds of Welsh and English immigrants arrived to work in the quarries. The quarries were closed by owners' consensus during World War I, and the workers shipped off to work in the Bethlehem steel mills.

The quarries reopened in 1930.

SLATE LICK

This town was so named because deer came here to lick salt from the slate rocks.

SLATINGTON

Quarrying for slate began in this area in 1845. The town that grew up around the quarries—there were more than twenty during Slatington's heyday—was named for its major industry.

SLIGO

Sligo was named for the Sligo Furnace, built here in 1745 by four Irishmen from Sligo, Ireland. The furnace was closed in 1873.

SLIPPERY ROCK

Originally called Ginger Hill, because the tavern-keeper gave away plenty of ginger with the whiskey he sold, the town's current name comes from the nearby creek.

Slippery Rock Creek was named, or so one legend goes, because Captain Samuel Brady, chased by hostile Indians, leaped across the twenty-three-foot stream in a single bound. However, the name obviously goes back to before the captain's time.

The Indians called the stream *wesch-ach-ach-apochka*, which translates to "slippery rock." The reference is to the presence in the stream of slimy, slippery rocks.

Slippery Rock was the scene, it is said, of the last Indian massacre in this region. In 1843, an old Indian named Sam Mohawk was drinking pretty heavily at the Old Stone House tavern. While James Wigton was away from his nearby farm, Mohawk went there and murdered Mrs. Wigton and five of her children.

SMETHPORT (East —)

Smethport was settled on land owned by the Ceres Land Company, managed by Captain John Keating. The investments in Ceres were, for the most part, derived from Frenchmen who fled their country at the outbreak of the French Revolution.

Because they were exiles, their finances were handled by two Dutch banking houses in Amsterdam. One of these firms was the house of Raymond and Theodore de Smeth. Though both men died before 1800, the name continued.

In 1807, when the new town was laid out in Keating Township, it was named by Keating in honor of the bankers.

SNOW SHOE

This town, within eyeshot of Snowshoe Mountain, takes its name, it is said, from the "Snow Shoe Camp Survey."

When surveyors were making their calculations here in 1773, they came upon a snowshoe hanging in a tree. The site was near an abandoned Indian camp along the Chinclacamoose trail.

Another bit of legend tells that a group of hunters were overtaken by a fierce storm and were forced to make snowshoes in order to make it through the snow.

This community was formerly known as Snow Shoe Camp.

SNYDERS (—burg, —ville, —town)

Snydertown, Northumberland County, and Snyder County were named for Simon Snyder, governor of Pennsylvania from 1808–17.

SOMERSET

In 1795, Adam Schneider laid out his own design for the county seat of the new Somerset County. He plotted the plan on land he had purchased from Ulrich Bruner. The place had been called Brunerstown since 1787, when Bruner laid out the town.

Somerset was ravaged by fire in 1833, and again in 1872, but each time continued to build and rebuild.

The town, then spelled Summerset, was named for the county, which took its name from Somersetshire, England.

SOUDERTON

Souderton, Montgomery County, though founded in 1876, was settled much earlier and named for early settlers.

The original log cabin church of the Indian Creek Reformed Church was built in 1753. Four successive buildings followed it.

SOUTH—

The "South" names came about just like the "north" names, only in the opposite direction. In this case we find South Bend, South Canaan, South Fork, South Heights, and South Mountain.

SPANGLER

At the time of its incorporation in 1893, this Cambria County village took the name of Colonel J.L. Spangler, of Bellefonte.

SPEERS

Speers, located on the west bank of the Monongahela River, was named for Apollos Speers.

SPRING HOUSE

Spring House, Montgomery County, was named for that particular bit of construction. A springhouse was a place where a homeowner could keep meat and produce cool during summer heat.

There was an inn located here that was used as a headquarters for the Pennsylvania and New Jersey militia during the 1798 Fries' or Hot Water Rebellion.

SPRING MILLS

Located on Penn's Creek, Spring Mills was part of the Penn family's Manor of Succoth until they passed the title on in 1791.

STANTON

Stanton bears the name of Edwin McMasters Stanton (1814–69), Lincoln's second secretary of war. He was dismissed from his post by President Andrew Johnson in 1868 because he demanded stricter Reconstruction efforts than those espoused by the president.

STATE COLLEGE

Farmers High School was founded in this Center County community in 1855. The school, sponsored for the most part by the State Agricultural Society, taught soil-conservation methods.

In 1862, Abraham Lincoln signed the Morrill Land Grant College Act, which provided for an institution of higher learning in each state. Two years later this school took advantage of the legislation and became the Agricultural College of Pennsylvania, and then the Pennsylvania State College in 1874. The town of State College was created in 1874 by incorporating the townships of Benner and Harris.

STEELTON

The Pennsylvania Steel Company began construction of its massive works in this Dauphin County area in 1865. The next year, Rudolph and Henry Kelker, of Harrisburg, laid out a town on land they owned adjacent to the works. They named it Baldwin, for Matthew W. Baldwin (1795–1866), owner of the Baldwin Locomotive Works and a major stockholder in Pennsylvania Steel. Baldwin was an abolitionist and, because of this belief, his locomotives were boycotted by Southern railroads.

When the post office was established here in 1871, it was called Steel Works. Nine years later, when the town was incorporated, Major Luther S. Bent, superintendent of the works, suggested the name become Steelton.

STONE HOUSE

When everyone else was constructing log cabins, this town boasted a house made of stone.

STOYSTOWN

In Somerset County, Stoystown was named for early settler and Revolutionary War soldier John Stoy.

STRASBURG (Upper —)

Strasburg, Lancaster County, is located at the eastern end of the Strasburg Road, which was authorized by the Pennsylvania legislature as a link between Philadelphia and York. The town was first settled by French Huguenots, but later became a community of German immigrants in the Pennsylvania Dutch county.

The earliest settlers, arriving in 1733, came from Strasbourgh, Alsace. The name translates to "the town by the road, or street." German settlers called their town Peddlehausie, which translates to Beggartown.

STRINESTOWN

Once the site of an Indian village, Strinestown was founded in 1800 and named for John Strine, an early settler. For half a century, the town was the center of cigar manufacturing in the state.

STROUDSBURG (East —)

Colonel Jacob Stroud, a veteran of the French and Indian War and a native of New Jersey, settled in this Monroe County area in 1769. He named the stockaded home he built in 1776 Fort Penn.

Stroud refused to sell building lots. After his death in 1806, his son Daniel laid out the town and sold off lots in the town site. One stipulation he set was that all houses be set back thirty feet from the street.

SUGAR (— Grove, — Hill, — Notch, — Run)

Sugar Notch, Luzerne County, was so named because settlers from New England found their favorite sugar maple trees growing here in the "notch," or gap, in Little Mountain.

SUMMERHILL

This Cambria County community took its name from old Summerhill Township, organized in 1810. The community was named Somerhill upon its founding for Joseph and David Somers, important local landowners. The name was apparently Americanized.

SUNBURY (West —)

Sunbury, Northumberland County, was once the center of Shamokin, a cluster of three Indian villages forming the Indian capital of western Pennsylvania. The first white visitors, the Moravian Count von Zinzendorf and the provincial government's interpreter Conrad Weiser, were greeted here by Shikellemy in 1742.

Fourteen years later, it was the site of Pennsylvania's largest frontier fort, Fort Augusta.

Three months after the formation of the county in 1772, Governor Richard Penn ordered that the surveyor general, John Lukens, "with the assistance of Mr. William Maclay lay out a town for the county of Northumberland to be called by the name of Sunbury." Penn apparently borrowed the name from Sunbury-on-Thames, England.

Sunbury also had one of the world's first three-wire central station incandescent lighting plants, built by Thomas Alva Edison in 1883. (See Menlo Park, Edison, New Jersey.)

SUSQUEHANNA

Susquehanna takes its name from the county, which took its name from the river. The Lenni-Lenape *suckahanne* simply translates to "water-stream." According to the writings of Captain John Smith (ca. 1608–12), the name of the river was drawn from that of the tribe, the Susquehanocks. The tribe was almost annihilated by the Iroquois in 1675.

This translation makes a great deal of sense, since -*hanna* translates from the Algonquian as "stream," and the combined name becomes "stream of the Susque-tribe."

SWARTHMORE

Swarthmore takes its name directly from Swarthmore College, around which it grew. The college was established in 1864 by members of the Society of Friends. It was named for Swarthmore Hall, the home of Friends founder George Fox.

SWISSVALE

The town of Swissvale, Allegheny County, was built around the farm of James Swisshelm. The first settlement took place before 1760, but the town was not incorporated as a borough until 1898.

In 1854, when the Pennsylvania Railroad decided to establish a station here, James Swisshelm donated half an acre for the site.

The owner's wife, Jane Gray Swisshelm, suggested the name, and the town which grew up around the station assumed that name. Mrs. Swisshelm was a noted abolitionist and suffragette.

SWOYERSVILLE

Swoyersville, located in Luzerne County, was named for John Henry Swoyer, who operated two large coal breakers at this site when the borough was incorporated in 1888.

SYLVANIA

Sylvania took as its name the second half of Pennsylvania. The word is Greek for "woods."

TAMAQUA (South —)

Berkhard Moser built a sawmill here in 1799. The town was laid out in 1829 by the Lehigh Coal & Navigation Company.

The Schuylkill County town takes its name from the Tamaqua Creek, the west branch of the Little Schuylkill. The name comes from *tamaque*, a Delaware Indian word meaning "beaver."

Berkhard Moser built a sawmill here in 1799. Eighteen years later, he discovered coal on his property.

TAMARACK

Tamarack was originally an Algonquian word for the larch tree, a tree generally found near water.

TARENTUM

This Allegheny County town was originally settled in the late eighteenth century when a gristmill was built on Bull Creek.

Judge Henry Marie Brackenridge and his wife, Caroline, owned the land on which Tarentum is currently located. The town was laid out and named in 1829 by the judge, apparently for the ancient city in southern Italy.

The judge's farm was once occupied by a Shawnee village called Chartier's Old Town, for Peter Chartier, a half-caste trader.

Tarentum was incorporated as a borough in 1842.

TATAMY

This Northampton County community was named for an eighteenth-century Delaware Indian chief of the same name.

TAYLOR

Taylor, a suburb of Scranton, was named for Moses Taylor, a New York merchant, shipbuilder, and banker who had holdings in the area.

TEMPLE

During the late eighteenth century, the King Solomon Tavern was in full operation here. Outside was a sign that read: "Stop at Solomon's Temple."

The tavern-keeper's Christian name was Solomon. It was a natural leap to name the town Solomon's Temple, then simply Temple.

TERRE HILL

The French *terre* is "land" or "earth," so this town's name translates to "dirt hill."

THROOP

Dr. Benjamin Henry Throop was a prominent physician in this Lackawanna County area. The good doctor built a small cottage here in 1847. Six years later, he was the postmaster in Scranton. In a short time, he purchased extensive tracts of land, sensing that coal would be the chief source of income in this area. He became even more wealthy by buying up farms and dividing them into townlots, which he always sold at a profit.

Dr. Throop not only founded Throop, he was also instrumental in the establishment of Blakely, and the formation of Lackawanna County.

TIADAGHTON

This town took the name of an Iroquois chief.

TIDIOUTE

Tidioute translates from the Indian with various meanings, such as "seeing far" or "straight water" or "cluster of islands."

The first settlers here were members of the Harmony Society. The group had large landholdings in this area. (See Harmony.)

TIOGA (— Junction)

Tioga, Tioga County, takes its name from its county. The county, on the other hand, took its name from the river.

The word translates from the Indian to mean either "at the forks," "swift current," "entrance," or "gate."

Settled in 1792 by Jesse Losey, a veteran of the Revolutionary War, Tioga had formerly been an outpost of the Six Nations.

TIONESTA

First called Goshgoshing and then Saqualinquent, Tionesta became this town's final name. The name came from the Tionesta Creek, which first appeared on a map dated about 1795.

The name seems to be a modification of the Iroquois *tiyohweno-isto*, "it penetrates the island." Another source says it means "home of the wolves."

David Zeisberger established a small Moravian settlement here in 1797, but it was short-lived. Zeisberger was aware of the presence of oil, but did not exploit it. In his journal he wrote that the oil could be taken "medicinally for toothache, rheumatism, etc. Sometimes it is taken internally. It is of brown color and burns well and can be used in lamps."

TITUSVILLE (East —)

Titusville, located in Crawford County, was named for Jonathan

Titus, owner of the town site. Local Indians used the slick film on Oil Creek to mix their warpaint. Later, European settlers bottled it, and sold it as Senaca Oil, a supposed medicinal concoction.

During the summer of 1858, Colonel Edwin L. Drake dug several wells with pick and shovel, trying to figure a way to obtain the oil from the ground. When one of his "wells" almost drowned several of his workers, Drake decided to try drilling.

With the aid of "Uncle Billy" Smith, a blacksmith from Tarentum who had worked at drilling salt wells, Drake was able to drill through solid rock. On 28 August, the next year, they noticed a brown liquid bubbling near the surface. With a pitcher-pump, they filled several barrels and road into town shouting: "Struck oil! Struck oil!" They had indeed drilled the first oil. The Drake Well Park and Museum here explains the early days of oil-drilling in America. The library at the museum also contains the papers of Ida M. Tarbell (1857–1944), one of the original journalistic muckrakers. Her family had ties to the early oil industry, which explains her strong interest in the subject. Tarbell wrote the famous 1904 exposé, *The History of Standard Oil*. (See Wattsburg.)

Pennsylvania was the nation's primary oil producer until 1891.

TOBYHANNA

The name of Tobyhanna, Monroe County, is not the combination of the names of a man and a woman. The community takes its name from the stream, which the Indians called *tobi-hanna* for either "dark waters" or "alder stream."

TOUGHKENAMON

This Chester County community was settled in the early eighteenth century, and takes its name from the Indian for "firebrand."

Firebrands, pieces of burning wood, were used as offensive weapons by the Indians. The name is used to commemorate a battle between two Indian tribes fought here.

Another source suggests that the firebrands were used as signaling devices from local hills, and thus the source of the name. The first idea is the most logical, however.

TOWANDA (North —)

Towanda, the seat of Bradford County, was laid out in 1812 by William Means. For many years, it was known as Meansville and Williamston; both names referring to one man.

These names, it is said, caused "considerable animosity," and when the town was incorporated in 1828, it was named Towanda, after Towanda Township. The township was named for Towanda Creek. Towanda is a corruption of *tawundeunk,* "where we bury the dead." The Nanticoke Indians, it is said, buried their dead here.

Towanda was the boyhood home of composer Stephen Collins Foster (1826–64) and the home of David Wilmot (1814–68), founder of the Republican party.

TOWER CITY

This Schuylkill County community was named in 1868 for Charlemagne Tower, Sr., the town's founder. The town was built on reclaimed marshlands. Tower had known as early as 1847 that there was coal in the area, but he could not take advantage of his knowledge because he did not have the money to exploit it.

He kept the coal a secret until he accumulated a small fortune during the Civil War; then he was able to mine for the fossil fuel. He purchased Brookside Mountain for four dollars an acre and tunneled into it. At first he was unsuccessful, but he finally hit pay dirt and became richer than his wildest dreams.

His son, Charlemagne, Jr., later served as U. S. ambassador to Germany.

TRAPPE

Depending on which legend you wish to believe, this Montgomery County town's name came from an early tavern's high stoop, which was called a *treppe* by German settlers, or "a step." Another contends the word is that the tavern's high steps were a "trap" for unsteady customers. A more reasonable suggestion indicates that the name was that of a French or Swiss hunter.

The Augustus Lutheran Church here was built in 1743 by Dr. Heinrich Melchior Muhlenberg (1711–87), the "Patriarch of the American Lutheran Church." Dr. Muhlenberg is buried in the adjoining graveyard, next to his son John Peter Muhlenberg (1746–1807).

It was the younger Muhlenberg who, while serving as a pastor to a church in Woodstock, Virginia, roused his flock to support the Revolution. In his farewell sermon, Muhlenberg concluded with "There is a time for all things—a time to preach and a time to fight—and now is the time to fight!" With that, he threw back his liturgical robes and showed his uniform: that of a Continental army colonel.

TREVESKYN

Treveskyn is supposedly named for an Indian chief.

TREXLERTOWN

Trexlertown, Lehigh County, was named for John Trexler.

Located at the site was a stone-and-log building, erected in 1731. Trexler enlarged it in 1760 and opened it as a hotel, to protect himself against the "burden of Travellers" who could find no "tavern or house of entertainment near."

TROY (East —)

Troy, Bradford County, was settled in 1793 by Nathaniel Allen, a veteran of the Revolution and a land agent for the Susquehanna Company. The town was named for the ancient Greek city.

TUNKHANNOCK

This village began in 1775, when Dutchman Jeremiah Osterhout built a cabin here. Located at the confluence of Tunkhannock Creek and the North Branch of the Susquehanna River, the town takes its name from the creek. The creek's name usually translates from the Indian *tank-hanne*, "small stream." Other sources provide a more plausible interpretation: the name is derived from *Tenk-ghanacke*, an Algonquian word that means "forest, or wilderness."

Tunkhannock was incorporated in 1842, and became the county seat.

TURTLE CREEK

Turtle Creek, Allegheny County, is the translation of the Delaware Indian name for the stream on which the town is located, Tulpewi-sipu, "turtle creek."

The town was settled about 1765, and was incorporated in 1892 after the completion of the Greensburg turnpike.

TYLER (— Hill, —sburg, —sport, —sville)

Tylersville, Clinton County, was named during a presidential campaign in honor of John Tyler (1790–1862), who was then running for vice president. Tyler became president when William Henry Harrison died, making him the first vice president to gain the office through death.

TYRONE

This area of Blair County was settled in 1850, but immigrants from northern Ireland had made their mark earlier. They named their township for their native county of Tyrone. In Erse, the Irish language, *tyrone* means "the land of Owen."

Two years later, Elia Bowen, in his *Pictorial Sketch Book of Pennsylvania,* described the forge at Tyrone as the "principal theatre" of the iron industry in the region.

Tyrone became a borough in 1857, the first house having been built just seven years earlier by Jacob Burley.

UNIONTOWN

Uniontown, the seat of Fayette County, was laid out by Henry Beeson, a Quaker, in about 1768. For years, the town was called Beeson's-town.

Shortly after the town was surveyed, the name commonly used for the area was Union. That name appeared as early as 1780. In 1783, when Union Township was formed with Union at the center, it became necessary to modify one name or the other to distinguish between the two.

Uniontown was the birthplace of General George C. Marshall (1880–1959). Marshall was the chief architect of the United States' World War II effort and the author of the Marshall Plan, which brought life back to the conquered lands of Europe.

UPLAND

One possible source for this place name is that many of the original Swedish settlers had come from the Swedish Upland; or it may be derived from a 1631 Dutch fortification, Optlandt, "on the land."

UPPER BLACK EDDY

This town takes its name from an eddy in the River which bollixed up rafts of lumber. The name was probably coined by frustrated rivermen.

The town, taking its name from the eddy, had its first post office in 1830, with David Worman postmaster.

Nearby are the Ringing Rocks. The rocks, when struck with a hammer, give off a loud ringing sound. The rocks vary in size and also in musical tone.

UPPER DARBY

The Delaware County community where this author grew up takes its name from its position north of Darby. As a kid, he referred to the neighborhood as "upper dump," or "West Philadelphia with its socks pulled up."

VALLEY FORGE. A solitary soldier stands guard over replicas of Washington's cannon at Valley Forge National Historical Park. (Valley Forge Convention & Visitors Bureau)

URBAN

The name signifies "city" as opposed to "country," or "rural."

URSINA

Ursina, Somerset County, was laid out in 1868 by Judge William J. Bear. The word is taken from the Latin, and means "belonging to the bear." One source suggests it was an attempt to avoid the name "bear," which was prominent in place naming in the area.

VALLEY FORGE

One of the most hallowed spots in America, Valley Forge, Chester County, began in the 1740s as a small iron forge built by Isaac Potts on the Valley Creek. Potts, son of Pottstown's founder John Potts, built his forge here before 1759.

By the time of the Revolution, a sawmill and gristmill were added, but were destroyed by the British in 1777.

VAN

The name is derived from that of President Martin Van Buren. (See Vanport.)

VANDERGRIFT (North —)

This Westmoreland County town was laid out in 1895 by Frederick

L. Olmstead, for the Apollo Iron & Steel Company. It was named for J. J. Vandergrift, of Pittsburgh, a major stockholder in the company.

Vandergrift was incorporated in 1897.

VANPORT

This Beaver County community was named during the 1836 presidential campaign for Martin Van Buren (1782–1862), called "Little Van" or "Matty Van" by his admirers.

Van Buren was noted for his political savvy. He was the last vice president—before George Bush—to succeed by election to the presidency from the office of vice president.

VENANGO

Venango, Crawford County, takes its name from Venango County. The Indian *in-nun-gah* refers to an indecent figure carved on a tree by the Erie Indians.

VERA CRUZ

The ever-popular Mexican War campaign spawned a great number of place names. This community must be added to the list. The name translates from the Spanish for "true cross."

VERSAILLES

Versailles takes its name from old Versailles Township. The township was named for the palace of the kings in Paris, France. It also stands as a reminder of strong, but unsuccessful, attempts made by the French to colonize and possess western Pennsylvania.

VESTABURG

Vestaburg was named for the Latin goddess of the hearth.

VILLANOVA

Villanova takes its name from Villanova University.

The university was founded in 1842 by the Augustinian Fathers, and was named for St. Thomas of Villanova, Bishop of Valencia during the mid-sixteenth century.

VINCO

Vinco is Latin for "I conquer."

VIRGINVILLE

Virginville is located on Maiden Creek! Both the town and the stream are varied translations of the Indian *ontelaunee*, "virgin, or maiden." Though the names are different, they really are the same.

WAMPUM

Wampum, Lawrence County, was settled in 1796 on the Beaver River. It was incorporated as a borough in 1876.

The name is a contraction of *wampumpeak*, "a string of shell beads"; in other words, the Indian form of currency.

WANAMAKERS

Wanamakers was named for John Wanamaker (1838–1922), who created the department-store concept in his store in Philadelphia. Prior to Wanamaker, people shopped in specialty shops. He changed all that in 1877 by establishing individual "departments" under one roof, where people could do "one-stop" shopping.

Wanamaker was one of the first American businessmen to use advertising and advertising agencies. He believed that the "customer was always right," and was the first to give a full refund on returns.

After fund-raising for the successful election of Benjamin Harrison in 1888, John Wanamaker was named postmaster general. He made many innovations that helped improve the system, but his effectiveness was reduced by his free use of the spoils system.

WANAMAKERS. Philadelphia's "Merchant Prince," John Wanamaker, provided summer camp for his employees. The camp was located at a place now called Wanamakers in his honor. This photo was taken by Duhrkoop ca. 1912. (Print and Picture Department, Free Library of Philadelphia)

WARREN (— Center, —dale, —sville, North —, West —)

Warren, Warren County, was laid out as early as 1795 on state land, by General William Irvine and Andrew Ellicott.

Warren is the county seat and takes its name from Warren County, formed in 1800, which was named for General Joseph Warren, who fell at the Battle of Bunker Hill. The town was incorporated in 1832.

North Warren and Warrensville, Lycoming County, was also named for the general.

WARRIORS MARK

According to tradition, this Huntingdon County location took its name from strange marks carved into trees by the Indians.

WARRIOR RUN
This town was so named because of its location on an Indian route known as the Warriors Trail.

WARWICK
Warwick, Chester County, was first settled by Samuel Nutt, an ironmaster from Warwickshire, England. He named his operation the Warwick Iron Works.

WASHINGTON (— Crossing, —ville, East —, North —)
Washington, the county seat of Washington County, was originally known as Catfish's Camp. The name did not come from the campgrounds of the bottom fish. Rather, this is where Delaware Chief Catfish lived about 1750.

Catfish's Camp became a popular stopping spot for people traveling from Redstone Old Fort (Brownsville) to Wheeling. David Hoge bought the land upon which the town later was built. In 1781, he built a log courthouse, and laid out the town, which he called Bassett-town for his friend Richard Bassett, who would later help frame the U. S. Constitution and serve as governor of Delaware.

Realizing that his place would become the county seat, he changed the name to Washington-town. The extra "town" was soon dropped. Washington was incorporated as a borough in 1810, and chartered as a city in 1924.

George Washington and 2,400 men crossed the Delaware River 25 December 1776 and attacked the Hessians at Trenton, New Jersey. The resulting area became known as Washington's Crossing.

George Washington's name is commemorated in North Washington, Fort Washington, Washingtonville, and elsewhere.

WATERFORD (East —)
Waterford, Erie County, dates back to the 1753 erection of the French Fort Le Boeuf, "the bull, or the buffalo."

Waterford was laid out in 1795 by Andrew Ellicott, and named for its township. Waterford Township was named in respect to the Irish settlers, many of whom came from County Waterford.

WATERLOO
Waterloo was named for the Belgian battlefield where Napoleon met his defeat in 1815.

WATER STREET

This town's name remembers the time when early wagons and the Pennsylvania Canal ran along the bed of a shallow stream here as they passed through the gap in the Tussey Mountains. The first road was actually a "water" street.

This Huntingdon County community takes its name from the Water Street Branch of the Juniata River.

WATTSBURG

Wattsburg, located in Erie County, was founded in 1796 as a fur and supply store by William Miles. He named the town that grew around his establishment for his wife's family.

Just south of Wattsburg is the home of Ida Minerva Tarbell (1857–1944). In 1904, she wrote *History of the Standard Oil Company,* an exposé of price-fixing and corruption led by the Rockefellers. Tarbell could rightfully be called the "Mother of Investigative Journalism."

WAUKESHA

This community adopts its name from the Potawatomi Indian word *wauk-tsha* for "fox."

WAVERLY (South —)

Waverly takes its name from Sir Walter Scott's *Waverley Novels,* very popular when this naming process was taking place.

WAYNE (—sboro, —sburg)

Waynesboro, Franklin County, dates back to 1749. John Brown taught Sunday school here before he achieved fame with his raid on Harpers Ferry. The town was laid out by James Wallace, Jr., in 1797. He named it for General "Mad" Anthony Wayne (1745–97), who died the previous year. Wallace had served under the general during the Revolution. Townspeople persisted in calling their site Wallacetown, but in 1818 the town was formally incorporated as Waynesborough. Postal authorities simplified the name.

Troops under the command of Confederate General Jubal Early entered the town on 23 July 1861 and demanded the women of the town bake bread for him and his troops.

The town of Wayne was founded in 1880 and also named for Wayne.

Waynesburg, Greene County, is named for General Wayne. It is the county seat. Laid out in 1796, and incorporated in 1816,

Waynesburg is home to Waynesburg College, one of the first colleges in the nation to grant degrees to women.

WEBSTER (— Mills)

Webster, Westmoreland County, was laid out in 1833 and named for Daniel Webster (1782–1852). At the time of naming, the orator and statesman was at the peak of his popularity.

"Black Dan," as he was known, was a strong supporter of national government as opposed to states' rights. He believed strongly that disunion was worse than slavery, and supported the Compromise of 1850. This position kept him from being nominated for the presidency in 1848.

WEISSPORT

Weissport, Carbon County, was named for Colonel Jacob Weiss, a wealthy Philadelphian who also settled in the Lehigh Valley.

Weiss organized one of the first coal companies here.

WELLSBORO

Wellsboro is the county seat of Tioga County, formed in 1804. The town was founded by Benjamin Wister Morris, a Philadelphia Quaker who had fallen on hard times. To recoup his losses, Morris became agent and manager of the Pine Creek Land Company. In 1799, Morris settled here with his wife and two children. He laid out the town in 1806, using Penn's plan for Philadelphia, and named it for his wife, Mary Hill Wells.

Mrs. Wells' brothers, Gideon and William Hill Wells, were large landowners in the settlement before the name was given. In 1806, Mary and her brothers successfully secured Wellsborough as the county seat, whose name by that point had been modernized to Wellsboro.

WESLEY (—ville)

Wesleyville, Erie County, was laid out by John Shadduck in 1828. Shadduck built a Methodist church here, and named his town for John Wesley, the founder of Methodism.

WEST CHESTER

West Chester, the county seat of Chester County, was named because of its location—some sixteen miles northwest of Chester.

The honor of becoming the county seat formed the basis of a

constant, sometimes violent, struggle for many years between West Chester and Chester.

The *Jeffersonian*, one of very few Northern newspapers to side with the South, began publication in West Chester in 1842. Because of its political stance, the *Jeffersonian*'s office was wrecked; the federal marshal suppressed it; and the postmaster general banned it from being carried by the mails.

WESTFIELD

The first post office in this Tioga County community was established in the woolen mill of Henry B. Trowbridge. Trowbridge named the post office and the town in 1821 for his hometown in Massachusetts.

WHEATLAND

James Wood, a staunch Democrat, laid out this Mercer County location in about 1865, and named it for the estate of President James Buchanan, located near Lancaster.

WHIG HILL

The town was named for the political affiliation of some of its residents.

WHITE HAVEN

This town in Luzerne County was begun in 1824. It was incorporated eight years later as White Haven, in honor of Philadelphian Josiah White, a principal stockholder in the Lehigh Coal & Navigation Company.

WHITE HORSE

White Horse, Chester County, took its name from a local tavern, the sign of "the White Horse."

WHITE MILLS

White Mills was the early transfer point for coal that had been hauled over land from Carbondale, and then rafted down Lackawaxen Creek and the Delaware River to Philadelphia.

The difficulty of the route, and the greater desirability of the New York market called for the creation of a canal from Honesdale to the Hudson River. That canal was constructed in 1826.

WILAWANA

Wilawana takes its name from the Delaware Indian word that means "head, headgear, horns." Most logically, the name refers to "chief village."

WILKES-BARRE

This Luzerne County town was named for John Wilkes and Isaac Barre, members of the British Parliament and sympathizers with the colonial cause.

Wilkes-Barre is the county seat. Its name was selected by Major John Durkee who built a fort here with a band of 100 settlers. The settlers called it Fort Durkee, but their leader, in 1769, combined the two men's names for the settlement.

In an interesting sidenote, almost two years before Durkee named the town, he named his newborn son Barre Durkee. The major's first cousin, Andrew Durkee, had a son, born in 1768 and named Wilkes Durkee. It would seem that the two boys were the main reasons for the naming.

WILKINSBURG

Wilkinsburg is one of the oldest towns in Allegheny County. It was originally known as McNairsville when it was settled in 1780. It was later called Rippleysville.

The name was changed to honor Judge William Wilkins, who opened a law office here in 1801. Fifteen years later, Wilkins was president of the town council. He had an illustrious record as a public official, culminating with his appointment as secretary of war under Tyler.

The borough of Wilkinsburg was incorporated in 1887 from Wilkins Township.

WILLIAM PENN

This town was obviously named for William Penn (1644–1718), Pennsylvania's founder.

The younger son of Admiral William Penn was ousted from Oxford University for his Puritan religious leanings. Sent to Ireland to oversee his father's properties, he fell under the spell of Thomas Loe, a powerful Quaker preacher. In 1667, he was imprisoned for attending a Quaker meeting.

When his father died in 1670, William Penn inherited a modest fortune and large claims upon the King for loans the admiral had made to the Crown. In 1681, he took advantage of lands he obtained in America to establish Pennsylvania, a haven for religious liberty, particularly those of the Quaker persuasion. Religious freedom was not officially preferred to Roman Catholics. In fact, Old St. Joseph's Church on Willings Alley in Philadelphia was hidden behind a wall so as not to offend the Quaker majority.

His experiment in America was less than joyous. His administrators were ill-chosen and his oldest son was a disappointment. In 1712, Penn had decided to sell Pennsylvania back to the Crown when he suffered a paralyzing stroke. (See Penn—.)

WILLIAMSPORT (South —)

Little League began in Williamsport.

The Lycoming County location was named for William Hepburn, one of the first associate justices of the county. Or was it?

An 1876 history of the town indicates that early settlers wanted their town to honor Senator William Hepburn, a member of the U.S. Senate and the person instrumental in the formation of Lycoming County. They wanted to call it Hepburn's Port, but the senator suggested William's Port. Another history indicates that Michael Ross, who laid out the town in 1795 on his 100-acre tract, named it for his son William.

To add greater confusion, the Williamsport librarian published an article in the local newspaper titled, "The Origin of the Name of Williamsport," in which he wrote that the name probably came from William Ross, a boatman who, before the town was founded, discovered—and used—a landing spot, a "port," located near the railroad station. Further, he wrote, when Michael Ross laid out the town, he simply continued using the popular designation.

The site of Williamsport was formerly occupied by an Indian village called French Margaret's Town, named for the daughter of Madame Montour. Though settlers arrived in the 1770s, a town was not laid out until 1796, when Ross sold off the first town lot at an ox roast. By that time, the name William's Port was in common usage.

South Williamsport, located across the river south of the city, was incorporated in 1886. There is no controversy over the source of this name.

The town was born of two older settlements, Rocktown and Bootstown.

WILLIAMSTOWN

The land upon which the town of Williamstown is located was once sold for 5,000 shingles, then traded for a span of horses.

Originally settled by Daniel Williams, the town was acquired by coal operators in 1826.

WILLOW STREET

This town is located on the main road south from Lancaster. At one time, the road was lined with weeping willow trees. The post office, established here in 1840, took that name.

WINDBER

This Somerset County community was named by the Pennsylvania Railroad in 1897 when the company opened a new station here.

E. J. Berwind, chief stockholder of the Berwind-White Coal Company, suggested the name by transposing the syllables of his family's name.

Shortly after the station opened in 1897, the company laid out the town and adopted the railroad name for the towns.

WINDHAM (— Center)

Windham was named for the English town, Wymondham. The name was mispronounced by colonists.

WOMELSDORF

Womelsdorf was founded by German settlers in 1723 and called Middletown. When the town was laid out in 1762, it was renamed for John Wommelsdorf, the leader of the immigrants from the Palatinate, and named for him—even with the missing "m."

WRIGHTS (— Corner, —town, —ville)

In 1730, surveyors from Maryland attemped to set up a ferry on the Susquehanna at Wrightsville—in opposition to the one that was already there. Benjamin Chambers was "one of the Principal Persons to turn off . . . Lord Baltimore's surveyors who were chaining up the River Side on John Wright's land with a Possey of men not Less than Thirty . . . which Possey was ordered to take up the Cupas and Begon, or we would Breake it and make them Befon to their cost."

In 1736, for this little act of bravery, Chambers was given a grant of 400 acres on "Fawlling Spring on Cannogogige," now Chambersburg.

WYALUSING

This community was first settled by members of the New England-based Susquehanna Company in the mid-eighteenth century. The company obtained the land by right of charter and purchased it from the Indians. After the sale, the Indians who remained became Moravians . . . due to the efforts of David Zeisberger and the help of Chief John Papunhank, who was a zealous convert.

The town's name comes from that of the county, and translates to "home of the warrior" or "the place of the old man" or "good hunting grounds." One has a choice!

WYNNEWOOD

Wynnewood was named for Thomas Wynne, president of the first colonial Assembly of Pennsylvania, and a native of Wales.

WYOMING

In July 1778, the isolated settlements of the valley were attacked by a force of more than a thousand men, made up of Butler's Rangers and a contingent of Iroquois. The settlers had appealed for help from Congress, especially since two companies of volunteers had been raised from the area. Their request was denied, and they had to fend for themselves.

The Tories and Indians had forced the settlers into Forty Fort, where women, children, and elderly men cowered in fear. Colonel Nathan Dennison organized the retreating troops and the others at the fort into a garrison. Recognizing that defense was fruitless, Dennison looked over the articles of capitulation and agreed when he realized that the document stipulated safety for the inhabitants of the fort. Unfortunately, when Major John Butler and his force marched into the fort, the Indians began to plunder and loot the place. In the resulting massacre, it was reported that 300 men, women, and children were murdered.

Following the battle, Queen Esther, the "white queen" of the Seneca, is reported to have placed sixteen captured settlers against a rock. With methodical skill, the queen crushed the skull of all but one or two. It was said that the death of her son in the battle drove her to this revenge. Queen Esther's Rock is located at Eighth and Susquehanna Streets.

Indian trouble was not new to the area. As early as 1742, Count Nicholas von Zinzendorf, leader of the Moravians, camped near here and antagonized the local tribe. They planned to kill him, but, as the story goes, at the moment when they were to put their plan into operation, a rattlesnake slithered harmlessly over Zinzendorf's arm. The Indians took this as a sign that he was protected by the gods. They left him alone.

Wyoming is the seat of Wyoming County and takes its name from the county. The county's name came from the Algonquian

273

meche-weami-ing, "big flats at," originally used to describe the Wyoming Valley.

WYOMISSING

This town takes its name from the Indian for "place of flats."

WYSOX

Wysox was named for a tributary of the Susquehanna. The name comes from an Indian word meaning "place of grapes."

YELLOW HOUSE

This village was named for a country tavern. The tavern was always painted yellow, and became known as the Yellow House.

YORK (West —)

In 1741, Richard, Thomas, and John Penn ordered the then-deputy surveyor of Lancaster County, which included today's York County, to "survey and lay off in lots a tract of land on the Codorus, where the Monocacy road crosses the stream." They further ordered that the name be York, or Yorktown.

No one is sure whether the Penns named the town for York, England, or for James Stuart, Duke of York and later James II, a friend to Admiral Penn, William Penn's father.

York was incorporated in 1787, and served as America's capital—the Continental Congress met here while the British occupied Philadelphia—from 30 September 1777 through 27 June 1778. The first Pennsylvania town founded west of the Susquehanna, York is the seat of its county.

West York, adjacent to York, was originally named Eberton, for an early family. It is now a modern section of York.

YOUNGSVILLE

Youngsville, Warren County, took its name from a local eccentric bachelor schoolmaster, Matthew Young. Young was one of the first settlers, pitching his tent here in 1796.

The town was settled the year before by John McKinney.

ZELIENOPLE

Zelienople was first populated by the Delaware and Seneca Indians. In 1753, the area was claimed by Virginia. By 1774, it was annexed by George III, an action listed in the Declaration of Independence.

In 1802, Baron Frederick William Detmar Basse, of Germany, purchased about 10,000 acres of land from the Philadelphia Land Company, laid out the town, and named it for his daughter, Zelie (Basse) Passavant. Zelie was the girl's nickname.

Basse usually signed his name "Dettmar Basse Muller," meaning Dettmar Basse, the miller. Histories sometimes refer to him as D. B. Muller. He sold half of his tract in 1803 to George Rapp, who built the town of Harmony on the site.

ZION (— Grove)

Zion was named for Mount Zion in ancient Palestine. The term is used as a figure of speech to mean the New Jerusalem or the Chosen People.

ZIONS VIEW

See Zion.

Delaware

Henry Hudson discovered Delaware and claimed it for the Dutch in 1609. The next year, Captain Samuel Argall named the colony for Virginia's governor, Thomas West, Lord de la Warr. This naming has caused considerable consternation on the part of place namers ever since. The state, the river, and the bay together give West an aura of importance that is far from justified.

Thirty-two years after Hudson's discovery, the Dutch tried, with little success, to settle the area. In 1638, the Swedes took a stab at the colony and established Fort Christina (now Wilmington). New Sweden, as they called it, fell to the Dutch, led by New York's Governor Peter Stuyvesant, in 1655.

The English could not let the Dutch and the Swedes continue to establish themselves without opposition. In 1664, the British took control. The Delaware colony was transferred to William Penn as the southern "Three Counties" in 1682. Not until the turn of the eighteenth century did Delaware become almost self-governing, and it fought as a separate colony in the Revolutionary War. Delaware was the first state to ratify the federal Constitution.

In 1802, Eleuthere Irenee du Pont created a gunpowder mill near Wilmington and began Delaware's still-massive chemical industry.

During the Civil War, Delaware, though a slave state, remained in the Union.

In addition to the chemical industry, Delaware developed and maintains fine agricultural and poultry industries. All three play a prominent role in the place-naming of the state.

ANGOLA

The name for this Sussex County site was already in use in the seventeenth century when Delaware began to receive slaves exported from Angola, then in Portugese West Africa.

Angola's first post office was opened in 1851, with Peter R. Burton serving as postmaster. A Burton served as postmaster until service was discontinued in 1937. The town was, for the most part, occupied by African Americans, many of whom worked for the Burton family.

ARDEN

The name of Arden, New Castle County, was chosen by the locals in 1950 to replace the 1884 town-name of Grubbs.

ATLANTA

Prior to 1873, this village was known as Horsey's Cross Roads, for storekeeper Nathaniel Horsey. As Atlanta, the village opened its first post office in 1893. Service was discontinued in 1900. The name is probably in imitation of the Georgia city of the same name.

BAYARD

The name of Bayard, Sussex County, recalls the Bayard family, whose most prominent member was Thomas F. Bayard (1828–98).

Bayard was born in Wilmington and, after earning his law degree, began to practice in Delaware. He was a Peace Democrat who opposed both secession and the Civil War. After his election to the Senate in 1869 to the seat once held by his grandfather and father, he became an outspoken opponent of Radical Reconstruction. Following the election to U.S. president of Grover Cleveland in 1884, Bayard resigned his senate seat to become secretary of state. During Cleveland's second administration, Bayard served as ambassador to Great Britain. He was the first man to hold the rank of ambassador; all previous American representatives abroad were called "ministers."

BEAR

This community first appeared on post office records in 1888. Originally known as The Bear, for the Bear Tavern that once was located here, the village was a travelers' stop on the King's Highway.

BELLTOWN

Like Angola, Belltown began as an all-African-American village. Its name has nothing to do with the device found in a tower.

Belltown was named for Jake "Jigger" Bell, a freeman who gave land in 1840 for the construction of a church and sold town lots. Though it supported the church, Belltown gained a reputation for its "Devil-Worshippers," a religious sect led by a man named Arnsy Maull. Maull developed a strong following among blacks and whites alike. On his deathbed, Maull allegedly denied his voodoo practices and asked his followers to get whips and lash out around his room to "drive off the Devil and let the Lord in!"

BETHANY BEACH (South Bethany)

Bethany Beach, Sussex County, was selected in 1898 by members of the Christian Church Disciples of Scranton, Pennsylvania, as the location for the summer activities of the Christian Missionary Society of Delaware, Maryland, and the District of Columbia.

On 12 July 1901, Bethany Beach opened and The Tabernacle was dedicated. As with many other resorts founded by religious groups, the original deeds restricted the sale of alcoholic beverages. The sale of beer, liquor, or wine would cause ownership of the property to revert to the developers.

The name has obvious religious significance, and in fact came from the village in Biblical Palestine.

BETHEL

This Sussex County community began in the early nineteenth century as Lewisville, for the wharf built there by Kendall Lewis. Lewis' name remained on the community until 1880, when the first post office opened. For many years, Bethel was a shipbuilding center of the Chesapeake Bay area. Like Bethany Beach, the name has Biblical roots, its namesake is also in Palestine.

BLACKBIRD

A former stagecoach stop on the King's Highway, Blackbird, New Castle County, grew up around a gristmill established in 1780 at the head of Blackbird Creek. The town took the name of the stream.

According to local tradition, the creek was originally called Blackbeard, for Edward Teach, the eighteenth century pirate. Sadly, as early as 1679, maps show a "Black Birds Creeke," and, of course, Teach did not make his move as a pirate until a good thirty years later. Blackbird was discontinued as a post office location in 1933.

BLACKISTON

Benjamin Blackiston purchased the Deer Park tract, 2,250 acres of Kent County, in 1733 for a grand total of 45 pounds 2 shillings. The town commemorates him and his family.

The Blackiston Methodist Episcopal Church located here sits on the site of the original chapel, which was built in 1787 from a design by Bishop Francis Asbury. Blackiston first appeared on the post office rolls in 1861, as Blackiston's Crossroads.

BOYDS CORNER

Boyds Corner, New Castle County, is situated on the "Old Man's Path," a road cleared by the Herman family around 1673 from the homes of Casparus and Ephraim Herman, on the Delaware River, to Bohemia Manor.

The name belongs to the owner of the store at the site.

BRIDGEVILLE

Bridgeville, Sussex County, began in 1730 with the erection of a bridge over a branch of the Nanticoke River. At that time, the collection houses along what is now U.S. Route 13 were known as Bridgebranch. The current name was adopted in 1810.

Bridgeville had an operating post office before 1832. Henry Cannon was the first postmaster.

BROADKILL BEACH

This Sussex County community was settled by the Broadkill Hundred in the latter part of the eighteenth century. The name simply describes the number of settlers and their location. The name refers to the waterway, the Broadkill River. The river's name is not as dramatic as it seems: *kill* or *kil* is Swedish for stream.

CAMDEN

Camden, Kent County, was laid out in 1783 on the Piccadilly tract by Daniel Mifflin, a Quaker. Mifflin's brother, Warner, was one of the first Americans to unconditionally free his slaves. The Cooper House, located on the north side of town, is supposed to have been a station on the Underground Railroad.

Camden provided service as a post office before 1832. In 1962, the U.S. Postal Service merged the Camden office with the Wyoming office and cleverly renamed it Camden-Wyoming.

CANTERBURY

Canterbury was once an important horse-changing station on the stage line down the Peninsula. Before Dover was laid out, this town was considered for the county seat. The name probably refers to the English city, but it has never been a popular name because of its association with the Episcopal Church. It is possible that our forefathers were displaying a sharp sense of humor: "canter"—as in a horse's gait.

CHESWOLD

From colonial days until 1888 this Kent County village was known as Moorton. The town was settled by a group of people whose skin color ranged from nearly white to dark yellow but who were known as Moors. They considered themselves superior to African Americans, and were quiet and industrious, and kept to themselves. They may have been descendents of the Nanticoke Indians.

The post office here dates back to 1888.

CHRISTIANA. Swedish Queen Christina was a young girl when her country established "New Sweden" in the New World. Her name once graced Wilmington but, in a chauvinistic move, her name was replaced with that of an English male. (Print and Picture Department, Free Library of Philadelphia)

CHRISTIANA

Christiana was the name of this New Castle County community before 1832. Once an important shipping spot on the Christina Creek, the town was originally called Christine (later Christiana) Bridge. The bridge was built around 1686.

The "Bridge" was also a popular meeting place. Surveyors Charles Mason and Jeremiah Dixon met here in 1765 with Maryland and Pennsylvania commissioners, and George Washington was a frequent visitor to the town. The current name, an anglicized version of Swedish Queen Christina's name, was adopted in colonial days.

CLAYMONT

The first post office opened at this New Castle site in 1850, under the name of Naaman's Creek. The surrounding community went by the name of Naaman's until 1852, when both the post office and the community renamed themselves Claymont.

No one is quite sure why the name changed, but the most popular choices for the origin are a "mountain of clay," or the Clayton family (see Clayton).

CLAYTON

Richard Tibbitt sold the original town lots for this Kent County locale. When Tibbitt died, William Wertenby of San Francisco claimed ownership, stating that Tibbitt's claim ended with his death. Tibbitt's heirs thought differently. A court case ensued, and Wertenby, represented by Thomas F. Bayard, won the case. Bayard, who later became Grover Cleveland's secretary of state, received one-quarter of the tract in payment for his services. The city is built on his land.

In 1855, the railroad station was known as Smyrna Station, but it was later changed to Clayton, in honor of John M. Clayton, a senator from Delaware, former secretary of state, and a principal in the promotion of the Delaware Railroad.

COKESBURY CHURCH

The name for Cokesbury Church, Sussex County, is a combination of the names of the first two bishops of the Methodist Episcopal Church, Thomas Coke and Francis Asbury.

COLUMBIA

Columbia, Sussex County, was previously known as Owens' Store, Mount Hermon, and the Cooper Neighborhood. The current name was coined during the Revolutionary War period, suggested by a name for the emerging nation.

A post office by this name opened in 1891, Edward J. Owens postmaster. Service was discontinued in 1907.

DAGSBORO

The settlement that grew up around the gristmill at the head of Pepper Creek, a branch of Indian River, was first called Blackfoot Town. The name was changed to Dagsborough around 1785, to honor General John Dagworthy.

The village rested on Dagworthy's Conquest, a 20,000-acre tract given him by Maryland as a reward for his command of Maryland volunteers during the French and Indian War, particularly his conquest of Fort Duquesne (later Fort Pitt, and now Pittsburgh, Pennsylvania) in 1758.

Dagworthy had received a royal commission as a captain in the British army prior to the start of the American Revolution. This commission took on great significance in 1756, when he refused to take orders from Colonel George Washington at Fort Cumberland, Maryland. Dagworthy contended that Washington was of inferior rank, as he was only a Virginia provincial officer and Dagworthy held a royal commission. Washington threatened to resign his commission over this confrontation. General Braddock supported Dagworthy's claim, but Washington would not let the matter drop. He went before General Shirley, Braddock's successor, pleaded his case—and won.

Following the French and Indian Wars, Dagworthy retired to his acreage, but came out of retirement to accept a commission as brigadier general of the Sussex County militia. In 1777, Congress made Dagworthy a brigadier general in the Continental army. Though a competent officer, he saw little service during the Revolution. Some suggest that Washington's animosity, not Dagworthy's age, was the cause.

The Dagsborough post office was in operation before 1832, and the name was shortened in 1893.

DELAWARE CITY

Between 1800 and 1825, Delaware City was a river wharf known as Newbold's Landing. Streets were laid out by landowners Daniel and William Newbold in 1826 at the junction of the Delaware River and the Chesapeake and Delaware Canal, which was being dug across the peninsula. Anticipating great economic growth, the Newbold brothers renamed the town Delaware City.

The name honors Thomas West, Lord de la Warr, governor and first captain general of Virginia.

DELMAR

Delmar rests on the border between Delaware and Maryland. In

DELAWARE CITY. Thomas West, Lord de la Warr, is remembered, mistakenly of course, in the name of the Delaware River, which was discovered by Henry Hudson, and the State of Delaware. Subsequent uses of his name include Delaware, New Jersey; Delaware and Delaware Water Gap, Pennsylvania; Delaware City and Delmar, Delaware; and Delmar, Maryland. (Philadelphia Municipal Archives)

fact, its main street, State, forms part of the border between the two states. The town's name reflects this schizophrenic plan.

Delmar was a pine forest in 1859 when the Delaware Railroad arrived. The Delmar post office was opened in 1863.

DEWEY BEACH

Dewey Beach, Sussex County, developed around the Rehoboth Life-Saving Station, established in 1879. It took on the name of Admiral George Dewey (1837–1917), hero of Manilla Bay in the Spanish-American War, in 1898.

DOVER

William Penn ordered the establishment of a town, which he named Dover, as the seat of Kent County in 1683. The town was built on part of the "Brothers' Portion" tract of John and Richard Walker, and laid out in 1717. It became Delaware's capital after the British captured New Castle in 1777.

Dover's name was adopted from the English town.

DOWNS CHAPEL

This village was named for a chapel built here in 1880. That edifice was replaced by a small brick building with a belfry in 1927. The settlement of the town can be placed even earlier, evidenced by a dated brick that shows the Downs House was built in 1773.

E

ELLENDALE

Ellendale, Sussex County, was laid out in 1867 by Dr. John S. Prettyman. He intended to create a community at the railhead that had just been established at this location and named the village in honor of his wife, Ellen.

F

FARMINGTON

Farmington was called Flatiron when the railroad built a station here in 1855. The next year, this Kent County community had its own post office; Jesse Kaenard, postmaster. The area residents were predominantly involved in farming, as the town's name suggests.

FELTON

This Kent County location first existed as Felton Station. The post office was established there in 1857, Robert W. Reynolds, Jr., postmaster. The name originated with the railroad.

FRANKFORD

Originally named Long's Store in 1808, this Sussex County community became Gum's Store after the enterprise was purchased by Manaen Gum. The name Frankford comes from the surname of Gum's successor.

FREDERICA

The town of Frederica lies on the Murderkill, a frightening name—or is it?

Kijhl is Dutch for creek, and a 1704 map calls the waterway Murtherkill, or Mother Creek. An earlier map, however, has it *Mordarek-ijhlen*, Swedish for "murder creek." These names probably refer to the report of a 1648 Dutch expedition which calls attention to the Indian massacre of several explorers near Lewes. Afterwards, the writer said, the place should be called "ye Murderers kill, that is Murders Creek."

The first name for this Kent County village was Indian Point, and it was built on the St. Collum tract, owned in 1681 by Benoni Bishop, who purchased the Indian rights from Chief Saccarackett. The town was laid out by Jonathan Emerson in 1770, and it acquired the name of Johnnycake Landing. The name appears to have been changed to Frederica Landing sometime before 1796.

A post office existed in this town before 1832. At one point, the post office had its name changed to Woodside (1869), but like its predecessors, Woodside did not last.

GEORGETOWN

Georgetown, seat of Sussex County, was created as a convenience to local residents.

In 1775, the boundary settlement with Maryland gave Delaware additional lands in the southern and western portions of the county. Residents of the area, accustomed to convenient county seats in Maryland (which were usually located in the center of the county, equi-distant from all points), protested. In 1791, the legislature acted, purchasing one hundred acres of land in the center of the county, "at the place called James Pettyjohn's old field." The next year, the new community was named Georgetown for George Mitchell, a resident and one of the commissioners who supervised the work.

G

GLASGOW

Glasgow shares a great deal of its history with Cooch's Bridge. According to postal records, Glasgow was discontinued as a post office before 1832. Another post office, known as Cooch's Bridge, with William Cooch as postmaster, served the same area. Glasgow in 1841 *was* Cooch's Bridge. Then something happened.

There appear to have been two competing post offices: Cooch's Bridge (later modified to Coochs Bridge by the post office), with William Cooch as postmaster, and Glasgow, with Robert Cann. Glasgow maintained its name until the present day; Cooch's Bridge lasted until the office was discontinued in 1934.

The Cooch family had a long history as postmasters/mistresses of their family-named office. In fact, they had a habit of setting up the post office in their name everywhere they went. There were Cooches in control from before 1832 until the office was discontinued, including Mary E. Cooch, who served under her maiden name as well as her married one: Mrs. Mary E. Dayette. The last member of the family to head that post office was her son J. Irvin Dayette, who closed the office.

Glasgow was originally settled in the early eighteenth century by residents of the Welsh Tract. The original name was Aikentown, for Matthew Aiken, who laid out the streets and kept a noted tavern. Aiken's tavern was used as headquarters for General Sir William Howe, from September 3rd through the 8th, 1777. Howe used the nearby Presbyterian Church for a hospital after the skirmish at Cooch's Bridge, the only "battle" to take place in Delaware during the Revolution.

The name Glasgow recalls the Scottish city.

GREENWOOD

The post office in Greenwood was known as St. Johnstown in 1834. The name was changed to Greenwood in 1862.

The town's development was inspired by the railroad.

GUMBORO

Originally spelled Gumborough, this Sussex County town was a forest at the end of the Great Pocomoke Swamp in 1840. Legend has it the town was named for a stately white-gum tree that stood by the road. Others suggest the name really was Gumburr, for the prickly seed balls of the gum tree.

Gumboro was partitioned from Broad Creek and Dagsboro in 1873.

HARBESON

Harbeson, Sussex County, was named for Harbeson Hickman, a local landowner who lived in the area when the railroad arrived in

1869. The town opened its first post office that same year, John C. Thompson postmaster.

HARDSCRABBLE

This town's name signifies a "hard place to scrape out a living." The nineteenth-century name was given to places where farming was difficult, but later shifted to refer to mining communities.

HARES CORNER

Hares Corner was originally a stop on the stagecoach line and a market for cattle. The Green Tree Inn, the watering spot for man and beast, was razed in 1931 to make way for a two-lane highway.

Hares Corner first appeared as a post office in 1863 with an apostrophe. It was discontinued in 1891. Its name commemorates an early family—not a rabbit's warren.

HARRINGTON

Harrington, Kent County, began as a railroad junction for the Delaware, Maryland and Virginia Railroad. In 1857, its post office was known as Clark's Corner, Matthew J. Clark postmaster. The name was changed to Harrington in 1859, in honor of Samuel M. Harrington, a state chancellor.

HARTLY

In 1870, William Slaughter became postmaster in the town of—guess what?—Slaughter. Twenty-two years later, the name was changed to Hartley.

Hartly (no one knows when the "e" was dropped, but one can assume it was a post office slip), Kent County, grew up at the crossroads of what was then the Oxford Branch of the Pennsylvania Railroad. Previously, the village had been called Arthurville and Butterpot. The latter name, legend has it, came from the practice by townswomen of cooling newly-churned butter in the nearby stream. Young swains would travel from house to house, singing "Butterpot gals, ain't you comin' out tonight?"

HENLOPEN ACRES

This name apparently was borrowed from Cape Henlopen. The cape was first recorded in 1633 as Hinloppen. The name translates from the Dutch *hin-loop* or *inlopen*, "run in." Most authorities cite it as a family name.

HICKMAN

Hickman, Kent County, is a village that grew up around a station of the Queen Anne's Railroad in the late nineteenth century. Hickman was the official post office name in 1886. The town's name probably was taken from a surname. Two possibilities are Hugh Hickman or Harbeson Hickman. (See Bayard and Harbeson.)

HOCKESSIN

The English word "occasion" was associated with a local Quaker meeting house. It is possible that over the years the word took on an Indian flavor, after the original meaning was lost. It is also possible that the name comes from the Indian word for "good bark."

Hockessin is built on part of what was called Letitia Manor, a 15,000-acre estate given by William Penn to his daughter, Letitia, in 1701.

HOLLANDSVILLE

Hollandsville had its first post office in May of 1861. Previously it was known as Whiteleysburgh, a community that existed in Kent County before 1832. The current name, most sources agree, came from the nationality of its settlers.

INDIAN MISSION CHURCH

Indian Mission Church, Sussex County, obtained its name from the obvious: a mission church for the Nanticoke Indians.

The Indian Mission M.P. (Methodist-Protestant) Church served a large congregation of Moors, or "yellow people." (See Cheswold.)

KENTON

Originally called Lewis Cross Roads, this Kent County community developed a reputation for supplying liquid refreshment to travelers between Maryland, Smyrna Landing, and Leipsic. The tavern that drew the crowds was built in 1809.

Lewis Cross Roads soon became Grogtown. Kenton appeared with a post office in 1857. William H. Taylor was the first postmaster. It appears that the name means "town in Kent," which makes sense.

KIRKWOOD

Formerly St. Georges Station, this New Castle County village was laid out in 1730 at a milldam on St. Georges Creek. A tavern was serving customers there by 1735. The name was changed in 1862 to Kirkwood, for Revolutionary War Captain Robert Kirkwood.

KITTS HUMMOCK

Legend has it that this Kent County town was really named Kidd's Hammock for famed pirate Captain William Kidd. A "hammock" (or "hummock") is a wooded knoll or high, fast land in a marsh or near a beach.

LEBANON

Lebanon, Kent County, was a thriving shipbuilding center in the mid-nineteenth century. As late as the 1880s, the town was still dispatching schooners to the East and West Indies, as well as Boston, New York, and Philadelphia.

There is no clear-cut reason for the name. It has been suggested, though, that the Lotus Lily Beds nearby hold the key. Legend has it that in an unknown year a sunken ship of an unknown design was found in Jones Creek. The vessel had strange markings that resembled Egyptian hieroglyphics. The characters in the markings suggested the Biblical cedars of Lebanon. More likely the town's name was given because of the cedar trees that once populated the creek.

LEIPSIC

A village was laid out by Jacob Stout in 1723 as Fast Landing, because this location had the first firm ground along the Leipsic River. Despite the legislature acting to change the name to Vienna in 1814, the townspeople called their town Leipsic, in honor of Leipzig, the German fur-trading city, a reference to the trapping being done in the Delaware area.

LEWES

The first village on this Sussex County site was founded in 1631 by settlers from Hoorn, Holland. They called their settlement Zwaandendael, "Valley of the Swans." It was destroyed by Indians a year after settlement.

Lewes is the name of the county seat in Sussex, England, just as Delaware's Lewes is the seat of Sussex County.

LINCOLN

Lincoln, Sussex County, was laid out in 1865 by Colonel Abel S. Small, from New York, on the proposed line of the railroad. When

LINCOLN. The Lincoln Memorial is one of the most visited shrines in the nation's capital. Following Lincoln's death in 1865, many towns and villages in the thirty-six states that were part of the Union at the time of his death honored him. Thus we find Lincoln Park, New Jersey; Lincoln, Pennsylvania; and Lincoln, Delaware. (Washington Convention & Visitors Bureau)

the railroad arrived two years later, he laid out streets and parks for the "future Metropolis of southern Delaware." Small's dreams, though quite grandiose, never materialized.

The town was named for Abraham Lincoln and, back in a slower-paced society, strangers to the general store were good-naturedly sent out in pursuit of a nonexistent statue of President Lincoln.

LITTLE CREEK

This Kent County town had a post office in 1850 under the name of Little Creek Landing. The name was changed to Bayview in 1883, but returned to a modified form of its original name.

Little Creek Landing was a sleepy village before 1857, when John Bell built a wharf and opened a store. The most excitement the town had experienced prior to that was when a boatload of British sailors arrived in 1813 on the schooner *Pilgrim* and attempted to obtain food supplies. The townspeople refused, and the tars spent the next day-and-a-half looting. They were finally driven off.

LITTLE HEAVEN

Little Heaven, Kent County, was the name for a group of cabins built about 1870 by Jehu Reed and his son, Jehu M. Reed. The cabins were for the families of Irish laborers who worked in the neighboring orchards. The brick Jehu Reed House was built almost a hundred years earlier.

While the Reeds were establishing Little Heaven, Jonathan

Willis, another orchard owner, established a settlement for his African American workers and their families. He called this one Little Hell. The stream that separated the two villages was called the River Styx.

MAGNOLIA

Magnolia, Kent County, is located on the Caroone Manor, a 10,000-acre tract that William Penn, when he arrived in 1682, ordered reserved for the Duke of York. A similar piece of land was reserved for the duke in each county. The portion of the manor where Magnolia sits was eventually sold to James Millechamp, and for a number of years was known as Millechamp Woods.

The name is derived from the tree, and indirectly from Dr. Pierre Magnol, the man for whom the species was named.

MARSHALLTON

John Marshall opened a rolling mill in this area in 1836. Marshall, besides providing employment, gave his name to the town.

Though Marshalltown grew with the opening of the mill, its roots go back farther. The oldest tombstone in the churchyard of St. James' Episcopal Church is dated 1726. In 1717, James Robinson donated land for a "Church and Schoolhouse." That same year the White Clay Creek Church was in full operation.

This community was established as a post office in 1878, John R. Bringhurst postmaster. Service was discontinued in 1952.

McDONOUGH

Formerly known as The Trap, McDonough was named for Commodore Thomas Macdonough (1783–1825), the Hero of Lake Champlain. Macdonough, a native of this town, captured the entire British fleet in the Battle of Platsbourgh in 1814. No explanation can be found for the difference in spellings of the name.

McDonough appeared as a post office site in New Castle County in 1856, with Zaddock Pool as postmaster. Service was discontinued in 1922.

MIDDLEFORD

This Sussex County community had a post office before 1832, Barkley Townsend postmaster. It was the "middle" ford of a branch of the Nanticoke River.

MIDDLETOWN

Middletown, New Castle County, was originally a tavern stop midway between the navigation head of the Bohemia River, in Maryland, and the Appoquinimink Creek. The community boomed between 1850 and 1875 from the profits of its peach orchards. The Middletown Academy was used chiefly as a private school when it was built in 1826. There is also reference to a tavern built there in 1761 by David Witherspoon.

Middletown's name appeared on the post office in 1831.

MIDWAY

When Midway was first established, it was on a dirt road "midway" between Lewes and Rehoboth.

Midway's post office opened in 1884, Edward L. Warrington postmaster. Service was discontinued in 1928.

MILFORD

North Milford, the older section of this Kent County town, stands on the Saw Mill Range. This section of land was taken up by Henry Bowman in 1680, but it was not until 1787 that any thought was given to establishing a community.

In 1787, Joseph Oliver, a local landowner and merchant, laid out streets on his plantation at Oliver's Landing. The same year, the Reverend Sydenham Thorne built a dam for a grist mill and a saw mill at a ford on the Mispillion River. It is from Thorne's mills—and others, as there were a number in the area—that the name of Milford is derived.

There was a post office in Milford before 1832.

MILFORD CROSSROADS

In 1764, Mason and Dixon set up "the post marked West," according to their journal, in the general vicinity of this New Castle County community before beginning their survey of the Mason-Dixon Line. Their survey would settle the dispute between the Penn and Calvert families over the boundaries between their properties. If the Penn boundary claim had been correct, Baltimore would be in Pennsylvania; if the Calvert claim was accurate, Philadelphia would be in Maryland. (See Milford for name origin.)

MILLSBORO

In 1792, Elisha Dickerson built a grist mill at what was then called Rock Hole, originally Rock Haul (for river rockfish), on the north shore of Indian River Hundred. Increased activity on the waterway prompted a tavern and a few stores to be built. The south shore of the river also saw a community develop.

In 1809, Rock Hole was renamed Millsborough, while the south shore community retained the name of Washington. Before 1832, there was a post office in this name in Sussex County, Thomas Wingate postmaster. In 1840, Rock Hole became Washington. The next year the name was changed to Millsborough. It appears that the post office simply shifted from one side of the Indian River to the other. The modernized spelling of the name was attached in 1893.

A major industry in Millsboro was a primitive blast furnace, built in 1817 by William D. Waples and in operation until 1836. It was the last furnace in Delaware to operate using local bog ore. The foundry, using imported bog iron, continued operation until 1879.

MILTON

James Gray received the patent for a 1,000-acre site in Sussex County in 1686, on which Milton stands today. North Milton, above the Broadkill, later belonged to the Conwell family; South Milton, below the stream, the Perry family.

The settlement that grew here took on an assortment of names: Osborne's Landing, Conwell's Landing, Upper Landing, and Head of Broadkill. Head of Broadkill was officially changed by a legislative act in 1807 to Milton, supposedly for the English poet. It is more likely the town was named for a local mill.

MINQUADALE

Minqua was the name of an Indian tribe. By adding "dale" to it, the meaning becomes clear.

MISSION

William H. Truitt was postmaster in 1884 when this Sussex County community opened its first post office. Service was discontinued in 1902. The name commemorates a "mission" to the Indians.

MONTCHANIN

Colonel Henry A. du Pont, of Winterthur, was president of the Wilmington & Northern Railroad (later a part of the Reading) when this New Castle County town was named. The colonel named it for Anne Alexandrine de Montchanin, mother of Pierre Samuel du Pont, the first du Pont in Delaware. Colonel du Pont used other

French names associated with his family, such as Granogue and Guyancort, for other railroad stations.

MOUNT PLEASANT

Mount Pleasant appeared as a New Castle County post office in 1868. Service was discontinued in 1951.

The town is situated on flat land, which belies its name.

MOUNT PLEASANT CHURCH

The church at this location was called Mount Pleasant, and the town that grew around it assumed the church's name.

N

NASSAU

Nassau, Sussex County, began its post office career as Rehoboth in 1870. The name was changed in 1873. In 1885, Rehobeth Beach took on the name Rehoboth. It seems likely that this community decided to avoid any possible confusion between the two.

NEWARK

Newark was the early crossroad of two well-traveled Indian trails. A village grew up around the St. Patrick's Inn, located there in 1747. A post office was in service in this New Castle County city before 1832. Newark received a town charter in 1852, and was reincorporated in 1887.

The source of Newark's name is quite interesting. Though it is a common English place-name, this particular Newark had a unique origin.

Valentine Hollingsworth took out a patent on a tract of land north of Wilmington which he called New Wark. Wark is Old English for "work" or "works." Hollingsworth later donated land for the creation of a Quaker meetinghouse which was also called New Wark, later written as one word.

NEW CASTLE

Established first as Fort Casimir in 1651 by Peter Stuyvesant and the Dutch, this New Castle County city served as the bulwark needed to regain the river trade from the Swedes. In 1654, the town was taken by a strong force led by Captain Johan Classon Rising, the Swedish governor, but the victory was short-lived. The next year, Stuyvesant ended the Swedish rule for good.

Fort Casimir became New Amstel, named for a suburb of

Amsterdam, in 1656. The British arrived in 1664 and demanded the town surrender. After a very brief battle, the British gained control of the fort and the town in the name of the Duke of York. Later that year, Colonel Richard Nicolls, the duke's deputy governor for New York and Delaware, visited New Amstel and renamed it New Castle, for either William Cavendish, the Earl of New Castle, or Newcastle-on-Tyne in England.

The Dutch regained the town in 1673, but lost it the next year. William Penn took possession in 1682.

New Castle appeared as the name for the post office before 1832. Between 1857–74, the post office streamlined it to Newcastle. It returned to its correct two-word version before the end of the nineteenth century.

NEWPORT

Before 1832, the post office listed at this location was New Port. The name was streamlined between 1857–74, in the same post office exercise that affected New Castle. Unfortunately, the name was never returned to its original two-word status.

This town's name points out one of the problems that affect place-name research. Without the postal records, one might think that the name came from a family, such as that of Christopher Newport of Virginia, rather than from the description of a new port on the Christiana River.

Newport was laid out in 1735 by John Justice, who called it Newport Ayre. It was also the birthplace of Oliver Evans (1755–1819), the first great American inventor.

OCEAN VIEW

Not from any spot in Ocean View can one see the ocean!

In 1833, this community was known as Hall's Store, the same year the post office opened, William Hall postmaster. Joseph E. Hall was postmaster in 1870 when the name was changed to Ocean View.

Legend has it the name stuck after a young boy climbed to the top of the highest pine tree, looked eastward and shouted, "I can see the ocean from here."

ODESSA

Cantwell's Bridge was settled in the early nineteenth century. In fact, it had a post office by that name before 1832.

Beginning in 1721, a toll bridge across the Appoquinimink Creek was operated by a son of Captain Edmund Cantwell, who, in

1664, obtained the confiscated lands of Alexander D'Hinoyossa, director of the Dutch settlement of New Amstel (see New Castle). By 1825, Cantwell's Bridge was a shipping center for grain, but thirty years later the grain trade collapsed. At the time of the collapse, the Delaware Railroad announced its intention to run a line through Cantwell's Bridge. Hoping to protect the shipping business, the town fathers refused the railroad's offer, instead, changing the town's name to Odessa in honor of the Russian grain port on the Black Sea. History proved their decision was the wrong one.

OMAR

Omar, Sussex County, was originally settled as Waplesville. The family name of Omar appeared on the post office in 1888. James K. Torbert was the first postmaster. Service was discontinued in 1902.

In 1927, Omar made headlines with the Hitchens murder. May Carey and one of her three sons murdered Mrs. Carey's brother for his $2,000 insurance policy. Mother and son were hanged; the first hanging in the state since 1869.

PEPPERBOX

The name of this Sussex County community may have come from a small weapon of the eighteenth century.

PETERSBURG

This Kent County site, operating as a post office in 1873, was not named for the great mine explosion of the Civil War, but probably for the first postmaster, Peter S. Frasher. Other sources suggest the name came from Peter Fowler, a local resident, but it seems more likely to have come from the postmaster.

PORT PENN

Stories tell of William Penn visiting this New Castle County community, but there is no documentary evidence to support them. Likewise, the tradition that has it that Casimir Pulaski, the Polish general in Washington's army, lived here cannot be proved.

The name Port Penn does not appear on maps prior to 1780, and it is probably the name given in 1774, when Philadelphia port officials ordered piers built in the area. A post office operated under this name in 1832.

PRIMEHOCK BEACH

The word *primehock* comes from the Dutch for "plum point," and describes the presence of wild plum trees at the founding site.

REDDEN CROSSROADS

There was a Redden post office in Sussex County in 1868, James A. Evans postmaster. Service was discontinued in 1933.

The name comes from Colonel William O. Redden.

REHOBOTH BEACH

Rehoboth is a Biblical word for "room enough" or "enlargement." The community took its name from the nearby Rehoboth Bay, which was named by the English before 1675.

The beaches at Rehoboth, Sussex County, remained virtually untouched until 1855, when the State of Delaware granted five acres of beachland to the Rehoboth Hotel Company to build a hotel. The company failed to do so.

In 1872, the Rehoboth Beach Camp Meeting Association of the Methodist Church purchased land along the beach line and laid out a town. A post office was established at the site in 1873.

The association held revival-type camp meetings in the town. The name was changed to Rehobeth in 1885, then back to Rehobeth Beach in 1911. The modern resort took shape in the 1920s. (See Nassau.)

RISING SUN

This town in Kent County had its first post office in 1884. The name apparently was taken from a tavern of the same name.

SAINT GEORGES

St. Georges, New Castle County, takes its name from the neighboring St. Georges Creek. The town was laid out before 1730 across the creek from a mill dam. A tavern was serving travelers by 1735.

SEAFORD

Seaford, Sussex County, was laid out in 1799 as Hooper's Landing on the Nanticoke River.

One of the earliest records of Seaford is an account of a "mercy killing." Shadrach Cannon, in 1818, tried to pull his dog out from under his house, but the rabid dog bit him. Within a few days, Cannon was a raging madman, and his doctor and friends decided to put him out of his misery: they smothered him to death between two beds.

The town's name is descriptive of a "ford at the sea."

SELBYVILLE

Selbyville began as a grist mill and blacksmith shop. It was known as Sandy Branch until 1842, when Samson Selby opened his store. The town stands on land once owned by Matthew McCabe, a blacksmith and veteran of the Revolutionary War.

Josiah Selby was the postmaster in 1848 when the post office opened.

SHORTLY

The post office at this Sussex County address first opened in 1883, George W. Records postmaster. Service was discontinued in 1902. Some wags suggest the name came about when someone inquired when the town would get its post office. The answer was "Shortly."

SLAUGHTER BEACH

Slaughter Beach, Sussex County, takes its name from the neighboring Slaughter Creek. The origin of the name of the stream, however, is uncertain. Some sources suggest the name was brought from England, where it is both a place name, in Gloucestershire, and a family name. Others propose a more grisly reason.

According to Delaware legend, in very early colonial times, the local Indians went on a rampage and threatened to kill every settler except one, a man named Brabant. Brabant settled the whole situation by borrowing a cannon from a nearby beached vessel. He called a general meeting and told the Indians that the Great Spirit would soon "speak" and punish all the "bad" Indians. He lined up the troublemakers in front of the weapon and the "Great Spirit" roared. Peace was restored.

SMYRNA

Smyrna, Kent County, was originally called Duck Creek Cross Roads. It was renamed in 1806 for the chief seaport of Asia Minor, as noted in the book of Revelation.

A post office was in operation before 1832.

STANTON

Stanton, New Castle County, is one of the oldest settlements in the region. It was called Cuckoldstown as late as 1768, but no one knows why—or if they do, they're not telling.

The village was named for George Stanton, a local property owner. The community appeared on the postal records as Staunton, similar to the town in Virginia. Its post office was in service before 1832. In the 1843–57 records, the "u" is crossed out, and the town became Stanton. Service was discontinued in 1958.

STATE ROAD

Ephraim Rittenhouse was the first postmaster of this New Castle County community when the post office opened in 1880. Service was discontinued in 1921.

The town is located on "State Road" 896.

STUMPS CORNER

The appearance of the "s" in this New Castle County town's original name suggests the name was drawn from a family name and not from the remains of some stately trees.

SWANWYCK

This name was adapted from the seventeenth century Dutch *swaenewyck*, "swan place."

TOWNSEND

Townsend, New Castle County, was known as Charley Town before 1850. The name came from Charles Lloyd, an African-American who lived in one of the shanties that made up the early settlement.

When the railroad arrived about 1855, the station and the town were renamed for Charles Townsend, a local landowner.

VIOLA

Viola, Kent County, was laid out in 1856 when the railroad opened its station. It is located on the Golden Thicket grant, patented to William Shores in 1681.

Charles C. Coolbaugh served as the first postmaster in this Kent County town beginning in 1878.

WILLIAMSVILLE

There was a post office in service in this Kent County community before 1832. The first postmaster was William Heather.

The Sussex County Williamsville began its existence as Tunnell's Store. Nathaniel Tunnell was postmaster when it opened in 1833. The name was changed to Williamsville in 1875. Service was discontinued in 1913.

WILMINGTON (Wilmington Manor)

Founded in 1638 by the New Sweden Company as Fort Christina, this city became known as Wilmington, New Castle County, in 1731, when William Penn's Quakers laid out town lots. A post office was opened in the name of Wilmington in 1831.

The name Wilmington came from Spencer Compton, Earl of Wilmington (1673–1743), a prominent English politician with an interest in the colonies. Another source suggests the name came from Thomas Willing, and the city's name is a corruption of Willington.

WOODLAND

This Sussex County location began as Cannon's Ferry, on the Nanticoke River. That name came from the ferry that connected this town with the road to Laurel. The settlement goes back to the early nineteenth century, when Jacob Cannon built a home here. Legend has it that Cannon was engaged and built the house for his future wife. But the romance ended abruptly, and the house lay vacant for twenty years.

In 1826, the Cannon's Ferry post office was opened, with William Powell as postmaster. Service was discontinued in 1861, but reestablished in 1880 as Cannon. It was reopened in 1881 as Woodland—the name being descriptive—Charlie F. Wright postmaster. Service was discontinued in 1907.

WOODLAND BEACH

Woodland Beach, Kent County, according to local legend, was selected by Captain Kidd as the hiding place for his plunder. Generations of locals and tourists have dug in vain.

The name is descriptive.

WYOMING

John T. Jakes (not the best-selling author) was the postmaster when the post office opened a branch in this Kent County town in 1863.

Wyoming developed after the arrival of the railroad in 1856. Originally called West Camden, the village was renamed Wyoming by the Reverend John J. Pearce, a Methodist minister from the Wyoming Valley of Pennsylvania.

Wyoming first appeared as a Delaware place-name in the shortened form of the Algonquian *meche-weami-ing,* "big flats at." Partly because it was descriptive, and partly because of the popularity of Thomas Campbell's 1809 poem "Gertrude of Wyoming," the name moved around the countryside.

Maryland

The Chesapeake Bay was explored by Captain John Smith. Twenty-four years later, Cecil (Cecilius) Calvert, Lord Baltimore, was granted a charter to the land by Charles I.

In 1634, the first wave of English Roman Catholics landed at what is now Blakistone Island. Religious freedom, the desire of Calvert and his fellow Catholics, was finally achieved, and put into law by "An Act Concerning Religion" passed by the Maryland Assembly in 1649. Christians, regardless of denomination, could worship openly. Religious freedom, however, was short-lived. Between 1654 and 1658, the Puritans revolted and toleration ended.

Religious intolerance was not the only problem Maryland faced. A dispute arose between the proprietors in Pennsylvania and those in Maryland over the boundaries between the two provinces. To settle the dispute, two surveyors, named Charles Mason and Jeremiah Dixon, surveyed the disputed area and established what has come to be known as the "Mason-Dixon Line," an arbitrary line that separates North from South.

In 1791, Maryland ceded a portion of land to the federal government so that that body could establish the District of Columbia, the federal city. During the "second" war with Great Britain, the British tried to capture the Baltimore seaport, but without success. The bombardment of Fort McHenry inspired Francis Scott Key to write our national anthem, "The Star-Spangled Banner."

During the Civil War, Maryland was a "border" state, and a hotbed of covert Confederate activity. It was because of Maryland, particularly Baltimore, that General Winfield Scott ordered martial law and the first suspension of the writ of *habeas corpus*.

Since its founding, Maryland has been a haven for seafood. In fact, the Chesapeake Bay produces more oysters, crabs, and clams than any other body of water of comparable size.

The place names of Maryland have a uniqueness due to the Chesapeake and its many estuaries, rivers, and creeks. At the same time, names there are similar to other states in that the settling fathers sought to honor themselves, their benefactors, friends, and relatives in their name selection. Maryland also has a penchant for spelling place names the way they sound, rather than the way they were originally spelled!

ABINGDON

Abingdon was named for the borough in Berkshire, England. The town was founded by Maryland governor and signer of the Declaration of Independence William Paca (1740–99) in 1779.

ACCIDENT

George II granted 600 acres of land anywhere in western Maryland to a George Deakins for "services rendered." Deakins, a man to be reckoned with, sent out two teams of surveyors. When they returned, both teams discovered they had started from a tall oak tree and ended up at the same spot. Deakins patented the land as "The Accident Tract." When a town was established, it took on the name, probably as early as 1774.

ACCOKEEK

Accokeek occupies the site of an old Indian village, called Moyaone, that Captain John Smith marked on an early map.

Settlers burned down the village in 1622 in revenge for the Indian uprisings.

The name comes from the Acquakick, a stream that flows nearby. The name is Algonquian, and probably means "at the edge (or limit) of the hill (or rising ground)."

ADAMSTOWN

This Frederick County locale was previously known as Adamsville, Adamstown Junction, and Davis' Warehouse. The name was changed to Adamstown in 1840 when Adam Kohlenburg became station agent for the Baltimore & Ohio Railroad.

ADELPHI

The name for this town comes from the Greek word *adelphia* meaning "brother."

AIKEN

Aiken takes its name from the Aiken, or Aitkens, family. Some sources contend the town was named for that branch of the family whose scion, a Scottish doctor who fought in the American Revolution, built "Galen Hall," the family estate. It is more likely, since earlier names for the town include Aikens or Aikenstown, that the name honors the man who operated the local hotel.

AIREY

The post office of Airey was in operation by 1856 under the family name of Airey's. The earliest member of the family to settle in the area was Thomas Airey of Kendall, Yorkshire. He came to Maryland in 1726 to serve as rector of Christ Church in Cambridge.

One of the minister's relatives, Henry Airey, allowed the first Methodist service in the county to take place in his home in 1780. The preacher, Freeborn Garettson, was subsequently arrested because Methodists were considered Tory sympathizers at the time.

ALLEN

In 1672, William Brereton built his plantation at this Wicomico County location. The small village that grew up near the plantation named itself Brereton and, later, Brewington in his honor.

Two hundred and ten years later, the town received its first post office, and those officials called it Upper Trappe. The postmaster felt there were an adequate number of Trappes in Maryland already, however, so he proposed the town be named after him and his family. Joseph S. C. Allen succeeded in changing the name.

ALLENS FRESH

"Fresh" usually refers to the upper end of a tidal creek that supplies fresh water. In this case, the fresh was located on Mr. Allen's land.

Allen's Fresh was the original name for this Charles County community. That name appeared on the village post office before 1832. The name was converted to one word in 1895, but reverted to two words after 1971.

The name probably arose in 1674, when John Allen built a courthouse and prison about four miles from Port Tobacco River. A reference to Allen's Mill, "now called Fresh," also exists.

ALTAMONT

One origin for the name of this town is strange and unlikely: a combination of *alta*, which in Italian means "high," and *mont*, French for "mountain." The name could also be a Spanish phrase that means the same thing.

AMERICAN CORNER

American Corner, Caroline County, was known by that name before 1872. The town name apparently carries a strong patriotic message. But does it?

According to several Maryland historians, the name could just have easily come from a modification of the Merriken family name.

ANDREWS

Charles R. Andrews was the first postmaster in this Dorchester County location. He opened the office in 1908 and gave his name to the town. Another source suggests the name had colonial origins.

ANNAPOLIS

A group of Puritan families from Virginia established a colony on the north bank of the Severn River in 1649. They called it Providence. Within a year, the population grew so large that a new county was created, and named Annarundell—for the wife of the second Lord Baltimore. By 1670, maps show Arundeton across the Severn from Providence. Fourteen years later, Anne Arundell Town was laid out on 100 acres in the same area.

In 1694, Maryland moved its capital from St. Mary's City to Anne Arundell Town, and renamed it Annapolis, in honor of Princess Anne, later Queen of England (1702–14).

ANNAPOLIS JUNCTION

Annapolis Junction, Anne Arundel County, began as a community in Howard County. Its first post office opened in 1844, though it was a "junction" two years earlier. The town was named by the Annapolis, Washington & Baltimore Railroad. (See Annapolis.)

ANTIETAM

Antietam, Washington County, takes its name from the name of the stream, which translates from the Algonquian to mean "swift water." A Civil War battle took place here on 18 September 1862, sometimes called the battle of Sharpsburg.

AQUASCO

The Delaware Indian word for this Prince Georges County community translates to "edge of grass."

ARCADIA

This name originally derives from the district of ancient Greece, romantically linked with rural simplicity and loveliness. The place may also have been named for an estate or tract of land, near St. John's Lane on Route 40, once called Arcadia.

ASHTON

Ashton was built amid a forest of ash trees: at least that's what one authority contends. Another has a more plausible idea: the name is a combination of Ash from Ashland and -ton from Clifton. Ashland and Clifton were the neighboring estates of the Thomas family. Ashton's first postmaster, in 1889, was Alban G. Thomas, a Quaker merchant.

ATHEL

The name of this town could be a misspelling of Atholl, a district in Scotland, or the name of James Murray, second Duke of Athol, or the Massachusetts town. Another source suggests the name was derived from Athel Neck, the name of a nearby tract of land.

AVILTON

This Garrett County village was earlier known as McKenzie Settlement and Pea Ridge. Between 1874 and 1885, it was St. Ann's, for St. Ann's Roman Catholic Church. According to county records, Auvil was a military lot in 1839. Other records indicate a land transfer of Avilton and an owner named Herman Auvil, both possible sources.

BALTIMORE

Baltimore was founded in 1726 by Act of the Provincial Assembly, and laid out on lands owned by Thomas Carroll. In 1745, the new city was consoldiated with Jones-Town (Old Town). It was incorporated in 1797.

It was named for Cecilius Calvert, Lord Baltimore, who founded Maryland in 1635. The original name was Baltimore City, to differentiate it from the county by the same name. The name is Gaelic and translates to "big houses, homesteads, estates."

BALTIMORE CORNER

The original name for this Caroline County village was Hogpen Bridge. The name was changed to Baltimore Corner in the late nineteenth century.

Before the Chesapeake Bay Bridge was built, the route to Baltimore took travelers from Denton to the intersection here, where they made a left on the Old Baltimore Road. This was the "corner" to Baltimore. (See Baltimore.)

BARRELVILLE

In 1852, Michael P. O'Hern opened a post office in Allegany County called Barralville. Service was discontinued in 1867, but in 1903, Otis P. Jewett, Jr., became postmaster and called the town Pamosa. The name was changed to Barrelville in 1909.

The name probably derives from the Burrell family, since many members of that clan were living in the area in the nineteenth century.

BARTON

John Jones was the first postmaster in Barton in 1853, about the same time coal was discovered in the area. By 1866, the Barton Mines and a Barton Coal Company were thriving. The town was founded by Andrew Bruce Shaw on land owned by his father, Major William Shaw. The major was born in Barton, England.

BASKET SWITCH

Basket Switch, Worcester County, was known by this name as early as 1901. Its location on the now-defunct Pennsylvania Railroad (even though the original line had been the Maryland, Delaware & Virginia), produced the "switch" part of the name. But what about the baskets?

By 1847, Chester Thomas, of Ocean City, was manufacturing baskets here, even though the industry began earlier. The area was once covered with gum trees, an excellent source material for the production of baskets.

BAYARD

This Anne Arundel County town opened its first post office in 1888, with Benjamin A. Norfolk as postmaster. The town was named for James A. Bayard, who helped negotiate the Treaty of Ghent that ended the War of 1812.

BAYVIEW

The original name for this Cecil County community was Shelemiah, the name of the local Methodist Church when the post office opened here in 1851. Elihu B. Hall was the first postmaster.

The name was changed to Bay View in 1856 . . . probably to make it easier to spell and more promotable to tourists and vacationers. Surprisingly, the bay is located several miles away.

BEALLSVIEW

The first post office in this Frederick County locale was established in 1834 in the name of Beallville. The name honors Colonel Samuel Beall, who later became sheriff of Frederick County, and served as a member of the Committee of Correspondence and a Justice of the Frederick County Court.

BEAUVUE

This town's name translates to "beautiful view."

BEAVERDAM

The name is taken from the nearby Beaver Dams Branch. It refers to a dam built by beavers during the settlement. There was also a Beaverdam in Anne Arundel County at one time.

BEL AIR

Bel Air is a French name that translates to "good air." The seat of Harford County, the town was originally known as Aquila Scott's Old Field, when the courthouse was located here in 1782. The town was not incorporated, however, until 1874.

The name was spelled Bellair in 1794.

BEL ALTON

The original name for this community was Cox's Station. Samuel Cox was the first postmaster when the office was established here in 1873. The name was changed in 1891 to Bel Alton.

Some sources contend that the Alton of the name may have been transplanted from another location, such as Alton, Illinois, or from Alton, Derbyshire, England.

BELCAMP

This Harford County community carried this name as early as 1900. Belcamp probably means "good camp."

BELLEVUE

Bellevue, Talbot County, was created in 1683, at the same time as Oxford, located across the Tred Avon River. The town's original name was Ferry Neck, but it was changed to Bellevue by Colonel Oswald Tilghman to honor his wife, the former Belle Harrison.

In other locations, Bellevue is taken from the French for "beautiful view."

BELTSVILLE

Beltsville, Prince Georges County, takes its name from a man named Truman Belt, who originally owned the land. In 1811, the town was called Vansville, and G-G. Van Horn was postmaster. In 1835, the post office moved three-quarters of a mile south and the name changed to Beltsville. That same year, the Baltimore & Ohio Railroad acquired a right-of-way and named their station in Belt's honor also. (See Chevy Chase.)

BENEDICT

Benedict, Charles County, was the port from which the British marched on Washington in 1814.

There was a post office operating here before 1832. In 1695, it was known as Benedict-Leonard Town. The name was shortened in 1747 to Benedict-Town. Both versions of the name honored Benedict Leonard Calvert, the fourth Lord Baltimore (1675–1715).

BENEVOLA

Benevola, Washington County, had an operating post office in 1850. The name is a corruption of "benevolent" and was used to describe a friendly community.

BENSON

Benson was named for a nineteenth-century politician and land developer, Oregon Benson.

BENTLEY SPRINGS

C. W. Bentley owned land from which natural springs flowed in this area. The springs were considered "highly medicinal."

BERLIN

This Worcester County community could have been named for the city in Germany. That is the easy answer . . . but not the truth.

Berlin began its life as Burley. The name became Ber'lin" by the early nineteenth century, when the Burleigh Inn began to accommodate stagecoach travelers. Postal authorities, unhappy with apostrophes, dropped the uniqueness of the name.

Early records call the community Burleigh Manor and Burleigh Cottage. When the land was patented by Captain William Stevens in 1677, he called it Burleigh Plantation. For a time, the settlement was called Stephen's Cross Roads, probably referring to the captain, though some think the name honored Stephen Decatur.

BERWYN HEIGHTS

This Prince Georges County village takes its name from the Berwyn Mountains and River in Denbighshire, Wales. The town came into existence in the late nineteenth century.

BESTGATE

Though legend has it that illegal harness racing took place near here, and this Anne Arundel County town was the "best gate" to the action, there is a more plausible and less interesting source.

The town formed around the station of the Washington, Baltimore & Annapolis Railroad in 1905 . . . on land once owned by a Dr. Best. His farm gate opened on a road that paralleled the railroad.

BESTPITCH

Bestpitch sounds like a modern-day shared-time community, or perhaps the home of a used car saleperson.

Jesse B. Wall opened this Dorchester County town's first post office in 1888. Four years earlier, a Best Pitch Ferry operated here.

The name comes from the Bestpitch family. In fact, Levin

Bestpitch was a first lieutenant in the Upper Battalion of the Dorchester County Militia in 1778, while John Bestpitch was an ensign in the Lower Battalion. One authority indicates the name came from "a man named Bestpitch, who had a farm in the vicinity early in the [nineteenth century]."

BETHESDA

The name of the pool in Jerusalem is mentioned only once in the Bible, but it became a popular designation for churches. The Bethesda Presbyterian Church in this Montgomery County community was built here in 1820, and gave its name to the town.

Bethesda was founded in the late seventeenth century by Scottish, English, and Irish colonists.

BETHLEHEM

Bethlehem, Caroline County, had a post office under that name as early as 1858. One source suggests the name was given by Methodist Bishop Francis Asbury. The town might have been previously called Brannock's Crossroads. (See Bethlehem, Pennsylvania.)

BETTERTON

Betterton was once a beach resort drawing sun worshippers from Baltimore via the steamboats that connected the two locations.

Laid out on the site of a farm called Fish Hall, the town fathers decided they needed a more attractive name to draw tourists. The town's developer, Richard Turner, came up with a winner: Betterton. Some sources believe the name is a play on words, i.e., "better town." In reality, Betterton was the maiden name of Turner's wife!

BIG POOL

The name of this Washington County town is descriptive. While building the Chesapeake & Ohio Canal, the workers encountered a difficulty: "opposite Fort Frederick the canal passed through a piece of low swampy land, which, immediately filling up to the canal level, formed the 'Big Pool'." Once, it has been said, the pool was 700 feet wide and filled with fish and water fowl.

BIRDTOWN

Birdtown, Somerset County, has nothing to do with our feathered friends. The name honors members of the Byrd family, who settled here in the early eighteenth century.

BIVALVE

Bivalve is located in Wicomico County. Originally known as Waltersville in 1877, the name was changed at the insistence of the postmaster, James E. Willing. The Bivalve Oyster Packing Company operated a shucking house here. (See Bivalve, New Jersey.)

BLACKHORSE

Blackhorse opened its first post office in 1834. The name was changed to Shawsville in 1846, but stronger heads ruled and the original name was returned. The name Blackhorse commemorates the fine team of black horses owned by the first innkeeper, who named his establishment The Black Horse Tavern. George Washington allegedly stopped here; but did he not stop everywhere?

BLADENSBURG

Bladensburg was named for Thomas Bladen, who served as Maryland's governor from 1742 to 1747. Early names included Garrison's Landing, and the original settlement was named Beall Town for John Beall (1688–1742), who owned the land.

BLOOMINGTON

Slangallen (or Llangollen—from the Llangollen Mining Company) was the original name of this Allegany County town when the post office opened in 1852, James Bell postmaster.

The name was changed to Bloomington in 1853. The suggestion came from Baltimore & Ohio Railroad workers who noticed the many spring wildflowers. Bloomington is now part of Garrett County.

BLUE BALL

At one time, the main roads from Lancaster, Pennsylvania, to New Castle met here. It was an ideal location for a tavern. Jacob Job founded just such an establishment here in 1710, known as the Blue Ball Tavern, after the blue circular object on his sign. (See Blue Ball, Pennsylvania.)

BOONSBORO

Boonsboro, Washington County, was settled in 1774 by George and William Boone. Legend has it they were related to Daniel Boone. The post office, opened in 1801, was called Boonsburg. Town lots were laid out in 1829.

BORING

Boring, Baltimore County, is not a ho-hum town; it was named for the Boring family, prominent in the area. In fact, when the office opened in 1905, the first postmaster was David Boring.

BOWIE

The main streets of Bowie were once the pastures of the famous Belair Stud Farm. Some sources suggest the name came from James A. Bowie, designer of the Bowie knife. The truth is not so exciting. Bowie was named for Ogden (or Odin) Bowie (1826–94), the seventh governor of the state. Bowie's father was William Duckett (see Ducketsville); his mother, Eliza Oden (see Odenton).

BOXIRON

Boxiron, Worcester County, takes its name from the Boxiron Creek. The name is a modification of bog's iron, a product formed in Eastern Shore bogs from stagnant water containing iron oxide.

BOZMAN

The town of Bozman was named for John Leeds Bozman (1757–1823), a prominent attorney and historian. He was the author of *The History of Maryland From Its First Settlement in 1633 to the Restoration in 1660.*

BRADDOCKS HEIGHTS

The spring here refreshed General Edward Braddock's troops in 1755 before he and the young George Washington traveled to their defeat near Fort Duquesne.

BRANCHVILLE

This Prince Georges County town is located near the Paint Branch stream. The name is taken from the waterway.

BRANDYWINE

The Dutch *brandewijn* suggests spirits. Perhaps the name came from the color of polluted water; perhaps for the memory of the Revolutionary War battle. Another possible origin is Andrew Braindwine, an early settler by the Pennsylvania creek. Most likely, the name for this Prince Georges County village was transferred from the town in Pennsylvania.

BRENTWOOD

At one time there were two communities at this location in Prince Georges County: North Brentwood, populated only by black people; and Brentwood, containing only whites.

Both places were settled immediately following World War I by commuters to the nation's capital. The name is drawn from the Brent family, of which Giles and Fulke Brent were in Maryland as early as 1638.

BRIDGETOWN

When the first post office opened in this Caroline County location in 1839, it was called Nine Bridges. The name was shortened to its present configuration in 1841. At one time, the town had nine small bridges; later, they were reduced to one single, large, concrete bridge. Why continue to call it nine, when there was only one?

BRINKLOW

Brinklow, Montgomery County, was named in the late nineteenth century by Hallie Lea, a local storekeeper. She named it for "a place in England because she thought it a pretty name and one not used anywhere in the United States."

BROAD RUN

The post office at Broad Run was first opened in 1868 with Daniel Grove as postmaster. The name comes from the waterway.

BROOKEVILLE

This Montgomery County village has a descriptive name: it was a village by a brook. One authority stated that origin, and the others followed suit.

Brookeville was founded in 1780 as an addition to Brooke Grove, surveyed by James Brooke in 1762. A latter-day postmaster said the town was "named by founding fathers for their three Brooke wives" (or was it to flatter father-in-law?).

BROOKLYN

Anne Arundel County's Brooklyn had its own post office in 1869, though the community was in existence long before that. It was named for the New York borough. R. W. Templeman, an employee of the Patapsco Company, saw geographical similarities and named it in about 1857.

BROOKVIEW

In 1856, William Brinsfield opened a post office in this Dorchester County locale. He called the site Crother's Ferry. Sometime before 1887, the name was changed to Brookview. The town overlooked a swampy region of the Marshyhope Creek.

BROWNING MILL

This Garrett County community indirectly honors the scion of the Browning family: Meshach Browning. He was one of the county's most renowned hunters in the early nineteenth century.

BROWNSVILLE

Brownsville, Washington County, had a post office in 1833. The town was named for Tobias Brown, son of Rudolph Brown, who was one of the first settlers in the county. Andrew Jackson appointed Rudolph's grandson John postmaster, and thus the name.

BRUNSWICK

Brunswick, Frederick County, began to develop in 1787 on Leonard Smith's land. Smith subdivided his land, called "Merry Peep 'o Day," and sold off part of his 280 acres. The majority of the purchasers were from Berlin, Germany, tradition has it, and so Smith named the community Berlin.

When the post office opened in 1832, it was called Barry, so it would not interfere with the town of Berlin in Worcester County. The town decided on one name in 1890, when the railroad arrived. It was called Brunswick, for the town in Germany from whence many of the townspeople originated.

BUCKEYSTOWN

This Frederick County village was established by George and Michael Buckey when they opened their Buckey Tannery here in 1775. The tannery was sold in 1834 to Daniel Baker, who opened a tile and brick factory. The post office was established before 1832.

BUCKTOWN

Greensberry Holt was the first postmaster at this Dorchester County location. The post office opened in 1856.

Two bodies of water near this town indicate that the town was named from an abundance of buck, or deer. The Backgarden Creek and Backgarden Pond are mispronunciations of buck garden.

Harriet Tubman was born near here in 1820. At the age of twenty-nine, she escaped slavery and began to help other slaves escape through the Underground Railroad. As legend has it, she was responsible for helping 300 black people reach freedom. During the Civil War, she served the Union as a spy and nurse.

BURNT STORE

The "store that burned down" became a natural landmark, and thus the name for this Charles County town. The name appeared on Martenet's Map of 1866. The name, some say, comes from a remark made by a black farmer giving instructions: "Used to be a store here but it burned down."

BURRSVILLE

Burrsville, Caroline County, received its first post office in 1832. According to most historians, the name has no reference to the neighborhood, but refers instead to a family. The family name might be Burroughes, Bussus, Burris, Borrows, or Burrows.

An earlier settlement here was called Punch Hall. The reference was to a building where fugitive slaves would hide, only to be poked or "punched" out of their holes by local townspeople wielding long poles.

CABIN JOHN

In 1819, this Montgomery County post office was called Captain John's Mills. The word "cabin" is apparently a corruption of "captain."

C

CALIFORNIA

This St. Marys County village was named for the western state. Originally known as Benitia, the name was changed shortly after the Civil War. Lumber was shipped here from California to build an estate called "California Farmstead."

CALLAWAY

James Calaway, reportedly a grandson of Daniel Boone, was the donor of this town's name; at least, that's one source's version. The name may have come from Frank Callaway, a late-nineteenth century land developer.

CALVERT. George Calvert, the first Lord Baltimore. (Enoch Pratt Free Library)

CALVERT (— Beach, —ton)

The original name of Calvert, Cecil County, was Brick Meeting House. It was known by that name following construction of a two-and-a-half-story addition to the Friends Meeting House in 1724. Later it was called East Nottingham. The name was changed to Calvert in 1880, in honor of Cecil Calvert, Lord Baltimore.

CAMBRIDGE

Cambridge, Dorchester County, was established by Act of the General Assembly in 1684, and named the county seat. The town's design was replatted in 1706. The town was incorporated in 1745.

The name apparently comes indirectly from the English town or county. More likely it was borrowed from Cambridge, Maine, founded in 1636.

Cambridge, Guernsey County, Ohio, was named for this Maryland town; both are located on a Wills Creek.

CAPITOL HEIGHTS

This Prince Georges County community is located next to the nation's capital. At an elevation of 100 feet, might one call it the "heights"?

CAPITOL HEIGHTS. The U.S. Capitol has found its way to the naming of Capitol Heights, Maryland, even though you can't see it from there. (Washington Convention & Visitors Bureau)

CARROLLTON

The name of this Carroll County village honors John Carroll of Carrollton, the only signer of the Declaration of Independence to jot down his home address—in case the King wished to discuss the document with him. The "Carrollton" in the address really meant his Carrollton Manor.

CARSINS

Carsins, Harford County, takes its name from the nearby Carsins Run. In 1878, the site was known as Carsin's Run Post Office, for a local farmer, William Carsin.

CARVILLE STATION

The Carvill, or Carvil, family goes back in Maryland's history. John Carvill was Kent County Commissioner in 1706; Edmund Carville, a Kent Island resident in 1805; and Thomas R. Carville, a founder of the Bank of Centreville in 1874.

This Queen Annes County community has also been known as Carville's Corner and Carville's Station.

CATOCTIN

Peregrine Fitzhugh opened the first post office in this community in 1851. The name at that time was Catoctin Furnace.

The name comes from the Algonquin word meaning "speckled mountain," because of the appearance of mottled rock in the area. Statuary Hall in Washington, D.C. has columns made of the speckled stone from the Catoctin Mountains.

CATONSVILLE

Catonsville commemorates Richard Caton, son-in-law of Charles Carroll, "of Carrollton." Caton was a ne'er-do-well who failed in several major business ventures and went into bankruptcy. The estate Charles Carroll gave his daughter and son-in-law makes up the current site of Catonsville.

The first name of this village was Johnny Cake. A local tavern, legend has it, made the best cornbread in the area.

CAVETOWN

Cavetown, Washington County, was once the site of the oldest known cave in Maryland. The cave, large enough to hold 1,000 people, contained a lake large enough to sail a small boat.

The cave became unsafe in 1912 because of quarrying in the area. It finally disappeared by 1920.

CAYOTS

The post office at Cayots, Cecil County, was opened in 1898. Eleven years earlier, it was known as Caryot's Corners. The name, some say, is for a Frenchman who lived here. The name might be a variance of a French family name.

CECILTON

The Cecilton, Cecil County, post office was in operation before 1832. The name is derived from Cecil Calvert, the second Lord Baltimore. Cecilton was one of several "Ceciltons" "planned" by the state legislature. Most failed; this one survived.

Earlier names for the town were Savington and Cecil's Crossroad.

CENTREVILLE

Located in Queen Annes County, Centreville was originally known as Chester Mill in 1782, when the town became the county seat. Fifteen years later, it was renamed Centreville to represent its accessibility to all citizens. Some authorities point out that the French "centre" and "ville" were used to honor the help America's ally provided during the Revolution . . . also to differentiate it from Middletown in Delaware.

Maryland has many Centrevilles, including those in Frederick, Charles, Prince Georges, Somerset, and Washington counties.

CERESVILLE

Ceresville, Frederick County, takes its name from Ceres, the Roman goddess of grain and the harvest.

Cornelius Shriver built the Ceresville Mill here in about 1745.

CHAMP

The earliest name for this Somerset County village was St. Peter's Peninsula. A local optometrist suggested the town's post office name be changed to his own. But postal authorities considered Beauchamp too long a name, so they dropped the "beau" from I. Frank Beauchamp's name and created the town of Champ.

CHANCE

Some sources have suggested this name came from some idea of luck; in fact, it is the shortened version of Last Chance.

As truth has it, when the first post office was opened, the postmaster adopted the name from the Chance Farms located here. Another source, however, thinks the name was given facetiously by Captain James Whitlock, who first suggested Rock Creek as the name. When that was rejected, he threw in Chance, never thinking the town had a "chance" at getting a post office.

One author reminds the reader that the name of several land grants included the word Chance, such as "Chance," a 1712 grant in Calvert County, "Come by Chance," and "Accident."

CHANEY

Thomas Webb opened the post office in Chaney in 1900. But the Chaney name goes back even further in Maryland history.

Richard Cheyney (or Chaney) arrived here from Kent County, England, in 1658. He settled in Anne Arundel County. The first Chaney to settle in Calvert County was Richard's grandson: Thomas Chaney.

CHANEYVILLE

The town of Chaneyville, Calvert County, bears the name of its first postmaster, Charles D. Chaney. Postal operations began in 1871 and ended in 1918. Chaney and Chaneyville share the same family roots. (See Chaney.)

CHAPTICO

This village takes its name from the Chaptico Creek. The waterway's name translates from the Algonquian to "it is a big (or deep) river." In 1651, the stream's name was spelled Choptico.

CHARLESTOWN

John N. Black opened the first post office at this Cecil County location before 1832.

Charlestown, named for Charles Calvert, the fifth Lord Baltimore, was another of the county's planned communities. It was laid out in 1742 by Act of General Assembly, because no settlement existed near the head of the Chesapeake Bay. For years it rivaled Baltimore and was considered a vital port. But fortunes dwindled, and the county seat was moved here with hopes of revitalizing the economy. Unfortunately, the location proved too remote, and the seat was moved to Elkton in 1786.

Descriptions of Charlestown in the mid-eighteenth century were not too flattering. In 1762, Benjamin Mifflin described it as "a miserable forlorn place. . . ." A great deal has changed since then.

CHARLOTTE HALL

Charlotte Hall was established in 1698, and became a health resort, usually called "Ye Cool Springs of St. Maries." The name honors Queen Charlotte, who married George III in 1761.

CHASE

Chase was not named for Supreme Court Justice Samuel Chase (1741–1811), as some authorities contend.

Chase, a native of Somerset County, was an ardent supporter of independence from England. He worked hard toward this end, representing Maryland in Congress and signing the Declaration of Independence. A delegate to the Constitutional Convention, Chase voted against ratification.

Samuel Chase, while on the Supreme Court, made a number of comments which Thomas Jefferson took personally. Jefferson convinced Congress to impeach the justice in 1804. After hearing the facts, the Senate voted him not guilty and strengthened the concept of the independence of the courts. But this Chase was not the source for this town's name.

The "real" Chase was one of Sam's relatives. A product of the early twentieth century, Chase was named for Charles Chase, a lawyer from New England who came south for his health. The town was first named Chase's Station, for its location on the now-defunct Pennsylvania Railroad.

CHESAPEAKE BEACH

The Calvert County beach on the Chesapeake takes its name from the bay. The name was first recorded in English in 1585 as Chesepioc. By 1608, it became Cheapeak. The English first used the name for a village, and then for the bay.

Captain John Smith was elated to find that the Chesapeake Bay offered so much, for so little effort. It was filled, he wrote, with "brettes, mullets, white Salmonds, Trowts, Soles, Plaice, Herrings, Rockfish, Eeles, Shades, Crabs, Shrimps, Oysters, Cockles and Muscles. . . . In summer no place affordeth more plentie of Sturgeon, nor in winter more abundance of fowle. . . . In the small rivers all the years there is good plentie of small fish, so that with hookes those that would take paines had sufficient."

Chesapeake Beach was named and incorporated by the Maryland Assembly in 1894. Six years later, the town took form as the Chesapeake Beach Railway Company completed its track work and opened a power plant, a water system, and an amusement area.

The post office here began after 1900, but under the name of West Beach. In 1960, the postal name was officially changed to Chesapeake Beach.

The most logical interpretation of the name is from the Algonquian *che-sipi-oc*, "big river at" the beach. Another source, however, suggests the name is derived from the Delaware Indian *kitshishwapeak*, "great salty bay."

CHESAPEAKE CITY

Chesapeake City came into existence because of the Chesapeake & Delaware Canal that links Chesapeake Bay across the Delmarva Peninsula. The waterway was predicted as early as 1661 by Augustine Herrmann, a Bohemian settler who drew up the first map for the Calverts. Herrmann originally called his 22,000-acre Cecil County land Bohemia Manor.

Work on the canal as Herrmann saw it, however, did not begin until 1804, under the guidance of Benjamin Latrobe. The early hamlet that grew up around the construction was known as Bohemia Village. The name was changed to Chesapeake City in 1830, even though the canal did not open until 1832. The completed project was often called the "$25 million ditch."

At one time, there was a Chesapeake Town post office located near Perryville. That post office was discontinued in 1834. An official post office was opened as Chesapeake City in 1839.

CHESTER (—town, —ville)

Chestertown, Kent County, began in 1707–08 as the port of entry for Cecil, Kent and Queen Anne counties, and called New Town. A legislative act of 1730 mentions it as "Chester-town or New-Town."

In 1774, Chestertown objected to the tea tax with its own "tea party" that predated the more famous Boston celebration.

Chestertown, Chester, and Chesterville are named after the Chester River.

CHEVERLY

Cheverly, Prince Georges County, was named in 1918 by Robert Marshall for Cheverly Gardens, near Landover Station. Marshall named the town, as his wife explained, "after a rich man's estate in England. It has no other significance except English sentiment."

CHEVY CHASE

This town did not receive its name from that of a popular comedian who first became famous on "Saturday Night Live."

Incorporated in 1914, Chevy Chase was developed on and around the estate of Joseph Belt (1690–1761). The name of Belt's estate, which he patented in 1751, was spelled "Cheivy Chace."

CHICAMUXEN

This Charles County village takes its name from the nearby stream. The name is Algonquian, but may also come from the Lenni-Lenape *shackamaxon*, "meeting ground of chiefs" or "meeting ground of the eels." Another suggestion is that the Indian word meant "fishing place at a weir."

Another suggestion brought forth was that the name came from *chingomuxon*, as that is how the name was spelled in 1650. That word translates to "here lies big or high ground."

CHILDS

William Harvey opened the post office at this Cecil County location in 1887. The town was named for Gary W. Childs, editor and publisher of the Philadelphia *Public Ledger*. Childs owned and operated a paper mill near this location for many years.

CHILLUM

Chillum is a suburb of Washington, D.C. Before a bedroom community arose in the area, this was the site of Chillum Castle Manor, a reference to the ancestral home of the Digges family in England. William Digges settled in Maryland in 1650.

CHICAMUXEN. The event depicted in Benjamin West's famous painting, "William Penn's Treaty with the Indians," allegedly occurred at the place the Lenni-Lenape called Sachamexin or Shackamaxon. This word may have been the source for this Maryland town's name. It translates as "meeting ground of the chiefs" or "meeting place of the eels," depending on the Indian dictionary.

The treaty was never signed. Penn, in fact, wrote that "a treaty never signed is never broken." (Print and Picture Department, Free Library of Philadelphia)

CHOPTANK

This name comes from the name of the nearby Choptank River, which is derived from an Indian tribal name. The best available translation suggests it means "tidal stream."

A post office was in service here in 1888. Earlier names for the town were Medford Wharf and Leonard's Wharf.

CHURCH CREEK

A post office was in service at this Dorchester County site before 1832.

The town grew up around the local Episcopal Church, founded in 1692, which lent its name to the local creek and the town itself. Prior to becoming Church Creek, the community was known as Dorset, Old Dorchester Town, and White Haven.

CHURCH HILL

This Queen Annes County community grew up around St. Luke's Episcopal Church. The "hill" was obviously added as a touch of class, since the highest elevation in town is only eighty feet!

CHURCHTON

Miss Lola Burr opened the first post office in this Anne Arundel town in 1885.

The obvious source of the name is that several churches existed here when the town got around to naming itself.

CHURCHVILLE

The source of the name for this community is quite obvious. The congregation of the Churchville Presbyterian Church was founded in 1739 after George Whitfield preached in the area. The community considered themselves as living in a "church village."

CLAGGETTSVILLE

Claggettsville, Montgomery County, remembers the Claggett family. The most famous Maryland member of the family was Lieutenant Levi Claggett, who was killed during the bombardment of Fort McHenry during the War of 1812.

The family's founder, Captain Thomas Clagett, came to Calvert County in 1670. Twelve years later he settled Clagett's Delight. He was originally from Claygate, England.

CLAIBORNE

The town of Claiborne, Talbot County, takes its name from Captain William Claiborne, the first permanent white settler in the state. He established a trading post on Kent Island in 1631.

The town of Claiborne, however, does not got back that far. It was created in 1886 by the Baltimore & Eastern Railroad as a ferry docking point on Tilghman Creek.

CLARKSVILLE

In 1837, John Morris opened a post office in the Anne Arundel County community of Owingsville. The name was changed to Clarksville in 1840, and the town became part of Howard County.

William Clark was "an extensive farmer of the limestone section of Clarksville." His father was David Clark, one of three brothers who came to this area from Ireland shortly after the American Revolution.

CLEMENTS

St. Clement's Manor was granted Thomas Jerrard by Lord Baltimore. Jerrard arrived in Maryland in 1637. The "Saint" was dropped from this St. Marys County village in response to Puritan pressure that began in 1643. It was truly amazing how much religious freedom this country provided . . . the question was for whom?

CLINTON

Clinton, Prince Georges County, was originally named Surratt's or Surrattsville, for John Surratt, the first postmaster in 1854. The post office was set up in his place of business, Surratt House and tavern.

John Wilkes Booth stayed in the Surratt House following his assassination of Abraham Lincoln. Three weeks after Lincoln's death, the townspeople changed the town's name to Robeystown. Mary Surratt was hanged as a conspirator in Lincoln's death because Booth stayed at Surratt House.

In 1878, the name was changed again—to Clinton, to honor Governor DeWitt Clinton of New York.

COKESBURY

Cokesbury's name is a combination of the names of two bishops of the Methodist Episcopal Church: Thomas Coke and Francis Asbury.

The lower Eastern Shore was one of the first footholds of the Methodist Church in America.

COLEMAN

The probable source of the name of this Kent County village is the Reverend John Coleman, a native of Dinwiddie County, Virginia. Coleman, known as "Parson Coleman," was an Episcopal minister and a former soldier in Washington's army.

COLLEGE GREEN

College Green, Cecil County, takes its name from the estate the Reverend John Beard gave to his sons prior to the American Revolution.

COLLEGE PARK

College Park, located in Prince Georges County, is the home of one of the University of Maryland's campuses.

The university was chartered in 1856 as a private institution, but by 1866 it appeared on maps as "Md Agr Coll/Agricultural College." Before a Washington developer turned the neighborhood into a subdivision, the community consisted of the college and College Station, an unscheduled railroad stop. The name was changed in 1890 to College Park.

COLORA

Colora, Cecil County, was known as West Nottingham in 1857, when Eli Coulson opened the post office. The name was changed to Colora in 1869, according to the postal records.

Documents at the Maryland Archives, on the other hand, suggest the name is much older, used in 1845 by Lloyd Baldeston. Baldeston called his estate "Colora." The town was probably known as Colora because of the estate, but it was not until much later that officials took note and processed the paperwork.

Colora is Latin for "breezy ridge."

COLUMBIA

Columbia, Howard County, is a planned community of seven villages. The first families moved into the bedroom community in 1967, which is built on an old village of the same name.

The first recorded use of the word Columbia was in Philip Freneau's 1775 poem, "American Liberty." The name, in this case, probably came from the Columbia Pike, on which the old town was located. The sixties developers conceived of the community as a "short" commute to the District of Columbia, another possible source for the name.

COMUS

This Montgomery County community's name is a shortened version of McComas or McComus. Louis E. McComas was the U.S. senator from Maryland in 1898.

CONCORD

This community was named for the battle of Concord.

CONOWINGO

Conowingo had a post office in operation before 1832.

The name comes from the Algonquian for "at the rapids," a reference to the mouth of a stream.

CONTEE

The first postmaster of Contee's Station, Prince Georges County, was C. S. Contee, in 1878. Colonel John Contee was the first member of the family to settle in Maryland. He was a member of the militia in 1707, and later a member of the Council of State.

CORDOVA

This Talbot County village was named for the city of the same name in Spain. It was chosen because it had a romantic-sounding name. Though Spain had nothing to do with the area, the new name was better than the original, which was Thimbletown.

A popular legend asserts that when the railroad was being built, there was a "cord" of wood left "over."

CORNERSVILLE

One would think that this village in Dorchester County received its name because it was a crossroads town. Let the truth be known!

In 1856, Samuel Corner opened the post office here and named the town for himself.

CRANBERRY

The post office is to blame . . . again. Cranberry, Carroll County, was originally named Cranbury in 1874, when the first post office opened. Fearing there were too many "Cranburys" around, the name was modified by postal authorities to its current spelling—and its misunderstood meaning.

CRAPO

The original name for this village was Woodlandtown, chosen in 1872. Eight years later, the name was changed to Crapo.

Though Crapo does not appear to be the greatest name for anything, the townspeople picked it to commemorate the numerous frogs that live in the local marshes. Crapo is an Americanized version of the French "crapaud," which translates to "toad."

CRELLIN

The village of Crellin, Garrett County, was originally known as Sunshine. In the late nineteenth century, a sawmill was built here by friends and associates of Rolland P. Crellin, an industrialist from Pennsylvania. In 1892, the post office became Crellin.

CRESAPTOWN

The post office at Cresaptown, Allegany County, was first opened by John Barnard in 1836. Service was discontinued a little more than a year later. In 1855, Samuel D. Brady opened a post office and called it Brady's Mill. The name of that office was changed to Cresaptown in 1876.

When Robert Derenier reopened the post office in 1877, he called it Brady's Mills. In 1880, it became Brady. In 1890, the name "Cresaptown" was back on the post office.

There is a possibility that Cresaptown was Cresapburg from about 1800 to 1823 and perhaps Cresap Station at one time. The name comes from the Cresap family. Daniel Cresap built his brick home here and was considered an influential citizen.

CRESWELL

This community was named in honor of then-Postmaster General John A.J. Creswell. He served from 1869–74.

CRISFIELD

It is said that Crisfield is built almost entirely on oyster shells.

The town was first settled in 1666 by Benjamin Somers, who called it by the Indian name Annemessex. That name was changed to Somer's Cove, which remained until the Eastern Shore Railroad came into town following the Civil War. The efforts to get the railroad were led by an attorney from Princess Anne County, John Woodland Crisfield. He was also the founder of the Eastern Shore rail system.

Crisfield is the site of the annual National Hard Crab Derby.

CROCHERON

Crocheron was named for—and by—its first postmaster, Eugene Crocheron. He opened the post office here in 1901. He was also a county commissioner after the state's "Constitution of 1850."

Another source suggests the name came from Nathan Crocherton, a nineteenth-century settler.

CROFTON

Of recent vintage, the village of Crofton, Anne Arundel County, was constructed by Hamilton Crawford in 1964. Legend has it that he used the pronunciation of the first syllable of his last name (Craw- became Cro-) and added the "-ton" for town at the end.

CROWNSVILLE

Crownsville, Anne Arundel County, had its first post office in 1857, with Octavius Diffendorfer as postmaster. In 1866, the name was spelled Cronsville, leading some authorities to suggest the name was derived from a family name: Crown, Crowne, or Cron.

Another Crownsville began as Waterbury with James F. Baldwin as postmaster. The name was changed in 1937.

CUB HILL

The spotting of a bear and her cub caused the townspeople to name their town "Cub Hill."

CUMBERLAND

First called Will's Creek, then Washington Town, Cumberland, Allegany County, took its name in 1787 from Fort Cumberland.

The fort, begun in 1754 as Fort Mount Pleasant, was headquarters for General Braddock and Lieutenant George Washington during the French and Indian War. The fort was renamed Cumberland by Colonel James Inness in honor of William Augustus, Duke of Cumberland (1721–65), the son of George II.

Cumberland was the western terminus of the Chesapeake & Ohio Canal and the eastern terminus of the Cumberland Trail, the National Road—now U.S. 40, the first American road built with federal funds.

D DAMES QUARTER

Some authorities like to think this Somerset County community took its name from a local family name, with "quarter" an indication of a section of the overall settlement.

A more attractive—and likely—story is that the seventeenth-century watermen called their community Damned (or Damnd) Quarter because Indians fished near the village, against the will of the townspeople. An apocryphal tale has them shouting, "There's some of those damned squattors."

Damned Quarter, due to the efforts of Methodist ministers, became Dames Quarter by 1794.

Another source thinks the name might have had something to do with the proximity of this town to Deal Island, which originally was called Devil's Island. The logic is that the "quarters" of the "damned" were close to the "devil's island."

DANIEL

There was a post office under the name of Daniel in this village as early as 1885, even though some think it was mapped out as a town in 1909. It was unheard of for the post office to begin operation before a town was functioning. The absence of an "s" from the corporate name would indicate that the town's name probably honors a man with the proper name of Daniel and not a family.

DANIELS

This community recalls the Daniels family, the most famous member of which was probably Josephus Daniels, Woodrow Wilson's secretary of the Navy. The town was settled as a mill site on the Patapsco.

DARLINGTON

The name of this Harford County village also appears in Beaver County, Pennsylvania, and South Carolina.

Darlington was the post office's name in 1818, but it was changed to Woodlawn in 1821, and to Battle Swamp in 1853. At another time it was called Red Door. Postal authorities say the name was suggested by a Quaker resident. This bit of information indicates some ties with England. It is possible that the name came from the Quaker's home, Darlington, Durham, England.

DARNESTOWN

The first name for this Montgomery County village was Darnes. By the 1820s, "town" had been added to the name.

Darnestown takes its name from the Darne family. William Darne was a frequent representative from the county to the state legislature and also a director of the Chesapeake & Ohio Canal.

DEALE

John J. Leatherbury opened the Deale, Anne Arundel County, post office in 1899.

According to an 1878 county atlas, the land on which Deale stands belonged to "J. Deale Heirs." "J." or James Deale owned tracts of land here as early as 1736.

DEAL ISLAND

The name of this Somerset County community is a corruption of the old name for the island: Devil's Island.

In 1783, the name was Devil's Island; in 1866, Deil's I., and Deil's P. O. The transition from Deil to Deal was a post office decision. Deil, by the way, is Scottish for "devil."

DELMAR

Located in Wicomico County, Delmar straddles the Delaware-Maryland state line. The town was founded in 1859, when the Delaware Railroad reached here. (See Delmar, Delaware.)

DENTON

The seat of Caroline County was originally named Eden Town, in honor of Sir Robert Eden, provincial governor (1769–76). Over the years the name was shortened by use to Edenton. When Eden fell out of favor and was sent back to England, the "e" was removed. Eden's wife Caroline is honored by the county's name.

A post office has operated under the name of Denton since before 1832.

DENTSVILLE

Francis A. Murphy was the first postmaster in this Charles County community. The post office was opened here in 1885.

John Dent (ca. 1645–1712), scion of the family for which the town was named, arrived in Maryland from Yorkshire, England. Dent served as captain of the Chaptico Hundred.

DETOUR

Most authorities suggest that the name of this Carroll County village is of English origin. That might be true of the word, but the name was not placed on the town until 1905. From 1837 to that date, the community was called Double Pipe Creek.

The Double Pipe Creek name was considered too long by officials of the Western Maryland Railroad—it would not fit on their signs or in their timetables, so the name was changed to Detour.

Perhaps the namers made the choice with tongue in cheek. The Double Pipe Creek is formed here by the meeting of the Little Pipe Creek and the Big Pipe Creek. A look at a map shows us that the Little Pipe Creek makes a sharp turn from its normal course to meet up with Big Pipe Creek at Detour. Is it possible that that veering action was called a "detour"?

DICKERSON

The Dickerson family is remembered in the name of this Montgomery County community. In 1878, W. H. Dickerson was postmaster and owner of the general store.

At the outbreak of the Civil War, one of the Dickersons joined Chiswell's Exile Band. The Exile Band, no relation to Sergeant Pepper and his Lonely Hearts Club Band, was a group of Marylanders from the county who deserted their homes to fight for the Confederacy.

DOWELL

This Calvert County community received its first post office in 1926. Mrs. Sadie McDowell was the postmistress. The name, however, is not an abbreviation of her married name.

Dowell honors a family of that name that first settled in this area in the eighteenth century. John Dowell was listed as a resident of Lyon's Creek Hundred, Calvert County, in 1733.

DOWNSVILLE

Downsville, Washington County, was founded in 1852 and named for Charles Downs, who died in 1857. Downs was a constable in the area and a lifelong Democrat.

DRAWBRIDGE

William D. W. Raleigh, in 1859, was the first postmaster in this community. It was named for the principal structure in town.

DUNDALK

Located in Baltimore County, Dundalk's name was inspired by the Irish seaside resort situated to the north of Dublin.

The name was suggested by Henry McShane who wanted a name for the railroad siding by his bell foundry. He chose Dundalk because he was born on Dundalk Bay.

DUNKIRK

The post office at Dunkirk, Calvert County, dates back to 1842, when Charles H. Johnson opened its doors. The town's name comes from Dunkirk, the seventeenth-century estate of William

Groome. Groome acted as adviser to many of the English merchants who dealt with county planters.

EAGLE HARBOR

Eagle Harbor is located at the head of the Patuxent River.

The town was incorporated in 1929. Some authorities feel the name came from the presence of eagles, or from a family name. It is possible the town was mistakenly named for the seagulls that fly around the area.

EAST NEW MARKET

Before 1832, there was a post office under the name of East New Market in Dorchester County. The reason behind the naming is simple: it was to differentiate this town from the New Market in the western part of the state. The post office at "East" New Market opened in 1803, and was called New Market until 1827.

The town was settled in 1660, and was known as Crossroads, then New Market. Another source suggests the name came from the New Market House, located here.

EASTON

Easton was settled in the late seventeenth century as Pitt's Bridge. The community grew up around the Third Haven Friends Meeting House, built in 1682–83. After the courthouse was built in 1711, the town was called Talbot Court House or just Court House.

The town was formally laid out in 1788 as Easton, but sources disagree as to the origin of the name. Some historians suggest it was called Easton because it was the governmental center "east" of Annapolis. Others contend it was so named because of its position near the head of the Tred Avon River—similar to the English town of Easton on the Avon River.

The first post office in Easton was opened in 1789.

EASTPORT

The first post office in Eastport, Anne Arundel County, was opened in 1887 with George W. Brock as postmaster.

During the War of 1812, the site of Eastport was occupied by Fort Horn. The community's name then became Horn Point. "Horn" came from Van Horn, a Maryland congressman. By 1887, the name became Severn Point, but that name did not take hold. The next year, postal authorities named the community Eastport. The name came from Eastport, Maine, the home of Charles Murphey, an Annapolis real-estate developer.

ECKHART MINES

When Joseph Womsley opened the post office in 1852, this Allegany County community was called Eckhart Mills. Less than a month later, the name was changed to Eckhart Mines.

The name comes from the Eckhart family, who owned the mines. The earliest members of the family to settle here were Adam, George, and John Eckhart who received military lots in Western Maryland in 1788.

EDEN

This Somerset County site is supposed to have a name with Biblical roots. One source waxed eloquent on how early settlers, seeing their verdant surroundings, sensed a similarity to that first garden.

On a more realistic note, Eden was probably named for Sir Robert Eden, the last royal governor of Maryland. The town of Denton once honored him, but, because of their anti-Tory feelings, the "e" was dropped from the town's name. The people here were more sympathetic to the crown, so Eden's name remained.

EDESVILLE

Originally called Forktown, because several roads converged here, Edes, Kent County, was named in honor of a late-eighteenth-century family, either Eads, Eades, or Edes.

EDGEWOOD

Edgewood, Harford County, was known as Edgewood Station in 1866. The name probably comes from the town's location near the 10,000-acre Cadwalader estate.

EDNOR

This Montgomery County village was either the victim of a post office goof or a local dialect.

Ednor was named for Edna, the eight-year-old niece of Dr. Francis Thomas, the town's first postmaster. Some authorities think the name was misread by postal authorities; others believe a Southern drawl slurred the name.

ELDERSBURG

The first post office in this community opened in 1873. Originally, the name was spelled Eldersburgh. Postal officials streamlined the name, as it did many others throughout the United States.

The town was named for John Elder, who owned a great deal of the land in the area and laid out the town in the late eighteenth century.

ELDORADO

Ezekiel W. Wilson opened the first post office at this Dorchester County location in 1880. Eldorado County, California, was the first place in which gold was discovered, and the name was used on a local farm, owned at the time by Becky Taylor.

Eldorado replaced the earlier name of The Ferry, given because people crossed the Marshyhope Creek to Brookview at this location.

ELKRIDGE

Elkridge was named for the elk once sighted in this Howard County locale.

When it was founded in colonial days, the town was known as Elkridge Landing and was the shipping point for tobacco grown in the watershed of the Patapsco River. In the mid- to late eighteenth century, the river was deep enough for ocean-going vessels and made the landing a center for imported goods.

Elkridge had its first post office in 1815. By 1866, it was known as Elkridge Landing P.O.

ELKTON

Elkton, Cecil County, opened the doors to its first post office in 1827 with Adam Whann as postmaster. Its name is descriptive of its location, a town on the Elk River. The name appears in nine different states. Previous names for this community include Head of Elk and Elktown.

Built on the Friendship Tract, the town was incorporated as Elktown in 1787, one year after the county seat moved from Charlestown.

Prior to 1938, Elkton was notorious as the East Coast's marrying capital; some called it the "Gretna Green of the East." Before Maryland law required a forty-eight-hour waiting period, the town attracted eloping couples from Philadelphia and New York and other points north and east. In fact, this author's father and mother were wed here! Elkton's business dwindled, but Elkton is still a sentimental spot for elopements.

ELLICOTT

See Ellicott City.

ELLICOTT CITY

This community was first known as Ellicott Mills for the Quaker brothers—Andrew, John, and Joseph Ellicott—who founded their gristmill on the site. The brothers had purchased water rights in 1774, and moved their milling works from Philadelphia.

In 1837, when John Butler opened the first post office in Ellicott's Mills, the town was part of Anne Arundel County. It is now part of Howard County.

Benjamin Banneker, a free black born in the area in 1731, and Andrew Ellicott were commissioned to lay out the city of Washington after Pierre L'Enfant left with the plans. Legend has it that Bannecker reproduced the drawings from memory.

EMMITSBURG

Emmitsburg, Frederick County, was called Emmettsburgh before 1832, with a post office in place at the turn of the nineteenth century. At various times before being called Emmitsburg, it was known as Silver Fancy and Poplar Fields.

It was named for Samuel Emmitt, an Irish immigrant who gained a patent on the land in 1757 and laid out a town twenty-eight years later.

EMORY GROVE

This village was once the site of the Emory Grove Camp Ground, named for Bishop John Emory of the Methodist Episcopal Church. The first camp meeting was held at nearby Glydon in 1868.

FAIRBANK

For fighting in the War of 1812, Edward Ned Fairbanks (1792–1863) was given bounty land in Talbot County. According to the post office, the area has been called Fairbank since 1848.

FAIRHAVEN

In 1876, George W. Long opened the post office in this Anne Arundel County town. Even then it was known as Fair Haven, a likely name because it was a "fair haven" on Herring Bay.

FAIRMOUNT

In the midst of low land in Somerset County sits the town of Fairmount, a good five to ten feet above the rest of the area. That

F

does not seem like too great a "mount," unless you compare it with nearby Flatland Marsh.

FAIRVIEW

During the Civil War, when Oliver Wendell Holmes traveled to Frederick to find his wounded son, he wrote, "In approaching Frederick, the singular beauty of its cluster spires struck me very much, so that I was not surprised to find 'Fair-View' laid down about this point on a railroad map."

FALLSTON

Fallston, Harford County, is just what its name implies: a town by the Little Gunpowder Falls. The post office here was known as White House, but was changed to Fallston in 1849.

The Little Falls Meeting House, located here, was built in 1843. Still standing, it has separate doors for men and women and a partition down the center to further segregate the sexes.

During the Civil War, Fallston was a stop on the Underground Railroad.

FARMINGTON

The post office at this Cecil County location was in service under that name before 1832. The name was changed in 1840, but the handwriting on official records is so faint that one is unable to determine what happened to Farmington. The original name appeared to be more popular than the faint name, because Farmington was returned as the official name in 1854.

Another source, with perhaps better eyes than this author, suggests that other names for this community included Principio and College Green.

FAULKNER

This Charles County community received its first post office in 1888 with James T. S. Tennison as postmaster.

In 1906, the Pennsylvania Railroad station was called Lothair, but the post office was named Faulkner. The name Faulkner is probably a misspelling of the family name Forkner, because there once was a Forkner's Mill on the Faulkner Branch.

FEDERAL HILL

A post office was in operation at this Harford County location in

1843. The elevation here is almost 600 feet, so the "hill" appellation makes sense. "Federal" is commendatory.

FEDERALSBURG

Originally situated in Dorchester County, this town is now part of Caroline County. Initially called Northwest Fork Bridge, the name was changed in 1812 following a large meeting of members of the embryonic Federalist Party.

Prior to that meeting, this community was known as Northwest Fork Bridge, and had grown around Clonsberry Jones' store, which was opened in 1789.

FINKSBURG

Finksburg, Carroll County, was originally called Finksburgh in 1834, when the post office opened. The name was modified in 1893.

The town commemorates the Fink family. One "authority" contends the town was named for Charles E. Fink, one of the founders of the Western Maryland Telephone Company.

FINZEL

This Garrett County village was named for John George Finzel, a German immigrant born in 1812, who came to America with his wife before the Civil War. Not long after they settled here, he joined up and fought for the Union.

FLINTSTONE

A post office has operated at this Allegany County location since before 1832. At that time the name was two words. The single word came into being in 1951.

Most authorities agree that the name came from the nearby Flintstone Creek, mentioned by Christopher Gist in his 1750 journal. The waterway came by its name because of "the abundance of Indian flintstones. . . ."

FLORENCE

The donor of the name for Florence, Howard County, is a mystery. According to an eyewitness to the naming, Gassaway Watkins Warfield named the town for some woman "who lived around here, but who she was and when she lived I don't know."

FORESTVILLE

A suburb of Washington, D. C., this town was, until 1854, known by the post office name of Long Old Fields. In that year, the community decided to change the name to Forestville.

A historian of the late nineteenth century was appalled by the name change, since he recalled the place as being covered by a series of old forested fields. Another source suggests, based on postal records, that the name was once spelled Forrestville—and suggests it is based on a family name. The contemporary suggestion is more likely correct.

FOUR CORNERS

Four Corners was once an important crossroads, and thus the name. It was listed by that name on an 1866 map.

FREDERICK

The first settlers to this area were German immigrants who arrived in the early eighteenth century. Frederick, seat of Frederick County, was the home of ninety-five-year-old Barbara Fritchie, who challenged Stonewall Jackson's troops to shoot her rather than harm her Union flag. John Greenleaf Whittier heard the tale and wrote another of his famous poems, "Barbara Fritchie."

Daniel Dulaney, a land speculator, laid out the town of Frederick in 1745, but by 1792 it was known as Fredericktown. Incorporated in 1817, its first post office was opened in 1837.

The source of the name, most historians agree, was Frederick Calvert, the sixth Lord Baltimore. One disagrees, saying that the Calvert boy was only fourteen at the time, and the name probably came from Lord Baltimore's friend, Frederick, Prince of Wales. This author votes with the majority.

FREDERICKTOWN

Prior to 1683, settlers were content with tobacco farming and did not care to create villages, towns, or cities. When the legislature got into the act, it spent more than half of the next century attempting to establish some planned communities. One of the first was Fredericktown, Cecil County.

Fredericktown was laid out in 1736, along with Georgetown, Kent County. The two cities face each other across the Sassafras River. The town was named for Frederick, brother of George III; thus the parallel between the two towns' names. The first permanent settlers were French neutrals, the Acadians, who fled Nova Scotia in 1755.

Fredericktown opened its first post office in 1891. Prior names include Pennington's Point and Happy Harbor.

FRIENDSHIP

There was a post office in operation in this Anne Arundel County community before 1832 with Cephas Simmons as postmaster.

The town, then known as Greenhead, was founded in 1804. The current name, local legend has it, was given following an incident that took place in 1807.

The Reverend Eli Towne fell ill after giving a sermon in the local meetinghouse. (Another version has it that he was beaten by the town drunk.) Too weak to leave, he spent the night on the floor, but was ministered to kindly by the townspeople. When he awoke the next morning, he felt much better and suggested the name of the town be changed to Friendship.

A more realistic source of the name was the presence of members of the Society of Friends, the Quakers, in the area.

FRIENDSVILLE

The name might suggest that the Society of Friends, the Quakers, named this town. That is not the case. The first postmaster of this Garrett County town was Garfield Friend, who named the town Friend's before 1832. The name was changed to Friendsville shortly after the post office opened.

John Friend (1732–1803) was the county's first settler, arriving in 1764.

FRIZZELLBURG

Frizzelburg, Carroll County, commemorates the Frizzel family. The town was originally called Frizzelburgh, beginning in 1869, until postal authorities got the "h" out of there.

The first house to be built here was constructed before the turn of the eighteenth century. In 1814, Nimrod Frizzell came to town and opened a blacksmith shop. Shortly after that, he opened an inn and general store. Because of his prominence, the town became known as Frizzell's.

FROSTBURG

Frostburg, Allegany County, was founded by act of Congress in 1806, because of the construction of the National Road.

The first resident in the area was Josiah Frost, who bought a tract across the designated route and cut it into town lots. In 1812, his son Meschach built a log house on Lot 1. The house was converted into an inn and named Highland Hall when stagecoach service began in 1818.

The town was formally named Frostburgh by the post office in 1820 when postal service began. Meshach Frost was the first postmaster. The name was modified to Frostburg in 1892.

FRUITLAND

Fruitland was originally called Disharoon's Crossroads. When this became too difficult to pronounce, the town changed its name to Forktown, another descriptive term for its location. In 1875, the townspeople voted to change the name. They rejected Phoenix, and took on the name Fruitland, because the town was a major distribution point for strawberries and other crops.

G

GAITHERSBURG

The first house to be built in what is now Gaithersburg, Montgomery County, was constructed in 1802 by Benjamin Gaither, farmer, blacksmith, and tavern owner. When he began construction, he was the sixth generation of the English-born Gaither family to live in North America.

Though founded by the English, Gaithersburg has taken on a growing minority population. Town fathers note they have begun a Hispanic newsletter, organized an annual ethnic festival, "and hired a Hispanic police officer."

GALENA

Galena, Kent County, takes its name from the Latin for "lead ore." The ore was discovered in 1813, but never adequately mined.

In 1789, the town was known as Georgetown Cross Roads and Down's Crossroads.

GAMBRILLS

The first post office in this community was opened in 1869, under the name Sappington, or Sappington Station. That name appeared when Mary M. Sappington was postmistress.

The name was changed to Gambrill's in 1885, then streamlined in 1895. According to local lore, the name came from Augustine Gambrill, who had a plantation near Annapolis from about 1723 to the time of the American Revolution.

GARRETT PARK

Garrett Park, Montgomery County, takes its name from Garrett County, which was named for John W. Garrett, president of the Baltimore & Ohio Railroad.

The town was settled in 1890, and incorporated a year later.

GEORGETOWN

Laid out in 1736, Georgetown, Kent County, was named in honor of the English prince who became George III. (See Fredericktown.)

GERMANTOWN

Germantown, Montgomery County, was founded in 1849 by German immigrants. The first man to buy land in the area was Jacob Snyder. When, in 1873, the Baltimore & Ohio Railroad arrived here, a farmer, F. C. Clopper, donated the land for the station. The station was named Clopper or Clopper's.

GIRDLETREE

The name of this Worcester County village has no relation to an overweight tree. The name was taken from the time a local resident killed a tree by cutting a ring of bark from it, or "girdling" it.

Most authorities accept that the "girdler" was Charles Bishop, who killed a large beech tree before constructing his home. He called his manor farm Girdle Tree Hill. The community gradually became known as Girdle Tree.

A minority view is that the "girdled" tree was a marker left by surveyors.

GLEN ARM

This Baltimore County village was named for the ancestral home of William Armstrong, a one-time treasurer of the Maryland & Pennsylvania Railroad. Historians are unsure whether the name came from Scotland or Ireland.

GLEN BURNIE

Glen Burnie has a name of fairly recent origin.

Samuel S. Tracey opened the first post office in the town, but under the name of Myrtle, later changed to Tracey's Station. The name was changed to Glenburnie in 1888, then to its present form in 1930. The name commemorates the town of the same name in Scotland. Perhaps.

Glen Burnie was also the name of the home of Colonel James Wood, who founded Winchester, Virginia.

GLENCOE

The name for this Kent County community, like the one in Baltimore County, comes from the writings of Sir Walter Scott; at least, that is one authority's opinion. Another suggests that the town was named by a homesick settler originally from the Scottish valley of Glencoe.

GLEN ECHO

During the late nineteenth century, Glen Echo was a center for Chatauqua meetings and a summer resort.

It was the last home of Clara Barton, founder and first president of the American Red Cross.

GLENELG

Glenelg takes its name from the Glenelg Manor. The manor was owned by General Joseph Tyson, assistant postmaster in 1845. He allegedly took the name from an old Scottish estate.

GLYDON

One of the many problems facing a growing community was by which name the town would be known: the railroad station, the post office, or the village name.

Glydon, Baltimore County, was earlier known as Reisters-Town Station by the railroad and Emory Grove by the post office. The townspeople in 1879 decided to draw lots for an "umbrella" name. Glydon was the winner.

Dr. Charles A. Leas laid out the town in 1871 and, local lore has it, selected the name Glydon from an English town.

GOLDSBORO

The people of Oldtown decided when the Delaware & Chesapeake Railroad arrived in 1867 that they needed a new name.

The name they selected was Goldsboro, in honor of Dr. G. W. Goldsborough, since he owned most of the land surrounding the town. In 1872, when the first post office opened, the name was spelled as it is today. Sometime later, the name was given status with the correct spelling of the good doctor's name. The town name was restored to its original form in 1892.

GOODWILL

The Worcester County community that grew up around the Goodwill Baptist Church assumed the name of the church.

GORMAN

Arthur Pue Gorman was the Maryland Democratic party's boss in the late nineteenth century. He was considered by many to be a political wizard. He served in the U.S. Senate for twenty-four years.

Senator Gorman was one of the founders of the Western Maryland Railroad. His name also appears in an ancient form on the West Virginia side of the Potomac River. (See Gormania, West Virginia.)

GOSHEN

Goshen takes its name from the Goshen Creek, named for the land where the Israelites lived in Egypt. The name usually conveys a hope for fertility. The name appears in many states.

GRACEHAM

Graceham, Frederick County, began as a village in the mid-eighteenth century. By 1832, it had an operating post office.

Local tradition suggests the name was given to the town by a visiting Lutheran bishop who said, "May this be a hamlet where the grace of God abounds!" Graceham as also been known as Gracetown.

GRANITE

In 1830, Captain Alexander Walters opened granite quarries in this Baltimore County area, calling them the Waltersville Granite Quarries.

Waltersville became Granite in 1873.

GRANTSVILLE

When Jesse Tomlinson opened the post office in this location, before 1832, it was known as Tomlinson's, located in Allegany County. In 1834, when James Burton became postmaster, the name was changed to Little Crossings. Six years later, the name became Grantsville. It is now part of Garrett County.

The name, we are told, comes from Daniel Grant, of Baltimore. Grant patented land here in 1785.

GRATITUDE

First known as Deep Landing, the town of Gratitude, Kent County, borrowed the name of a steamboat from Philadelphia that docked here regularly in the late 1880s.

GREENBELT

Greenbelt, Prince Georges County, was developed in 1935–38 as a social experiment funded by the federal Resettlement Administration, employing out-of-work men on relief. Originally, the town enforced strict rules of behavior for residents.

The Greenbelt Museum, located at 10B Crescent Road, contains furnishings from 1937 and presents a view of what life was like in Greenbelt in the beginning.

The name comes from the Roosevelt Administration policy designed to curtail unwanted urban expansion by creating a permanent barrier, or belt, of green parkland or forests.

GREENSBORO

In 1832, when the first post office was opened in this Caroline County locale, it was called Greensborough, named for a local family. In 1893, postal authorities streamlined the name to its present configuration.

Earlier names for this town, founded in 1732, include Bridgetown, for the first bridge across the Choptank River, which was built here in the same year; Head of Choptank, and Choptank Bridge.

GUILFORD

Guilford was named for the Earl of Guilford, father of Lord North. At least that's what those outside of Maryland contend.

In reality, Guilford was named for the nineteenth-century estate of a wealthy local sportsman.

HAGERSTOWN

Jonathan Hager (1719–75) settled in this area in the mid-eighteenth century. In 1762, he laid out a hamlet in Washington County which he called Elizabeth Town, after his wife, Elizabeth Kershner Hager. When other settlers arrived, they began calling the settlement Hager's Town. That name became official in 1814 when the people petitioned a change in name, and the legislature went along with it.

Hagerstown's library was the first in the world (after 1901) to have a bookmobile: a two-horse cart, fitted with bookshelves, traveled around to rural areas.

HALETHORPE

Halethorpe was named by the mother of State Senator Carville D. Benson. The name means "healthy village."

HALF PONE POINT

The reason behind this naming is clouded. By looking at a map, one can see that Half Pone Point juts into the Patuxent River roughly halfway between Cornfield Point and where the river narrows. Half Pone is also the name of an island in the state.

Another possibility is the Algonquian word for "bread," *apones*. One can almost hear the corruption of that word, to 'alf pones, in progress.

HALFWAY

Halfway, Washington County, is the midpoint between the West Virginia and Pennsylvania state lines, or Williamsport, Pennsylvania, and Hagerstown, Maryland.

HAMPSTEAD

Hampstead, Carroll County, has used that name since 1834.

According to a historical marker in the town: "Spring Garden. Christopher Vaughan laid out the town of Hampstead in 1796 on land called Spring Garden, located along the Indian path from Patapsco (Baltimore) to Letort's Spring (Carlisle). . . ."

Both Spring Garden and Hampstead were well-known locations in London.

HANCOCK

Hancock, Washington County, might honor the memory of John Hancock (1737–93), the first signer of the Declaration of Independence. Hancock wrote his name boldly so the king would not have to use his spectacles to read it.

But it does not!

By 1794, this community was called Hancock's Town. The first settlers began to arrive in 1732, but as a publication by the town's government states, a Joseph Hancock owned a royal grant and settled here himself about 1749.

Hancock was incorporated in 1853.

HARMONY

The post office at Harmony was opened by Henry Nicodemus in 1870. The name is probably drawn from the Harmony Society in Pennsylvania, or may simply denote peace and tranquility.

Prior to getting a post office, the town was called Beallville, from 1834–42.

HARNEY

The name of this Carroll County community dates back to 1856, when the townspeople applied for a post office. They had been calling their town Monocacyville, and that is the name they proposed for the post office. Unfortunately, there was another town in Maryland by that name.

They asked James Elder, postmaster at Eldersburg, to help them find a name. He mentioned that he had just read an article about a conflict between the federal government and the Mormons in Utah. Elder suggested the town name itself Harney, for General W. S. Harney (1800–89), the commander of the troops that quelled the disturbance.

HARRISONVILLE

Richard Harrison was the first member of the Harris family to settle in Maryland. He arrived at Anne Arundel County in about 1651. The post office in this locale was in operation by 1843.

According to postal records, another Harrisonville existed, in Dorchester County. That post office was established in 1856, and was named for a local family. The first member of that family to settle in the area, Thomas Harrison, arrived in Maryland in 1742.

HAVRE DE GRACE

Though Havre de Grace, Harford County, was settled before the American Revolution, it did not become a mercantile center until the mid-nineteenth century.

The town was laid out in 1658 for Godfrey Harmer, who called his settlement Harmer's Town. The next year, Harmer passed the property to Thomas Stockett. He changed the name to Stockett's Town. A ferry had been in operation here, known as The Lower Ferry. After 1700, it was called Susquehanna Lower Ferry.

Havre de Grace, the name given to the town in 1785, translates from the French as "haven of grace." Lafayette, legend tells us, visited here in 1782 and remarked on how much the port resembled Le Havre, France. He was also told the story of a French traveller who, upon seeing the area, remarked *"C'est Le Havre. Le Havre de*

Grace!" The French seaport of this name was named in honor of a chapel dedicated to *Notre Dame de Grace, "*Our Lady of Grace."

HEBRON
Hebron bears the name of the ancient city (sometimes spelled Hebron, or Hevron) of Palestine. Other sources contend that the name really was slang for "heaven," since some early residents considered their community to be "heaven on earth."

HELEN
Helen, St. Marys County, was named by the first postmaster, Oscar Hancock, for his daughter. The post office was first opened here in the early twentieth century.

HEREFORD
The original name for this Baltimore County town, Loveton, was changed to Hereford in 1821.

John Merryman, of the Clover Hill estate in Baltimore, took title to the land in 1714. The Merryman family had immigrated to the colonies from Herefordshire, England, and borrowed that name for their new community.

HICKORY
In 1831, Hickory, Harford County, was simply the Hickory Tavern post office. It seems likely the tavern and the town were named for President Andrew Jackson, "Old Hickory." He won re-election in 1832. At the same time, one cannot rule out the presence of hickory trees as the place-name origin. The date, however, makes the reference to the president seem more likely.

HIGHLAND (— Beach)
Highland Beach had its post office opened in 1916 with Augustine Lewis as postmaster. The beach is located on high land, which helped establish Highland Beach as a summer resort town.

Charles Douglass, son of Frederick Douglass, the famed black abolitionist, purchased land here in 1892.

HILLSBORO
When the first post office was opened in this Caroline County locale, it was called Hillsborough, after the Hill family. Postal

authorities streamlined the name in 1893.

Another authority, however, suggests the name was derived from a relative of one of the Lords Baltimore, a certain Lord Hillsboro. An earlier name for Hillsboro was Tuckahoe Bridge, for the structure spanning the Tuckahoe Creek.

HOLLYWOOD

Hollywood was named for the American holly, a shrub that grows in abundance on the Delmarva Peninsula.

HONGA

The town of Honga, Dorchester County, received its first post office in 1913. The town's name is derived from the Honga River, whose name comes from the Algonquian word for "goose."

HOOPERSVILLE

Henry Hooper was postmaster in 1860 when the office was opened at this Dorchester County location. Another Hooper, William E., was Baltimore's Cotton Mill King in the nineteenth century.

The town, located on Upper Hooper Island, cropped up between 1852 and 1866. The Hooper family goes back to 1667 in this county, though the original member came to Maryland from England a number of years earlier.

HORSEHEAD

In 1819, this Prince Georges County village was known as Horse Head. There once was a Horsehead Store located in town, so named because the wooden sign, designed to be recognized even by those who could not read, showed the head of a horse. There also was a Horsehead Tavern here, the more likely choice as the name origin.

John Wilkes Booth, according to local lore, is supposed to have visited this tavern twice.

HOYES

William Waller Hoye (1768–1836), an Irishman who lived at Frog Harbor Manor on the Potomac near Williamsport, moved with his family and slaves to Ginseng Hill, Garrett County.

The post office opened here in 1841 under the name of Hoyesburg. Later it was called Hoyestown and Johnstown. The Hoye family name in Ireland is spelled O'Hoye.

346

HUGHESVILLE

Thomas P. Boarman opened the first post office at this Charles County site in 1866, but the name comes from the Hughes family. The most famous member of that family is probably Christopher Hughes, an artist of the late eighteenth century.

HUNTINGTOWN

There was a post office in operation at this Calvert County location as early as 1802. Located on Hunting Creek, the first town by this name was established in 1683 when the legislature passed an act to lay out the town. The "old" Huntingtown was torched by the British in 1814, and the village was totally destroyed. Huntingtown, the present village, sits near the old site.

HURLOCK

The town of Hurlock, Dorchester County, was named for—and by—its first postmaster, John M. Hurlock, who opened the post office here in 1870. Three years earlier, the railroad had arrived.

John Hurlock also built the town's first store (1869) and house (1872). However, the reason the town bears his name is because he won a tree-chopping contest!

HUTTON

John Conel opened the first post office in what was known as Hutton's Switch in 1865; it was located on the Baltimore & Ohio Railroad. The town was named for either the railroad stationmaster or for a local family. Since there were no Huttons in this county, it would seem likely that the railroad had something to do with the naming.

Originally located in Preston County, Virginia, Hutton's Switch became part of Allegany County until the formation of Garrett County, where it presently resides.

IDLEWILDE

The name of Idlewilde, Anne Arundel County, is probably a fanciful variation of Idyll-wild.

One source, however, suggests the name has a different derivation. Apparently, a German family by the name of Wilde settled here in the late nineteenth century. If that is the case, the family would break the stereotypical description of Germans as hard-working. Were members of the Wilde family really "idle"?

IJAMSVILLE

Plummer Ijams opened the post office in this Frederick County community in 1832.

While the post office was called Ijamsville, the community went by Ijams' Mill, as John Ijams had built a gristmill at this location. The two names merged when Plummer allowed the Baltimore & Ohio Railroad to run its line through his property.

The Ijams name may be a corruption of the English James or Ian, or it may reference a Dutch or Flemish name.

INDIAN HEAD

A tale told in a poem by Dorothy Beecher Artes talks about an Indian brave from Virginia who fell in love with an Indian princess who was promised to a prince of the Algonquian tribe. Her father told them to cease and desist. They did not and, fulfilling the dream of fathers far and wide toward unwanted suitors, he chopped off the brave's head, and stuck it on a spear to warn other Indians not to trespass on his turf. Believe it or not.

Indian Head is located on the Potomac River. A post office was opened in this Charles County community in 1896.

INGLESIDE

"Ingle" is a sentimental term from the Scotch, meaning a "nook" or "corner," and Ingleside was a popular name in the nineteenth century. This village was named in 1812. Prior names for this location included Long Marsh ("Tappahanna or Long Marsh") and Beaver Dam, after two local streams. Long Marsh became a post office address in 1837, and the name was later changed to Ingleside. Some sources think the name belonged to a local farm.

IRONSHIRE

It might seem a likely guess to say that this Worcester County town took its name from the presence of iron ore deposits in the county streams. That was not the case. The town, originally called Poplar Town, was renamed in honor of the Ironshier family.

IRONSIDES

John W. Clements opened the post office in this Charles County community in 1897. It has been said that the name came from "Old Ironsides," the nickname of the U.S.S. *Constitution*.

Another source, however, suggests a much better idea! A house in the town, built about 1886, was renovated, and the owner

348

used tin (an earlier version of aluminum siding) to cover the exterior walls of his home.

ISLAND CREEK

Island Creek, Calvert County, opened its first post office in 1878 with John C. Parker as postmaster.

The town is named for the Island Creek and located on the headwaters of that stream. A more proper name for the creek would be Islands, since it begins near Solomons Island and goes past Broomes Island into the Patuxent River.

ISSUE

The town of Issue, Charles County, opened the doors to its first post office in 1885.

According to town tradition, the name came from the issue of where the post office should be located . . . to the north or the south end of town. The post office department referred to the town's discussion as a matter of issue in its correspondence. A compromise made the name official.

JACKSONVILLE

Jacksonville, Baltimore County, most probably honors the memory of President Andrew Jackson.

J

JARRETTSVILLE

The original name of this Harford County town was Carmen's. The name was changed to Jarrettsville in 1838.

The Jarrett family had strong roots in the county. Jesse Jarrett was the county's real-estate assessor in 1798. In 1858, A. Lingan Jarrett was one of the county commissioners who contracted for the new courthouse in Belair.

JEFFERSON

The original name for Jefferson, Frederick County, was Newtown Trap. That name was bestowed in 1829. "Trap" was apparently used to differentiate between this town and Newtown in Worcester County. Or was it because the town was the site of a number of highway robberies, and the people began to think of it as a "Trap"?

The change to Jefferson, in honor of President Thomas Jefferson, took place in 1832—six years after Jefferson's death.

JEFFERSON. Thomas Jefferson, author of the Declaration of Independence and one of this nation's most influential thinkers, is remembered in the Jefferson Memorial, Washington, D.C., and in the names of Jefferson, New Jersey; Jefferson, Maryland; and Jefferson and Jeffersonton, Virginia. (Washington Convention & Visitors Bureau)

JESSUP

In 1863, James Kelly opened a post office in Hooversville, Anne Arundel County. While the post office was Hooversville, the Baltimore & Ohio Railroad station was called Jessup's Cut. A "cut" was a channel allowing the railroad to pass; Jessup was for Jonathan Jessup, a railroad contractor.

By 1871, it was officially known as Jessup's Cut. The name was simplified to Jessup's in 1877, and for a period of time, the community existed in Howard County. Sometime after 1931, the name was further simplified to Jessup.

JOHNSVILLE

Basil Root opened the post office at this location in 1832.

The name, it is suggested, commemorates members of the Johns family. Richard Johns II and members of his family moved from Calvert County in the late eighteenth century and settled in Prince Georges, Anne Arundel, Montgomery, and Frederick counties.

JONES (—town)

Jonestown, Caroline County, was named for the couple that almost single-handedly created the town. Sarah and Jenkins Jones first built a log cabin here in the late nineteenth century, then proceeded to raise ten children.

JOPPA (—towne)

Joppa took its name from the Biblical seaport in Palestine. The name translates from the Hebrew to mean "beauty."

Joppatowne, Harford County, bears a similar origin.

KEEDYSVILLE

Before 1852, this Washington County community was known as Centerville. But, due to confusion with a town by the same name in Queen Annes County, the townspeople asked postal authorities for a new name. Folklore tells us that so many members of the Keedy family signed the petition that the post office department had no choice but to name the town Keedysville.

Another source, however, indicates the name was selected to honor John J. Keedy, who built the Baker Mills, located here.

KEMPTOWN

Jack Kemp, former quarterback for the Buffalo Bills and secretary of the U. S. Department of Housing & Urban Development, had nothing to do with the name on this Frederick County village. The name was given when the post office opened here in 1853.

The name obviously comes from the Kemp family. The first member of that family in the area was David C. Kemp, who fought in the American Revolution. He built a mill and distillery, and also built the first grain elevator in Frederick County.

KENNEDYVILLE

The name of Kennedyville, Kent County, does not reflect on the memory of President John F. Kennedy. It commemorates another Kennedy family. One possible source is Captain William Kennedy, a wealthy Baltimorean who built the "Oak Hill" estate.

Founder of the Mount Vernon Cotton Mills, Kennedy was devoutly religious. When he was rescued from sure death during a storm in the Gulf of Mexico, he lived up to the vow he took when he thought he was a goner: he built St. Ann's Church.

Another possible source is a Pennsylvanian by the name of Kennedy who purchased land here, expecting the railroad to come through town . . . and it did.

KEYMAR

Keymar was originally known as York Road in 1871, when a post office was established in this Carroll County community. The name was changed in 1909. The name signifies that this town is the "key" to "Maryland," according to one authority.

John Ross Key, father of Francis Scott Key, owned a large estate on Pipe Creek near here. In 1822, the son sold the estate. Keymar, it is said, was the name of the family's estate. "Key-" obviously comes from the family; "-mar," from Maryland.

KEYSERS RIDGE
Keyser's Ridge, Garrett County, went by that name in 1852. The name probably recalls John Kiser, who was a squatter on the Savage River in 1787. Another source, however, thinks the town was named for an official of the Baltimore & Ohio Railroad.

KEYSVILLE
Keysville, Carroll County, commemorates the Key family. The most famous Key, of course, was Francis Scott Key, the lyricist of "The Star-Spangled Banner." A post office was opened here in 1886.

The land on which Keysville was built was part of the patent received by Key's grandfather, Philip Key. The Key scion built Terra Rubra, the family mansion, where Francis was born 1 August 1779. (See Keymar.)

KINGSTON
Kingston, Somerset County, takes its name from Kingston Hall, built here before 1750 as the country home of Robert King III.

KINGS TOWN
Located on the Chester River in Queen Annes County, Kings Town was named for the "reigning monarch" when the General Assembly ordered it to be built in 1732. The original name was Kingston, but was changed to avoid postal confusion with Kingston, Somerset County.

KINGSVILLE
Some historians create a plausible explanation for the naming of this Baltimore County village.

The original (1740) owner of the house that became part of the Kingsville Inn, which was named after the town, was the Reverend Hugh Dean of St. John's parish. After his death, his son-in-law, John Paul, acquired the property. Paul was a Quaker suspected of loyalty to the crown. In fact, he was arrested in 1781 for supplying flour to British troops.

According to postal records, another origin could be the postmaster in 1834, George King. Another source indicates the name came from Abraham King, who came to Maryland from Willistown, Pennsylvania. Other records show that the town was called King's Tavern before 1829, when the name was changed to Kingsville. Kingsville was changed to Fork Meeting House in 1839. Fork Meeting House, however, was the name of the post office—not the town.

KITZMILLER

The original name for this Garrett County village was Military Lot 300. It was purchased in 1796 by Thomas Wilson II. Ebenezer Kitzmiller married Wilson's granddaughter and operated his in-laws grist- and sawmills.

KNOXVILLE

Knoxville was the original name of this Frederick County town. When a division of Frederick County took place in 1842 and the town became part of Washington County, the name was changed to Weverton. In 1870, Weverton returned to Frederick County, and its original name was restored.

The town was laid out in 1772 on part of the Merryland Tract, and received a post office in 1829. The name comes from the Knox family which was in evidence here.

LADIESBURG

Legend has it that this town, founded in 1820, received its name because of the large number of women in the early population. According to one source, the name was given due "to the disproportion of seven women to one man in its early population." More likely, it came from a family name.

John A. Baker was the first postmaster of this Frederick County village. He opened the office in 1835.

LAKESVILLE

There are no lakes anywhere near this Dorchester County town, but members of the Lake family did live here.

During the American Revolution, the town was called Lake's. The most famous Lake was Lavinia (Lovey) Lake who held off a band of Tories who were looking for her father, Captain Henry Lake of the Dorchester County Militia.

In 1878, the postmaster was lumber dealer Charles Lake.

LANDOVER (— Hills)

This Prince Georges County community has been called Landover, Landover Depot, and Landover Road. Most sources agree the name comes from Llandovery, a market town in Carmarthenshire, Wales.

LANGLEY PARK

Samuel Pierpont Langley (1834–1906) was an aviation pioneer who experimented in 1896 with pilotless, heavier-than-air planes that actually flew.

It is believed by most aviation historians that Langley would have exceeded the accomplishments of the Wright Brothers if his experiments had not been beset by unfortunate accidents. This community remembers him, as does Langley Field in Virginia.

LANHAM

Lanham was named for the Lanham family. There are still members of the family living in this Prince Georges County community.

One of the first members of the family, Aaron Lanham, was a member of the first Montgomery County grand jury in 1777.

LANSDOWNE

Lansdowne, Baltimore County, was named for the British lord.

LA PLATA

Robert F. Chapman opened the post office in this community in 1873. The town's name is Spanish for "mountain of silver."

The La Plata name appeared on an 1866 map, and when the Pope's Creek railroad came through here, the station was called La Plata. The name comes from La Plata, the name of the Chapman farm.

LAPPANS

Located in Washington County, Lappans was known as Lappons Cross Roads post office in 1843. It is also referred to as Jones' Crossroads about the same time. Most sources agree that the name comes from a family, most likely the Lapins.

LAUREL

Laurel, Prince Georges County, was once a small industrial center.

The town stands on land patented in the seventeenth century

to Richard Snowden. The Snowdens played a major part in the development of the area. In 1811, Nicholas Snowden built a gristmill. Thirteen years later, he converted it to a factory. His son-in-law, Horace Capron, founded the Patuxent Company in 1835, a cotton mill that employed nearly 400 people. The post office was called Laurel Factory in 1837.

In 1900, the town boasted a shirt factory, cotton mill, foundry and gristmill. It promoted itself as "destined to become an important center." Unfortunately, by 1911, the textile mills had closed down. The town expanded again with the growth of nearby Fort Meade during World War II. The name comes from the local abundance of laurel bushes.

LA VALE

In 1901, when Fannie S. Kelley opened the first post office in this Allegany County town, it was known as Long. The name was changed to La Vale, "the valley," in 1947.

One authority contends the town was named by a local resident for the place of his nativity, a farm in Pennsylvania.

LEITERSBURG

George Poe was the original owner of the Well Taught tract, on which Leitersburg now resides. He sold some of his Washington County holdings in 1762 to Jacob Leiter. Leiter's grandson Andrew inherited the land in 1811, and laid out the town four years later.

Leitersburg was the name on the post office when it opened in 1826.

LEONARDTOWN

The earliest name for this St. Marys County community was Seymourtown, named in 1652 for John Seymour, a provincial governor. The name was changed to Benedict Leonard Town in the late seventeenth century.

The present name was given in 1733, to honor Benedict Leonard Calvert, fourth Lord Baltimore. At least one source attributes the name to Leonard Calvert (1608–1746), brother of Cecilius Calvert, second Lord Baltimore. By 1797, Leonardtown had a post office by the same name.

LEXINGTON PARK

Lexington Park is a community of recent origin. In the early twentieth century, it was called Jarboesville. The name was a reference to John Jarbo, one of Maryland's earliest French pioneers.

In 1942, the government built a $90 million naval air flight center. The name was changed to Lexington Park in that year, and commerates the World War II aircraft carrier, the U.S.S. *Lexington*.

LIBERTY GROVE

Liberty Grove, Cecil County, was established as a post office in 1871, with Robert A. Saunders as postmaster. The name conveyed the patriotic spirit of the settlers.

LIBERTYTOWN

Libertytown, Frederick County, existed as a post office prior to 1832. The town was laid out on the Duke's Woods tract in 1782. The source of the name seems to be patriotic, especially with the proximity of nearby Unionville. Another origin could be the early English concept of "Liberty." Liberties were areas that did not come under the legal jurisdiction of a sheriff or other law enforcement

LIBERTY GROVE. The Liberty Bell, which once "proclaimed Liberty throughout the land," was once housed in Independence Hall. Fearful that the bell's location would interfere with the interpretation of the building and because of the large number of tourists who visited the hall only to touch the bell, the Department of the Interior moved it across Chestnut Street in Philadelphia on New Year's Eve 1975. The concept of liberty is perpetuated in Liberty and Liberty Corners in Pennsylvania, and Liberty Grove and Libertytown in Maryland. (Convention and Tourist Bureau, City of Philadelphia)

authority. In Philadelphia, the section above the "old town" was known as Northern Liberties and was a haven for the lawless.

At one time it was considered a "storybook hilltop village" by young Marylanders who saw in Libertytown "a better way of life." (See Liberty Grove.)

LILY PONS

Lily Pons, Frederick County, was named for the famous opera singer, but with tongue in cheek. The area is also greatly involved in the production of pond lilies.

In 1917, G. L. Thomas opened a business to hatch goldfish and raise water lilies; 43 years later there were 800 ponds! A post office was established here in 1930 as Lilly Pons.

LIME KILN

G. J. Grove opened the first post office at Lime Kiln, Frederick County, in 1871. As late as 1866, the town's name was Slabtown, for the "slab houses" built for railroad workers.

The presence of a kiln—or oven—for making lime is the reason behind the renaming. When the Baltimore & Ohio Railroad opened its station here, lime production was at its peak.

LINKWOOD

When the first post office was opened in 1841, this locale was called Hicksburgh. The name was changed to Linkwood in 1870.

At one time, as one historian puts it, this town was a connection, a link between two forested areas.

LINTHICUM

The land on which this Anne Arundel County town rests was purchased in 1801 by Abner Linthicum, a descendant of the Welshman who arrived in the county as early as 1658.

Another source opines that the town was built on the farm of Sweetser Linthicum, Sr., a descendant of Abner. The town was platted and recorded as Linthicum Heights in 1920.

LOCH LYNN HEIGHTS

Located near Mount Lake Park, the use of loch in this town's name indicates "lake," and the family name Lynn gives us the key to the ownership of this Garrett County community.

In about 1827, a Captain David Lynn, the owner of nearby

"Lynn Pastures," sold a Military Lot. The land was used to build the Loch Lynn Hotel in 1894.

Another source thinks the name comes from Loch Lein, near Killarney, Ireland.

LONACONING

The first post office in this community was opened in 1873.

Lonaconing takes its name from the nearby Georges Creek. Figure that one out! The original name for the creek was Lonaconin.

The waterway's name is Algonquian, of uncertain meaning. According to local legend, the Indian name translates to "where many waters meet." But, according to an authority on Indian names, the name may mean "where there is a beautiful summit."

LONDONTOWNE

Londontowne, located in Anne Arundel County, was founded in 1680 by William Burgess. For a while it was known as Burgess' Wharf, but the Act of Assembly establishing the town as a port of entry in 1683 called it London Town.

LOTHIAN (MOUNT ZION)

The post office at Lothian opened in 1876 with John Bevan as postmaster. Lothian is the postal name for Mount Zion.

Philip Thomas, local tradition has it, built Lothian about 1804, giving it a name based in English history. In the eleventh century, Lothian was used to designate the English part of Scotland.

LOWER MARLBORO

There was a Marlborough post office in operation in this community in 1796 (an earlier name, some suggest, was Coxtown, but postal records do not reflect this). The name was modified in the late nineteenth century, and "Lower" added to differentiate this locale from Upper Marlboro. There is no Marlboro in today's Maryland.

Lower Marlboro's name honors John Churchill (1650–1722) who was victorious at the battle of Blenheim.

LUKE

When first established, Luke was known as West Piedmont—to differentiate it from Piedmont, West Virginia, which lies across the Potomac River from this town.

The name comes from the Luke family, who arrived in America in 1850 from Scotland. The family later founded the West Virginia Pulp & Paper Company.

In 1897, Samuel A. Rowe opened the post office in Luke.

LUTHERVILLE

The name for this Baltimore County community, once known to the railroad as Timonium Station and postal authorities as Lutherville, honors Martin Luther (1483–1546).

The Lutheran Church had great influence in the town. In fact, the Lutherville Female Seminary offered education to women here during the early nineteenth century.

The seminary became the Maryland College for Young Ladies, chartered in 1853 by a pair of Lutheran ministers. The college closed following its 1952 graduation.

MACKALL

The first postmaster in this Calvert County village was John B. Mackall. He opened shop in 1876.

The Mackall family, in the person of James Mackall, arrived in Maryland in 1666. Some suspect that Mackall was a Scottish prisoner of war.

MADISON

When Joseph Stewart opened the first post office in 1837, this Dorchester County village was called Tobacco Stick. The name was changed in 1879 to Madison, in honor of President James Madison.

According to local legend, an Indian was trying to escape a mob of angry townspeople when he came to the Corsey Creek. He is supposed to have vaulted the river with the aid of a long stick of tobacco, and thus the name.

MADONNA

This town was not named for the patron saint of the "wannabes." Rather, it is the Italian name for the Virgin Mary, the original Madonna. This origin does not hold true for Madonna, Harford County.

The name, according to local historians, is supposed to have been donated by Madonna McCurdy, daughter of a former postmaster. Earlier names for Madonna include King's Corner and Cathcart.

MANOKIN

Manokin, Somerset County, takes its name from the Manokin River. The name is Algonquian for either "people who dig the earth" or "where there is a fortification."

The area was the location of an Indian village.

MARBURY

Charles Marbury came here from Chestershire, England, and settled near Piscataway. He received a deed to Carroll's Kindness tract on the Piscataway Creek in 1693. Five years later, he received a second grant on the creek; this time for the Marbury's Chance tract.

MARDELA SPRINGS

The name of Mardela Springs, Wicomico County, is made up of "Mar-" from Maryland and "-dela" from Delaware. The other portion of the name comes from the local springs. Unlike Delmar, Mardela Springs is several miles from the state line.

The original name for this community was Barren Creek. The name was changed to Mardela Springs in 1906.

MARION

When the railroad extended into this Somerset County area, John C. Horsey, because he donated a great deal of land, was given the right to name the new railroad station. Horsey selected Marion, the name of his youngest daughter.

MARRIOTTSVILLE

There was a Marriottsville in Howard County in 1834. The name comes from General Richard Marriott's estate.

His ancestor, John Marriott, lived on Peter Porter's plantation, Indian Landing, in 1681.

The Marriott name is best known for its present-day hotel chain.

MARSHALL HALL

James Little was the postmaster in this Charles County village when the first post office opened in 1868.

William Marshall had a 500-acre tract surveyed in 1651, and called it "Marshall." In another era, Marshall Hall featured a popular amusement park frequented by Washingtonians.

MARYDEL

Since this Caroline County village is located on the Maryland-Delaware border, it seemed logical to combine the two state names into the town name. It was spelled Marydell when the town's name was given in 1853. In 1905, they got the "l" out of there.

An earlier name was Halltown, for landowner William Hall, who purchased the land in 1850. His purchase included parts of Caroline County and Kent County, Delaware.

MASON SPRINGS

The post office at this site opened in 1890 as Mason's Springs. The "'s" was dropped by postal authorities three years later. The name describes the springs owned by the Mason family.

MATAPEAKE

Queen Annes County. See Mattapex.

MATTAPEX

Mattapex takes its name from the Algonquian for "junction of waters." English settlers decided that the plural of the word was Matapeake, and thus we have two rural communities, located five miles apart, sharing the singular and plural of the same word.

MATTAWOMAN

The first post office in this locale was opened in 1873.

The name of the village comes from the Mattawoman Creek, a tributary of the Potomac River. The name comes from Captain John Smith's 1608 reference to Mataughquamend, which translates to "where one goes pleasantly."

MAYO

When Thomas E. Collison opened the post office in this Anne Arundel town in 1879, it was known as Rhode River. The name was changed to honor the Mayo family in 1891.

The earliest Mayo in this county was Joshua Mayo, who married Hannah Learson here in 1707. The most famous member of the family, however, was Commodore Isaac Mayo (1795–1861) who served under Captain James Lawrence in the War of 1812.

Shortly before his death in 1861, the much-decorated Mayo protested Lincoln's denial ". . . to millions of free men the rights of the Constitution. . . ." For this act, he was dismissed from the Navy "with prejudice." Later the "dismissed" was changed to "resigned."

McHENRY

This Baltimore County community was named for James McHenry (1753–1816), secretary of war under Presidents Washington and Adams. McHenry also gave his name to Fort McHenry, in Baltimore Harbor, Francis Scott Key's inspiration for the national anthem.

In 1810, James McHenry purchased land in Locust Tree Bottom that included the Buffalo Marsh, and this is the site of the town.

MECHANICSVILLE

Mechanicsville, St. Marys County, got its name because all the businesses in town required mechanics.

The village began when the Adams brothers built a tavern here. Later they added a forge and blacksmith shop. (See Mechanicsville, Pennsylvania.)

MELITOTA

This community's name is from the Greek *melitoutta,* and means "sweetened with honey." Most authorities believe this name was used to avoid the more mundane "Harmony" or "Pleasant."

MEXICO

This Carroll County village was listed as Brummel on an 1873 map for first postmaster Elisha Brummel, who served from 1883 to 1889.

Some sources suggest the name was taken from the home of a man named Santa Ana who came from Mexico and used that name for his homestead. Others contend the name really comes from the Mexico House, a hotel built here in the early 1870s by a man who had lost a relative in the Mexican War.

The name translates from the Aztec *Mexitili,* and could refer to the name of a deity, or "home of the war god."

MIDDLEBURG

Middleburg had its own post office before 1832, but with an "h" at the end of its name. The town is located in the middle of Frederick County. It was part of Baltimore County before 1837.

MIDDLETOWN

Before 1832, Middletown, Frederick County, had its own post office. It was the "middle town" between Boonsboro and Frederick on the National Road (U.S. 40).

MIDLAND

Mullan was the first name for this Allegany County town when its post office opened in 1891 with Jonathan C. Mullan as postmaster. The name was changed to Midland in 1894.

The Midland name was given to describe the town's location between Lonaconing and Frostburg.

MILFORD

Milford, Kent County, began its existence following the enaction of the Supplementary Act of 19 November 1686, which established an additional town in the county. Milford Town was built on the land of William Stanley.

The name describes a ford at a mill site.

MILLINGTON

Founded in 1794 by Thomas Gilpin on the tract known as London Bridge, the name probably honors Richard Millington. Millington owned farmland where a portion of the town was built. Another possibility notes that Millington was a "milling town" for many years, with several mills in operation.

Millington was also called Bridgetown and Head of Chester.

MILLSTONE

It has been suggested that stones found in this area were suitable for milling. The name of this Washington County village commemorates those necessities.

MONIE

This community takes its name from a tribal or village name.

The name, coming from the Monie Creek, appears in numerous forms, including Mannij (1605) and Manaye (1780). Some suggest it was drawn from Virginia's Nominy Bay.

MONKTON

Monkton has no relationship to an order of religious brothers.

Monkton's name comes from Monckton, Nova Scotia. Pennsylvanian Robert Cummings visited Nova Scotia in the 1770s and, while there, apparently fell in love with Rosanna Trites, a woman from Monckton. When he returned to his uncle's estate in Baltimore, he settled there and called his new home Monckton Mills. Postal authorities, not known for their romantic gestures, changed the spelling at a much later date.

MONROVIA

Jacob Cronise opened the post office in Monrovia, Frederick County, in 1833—two years after President James Monroe's death.

MONTGOMERY VILLAGE

A new community, Montgomery Village began in 1966 and was completed the next year. The builders were Kettler Brothers, Inc., and the name simply signifies a village in Montgomery County.

MORGANZA

The Morganza post office opened here in the late nineteenth century and took its name from the Morgan family, large landholders.

According to one source, the name comes from George W. Morgan, who owned Goodrick Farm. The "-za" at the end gives a decided Mexican or Spanish flavor to the name.

MORNINGSIDE

Morningside, Prince Georges County, grew up during the war years of 1940–49. The builders called it Morningside for no other reason than that they thought the name sounded "romantic."

MOSCOW

Willis D. Shaw was postmaster in this Allegany County town when the post office opened in 1891 as Moscow Mills.

Moscow Mills appears on a 1876 map. The land was originally owned by Englishman William Burns Shaw. His son, Andrew Bruce Shaw, developed the area by building a gristmill and a lumber mill. He also laid out the town.

The name was selected because it sounded exotic.

MOUNTAIN LAKE PARK

This Garrett County community was originally Hoyes Big Pasture.

In 1881, the Mountain Lake Park Association created a vacation community here.

The village is located in the Little Youghiogheny glades; the park was an oak forest; and the lake is formed by Broad Ford Creek and Crystal Spring.

MOUNT AIRY

Before the Baltimore & Ohio Railroad arrived in this Carroll County area, Mount Airy was called Parr's Spring Ridge.

The Mount Airy Coal & Iron Company was established here in 1854. A post office opened under this apparently descriptive name in 1869; Mount Airy sits on an airy loft 800 feet high.

MOUNT HARMONY

This Calvert County village received its first post office in 1890. The name could have come from the Harmony Society of Pennsylvania.

MOUNT PLEASANT

Mount Pleasant had its own post office before 1832. The town sits 450 feet above sea level and commands a pleasant view.

MOUNT RAINIER

Virtually a suburb of Washington, D.C., this Prince Georges County community was formed by a group of Army officers from Seattle, Washington. They took their 100 acres and called the package Mount Rainier, for the peak back home.

Six men bought the acreage in 1902, and incorporated the community as Mount Rainier eight years later. According to local historians, the unpaved streets often became so muddy that the nickname for the community was Mud Rainier.

MOUNT SAVAGE

In 1840, the post office in this Allegany County location was called Jennon's (or Jenning's) Run. John J. Murrary was postmaster. The name was changed to Mount Savage in 1847. In 1906, the post office name was Corriganville; the railroad station, Mt. Savage Junction.

During the heyday of the Mount Savage Iron Works, 1839–47, the town flourished. The name obviously comes from the iron works, which took its name from the nearby Mount Savage.

MOUNT VERNON

Mount Vernon, Somerset County, was named for George Washington's plantation home on the Potomac. There are three other Mount Vernons in Maryland.

MOUNT VICTORIA

The original name of this Charles County community was Cooksey. The first post office opened here in 1891 with Robert L. Cooksey as postmaster. The name was changed to Mount Victoria in 1914.

The name is drawn from the home of Robert Crain. The home, a "huge structure," was built in 1905, just four years after the queen died.

MYERSVILLE

William Metzger opened the post office in this locality in 1848.

According to local tradition, the first home to be built here was a log cabin, in 1742. It was crafted by James Stottlemyer, and he was joined later by other members of his family. The name has been spelled "-myer" or "-meyer."

NANJEMOY

Nanjemoy, Charles County, was known as Cross Roads before 1832, then Nanjemoy Cross Roads before 1890. The current name comes from the creek, whose name, it appears, can be translated from the Algonquian to mean "they go down to the river" or "one goes on downward."

NANTICOKE

Nanticoke, Wicomico County, is located on the Nanticoke River and takes its name from the stream. The name is an Indian tribal name that can be translated as "tide-water people."

NEWARK

Almost every state on the East Coast has a Newark. Some are named for Newark-upon-Trent; others, because they were a "new work." In the case of Newark, Worcester County, local tradition says the name was taken from a Civil War-era house, The New Ark, a boat-shaped home design.

Postal records, however, list Newark as a post office in 1824, a mite too "antebellum" for the house suggestion. The best bet is that the name was brought from England.

NEWBURG

In 1860, Newburg, Charles County, was called Newburgh. Postal authorities, in an effort to streamline place names, dropped the "h" in 1892. By so doing, they removed the English influence and added a decided German slant to the name. The town name, of course, was transported from England.

NEW CARROLLTON

New Carollton, Prince Georges County, was called "new" to separate it from the Carrollton in Carroll County.

NEW MARKET

New Market, Frederick County, was founded in 1793 along the National Road (U.S. 40) between Baltimore and Frederick, and served as an important stop for nineteenth century travelers. Its first post office was in operation in 1800. (See East New Market.)

NEWPORT

Newport, Charles County, was called New Port in 1806, when the post office opened. By the mid-nineteenth century, the name was hyphenated. The current one-word name is another example of post office streamlining.

This community lies at a distance from the Wicomico River, and suggests that the river is now much narrower than it once was.

NEW WINDSOR

New Windsor, Carroll County, was once part of Frederick County, with a post office established here in 1828.

Isaac Atlee, of Philadelphia, opened a tavern here in about 1788. Eleven years later, town lots were laid out, and the town was named Sulphur Springs. When townspeople approached Atlee about naming the town after him, he demurred, and suggested the name of a friend who was visiting from Windsor, England. Rather than name the town for the friend, whom they did not know, they named it for whence he came.

NORRISVILLE

Benjamin Norris "the elder" settled in Baltimore County in about 1690 and established a farm he called Everly Hills. Norrisville is now part of Harford County.

NORTH BEACH

The post office at North Beach opened in 1909. The town is the northernmost beach in the county.

NORTH EAST

North East is located at the head of the Northeast River, and takes its name from the waterway. The river was named by a group of early explorers who were searching for the Northeast Passage. The name came from the direction the stream flowed: northeast.

North East could easily have been called Shannon, the name favored by George Talbot, owner of the Susquehanna Manor Land Tract. He wanted to name the town after the river of his Irish homeland, but the idea never caught on.

North East was the site of a flour mill and bloomery—perhaps the first in Maryland—in 1716. The town had an operating post office prior to 1809.

It is the northeasternmost spot on the Chesapeake Bay.

NORTH POINT

North Point, Baltimore County, is located at the northernmost point of the harbor on Sparrows Point.

NORWOOD

Norwood was named for an ivy-covered brick house.

When Robert R. Moore came here for his health in 1867, his son Joseph bought the house. Why was the house called Norwood? Two possible sources are a town in Middlesex, England, and a family name.

OAK—

The prefix "oak" in place names is most often used directly or indirectly for the oak tree. In some cases, the name is drawn from an estate or manor house. We find this prefix appearing in Oak Grove, Oakland, Oaklawn, Oakley, Oakton, Oakview, Oakville, and Oakwood. (See Royal Oak.)

OAKLAND

When John Armstrong opened the first post office here in 1831, it was called Yough Glades and was located in Allegany County. The name was changed to Oakland in 1853, and the town is now located in Garrett County.

Oakland went by other names, such as Yox Glades, Armstrong's, Armstrong's in the Green Glades, and Green Glades. The Baltimore & Ohio Railroad named its station here McCarty's Mill.

OCEAN CITY

This Worcester County town's name is purely descriptive. It is located on the Atlantic Ocean.

When settlement began in the late nineteenth century, the village was called The Ladies Resort to the Ocean. That was not a promotable name for either real-estate development or tourism, so the name was shortened.

According to local tradition, the town was "founded by a company of well-meaning Eastern Shoremen and was formally open to visitors on July 4, 1875."

ODENTON

Odenton was founded in 1867. It was named for former Governor Oden Bowie, but not during his two-year term of office.

At the time of naming, Bowie was president of the Baltimore & Potomac Railroad, and a new station had just been established here.

OLDTOWN

An Old Town post office existed in Allegany County in the early nineteenth century, with John Read as postmaster. The post office was discontinued in 1864, and reestablished and discontinued again in the 1870s. In 1886, William Carden opened the Old Town post office still there today.

According to some authorities, the original name was Skipton, a name that existed until 1807. It is considered the oldest town in the county, settled by Colonel Thomas Cresap and others in 1741.

OLIVET

Olivet opened its first post office in 1893 with George B. Lusby as postmaster. The office was closed in 1868. Most sources suggest that the name comes from the Biblical Mount Olivet.

OLNEY

This Montgomery County town, according to some "authorities," was named for its counterpart in England.

In reality, the town name goes back to 1832, when the post office was called Mechanicsville. The current name is derived from Mount Olney, the Farquhar family's home, built in 1800. The family enjoyed William Cowper's poetry, and he often referred to Olney in his writing. Cowper himself lived for several years in Olney, Buckinghamshire, England.

The "mount" comes from Olney's elevation. At 544 feet above sea level, Farquhar considered it one of the highest spots in lower Montgomery County.

ORIOLE

The state bird of Maryland is the oriole, from which this town takes its name.

Oriole, we have learned, was not the first choice of the townspeople when they were deciding on a post office name in the late nineteenth century. The leading citizen's (William Thomas Smith) first choice was St. Peter's, but that was already in use, so they settled for Oriole.

OVERLEA

Once called Lange's Farm, the name of this Baltimore County village was changed to Overlea to signify "over the meadow."

OWINGS MILLS

There was a post office at this Baltimore County location in 1833. Samuel Owings had been appointed in 1733 as overseer of "the roads from Henry Butlers up by the Garrison to the North Run and from said Butlers . . . to Gwynn's Falls. . . ." On the falls, Owings built three gristmills and prospered.

OXFORD

Oxford, located on the Tred Avon River, was the official port of entry for the Maryland colony in 1683. It was laid out as one of the port towns Lord Baltimore planned for his colony.

Notorious pirates such as Blackbeard Teach and Stede Bonner patronized the nearby Skillington Shipyard.

Oxford, Talbot County, takes its name from the town and university in England. It was known as Williamstadt from 1695–1702, in honor of William of Orange. When Anne assumed the throne, the name returned to Oxford.

Previous names for the village include Thread Haven and Third Haven, both corruptions of the river's name.

OXON HILL

Oxon Hill, Prince Georges County, has been associated with the estate (Oxon Hill Manor) belonging to the Addison family since the seventeenth century. The house was built by Colonel John Addison, a privy counsellor to Lord Baltimore.

The origin of the name is Oxford, or Oxoniensis, "of Oxford."

John Hanson, president of the Congress of the Confederation (Swedish descendants ballyhoo him as the first president of the United States), is buried on the grounds of the old Oxon Hill Manor.

PARK HALL

There was a time when this St. Marys County's name did not sound so prestigious. By 1640, a reference was made regarding Snow Hill Manor, extending northward "as far as Porke Hall, now Park Hall." It continued that at the village was "Gerrard's Freehold" or "Porke Hall Freehold." The land had been surveyed for Thomas Gerrard in 1640.

Most authorities think that "porke" and "park" are one and the same; the difference lies only in the way Marylanders say it.

PARKVILLE

In 1874, Simon J. Martenet began to develop this area of Baltimore County. Martenet called the development Parkville because he intended to construct a 360-foot-long park along Towson Avenue, between Chestnut and Oak avenues.

PAROLE

This Anne Arundel County town took its name from Camp Parole, where, during the Civil War, soldiers of dubious status and loyalty were kept. Some of the men were draftees, substitutes, and those who had been released by the Confederates on "parole."

PARRAN

The post office at Parran opened in 1886.

The name comes from the Parran family. The first member to settle in Calvert County was Alexander Parran, a French Huguenot who settled near the head of St. Leonard's Creek. He was granted a landed estate, Parran's Park, in 1706. Former state senator Thomas Parran, though a lumberman, was known as Maryland's Alfalfa King.

PASADENA

In 1874, the name Pasadena was transported from Indiana to California by fruit growers. The name, some contend, is Algonquian for "a gap between mountains." Others think it comes from *passadina*, "there is a low place between mountains, a valley."

There are no mountains here, but Pasadena is near the Mountain Road; a far-fetched origin story. More likely, the name went out west, then came back east.

When Clarence S. Johnson opened the first post office in this Anne Arundel County town, it was known as Elvaton. The name was changed to Pasadena in 1914, taken from the California town based on the Indian word meaning "crown of the valley."

PATAPSCO

Patapsco, Carroll County, takes its name from its location on the North Branch of the Patapsco River.

According to one source, the river's name comes from that of an Indian village and translates to "jutting (ledge of) rock at." Another source considers the translation to be "black water."

When the first post office opened here in 1873, the town was called Carrollton. The name was changed to Patapsco in 1878.

PATUXENT

There was a Patuxent City in Charles County before 1853.

The name is derived from the town's proximity to the Patuxent River, and means "at the falls or rapids."

PEKIN

The post office at Pekin was opened in 1874.

The town was named for the Pekin Mine, a coal mine named by the Atlantic & George's Creek Coal Company. In fact, the town is listed in 1866 as Pekin Mine.

As an interesting aside—in 1919, a new post office opened in Allegany County called Nikep: Pekin spelled backwards.

Pekin is another spelling of Peking or Beijing, China. It was a popular custom in the nineteenth century to name new communities after large cities elsewhere.

PERRY HALL

In 1774, Henry Dorsey Gough bought a very large estate in Baltimore County. He quickly changed the name of the estate from

The Adventure to Perry Hall, the name of his family's English seat in Staffordshire.

PERRYVILLE

Perryville opened its first post office in 1837 with John J. Heckart as postmaster.

The name comes from Commodore Oliver Hazard Perry (1785–1819), the hero of the battle of Lake Erie during the War of 1812, some say. Others think a more likely candidate would be Captain Richard Perry, who settled the area in the early eighteenth century. Sadly, we will never know the true origin of this name; Perry Point was surveyed as early as 1658, neatly eliminating both Oliver and Richard.

Earlier names for the community were Perry Point, Susquehanna, Chesapeake, and Lower Ferry.

PHOENIX

The name of the mythical bird that rose from its own ashes usually symbolizes "new growth."

Phoenix, Baltimore County, apparently takes its name from a local cotton firm, the Phoenix Manufacturing Company, built in the early nineteenth century. It went out of business about 1930.

PIKESVILLE

Settled before the American Revolution, this Baltimore County community opened its first post office in 1817.

A local landowner, Dr. James Smith, named it for his friend, Brigadier General Zebulon M. Pike (1779–1813). Pike was killed during the War of 1812 while leading an assault on Fort York, Toronto.

PINTO

Pinto, Allegany County, opened a post office in 1891.

At one time, this town was a stagecoach stop. The name, some think, refers to the pinto ponies stabled here at that time. Another source indicates, without elaboration, that some episode took place here concerning pinto ponies of the Southwest.

PISCATAWAY

Piscataway, Prince Georges County, takes its name from the nearby

Piscataway Creek. The creek's name was borrowed from that of an Indian tribe, and translates from the Algonquian as "fork (of) river at." The word indicates where a village was located.

A post office was opened here in 1792.

PISGAH

The original name for this Charles County community was Sandy Bottom, a name that graced the town's post office from 1856 to 1857. The Pisgah name first appeared on a local church, then on the town. It recalls the Biblical Mount Pisgah.

PITTSVILLE

Local legend has it that this Wicomico County community's name was too long to fit on the railroad sign. So, when the Wicomico & Pocomoke Railroad arrived in 1868, Derrickson's Cross Roads was changed to Pittsville. Dr. Hilary R. Pitts was the president of the railroad at the time.

POCOMOKE CITY

Some think Pocomoke City's name is the southern form of *poquo-mock*, which appears in Massachusetts. The name translates from the Algonquian to "small farm." Another source considers this Worcester County community's name to mean "broken by knolls."

Since its original settlement in 1670, this town has been known as Steven's Ferry and then Steven's Landing, for its founder Colonel William Stevens. Other names that followed included Meeting House Landing, Warehouse Landing, New Town (or Newton), and Pitts Creek.

Perhaps not liking to say he "hailed from the Pitts," the Reverend I. O. Ayers, a clergyman in the Methodist Episcopal Church, lobbied to have the name changed. In 1878, the town became Pocomoke City.

POINT LOOKOUT

The "point" juts out into the Chesapeake at the mouth of the Potomac. Earlier names included Smith's Sparkes Poynt and St. Michael's Point.

According to one Maryland historian, early settlers believed that if they stood at this point, on a clear day they could see to the Virginia Capes.

POINT OF ROCKS

Alexander H. Brown opened the first post office at this Frederick County location in 1832. Point of Rocks is located on the Potomac River, and appears to be a natural barrier formed by the Catoctin Mountain and the granite walls of the riverbanks.

POMFRET

Is it possible this is a modification of Pomphrey, Anne Arundel County? The post office there was opened in 1880 by Thomas W. Pomphrey. The Earl of Pomfret was prominent in the court of George II.

Pomfret, Charles County, opened its first post office in 1879, and most authorities believe it was named for Pontefract, Yorkshire, England. The British pronounce the name Pomfret.

Pomfret began to grow in 1763, after the Catholic Church built a "small frame chapel" on what was called "Pomfret Chapple Land."

POMONA

The Roman goddess of fruit trees and a city in Los Angeles County, California, share the name of this Kent County community.

POMONKEY

Pomonkey is the name of an Indian village or tribe.

Henry M. Hannon opened the post office in this locale in 1832. Earlier it had been known as Pomunkey Quarter.

POOLESVILLE

This Montgomery County community recalls the Poole family. The most famous member of that Maryland clan was Robert Poole, an Irish foundryman and ironmaster. Poole cast the iron capitals for the U. S. Capitol and Treasury buildings.

Postal records state the town name Poole's Store was changed to Poolesville between 1823 and 1825. Local tradition has it the town was named in 1793 for John Poole, who built the first house.

POPES CREEK

The name on the post office in this Charles County village dates back to 1882. It has no relationship to the Bishop of Rome, but commemorates the Pope family.

The name goes back to the mid-seventeenth century when the county sheriff ordered a ducking stool be erected "at Mr. Pope's Creek." The Pope in question was Francis Pope. It is said that Mr. Pope was the first in the seventeenth century to import slaves into the county.

PORT DEPOSIT

Before 1832, there was a post office in operation in this Cecil County town.

The name was given when the town was laid out by Philip Thomas in 1812, because the Susquehanna River shipping point was an active "port of deposit" for lumber and other commodities. When discussing possible names, one wag turned and said, "It is a port of deposit for lumber, why not call it Port Deposit?"

Port Deposit saw great growth following the arrival of Jacob Tome in 1833. Tome single-handedly developed the lumber and banking business in town. His 1898 death marked the end of the town's development.

Prior names included Cresap's Ferry, for Thomas Cresap, who started the first regular ferry across the river to Lapidum in 1725; Creswell's Ferry, for Colonel John Creswell, who succeeded Cresap; Rock Run, Smith's Falls, and Smith's Ferry—in honor of Captain John Smith.

PORT HERMAN

Thomas C. Marshall opened the first post office at Port Herman, Cecil County, in 1852.

The name commemorates Augustine Herrman, whose name and place of origin are recalled in the Bohemia River, Bohemia Manor, St. Augustine Church, St. Augustine Manor, and this town.

PORT TOBACCO

Port Tobacco, seat of Charles County, had a post office by that name before 1832. The name has nothing to do with the plant, but takes its name from the Port Tobacco Creek.

Port Tobacco is a corruption of the Indian *pautapang*, a "bulging out," "bay" or "cove." Earlier spellings of the name are Potopaco and Portobacke.

The town was previously named Chandler's Town, but that was changed to Charlestown in 1728. In 1820, the name became Port Tobacco.

POTOMAC (— Heights, — Park)

Potomac, Montgomery County, takes its name from the Potomac River, which was recorded by John Smith in 1608 as Patawomeck. He gives no meaning for the word, but it may translate from the Powhatan for "where one comes in."

The earliest name for this community, according to postal records, was Section 8, but that was quickly changed. Section 8, of course, is the military designation given to people with mental problems.

PRATT

Henry O. Robinett opened the first post office in this Allegany County community in 1893.

The name commemorates Maryland legend Enoch Pratt, hardware king of the nineteenth century and donor of Baltimore's first public library system.

PRESTON

From 1842 to 1859, this Caroline County village was known as Upper Hunting Creek, for its location. Later it was known as Snow Hill, but another Snow Hill existed in Worcester County. The name was changed to honor a local family. The best-known member of that family was a prominent Baltimore lawyer, Alexander Preston.

PRIEST BRIDGE

Priest Bridge takes its name from the bridge over the Patuxent River. The "priest" in question is up for grabs.

PRINCE FREDERICK

Named for one of King George I's sons, this town has been the seat of Calvert County since 1725. The town has been destroyed three times in its history: in the 1740s, during the War of 1812, and in 1882.

Known as Old Fields, or Williams' Old Fields (the land had been patented to William Williams) until 1725, then as Prince Fredericktown, Prince Frederick had its first post office opened before 1832. The name was changed to the current version in 1911.

PRINCESS ANNE

The General Assembly created Somerset County's seat in 1733 and named it for Princess Anne, the daughter of George II. Some seem to believe the city was named for Princess, later Queen, Anne of England, the last of the Stuarts. Documents, however, show that George's girl was the right one . . . even though a portrait of the wrong Anne hangs in the courthouse.

PRINCIPIO FURNACE

Principio Furnace, Cecil County, takes its name from the Principio Iron Works, named because it was the first of its kind in the region. The works were established around 1715 by Joshua Gee. A post office by this name, however, was not opened until 1950.

Some historians prefer to think the town was named from the Principio Creek, called Back Creek until about 1715, when iron became a major county industry. They ignore the (ca.) 1715 letter from English entrepreneur Joshua Gee to Joseph Farmer, an English ironmaster: ". . . I will charge thee to change the stream's name from Back to Principio. That means 'first' or 'in the beginning' if thou knowest thy Latin." It would appear that the creek's name and that of the ironworks developed at the same time, but with the works getting precedence.

PUTNAM

Putnam, Harford County, bears a family name, perhaps that of General Israel Putnam, Revolutionary War officer.

Q

QUAKER NECK LANDING

Used as a landing spot on the Chester River in Kent County, Quaker Neck Landing reflects the settlement of this area by members of the Society of Friends. The house Providence Plantation was built by a Quaker couple, William and Mary Trew, in 1781.

QUANTICO

This Wicomico County village comes from the Indian word that translates to mean "dancing" or "place of dancing." Another source suggests it is Algonquian for "long reach at." Some authorities suspect that an Indian village once existed on this site. (See Quantico, Virginia.)

QUEEN ANNE

This Queen Annes County community was settled in 1857, long after the reign of the queen. The town received its name when the railroad arrived in 1878, allegedly because the town was the only point where the railroad ran in the county. The county bears the name of Queen Anne of England (1665–1714).

QUEENSTOWN

Queenstown, Queen Annes County, takes its name from the county. The town was established in 1707 as the first county seat, and named "Queenstown" or "Queen Anne's Town." A 1710 act refers to it as "Queens-Towne." A post office opened under that name in 1800.

The name of both the county and town honor Queen Anne of England, Scotland, and Ireland.

RAWLINGS

Newton T. Rawlings opened the post office at Rawling's Station, Allegany County, in 1856. The name was changed to just Rawlings in 1880, when Charles M. Rawlings was postmaster. The scion of the Rawlings family was Colonel Moses Rawlings, a "pioneer resident" who was commissioned a lieutenant colonel in a Maryland rifle regiment 1 July 1776.

The earliest name for this village was Hickory Flats.

RED—

When used as a prefix to a place name, "Red" usually refers to some sort of landmark of that color. The following Maryland communities bring this to mind: Redgate, Redhouse, and Redland.

REDHOUSE

Redhouse, Garrett County, recalls The Red House, a tavern painted dark red built about 1830, and used as a stopping spot for cattlemen traveling the Northwest Pike (U.S. 50).

REHOBETH

Rehobeth, Somerset County, began as a "planned" community in 1668. It took its name from the plantation of William Stevens (1630–1687) who owned the land on which the town grew—as well as hundreds of acres through the lower Eastern Shore. In 1708, the town is referred to as "Pocomoke Town Called Rehobeth." The word "Rehobeth" is used in the Bible to indicate "room for all."

Stevens donated the land on which the first Presbyterian church in America was built in 1706 by Francis Mackemie. See Rehobeth Beach, Delaware.

REISTERSTOWN

Legend has it that when George Washington visited this Baltimore County village, he was asked to name it. Of course, the general named it Washington. That name, however, only graced the northwestern part of town. The southwestern portion was called Reisterstown, for the Reister family.

Three-quarters of the residents of Washington and Reisterstown were members of that family, so it seems logical that their name would be used for the entire town. When the Calverts granted land to German immigrant John Reister, he called his land Reister's Desire.

RHODES POINT

Rhodes Point, Somerset County, was once called Rogue's Point. It is possible that the name was simply cleaned up at a later date.

RIDGELY

This Caroline County village opened its first post office in 1870. An earlier attempt to create this town in 1867 was a failure.

The town commemorates the Ridgely family, long considered one of Maryland's first families. Charles Ridgely was a two-term governor of the state and the family's manse, "Hampton," is now a national monument.

Another authority, however, suggests the name came from the Reverend Greenbury W. Ridgely and the Maryland Baltimore Land Association. The minister, a law associate of Henry Clay before ordination, and the company, were the ones who convinced the railroad to come to town. Ridgely also owned a great deal of land in the area, and built his home, Oaklawn, here.

RIDGEVILLE

The original name of Ridgeville, Carroll County, was Parrsville, but it only held that name for about two weeks in 1837. Then the name was changed to Ridgeville. The reason the change took place, we must assume, was because Frederick County was divided, and this town was shifted to another county.

Another source indicates the original name was Ridgeville, then changed to Parrsville, then back again. The name comes from Parr's Ridge.

RINGGOLD

Major Samuel Ringgold (1800–46) was the first American officer to be killed in the Mexican War. Ringgold was an artillery man who fell at the battle of Palo Alto.

The original name for this Washington County village was Ridgeville. When the post office was opened in 1850, it was changed to Ringgold.

RISING SUN

In the early eighteenth century, Henry Reynolds settled in this area and built a tavern at the crossroads between the markets in Lancaster, Wilmington, and Philadelphia. His sign was a painting of the sun at dawn, and he called his establishment "The Rising Sun." Some sources suggest the business was really called "Sunrise Tavern." Others think the name originated with deliverymen who brought produce to Port Deposit each morning. They would pass this village as the sun began to rise. Rising Sun was, however, a popular tavern name about this time.

Originally named Summer Hill, the community changed its name to Rising Sun by 1817, giving in to popular usage. The Rising Sun name graced this Cecil County post office before 1832.

RISON

Rison, Charles County, opened its first post office in 1906 with Jessie F. Rison in charge. The folk legend that says the name—pronounced RISE-n—refers to the morning sun is a lot more interesting, but wrong.

RIVA

Riva was Riverview in 1886, when the town's first post office was opened. It appears the name was changed to reflect the name's pronunciation with a Southern drawl, though one "expert" tries to tie it to the Latin *rivus*, "a small stream of water, a brook."

RIVERDALE

Riverdale, Prince Georges County, carries a descriptive name. That is, if you believe some of the "experts."

In reality, Riverdale was named after Riversdale, a mansion owned by the Calvert family that is currently used as headquarters for the Prince Georges County Delegation. The mansion, fashioned after the Chateau du Mick in Belgium, was built in 1801–02 and housed Henri Joseph, Baron de Stier. His daughter Rosalie Eugenia (1778–1821) married George Calvert (1768–1838) and they moved into the house in 1803.

By 1927, the Riversdale mansion was known as the Calvert Mansion.

RIVERTON

This Montgomery County village was not named because it was a "river town," as some authorities suggest.

Riverton's name before the Civil War was Brooke Black Meadow, for landowner James Brooke, who died in 1784. Elisha Hall moved into the property about 1860 and renamed the house at Black Meadow (the name had changed slightly by then) Riverton, because it was located next to the Rawlings River.

RIVIERA BEACH

Riviera Beach is located on the Patapsco River. The original name, ca. 1947, was Rivera Beach—to signify a "beach on the river." The name changed to Riviera Beach sometime before 1962.

That derivation took place in a rather roundabout way: in the 1920s, when T. W. Pumphrey and his brothers developed the area, they called themselves the Riviera Beach Development Company.

ROBERTS

Roberts, located in Allegany County, bears the name of one of the most widely scattered families in the colonies.

This particular location was probably named for either William Milnor Roberts I or II, because the site was a Baltimore & Ohio Railroad station. Both Roberts were railroad builders.

ROCK— (—dale, — Hall, — Point, —s, —ville)

Rock Hall is the seafood capital of the county. Authorities who postulate on the source of the name have come up with some strange notions: the name is a modification of "Rock Hole," for the number of rockfish seen; "Rock Haul," for the number of rockfish caught; or "Rock Hall," from an early estate by that name.

The most logical source is the old estate.

Rock Hall was changed to Eastern Neck in 1840, but the name was returned the next year.

Eugene Mitkiewiez opened the first post office at Rock Point, Charles County, in 1883.

Rockland was a nineteenth-century mill village. The Rockland Grist Mill, built here in 1813, was purchased in 1978 by the Azola

Building Company, which restored the mill and constructed expensive stone homes nearby. The name is descriptive.

Rockville's place in American history goes back to 1774, when a group of irate citizens gathered at Hungerford's Tavern in Montgomery County and resolved to cut off all trade to England until the tea tax was lifted. The original name was Montgomery Court House; after 1774, it was known as Hungerford's—for the tavern. In 1784, after William Prather surveyed the site, streets were laid out and the village was renamed Williamsburg. Williamsburg became Rockville in 1817, probably a reference to Rock Creek.

RODGERS FORGE

Rodgers Forge, a suburb of Baltimore, sits on farmland where F. Scott Fitzgerald once lived. Following World War II, "it became a maze of brick, each block with its garbage-truck mews."

ROHRERSVILLE

Located in Washington County, Rohrersville honors the Rohrer family. The first member of the American branch of the family, Frederick Rohrer, arrived in the county in 1766.

This town, however, was founded by his son David. Other members of the family have served as town postmaster, railroad agents, merchants, and millers.

ROMANCOKE

The Algonquian word for "low ground there" was first used in Virginia. Colonel William Claiborne adopted the name for his plantation on Kent Island. The name in Virginia was originally spelled Romangkok, and the colonel, "Claiborne of Romancoke."

The name probably translates to "where there is low-lying ground."

ROSARYVILLE

This Prince Georges County community bears a religious name.

The Church of the Holy Rosary, built here in the late 1850s, loaned its name to the village. The church was destroyed in a 1920s storm, but was replaced by the current Holy Rosary Church.

ROSEMONT

The name for this Frederick County village translates to "mountain of wild roses."

ROYAL OAK

This Talbot County village was named for a large oak into which the British shot a cannonball (or two, or was it chain-shot? It all depends on the historian!) during the War of 1812.

Others seem to think that the name was given earlier, because of an oak seedling that was brought over from England and planted. Still others think the tree the British hit was the same tree grown from a seedling. (See Front Royal, Virginia.)

RUMBLEY

There is no agreement as to the source of the name for this Somerset County town. One side has it that the name comes from a family name, such as Rumbley, Rumbly, or Rumble; the other side says the name is from the sound of the thunder that "rumbles" across the Bay, or the sound of the water, or the sound of the wind.

The name comes directly from Rumbley Point, Pocomoke Sound.

RUTHSBURG

The name for this Queen Annes County community does not honor a woman by the name of Ruth. The name honors instead the Ruth family. Christopher Cross Ruth was a county justice in 1765.

An earlier name for the town was Cross Roads by Henry Pratt's. The Ruthsburg or Ruthsborough name appeared in 1861.

RUXTON

Toward the end of the eighteenth century, Nicholas Ruxton Moore owned farmland west of the town's railroad bridge. Moore was a Revolutionary War officer and a Maryland congressman.

In 1885, when the Northern Central Railroad built a station here, the town's name became Ruxton.

S SABILLASVILLE

Many sources suggest that this Frederick County village bears the name of a family, most likely Sibley. The basis for this conjecture is the appearance in records of Siblysville and Sybilisville, early spellings for the town. In 1830, the name stabilized as Sabillasville, occasionally appearing as Sabillisville.

One authority suggests another theory: Could the name possibly come from a personal name? In 1792, a Captain Carberry married the "amiable Miss Sybila Schertzell of Frederick County."

ST. AUGUSTINE

St. Augustine had an operating post office before 1832.

The name, most Maryland authorities contend, honors Augustine Herrmann, who founded Bohemia Manor near here.

At the same time, taking into consideration the religious roots of the state, it might also honor the fourth-century Christian philosopher.

ST. CHARLES

St. Charles is a planned community of fairly recent origin. It was developed in the late 1960s and, according to some, carries the name of the county . . . with "saint" added for class.

ST. GEORGE ISLAND

A part of St. Marys County, St. George Island can be found in the Potomac River. St. George was patron saint of England, and the name may have been brought over. Another possibility is that it came from the St. George's River, now St. Marys River.

ST. INIGOES

The village of St. Inigoes opened its first post office in 1801. St. Inigoes Manor was patented to the Reverend Thomas Copley, a Jesuit. He named the area for St. Ignatius of Loyola (1491–1556), the founder of Copley's religious order, the Society of Jesus.

Ignatius of Loyola spelled his name both Ignatius and Inigo.

ST. LEONARD

Before 1832, this Calvert County community was known as St. Leonard's. Postal authorities dropped the "'s" in 1894.

The village takes its name from St. Leonard's Creek. It was reestablished in 1683, and an Act of Assembly of 1735 further authorized a "new and enlarged St. Leonard's Town." It is probable that the creek had lost some of its depth, so they kept moving the city downstream.

St. Leonard's name, some say, comes from St. Leonard, patron saint of captives. A more likely source would be Leonard Calvert.

ST. MARYS CITY

St. Marys City takes its name from the its county in which it resides, St. Marys. Governor Leonard Calvert laid out the original site in 1634. The first settlers arrived in the *Ark* and *Dove* on 25 March 1634, on the Feast of the Annunciation, which gives credence to the argument that the town was named for Mary, mother of Christ.

The settlers purchased land from the Indians, including the village of Yaocomico, which they renamed St. Maries.

St. Marys City served as the capital of Maryland until 1694, when that honor moved to Annapolis.

ST. MICHAELS

St. Michaels, Talbot County, was an active community as early as 1632, when Captain Claiborne from Kent Island recorded trading there. The town was originally known as Shipping Creek.

There are several possibilities for the name of this town. One suggests that St. Michaels took its name from the river on which it is located, now called the Miles River. The river's name was changed because Quaker settlers were irate at the apparent sanctification of the river and demanded the name be changed to Michaels and then to Miles.

Another source contends that Lord Baltimore liked the name St. Michaels because most of his rents came due on St. Michael's Day or Michaelmus.

The final possibility we know of contends that Edward Elliott, who came to Maryland in 1667, donated land for St. Michael's Church, and the town grew around the church.

The first post office opened here in 1801.

SALEM

Before 1832, this Dorchester County community was known as Big Mills. In 1862, the name was changed to Salem.

The town grew up around the local Methodist church, known originally as Ennal's Chapel and then as Salem Methodist Church. (See Salem, New Jersey.)

SALISBURY

Chartered and laid out in 1732, Salisbury Town was originally settled at the intersection of several Indian trails and the Wicomico River. As early as 1665, Colonel Isaac Handy opened a wharf here and called his settlement Handy's Landing. The city was named for either Wiltshire, England, or the Earl of Salisbury, a friend of the first Lord Baltimore. The more likely source is the English town, because many of the settlers traced their roots there.

In 1832, when Worcester County was formed, its border with Somerset County ran through the middle of Salisbury, much to the dissatisfaction of its residents. In 1867, Wicomico County was formed and Salisbury became that county's seat.

SANDY HOOK

Sandy Hook, Washington County, came into existence in 1832 when the Chesapeake & Ohio Canal was completed.

The original name was Keep Tryst. Sandy Hook was chosen instead after a team of horses was lost in a nearby quicksand pool.

SANDY SPRING

This Montgomery County village was founded in 1728 by James Brooke, of the De la Brooke Manor. In earlier times, a spring bubbled up through the white sand here. That spring is gone.

The first post office opened here in 1817.

SANG RUN

The Sang Run post office dates to 1837, when Elijah Friend became the first postmaster. The Allegany County town was then called Sangrun, and named for the waterway. The original name for the Sang Run was Ginseng Run.

Because of the abundance of the ginseng root, the area was called the "Sanging Ground."

SASSAFRAS

Sassafras, Kent County, is located on the Sassafras River and takes its name from the stream. The name is the English version of the Indian *winakhanne*. The town's original name was Head of Sassafras.

The sassafras tree was once abundant in this area, and many housewives harvested the root, dried it, and brewed it with water to make sassafras tea.

SAVAGE

Amos A. Williams opened the first post office in this community in 1834.

Joseph White purchased the land, the Mill Land Tract, on which Savage stands in 1753. Seventy years later, his son Gideon sold the tract, then called Mill Land, and 500 acres of another tract, White's Contrivance, to John Savage, a merchant from Philadelphia.

Savage and the Williamses developed a cotton mill which they named the Savage Manufacturing Company, at the falls of the Little Patuxent River in 1821–22. In 1835, when the Baltimore & Ohio's Washington Branch was completed, the station was called Savage Station.

SEAT PLEASANT

The original name of this Prince Georges County community was Chesapeake Junction, because it was at the junction of the railway line to the Chesapeake beaches.

Roughnecks in the area gave Chesapeake Junction a bad name, so townspeople, in an effort to change the image of the town, decided to change its name. From a list that included Gregoryville, Seat Pleasant, Advance, Pine Pond, and District Line, they decided on 20 May 1906 to rename Chesapeake Junction to Seat Pleasant . . . because it sounded like a nice place to live.

SECRETARY

Secretary, Dorchester County, opened its post office in 1890 with James H. Howard as postmaster. The town was named for Lord Henry Sewall, secretary to George Calvert, the third Lord Baltimore.

In 1661, Sewall was granted several thousand acres on which he built Carthegena, better known as "My Lady Sewall's Manor." Shortly after construction was completed, Lord Sewall died and Lady Jane Sewall married her husband's boss: Charles Calvert. The nearby Warwick River was once called Secretary Sewall's Creek. Sewall was later dropped from the name.

SELBYSPORT

Moses A. Ross opened the first post office in this community in 1833.

The name comes from Evan Shelby (or Selby), who surveyed the land here in 1772 and laid out town lots six years later. The "-port" comes from the pioneers' intention to use the Youghigoheny or a canal for transportation.

SENECA

Seneca is a village which lies within a mile of Seneca Creek, from which it takes its name. An earlier name was Middlebrook Mills.

The current name is from the Algonquian and means "stony, and activity in regard to stones." The area was known in 1866 for its fine red sandstone and the nearby Quarry Point.

Seneca is also the name of one of the Iroquois tribes.

SEVERN (— Grove, — Park)

The post office at Severn was first opened in 1875 by Benjamin F. Clark. Service was discontinued, and then returned in 1881.

In 1914, when Edward Grotzky was appointed first postmaster of Severn Park, Anne Arundel County, the community's name was Boone. The name was changed to Severna Park in 1925. Sometime later, the postal service streamlined the name.

The source of the town's name is obviously the Severn River, though some historians think there is a different source. One source says the name is derived from Wallis T. Severn, a nineteenth-century leader of Baltimore's bar. Loyal to the Union at the outbreak of the Civil War, Severn never forgave the federal government for imprisoning dissenters, himself included.

This origin is unlikely because the name preceded the attorney by many years. As early as 1670, Augustine Herrmann referred to the stream as "Seavorn R." The namer was probably Colonel Edward Lloyd, a Scotsman who commanded armed forces in the area in 1650. He bestowed Scottish names on other waterways, such as the Wye and the Tred Avon.

SHADY SIDE

Shady Side has one of those names the post office seems to enjoy changing. When the post office was opened in 1886, the town was called Shady Side. Later, it was changed to Shadyside. Sometime after 1971, it reverted to its original form.

The name is descriptive of the area. Before the coming of the post office, the town was known as Sedgefield, after the sedge grass common to marshy areas. One source contends that, in earlier times, the town was called Parrishe's Choice and Rural Felicity. Those two names appear to be fanciful names for local land tracts, not actually the name of the town.

SHARPSBURG

Sharpsburg was the site of the Civil War battle of Antietam. Union army officials identified battles by the name of the body of water near to the action; the Confederates, the nearest town.

Joseph Chapline, a real-estate investor, laid out a town on Joe's Tract in this area in 1763. He called the development Sharpsburg, for Governor Horatio Sharpe, the Calvert's representative in Annapolis. Sharpe served as governor from 1753–69.

SHARPTOWN

The original name of this Wicomico County community was

Twiford's Wharf, and then Slabtown. The name Sharptown honors Governor Horatio Sharpe. (See Sharpsburg.)

SHAWAN

This Baltimore County town's name was first mentioned in a 1714 land grant as "Shawan Hunting Ground."

The name is derived from the Indian word for "south." One source, however, considers it a variation of the tribal name Shawnee. This makes a great deal of sense when one considers the use of "hunting ground" in the original land grant name.

A post office opened under this name, and went through a variant spelling or two, in 1837.

SHELLTOWN

The name of this Somerset County village was derived the same way as Wicomico County's Bivalve . . . from the presence of oysters.

When the post office opened here, the community was already harvesting the oyster beds along the Pocomoke River, and calling itself Shell Town.

SHERWOOD

One of the first settlers to this Talbot County area was Major Hugh Sherwood (1632–1710), who arrived in Maryland in 1661. He later served with the state militia and the Maryland General Assembly.

SHERWOOD FOREST

Sherwood Forest, Anne Arundel County, opened its first post office in 1933 with William E. Hoffman as postmaster.

Local residents refer to it as "The Forest," and most suggest the fanciful name to originate with the domain of the Sheriff of Nottingham, Robin Hood's nemesis.

SHOWELL

The original name for this Worcester County community was St. Martin's. The name was changed in the late nineteenth century to honor Lemuel Showell III, an early developer of Ocean City who was instrumental in bringing the railroad to Worcester County.

One source suggests the Showell family was one of the largest slave-owning families in Maryland, but Lemuel's descendants, Eli and Samuel Showell, of Worcester County, were not slave holders.

SILESIA

Silesia takes its name from the European district.

SILVER HILL

Tradition has it that the name of this community came from an incident that took place in the early days.

As rumor has it, a country-store customer lost a silver buckle, and the townspeople spent the better part of a day searching for it.

SILVER RUN

This Carroll County community's name first appeared on a post office door in 1871. The name came from the presence of mica in the nearby stream. See Silver Spring.

SILVER SPRING

Another bedroom community of Washington, D.C., this Prince Georges County locale was named for a nearby spring.

According to local tradition, there were mica flakes scattered across the bottom of the spring, and when sunlight touched the water, it looked like glittering silver.

Another story has it that the town grew around the mansion of Francis Preston Blair (1791–1876). Blair's horse ran away and was caught at the spring, which Blair noticed had "very cold water bubbling up with white sand in it which looked like silver." Blair, captured by "the beauty of the spot, and with its fine timber," bought the land and built his house.

SINEPUXENT

Sinepuxent, Worcester County, takes its name from the Sinepuxent Neck. The word comes from the Algonquian *sine*, meaning "stone." The rest of the name probably refers to a "watered place, swamp."

SNOW HILL

Snow Hill was founded in 1642, laid out by order of the General Assembly four years later, and named for a section of London. In 1742, Snow Hill became the seat of Worcester County.

Colonel William Stevens, who helped develop both Berlin and Pocomoke City, named the land he owned here Snow Hill—for his home in England. Another source, Civil War author George Alfred Townsend, states in his book *The Entrailed Hat* that Snow Hill got its name from the tons of white sand that piled up here after a violent storm. Townsend's book, however, was a novel.

A post office was opened under the Snow Hill name in 1792.

SOLOMONS

When Charles B. Solomon opened the post office in this Calvert County location, he called the town Solomon's Island. The name was shortened by postal authorities in 1884.

Another source contends the original name of the island was Somervell's Island, named for the plantation of Alexander Somervell. The postmaster's name is the more likely choice.

SPARROWS POINT

The community of Sparrows Point was created early in the twentieth century, complete with a planned company town and golf course. The name, however, has a much earlier origin.

In 1652, Lord Baltimore granted land at the Patapsco River Neck to Thomas Sparrow, and since that time, the area has carried his name.

SPENCE

One of the earliest settlers in this Worcester County area was Adam Spence, but the town remembers one of Adam's descendants: Judge Ara Spence (1793–1866), who lived in Mansion House. He was a community leader, and after his death, the town was renamed in his honor.

STATE LINE

State Line, Washington County, sits on the boundary line between Maryland and Pennsylvania.

STEVENSVILLE

Stevensville, Queen Annes County, is located on Kent Island. It is considered the oldest town within the county.

The original name was Broad Creek, so named because it is near that waterway. The name was changed, we are told, "in recent years to honor Maryland's twentieth governor, Samuel Stevens (1823–25)."

STILL POND

This community takes its name from the nearby Still Pond Creek.

The waterway's name is a corruption of "Steele's Pone." Steele refers to an early English settler who "favored" this stream. "Pone" was an old English word used to describe "favorite" or "pet."

Because Still Pond was at the intersection of several roads, its original name was Four Corners. Still Pond was incorporated in 1908.

STOCKTON

Stockton was named for New Jersey's Richard Stockton, one of the men who signed the Declaration of Independence. At least, that is the origin proposed by one of the leading authorities.

Stockton was known as Sandy Hill in its earliest incarnation, and then as Ticktown. It became Stock Town by the Civil War. Before the railroad reached here, cattlemen herded their livestock to a nearby assembly spot. When the railroad finally arrived, the town fathers tried to change the name to Hursley, but the name never stuck.

STREET

In 1774, a group of Scotch-Irish Presbyterians settled in this area and called their settlement Highland . . . for obvious reasons. When the post office opened, it called itself Street. Townspeople who lived in Highland gave their address as Street, a right confusing situation. As in many cases, the post office triumphed.

Records indicate that before the Revolution, Thomas Streett patented a local tract and called it Streett's Hunting Ground, above the Rocks of Deer Creek. He was living on his land in 1774.

SUDLERSVILLE

One of the first members of the Sudler family to settle in the Queen Annes County area was Joseph Sudler, a member of the grand jury in the late seventeenth century. The town was called Sudler's Cross Roads when the post office opened in 1811.

The name was reduced to its present size in 1839, when the railroad arrived.

SUITLAND

Suitland, Prince Georges County, is the home of Andrews Air Force Base, best known by Americans as the base of Air Force One.

The name came from Colonel Samuel Taylor Suit. Suit, a state senator, lived in the area from 1834 until his death in 1888.

SUNDERLAND

The post office at this Calvert County location was opened in 1840 by its first postmaster, Richard Sunderland. He called it Sunderlandville. The name was changed in 1842 to Sunderland. In 1856, the name reverted to Sunderlandville. By 1868, the name was changed to Chestnut Hill. Fourteen years later, it became Sunderland.

Some suggest the name came from Charles Spenser, the Earl of Sunderland, who in 1718, became Great Britain's prime minister. Unfortunately for those individuals, Richard Sunderland was the name donor.

The Sunderland family traces its roots back to John Sunderland, who arrived in the county before 1669 and settled on his Hopewell Tract. The tract is not far from the center of the present town.

SUNNYBROOK

Tradition has it that this Baltimore County town was named Sunnybrook when the post office opened in King's Hotel in 1870. The name was selected to reflect the best aspect of Overshot Run, a nearby stream.

SWANTON

This Garrett County community began its existence as part of Allegany County in 1857, when Thomas W. Archer opened the post office here and called it Swantown. The name was later changed to its current spelling.

In 1823, the town was noted as Swan's Mill, which suggests the name was reflective of a family name.

SWEET AIR

Sweet Air, Baltimore County, takes the name of one of Charles Carroll's family estates in Ireland.

The Sweet Air estate was part of a 1704 grant to Carroll. The 5,000-acre grant was divided into "Ely O'Carroll," "Litter Luna," "Clynmalira," and "Sweet Air." All were Carroll landholdings back home.

TAKOMA PARK

Takoma Park was named by Benjamin Gilbert on the advice of his friend Ida Summy in 1883–84. Gilbert was the creator and developer of this Washington, D. C., bedroom community.

The name, according to local historians, was drawn from Washington State's Mt. Rainier. Before 1902, the mount was called Mt. Tacoma. This community's name has also been spelled with a "c" instead of a "k." See Mount Rainier.

TANEYTOWN

Taneytown, Carroll County, was once part of Frederick County, where a Taneytown post office was opened before 1832, probably around 1795.

The most popular choice for the name source is Roger Brooke Taney (1777–1864), chief justice of the United States. At the time of the naming, he was attorney general. Throughout his career, Taney was a proponent of federal supremacy over states' rights. In the 1857 Dred Scott decision, Taney held that Congress could not forbid slavery in the territories and that slaves did not have the rights of citizens. But Maryland historians do not agree with this origin.

There were members of the Taney family (originally de Tani) in Maryland before 1655. The first American member of the French Huguenot family was Michael. The town was founded in about 1740–50 by either Frederick or Augustine Taney. Most lean toward Augustine who was the better-known member.

TANYARD

The name of this Caroline County community recalls an early industry: the use of tannin bark to change hides into leather.

TASKER CORNERS

This Garrett County community was sometimes referred to as Tasky Corners, but the name goes back to members of the Tasker family. Records show that Thomas Tasker, who died in 1700, settled in Calvert County in about 1668. His son, Colonel Benjamin Tasker, helped develop the iron mines in Anne Arundel County.

T.B.

The local legend in Prince Georges County is that early settlers found initials carved in either a tree or rock. One theory was they were put there by Thomas Blandford, an early landowner.

Others are not too sure about Blandford. The first postmaster, Francis T. Monroe, was appointed in 1862. He contended that the initials were carved into a boundary stone, with "T" on the west, and "B" on the east. He claimed the stone marked the boundary between the land of his great-grandfather, William Townsend, and the land of Major Thomas Brooke.

TEXAS

It is usually accepted that the name for the Lone Star State is the translation of an Indian word for friendship.

This Baltimore County community took the name of the state, some say, because a number of Marylanders were stationed in Texas during the Spanish-American War. Unfortunately for that theory, the town was named about twenty-five years before that war.

A more realistic theory gives the name to the town for the men from Maryland who fought for Texas independence.

Before being named Texas, the community was known as Taylor Hall, then Ellengowan in 1850.

THOMAS

Wildy Jackson Cook was the first postmaster of Thomas, Dorchester County, when the office opened in 1903. The town was named for one of the many members of the Thomas family that settled here. The Thomases were a popular family; there are eleven places in Maryland that include Thomas in their name.

Another source cites Philip E. Thomas, first president of the Baltimore & Ohio Railroad, as the name source.

THURMONT

Legend has it that Jacob Weller and his family, while traveling west, stopped here in Frederick County in 1751 to nurse a sick child—and stayed. Weller family members developed industries that required mechanics and, by 1811, the town was being called Mechanicstown —with its own post office by 1815.

After the railroad made the area accessible around 1894, the town became a popular resort. The townspeople renamed their home Thurmont, "gateway to the mountains." Thurmont is also the entrance to Camp David, the White House retreat.

One source suggests the name was drawn from a local family, named Thurman, Thurmand, Thurmon, or Thurmond, but the earliest listings of families with that name are in the late 1960s.

TILGHMAN

This community was named for Tench Tilghman (1744–86).

Tilghman was one of Washington's trusted aides. The general honored Tilgham by rousing him from his sickbed, and sending him to bring the news of the British surrender at Yorktown to Congress in Philadelphia. He arrived in Philadelphia at 3 a.m. 22 October 1781, and was almost arrested for disorderly conduct: Congress already knew of the surrender—the French had alerted them. Regardless, Congress voted Tilghman "a horse properly caparisoned, and an elegant sword, in testimony of their high opinion of his merit and ability."

Tilghman died a few days shy of his forty-first birthday due to "hardships encountered during the war."

The earliest member of the Tilghman family in Maryland was Dr. Richard Tilghman, who came to Maryland in 1657, and became the county sheriff three years later.

TILGHMANTON

The name of Tilghmanton, Washington County, honors the tale of the patriotic Dr. Frisby Tilghman. In 1807, the doctor became Captain Tilghman of the Washington Hussars. A year later, he was elected a delegate to the state legislature.

TIMONIUM

The name of this Baltimore County community, we are told, comes from the name of Mrs. Archibald Buchanan of Timonium Mansion.

Mrs. Buchanan, as the story goes, lost a very close friend at sea, then went blind. Known locally as "the lady of sorrows," she allegedly named her house for the tower near Alexandria, Egypt, where Mark Anthony took refuge following Actium and the desertion of his friends. Another source suggests that the morose Mrs. Buchanan likened herself to Shakespeare's Timon of Athens, another person who drew bad luck.

TOLCHESTER BEACH

A popular turn-of-the-century beach resort, Tolchester Beach, Kent County, is said to be a combination of names: "Tol-" from Tolson, for the seventeenth-century surveyor William Tolson, and "Chester" for the Chester River. Tolchester Beach sits on the Chesapeake Bay, but is several miles from the river!

TOWN POINT

Town Point sits on a "point" of land that juts into the Patuxent River in St. Marys County.

TOWSON

Established in 1685 as a stagecoach stop, Towson became the county seat for Baltimore County in the mid-nineteenth century. It was named for the Towson family, specifically Nathan Towson, who commanded the guns in the War of 1812. He also commanded artillery at the battle of Chippewa.

The town, then called Towsontown, had a post office in

service in 1827, adequate time for the tale of Nathan Towson to become legend. Others would like to confer the honor on Ezekiel Townson, who allegedly settled here in 1750, or William Towson, an innkeeper.

TRAPPE

There are several suggestions as to the source of this Talbot County community's name. On one hand, we have historians who suggest the name comes from a modification of Trappist, since French clerics built a monastery here during the early settlement.

Others think the name came from the Partridge Trap, a popular local tavern. Still others contend that the town's name came from the local practice of using traps to capture wolves and other beasts. (See Trappe, Pennsylvania.)

TRAVILAH

Travilah, Montgomery County, opened its first post office in 1883. The origin of the name is a mystery. Some authorities think it comes from a family, such as Travilla. Others think the name may originate in Travillick, Cornwall, or Treville, Herefordshire, England.

TULLS CORNER

Tulls Corner, Somerset County, takes its name from a member of the Tull family, but which one?

Even though this village did not have its first post office until 1904, it appears its history goes back a bit further. Rumbley Point in Pocomoke Sound was once Tull's Point, and there is also a Tull's Creek. In documents regarding the waterway, there is mention of a John Rhodes selling the the Salisbury Tract to Thomas and Richard Tull. The date for that transaction is 1671.

TUSCARORA

Tuscarora takes its name from the Tuscorora Creek, which empties into the Potomac River here. The waterway's name is from the tribal name for one of the confederated Iroquois tribes.

There was a time when this town was known as Licksville and the post office as Tuscarora. Around 1925, the post office moved from Tuscarora Station, but the name stayed.

TWIGGTOWN

While some might think this town was named for woody scraps of trees, that is not the case. Twiggtown, Allegany County, was named for its first postmaster, Austin D. Twigg. He opened the Twiggtown post office in 1893.

Those who like to trace the origin back far enough to be sure the name was given for a first family say that the first Twiggs moved into this area as early as 1787. These same people also contend that it was never a town or a village, merely a neighborhood.

TYASKIN

Tyaskin takes its name from the Tyaskin Creek. The name of the stream is from the Algonquian word for "bridge." The name referred to an obstruction in the stream built to assist in catching fish.

TYLERTON

Tylerton commemorates President John Tyler. President Tyler usually gets a bad rap because, as a Virginian, he supported the South during the Civil War.

UNICORN

The unicorn is a mythical animal. How it ended up as this town's name is pure conjecture. It appears the residents wanted a name that was unique, and "unicorn" is certainly unique. More likely, the name was adopted from the local Unicorn Woolen Mills, after the town grew up around the factory.

UNION BRIDGE

Union Bridge, Carroll County, was once part of Frederick County. Earlier names for the settlement include Little Pipe Creek Settlement, because the village is located on that stream, Buttersburg, because of the quality of butter the community churned and sold, and Union Bridge.

The Union Bridge name came into being in 1810, when the post office opened. Unlike almost every other "union" in Maryland, its name commemorates a bridge across the creek.

UNION MILLS

Union Mills, Carroll County, was once part of Frederick County. There was a post office in service here as early as 1803.

In the earliest days of settlement, the town was known as Meyersville, for the Peter Meyers family. About the time of the

American Revolution, Adam and Daniel Shriver built a sawmill here that was still in operation in 1878.

The name comes from the general feeling of the townspeople toward the new nation following independence.

UNIONTOWN

Uniontown, Carroll County, had a post office in operation under that name about 1815. The first recorded use of the name was in 1813; before that, the town was called The Forks. The same enthusiasm for independence expressed by the naming of Union Mills existed here.

UNIONVILLE

This Talbot County community was built around a settlement of blacks emancipated during the Civil War. The name suggests the freedmen's support of the federal Union.

UNIVERSITY PARK

The University of Maryland has a campus in this Prince Georges County location.

UPPER—

"Upper" is a locator prefix for a place-name. The word is used to indicate the northern location of a place of the same name situated to the south. We find this in Upper Crossroads, Upper Fairmount, Upper Falls, Upper Hill, and Upper Marlboro.

UPPER MARLBORO

Upper Marlboro is the seat of Prince Georges County. It was named "upper" to differentiate it from Lower Marlboro. The name for both came from John Churchill Marlborough (1650–1722), the hero of Blenheim, who was very popular in the colonies. The post office name was given in 1792, while the village's name is much older. It was bestowed the year before Marlborough died. (See Lower Marlboro.)

URBANA

Lorenzo B. Windsor opened the first post office at this Frederick County address in 1833. The name is derived from "urban," or "pertaining to a city." The town was settled in about 1830.

VALE SUMMIT

Walter Martin opened the first post office in this Allegany County community in 1882.

The name comes from the nearby Vale Run, or the nearby Vale Farm. But if one looks at a topographical map, the town's elevation is 1,987 feet above sea level, and the surrounding Dan's Mountain is at 2,898 feet. One might suspect that the town is in a small valley, or vale.

VIENNA

There was a post office in this Dorchester County locale before 1832.

The name comes from the capital of Austria, or so says one authority. He is wrong.

Vienna, in the late seventeenth century, was an Indian village called Emperor's Landing. The "emperor" in the name was the chief of the Nanticokes. When the white settlers arrived, the name of the tribe's current chief was Vinnacokasimmon. The chief negotiated a peace treaty with the settlers, but they had trouble fitting his whole name into their correspondence. Ever resourceful, the settlers abbreviated his name to Vnna—pronounced Vee ANNA. After the Indians were moved out, a town was laid out in 1706. The townfolk wanted to call it Baltimore, but since that was already in use, they settled for Vienna.

WAGNERS CROSSROADS

The name of Wagners Crossroads commemorates the Wagner family. Family member Frank Wagner was the king of the canning industry.

WALDORF

When a post office opened at this Charles County location in 1844, it was called Beantown, and Edward D. Boone was postmaster. The name was changed to Waldorf in 1880. In 1868, when the Pope's Creek Branch of the Pennsylvania Railroad opened, the station's name became Waldorf.

Some suggest the name was used to describe a "town in the woods," but a more likely source for the name is the railroad. Financier John Jacob Astor (1763–1848) was born in Walldorf, near Heidelberg, Germany, and the railroad might honor his memory with the name. His great-grandson was William Waldorf Astor. At one time the family owned the Waldorf-Astoria Hotel in New York.

WALKERSVILLE

A post office was in operation in Walkersville, Frederick County, before 1832. The name came from a local family.

The Walker family includes Patrick Henry Walker, who farmed at "Dumbarton," his Pikesville farm. He was the son of Noah Walker, who commanded the Baltimore dry goods business for years.

WANGO

This Wicomico County town takes its name from a shortening of the Indian *nassawango*, a "place between streams." A nearby stream continues to carry that name. The streams in question were the Beaverdam and Nasawango creeks.

WARWICK

Before 1832, Warwick, Cecil County, had its own post office. The name source was Sir Richard Rich, second Earl of Warwick (1587–1658); at least, that is what one "reputable" source suggests.

It is more likely that James Heath, the town's first settler, named the community. Heath, a native of Warwick, England, purchased several tracts in 1711.

WASHINGTON GROVE

Washington Grove, Montgomery County, is yet another community named for the first president.

WATERLOO

Waterloo, Anne Arundel County, had a post office in operation before 1819. The town's name comes indirectly from Napoleon's 1815 defeat at the Belgian battlefield of the same name.

The original name of the town was Spurrier's Tavern, followed by Waterloo Tavern. The name came from the tavern.

WEBSTER

Some authorities claim that this Harford County village was named for the famed orator and statesman, Daniel Webster (1782–1852). A more logical choice for the source might be Lieutenant John Webster, who repelled the British when they attempted to land on the Fort McHenry peninsula in 1814.

WELCOME

Welcome, Charles County, may take its name from the ship on which William Penn's settlers arrived in the New World, the *Welcome*. At the same time, it may not.

The name may originate with a family, since several families of that time were named Welcome and Wellcome.

WENONA

This town's name is a variation of Winona. Longfellow, in *Hiawatha*, spelled it Wenonah. The name translates to "first-born daughter."

The town, located in Somerset County, was named by postal authorities in 1883—no reason given for the choice.

WESLEY

This Worcester County village was named in honor of John Wesley (1703–91), the founder of Methodism.

WESTERNPORT

James Paris opened the Western Port post office in this Allegany County town before 1832, and the name became one word in 1953. The town is located in the western part of the state, on the North Branch of the Potomac River.

Earlier names include Western Port or George's Creek (1803), and Western Port (1825). One source decided the town had been laid out at the beginning of the nineteenth century and called Hardscrabble.

WEST FRIENDSHIP

This Howard County community had a post office in full operation before 1832. The name was given to differentiate it from the Friendship in Anne Arundel county. Samuel Gaither was postmaster. (See Friendship, Gaithersburg.)

WESTMINSTER

Originally named in 1764 for the town founder, William Winchester, the name changed around the beginning of the Revolution. However, there was a post office at this Carroll County address—by the name of Westminster—by 1800. The name apparently comes from the London borough. The town was incorporated in 1837.

The name-change took place to reduce confusion with Winchester, Virginia.

WESTOVER

The name of this Somerset County village came from a local mansion, the Westover Manor or Westover Farm.

WEVERTON

One authority tells this story about Weverton: In about 1835, Caspar W. Wever established a file factory and marble works at this site. After Wever's death, the venture collapsed.

Another tells us that the superintendent for construction of the Baltimore & Ohio Railroad in the area was another Wever. He built a great deal of the road through Ohio.

Which story is correct, no one knows for sure.

The original name for the site, postal records assure us, was Wever's Mills, but the name was changed to Knoxville in 1828. That would have been about seven years before Caspar Wever opened his mills. The name was changed back to Weverton in 1848. It appears there must be a third explanation for this town name's origin.

WHALEYSVILLE

First known as Mitchell's Store, this Worcester County village later became Turn in the Road. By 1850, the name was changed to the present one. In fact, a post office was located here under the name of Whaleysville in 1836.

It honored Peter Whaley, a local businessman, politician, and sea captain. Whaley's ancestor, General Edward Whaley, supported Oliver Cromwell and found himself on the death list when Charles II returned to the throne. Using his own funds, General Whaley established and maintained this community. Another source contends the descendant was actually Captain Seth Whaley, an eighteenth-century settler. Edward Whaley (Whalley) is buried here.

WHITEFORD

Whiteford commemorates the White family, who operated a ford here in Harford County. Or does it?

Charles Whiteford was a power in the Democratic party in the late nineteenth–early twentieth century. Could he be the source?

WHITE HALL

White Hall was the name of a famous Baltimore tavern. This town, located in Baltimore County, gained an official post office in 1833.

WHITEHAVEN
Colonel George Gale, stepfather of Augustine Washington, George Washington's father, named this Wicomico County town for his hometown in England.

The first official post office at White Haven was opened in 1809.

WHITE PLAINS
When Elizabeth Duffield opened the first post office in this community in 1849, the town carried her family name. The name was changed to White Plain in 1866, then White Plains in 1873.

Part of the name obviously is drawn from the lay of the land. The source of the name White is a little more difficult to pin down, but this area was rife with members of the White family.

One authority suggests the name commemorates the Revolutionary War battle of White Plains, New York, that took place in 1776. The authority sees this as a reasonable reference in view of the Brandywine in Prince Georges County, but this author thinks that is stretching things a little far.

WHITON
It is possible that when they changed the name of Locustville, the townspeople were honoring a local family with a rare name, Whiton. It is more likely that they named it for a family by the name of White. The townfolks pronounce this Worcester County location as WHITE-n.

WIDGEON
The widgeon is a freshwater duck that breeds in this area and is a fairly popular game bird.

This Somerset County village carries that name.

WILLARDS
Located on the edge of the Great Pocomoke Swamp in Wicomico County, Willards was originally known as Holly Swamp. In 1875, Ebenezer Davis, a rich and influential citizen, petitioned that the town be renamed to honor his son Grover. Sadly for Mr. Davis, another Grover already existed in Maryland.

A few years later, when the railroad arrived, the name was changed to Willards. The railroad's general manager was Captain Willard Thompson.

WILLIAMSBURG

In 1893, postal officials got the "h" out of Williamsburgh, Dorchester County. The original name had been official since 1858, when Isaac H. Lowe opened the post office here, though the Williamsburgh name had been in place since 1840.

Earlier names for this town included Bunker Hill and Slabtown. The town was called Bunker Hill because, as local legend has it, the battles in a local tavern rivaled those of the Revolutionary War.

WILLIAMSPORT

Following the Revolution, in 1786 to be exact, General Ortho Holland Williams (1749–94) laid out the streets of this Washington County town and gave it his name. Williams was General Horatio Gates' deputy adjutant-general.

Williamsport petitioned Congress to become the federal city. In 1791, George Washington inspected the site, and that was the end of Williamsport's race for glory.

WOOD—

Just as we saw with "Oak" and "Pine," early namers developing descriptive names tried to be specific. There were times, however, that the variety of trees prevented them from doing so. Rather than favor one tree and slight another, they used the generic "wood." In Maryland, we find this in Woodfield, Woodlawn, Woodmore, Woodstock, and Woodvile. Sometimes, such as in the case of Woodsboro, the name commemorates a family, or as with Woodstock, another location.

WOOLFORD

In the earliest days of settlement, this community was called Loomtown, because each home had its own weaver's loom. The looms were used by local housewives to transform wool into cloth. But that is not how the name came about.

One of the early postmasters balked at the name the postal authorities gave the town: Milton. He decided there was a better name, and Postmaster Samuel W. Woolford won. Woolford's ancestors arrived in the area as early as 1662.

WORTON

Worton, Kent County, was probably named for a local family, but it is also possible the name was transported from England, since the earliest records for the town under this name are dated 1765.

In England, there are Worton, Nether Worton and Over Worton, all in Oxfordshire.

WYE MILLS

This town grew up around old Wye Mill, which produced flour for George Washington's troops at Valley Forge. The name comes from the nearby Wye East River.

ZIHLMAN

The name most authorities tie to this community is Frederick N. Zihlman, a member of Congress from the sixth Maryland District in 1916.

Virginia

The history of the United States and the history of Virginia are tightly intertwined. It was at Jamestown, Virginia, in 1607 that the first English-speaking settlement in North America was established. It was also at Jamestown, twelve years later, that slavery was introduced.

Virginia was the scene of the surrender in two major American wars: the American Revolution ended at Yorktown; the Civil War, at Appomattox. Virginia is also the only state in the Union in which resides a former foreign government's capital: Richmond, seat of the Confederacy.

The Civil War took its toll on the Commonwealth. In fact, the majority of Civil War battles took place on Virginia soil. Civil War historians can hear the echoes of cannon and musket, the whiz of Minié balls and the cries of the wounded and dying at Manassas, The Wilderness, Fredericksburg, Spotslyvania, and other familiar place-names.

Virginia is known as the "Mother of Presidents," because eight United States presidents were born in the Old Dominion—George Washington, Thomas Jefferson, James Madison, James Monroe, William Henry Harrison, John Tyler, Zachary Taylor, and Woodrow Wilson. To many, Virginia is more important for another individual, a man who never was president: Robert E. Lee. Lee is held with more respect perhaps than any other Virginian save George Washington. We find Lee and Lee's lieutenants remembered in countless places throughout the state.

Tobacco has always been a major part of the state's economy, but it is one industry that has very few place names. More frequently one finds towns and villages named for land- and plantation-owners; the local postmaster; the English gentry that came to visit. And, we find a basic love of the land in the pioneers' choice of names for their homesites.

Virginia, perhaps more than any other state in the mid-Atlantic area, has a propensity toward names that came from classical literature. But, like the others, the state's names are imbued with a unique tang that is Virginia.

ABINGDON

First named Wolf Hills, because of an attack by wolves in 1760, this community became Black's Fort in 1774.

Abingdon was founded in 1778 at the junction of two Indian trails. It is the oldest incorporated town on waters draining into the Mississippi, and the county seat of Washington County.

How did it get its name? It all depends on which source you prefer. There are some who say it was named for the hometown of George Washington's mother, Mary. Some feel it was named in honor of Lord Abingdon. And, finally, others like to think of it as a remembrance of Daniel Boone's former home in Pennsylvania. Whichever the case, Abingdon is also a town in England.

ACCOMAC

The county seat of Accomac County, Accomac takes its name from the Accomacs, an Indian tribe that lived on the Eastern Shore. The

Algonquian word *accomac* (*accomack*) means "other side at." In this case, this village would be on the "other side" of the Chesapeake Bay from the other Indian villages.

In 1614, the town was known as Dale's Gift in honor of Governor Dale, who gave the land to a group who were "kerning salt." It has also been called Freeman's Plantation, Metompkin Court House, Drummondtown (for eighteenth-century landowner Henry Drummond), and Accomac Court House. The name Accomac became permanent in 1893.

ACCOTINK

Accotink is located in Fairfax County. In Algonquian, *accotink* means "uncertain."

AFTON

Afton was named by the wife of the first postmaster. Mrs. David Hansbrough, a native of Scotland, saw some resemblance in this Nelson County area to her homeland.

ALBERTA

The first name given to this Brunswick County town was Walthall's Store. Is it possible the owner was Walt Hall? The source of the current name is questionable. Some feel it was adopted from the Canadian province; others, that it was borrowed from an official of the Seaboard Air Lines Railroad.

ALDIE

In 1810, Charles F. Mercer laid out this Loudon County town. The Mercer family believed they were descended from the Mercer family that lived in Aldie Castle, Scotland.

ALEXANDRIA

The land where Alexandria sits was patented in 1657. In 1731, a warehouse was built and the village that grew up around it was named Bellhaven. The city of Alexandria was established in 1749 by a group of Scottish merchants, and named for John Alexander, who purchased the land in 1669.

Alexandria's *Gazette* is the oldest daily newspaper in continuous publication in America. It dates from 1784.

ALGOMA

The name of this Franklin County town could have ties to a region in Canada. H. R. Schoolcraft manufactured the name to represent a region bordering Lakes Superior and Huron. The *al-* is from Algonquian, and the *goma* is "lake" in Algonquian.

ALMA

The name of this village appears with some frequency across the United States. In some cases, it commemorates the 1854 battle of the Alma River in the Crimean War; in others, female children.

ALTAVISTA

This Campbell County community was named for the farm owned by Henry Lane. The name is a combination of Spanish words that translate to "high view."

AMELIA

Amelia is the county seat of Amelia County. It takes its name from the county, which honors Princess Amelia Sophia, the youngest daughter of George II.

AMHERST

Amherst derives its name from the county in which it resides.

Amherst County was named for Lord Jeffrey Amherst (1717–97), the successful British commander in the French and Indian War. It became the county seat in 1807.

ANNANDALE

The name for this community is supposed to remember the Earl of Annandale, a thirteenth-century Scottish knight.

APPALACHIA

This Wise County town takes its name from the Appalachian Mountains. Cabeza de Vaca recorded Apalachen in 1528 as the name the Indians gave to one of their provinces. It eventually became a vague name for the mountainous interior.

The town site was wilderness until 1891. The town was chartered in 1906.

Real estate developers tried to name this town Mineralville, but the South Atlantic & Ohio Railroad called their local yards

Intermont. The Louisville & Nashville named their boxcar station Appalachia. That name, tied in with the mountains, took hold.

APPOMATTOX

One of the most famous towns in Virginia, Appomattox is the site of the McLean House, where Confederate General Robert E. Lee surrendered his Army of Northern Virginia to Union General Ulysses S. Grant on 10 April 1865.

Appomattox, which became county seat for Appomattox County in 1845, takes its name from the county, which takes its name from the Indian tribe that lived along the James River, the Appomattox. Coming from the Algonquin word *apamutiky,* it translates to "a sinuous tidal estuary" or "tobacco plant country." The latter translation seems to fit the area better than the former.

Another source suggests that the name was first recorded in 1607 as Apumetec, making the name of the river Apumetec's.

ARK

This locale grew up around, and was named for, the Old Ark farm. Why the farm carried that name remains a matter for conjecture.

ARLINGTON

Arlington was brought to Virginia about 1650 as the name for the house or estate of John Custis II in Northampton County. The name was transferred to an estate bought by the Custis family in 1778, which is the site of the present-day Arlington.

ASHBURN

Ashburn was the name of the Lee family's farm in Loudon County. When a family member donated land in 1869 for the Washington & Old Dominion Railroad right-of-way, the station's name became Ashburn. The town previously had been known as Farmville.

ASHLAND

Ashland, Hanover County, began as a community when the president of the Richmond, Fredericksburg & Potomac Railroad bought land in the area. The discovery of a well that produced mineral water led to the establishment of a health resort, Slash Cottage. In his boyhood, Henry Clay lived at the cottage. The town assumed the name of his estate.

ARLINGTON. The Tomb of the Unknowns (formerly The Tomb of the Unknown Soldier) at Arlington National Cemetery is guarded twenty-four hours a day by the first Battle Group, Third Infantry (The Old Guard), U.S. Army. The site of the cemetery was once the estate of Confederate General Robert E. Lee. (Washington Convention & Visitors Bureau)

ATLANTIC
This village derives its name from the Atlantic Ocean, which is named for the Greek for "sea beyond Mount Atlas."

AUGUSTA SPRINGS
This Augusta County community takes its name from the county. The county, formed in 1738, was named for Augusta of Saxe-Gotha, mother of George III. In the early nineteenth century, the springs were reputed to have strong medicinal value.

AVON
A Shakespearean connection provided the name of this town.

AXTON
The early name for this Henry County village was Old Center. Axton Lodge, the home of a congressman, apparently was the source of the town's current name.

B BACONS CASTLE
The name of this Surry County village comes from the fact that the plantation house at this location was taken over by Bacon's followers during the rebellion of 1676.

BACOVA

Bacova, in Bath County, is a made-up name. It comes from BA for Bath, CO for county, and VA for Virginia.

BAILEYS CROSSROADS

Baileys Crossroads, Fairfax County, was named after Hachaliah Bailey, of Barnum and Bailey Circus fame. He owned land nearby and used it for winter quarters for his troupe.

BARBOURSVILLE

Barboursville was named for the estate of a Virginia governor, James Barbour. His home burned to the ground Christmas Day of 1884, and was never rebuilt. Barbour also served as a United States senator, secretary of war and represented this nation in England.

A future Supreme Court justice, Philip Pendleton Barbour (1783–1841), was born here.

BEALETON

The Fauquier County right-of-way for the Orange & Alexandria Railroad was given in 1850 by the Beale family. Supreme Court Chief Justice John Marshall (1755–1835) was born in Germantown, an earlier name for Bealeton.

BEAVERDAM

Sometime in the past, beavers apparently built a dam near this Hanover County location, and thus the name. It could also have been named after a local plantation. Beavers, however, were of great importance in the early days of the nation. They were so important, in fact, that there are more than 1,000 locations nationwide whose names celebrate the beavers and/or their dams.

BEDFORD

The county seat for Bedford County began its existence in 1782 as Liberty. In 1890, it became Bedford City. The "city" was dropped in 1912. The name is drawn from the county, which was formed in 1747, and named in honor of the fourth Duke of Bedford.

BELLE HAVEN

In the early eighteenth century, a Mr. Bell baked for the community in an outdoor oven, so the first name for this village was Bell's

Oven. In 1762, a plantation was created there and named Belle Haven. The town assumed the name of the plantation.

BELSPRING

The water rushing from a large local spring produced a ringing sound, much like that of a bell. The early residents of this Pulaski County area called the spring Bell Spring. The name was shortened to Belspring when they gave the name to the town.

BENHAMS

Benhams was named for an Indian warrior who, in 1790, warned the settlement at Castle Woods of an impending Indian attack.

BEN HUR

A friend of Lew Wallace named this Lee County town for the author's book, *Ben Hur.*

BENT MOUNTAIN

The source of the name for Bent Mountain could best be settled by a coin flip. The choices are: (1) the mountain has the shape of a horseshoe, or (2) the Bent brothers from Pennsylvania did a great deal of surveying in the county.

BENTONVILLE

Benton Roy, chief of staff of Union General James Allen Hardie's corps, donated his name for this Warren County community. His first name was used for the honor to differentiate him from his father, Gibson Roy, who was superintendent of schools.

BERGTON

Bergton, in Rockingham County, is a merger of two worlds.

The German *berg* means "mountain." The English "ton" signifies town. So, Bergton really is a "mountain town." An earlier name was West Gap, for a settler family named West. The Wests were evidently not too well-liked, since community dissent escalated to the point that the name was changed to Dovesville, for a more popular family.

Postal authorities rejected the name Dovesville, because they felt the name would conflict with Covesville, so the community made up Bergton.

BERMUDA HUNDRED

This town was named about 1613 in memory of the Englishmen who died in a shipwreck at Bermuda Town, established on the James River at the mouth of the Appomattox in 1611.

BERRYVILLE

Several paths to Winchester crossed in this location, and young men would get together at the crossroads and drink and fight. The first name for this community was Battletown. Berryville was established by the General Assembly in 1803, and named for Benjamin Berry, who divided some of his land into town lots. It serves as the Clark County county seat.

BEULAHVILLE

In Isaiah 62:4, Beulah was that vague but blessed land of the future. The concept of "Beulah" was more directly seen in John Bunyon's *Pilgrim's Progress*. This King and Queen County community's name comes from the latter source.

BIG ISLAND

The name for this Bedford County locale is simple. It is the largest island in the James River.

BIG ROCK

This site is named after, of all things, a large local rock.

BIG MEADOWS

This Page County community takes its name from the view seen from the summit of the Blue Ridge in Shenandoah National Park.

BIG STONE GAP

Big Stone Gap, first known as Imboden, for John D. Imboden, the first settler, was established at the junction of three forks of the Powell River, which created a pass, or gap, through Stone Mountain. This Wise County site replaced Imboden with Three Forks, followed by Mineral City.

When the Duke and Duchess of Marlborough visited the area, the Duke suggested Woverhampton. Thank goodness, calmer minds prevailed.

This area was the setting for John Fox, Jr.'s novel, *The Trail of the Lonesome Pine.*

BIRDSNEST

Birdsnest was originally called Bridgetown Station, but the postal people in Washington declined to accept that as the name of the post office because there was another Bridgetown in the same county. The name probably comes from one of two sources. The first possibility refers to "birdsnest" as the name given to a low-ceilinged room in a three-story house. The second probable name source is a Northampton County plantation, sold in 1842, called Birdsnest. The second is the more likely.

BLACKSBURG

A Colonel Patton settled the site of Blacksburg, Montgomery County, in 1745, calling it Draper Meadows. That settlement was destroyed by the Shawnee massacre of 8 July 1755.

The current name honors William Black, who donated land for the town, which was incorporated in 1798. It is the location of Virginia Polytechnic Institute & State University.

BLACKSTONE

Originally, this Nottoway County city was called Black and Whites because there were two taverns, one owned by a Schwartz ("black" in German), the other by a White.

The townspeople later settled on Bellefonte, but that name had already been used in Pennsylvania. Tradition has it that the city was renamed for Sir William Blackstone when it was incorporated in 1885, but the probable allusion to the Schwartz family carries more weight than the name of a British jurist.

BLACKWATER

The sawdust from the sawmills along a nearby stream turned the water black as it decayed. This Lee County town assumed the name of that gunky river.

BLAIRS

John Blair, owner of large quantities of land and member of the Virginia House of Delegates, donated the land for a Southern railroad station—and his name to the town. The "s" was added to distinguish this community from Blair, West Virginia.

BLAND

The county seat of Bland County, this community was originally called Crab Orchard Creek, then renamed Selden for James Alexander Selden. In 1891, the name was changed to match the county. Bland County, formed in 1861, honors Richard Bland, a Revolutionary War leader.

BLUEFIELD

This Tazewell County city was named, tradition tells us, for the bluegrass valley in which it is situated. The city receives its water from the Bluestone River, so there might also be a connection there.

BLUE GRASS

Blue Grass was named by the U. S. Board of Geographic Names in the early 1950s. It had formerly been called Hull's Store, and later Crabbottom. No reason for the change was given.

BLUEMONT

Originally named Snickersville, for landowner Edward Snickers, this Loudon County community decided to change its name in 1901. The name selected, Bluemont, describes its location on the Blue Ridge Mountains.

BON AIR

A popular family resort in the late nineteenth century, this town takes its name from the French for "good" and the English "air."

BOONSBORO

This village was allegedly named to commemorate a visit by Daniel Boone. Boone visited a friend before they took a trip to Kentucky.

BOWLERS WHARF

Thomas Bowler settled in Essex County in 1663, and the house he built is still standing. He established a ferry across the Potomac, and by 1730 the town was known as Bowler's Ferry. Still later, it became Bowler's Wharf.

BOWLING GREEN

The county seat for Caroline County was named for the Hoomes' family estate in England. The oldest house in town was built by Major Thomas Hoomes after he received a land grant in 1670. He donated the land for the courthouse.

BOYDTON

Boydton has been the county seat of Mecklenburg County since 1765. The town was laid out in 1812, and named for Judge Alexander Boyd, who died in his courtroom.

Randolph-Macon for Men was founded in Boydton in 1832, but moved to Ashland in 1867.

BRANDY STATION

This location was an early crossroads, called, interestingly enough, Crossroads. According to local lore, there was a tavern in town that served hard liquor. High-proof brandy was highly prized by travelers, but during the War of 1812, the supply diminished a bit. Disgruntled soldiers showed their anger, it is said, by emblazoning the word "BRANDY" in large letters on a wall of the inn. The tavern and inn became known as Brandy House.

In 1854, the Southern Railroad drove its right-of-way through town and called the station Brandy Station.

BREAKS

The ravine or gorge that cuts through the Cumberland Mountains was called "The Breaks." This community adopted that name.

BREMO BLUFF

The Bremo grant was given to General Carey C. Cooke during the Revolutionary War. The Cooke family brought the name from the village of Breamore, County Wilts, England.

BRIDGEWATER

The original town was situated on twenty acres of land owned by John and Jacob Dinkle. At one time it was called Bridgeport because it was situated near a bridge at a North River flatboat port.

Bridgewater, established in 1835, took its modified name from the covered bridge that was considered a community necessity. It is home to Bridgewater College, the first co-educational college in

Virginia, founded in 1880 as Spring Creek Normal and Collegiate Institute. The institution moved to Bridgewater in 1887 and was chartered as Virginia Normal. It became Bridgewater College in 1889. It is the first college of the Church of the Brethren to confer degrees.

BRISTOL

Sapling Grove was the name of this Washington County community in 1765. It was incorporated as Goodson, for Colonel Samuel E. Goodson, in 1765. The Virginia General Assembly changed the name to Bristol and granted a new city charter in 1890.

State Street, the main thoroughfare of Bristol, geographically bisects the boundaries of Tennessee and Virignia.

BRISTOW

Apparently, an Englishman who owned an estate in Prince William County lost it during the Revolution. The land was acquired by the state, and the community took on the estate's name.

BROADFORD

This Smyth County community is now situated next to the Laurel Creek. The earlier community was located at the widest spot on the Holston River with a valley road crossing.

The community moved about a mile to reach its new location. The older spot is now called Old Broadford.

BROADWAY

According to local legend, Broadway's name originated with a group of young hellions who liked to party in this Rockingham County area. People who were offended by their activities suggested they were on the "Broadway to Destruction." The name stuck. When the railroad arrived, the town was called Broadway Depot and, in 1854, when the post office was opened, it was shortened to Broadway. Broadway was incorporated in 1880.

BROOKE

A Colonel Brooke, a leading colonial figure, lived near this contemporary village in Stafford County. He donated his name.

BROOKNEAL

This Campbell County town commemorates the intermarriage of two families: the Brooks and the Neals.

BROWNSBURG

A petition went to the legislature in 1793 for the establishment of a village in this area. Five years later, that town had been settled by the Brown family, headed by the Reverend Samuel Brown, who was pastor of New Providence Church from 1796–1818.

BRUNSWICK

Brunswick was named for its county, formed in 1720 and named for the House of Brunswick. George I held the title of Elector of Brunswick-Luneberg.

BUCHANAN

Buchanan began its existence as Pattonsburg, for Colonel James Patton, a local landowner. The name was changed to honor Colonel Patton's son-in-law, John B. Buchanan. Buchanan was the deputy surveyor of Augusta City.

BUCKINGHAM

When first established, this town was called Mayville, then Buckingham Court House, because it was the county seat for Buckingham County. It draws its name from the county, formed in 1761, and named for the Duke of Buckingham.

BUCKROE BEACH

One tale has it that Frenchmen sent over to this continent in 1620 to plant mulberry trees and grape vines settled here. Records dating to 1617 call the area Buck Row.

There was a plantation on the site that drew its name from Buckrose, Yorkshire, England.

BUENA VISTA

The iron furnace in this area supplied cannon balls which were used by federal forces at the Battle of Buena Vista during the Mexican War. The furnace's name was adopted by the town.

Buena Vista is Spanish for "beautiful view."

BUFFALO (—Gap, —Springs)

Buffaloes once used the "gap" in the Shenandoah Mountains to move from one side to the other. A highway and railroad tracks now go through the gap. Buffalo Gap and Buffalo Springs draw their names from that memory.

BUFFALO JUNCTION

An early resort in this Mecklenburg County locale was called Buffalo Springs. After the Norfolk, Franklin & Danville Railroad was built, the area of the spur line from the station to the springs where a town grew was called Buffalo Junction.

BUMPASS

This village in Louisa County is named for one of the community's postmasters, John T. Bumpass. There have been other suggestions for this name's origin, based on the pronunciation of the word—or words.

Before Bumpass took over the job in 1860, the town was known as Second Turnout. A post office had been established in that name in 1847, at the time when the Chesapeake & Louisiana Railroad came through. The name Bumpass is actually from the French *bonpass*. Unfortunately, the French word transmogrified into Bumpass.

BURKES GARDEN

There is a charming legend about this Tazewell County site. In 1748, a group of explorers entered this area. One of them, an axman or chain-carrier by the name of Burke, planted peelings from his breakfast potatoes. A year later, when the party returned, they found a bed of potatoes growing. Voilá! Burke's Garden. Burke's Fort was located here in 1774.

BURNT CHIMNEY

This Franklin County community takes its name from the chimney that was left standing after a fire. It became a local landmark.

CALLANDS

Until 1777, this village, then called Chatham, was the seat of Pittsylvania County. The name changed to Callands for storekeeper Samuel Callands.

CALLAO

Jacob Callaway owned the store in this Northumberland County locale. When the post office was established, he wanted it to bear the name Callaway. Unfortunately, that name already applied to a Franklin County town. Callaway settled for a condensation of his surname. Callao is also a seaport in Peru.

CALVERTON

First known as Owl Run, then Warrenton Junction, this Fauquier County community was named by a family who came from Calvert City, Maryland.

CANA

When it came time for the townsfolk to select a name for the post office in this Carroll County town, they selected the Biblical name.

CAPE CHARLES

The harbor at this Northampton County site was built in 1884 and used by large steamers. The town was named for the cape, which colonists named about 1610 "in honor of the worthy Duke of York." The duke became Charles I.

CAPEVILLE

Capeville is located on the Atlantic Ocean side of Cape Charles. It is possible that, since the name Cape Charles was already in use, the townspeople settled for second-best.

CARET

The first courthouse in Essex County was near this town, circa 1665–93. The name Caret was selected by the post office. In printing, a caret is a mark showing where something is to be inserted.

CARSON

Legend has it that at the time of an Atlantic Coast Line railroad wreck in Dinwiddie County, a telegram was sent. It read: "Cars off and cars on." The last two words became the name of this community.

CARTERSVILLE

Cartersville was an overnight stop for James River traffic in the late eighteenth century. This Cumberland County community was named for a descendent of King Carter, of Carter's Grove.

CATAWBA

The origin of the name of this Roanoke County village is from an Indian tribe. There is a Choctaw word, *katapa*, which means "cut off" or "separated."

CENTER CROSS

At the spot where two highways cross near the center of Essex County is a town called Center Cross.

CENTRALIA

Centralia, Chesterfield County, was named for its location.

CENTREVILLE

The location of this Fairfax County village is equidistant from Leesburg, Middleburg, Warrenton, Georgetown, and Alexandria.

CERES

This farming community is the oldest settlement in Bland County. It was named in 1879 for the Roman goddess of agriculture.

CHAMPLAIN

Champlain, Essex County, was the early seat of the Garnett family. The farm there retains the name. Samuel de Champlain discovered the lake in 1609, so it is probable that the town took its name from the·lake and the man.

CHANTILLY

The early name for this Fairfax County community was Ox Hill. Chantilly, the name of an 1816 farm in the area, was later given to the town. The farm's name came from a French town and estate.

CHARLES CITY

Charles City is the site of the original courthouse of Charles City County, built about 1730 and named for the county. Charles City County was formed in 1634, and named for the king's son, later Charles I.

CHARLOTTE COURT HOUSE

In 1756, this town served as a storage spot for munitions and was called The Magazine. Three years later, it was called Daltonsburgh, for Catherine Dalton, wife of Lieutenant Governor Francis Fauquier. In 1836, it was again renamed. This time it was called Maryville. By 1874, it was dubbed Smithville, for a local family.

In 1901, it became Charlotte Court House, for the county which was formed in 1764 and named for Charlotte Sophia, wife of George III.

CHARLOTTESVILLE

Charlottesville, Albemarle County, was patented in 1737 by William Taylor, and established as a town in 1762. It was named for Princess Charlotte Sophia of Mecklenberg-Sterlitz, the bride of George III (see Charlotte Court House). Charlottesville was the county seat in 1761, and from May to June 1781 served as the temporary capital of Virginia. It was home to Thomas Jefferson and James Monroe. The University of Virginia, Jefferson's dream-come-true, resides here.

CHASE CITY

The village of Christiansville existed here in Mecklenburg County until 1870. In that year, new residents argued for a name change. The name agreed upon was Chase City, in honor of Supreme Court Chief Justice Salmon P. Chase (1808–73).

Chase had been the chief architect of American banking during the Civil War, and was instrumental in the issuance of "greenbacks," the paper money that helped finance the Union cause.

CHATHAM

Chatham, the county seat for Pittsylvania County, was first named Competition in 1777, when the seat was moved here from Callands.

The name was changed to Chatham in 1874, in honor of William Pitt, Earl of Chatham.

CHECK

One story claims that this village was named Check because of a local store that was a popular haunt for checker players.

CHERITON

Cheriton was once called Townfield, then Sunnyside. The current name was selected by Dr. William Stratton Stockley, a landowner. It is a modification of his first choice, "Cherry Stones."

CHESAPEAKE

Though one of the first areas explored by Captain John Smith, and settled about 1620, Chesapeake was not created until 1963, when Norfolk County and the City of South Norfolk merged.

The town, of course, takes its name from the bay. The name was first recorded in 1585 as Chesepioc; in 1608, it had become Chesapeak. It was first the name for a village, then transferred to the bay. In Algonquian, *che-sipi-oc* means "big river at."

CHESTER

It seems probable that this Chesterfield County location took its name from the county.

CHESTERFIELD

The county seat for Chesterfield County draws its name from the county, formed in 1748 and named for English politician Philip Stanhope, the Fourth Earl of Chesterfield (1694–1773).

CHILHOWIE

Chilhowie is derived from an Indian phrase used to describe the nearby valley: "valley of many deer." The Cherokees had an important village by that name in Tennessee.

The earliest name for this Smyth County community was Town House—the first frame house was built about 1748. When the railroad came through, it called the station Greever's Switch.

CHINCOTEAGUE

This Accomac County town derived its name from the Cingo-Teague tribe. The Indian name translates to "Beautiful Land Across the Water." Another possible suggestion is that the Algonquian meaning is "big stream."

The town is known for an annual roundup of wild horses. Chincoteague Island is connected to the mainland by a bridge, and is the largest inhabited island in Virginia.

CHRISTIANSBURG

Originally known as Hans' Meadows, this town was established in 1792. The city is named for Colonel William Christian, a Revolutionary War soldier who was murdered by Indians in Kentucky in 1786. Christiansburg is the county seat for Montgomery County.

In 1964, the neighboring community of Cambria consolidated with Christiansburg. Cambria formerly had been Bangs. When the legislature incorporated the town in 1878, the town changed its name to Cambria, because it sounded better.

CHUCKATUCK

This village takes its name from the Chuckatuck Creek. The name is of Indian origin and was mentioned in a land grant of 1635. A loose translation from the Algonquian comes out to "tidal basin."

CHULA

The word "chula," as in this village, is Choctaw for "red fox."

CHURCH ROAD

The community in Dinwiddie County that grew up on the road that led to a country church became known as Church Road.

CHURCHVILLE

During its settlement days, this village had one small log church used by several denominations. Later, when each denomination built its own church in this locale, the community decided to name itself Churchville, for so many churches in such a small town.

CISMONT

Nicholas Meriwether built a home on top of a hill and named it Cismont. The name is from the Latin and means "on this side of the mountain." In the late nineteenth century, however, the village was named Bowlesville for the local blacksmith, then Brown's Store, until it took the name of the nearby estate.

CLAREMONT

English settlers arrived at Claremont, Surry County, in 1607, and named the village for the royal residence in Surrey, England.

CLARKSVILLE

John Lederer visited this Mecklenburg County locale in 1669, and found Indians trading corn, pelts and tobacco. Incorporated as a town in 1818, Clarksville is named for Clark Royster, who owned property on the west bank of the Roanoke River. Clarksville is the oldest continuous tobacco market in the world.

CLEVELAND

The owner of the town's land when the post office opened in 1890 suggested the name of President Grover Cleveland.

CLIFTON

The two popular ideas on the naming of Clifton, Fairfax County, are, first, that the Wyckliffe family from England were large landowners in the county. Their name means "Cliff by the Ye"; or that the town was named by Harrison Gray Otis, whose family came from Orange-Clifton, New Jersey.

Otis was born in Marietta, Ohio, and spent the main portion of his life in that state. His rise to fame, however, did not take place until 1876 when he moved to California and he gained control of the Times-Mirror Company in Los Angeles. Otis did actually spend a few years reporting for Ohio newspapers from the nation's capital.

The name of the town may be a combination of both origin stories.

CLIFTON FORGE

This community in Alleghany County was named for James Clifton's iron furnace at Iron Gate Gorge. Before it was incorporated in 1884, it was known as Williamson.

CLINCHCO

The railroad station in this Dickenson County locale was called Clinchfield, after the Clinchfield Coal Company. The town's name is a shortened version.

CLINCHPORT

Clinchport, Scott County, is located at the confluence of Stock Creek and the Clinch River. The namers expected the Clinch to be navigable. The name of the Clinch River was, according to a quote by Dr. Thomas Walker in 1750, named for "one Clinch, a hunter."

CLINTWOOD

The early name for this community was Holly Creek. Holly Creek was renamed for Senator Henry Clinton Wood of Scott County. Clintwood became the county seat for Dickenson County in 1882.

CLOVERDALE

The Furnace Plantation, which supplied iron beginning in 1808, included John Breckenridge's plantation, Cloverdale. The community that grew up around it in Botetourt County became Cloverdale.

CLUSTER SPRINGS

This community was early called Black Walnut. Within a three-mile radius of the town are 75–100 mineral water springs.

COEBURN

Christopher Gist (Guest) was the proprietor of Guest Station, a popular stopping spot on the Guest River. The first settlement around this Wise County community was established about 1770.

The name was changed to Coeburn when the Norfolk & Western Railroad arrived in 1891. The name, as a local story goes, was a combination of the names of the railroad's chief engineer, W. W. Coe, and that of Judge W. E. Burns, of Lebanon.

COLLINSVILLE

In 1931, a member of the Collins family opened a battery-less flashlight company in this Henry County location. When the post office was established in 1945, it took the name of Collinsville.

COLONIAL BEACH

Colonial Beach is located on the Potomac, and was earlier known as White Beach. Part of the present-day Westmoreland County city is on land that was patented about 1650 by Samuel Bonum.

In the late nineteenth century there was active development of the waterfront property, and it was called Colonial Beach. By 1909, this was a flourishing resort. It has been nicknamed "Las Vegas on the Potomac."

COLUMBIA

Until 1788, the Fluvanna County village that existed at the point formed by the Rivanna emptying into the James River was called Point of Fork. The General Assembly named it Columbia.

COLUMBIA FURNACE

This community was named in 1803 when Columbia was a popular name. The word was coined during the Revolution as a Latinized version of Columbus, a heroic figure in that period. It first appeared in Philip Freneau's 1775 poem "American Liberty."

The furnace was in business for almost a century, even after being destroyed twice by Union troops during the Civil War.

CONCORD

The Old Concord Furnace supplied military supplies during the American Revolution. The name for this Campbell County community comes from three Presbyterian churches in the neighborhood: Old Concord, New Concord, and Little Concord.

COPPER HILL

A Mr. Tonycrafty was supposed to have prospected for copper in this Floyd County area.

COURTLAND

The name of the county seat for Southampton County makes sense. It is the "land of the court (house)."

Named Jerusalem from about 1750, Courtland was renamed in 1788 when it became the county seat.

COVESVILLE

This Albemarle County village drew its name from the Cove Presbyterian Church, which was established about 1769.

COVINGTON

Originally called Merry's Store for Dr. James Merry who surveyed and plotted the town, this Alleghany County town was incorporated as Covington in 1833. Merry, it seems, was related to the Covingtons of Prince Edward County, and named it for a relative.

CRADDOCKVILLE
The area in Accomack County was settled in June 1614 and, by 1820, was known as Farmer's Interest. Craddock was the name of the estate of the first rector of St. George's of Pungoteague.

CRAIG SPRINGS
This town took its name from the county, formed in 1851, which honored Congressman Robert Craig.

CRIMORA
In 1881, a landowner was approached by the Norfolk & Western Railroad to donate land for the new station. He agreed, as long as the station—and the village—was named for his sweetheart.

CROSS JUNCTION
For many years, this Frederick County town was known as Cross Junction, for its location. When a post office was established, the name naturally went along.

CROZET
Originally Waylands, for the landowners, this community honored Colonel Claude Crozet, who engineered the construction of the Chesapeake & Ohio Railroad tunnel under the Blue Ridge Mountains. He later served as president of the Virginia Military Institute.

CROZIER
When Sergeant John Abbott retired from the Army and became postmaster in this community, he requested the post office and town be named for his former commanding officer.

CULPEPER
In colonial times, this county seat was called Fairfax. But, because of confusion with Fairfax Court House in Fairfax County, this town's name was changed in 1870 to Culpeper, after the county.

Culpeper County was formed in 1748, and named for Lord Culpeper, governor of Virginia, 1680–83.

In 1749, when he was seventeen, George Washington surveyed the town for proprietor Lord Thomas Fairfax. Washington received his surveyor's license there.

CUMBERLAND

The seat for Cumberland County, this city was named for the county. Cumberland County was formed in 1748, and named for Prince William Augustus, Duke of Cumberland and second son of George II. The duke was famous for his victory at Culloden in 1746.

DAHLGREN

D

The U.S. Navy Proving Ground, in King George County, was named for Admiral John Adolphus Bernard Dahlgren.

Dahlgren was the inventor of the Dahlgren gun during the Civil War. He learned through testing that the pressure within a cannon was strongest at the breech. He had cannons built that were reinforced at that end. They were nicknamed "soda-water bottles."

Dahlgren saw service during the Civil War, and later served as chief of the Bureau of Ordnance and superintendent of the Washington Navy Yard.

DANVILLE

The earliest settlement for this Pittsylvania County city was The Ford at Wynn's Falls. William Wynne was a pioneering settler who gave his name to Wynne's Creek and Wynne's Falls.

The town was chartered in 1793 and, at that time, took on the name of the Dan River, which flows through the city.

The auction method of selling tobacco in piles of loose leaves began in 1858 at Neal's Warehouse, Danville. It was also the last capital of the Confederacy. Jefferson Davis arrived 3 April 1865, and stayed one week.

DAYTON

In the early days, this town was called Rifeville or Rifetown. Daniel Rife and his family held large quantities of land in the area. The town of Dayton was established in 1833. The origin of the name change is not clearly identified, even though there are a number of towns named for New Jersey's Jonathan Dayton (1760–1824), the youngest signer of the Constitution and the founder of Dayton, Ohio. A nephew of his lived in this area.

Fort Harrison, one of the oldest houses in Rockingham County, was built in 1749 by Daniel Harrison, as his home and also as a defense against Indians.

DEERFIELD
Deerfield was named for the local abundance of deer.

DELTAVILLE
The original name for this site was Unionville, named for the union of two churches. The name was changed when the post office was established. The land forms a delta on the Chesapeake Bay.

DENDRON
A village began in this locale in the late nineteenth century. It grew around the lumber interests near the Blackwater River. The name is taken from the Greek word *dendron*, which means "tree."

DINWIDDIE
The county seat, Dinwiddie was named for the county. Dinwiddie County was formed in 1752 and named for Robert Dinwiddie, governor of Virginia from 1751–56. Lieutenant General Winfield Scott was born here in 1786, and practiced law in this community in his younger days.

DISPUTANTA
There apparently was a great deal of dissension over the naming of this town. Someone, legend has it, suggested Disputanta—a name quickly accepted without, we fear, tongue in cheek.

DIXIE
One legend has it that this village was so-named because the good old boys used to gather there to sing Dixie.

DOE HILL
A store was in operation in this Highland County village before 1850, and the name seems to recall a day when female deer were seen here. In some localities, "doe" is given to a smaller site; "buck" to a larger one.

DOGUE

The name for this village comes from the Dogue (Doeg) tribe. The tribe had a very uncomplimentary reputation. Their name, so it is told, survives as "dawg," as in "mean as a dawg."

DOSWELL

Doswell is supposed to have the largest truck stop in the world.

The town was named for the family of Bernard Doswell, who operated a racetrack and was the largest landowner in Hanover County.

DRAPER

Draper was named for the family of Mary Draper. She apparently married a member of the Ingalls family (television's "Little House on the Prairie") and was captured by the Indians.

DRY FORK

Two small streams run together—or fork—at this location. When there is a long period without rain, the forks dry up.

DUGSPUR

An east-west road in Carroll County crossed mixed terrain, and was built with hand labor. This particular town grew up on a hand "dug" "spur" leading from the main road, and thus the name.

DUMFRIES

A tobacco warehouse, built in 1730, was the first structure in this community. The town itself was established nineteen years later.

Dumfries is the first and oldest town in Prince William County. Its name was given by John Graham, one of the first trustees, for his old home in Scotland.

Bookseller Mason Locke "Parson" Weems (1759–1825), the Anglican minister who contrived the legend of George Washington, the cherry tree and the hatchet, launched his 1808 *Life of George Washington* at 300 Duke Street (now the Weems-Botts Museum). By the time Weems died, the book had gone through 29 editions, and people everywhere believed that little George "could not tell a lie."

Benjamin Botts was the lawyer who represented Aaron Burr at his 1807 treason trial. The trial, presided over by Chief Justice John Marshall, ended, because of a lack of evidence, in an acquittal for Burr.

DUNDAS

A local story tells about a black worker on the Virginian Railroad who remarked at the end of a day's work that "We have done dis." When the railroad station was built in this Lunenburg County town, it was called Dundas.

DUNGANNON

This Scott County town was named by Captain Patrick Hagan for his ancestral home in Ireland.

DUNN LORING

Originated in 1885, Dunn Loring was developed by the Loring Land Improvement Company. The chief officers were General Lanier Dunn and a Dr. Loring, a Washington, D. C., ophthalmologist.

EAGLE ROCK

Earlier known as Eagle Mountain, this village became Eagle Rock, named for an eagle-shaped rock that overlooks the town.

EASTVILLE

The courthouse at Eastville has the oldest continuous records in the United States, dating to 1632. Earlier names for this town were Peachburg and The Horns. Eastville, incorporated in 1896, was so-named because it once was "east" of other settlements.

EDINBURG

In 1828, this Shenandoah County community was known as Shryock, for the landowner. By the middle of the nineteenth century, the post office was called Stony Creek.

Edinburg was incorporated in 1852. Early settlers, the story goes, thought they had found a second "Garden of Eden." Sadly, they did not spell it correctly.

During the Civil War, Edinburg was called the "Granary of the Confederacy." During the war, Edinburg Mills was spared when other buildings in town were burned.

EDOM

The name of this community is drawn from the Biblical country.

ELBERON

The first postmaster of this Surry County community was O. J. Cocke, who called the village Cocke's Crossroad. The current name is believed to have been transported by New Jersey natives; in New Jersey, it is a coined word for E. L. Brown, a town founder.

ELK (CREEK, Garden)

The oldest house in Grayson County was built in this Elk Creek about 1760. The town takes its name from the nearby stream, where settlers once shot an elk. English settlers were not aware of the European elk, and referred to any large-antlered animal of the deer family as an elk.

When early settlers came to Elk Garden locale they noticed elk dining in a natural "garden."

ELKO

This village takes its corporate name from that of a plantation.

ELKTON

Until the end of the nineteenth century, Elkton was known as Conrad's Store. It was named Elkton for the Elk Run, which runs through this Rockingham County town.

ELKWOOD

Elkwood was the name of the Cunningham estate. The estate, Elkwood Downs, is currently owned by Lee Sammis, a California developer.

ELLISTON

Originally Big Springs, the name was changed during the economic boom of 1880 to Carnegie City, because it had been proposed as a major steel center. In 1890, the name was changed to honor Major Ellis, who married President Tyler's daughter.

EMORY

This Washington County city was named for Bishop John Emory.

Emory is the site of Emory & Henry College, founded in 1836 by the Holston Conference of the Methodist-Episcopal Church and named for Bishop Emory and Patrick Henry, whose sister brought Methodism to the Valley.

EMPORIA

The first name for this community was Hicksford, for Captain Robert Hix, an Indian trader. The town grew where the Fort Road crossed the Meherrin River. In 1796, the town of Belfield began across the river. The two towns merged in 1887, and called the new town Emporia. The name, the plural of "emporium," means "centers of trade."

ESMONT

Esmont, Albemarle County, was named for an early house. The community was established in 1905–06.

EVINGTON

The Southern Railroad built on Campbell County land owned by Miss Evie Smith. Her name adorns the community.

EXMORE

The tradition about the naming of this Northampton County city is that it was the tenth station on the Pennsylvania Railroad south of Delaware. Ten, using Latin numerals, is "X" or, spelled out, "ex." The name Exmore more probably comes from a place in England.

FAIRFAX CITY

Fairfax (the "City" is rarely used by residents) is the seat of Fairfax County. It was named for the county, formed in 1742 and named for Lord Fairfax (1693–1781), the grandson of Lord Culpeper and proprietor of Northern Neck. When Alexandria became part of the federal city of Washington, Fairfax became the county seat.

Fairfax became an independent city in 1961, and its judicial center is the repository for the original wills of Martha and George Washington.

FALLS CHURCH

The Falls of the Potomac lent its name to The Falls Church, founded in 1732, then to the town. Falls Church, Fairfax County, was incorporated in 1875, and became an independent city in 1948. The earlier use of "falls" usually indicated "rapids."

FALLS MILLS

Tazewell County. (See Falls Church.)

FALMOUTH

This area was visited by Captain John Smith in 1608. The town was founded in 1727 and named for Falmouth, England.

Falmouth was a major trading center for the Northern Neck.

FANCY GAP

As a young man, Colonel Ira Coltrane drove wagon teams across the Blue Ridge Mountains. He always figured there was a better route than the "Good Spur Road." His choice commanded a fantastic view of the countryside, and he called it "The Fancy Gap." The village and post office adopted Coltrane's descriptive title.

FARMVILLE

Earlier known as Rutledge's Ford, Farmville was founded in 1798 as a trading and distribution center for the flat-bottomed boats that traveled up and down the Appomattox River.

It is the county seat of Prince Edward County, and the home of Longwood College, the first institution of higher learning for women in Virginia.

FERRUM

This village in Franklin County began in 1889, when the Norfolk & Western Railroad came through. The railroad surveyors were interested in an iron mine nearby. The Latin word *ferrum* means "iron."

FIELDALE

Fieldcrest Mills, a leading towel manufacturer, was located in this Henry County town in 1919. The Marshall Field group built a model community near the mills for workers.

FIRST NAMES

In the course of our research a number of place names appeared that were obviously personal names of individuals, with little more information available. Perhaps in the future we—or other researchers—will find out more about Bertrand, Colleen, Edgerton, Leda, Susan, and Vera.

FINCASTLE

This county seat was called Botetourt (County) Court House for two years. The community was planned by Israel Christian in 1770. In 1772, the legislature established the new town on forty acres of land and named it for George, Lord Fincastle.

FIVE FORKS

Five Forks, in James City County, is a crossroads town.

FLAT —

Flat Gap, Wise County, was named for that geologic cut through the mountains. Flat Rock, Powhatan County, was named for a level rock. Flat Run, Orange County, was named for the nearby stream.

FLINT HILL

Because of the presence of white flint near this Rappahannock County village, the town was named Flint Hill.

FLOYD

Originally named Jacksonville for President Andrew Jackson, this town became the county seat and was subsequently named for the county. Floyd County was formed in 1831, and named for John Floyd, Virginia governor from 1830–34.

FORD

Ford, Dinwiddie County, was named for Fred Ford, the first station agent for the Norfolk & Western Railroad. The town was sometimes called Ford's Depot.

FOREST

Established in the 1850s, this community draws its name from "Poplar Forest," Thomas Jefferson's home, which was nearby.

FORK UNION

At one time, several denominations worshipped in the same church, a "union" church, in this area. The town is situated not far from the fork of the James and Rivanna Rivers, ergo the name!

FORT BLACKMORE

Fort Blackmore, Scott County, was named for Captain John Blackmore, a member of the family that first settled at the mouth of Stony Creek on the Clinch River in 1774.

FORT DEFIANCE

The Augusta County community of Fort Defiance was named when the Chesapeake Western Railroad built through the community in 1874–75. The name commemorates a fort built around the Old Stone Church in 1755. According to local residents, there was an escape chamber in the floor of the church.

FORT MITCHELL

Local legend has it that a most popular lady by the name of Mitchell lived there. When curious about the location of her current heart-throb, people would ask: "Who's holding down the fort?" This question is supposed to have created the name.

FRANCONIA

The owner of Franconia Farms, Fairfax County, granted right-of-way to the Richmond, Fredericksburg & Potomac Railroad and had the station named after the property. Franconia was the name of a medieval German duchy.

FRANKLIN

There are several suggestions about the source of this town name.

Some suggest that a man named Franklin operated a store here. After all, the previous name was Franklin Depot. Another source thinks that a railroad foreman announced "This shall be Franklin." Yet a third source claims that it was named for Benjamin Franklin, America's Renaissance Man.

FRANKTOWN

When this Northampton County town was first settled in 1764, it was called New Towne. When the village grew, Frank Andrews opened his store in 1764 and the town became Frank's Towne, which was shortened to accommodate postal authorities.

FREDERICKSBURG

Though officially founded and given its name in 1727, a grant for the town had been made in 1671. Fredericksburg had been settled as early as 1676, when settlers began to build a fort there. The city was named for Frederic, Prince of Wales and father of George III. Frederic(k) is the Anglicization of Friedrich. Fredericksburg was the Spotsylvania county seat from 1809–38.

It was George Washington's boyhood home, and the site of a bloody Civil War battle. The first drugstore in America was opened in Fredericksburg, and the site is now the museum of the American Pharmaceutical Association. Mary Washington College is also located in this town. Named for George Washington's mother—her home and tomb are nearby—the college was created by the Virginia legislature in 1908.

FREDERICKS HALL

Fredericks Hall, Louisa County, was named for Frederick Overton Harris, the first president of the Louisa Railroad.

FREE UNION

When founded, this Albemarle County village was Nicksville, named for an African-American blacksmith. The name changed when a free union church was established.

FREMONT

This Dickenson County site may be named for General John C. Fremont, explorer, presidential candidate, and Union general.

FRONT ROYAL

Front Royal, Warren County, began as a frontier village called Hell Town. Until 1788 it was known as Lehewtown. Peter Lehew owned 200 acres where the town stands.

In 1788, it became Front Royal. A giant oak stood in the public square; the "royal" tree of England. The square was used for drilling militia, and local legend says that frustrated military officers would order their unruly troops to "front the royal oak," or face it. Jokesters in the audience would repeat the command over and over again. This, they say, is how Front Royal got its name.

Belle Boyd, the Confederate spy who charmed Union secrets from her lovers, lived here.

G GALAX

A decorative mountain evergreen called galax thrived in this Carroll County area. The town originally was called Bonaparte.

GATE CITY

This town has gone through a succession of names, starting with Winfield. It later became Estillville, for Judge Estillville of Abingdon. The postal authorities made the community change the name because it feared confusion with Esselville. The name selected, Gate City, was suggested because the town and the nearby Mocassin Gap were really "gateways" to the western coal fields.

GLADEHILL

This name equates to an open place in a forest atop a hill.

GLADE SPRING

The Norfolk & Western Railroad called the station at this site Passawatomie. Unfortunately, that name did not take hold with the community. The townspeople called it Glade Spring, for a spring that erupted in the middle of a glade. They even named their community church Glade Spring Presbyterian Church.

GLADYS

First called Connelly's Tavern for a local watering spot, this Campbell County town became Pigeon Run, because pigeons visited each year to feast on acorns and nuts in neighboring forests. In 1890, when the Norfolk & Western Railroad opened its station, the station was called Woodlawn. Later it was changed to Gladys in honor of a railroad stockholder's daughter.

GLASGOW

Part of the town of Glasgow was developed in 1890 on the Glasgow family homestead. Novelist Ellen (Anderson Gholson) Glasgow (1874–1945) was a descendant of that family. In 1897, Glasgow wrote *The Descendent*, the first novel in a series that mirrored Virginia's social and political history during her lifetime. She received the 1941 Pulitzer Prize for the last novel in the series, *In This Our Life*. Another authority suggests this particular town was named in anticipation of the settlement becoming a manufacturing town.

GLEN ALLEN

In the late nineteenth century, Benjamin B. Allen built a resort, Glen Allen, in the northwest corner of Henrico County. The name of the resort ultimately became the name for the community. The word "glen" was very popular in the nineteenth century—introduced through the writings of Sir Walter Scott.

GLEN LYN

Parkinson Shumate's Ferry was the original name of this Giles County town. John Toney settled here in 1750 and called it Montreal, then Mouth of East River. Later, laborers building the Norfolk & Western Railroad called it Hell's Gate. It became Glen Lyn, "lovely glen," in 1883.

GLEN WILTON

This town in Botetourt County was named by out-of-town iron workers where a furnace was established.

GLOUCESTER

When first established, this town was Botetourt Court House; its courthouse dates back to 1761. The old Debtors Prison at Gloucester dates from the mid-eighteenth century. It was named for the county, which was formed in 1651 and named for Gloucester, England.

GLOUCESTER POINT

In colonial times, this Gloucester County location was called Tyndall's Point. A fort was built there as early as 1607. Lord Cornwallis used it as an outpost at Yorktown in 1781.

GOLDVEIN

The name on this site is all that remains to remind the modern generations of the gold rush that took place in this area.

GOOCHLAND

Goochland is the seat of Goochland County, and drew its name from the county. Goochland County was formed in 1727, and named for Sir William Gooch, Virginia governor from 1727–49.

GORDONSVILLE

Beale Tavern was located at what is now the junction of Routes 15 and 33. In 1787, Nathaniel Gordon arrived, purchased more than a thousand acres and built the Gordon Inn. The Orange County community that grew up around the inn became known as Gordonsville. The railroad reached Gordonsville in 1840.

GOSHEN

This settlement was originally called Goshen Bridge. The name is a Biblical allusion referring to fruitfulness and fertility—at least, that is what the settlers wanted to convey. Goshen was the land of the Israelites in Egypt. The Bible refers to it as a country for sheep.

GRAFTON

Formerly called Cockletown, the name of this town was changed to Grafton in 1890. It seems that a traveling Baptist preacher established a congregation here in 1783 and named the Grafton Baptist Church after his Massachusetts hometown. The Virginia town adopted the church's name.

GREAT FALLS

This Fairfax County community takes its name from the thirty-five-foot-high "cataract" on the Potomac River. The river crashes down seventy feet at this location as part of a series of rapids. It is quite a popular area for white-water rafting and canoeing.

GREENBACKVILLE

According to a local origin story, an acre of ground or an acre of marsh in this area was sold in 1866 for $100, and the buyer covered the amount with "greenbacks," the paper currency issued by the U.S. government in 1862.

GREEN BAY

When the Southern railroad station was first opened, the company looked around the area for a fitting name. One official noticed a small lake nearby—covered with green moss. They created that name for the station, and when the post office opened, it followed suit.

GREENVILLE

Located in Augusta County, this community was named for Revolutionary War General Nathanael Greene (1742–86), of Warwick, Rhode Island. Washington & Lee College began near here.

GRETNA

Gretna suffered from schizophrenia before receiving its present name. At the same time that the post office was called Elba, the railroad station was known as Franklin Junction. The name Gretna comes from the Scottish town of Gretna Green, famous as the marrying place for eloping English couples.

GROTTOES

In its earlier days, this Rockingham County community was called Mt. Vernon Forge, then Shendun. In 1890, it was changed to Grottoes, from the Grottoes of Shenandoah.

GRUNDY

When the post office was opened in 1857, this community was called Mouth of Slate. The name was changed a year later to Grundy when the town became the county seat. It was named for a Texas senator who was in office when the county was formed.

GUINEA

This Caroline County town was sometimes called Guiney's, for a family from Guinea. In the colonial period, the word "guinea" was first used to describe natives of the Guinea Coast. Later, it became a catchall phrase referring to anyone with African-American origins.

General Thomas J. "Stonewall" Jackson (1824–63) died in a nearby house, after being wounded at Chancellorsville.

GUM SPRING

On old Three Chopt Road in Louisa County ran a spring where many travelers stopped to water their horses. Near the spring was a gum tree, and people used it as an identifying sign. The town took on that name.

GWYNN

Gwynn's Island was named for Hugh Gwynn, a member of the House of Burgesses. Lord Dunsmore and his troops were driven from the island in 1776.

HALIFAX

Established in 1792 as the county seat for Halifax County, this town was named for the county. Halifax County was formed in 1752, and named for George Montaga Dunk, the Earl of Halifax.

HALLWOOD

The land about Hallwood had been acquired by the Shae family in the eighteenth century. When Henry Hall married Mary Shae, he received a portion of land in Accomack County, which became Hallwood. The town was incorporated in 1958.

HAMPDEN-SYDNEY

Hampden-Sydney was named for two martyrs: John Hampden (1585–1643), member of the English Parliament, and The Reverend Algernon Sidney. It is possible that the townspeople did not think the "i" in Sidney carried as much snob appeal as the "y."

HAMPTON

Before the English settled this area, the Indians called it Kecoughtan, or "inhabitants of the great town." The city was established by law in 1680, and named—in a shortened version—for the Earl of Southampton.

Settled in 1610, Hampton is the oldest continuously English-speaking settlement in America. In 1619, it was one of the original boroughs in the Virginia legislature. It was established as a town and port in 1705, and incorporated in 1849.

HANOVER

John Sheltons, whose daughter married Patrick Henry, operated the Hanover Tavern. The courthouse dates to 1735.

The county seat for Hanover County, this town was named for the county. Hanover County was formed in 1720, and named for the Electorate of Hanover, the province of England's George I.

HARBORTON

Originally Hoffman's Wharf, the name of this Accomack County town was changed in 1893. It was an important landing for steamers until the arrival of the railroad.

HARMONY

Halifax County. (See Harmony, Pennsylvania.)

HARRISONBURG

About 1739, Thomas Harrison settled at the crossroads of an Indian path and the Spotswood Trail. In those days, the town was called Rocktown.

Harrisonburg was established in 1780 on fifty acres of land donated by Harrison. The town was incorporated in 1849, and became an independent city in 1916. It is also the county seat for Rockingham County.

Harrisonburg is the home of James Madison University, established in 1908 as the State Normal and Industrial School for Women. After a number of modifications of its name, it became Madison College in 1938. In 1967, Madison went coeducational.

HARTWOOD

Hartwood, Stafford County, reflects what life was like in this area before settlement. The name is a combination of "hart," for the male deer or bull elk, and "wood," for the area the deer once ran.

HAYES

Originally called the "Hook," the name of this Gloucester County community was changed when a store opened. It was then called Hayes' Store. The store has been eliminated from the name.

HAYFIELD

There is a tale told of an incident that took place shortly after the French and Indian War. Several men were cutting grass for hay, near the present-day location of Hayfield's post office, when they were set upon and murdered by Indians. Throughout the years, no other version of the naming of this Frederick County town has been accepted as a possibility.

HAYMARKET

In the eighteenth century, this town was called Red House.

William Skinner, who had received a large amount of land through an inheritance in 1752, laid out the town in 1798. He named it a year later for a famous racecourse in London.

HAYSI

Though this Dickenson County community sounds like a Japanese car, its name comes from Charles M. Hayter and his store partner, a Mr. Sypher. Together, they became Haysi.

446

HEALING SPRINGS

This community was named for its mineral springs. The naming probably was influenced by the Biblical story of the pool of Siloam.

HENRY

This site was first called Alumine. The railroad station opened as Henry, for the Henry County line, even though the post office is in Franklin County.

HERNDON

This Fairfax County spot was named for Captain William Herndon, who was lost at sea in 1857.

HIGHLAND SPRINGS

Highland Springs is located in an elevated area blessed with a number of springs that run down the hills and slopes. Apparently the townspeople took that into consideration in their naming.

HIGHTOWN

At an elevation of 3,200 feet, Hightown is the "highest" town in Highland County.

HILLSBORO

This Loudon County village is named for its location in the gap of Short Hill Mountain.

HINTON

Because of sympathy for the Union cause during the Civil War, this Rockingham County community had its name changed. Originally named Karicofe, for a local family, the name was changed to honor Confederate Colonel Hinton, who lived on nearby Muddy Creek.

HIWASSEE

Hiwassee, in Pulaski County, derives its name from a Cherokee Indian word that translates to "meadow."

HOLLAND

The first merchant in this locale was Z.T. Holland. The first Ruritan

Club was formed here in 1928. A Ruritan group, half of which must be farmers, strives through community service, fellowship, and good will to improve life in rural communities.

HOLLINS

Hollins, Roanoke County, was named to honor Mr. and Mrs. John Hollins, of Lynchburg. The Hollinses were financial supporters of the coeducational Valley Union Seminary, founded in 1842. Ten years later, the seminary became Hollins Institute, the state's first chartered college for women. It is now Hollins College.

HOPEWELL

Hopewell is an outgrowth of the old City Point, founded in 1613 by Sir Thomas Dale as the second English settlement in America. City Point was previously Charles City Point, and before that Bermuda City. In 1622, Indians wiped out the population. The town was revived during the Civil War and then again waned.

Frances Epes patented a large tract of land in 1735, including the original Charles City Plantation. A portion of the Epes' estate was called Hopewell, for *Merchant's Hope*, the ship that brought Epes to this continent.

Hopewell annexed Old City Point in 1923. Prior to America's entry into World War I, E.I. DuPont, with contracts for gun cotton from England and France, built a plant on the site of Hopewell Farms, and again restored life to the community.

HORNTOWN

The most logical explanation for the naming of this Accomack County town is its location, where two branches of the Savage Creek resemble a pair of horns. Another legend suggests that the local peddlers tooted horns to draw attention to their wares.

HORSEPEN

At an earlier time, a horse corral occupied this location.

HOT SPRINGS

This Bath County town draws its name from the mineral springs that were supposed to have medicinal qualities. The temperature of the springs at Hot Springs ranges from 90–103.8 degrees Fahrenheit. The earliest hotel was built in 1766, and the major industry of this town is currently The Homestead, a world-class hotel.

HUDDLESTON

This Bedford County community, though the name is misspelled, was named for Henry Huttleston Rogers, financier of the Virginian Railroad. It was named for him upon his death in 1910.

HUNTLY

The area of Rappahannock County where Huntly is situated was once well known for its fine hunting.

HURLEY

This Buchanan County town was named for the family of S.B. Hurley, the founder of the Mountain Mission Home for underprivileged children and orphans.

IDA

Two suggestions for this Page County site are that it was named for a woman, or for Mount Ida, from Greek mythology.

INDEPENDENCE

In 1849, a fight raged between Old Town and Elk Creek about which town should be selected as the county seat. A third group stood detached, and when asked where their loyalties rested, their spokesman said, "We're independent. We are not taking sides." County officials decided, based on that statement, the story goes, to locate the courthouse where the independent people lived. The county seat was then named Independence.

INDIAN VALLEY

Tradition has it that this area was once the summer hunting grounds of the Cathaway Indians, who lived in what is now West Virginia. Archeological research, however, proposes that the artifacts indicate the Indians came from a Cherokee tribe in North Carolina.

IRON GATE

The Jackson River cuts a gap through White Mountain. The Alleghany County town downstream takes its name from that gap.

ISLE OF WIGHT

County seat for Isle of Wight County since 1800, this city was named for the county. Isle of Wight County was originally named Warrascoyak, for Indians who lived there, when it was formed in 1634. Three years later, the county's name was changed to that of an island in the English Channel.

IVANHOE

Ivanhoe was named for the novel by Sir Walter Scott.

IVOR

This Southampton County town was named by the wife of a Norfolk & Western engineer in honor of a Sir Walter Scott novel.

IVY

The town of Ivy, Albemarle County, takes its name from the Ivy Creek, so-named as early as 1750.

INDEPENDENCE. Independence Hall, the old State House in Philadelphia, personifies the concept of independence manifested in the names of countless towns and villages across America. In the mid-Atlantic region, we find Independence in both Pennsylvania and Virginia. (Convention and Tourist Bureau, City of Philadelphia)

There was an abundance of kalmia, an evergreen that is often mistaken for ivy, growing in the area. The town originally was Woodville, then Ivy Depot, and finally Ivy.

JAMESTOWN

Jamestown, in James City County, was the first permanent English settlement in the new world, founded 13 May 1607. The name signifies it was the primary settlement on the James River.

Jamestown was the colonial capital until Bacon's Rebellion in 1676, when the town was burned. Williamsburg became the capital in 1699.

Jamestown was the site of another first in the new world, but an unfortunate one. The first slaves in the colonies arrived here in 1619.

JARRATT

The Jarratt family arrived in this county in 1652, but this Greensville County community did not get its name until William Nicholas Jarratt gave land to the Petersburg-Weldon Railroad for its right-of-way. Jarratt's Station, half-a-mile south of Jarratt, was burned to the ground by Union cavalry in May, 1864.

JASPER

There are two possibilities for the name of this Scott County community. A local family may have given its name, or the town may honor the heroic Sergeant William Jasper (1750–79). Jasper provided military intelligence to the Revolutionaries as a scout under Generals Moultrie, Marion, and Lincoln. In 1776, he dodged British artillery to replace the flag at Fort Sullivan (Fort Moultrie), and was killed while planting the 2nd South Carolina's colors during the assault on Savannah.

JAVA

Java, in Pittsylvania County, was named by the railroad. The railroaders liked the name because it was unusual and short.

JEFFERSON

Jefferson was named for Peter Jefferson, father of President Thomas Jefferson. The elder Jefferson owned land nearby.

JEFFERSONTON. Thomas Jefferson, as seen on our $2 bill. (U.S. Bureau of Engravings)

JEFFERSONTON

This Culpeper County town commemorates Thomas Jefferson. The post office was established in 1779, with the "-ton" added to distinguish it from Jefferson in Powhatan County.

JENNINGS ORDINARY

An "ordinary" was a tavern, and this one, in Nottoway County, was owned and operated by the Jennings family.

KEEZELTOWN

As early as 1777, George Keezel (Kiesell) built himself a fine stone house. He thought that the land around his home would make an excellent town, so he drew up plans and laid out the streets, and in 1791, Kiesell's Town was established.

Keezel was one of the first men in the area interested in organizing a county government, and he wanted his town to be the county seat. But he was not the only one.

Local tradition suggests that Keezel and Thomas Harrison of nearby Rocktown (now Harrisonburg) competed in a race to Richmond to see who could gain approval for his town as county seat first. One version of the tale has Keezel stopping for the night at an inn at Swift Run Gap. Harrison, seeing his adversary's horse tied up for the night, struggled on and won approval. Other versions of the legend say the disagreement was settled in an ordinary horse race.

KELLER

The original name for this Occomack County community was Pungoteague Station. The name was changed in honor of the contractor who built the Pennsylvania Railroad through the area.

KENBRIDGE

This Lunenburg County city was originally named Tinkling Spring. When the town was laid out, it was on land owned by two families, the Kennedys and the Bridgeforths. The merger of the names became the name of the community.

KEOKEE

Until 1905, this Lee County town was called Crab Orchard. Nearby land was leased by the Keokee Coal and Coke Company, and a mine was opened. The village became Keokee. Keokee Perrin, wife of one of the coal company's officials, was part Indian.

KESWICK

Originally called Turkey Hill, for an abundance of wild turkeys, the name was changed to Keswick Farm and then simplified to Keswick. It is supposed to have been drawn from the Cumberland, England home of the poet Southey.

KIMBALLTON

E. J. Kimballton, president of the Norfolk & Western Railroad, visited this Giles County area in 1881. He spoke to the residents about building a railroad to the coal mines, and a branch line ran into Kimballton.

KING AND QUEEN COURT HOUSE

County seat for King and Queen County, this village was named for the county. King and Queen County, formed in 1691, was named for King William and Queen Mary.

KING GEORGE

King George is the county seat for King George county, and named after the county. King George County was formed in 1720, and named for George I.

KING WILLIAM

This community is the county seat, and named after its county. King William County was formed in 1701, and named for William III.

LA CROSSE

L

Located at the junction of Pine Road and St. Tammany's Ferry Road, this Mecklenburg County village was first called Old Piney Road. It is reported that a local resident, a Miss Northington, was the selector of the current name: she was impressed by the name of the old Indian game lacrosse.

LANCASTER

Lancaster is the county seat of Lancaster County, and takes its name from the county. Lancaster County was formed in 1652, and named for Lancaster, England.

LANEVIEW

Local residents suggested this name for a long straight road, or lane, to the Rappahannock River.

LAWRENCEVILLE

James Rice agreed to donate land for this townsite, provided he be given the privilege of naming the town. They did, and he did. He named it Lawrence after a favorite horse, or so the legend goes.

Another possibility is that the name was selected to honor Captain James Lawrence, who is best remembered for his 1813 cry of "Don't give up the ship!"

LEBANON

A deed, dated 10 May 1816, allocated twenty acres of land for the county seat for Russell County. The name was selected in 1819, and refers to the area's profusion of cedar trees. The name, of course, also has strong Biblical overtones.

LEBANON CHURCH

The reason for the naming of Lebanon Church, Shenandoah County, is similar to that of Lebanon, Russell County: the large number of cedar trees in the vicinity.

Lebanon Church was first named Cottontown, for the Cotton family who lived in the area. Another story has it that most of the children in the area had blond hair. The Lebanon Church was dedicated in 1871.

LEEDSTOWN

Two possibilities arise for the name of this community: a local family, or Leeds, England, a town noted for its iron industry.

LEESBURG

Before Loudon County was formed, there was a settlement here called Georgetown. In 1758, the Virginia House of Burgesses passed a bill authorizing the establishment of a town at this site and naming it for Francis Lightfoot Lee (1734–1797). The Lee family jokingly called Francis Loudon or Colonel Loudon, because of the time he spent there. In a family noted for its aggressive behavior, he was "calmness and philosophy itself."

Leesburg is the county seat of Loudon County.

LENAH

It is possible that this Loudon County town's name was derived from the Shawnee *lenawai,* meaning "man."

LENNIG

Lennig was named for the daughter of a railroad official.

LEON

Originally called James City, for the James family, this village was established in 1810. As tradition has it, Jesse and Frank James were part of the founding family. In 1840, the postal department changed the name to Leon, Spanish for "lion." It was the second post office opened in Madison County.

LEXINGTON

This city was named shortly after the Battle of Lexington.

Lexington is the home of Virginia Military Institute and Washington and Lee University. Founded in 1839, VMI was the first state military college in the nation.

Washington and Lee, established in 1749 as the Augusta Academy in Staunton, was the first classical school in the Shenandoah Valley. In 1776, it became Liberty Hall, then Liberty Hall Academy in 1782. After receiving some financial help from George Washington, the name was changed to Washington Academy in 1798. In 1813, it became Washington College. Robert E. Lee served as president of the college, and a year after his death in 1870 the school became Washington and Lee.

LIGNUM

This Culpeper County village was established in a wooded area. *Lignum,* Latin for "woods," was suggested as the town name in 1880 by the Reverend Frank P. Robertson.

LITTLETON

The name of this Sussex County community is apparently a

contraction of "Littletown," the name of a nearby eighteenth-century plantation.

Littleton must have been a wild town in the early nineteenth century, because poor John R. Wyche complained that the stage and post office were noisy. He obviously received no response to his complaints, because in 1825 he moved, building a new home a mile from the village.

LIVELY

One might think this was a rock 'n' rollin' town by its name. But Lively, in Lancaster County, takes its name from an earlier town called Lively Oak. Perhaps as time passed and pollution came, the oaks died and all that remained was "lively."

LORETTO

The town-name of Loretto, Essex County, was in use as early as 1861. It is derived from the Italian shrine city, and communities by that name are usually named by Catholics. (See Loretto, Pennsylvania.)

LORTON

Lorton, Fairfax County, was named in 1875 for the postmaster's home in Cumberland County, England.

LOUISA

The county seat, Louisa was named for the county. Louisa County, formed in 1742, was named for the Queen of Denmark, the daughter of George II.

LOW MOOR

Low Moor, Alleghany County, remembers the Low-Moor Iron Company that operated nearby. Augustus Low, from New York, owned the iron ore-lands, and Moor (or Moore) was the name of his partner, a Cincinatti engineer.

LUNENBURG

Earlier known as Lewiston, this town became Lunenburg Court House when it became the county seat. It is named for Lunenburg County, formed in 1746, and named for George II, who was Elector of Brunswick-Luneberg (the "n" is usually added in English spellings).

LURAY

Luray was settled in the early eighteenth century by a group of German-Swiss. We cannot boast of even that much knowledge about the source of the town's name.

One suggestion is that the Page County blacksmith shop of Lewis Ray was a popular stop-off for the stage, therefore, Lew Ray's. Another source suggests that Luray is a corruption of the name Lorraine, and comes from the Lorrain Run, recorded in 1734 and of some unknown Indian origin. Another source claims that William Staige Marye named the town, and his family came from Luray, France.

LYELLS

Charles Lyell (1797–1895) was a British geologist. His name appears on this Richmond County community.

LYNCHBURG

The ferry house built by John Lynch in 1756–57 was the center of the original settlement. In 1786, the town applied for a charter as Lynch's Warehouse. Lynch's warehouse was the first tobacco warehouse in the nation. Lynchburg became the modified name at a later date.

LYNDHURST

This community was named for Lord Lyndhurst.

MACHIPONGO

The name of this Northampton County village is a corrupton of the name of an Algonquian tribe, the Matchapungoes. The name translates to "much dust" or "bad dust."

MACON

The Macon family settled in this Powhatan County area in 1753, established a tavern for the stage, and operated a stable, gristmill, sawmill, and store. What little else in town that did not bear their name conformed with the opening of the post office.

MADISON

The first post office in Madison County was located here, at what was then called Madison Court House, in 1801. Madison is named for the county. Madison County was formed in 1792, and named for James Madison (1751–1836), president of the United States and "Father of the Constitution."

MADISON HEIGHTS

This Amherst County community was an early river town. It draws its name from a storage spot for tobacco, the Madison Warehouse.

MADISON RUN

Madison Run is just downstream of Madison Mills.

MADISONVILLE

This town was not named for James Madison. Rather, it bears the name of Henry Madison, a legislator from that city.

MAIDENS

Originally called Maiden's Adventure, this Goochland village name is drawn from a legend. It seems that a young woman crossed the James River to rescue her lover from the Indians, and, in the memory of her adventure, the town was named.

MANAKIN

The earliest name for this village in Goochland County was Manakintown, the town of the Monocan or Manocan Indians. The land had been given to a French Hugenot colony.

MANASSAS (Park)

In 1852, the county seat for Prince William County was called Manassas Junction. Incorporated as Manassas in 1873, it took its name from the Biblical Manassah.

MANGOHICK

There is a great legend attached to this King William County village. The way the story is told, there was a drunken white man who was confronted by a sober Indian. The Indian looked at the settler and said: "Man go hick." It is a great story, but is it true? It is more likely that the name comes from an Algonquian word with uncertain meaning.

MANQUIN

The early name for this King William County town was Brandy-wine. It is possible that the town's current name is a corruption of the name of the local stream: the Moncurin Creek. Manquin is also a corruption of the Algonquian *manakin*, a tribal name, or *manokin*, "fortification at."

MARION

This Smyth County community was named for General Francis Marion (1732–95), the "Swamp Fox" of Revolutionary War fame. It became the county seat in 1832. Francis Marion's name became quite popular as a place name after "Parson" Weems wrote his biography in 1809.

MARKHAM

Originally, this Fauquier County town was The Hollow. Later on it became Farrowsville. The name was finally changed in 1854 to Markham for James Markham Marshall, the first president of a branch of the Southern Railroad.

MARSHALL

Early known as Salem, land in this Fauquier County area was purchased in 1773 by Thomas Marshall, father of Chief Justice John Marshall. The name was changed to Marshall in 1882.

MARTINSVILLE

Established in 1791 and named county seat of Henry County in 1793, Martinsville was named for General Joseph Martin, who was brigadier general of the state militia at the time the town became the seat.

MATHEWS

Mathews is the county seat, and was named for the county, which was formed in 1790. It was named for the man who resolved that the county should be formed: Colonel Thomas Mathews, a Revolutionary War veteran.

MATOACA

Located in Chesterfield County, Matoaca is the proper name for the Indian "princess" Pocohontas. (See Pocohontas, Pennsylvania.)

MAX MEADOWS

Max Meadows probably was named for an early settler, William Mack—Mack's Meadows. An alternative suggests the name originated with a McGavocks family that lived in the area, thus Mc's Meadows. The Mack name seems to be more logical.

McDOWELL

Named for a former governor of Virginia, James McDowell, this is the oldest village in Highland County. Its earlier names include Sugar Tree Bottom and Crab Run. Stonewall Jackson beat off a Union advance just south of here on 8 May 1862.

McKENNEY

William R. McKenney was a lawyer for the Seaboard Air Lines Railroad, and the owner of large landholdings in Dinwiddie County.

McLEAN

Edward McLean was one of the original founders of the Great Falls and Dominion electric line. This town bears his name.

MECHANICSBURG

A mechanic used to be anyone who worked in a factory. This community commemorates those workers. (See Mechanicsville.)

MECHANICSVILLE

Mechanicsville derived its name from the occupations of its early residents. At one time, there was a wheelwright and blacksmith operating at the crossroads.

MEHERRIN

This village exists in both Lunenburg and Prince Edward counties. Its name comes from an Indian tribal name meaning an "island."

MENDOTA

The earlier name for this Washington County village was Kinderhook, named for a resident's former home in New York. The name was changed to Mendota for a local merchant. The first use of Mendota as a place name was in 1837 in Minnesota, used to

460

describe where the Minnesota River joins the Mississippi. The word is Siouan, and means "where one river flows into another." The name has migrated to a number of states.

MEREDITHVILLE

David Meredith petitioned for a post office in this location. He simply seized what was a great opportunity, because the stage-coach drivers were forced to change horses near this town.

MIDDLEBROOK

A clear stream crossed Main Street near the center of this Augusta County community. A post office was operating as early as 1840.

MIDDLEBURG

The earliest name for this fox-hunting community was Chinn's Crossroads, for Joseph Chinn. The name Middleburg was selected because the town is located midway between Alexandria and Winchester. (A name containing the word "middle" usually indicates something located between two others of similar nature.)

The Red Fox Tavern in Middleburg claims to be the oldest tavern in the United States. Because of a "gone-to-the-hounds" reputation, the town has been called the "Leicestershire of America," after the hunting area of that name in England.

MIDDLETOWN

There was a fort built near this location in 1755. In 1796, Dr. Peter Senseny applied for a charter, and the town was called Senseny Town. The current name originated either because Middletown is near the south boundary of the county, or because it is located between the county seats of Winchester and Woodstock.

MIDLAND

Located in Fauquier County, Midland was named for the Virginia Midland Railroad.

MIDLOTHIAN

This Chesterfield County community was a coal-mining center from 1730–1865, and may have been named for a county in Scotland. On the other hand, Sir Walter Scott published *The Heart of Midlothian* in 1818 to great public attention.

MILFORD

At least two possible sources exist for the name of this Caroline County village: it could have derived its name from a mill located here, or been named by people who came from Milford, England.

MILLBORO

About 1829, the Loman family built the Millboro Roller Mills for grinding wheat and corn. The post office in this Bath County community took its name from the mill.

MILLBORO SPRINGS

Millboro Springs is named for the springs located near Millboro.

MILLWOOD

Colonel Nathaniel Burwell and General Daniel Morgan (1736–1802) built a gristmill at this location before 1798. There were also mills in the area before 1769, however. Millwood was the main outlet for wheat-growing neighbors in this area until 1953.

MINERAL

This Louisa County community was first known as Tolersville, for storekeeper Adam Toler. It kept his name until 1810, when the name was changed to Davis Turnout. The final name change came with the arrival of the Chesapeake & Ohio Railroad, which named its station Mineral for the variety of minerals in the area. Iron pyrites—also known as fool's gold—a source of sulfur, were mined here from before the Civil War until the turn of the century.

MOBJACK

This town was probably named for Mobjack Bay, which lies between Mathews and Gloucester counties. A 1657 will refers to the body of water as Mock Jack Bay, but some sources feel the name is a corruption of an Algonquian Indian word meaning "badland."

MODEST TOWN

In the late eighteenth century, this Accomack County town was known as Sunderland Hall.

Legend has it that two prim and proper ladies ran a boarding house when the town was a stagecoach stop, and that the post office was named for them. Court records show a Helltown about a mile to the west—Modest Town may have been so-named to counteract Helltown.

MONROE
A post office at this Amherst County location was opened in 1897, and named Potts. The name was changed to Monroe in 1905. James Monroe Watts was postmaster at the time of the change.

MONTEBELLO
This Nelson County community was named for the Massie family summer home located near there. Montebello is Italian for "mountain-beautiful."

MONTEREY
Bell's Place was the early name for this city, named for a 1774 settler. When it became the county seat, the name was changed to Highland, after the county which was formed in 1847 and is the "highest" of all Virginia counties. When Zachary Taylor was elected president, the town changed its name to commemorate Taylor's victory at Monterey during the Mexican War. Monterey means "mountain of the king," a fitting description of the glories of nature in the area.

MONTPELIER
This Hanover County community was probably named in honor of James Madison's home Montpelier in Orange County. Montpelier was first a Vermont town that took its name from the French city.

MONTVALE
Montvale was originally named Buford Gap, for Captain Paschal Buford, a hero of the War of 1812 who owned land in this Bedford County area. It became Bufordville when the owner gave land to the Norfolk & Western Railroad. It is located in a large basin surrounded on three sides by spurs of the Blue Ridge Mountains.

MOUNTAIN FALLS
Located about a mile-and-a-half from this Frederick County location are beautiful falls on North Mountain.

MOUNTAIN LAKE

The lake on Salt Pond Mountain, from which this Giles County community takes its name, was discovered in 1751.

MOUNT CRAWFORD

Mount Crawford was the first town in Virginia's Rockingham County, established by law in 1825. It is the smallest municipality in the county with a 1991 population of 228. (See Mount Sidney.) The name comes from a local resident called Crawford.

MOUNT JACKSON

This town, known in 1812 as Mount Pleasant, was renamed in 1826 to honor General Andrew "Old Hickory" Jackson, a frequent visitor to the area. Large burial mounds south of town indicate that the area was once the permanent home of the Senedo Indians.

MOUNT SIDNEY

A popular local tale speaks of two weary travelers who share a horse; while one rides, the other walks. The tale relates that when Mr. Crawford reached Ten-Mile Stage, Mount Sidney's original name, he called out "Mount, Sidney." The same tale is told about Mount Crawford (see Mount Crawford). The truth of the matter is that this Augusta County community was named by Samuel Curry to honor Sir Philip Sidney. Curry also named Mount Solon.

MOUNT SOLON

This Augusta County town grew around a distillery, a gristmill, a tanyard, two stores, and a crossroad. It was named by Samuel Curry, a local stonesman who was well read in the Greek and Roman classics. Local legend suggests he was finishing a neighbor's chimney when someone asked him to name the town. He chose Mount Solon, tradition has it, because of Solon, the sixth-century B.C. Athenian statesman and constitutional reformer, and because of the nearby hills covered with cedar.

MOUNT VERNON

Lawrence Washington, George's half-brother, named his estate for his commanding officer, Admiral Edward Vernon, commander of the disastrous expedition against Cartegena in the Spanish colonies, and for its position above the Potomac.

George Washington gained control of the property in 1752.

MOUTH OF WILSON

The Grayson County community located where the Wilson Creek joins the New River was named, quite practically, Mouth of Wilson.

NARROWS

There is a deep gorge where the New River cuts through the Alleghenies. This Giles County community, located about a mile-and-a-half south of the gorge, was called The Narrows of New River, then The Narrows. It has been shortened to simply Narrows.

NASSAWADOX

First settled in 1656, Nassawadox takes its name from an Algonquian Indian word meaning "a stream between two streams."

NATHALIE

This town was named for Nathalie Otey, daughter of the president of the Lynchburg & Durham Railway Division. The woman who donated the land for the right-of-way selected the name.

NATURAL BRIDGE (— Station)

A natural rock formation in Rockbridge County resembles a modern span and was worshipped by the Monocan Indians as "The Bridge of God." George Washington surveyed the site and scratched his initials in the bridge. Thomas Jefferson bought the bridge from the Crown in 1774—for twenty shillings. The town that grew up around this natural phenomenon took on its name.

NAXERA

The name of this village means nothing. The name was created to be different from other post offices in the country.

NELLYSFORD

The traditional story behind the name of this Nelson County community is that a girl named Nelly drowned crossing a nearby ford. Another source points out that the ford was in Nelson County, and suggests the locals modified the name.

NEW—

Early settlers tried to recall their old homes by creating new settlements, using the familiar name, and calling them "new." We find this phenomenon in New Baltimore, Newbern, New Bohemia, New Canton, and New Castle. Others were named for more obvious reasons, such as New Church, New Kent, Newland, New Market, New Point, Newport, New Post, and Newtown; some for clouded ideals, such as New Hope and Newport News.

NEWBERN

The first county seat of Pulaski County, Newbern was originally settled by Swiss pioneers. They named their community New Bern. The postal authorities streamlined the name.

NEW CANTON

When a post office was opened on lands owned by William Cannon, the community was named New Cannon, then New Canton.

NEW CASTLE

Established as a fort in 1756 by Governor Dinwiddie, this town was first called New Fincastle. Because of the confusion with the Fincastle, the name was changed to New Castle.

NEW CHURCH

New Church commemorates the last Anglican Church built in Accomack County during the colonial period.

NEW HOPE

According to a local legend, the wife of an early settler was determined to leave the clearing and start afresh. Her husband was confident they could make it where they were. Apparently, if the legend is true, they did. New Hope is located in Augusta County.

NEW KENT

New Kent is the county seat for New Kent County. The county, formed in 1654, was named for either the English county or Kent Island. Colonel William Claiborne allegedly selected the name after Lord Baltimore drove him away from the island.

NEW MARKET

New Market, named after a racing center in England, was founded by General John Sevier (1745–1815), who later moved from the area and became the first governor of the State of Tennessee.

An earlier name for this village, laid out in 1784, was Crossroads, for the obvious reason. New Market, scene of the 1864 Civil War battle that pitted cadets from the Virginia Military Institute against seasoned Union troops, was incorporated in 1796.

NEW POINT

Long before this town existed in Mathews County, there was a New Point Comfort Light House in service here. The town took the name of the lighthouse.

NEW PORT

In 1858, this Giles County site was considered the gateway to frontier lands, a door or "portal" to adventure. Mail and stage passengers would travel to Newport, which functioned as a central location for connections to all points west.

NEWPORT NEWS

The town, some say, was named for Captain Christopher Newport and Sir William Newce. The earliest name for this city was Point Hope, but by 1619, it was New Port Newce. This earlier naming seems to preclude Christopher Newport's role in the name. It would appear that the town was actually called "the new port of the Newces." The "new" may come from the fact that the Newce brothers had already founded Newce-town in Ireland.

NEWTOWN

The obvious is true about this town in King and Queen County. It was named "New" town because there was an older one nearby.

NINEVEH

Nineveh appears to have been named for that ancient Assyrian capital . . . even though the Bible condemns it as a den of iniquity.

NORA

This town served as the earliest county seat for Dickenson County when it was called Mouth of Open Fork of McClure River. Later it was renamed Ervinton. Finally, it became Nora, for Nora Dorton, the first postmistress.

NORFOLK

The area was first settled in 1682 when fifty acres of the site were purchased for 10,000 pounds of tobacco. As early as 1728, the post traded with the West Indies. The name was provided by Colonel Thorogood, one of the earliest settlers, for his native county in England.

During the Civil War, Norfolk was the chief naval station of the Confederacy.

NORGE

Settlers from Wisconsin and the Dakotas moved to this James City location and named it for their native home: Norway.

NORTH GARDEN

North Garden, Albemarle County, was named for the local flora.

NORTON

The first name of this Wise County settlement was Prince's Flats, when it was settled by Henry Frazier. William Prince, legend has it, was an early, if only temporary, resident.

The post office, established in 1883, was first called Eolia, then later Dooly. It became Norton in 1890, named for Eckstein Norton, president of the Louisville & Nashville Railroad.

NOTTOWAY

Nottoway is the seat of Nottoway County, and was named in its honor. Nottoway County, formed in 1788, derives its name from the Indian tribe Mangoac, or Nadowa. The English version is Nottaway. The name translates to "snake" or "enemy."

O

OAK HALL

This Accomack County site was named for the nearby plantation, "Oak Hall," that dates from 1671.

OCCOQUAN

In 1729, at the falls of the Occoquan River, "King" Carter built a landing in Prince William County from which he could ship copper ore. A town called Colchester was established there in 1753.

Occoquan was founded there in 1804. The name of this community comes from the Dogue Indian word meaning "at the end of the water" or the Algonquian for "hooked inlet."

OILVILLE

In the late nineteenth century, a sassafras-oil pressing business was established at this town in Goochland County.

OLD —

When progress took over, it was up to the place-namers to recall where things began. They rose to the challenge and dubbed places "old," as in Old Church, Old Cold Harbor, and Old Somerset.

ONANCOCK

In 1670, this Accomack County community was an Indian village. Ten years later, it was Port of Entry. It derives its current name from the Algonquian Indian *auwannaku,* a "foggy place."

ONLEY

Onley was named for the home of Henry A. Wise, a Virginia governor. It was incorporated in 1950. Onley is the base for the Eastern Shore Produce Exchange, which was organized in 1899.

OPEQUON

This community takes its name from the Opequon Creek, a tributary of the Potomac River, that flows nearby. The creek takes its name from the Algonquian Indian word for "white-pool-stream."

ORANGE

The county seat for Orange County was first located at this site in 1749. Orange County was formed in 1734, and named for the Prince of Orange who, in that year, married George II's daughter, Princess Anne.

ORDINARY

The tavern on the stage line from and to Yorktown was built before 1730 and called Long Bridge Ordinary. Before the Revolution, it was Seawell's Ordinary. The post office reduced the name to fit a standard-size envelope.

ORKISANY

Iron ore from this Botetourt County area, smelted in Richmond, was used to make armor for the iron-clad *Merrimac*. The name is Iroquoian for "nettles."

ORKNEY SPRINGS

Originally called Yellow Springs, and touted for its healing powers, this Shenandoah County site was chartered as Orkney Springs in 1858. It was named for the Earl of Orkney.

ORLEAN

Orlean grew up around a large estate that bore that name.

OTTERVILLE

This Bedford County village is located near the Peaks of Otter. The peaks were named for a similar ridge in Scotland. Another possibility is the Cherokee word *otteri*, which means a "mountain" or "high hill."

OTTOMAN

When the townspeople of this Lancaster County community were trying to get approval from Washington for their post office, they submitted the name Corotoman, after the Corotoman estate which lasted in the county until 1886. The post office returned the papers with the approved name: they had modified the estate's name.

OYSTER

This area of Northampton County is rich in oysters and clams, therefore the name.

PAINT BANK

Paint pigment, either cinnabar or red iron ore, was discovered in a bank of a nearby creek. It was mined to some degree during World War II. This community takes its name from that feature.

PALMYRA

This Fluvanna County city grew up around the courthouse, and was named for the ancient city of Greece. The name is popular

470

because of the story of Zenobia, "Queen of the East," who, around A.D. 265, conquered many Eastern empires, including Egypt and Alexandria, greatly expanding the power of her capital, Palmyra.

PAMPLIN CITY

This Appomattox County community took its name from the Pamplin Pipe Company, once a major clay pipe factory.

PARIS

Ideas often abound regarding the source of a community's name. In the case of Paris, Fauquier County, some suggest the name was given by a Revolutionary War soldier who served under Lafayette and founded the town. Others contend that the Marquis, while visiting, was taken with the beauty of the village and asked it be named after Paris, France.

PARKSLEY

Parksley, Accomack County, was laid out on land owned by Edmund Bailey Parkes in 1742. When the Pennsylvania Railroad moved into the area, they named the railroad station Matomkin, which conflicted with the local post office. The post office won.

PARNASSUS

The name Parnassus is reminiscent of the Greek mountain, sacred to Apollo and the Muses.

PATRICK SPRINGS

Patrick Springs, Patrick County, was once the site of a summer hotel resort that touted the medicinal qualities of the local mineral springs. The hotel burned to the ground, and was not rebuilt.

PEMBROKE

Sometimes legend and tradition are more fun than learning the truth. A prime example is this town in Giles County. It is probable that the name was given by Welsh settlers, and named for Pembroke, Pembrokeshire, Wales. On the other hand, early residents of the location were members of the Lybrook family. Some say that one of the family members, Pem Lybrook, suggested a merger of his two names: Pem and brook. Unfortunately, though it is a cute story, it does not account for the change from "brook" to "broke."

PENN LAIRD

The Lairds were early settlers in this Rockingham County locale near Massanutten Mountain, in an area near Laird's Knob. "Penn" translates to "the place on a hill."

PETERSBURG

Petersburg began in 1645–46 as Fort Henry, a frontier fort and trading post. When Peter Jones succeeded Abram Wood as the owner of the trading post, it became known as Peter's Point.

In September of 1732, Colonel William Byrd II proposed the name Petersburg. A village was laid out in 1748 and by 1784 four settlements united into Petersburg.

At the end of the Civil War, Mary Logan, wife of Union General John A. Logan, saw schoolgirls laying flowers on the graves of Petersburg defenders. She noticed the practice was repeated the next year at the same time. She told her husband, and he took steps to gain national holiday status for Memorial Day.

PHENIX

Since it was founded, this town in Charlotte County has had a number of major fires. In 1906, when discussing possible names, someone suggested this one. "Phenix," a simplification of "phoenix," refers to the mythological bird that "rose from its own ashes"—quite descriptive of the town.

PHILOMONT

Located in Loudon County, Philomont was settled by Quakers. It is possible that the name was drawn from the Greek *philos*, "love of" and *mont* for mountain. In other words, "love of mountain."

PHILPOTT

Philpott, in Henry County, is the exception to the rule. In most cases, we find that a town takes the name of a nearby body of water. That is not the case here.

The Philpott family were early settlers who founded the town that bears their name. Later, the Philpott Dam—now Philpott Reservoir—assumed the name of the village.

POCOHONTAS

This Tazewell County community was named for the Pocohontas Coal Mine, opened in 1883 and operated until 1955.

POQUOSON

The name for this community is from an Algonquian (*pocosin* or *poquoson*) word that means "swamp" or "overflowed land."

PORT HAYWOOD

Tradition has it that during a bad storm, a sea captain by the name of Haywood was able to bring his ship into the Mathews County harbor of the East River. He recommended it to other sailors, and from then on it was called Port Haywood.

PORT REPUBLIC

Port Republic was once the county seat of Augusta County, when the county extended to the Mississippi River. Established in 1802, it is now part of Rockingham County. In its earliest days, Port Republic was a terminal for flatboat transportation of goods to Alexandria.

PORT ROYAL

Established in 1744, Port Royal was one of the principal shipping ports on the Rappahannock River. The town was founded by Thomas Roy, and for years was called Port Roy.

PORTSMOUTH

The site of the city of Portsmouth was patented in 1659 by Captain William Carver. In 1716, a grant in the amount of 1,120 acres was made to Lieutenant Colonel William Craford (Crawford), who laid out the streets. Portsmouth was established as a town in 1752 and named by its founder. It was the county seat for Norfolk County, and in 1858, Portsmouth was chartered as a city.

The name has a double source: it was named for the English town, but is also quite descriptive of its location.

POST OAK

The way the local story goes, this town in Spotsylvania County received its name from a post and an oak tree near the post office.

POUND

A horse-powered mill at this Wise County crossroads gave rise to the name. Farmers brought their grain to be "pounded" into meal.

POUNDING MILL
An early mill at this location pounded corn into meal.

POWHATAN
For many years, the Powhatan County seat was known as Scotts-ville, for General Charles Scott, a resident of the county and a Revolutionary War veteran. The name was changed to Powhatan Court House, and then to Powhatan. Powhatan County, formed in 1777—the same year the courthouse was built here, was named for that famed Indian chief whose life was interwoven with Virginia's beginnings.

PRINCE GEORGE
The courthouse building here dates from 1810. Prince George takes its name from its county, which was formed in 1702 and named for Prince George of Denmark, husband of Queen Anne.

PROVIDENCE FORGE
A group of Presbyterian settlers arrived at this New Kent County area about 1770. Their principal industry was the forging of farm tools. Remnants of the old forge still exist on a nearby estate.

PULASKI
The original name for this town was Martin's Tank, named for the family of the prominent resident. In 1877, the name was changed to Martin's. When Pulaski became the county seat, the name was changed to reflect the county. Pulaski County, formed in 1839, was named for Count Kazimierz (Casimir) Pulaski (1747–79), a Polish cavalryman who was killed during the siege of Savannah in 1779. If not for his valiant death, Pulaski might have only been remembered for his failures.

PUNGO
Located in Princess Anne County, Pungo was the name of an Indian chief who established a trading post here. The name seems to be a shortening of an Algonquian name such as Pungoteague.

PUNGOTEAGUE
This community dates from 1660. It was the first county seat for

Accomack County, and was the site of the first dramatic performance in the New World, 27 August 1665.

The name is derived from the Algonquian *pongotecku*, "river of the sand fly."

QUANTICO

Best known as the U.S. Marine Corps training facility, Quantico was incorporated in 1874, though it was used during the Revolution as a service location for ships of the Potomac Navy.

The Marine Corps facility opened in 1917, and became a permanent post a year later.

The name for this Prince William County area derives its name from the Algonquian for, depending on the root word, a "long reach at," or "place of dancing." But don't ever tell it to the Marines.

QUINBY

Quinby, in Accomack County, is named for a prominent attorney who inherited lands from the Upshur family through his mother. She was a descendant of the original landowners. The area is still known as Upshur's Neck.

RADFORD

Incorporated in 1887, this Montgomery County city was formerly known as Ingle's Ferry, Lovely Mount, and Central Depot after the Norfolk & Western Railroad came in 1856.

Radford, home of Radford University, was named for Dr. John Bane Radford, who owned the land on which the town grew.

RAPHINE

This Rockbridge County town was the birthplace of James Gibbs, inventor of the sewing machine. The town's name is a play on Gibbs' invention: the Greek *raphes* means "needle."

RAPIDAN

The Rapidan River "loaned" its name to this Culpeper County town. There are some who say the river was named in honor of Queen Anne, or "rapid Anne." More likely, the name is derived from the Algonquian *hanne*, "stream," or *hanough*, "people." A "rapid hanne" really makes more sense.

RED ASH

Red Ash, Tazewell County, is named for the type of coal that was mined there. When burned, this particular coal left a reddish ash.

REMINGTON

Until 1850, this town in Fauquier County was called Millview, then Bowenville. In 1853, the Southern Railroad named its station Rappahannock Station, and in 1890, Remington.

RESTON

Reston was a prototype of modern planned communities. It was developed by Robert E. Simon. The initials of his name form the first syllable of the town's name. His concept was to establish seven villages, each having a "town center" as a retail area, but separated by woodlands. The first resident moved into Reston in 1964.

RICE

William Rice built a church for religious dissenters near the present-day location of this town in about 1775. The first name for this Prince Edward County community was Rice Meeting House, which has been much abbreviated for postal purposes.

RICHLANDS

Kentucky cattle drivers found high-quality pastures along the Clinch River and gave this Tazewell County village its name.

RICHMOND

Captain John Smith bought a tract of land from Chief Powhatan in 1609 and founded the settlement of "None Such." By 1634, Richmond had a population of 419 people. The city was named in 1733 by Colonel William Byrd. The name was given because Byrd thought this new town resembled Richmond-on-Thames, England.

Richmond was the county seat of Henrico County in 1752, and became the state capital in 1779. During the secession, Richmond served as capital of the Confederate States of America.

RIDGEWAY

Samuel Sheffield, keeper of a local store, named this Henry County village. Ridgeway was formerly a tobacco market.

RINGGOLD

Gold was discovered in this Pittsylvania County area, and a mine was started to exploit it. The mine was not very fruitful. In fact, as tradition tells it, there was barely enough gold for a single ring. A more likely name-source would be Major Samuel Ringgold, the first American soldier killed in the Mexican War.

RIPPLEMEAD

This town is reputed to be named for the rippling effect of the New River and the waving grasses in the meadows along its banks.

RIVERDALE

Located near the Back River, this housing development was named for the Riverdale Shopping Center.

ROANOKE

When the post office opened here, the town was called Big Lick, for the nearby salt marsh where animals gathered for that mineral. Big Lick was incorporated in 1874.

The town's name was changed to Roanoke in 1882, and two years later, the legislature chartered the city. The name is drawn from the county, formed in 1838. The name is derived from the Algonquian for "shell money" or "wampum." Recorded in the 1584 Amadas and Barlowe Expedition, *roanoke* was the first Indian word to be taken over by the English—and survive.

A dramatic feature of the city is a man-made star that shines atop Mill Mountain, making Roanoke "The Star City of the South."

ROCHELLE

Rochelle was originally Jack's Shop, named for the man who operated the local store. The name was changed to the French La Rochelle when the post office was established in 1854.

ROCKBRIDGE BATHS

Rockbridge Baths, located in Rockbridge County, was a very popular resort. People were supposed to apply the algae from the water to infections. There were even some cures reported.

ROCKY MOUNT

Since about 1760, there were two villages in this Franklin County area: Rocky Mount and Mount Pleasant. Rocky Mount became the county seat in 1786; in 1873, the communities merged into one. The name comes from a craggy spot near the town.

ROSEDALE

Rosedale was the name of the plantation where the first post office was opened in this Russell County community.

The name was changed to Elway in 1897, but returned to its historic name in 1941.

ROSSLYN

Rosslyn is a community in Arlington County—which does not have any incorporated towns. Rosslyn derives its name from the Rosslyn Farm, the property of Caroline Lambden and William Henry Ross. They merged the two names together.

ROUND HILL

A geological outgrowth, a round hill, of the Blue Ridge Mountains near this Loudon County locale was a landmark for early hunters and travelers. Settled about 1735, it had its first post office in 1868.

ROXBURY

Roxbury could have been named for the Massachusetts town of the same name that was named in 1630 for the condition of the town site. There is no Roxbury in England, only a Roxborrow, in Middlesex. Roxbury is in Henrico County.

RURAL RETREAT

Originally named Mount Airy, Rural Retreat, in Wythe County, takes its name from an old tavern in the area which stagecoach passengers used as a "retreat."

RUTHER GLEN

When first established, this Caroline County community was called Chesterfield Station. It was later changed to Ruther Glen to avoid confusion with Chesterfield, in Chesterfield County. The Scottish Ruther Glen was associated with Sir William Wallace and Robert the Bruce. Near the village is the old home of the Moncure family, "Ellerslie," named for the Scottish home of Wallace. The railroad station was called Ruther Glen by the railroad superintendent.

S

ST. CHARLES

This village was named for Charles Bondurant, an early operator of a coal mine and, as can be seen by the place-naming, a very successful promoter. But no one ever said he was a saint.

ST. STEPHENS CHURCH

When King and Queen County was established, it had three parishes, or governing units. One of these parishes was called Saint Stephen's. When a Baptist congregation became organized in 1842, it took on the name St. Stephen's Baptist Church. The town picked up the name, minus the "Baptist."

SALTVILLE

Saltville is named for the vast salt deposits found there.

Fifteen thousand years ago, what is now called the Saltville River flowed through the valley. The valley later was filled by Lake Totten. The salt deposits attracted prehistoric beasts, which makes this area a great location for archeological digs. Arthur Campbell, founder of the first commercial salt works at this location, sent Thomas Jefferson a fossil in 1782.

Lacking means of transportation, the salt originally mined here had limited distribution, but the arrival of the railroad in 1856 changed that. So, too, did the advent of the Civil War. Because of strong Union navy blockades and the loss of territory, the Confederacy relied more and more on salt from this locale. In fact, Saltville was called "The Salt Capital of the Confederacy."

Saltville was also the site of one of the worst atrocities of the war. Following an unsuccessful October 1864 attack, Union forces left Saltville—and their wounded—behind. Confederate troops massacred the men left there, more than one hundred black soldiers.

One of Saltville's famous residents was Elizabeth Russell, sister of Patrick Henry, who brought Methodism to the area.

Saltville's original name was Preston's Salines. General Francis Preston lived there and mined salt. In 1748, it was known as Buffalo Lick. The town was incorporated as Saltville in 1896.

SALUDA

Saluda is the seat of Mecklenburg County, with court records dating it back to 1673. A small Indian tribe from South Carolina lived here until they reportedly moved to Pennsylvania in the early eighteenth century. The name is apparently a corruption of an Indian word.

SANDY POINT

Sandy Point, Westmoreland County, is an exercise in futility. Whenever a storm blows in from the north or northeast, sand accumulates here in prodigious amounts. The more they take away, the more is delivered by the next storm.

SAXE

Originally, this community was called Carrington's Mill, for Judge Carrington. The name was changed to Saxe by an individual from Vermont who wanted to honor the poet of his state.

SAXIS

The name of Sikes Island can be traced to an island owned by Robert Sikes in 1666. It became Saxis in 1896, the corrupted name being established by the post office.

SCOTTSBURG

Located in Halifax County, Scottsburg was named for John Baytop Scott, a member of George Washington's staff during the Revolution, vice president of the Society of the Cincinnati, and a veteran of the War of 1812. His remains are buried in the neighborhood.

SCOTTSVILLE

This town was founded by John Scott, the owner of Scott's Ferry. David Scott donated the land upon which the first Albemarle Court House was built, and Scottsville was the county seat from 1744–61.

SEAFORD

Seaford, in York County, was named by E. E. Slaight. His reasoning for the name was simple: the location was near Sand Box, a sandbar that connected the York River with Back Creek.

SEBRELL

This Southampton County town was named in 1908 for James Sebrell, who represented the county in the state legislature.

SEVEN CORNERS

This town was named for the number of roads and highways that converge on this single intersection in Fairfax County.

SEVEN FOUNTAINS

The post office at this Shenandoah County location was established in 1853, and named Burner's Springs. The Burners were among the early settlers in Fort Valley.

The name was changed to Seven Fountains because seven different kinds of mineral water flow from seven different springs, all within half an acre.

SEVEN MILE FORD

Seven Mile Ford was so named because it was a ford on the river, just seven miles from another settlement, Royal Oak.

SHARPS

Originally called Milden, this Richmond County spot functioned as a shipping point from colonial times. Milden commemorated a local home. The Sharps family, on the other hand, were managers of the local wharf and large landowners. The post office name was changed to reflect the Sharps' contribution.

SHAWSVILLE

Much history has been lost because of postal department and railroad renamings. Shawsville is a good example.

In 1756, Mary Draper Ingalls and her husband arrived at Fort Vaux (Vass), a fortification built on the plantation of Captain Ephraim Vaux in the present village of Shawsville. The current name, however, is that of a Norfolk & Western engineer.

SHENANDOAH

Founded as Shenandoah Furnace, a settlement around the iron-smelting operation of William Milnes, the town grew in the 1880s as a result of mining and the introduction of railroads. Incorporated in 1884 as Milnes, for the pig iron manufacturer, the name was changed to Shenandoah, for the county, in 1890. Shenandoah is Algonquian for "spruce-stream."

SHIRLINGTON

Like Rosslyn, this Arlington County community is not an official municipality. It draws its name from its shopping center, so named because of its closeness to the Shirley Highway (Virginia Route 350). The highway was named for Henry G. Shirley, a former Virginia highway commissioner.

SINGERS GLEN

Before 1860, this Rockingham County community was called Mountain Valley. The name was changed to Singer's Glen when the post office arrived. Local resident Joseph Funk was known as the "father of song in Northern Virginia." In 1868, he established the Singers Glen School in the community.

SINKING CREEK

The town of Sinking Creek, in Craig County, was named for the Sinking Creek. The creek, which runs through both Craig and Giles Counties, goes underground near Hoges Chapel. Its disappearance gives rise to the name.

SKIPPERS

Depending on the source, Skippers, Greensville County, took its name from the nickname, "skippers," given to railroad signalmen; or from a Mrs. Skipwith who lived nearby.

SKYLAND

When first established, this site was a "dude ranch" called Stony Man Camp. Unfortunately for postal purposes, there was a Stony Man post office at the base of the ridge. Because it was on a higher plane, the new name became descriptive of the location.

SMITHFIELD

Though this Isle of Wight County community took its name in 1662 based on the fact that it was built on land owned by Arthur Smith, it had been settled perhaps ten years before.

Smithfield is well-known for the delicious hams it produces from peanut-fed hogs raised in Virginia and North Carolina. It was incorporated in 1752.

SNOWVILLE

Snowville, Pulaski County, was founded by Asial Snow, who developed industries in the area which prospered from 1830–50. The first Christian church in the area was opened in Snowville.

SOUTHANNA

Southanna, in Louisa County, takes its name from the South Anna River. The stream was named for Queen Anne.

SOUTH BOSTON

Captain E. F. Jeffries suggested that they change the name of Dabb's, Halifax County, to Boston when the post office was opened. The post office refused to accept that name because there was a Boston post office already—in Culpeper County. So Jeffries tried South Boston . . . at least, that is how the story goes.

SOUTH HILL

When South Hill, Mecklenburg County, was named, there was a small hill—rare in this area—north of the community. The town, because it was below the hill, was called South Hill.

There was a South Hill Methodist Church and school located nearby in 1800. In 1814, when the post office was established, it also took the name South Hill. The city was incorporated in 1900.

SPEEDWELL

Speedwell, in Wythe County, acquired its name from the nearby Speedwell Furnace. There was an association between the furnace on Cripple Creek and the Speedwell Furnace in North Carolina.

SPOTSYLVANIA

Spotsylvania is the seat for the county of that name.

Spotsylvania County was formed in 1720 and named for Alexander Spotswood, lieutenant governor of Virginia (1710–22). The name combines part of the governor's name and the Latin sylvania, "forest place."

SPRINGFIELD

Springfield was named for large springs in the vicinity.

SPRING GROVE

Richard Pace settled near this locale in 1620, in the midst of a grove of trees and a spring. Chanco, an Indian boy, lived at Spring Grove; he is the one who warned of the plot to massacre settlers in 1622.

STAFFORD

Stafford is the county seat. Stafford County, formed in 1664, was named for Staffordshire, England. Another source suggests the name actually came from the Viscount Stafford.

STANLEY

Stanley was developed after 1881 at the intersection of the Shenandoah Valley Railroad and the New Market-Gordonsville Turnpike.

Stanley was incorporated in 1900, and named for Stanley McNider, son of the president of the land development company.

STANLEYTOWN

Competition for the Bassett chair factory in Bassett was located a short distance away. Thomas Bohnson Stanley built his furniture factory, and a community grew up around it.

STAUNTON

One of the oldest cities west of the Blue Ridge Mountains, Staunton was settled by John Lewis in 1732. Named for Lady Staunton, wife of Virginia Governor William Gooch, the town was laid out in 1748–49. Chartered in 1749, Staunton was incorporated in 1871. Staunton, in Augusta County, was known as Mill Place after 1738, when William Beverly donated twenty-five acres "at his mill-site" near the center of his "Manor of Beverly" for the courthouse and jail. Staunton was birthplace to President Woodrow Wilson. It was also home—for a time—to Grandma Moses.

STEELES TAVERN

Steeles Tavern, in Augusta County, was named for David Steele, a Revolutionary War veteran who operated a tavern here. The earlier name for the community was Midway.

STERLING

The earliest name for this Loudon County community was Guilford, but that caused confusion with another Guilford, in Accomack County, also in Virginia. A miller, Ben Cockerill, suggested using the name of the Sterling Farm, which was located nearby.

STEVENSBURG

During colonial days, this town was known as York. The oldest town in Culpeper County, it was named Stevensburg for General Edward Stevens, the Revolutionary War hero of Culpeper.

STONEGA

Stonega was named for Stone Gap . . . without the "p."

STONY CREEK

This Sussex County community was named by the wife of Norfolk & Western engineer Mr. Mahone. She also named Wakefield.

STRASBURG

German settlers were drawn to the Bavarian-like countryside in the late eighteenth century.

At times, this Shenandoah County town was known as Staufferstadt (Stovertown) for Peter Stauffer (Stover) who purchased land in 1749; also as Funktown, Funk's Mills, and Shenandoah River. It was finally named Strasburg for a city in Alsace. Josiah Hite brought the immigrants to populate the village.

Between 1854 and 1870, Strasburg became a railroad crossroads. Today, it is at the crossroads of Interstates 81 and 66.

Excellent pottery was made here during the nineteenth century. It received widespread notice, and the town became known as "Pot Town." In 1908, the potteries all closed down.

STRATFORD

Stratford is hallowed ground to native Virginians. It was the boyhood home of Robert E. Lee—Marse Robert was born there 19 January 1807, a holiday still enjoyed by most Virginians as Lee-Jackson Day. In recent years, in an ironic twist of fate, the day is also shared by the commemoration of the Reverend Martin Luther King, Jr. Stratford was established in 1727 by Thomas Lee. The Lee homestead is controlled by the Robert E. Lee Memorial Foundation.

STUART

The earliest name for the Patrick County seat, established in 1792, was Taylorsville, but it was more often called Patrick Court House. The name was changed to Stuart, for General James Ewell Brown "Jeb" Stuart (1833–64), who was born in Patrick County.

Several years after his 1854 graduation from West Point, Jeb Stuart served as an aide to then-Colonel Robert E. Lee. Later, after the secession, Stuart became a trusted officer of the Confederacy. Lee thought highly of the man as an "intelligence officer of foremost ability." Stuart was promoted to major general and commanded all Confederate cavalry. After the death of General Thomas J. "Stonewall" Jackson, Stuart assumed Jackson's command. His role at the Battle of Gettysburg has always been controversial because it appears he did not follow orders. He died of wounds received at Yellow Tavern.

STUDLEY

Studley, Hanover County, was named for Patrick Henry's ancestral home in England.

SUGAR GROVE

A grove of sugar maple trees near the town gave this Smyth County community its name.

SUNNYBANK

This village was named by an admirer of writer Albert Payson Terhune. Terhune's home was called Sunnybank.

SURRY

The earliest names for this Surry County seat were The Crossroads and McIntosh's Cross Roads. In 1796, tavernkeeper Robert McIntosh donated the land for the county courthouse. The earlier courthouse was located about two miles west, at Troopers.

Surry is named for its county, formed in 1652 and named after Surrey County, England—with the alternate spelling: no "e."

SUSSEX

County seat of Sussex County, this community's courthouse was completed in 1815.

Sussex County, formed in 1753, was named for the English county.

SWEET BRIAR

Elijah Fletcher taught at the Clifford Academy, and married one of the young women he tutored. While he lived in Lynchburg, he managed the Sweet Briar Plantation. His daughter, Indiana Fletcher-Williams, provided for Sweet Briar College in her will. Located in Amherst County, the college opened in 1906. The plantation took its name from the large number of sweet briar roses that grew there.

SYLVATUS

Sylvatus Smith was a prominent resident of this Carroll County town when it blossomed following the opening of local mines. The post office was named for him.

TACOMA

The name of Tacoma in Wise County comes from the Algonquian for "high ground."

TANGIER

Discovered and named by Captain John Smith in 1608, Tangier Island was settled in the 1680s by John Crockett and his sons' families, fishermen from Cornwall, England. The name is derived from *tanja*, small clay bowls the Indians made which Smith thought looked similar to those he made when captive in Turkey.

TANNERSVILLE

At an earlier time, there was a tannery at this Tazewell County site.

TAPPAHANNOCK

The first name for this Essex County community was Hobb's Hold; a "hold" was land held under a grant. Some people believe the original name was Hobb's Hole, but this is erroneous.

In 1680, the General Assembly passed an act of "cohabitation," creating this and fifteen other towns. The act was vetoed by King Charles II, but revived under William and Mary. The 1682 port at this location was called New Plymouth.

The first permanent county courthouse was located here in 1728. The name itself is a variation of Rappahannock, derived from the Algonquian word meaning "on the rise and fall of water" or "on the running water."

TASEY

The name for this town is a corruption of Tazewell. The Tazewell family owned land on which Cape Charles was built. Littleton Waller Tazewell was Virginia's governor in the 1830s.

TAZEWELL

Tazewell acquired that name when it became the county seat in 1800. Before that, it had been known as Jeffersonville. The Tazewell name was selected to satisfy a Tazewell relative who opposed another name, for a legislator from Russell County.

Tazewell County, formed in 1753, was named for an English county.

TEMPERANCEVILLE

Temperanceville was originally Crossroads. The name of this Accomack County village was changed in 1824, when four land-owners purchased it on the provision that it would be a dry town.

TENTH LEGION

Thomas Jefferson is given credit for the name of this community. He referred to the Shenandoah Valley as "the Tenth Legion of Democracy," an allusion to Caesar's *Commentaries*, in which the Roman leader stated he could always count on his tenth legion.

THE PLAINS

Originally called The White Plains, local residents feared their community might be confused with White Plains, New York. The name was shortened.

THORNBURG

Before 1863, this location was known as Mud Tavern. At about the same time, another tavern, Thornburg's, operated on the Ta River further south. Thornburg was moved to take over Mud Tavern.

TIMBERVILLE

A log cabin constructed in the late eighteenth century was the start of Timberville, Rockingham County.

First known as Williamsport—the storekeeper was Abraham Williamson—then Thompson's Store, and Riddle's Tavern. A post office was opened in 1827 with the name Timberville, drawn from the vast local timberlands.

TOANO

This James City County site was once called Burnt Ordinary, after a local tavern burned. It was later called Toano, an Indian word which might mean "pipe camping place."

TOMS BROOK

The namesake for this town was a free African-American man who lived along the creek west of the town. They called the area Tom's Creek. Later, it became Tom's Brook, when a town was founded by William Border, Sr.

TOMS CREEK

Toms Creek, in Montgomery County, is a tributary of the New River, and was originally called Jones Creek. The local idea is that the donor of the name was Thomas Jones, and so that the name change did not affect the intent. This town, in Wise County, is nowhere near that stream.

TRAMMEL

This Dickenson County town was named for the Trammel Creek. Early hunters found the name of a man called Trammel carved in a beech tree, and named the stream for him. Legend has it he was captured by Indians and spirited away to Kentucky. There is some substance to this tale, since there is also a Trammel, Kentucky.

TRIANGLE

This community is located at the junction of several highways. A look at a road map will show how descriptive the town's name is.

UNION LEVEL

The stages on the Plank Road crossed the "union" of the Miles and Allens creeks on "level" ground. Local legend says that the stage drivers had a description for this Mecklenburg County area: "The wheel horses would brake the stage to Miles Creek, the lead team would get them over the hump of the level; then with my feet on the spatterboard, I blow my horses on the level."

UNIONVILLE

Unionville was named for the first church in its community.

UPPERVILLE

Upperville is located in a village in the upper part of Fauquier County; therefore, the name. The Piedmont Hunt, dating back to 1840, is located there. It is believed to be the oldest event of its kind in the country.

URBANNA

Urbanna, Mecklenburg County, was originally named Nicock, after the Nimcock Creek, and established in 1705. Half a century later, the town's name was changed to Urbanna, in honor of Queen Anne plus *urbe* for city. The creek's name was also changed.

Another source suggests that the name was influenced by the area's nearness to Fluvanna and Rivanna.

VANSANT
This Buchanan County town grew up around the Vansant Kitchen Company, a lumber company specializing in yellow poplar. The company's name was drawn from one of the partner's names.

VARINA
There is really no reason for the name, except it is mentioned in a lease dated 21 March 1633, as "Varina Parish." Varina, which might be a variation of Virginia, was the name of the plantation where John Rolfe lived with Pocohontas after their 1614 marriage.

VERNON HILL
The 1836 Quaker meetinghouse on Mountain Road was named Mount Vernon. This village took its name from the meetinghouse.

VERONA
The earliest post office in this Augusta County village was called Bowling's Mill. It was renamed Rolla when a roller mill was established locally. The post office was then Rolla, but the Chesapeake & Western Railroad station was called Verona. When another post office in Virginia called Verona closed, Rolla became Verona.

VESTA
Vesta is probably named for the daughter of a leading family. Vesta was also the name of the Roman goddess of the hearth.

VESUVIUS
This Rockbridge County town took its name from a local iron furnace, which operated there in the early nineteenth century.

VICTORIA
This Lunenburg County town was named for Queen Victoria.

VILLAGE
Originally Union Village, this Richmond County town is located

not far from the "union" of two county lines. The name was modified following postal confusion regarding the full name.

VINTON

Vinton's name before 1860 was Gish's Mill, founded in 1794 by David Gish. The name became Gish when the railroad arrived.

Vinton became the official name in 1884, and commemorates two prominent families: the Vinyards and the Prestons.

VIRGILINA

This Halifax County town is located on the state line, the border between Virginia and North Carolina. Earlier known as Tuck's Cross Roads, for an early family, the name combined the two states when the post office opened.

VIRGINIA BEACH

In the 1870s, Virginia Beach was a desolate strip of sand known as the graveyard for ships lost along the Atlantic coast. Congress authorized four lifesaving stations to be built on the beach. One of these stations, Seastack Lifesaving Station, developed into Virginia Beach.

Virginia Beach became an independent city in 1952. The name is descriptive: it is Virginia's beach on the Atlantic.

VOLNEY

When E. C. Hash submitted a list of names to the post office for his Grayson County town, he added his son's name. Volney Hash's name was the one selected.

VIRGINIA BEACH. The Adam Thoroughgood House at Virginia Beach was built in ca. 1680. It is a modified hall and parlor house. Its architecture is similar to what one might see in an English cottage. [CREDIT: City of Virginia Beach, Virginia]

WACHAPREAGUE

Originally called Powellton for the Powell brothers, who owned the land in Accomack County. There was confusion with another town by the same name in Brunswick County, so the name was changed to Wachapreague. The name translates from the Algonquian as "little city by the sea." It was incorporated in 1902.

WAKEFIELD

Local legend has it that Mrs. Mahone, wife of a Norfolk & Western engineer, named this Sussex County village for a Sir Walter Scott novel. Unfortunately, Scott did not write a book about Wakefield; it was Goldsmith who wrote *The Vicar of Wakefield*. Wakefield had been called Blackwater Depot in 1838, and the town was chartered as Wakefield in 1879.

Another possibility is that the town was named for George Washington's birthplace: Wakefield, in Westmoreland County.

WALTERS

Earlier known as Fraiser's Siding, Walters, in Isle of Wight County, took on the first name of Walter Joyner. In 1909, Joyner successfully brought a railroad station to the town. Another station was already named Joyner, but he got his name on the town in the end.

WARM SPRINGS

Warm Springs, county seat for Bath County, held court for the first time in 1791. Its medicinal springs are cooler than those at Hot Springs. The springs' temperature ranges from 94–95.2 degrees Fahrenheit.

WARNER

The first postmaster of this Mecklenburg County village was Robert Warner Allsworth, and his middle name became the town's.

WARRENTON

Warrenton, the county seat for Fauquier County, was established in 1760. The town was laid out in 1790, and incorporated in 1810.

Formerly known as Fauquier Court House, it was renamed for Dr. Joseph Warren (1741–75), who started Paul Revere and William Dawes on their famous ride. Warren was commissioned a major general of the militia, but was killed at the Battle of Bunker Hill before he received the rank.

WARSAW

The original name for this community was Richmond Court House. It was renamed in 1845 in sympathy with the Polish revolution.

WASHINGTON

The county seat of Rappahannock County was surveyed, platted, and established by George Washington in 1749. The name was chosen by Thomas, Lord Fairfax. It was incorporated in 1792.

WAVERLY

In 1838, this Sussex County community was known as Blackwater Depot. Then, along came the wife of Norfolk & Western's engineer Mahone. She supposedly named it for another of Sir Walter Scott's novels, *Waverley* (1814). (See Wakefield.)

WAYNESBORO

Earlier known as Teesville, for the early settlers the Tees brothers, the name was changed in 1801 to honor Revolutionary War General "Mad Anthony" Wayne. This Augusta County community was incorporated in 1834, and became an independent city in 1848.

WEBER CITY

The way the story is told, a filling-station owner in Scott County wanted to increase his business. An avid listener to the "Amos 'n'

WASHINGTON. The most popular name in the naming of American cities, towns and villages is Washington, for George Washington, "the father of his country." The Washington Monument, rising 555 feet over the skyline of the nation's capital is the first sight seen by many tourists to Washington, D.C. [Credit: Washington Convention & Visitors Bureau]

Andy" show, he recalled they lived in the made-up town of Weber. So he painted the name "Weber City" on the sides of his station: the area grew, and the name remained.

WEEMS

This town was the site of the Corotaman estate. After the estate was disposed of in 1886, an arrangement was made with a steamboat to stop there. The steamer owners agreed; but only if the townspeople would build a wharf, at their own expense . . . and name it after the boat, the *Mason L. Weems.* The steamer's name, one will note, is for that imaginative biographer of George Washington.

WELLFORD

Wellford was once a ford on a tributary of the Rappahannock.

WEST POINT

The first name for this port city, built on land granted to Captain John West, was King and Queen, and dates from about 1691. The name was changed to Delaware in 1705. In an interesting twist, Lord de la Warr was Thomas West.

By the eighteenth century, the port of entry was called The Point. Local residents, it is said, added the West family name to it.

WEYERS CAVE

In 1806, a man named Bernard Weyer was trying to rid his property of ground hogs. On one particular day, he started to use a shovel to dig out one of the varmint's escape tunnels. He discovered vast caverns beneath. The caverns became known as Weyer's Cave until the name was changed to Grand Caverns . . . to attract a larger number of tourists.

The name of the Chesapeake & Western Railroad station at this Augusta County village, however, remained Weyer's Cave.

WHITE MARSH

The name of a colonial mansion in Gloucester County, White Marsh, was assumed by the community. The land was mentioned in a patent of 24 August 1637.

WHITE POST

This Chesterfield community takes its name from a white post, erected about 1748 by surveyor George Washington, to mark the route to Lord Thomas Fairfax's manor, Greenway Court. The manor was torn down in 1858.

WHITE STONE
This location in Lancaster County was called The White Stone, and is located near White Stone Beach.

WICOMICO
An Indian settlement, Werowocomoco, existed at this Gloucester County site. The Wicocomoco was the tribal name of a member group of Powhatan's confederacy. *Moco* means a "fortified village." Another translation of the Algonquian results in "pleasant village."

This particular place, legend has it, is where Pocohontas saved Captain John Smith.

WICOMICO CHURCH
This village in Northumberland takes its name from the first church of Richard and Anne Lee, scions of the Lee family of Virginia. The original spelling of the name was Wicocomico Church, for the tribal group in Powhatan's confederacy. In 1653 it became Lee Parish.

WILLIAMSBURG
This restoration of a colonial town began in 1633 as Middle Township, an outpost of Jamestown. It was renamed in 1699, when it became Virginia's capital, to honor King William III. For eighty-one years, it was the seat of government. In 1780, Governor Thomas Jefferson moved the state's capital to Richmond.

Williamsburg is the oldest incorporated city in America; it received a royal charter as "city incorporate." The restoration of Colonial Williamsburg, which is only one part of the city, was instigated by John D. Rockefeller, Jr., and the rector of Bruton Parish Church.

WINCHESTER
The first white residents to this Frederick County location arrived in 1738. They called their settlement Opequon; then Old Town; and Fredericktown, since it was the county seat.

It finally became Winchester in 1752 (or 1744), named for the home of founder John Wood. Winchester played a major role in the French and Indian and Civil wars.

WINDMILL POINT

Windmill Point is situated at the confluence of the Rappahannock River and the Chesapeake Bay. There is a creek by the same name nearby, but no one is sure which came first. The name probably refers to the number of windmills that were once in the area.

WINDSOR

The name for this Isle of Wight community was chosen by a Mrs. Mahone, who had a fascination with the novels of Sir Walter Scott. (See Wakefield, Waverly.)

WINGINA

Wingina, Nelson County, is supposed to be the name of an Indian chief, the son-in-law of Powhatan. His name was mentioned in the Amadas and Barlow narrative of their 1584 voyage. An Indian village once sat on this site.

WISE

When it was first settled, this town was called Big Glades. Not because it was a "big glade"; the name was derived from an archaic word, "gladly," which meant attractive. Or was it? The Gladys Creek, which sounds like "glad," flows nearby.

In 1856, the name became Gladeville, but that caused confusion with the West Virginia town of the same name. When it became the county seat, it was known as Wise Court House, for the county. Wise County was formed in 1856, and named for Henry Alexander Wise, Virginia's governor from 1856–60. The name was shortened to Wise during the Cleveland administration.

WOODBRIDGE

The first name attached to this community was Occoquan Plantation, owned by George Mason. Its current name was given by Mason's son Thomas, who commemorated the "wood bridge" that replaced the ferry across Occoquan Creek in 1798. The wooden bridge lasted until it was replaced in 1927.

WOODFORD

For many years, the Richmond, Fredericksburg & Potomac Railroad station at this Caroline County stop was called Woodslane. It was changed to Woodford for General William Woodford, who was born in the community.

WOODLAWN

This community in Carroll County was named for Colonel James Wood, who received a grant of 2,800 acres from George II.

WOODSTOCK

Originally called Muellerstadt, after its founder Jacob Mueller (Miller), the town became Woodstock—legally—in 1761. In fact, Mueller named it himself. Woodstock possesses one of the oldest county courtrooms in continual use in Virginia, built in 1791.

WOODVILLE

Woodville, in Rappahannock County, was named for the Reverend John Woodville, the last rector of St. Mark's parish.

WYTHEVILLE

Wytheville has been the county seat since the formation of Wytheville County in 1789, and takes its name from the county. In earlier times, it was known as Abbeville and Evansham.

Wytheville County commemorates George Wythe, prominent lawyer and signer of the Declaration of Independence. He was born in Elizabeth City County, now the city of Hampton.

The area around Wytheville is peppered with valuable lead and salt mines. During the Civil War, Molly Tynes rode forty miles over the mountains to alert home-guard members to return to fight off Union forces attempting to take Wytheville.

YALE

The only possible suggestion for the name of this Sussex County community is that some railroad official, because that is who named it, was from Old Eli.

YORKTOWN

The land on which Yorktown was built was patented by a French engineer in 1630. The Virginia Assembly authorized the establishment of a port here in 1680. Yorktown is the county seat of York County, formed in 1634 as the Charles River County but renamed in 1643 for Yorktown, England.

Its courthouse dates back to 1697. Its custom house, built in 1706, is the oldest in America.

Yorktown hosted the 19 October 1781 British surrender during the Revolution.

ZION CROSSROADS
This Fluvanna County community takes its name from the Biblical hill in Jerusalem.

ZUNI
No one knows for sure the origin of this village name. One suggestion is that it came from a novel by Sir Walter Scott.

Scott's fiction also helped name Windsor in the same county, so this suggestion is possible. Another possibility is that the name comes from an Indian tribal name.

West Virginia

West Virginia shares its history, from about 1609 until the Civil War, with Virginia.

West Virginia was the western section of Virginia until that state seceded from the Union in 1861. Following secession, delegates of the forty western counties formed their own government. West Virginia was granted statehood in 1864.

The Civil War brought pain and suffering to the "Mountain State." In fact, what has become known as the first overt act of the war took place in what is now West Virginia, at Harpers Ferry. This was where a young Robert E. Lee arrested John Brown for his assault on the federal arsenal. Little did his contemporaries realize that the young military officer who stood up for the Union would lead the Army of Northern Virginia against his former comrades.

West Virginia's first settlement was founded by Morgan Morgan at Mill Creek in 1731. Twelve years later, coal was discovered on the Coal River, and that discovery, more than anything else, helped mold the future of this state. The desire to exploit the land and its natural resources created towns and villages that bore the name of the exploiters and the ore they tore from the earth. Some of these towns are still in existence, though the need for coal has greatly diminished over the years.

Coal mining brought the railroads to West Virginia. These roads transported the "black gold" from mine to market. The names that dot the West Virginia soil carry the name of the railroaders, the coal mine operators, and the federal officials who helped make it all possible. Senator Henry Gassaway Davis proved especially prominent, single-handedly naming a great deal of West Virginia for himself, his family, his friends, business associates, and fellow members of Congress.

West Virginia is, as its nickname implies, a mountainous area. Man's reverence of nature and its beauty is also represented in countless West Virginia place names.

ACCOVILLE

This village takes its name from the name of one of the three mines that once operated here, the Amherst Coal Company.

ACME

Acme describes a high point.

ALDERSON

This Monroe County town was named for the Reverend John Alderson, a frontier minister who organized the first Baptist Church in the Greenbrier Valley. Alderson apparently settled here in 1777 and started a ferry service under his name.

ALLOY

This town, formerly a coal-mining community, came to depend on the Electro-Metallurgical Company, manufacturer of ferroalloys. The original name of this town was Carbon, but the name was changed sometime between 1917–20 to Boncar, to avoid any conflict with the nearby community of Mount Carbon. Boncar, by the way, is "carbon" spelled backwards. The town became Alloy in 1931.

Alloy stands on the site of the Paddy Huddleston Farm. Paddy and Daniel Boone trapped beaver together at Kanawha Falls.

ALPENA

When this Randolph County community developed about 1880, it was called Alpine. The name was given by a group of Swiss immigrants to the area who established a dairy industry. The name was soon modified to Alpena.

ALTA

The Latin word *alta* signifies a high location.

ALUM BRIDGE

At an earlier time, a bridge spanned the Alum Creek. The town that grew around this area assumed the name of that structure.

ALVON

The name of this Greenbrier County community goes back to the mid-nineteenth century. The town, local tradition has it, was named for the steamer *Alvin Adams*, also the name of the president of the Adams Express Company.

AMEAGLE

A mining town in Raleigh County, Ameagle takes its name from the coal company that operated there, American Eagle Colliery.

AMMA

Amma was suggested to postal authorities as Amie, the name of the eleven-year-old daughter of John M. Geary, a leader in this Roan County community. The post office modified the name.

ANJEAN

The name of this Greenbrier County town is a combination of the names of Ann and Jean Leckie, the mother and daughter of the owner of the Leckie Coal Company, which was established here.

ANSTED

Originally settled in 1790 by a group of Baptists, this Fayette County community was named New Haven by a group of New England Spiritualists who arrived in 1830. It was renamed about 1873 for British scientist David T. Ansted, who interested English investors in the coal-mining operations in the area. He apparently also owned some land in the vicinity.

Some sources suggest Ansted had prior names, including Mountain Cove and Woodville. These names do exist—near the site of Ansted.

Confederate General Thomas "Stonewall" Jackson's mother, Julia Neale Jackson, is buried in Ansted, in Westlake Cemetery.

ANTHONY
Anthony, Greenbrier County, takes its name from the Anthony Creek. The creek was named after an Indian, John Anthony, who hunted in the woods nearby.

ANTIOCH
Before 1800, Antioch, was called Old Rodgers Mill, then Jone's Mill. It became Harrison's Mills until about 1880. To some extent, during the same period, it was also known as Grayson's Gap.

The present name, it is reported, was given by Marcus L. Mott and Abe Chamberlain, for the ancient capital of Syria. A more likely origin is the fact that the town grew up around the Antioch Woolen Mill.

ARBOVALE
By the end of the nineteenth century, this town was named Arbovale. The naming appears to honor Adam Arbogast, who owned the land on which the post office was built. A combination of his name and "-vale" for valley create Arbovale.

ARCOLA
When first settled, this town was called Hardwood.

In the early twentieth century, the Lilly Coal Company opened a mine here and lobbied to have the name changed. The lumber people wanted it to be Lumberport; the coal compay, Arcola or "our coal." According to local tradition, the coal company "influenced a majority" of townspeople, and their name was accepted.

ARISTA
This Mercer County village experienced the age-old struggle between men and women. The town was often called Patterson, after the president of Patterson Coal Company. Arista was his wife's given name. The best man . . . er, woman, won.

ARLINGTON

The name for this Upshur County town came from Alfious [sic] Arlington Fidler, the first postmaster. It was known as Fidler's Mill before the Civil War.

ARMILDA

Kim Mills, the man responsible for establishing the first post office in this Wayne County village, named it for his deceased wife.

ARNOLDSBURG

Arnoldsburg, Calhoun County, was settled by Phillip Starcher in 1810, but the town was named for Charles Arnold, the town's schoolteacher when the post office opened in 1832.

ARTHURDALE

The site of this community was originally the plantation of Colonel John Fairfax, one of George Washington's close friends. The land was later sold to Richard M. Arthur, of Pittsburgh, Pennsylvania. Arthur apparently gave his name to the location.

Arthurdale was one of three federal resettlement programs of the Roosevelt administration, a 1934 experiment to rehabilitate selected families.

ASHLEY

This Doddridge County community was named Ashley in 1894. It takes its name from the Ash family, numerous in the area. They would have preferred Ash, but that version was already in use.

ASHTON

This neighborhood was originally known as Mercer's Bottom. In 1881, the post office was organized in this Mason County town and the name selected was Ash, for the ash tree. Unfortunately, that name was already in use, so a young woman, Ella Belle Hill, suggested, "If you are going to have ashes, make it a ton of them." The "-ton" was added to the "Ash," and the name stuck.

ATHENS

For most of the nineteenth century, this Mercer County locale was called Concord Church. The local church had been built (1837) and used by a number of different denominations, and so the name. Because Concord proved to be such a popular name, postal authorities suggested replacing the name in 1873. C.A. Fulwider proposed Athens, because he felt the Concord State Teachers College helped the town resemble Athens, a "seat of learning."

AUGUSTA

This town revived the colonial name of Augusta, the county from which part of Hampshire County was formed. The county was named for the Princess Augusta, wife of Frederick, Prince of Wales, the eldest son of George II.

Augusta had earlier been called Barrettsville, after a local family. The name change took place in the late nineteenth century.

AURORA

The first settlement in this Preston County area was founded by the Reverend John Stough in 1787. His colony was called the German Settlement. In 1800, John Wheeler moved here from Lancaster, Pennsylvania, and established Carmel (or Mount Carmel). Forty years later, the two cities merged and became West Union.

In 1875, West Union became Aurora, at the suggestion of Dr. F.V.N. Painter, who thought the name quite descriptive of the town's altitude.

BALD KNOB

From 1800 until 1875, this Boone County area was called Bald Knobs. The "s," unfortunately, was dropped for some unknown reason. That consonant provides us with an inkling of the name source. The town is surrounded by five "bald knobs," five high rock-capped peaks.

BARBOURSVILLE

This Cabell County village was established in 1813, and named for Philip Pendleton Barbour, a Virginia lawyer, for whom Barbour County was also named.

BARNABUS

An earlier name for Barnabus was Cow Creek, taken from the nearby waterway. The current name, once spelled Barnabas, appeared in 1910. It honored local resident Barnabus Curry.

BARTLEY

Bartley takes its name from Bartley Ross, the owner of this land, surveyed by Virginian John Charles in the early nineteenth century.

BARTOW

In the eighteenth century, Bartow was known as Traveller's Repose. In 1904, with the approach of the railroad, the name was changed.

Legend has it that during the Civil War, a Camp Bartow was located here. This is possible, because a minor skirmish took place here in 1861. The Bartow who gave his name was Confederate General F. S. Bartow, also gave his life at the first Battle of Bull Run.

BASS

In 1908, G.V. Wolfe, the first postmaster, suggested the town be named bass because it was located on a stream full of that fish.

BAYARD

The Grant County village was named in 1882 for Thomas F. Bayard, a member of Grover Cleveland's cabinet. He was also a stockholder in the Western Maryland Railroad.

BEATRICE

Beatrice Haught, niece of local resident C.M. Deem, was the source of the name of this Ritchie County community.

BECKLEY

The county seat of Raleigh County was once called Raleigh, after its county. Originally in Fayette County, the city was established by the legislature in 1837. At one time, it was known as "the smokeless coal capital of the world."

It was named for General Alfred Beckley, who had served under Winfield Scott in the Mexican War and later became clerk of the House of Representatives. His father had been a congressman during the administrations of Washington, Adams, and Jefferson. Beckley settled here in 1838, but the community was slow to grow. It was not until 1850 that the first business, a blacksmith shop, opened. In that year, the state legislature created the county and named Beckley as the county seat.

BEDINGTON

Originally called The Lick, for the sulfur spring nearby where deer came for their dose of salt, this Berkeley County town was named for Major Henry Bedinger.

The major was born in Little York, Pennsylvania, and was brought to the county in 1758. In 1775, he began a military career under Captain Hugh Stephenson. After the war, he became a merchant. He died in 1843 at his estate, "Protumma," five miles south of Martinsburg. Years ago, townspeople felt the name should be Bedingerton, but that did not work out.

BELINGTON

Belington, Barbour County, formerly known as the Barker Settlement, was named for John Bealin, a native of the town of Philippi who built a store here before the war.

The Civil War battle of Laurel Hill took place in the neighborhood of Belington in July 1861. By a series of moves, General George B. McClellan was able to deceive Confederate General Robert S. Garnett, who was in command of Laurel Hill. Garnett did not realize he had been outflanked. Faced with hunger and a retreat through hostile territory, 555 Confederate officers and soldiers surrendered when offered a wagonload of bread.

BELLE

The post office at this location was organized in 1902. The first postmistress was Miss Belle Reynolds (later Mrs. Gardner).

BELLEVILLE

Fort Belleville was erected in this Wood County location during the winter of 1785–86, under the command of Captain Joseph Wood and ten laborers from Pittsburgh. Wood gave no reason for the naming, but the name combines belle, "beautiful," with -ville.

BELLWOOD

A coal camp was established in this Fayette County location in 1918. The name is a combination of the surnames of the founders: J. Wade Bell and J. E. Wood.

BELMONT

The name of Belmont was meant to infer a "beautiful mountain."

BELVA

Belva honors Belva Lockwood, a pioneering feminist who twice ran for the presidency as a candidate on the Equal Suffrage ticket.

BENWOOD

This Marshall County community was legally established in 1853. The name comes from Benjamin McMechen, who owned the land on which the town was built. The acreage had formerly been known as "Ben's Woods."

BEREA

The first settlers arrived at this location in 1848—the name came later. This Biblical name was suggested during a revival meeting.

BERKELEY SPRINGS

In a March 1747 diary entry, George Washington referred to this locale as "Warm Springs," but that name did not last. In fact, it was his enthusiasm for "y Fam'd Warm Springs" that made the springs well known.

The state legislature established the town in 1762 as "Bath, now in the county of Berkeley." The post office, however, was called Berkeley Springs.

The town was settled as a health resort in 1776 and named Bath, which is still its official name. The name Berkeley Springs settled into place again following the Civil War.

The name Bath has one of two origins: the bathing that took place in the springs at this Morgan County locale, dating back to the Indians; or from Bath, England, a place renowned for its mineral springs. The Berkeley name recalls the county, which honors Norborne Berkeley, governor of Virginia from 1768–70.

BESOCO

Besoco is another West Virginia community whose name is derived from letters of the name of its major industry, in this case Beckley Smokeless Coal Company. The name originated in 1915.

BETHANY

This community was founded before 1818 by Alexander Campbell. Campbell, the son of a Presbyterian minister, established Buffalo Academy (1818–23), which became Bethany College.

Twenty years later, he laid out the town on his land and called it Bethany. Campbell also founded one of the largest religious movements in the United States. Until 1830, Campbell and his followers were basically Baptists. That movement then developed into the Christian Churches, the Christian Church (Disciples of Christ), and the Church of Christ.

BEVERLY

The earliest name for this Randolph County village was Edmundton, named for Edmund Randolph, governor of Virginia (1786–88), for whom the county was also named. When the legislature legally established the town in 1790, it changed the name to Beverly.

Several sources suggest that Beverly came from Beverly Randolph, Edmund Randolph's mother—in fact, her name was probably Arena. Other sources think it came from William Beverly, original owner of Beverly Manor.

Beverly was settled by Robert Files and his family in 1753. A few weeks after they arrived, Indians attacked the family, and only one son escaped. No new settlement was attempted for more than twenty years. In 1774, the six Westfall brothers built a fort at the mouth of Files Creek.

BIGBEND

At this point in the Greenbrier River, there is a "big bend." That name was given to the mountain, the Chesapeake & Ohio Railroad tunnel through the mountain and, probably, this town.

BIG CHIMNEY

This Kanawha County community took its name from the stone foundation of a brick chimney; all that remained of an eighteenth century salt works around which the town grew.

BIG SPRINGS

The name for this Calhoun County village comes from two large springs at the site. The town was earlier called Chestnut Stove.

The town occupies the site of Fort Evans, which John Evans built in 1755. A year later, Indians attacked while the men were away. Evans' wife, Polly, rallied the women, who pretended to have a superior force and scared the Indians off after exchanging a few shots.

BLACKSVILLE

Shortly before the American Revolution, this Monongalia County location was the site of Fort Baldwin (Baldwin Blockhouse). In 1797, it was known as New Hampshire or Hampshire Town, a reference to the origin of the settlers. The town was settled by Bruce and Nathan Worley. Bruce Worley also settled Pentress in 1766.

In 1829, David Black laid out town lots on his farmland. The current name is obviously his. Before 1831, however, the area was called Dunkard, then Thomas. The name Dunkard returned in 1832 and lasted until 1840, at which time the town became Blacksville.

BLAINE

James G. Blaine, a stockholder in the business adventures of Henry Gassaway Davis, gave his name to this Mineral County village.

Blaine (1830–93) was a leading politician of the late nineteenth century and headed up the Pan-American movement to foster closer ties with Latin American counties. He was the 1884 Republican presidential candidate.

BLOOMERY

A "furnace and forge in which wrought-iron blooms are made" is called a "bloomery." As early as 1742, a "bloomery" was in operation at this Hampshire County site, run by Thomas Mayberry.

BLOOMINGROSE

Until 1902, this Boone County town was known as Toney's Branch, a reference to the waterway situated there.

The current name appears to refer to an area of Western Maryland known as Blooming Rose, because of the abundance of flowers there.

BLUEFIELD

Bluefield, Mercer County, was named for the fields of chicory, a native wild flower with distinctive blue blooms, that cover this area. Its sister city, Bluefield, Virginia, lies to the southwest.

BOAZ

In 1878, when the post office in this village was being organized, William Johnson submitted three possible names: Johnson, Ruth, and Boaz. Postal authorities selected the Biblical name of Boaz.

BOLAIR

"Beau Clair" was a popular song among settlers and wagoners of the era. They corrupted the French title into Bolair, the name of their town. There are, however, other suggestions of corrupted words that may have become the name of this village.

One source suggests the name came about after a traveler commented on the brisk wintery air: "What a bold air!" Another contends that the song was "Beau Laire."

BOLIVAR

The name for this town in Jefferson County was given by a Major Pauls, who owned the land during the first half of the nineteenth century. The town was established by law in 1825. The name probably refers to Simon Bolivar (1783–1830), who liberated South America from Spanish domination. Bolivar was well-respected in this country, and was seen in the same light as George Washington.

BOMONT

Bomont is a misspelling of "beaumont."

BORDERLAND

Borderland, Mingo County, "borders" on the Kentucky state line, a logical reason for the naming. However, the Borderland Coal Company was located there and some historians suggest the company provided the name. It seems the opposite is more likely.

BRAMWELL

The name for this Mercer County site came from the English engineer and coal-mine operator who once lived here.

Bramwell was once considered the richest town in the United States, with fourteen millionaires in residence. During World War I, the Bank of Bramwell floated the largest Liberty Bond of the war. In the 1920s, a popular phrase was "solid as the Bank of Bramwell." The Depression and the stock market collapse ended prosperity and the Bank of Bramwell.

BRANCHLAND

Located on both sides of the Guyandot River, Branchland was once two towns: Branchfield on the west, Branchland on the east. Local tradition holds that the town was named for Colonel Branch when he began to operate coal mines here in 1903. Another source indicates that Branchland was originally called Hadley.

BREEDEN

Previous names for this Mingo County town include: Breding, Breeden, Breeding, Logan, and Randolph.

A George Bredin (Breeding) was a resident of Randolph in 1785. It appears that this man's name was chosen for the town.

BRIDGEPORT

The building of a bridge across Simpson Creek in 1803 was reason enough to name this Harrison County community. This was the first bridge built in the county.

Before the bridge arrived, Bridgeport was known as Powers Fort, in 1771, for the small structure built by John Powers. However, John Simpson, the first white man in the territory, camped on the site in 1764. The town was patented by Daniel Davisson.

In 1816, the town was legally established as Bridgeport on the lands of Joseph Johnson. Johnson was the only governor of Virginia from west of the Allegheny Mountains. Bridgeport was also home to Colonel Benjamin Wilson, a legendary figure in his own way: he fathered thirty children!

BRUCETON MILLS

The village of Bruceton Mills, Preston County, was called Morton's Mill in 1791 when Samuel Morton built his gristmill here.

The name change came about in the mid-nineteenth century when John M. Huffman named the town for his stepfather, Colonel George Bruce. This town also may have been called Bruceton and New Bruceton.

BUCKEYE

In 1784, John and James Bridger were murdered by Indians near a horse-chestnut (buckeye) tree. That event is apparently commemorated in the naming of this Greenbrier County community.

It has also been known as Swago, from the Swago Creek. When the post office was established in 1866, and up until 1877, the name was Buckeye Cove.

BUCKHANNON

The first settlement at this Upshur County location was called Bush

Fort. It was destroyed by Indians in 1782. The town was platted by Colonel Edward Jackson in 1815, on land owned by his mother, Elizabeth Cummings Jackson. It was legally established a year later, and named for the Buckhannon River on which it is located. The river's name came from either a Delaware Indian chief by the name of Buck-on-ge-ha-non, or an English family.

There is merit to both ideas. The chief was a figure during the border wars and was known as the "Washington of the Delaware." Census records report a Hannon family living in Harrison County. Since the town was once called Buckwheat, it is possible that the name was a merger of "Buck" and "-hannon."

BUD

Before the Virginian Railroad was built, Bud Adams had a logging camp on Barker's Creek. His name is recalled in this village.

BUFFALO

This town, established between 1834 and 1839, was named "for the American bison whose trail cuts through this valley."

A famous resident of Buffalo was William Hope "Coin" Harvey (1851–1936). Harvey politicked for the free coinage of silver, an issue that rocketed William Jennings Bryan to his place in history. When the Democratic Party dropped the "free silver" issue in 1900, Harvey moved to Arkansas and built a resort town, Monte Ne, and opened a hotel.

Harvey felt civilization was doomed, and began building a gigantic pyramid that would be the depository for the wealth of American culture. Apparently, he decided there was still hope when he halted work in time to run for president in 1932. He carried the standard of the Liberty Party, and garnered 800 votes!

BUNKER HILL

Bunker Hill, Doddridge County, has a name that might commemorate the famous Revolutionary War battle, misnamed by chance, of Breed's Hill in Boston.

Morgan Morgan, a native of Wales, came from Delaware and built the first Episcopal church in West Virginia at "Bunker's Hill" in 1740—slightly earlier than the battle. Chances are the name commemorates a settler. In fact, there are some records extant that call the early settlement "Bunkersville." The "s" provides a hint at the possessive. If it had not been included in the name, historians might have concluded that the derivation was from an underground fortification.

BURLINGTON

Burlington, Mineral County, was a settlement as early as 1833. It is possible the name originated with settlers from the New Jersey town of the same name.

The oldest structure in town, the old Homestead Tavern, was built about 1785 and rebuilt in 1925.

BURNING SPRINGS

One of the legends attached to this town is that an Indian struck a flint too close to an oil-covered spring. The "water" caught fire and the Indians, in awe, named the site Burning Springs.

Other tales with more substance include the following:

Mathew Arbuckle and his band came upon a spring in 1773, found gas bubbling through it, and ignited it. Two years later, the land was patented by George Washington and General Andrew Lewis.

Another describes the "burning springs" as just "a hole in the ground through which gas escaped and which in rainy weather filled with water." In 1841, salt makers used the gas to boil down the salt brine. This seems to be the most logical source for the name.

BURNSVILLE

Before the 1870s, this village was known as Lumberport.

In 1866, Captain John Miller Burns and his brothers bought up large tracts of land, and operated the first sawmill in this part of West Virginia. The name came from the captain and his family.

BURNT HOUSE

A major stagecoach stop in the late nineteenth century was the three-story Harris Inn, located at this site. It burned to the ground one Sunday night amid a great deal of mystery and intrigue.

The gossip mill of the day was fueled by the disappearance of a Jewish peddler and the subsequent mysterious flight of John Harris, the owner of the inn. The fire, by the way, was supposedly started by an angry female slave.

After the fire, the town became known as "The Place of the Burnt House."

BURNWELL

The name of this Kanawha County village is purely descriptive. It was a "coal camp," and the name describes what coal does.

BURTON

The origin of the name of Burton, Wetzel County, is hard to pin down. Local tradition says it was named for George Bartrug, who settled the area in 1812. How the name transforms from Bartrug to Burton escapes this author.

CABINS

The previous name of this village was Corners. The name was changed to Cabins in 1935 by postal authorities. Why? No one knows.

The name might have been derived from the number of "white tourist cabins"—as they called the segregated bungalows—that were located here in the pre-World War II period.

CAMDEN

Camden, Lewis County, was named for Johnson Newlon Camden (1828–1908), a U.S. senator and railroad builder. His name is also recalled in Camden on Gauley and Jayenne. Some suggest the town was actually named for the senator's nephew, Richard P. Camden.

CAMDEN ON GAULEY

Originally called Camden, for Senator Camden, this Webster County town changed its name to avoid being confused with the "other" Camden. It is located on the Gauley River.

The original name, Lanes Bottom, lasted until the town was incorporated in 1904.

Senator Camden built a large resort hotel and also managed the Gauley Lumber Company at this location. He was deeply involved in the oil industry during his senatorial tenure, particularly during the time when Rockefeller's Standard Oil Company was receiving large secret rebates from the Pennsylvania, New York Central, and Erie Railroads to transport petroleum products. This rebate practice was later declared illegal. In 1875, Senator Camden, along with a number of other independent oil men, conceded to the government's objections and traded off his oil holdings for Standard stock. This transaction allowed Rockefeller's firm to receive rebates from the Baltimore & Ohio Railroad. Camden was a strong defender of Standard's practices. Later, he championed legislation that precluded a railroad from charging more for a short haul than for a long one. This allowed his coal and lumber holdings to compete more aggressively with his western competition.

CAMERON

This area was first settled in 1788 by Joseph, Christopher, and John Himes. They erected a blockhouse for their protection, but soon learned that a timely "bribe" to the Indians (a side of bacon, a hog, etc.) was much more effective than a fortified position.

The settlement grew. In 1852, following the completion of the railroad, an Irish merchant named David McConaughey named the town after his good friend, railroad official Samuel Cameron. At the time McConaughey owned the land on which the town rested.

CANAAN

Located in Upshur County, Canaan was near the hamlets of Goshen and Eden, both of which have disappeared. It appears that the naming was strictly Biblical.

CANEBRAKE

This village was named for the existence of a thicket of canes.

CAPON BRIDGE

Capon Bridge, located on the banks of the Capacon River, was settled in the late 1740s. Following George Washington's survey of the area for David, Joseph, and Thomas Edwards in 1750, Fort Edwards was built. The town takes its name from the river.

It was at Capon Bridge in 1756 that almost 100 members of Washington's command were massacred by Indians. In his after-action report, the future commander-in-chief wrote, ". . . I could offer myself a willing sacrifice to the butchering enemy, provided that would contribute to the people's ease."

CAPON SPRINGS

Capon Springs is located on the Capon Springs Run. The name is apparently descriptive of the town's location. Both the town and the run owe their names to the Capacon River.

Earlier names for this village include Watson, established in 1787, and Frye's Springs, for local resident Henry Frye.

CAPTINA

Prior to the Revolution, the creek opposite this Marshall County town was known as Caapteein, "the captain's creek." It is probably from this waterway that Captina took its name.

514

Others suggest the name came from the "Captina Affair" which precipitated Lord Dunmore's War in 1774.

Captina had its "moment in history" in 1849 when Zachary Taylor, on his way to his inauguration in Washington, was stranded here when his packet boat was unable to continue because of the frozen river. Taylor made his inauguration, but only after traveling by sled from Captina to Wheeling.

CARETTA

The name for this village was given "when [the] camp was built." It comes from the syllables of a woman's name: Etta Carter.

CARL

This Nicholas County community got the name of the Hominy Falls postmaster's son. Before Carl received its own post office, the mail was delivered to Hominy Falls.

CASCADE

Cascade takes its name from the cascades in Deckers Creek.

CASSITY

Cassity, Randolph County, is located on the Cassidy Creek. It appears that the town's name is a misspelling of the man's name.

Cassidy was a hunter who, in the mid-nineteenth century, camped at the head of the stream.

CASSVILLE

The earlier name for this Monongalia County village was Jacksonville, named by Peter Layton, who built a tannery here in 1827 and named it for the popular president.

To avoid postal conflict, the name was changed in 1852 to Cass, in honor of General Lewis Cass, the Democratic party's presidential candidate in 1848. (See Cassville, Pennsylvania.)

CEDAR GROVE

The first white settlement in this Kanawha County area began in 1773, when Walter Kelly came from North Carolina to try his luck.

Even after learning that the local Indians were on the warpath, Kelly brought his family to his town. A few hours after their arrival, Kelly and a black servant were killed and scalped. The next year,

William Morris assumed the Kelly claim. Morris, his seven sons, and several daughters built Kelly's Fort and established the first permanent settlement. Morris is remembered in this town by the William Morris Memorial Boulder.

In 1884, Rachel M. Grant Tompkins, wife of the owner of Tompkins Mansion and aunt to Ulysses S. Grant, named the settlement Cedar Grove for the obvious: there was a large grove of cedar trees near her new home.

CENTERVILLE/CENTER POINT

Both Centerville and Center Point indicate their location within the state.

CENTRALIA

On one hand, this village, was named thusly because it was situated in the "center" of a coalfield. On the other hand, its name may reflect its position near the center of its county and the state.

CENTURY

Originally named Big Run, for the waterway it is on, this Barbour County village underwent a name change in 1900. The logic of the renaming comes from the fact that 1900 marked the beginning of a new century, and also that the town's main commodity, coal, was destined to last another century.

CEREDO

Massachusetts congressman Eli Thayer platted this Wayne County town site in 1857. Thayer and a group of New England abolitionists came here to establish a free colony in a slave-holding state.

Thayer and his group dreamed of Ceredo as an industrial center, but the Civil War and the rapid growth of nearby Huntington, due to the arrival of the Chesapeake & Ohio Railroad, forever destroyed those hopes.

Thayer named his town, because of its rich farmland, for Ceres, the Roman goddess of agriculture. Ceres had already been used in Virginia, and West Virginia had not as yet become a separate state.

CHARLESTON

The state capital, Charleston was founded in 1794. The earliest name, however, was either Clendenin's Settlement or The Town at the Mouth of the Elk. The settlement grew around Fort Lee, or Clendenin's Fort, located in this location from 1788–95.

In 1794, the name was Charlestown. Two years later, an official deed showed the name as Charleston. The name was obviously changed to eliminate confusion over other Charlestowns or Charles Towns in the territory. Sometimes, this location was even referred to as Charleston-on-the-Kanawha.

The name of Charles-(whatever) comes from George Clendenin, who named it for his father.

The first white people to reach the site of Charleston were Mary Ingles and Betty Draper. The young women had been captured by Indians during the Ingles-Draper massacre at Draper Meadows (Blacksburg), Virginia, in 1755. They were taken to the Shawnee village at Chillicothe, Ohio.

CHARLES TOWN

Charles Town was established in 1786 on land laid out by George Washington's brother, and named for him. The name of the town was spelled as two words from the day of establishment—"to avoid confusion with Charleston, Kanawha Co." Many of the streets in this town carry the names of Washington family members. In fact, the main thoroughfare is named Washington Street.

John Brown was tried and hanged here in 1859 after his raid on Harpers Ferry. At the outbreak of the Civil War, the residents of Charles Town pledged support to the South and, as a result of this action, suffered greatly during the conflict. Charles Town was savaged by the constant invasion and withdrawal of troops. Charles Town, formerly the county seat, lost its courthouse to Shepherdstown, and consequently suffered a decided loss of prestige and revenue. There was also great rancor over the annexation of Jefferson County by the new state of West Virginia, since the majority of residents had been disenfranchised by supporting the South and were thus unable to vote on this critical issue. For years, Charles Town residents referred to themselves as from "Jefferson County, Virginia."

CHARMCO

This Greenbrier County village does not take its name from a modeling and charm school. Rather, its name is formed from the letters in the name of its principal employer at the time of naming: Charleston Milling Company.

Up to 1926, when the post office was established in the name of Charmco, the town was named Laurel Creek, for the stream on which it is located.

CHATTAROY

Chattaroy takes its name from a modification of the Indian name for the Big Sandy River, on which the village is situated.

CHEAT BRIDGE

The post office established in this community was named Winchester, for A.H. Winchester, owner of a lumber camp located here.

Several years later, the name was changed to avoid confusion with Winchester, Virginia. There is a bridge across the Cheat River here, so the name makes sense. The river took its name, perhaps, from the deceptive qualities of its waters. Would it not have been more fun if the name had something to do with a card game?

CHELYAN

In the 1880s, Chelyan, Kanawha County, took the name of Chelyan Calvert, daughter of the town's first postmaster. Previously it had been known as Slaughter's Creek and Peerless.

CHESTER

The first post office at this Hancock County location was called Mercer. In 1898, the name was changed to Chester.

It appears the town was laid out in 1896 by J.E. McDonald, who chose the name "solely because it was a short name, easy to remember." Chester was incorporated in 1907.

CHURCHVILLE

Churchville was named for the same reason as Churchville, Virginia: there were a number of churches located here.

CICERONE

The translation of this Roane County village name is "a guide who conducts sightseers." The name was suggested when the townspeople had trouble deciding on a name.

CINCO

Earlier known as Perryville, this Kanawha County village underwent a name change at the request of postal authorities. The new name was suggested by a local coal-company official. Cinco was the brand of cigar he smoked!

CIRCLEVILLE

Strange as it may seem, this Pendleton County village was named for the Zirkle family, who operated a store here. The town was settled about 1820 by Scotch-Irish immigrants.

CIRTSVILLE

Cirtsville was named in 1889 for Curtis "Curt" Vass, one of the oldest residents at the time of naming.

CLARKSBURG

In early postal records, this village ended in an "h."

The first white settler to the Clarksburg site was John Simpson, a trapper who camped here in 1764. In 1773, Simpson acquired a claim of 400 acres. He was followed by others. At the first formal town meeting in 1781, a Mr. Shinn suggested the name be Clarksburg, in honor of General George Rogers Clark, whose name is also used for Clark Township, in which this town resides.

Clarksburg is the birthplace of Confederate General Thomas J. "Stonewall" Jackson. He was born here 21 January 1824. Six years later, he moved to his grandfather's farm, now Jackson's Mill.

CLAY

Originally incorporated as Henry, this community became known as Clay Court House, since it was the seat of Clay County. The names of the county and the town honor Henry Clay.

For one brief period, Clay was known as Marshall. It is the home of the original Golden Delicious apple.

CLAYTON

In 1879, balloonist Richard Clayton rose from Cincinnati, Ohio, and floated into a windstorm. Before he could land safely, he soared past the Allegheny Mountains, making the first balloon flight west of the mountains. When he finally landed, as legend has it, he walked miles to find food and help. He found both at a house where the residents were deciding on a name for their town.

Clayton's arrival, or so they say, saved the residents a great deal of bickering over the town's name.

CLEARCO

This site was developed in 1929–30 by the Clear Creek Coal Company. When the post office was established in 1930, the townspeople elected to use a shortened version of the company's name.

The coal company, by the way, took its name from the creek on which the town is located. Because Clear Creek already existed as a community name, the Clearco name avoided any confusion.

CLENDENIN

The first name of this village was Chilton. It was laid out by William E. Chilton in 1877 and named in honor of his father, Black Chilton.

The name was changed to recognize Charles Clendenin, the first settler at the mouth of the Elk River and the real founder of Charleston in 1788.

CLEVELAND

Earlier named Point, the name of this Webster County village was changed to commemorate President Grover Cleveland.

CLOVER LICK

This Pocahontas County community received its name in 1875 when a post office was opened. It carries the name of a local farm, Clover Lick, owned by John Warwick. Warwick's farm was named before the Revolution by the first white men in the area, who saw deer licking the moisture from clover growing in a field.

COAL CITY

The presence of coke ovens in this town caused the townspeople to change the name of Dabney to Coal City in the late 1920s.

COALTON

The original name for this coal center in Randolph County was Womelsdorf(f), named for O.C. Womelsdorf, the area's first coal operator and a native of Pennsylvania. The name change was descriptive of the community's major occupation.

CORINTH

The name of this Preston County community was Spencer until 1890, when postal authorities asked the town to change its name to avoid confusion with another West Virginia town. The name selected comes from the Biblical city.

CORNSTALK

The name of Chief Cornstalk (1727–1777), leader of the Shawnees, is carried on by this Greenbrier County town. Cornstalk was an honorable man who kept his peace treaty with the English only to be murdered at Point Pleasant in 1777.

COTTAGEVILLE

When the post office was established here, the majority of houses did not reach two stories.

CRAWLEY

Crawley takes its name from Crawley Creek, named for James Crawley, who was killed while surveying on the stream in 1783.

CRESSMONT

Cressmont began in 1907, when the Crescent Lumber Company opened a lumber camp in this Clay County area. The name has something to do with the "Crescent" in the company's name.

CULLODEN

The Chesapeake & Ohio asked L. R. White, who had lost a leg working on the railroad, to come up with a name for their station in this Cabell county community. White selected Culloden because there were few, if any, towns with that name in the United States.

CUNARD

At one time, this village had two names: Coal Run for the village, after the waterway, and Cunard for the post office. The post office name was selected by an official of the Coal Run Coal Company who had an interest in the Cunard Line of steamships.

CUTLIPS

Cold weather had nothing to do with the naming of this Braxton County village. The name comes from E. W. Cutlip, a state representative in 1897.

CUZZART

Cuzzart, Preston County, seems to be a phonetic pronunciation of the family names of Thomas Coser and Jacob Cozar, settlers in the late eighteenth century.

Prior to 1886, when Cuzzart was chosen as the town's name, the church was called Pleasant Valley, and the school Chidester.

CYCLONE

Cyclone took its name from that destructive natural phenomenon. The name was given in 1888, after a cyclone ripped through this Wyoming County area and laid bare a strip of forestland 300 yards wide and 600 yards long.

CZAR

The postal authorities selected the name for this Randolph County village from a list submitted by A. D. Lewis, the first postmaster. The most likely source is that the name was that of an individual. For example, there was a Zar Beerbower for whom the Preston County town of Zar was named.

DALLAS

Dallas was first called Haney Town, for Thomas Haney who, in 1816, built the first house in this Marshall County location. Later the name became West Union.

In 1865, postal authorities made the change to Dallas to avoid confusion over West Union, Doddridge County. The name is perhaps a surname, since there were a number of Dallas families in West Virginia at the time.

DALLAS. George Mifflin Dallas was the only Pennsylvanian ever to be elected vice president of the United States. Though virtually forgotten in political circles, Dallas is recalled in the names of Dallas and Dallastown, Pennsylvania, Dallas, West Virginia, and—of course—Dallas, Texas. [CREDIT: Print and Picture Department, Free Library of Philadelphia]

DANESE

When the post office was established in this Fayette County location, it was named Noel. Two years later, the name was changed to that of Danese, the daughter of Sherman G. Bowyer.

DANVILLE

Earlier names for Danville were Newport and Red House. The current name comes from Dan Rock, the first postmaster.

DARKESVILLE

This town was established by the legislature in 1791. It had two previous names: James Town, then Buckle Town (or Bucklestown, Buckelstown, Buckellstown), for a General Buckel(l)s.

The name was changed to Darkesville in 1797 when the town was incorporated. The name commemorates General William Darke (1736–1801), a veteran of the Revolutionary War and a magistrate in Berkeley County. Darke spent his boyhood in this town, and his family's log cabin has been incorporated into the Adam Link House.

In 1862, Darkesville was the staging ground from which Confederate General J.E.B. Stuart and almost 2,000 troops successfully raided Chambersburg, Pennsylvania. They destroyed $250,000 worth of Union property, captured 30 men and 1,200 horses. Stuart lost two men and two horses in the conflict.

DAVIS

Established in 1885, Davis was one of the first lumber towns in the state. But lumber had nothing to do with its naming.

The town was named for Henry Gassaway Davis, president of the Western Maryland Railroad in 1881, a two-time U. S. Senator and coal magnate. Since the town was incorporated in 1889, the timing seems to indicate that he was the name donor.

DAVIS CREEK

Davis Creek, Kanawha County, takes its name from the waterway, which was named for Thomas Davis. Davis bought land at the mouth of the creek in 1790. For five shillings, he got 245 acres!

DAVY

This McDowell County town was once schizophrenic. The post office and town were called Hallsville before 1901; the station of the Norfolk & Western Railroad, on the other hand, was named Davy in 1893. Hallsville came from Henry Hall, who owned the townsite; Davy, from the nearby Davy Creek. When another Davy post office in northern West Virginia was cancelled in 1901, this community became one with its railroad station.

DEEP WATER

Earlier known as Loop Creek, because of its proximity to the waterway of that name, this Fayette County village changed its name in about 1880. James Gilespie Kincaid, Jr., named it Deep Water for a deep pool of water here caused by a temporary rise in the Kanawha River.

DEERWALK

Before 1875, this Wood County community was known as Pleasant Hill, but to avoid confusion with the other Pleasant Hill, the townspeople were asked to select a new name. With the establishment of the post office in 1875, the town selected Deer Walk. Apparently, during earlier days, the deer used to cross here.

DeKALB

William Stalnaker, the richest landowner in the area, used his position in 1835 to honor a boyhood hero, Baron DeKalb.

DELLSLOW

Dellslow is the result of a postal slip-up. When the post office was established, the name Delsloh was submitted. It was to honor Louis Hageborn, who owned the local mill and was from Fredelslow, Hanover, Germany. The postmark came back Dellslow.

Previously the town had been Valley Furnace, for an iron furnace and nail mill built in 1798 by Samuel Hannaway; Guesman's (or Guseman's) Mills in 1854, for a grist- and woolen mill set up by Abraham Guesman; and Hageborn's Mills in 1864, for Louis Hageborn. In 1884, the post office was established as Louisville, again for Hageborn. Finally, because of conflict with another Louisville, the name became Dellslow.

DENMAR

Tradition has it that Denmar was founded in 1910 by a Mr. Dennison from Hagerstown, Maryland. The name is supposed to be a combination of Dennison and Maryland.

DINGESS

Dingess takes its name from Dingess Trace Branch. The waterway recognizes the Dingess family. Peter Dingess, from Germany, made the first settlement in Logan County, about three miles from this town, in 1799. His son, William, was a noted Indian fighter.

DODRILL

Dodrill was once called The Mouth of Rush Run. The church there is still called Rush Run Church. The name Dodrill derives from the surname of William Christian Dodrill, the author of a 1915 book of West Virginia sketches entitled *Moccasin Tracks and Other Imprints*.

DOTHAN

Tradition has it that Dothan is a Biblical name. The post office here was called Armstrong from 1894–1898, for a family of early settlers. It is possible the current name also comes from a family name.

DUNBAR

Dunbar was incorporated in 1921. Its growth resulted from the expansion of the chemical industries in the area during World War I. It was named for Dunbar Baines, a Charleston lawyer and banker.

DUNMORE

Dunmore, Pocahontas County, was named by Major Jacob Warwick for Lord Dunsmore, the last colonial governor of Virginia.

An alternate story, more fanciful but less truthful, speaks of the town being called Matthewsville until 1840 or 1850, for the sole resident. He sold the land in 1845 to a Mr. Moore and a Mr. Dunn, and the name became Dunmore, or an amalgam of their two names. Sadly for the veracity of this story, the town was named Dunmore before the American Revolution.

DUO

When Albert Williams and his family settled in this Greenbrier County village, there were only two houses. One family member decided to call their settlement Duo, for "two."

DURBIN

This town name points out that when making a bank loan, it is always important to read the fine print.

In 1890, John T. McGraw bought this townsite, borrowing money from a Grafton bank to do so. He got the loan; then named the town after the bank's cashier, Charles R. Durbin, Sr.

EAST LYNN

When the community was settled, it was called Twin Creek, for the obvious reason: two streams enter the Twelvepole Creek at this point in Wayne County. One stream was called Lynn Creek; the other, Little Lynn.

Since this village was nearer Little Lynn, which comes in east of town, it was called East Lynn.

EASTON

According to local tradition, Tom Anderson named this community in about 1865. He named it Easton because it was east of Morgantown. Another source, however, implies that Dr. Charles McLane suggested the name when the post office was established in 1860.

Easton rests on the site of Fort Pierpont, built by John Pierpont in 1769. He was the son-in-law of Zackquill Morgan, for whom Morgantown was named. Francis H. Pierpont, governor of the Restored Government of Virginia (as West Virginia was known after Virginia seceded from the Union), was born here.

EDRAY

Edray is located on the site of Fort Drennan, built in 1774 by Thomas Drennan.

Fort Drennan was attacked by Indians, and Drennan's wife was murdered; his son, taken captive. Mentally destroyed, the man joined General Lewis' expedition against the Indians and fought at Point Pleasant. After the war, he wandered through the Northwest, still fighting Indians. Years later, he found his son, who had been ransomed by a trader.

ELEANOR

Along with Tygart Farms and Arthurdale, Eleanor was a social experiment created by the Federal Homestead Administration of Franklin D. Roosevelt. All three locations were designed as self-sufficient suburban communities, providing affordable housing and industrial rehabilitation for 150 West Virginia families. The residents' names were drawn from the relief rolls. The town was named for President Roosevelt's wife, Eleanor.

The first homesteaders took up residence in 1935 and formed the Red House Association. The group took its name from a local brick house, built before 1825 for Joseph Ruffner.

ELGOOD

Postal authorities named this Mercer County locale for L. Goodwin, whose suggestion for the post office's name was rejected.

ELIZABETH

This village was settled in 1796 by William Beauchamp. Until his marriage, it was known as Beauchamp's Mills. In 1817, it became Elizabeth, in honor of his bride Elizabeth Woodyard.

ELK GARDEN

When the first settlers arrived, it is said, they were greeted by herds of elk around a pond. With that image in mind, they named their settlement Elk Pond. Later, they changed the name to Elk Garden.

ELKHORN

This village takes its name from the Elkhorn River.

The waterway was so named because a hunter, after killing a large bull elk, stuck the animal's horns on a pole at the mouth of the stream.

ELKINS

This Randolph County community was named for U. S. Senator Stephen B. Elkins, who founded the current town in 1889. The honor was given Elkins possibly because he was a director of the Western Maryland Railroad, on whose route the town was located. More probably, the town was named because Elkins had located his country house on a hill overlooking the town.

Elkins was son-in-law to Senator Henry Gassaway Davis, who single-handedly named much of West Virginia for himself, his family, friends, and business associates. Davis' son-in-law was a powerful political figure in his own right. He served as secretary of war under President Benjamin Harrison and, as a senator, chaired the powerful Interstate Commerce Committee. As chair, he was entrusted by President Theodore Roosevelt to shepherd through the red tape of Capital Hill a controversial bill that would have empowered the ICC with greater power over railroad rate regulation. After the bill passed the House of Representatives, Elkins refused to sponsor it in the Senate.

Roosevelt was enraged, and made a number of speeches against the "evil practices" of the railroads. Faced with public support of the president, Elkins made one of his famous about-faces. He supported the bill, saying that when the "political horse is running away," he preferred to be "on the seat with the driver, ready to grab the reins."

Previously, Elkins was called Joans Friend's, Leadsville, and Leedsville—both names were pronounced with a long "e."

ELKWATER

Elkwater is located where the Elkwater Fork meets the Tygart River.

The original settlement was a fort, erected about 1774 by the Hadden family. Elkwater saw fierce fighting during the Civil War, and Colonel John Augustine Washington, grandnephew of George

Washington and aide-de-camp to General Robert E. Lee, was shot from his horse here and died 13 September 1861.

ELLENBORO

When the Baltimore & Ohio Railroad was built in this Ritchie County neighborhood, it needed to go through the property of the Williamson family. As a reward for granting right-of-way, the railroad allowed the family to name the station and, ultimately, the village. They did, for Ellen Mariah Williamson, the eldest daughter.

Ellenboro served as a trading center for speculators when oil was discovered nearby. An earlier name for the town was Shumley.

ENON

Local legend suggests that this village was named in 1861 by David and William Carden, after a town in Goochland County, Virginia. On the other hand, Enon spelled backwards is "none."

ENTERPRISE

Enterprise, once a thriving mining town—thus the name—was built on the farm of John McIntire. McIntire and his wife were murdered by Indians.

ERBACON

When the hotel-keeper in this village asked workers on the Baltimore & Ohio Railroad what they wanted to order, they responded "Beans er bacon." At least, that is how the legend goes.

A more likely source for this name is the initials and last name of Edward R. Bacon, a director of the B & O, and president of that company's Southwestern Division.

ERIN

Opinion on the reason behind the name of this village is divided: is it the name of Ireland? Or is it the name of a young woman?

EXCHANGE

The owner of the local mill gave this Braxton County village its original name of Millburn. Mrs. Samantha Duffield, the first post-mistress, changed the name to Exchange because the town's stores, blacksmith shop, and mill constantly changed hands.

F

FAIRMONT

This locale began to be settled in the late 1770s, but not until 1793 did any real development take place. In that year, Jacob Paulsley (Polsley) built a cabin on the east side of the river. His village carried his name. In 1838, his village was incorporated as Palatine.

In 1819, Virginia built a road connecting Clarksburg and Morgantown, but needed a halfway station. The land on the west side of the river, owned by Boaz Fleming, was selected because it was too rough for agriculture. This area became Middletown. The two Marion County towns, Palatine and Middletown, were merged into Fairmont, and incorporated in 1843. In 1852, the railroad reached Fairmont and built a suspension bridge connecting the east and west sides of town.

Tradition says the town was named for its scenic beauty. More likely, it was named for the district in which it resides.

FALLING ROCK

Falling Rock, Kanawha County, gains its name from the Falling Rock Creek on which it is located. In the late 1890s, Falling Rock was the name of the Baltimore & Ohio Railroad Station; the post office was named Weir. In the 1940s, the post office and the station became one and Falling Rock became the official name.

Sutton Mathews discovered the first cannel coal mines in the state when a rich vein was found at Falling Rock in 1846. The name "cannel" is a corruption of "candle" coal, because this particular coal is rich in gas and burns with a bright flame.

FALLS MILLS

The village of Falls Mills, Braxton County, was named for the mill that stood near the falls of the Little Kanawha River from 1840 to 1925. Falling Waters was the site of the July 1863 Civil War battle between the remnants of Lee's army retreating from Gettysburg and General George G. Meade's Union force. Lee's troops were able to cross the swollen Potomac River by ripping down warehouses along the Chesapeake & Ohio Canal and making a pontoon bridge. Meade vacillated, and lost his opportunity to shatter "the matchless Army of Northern Virginia."

FARMINGTON

Farmington, in Marion County, was named for the main occupation of the population, farming.

Prior to Farmington, the community was named Willeytown (or Willeyville) for the town's founder. William Willey laid out the town in the early nineteenth century. His son, Waitman T. Willey, led the movement to gain statehood for West Virginia. He was born in a log cabin here in 1811.

Farmington was also called Underwood, for Frederick Underwood, then president of the Erie Railroad.

FAYETTEVILLE

Settled in 1818, Fayetteville was named in 1839 for its county, which honored the Marquis de Lafayette.

Fayetteville was originally named Vandalia, for Abraham Vandal, who settled here in 1818. In 1836, the town was platted on his land. The next year, the town was named the seat of Fayette County, and chose the name of its county as its own. The first county court was held in Vandal's tavern.

Fayetteville was the first place where the military tactic of indirect fire—firing over the heads of friendly troops to reach enemy positions—was employed. This occurred during the Civil War.

FLAT TOP

The Flat Top area was originally settled in 1732 by "Father" Robert Lilly, who left Maryland with his wife, Mary Fanny Moody, and four sons. They settled about ten miles from town at the mouth of the Bluestone River. Lilly died in 1810, at the age of 114; his wife, seven years later, at the age of 110. Tens of thousands of Lilly family members attend a family reunion at this town each year.

FOLLANSBEE

Located in Brooke County, the village was named for a large steel mill located here, the Follansbee Brothers Mill Company.

FORT ASHBY

This Mineral County locale was first settled about 1735, and called Patterson's Creek. The name was changed to Fort Ashby in 1755 when the fort of the same name was built. When Fort Ashby received its charter in 1787, it became Frankfort or Frankford, ostensibly for Frankfurt, Germany.

At one point, the village was forced to change its name to Alaska—a bit of post-office-naming whimsy—because of conflicts with other Frankforts.

The current name was restored in 1932 and comes from the fort, which was built on the banks of Pattersons Creek by order of

George Washington, in 1755. The fort was named for Captain John Ashby, who made a miraculous escape from the Indians in 1756. Regional troops were mustered here when President Washington came to suppress the Whiskey Rebellion in 1791.

FORT GAY

Until 1900, when the post office was established, this Wayne County village was called Cassville. Due to a conflict with Cassville, Monongalia County, the name changed to Fort Gay—for a Civil War fort that once overlooked the town.

FRANKFORD

Frankford, Greenbrier County, was settled in 1769 by companions of William Renick and Captain Robert McClanahan. The town, when legally established in 1823, was called Frankfort, in honor of Frank Ludington, an early settler.

FRANKLIN

The original name for the county seat of Pendleton County was Frankford (or Frankfort), named for Francis (Frank) Evick, who, with his brother George, surveyed the land here in 1769.

Between 1794 and 1800, the legislature established the town as Franklin, changing the original name because of conflicts with Frankfort, Hampshire County, and Frankfort, Kentucky. The name is supposed to commemorate Benjamin Franklin, but Evick is the obvious name donor.

FRENCH CREEK

French Creek, Upshur County, was first settled in 1808 by a party of settlers from Massachusetts led by Aaron Gould.

The name for the stream on which this village is located got its name from a local legend about three Frenchmen who prospected for gold in 1725.

FRIARS HILL

This village in Greenbrier County carries with it no religious significance; in fact, just the opposite. It was named for a Mr. Friar who came to live here with another man's wife. One winter, he was finally tracked down by her husband's friends, who shot him and buried him in Friar's Holes.

The post office was named Friars Hill in the 1870s.

FRIENDLY

Located at the Ohio border, this town was named for Friend Cochran Williamson, grandson of Thomas Williamson, who first settled the area in 1785.

FROST

This area of West Virginia frustrated early farmers with its late spring and early autumn frosts.

G

GALLIPOLIS FERRY

William Clendenin settled this Mason County village in the 1790s. It is located opposite Gallipolis, Ohio, to which, at a later date, it was connected by a steam ferry.

Gallipolis Ferry was at one time the home of John Bryan and his wife. They were the grandparents of William Jennings Bryan.

GAP MILLS

From about 1775 to 1850, this Monroe County village was named Moss Hole, probably for James Moss, a settler.

A mill pond was located here in the narrow break—or gap—that forms Gap Mountain. Apparently, then, the name commemorates a mill or mills on or near Gap Mountain.

Gap Mills was the birthplace of Andrew Summers Rowan. Rowan, as a young second lieutenant, was given the dangerous task of delivering a message to General Garcia, leader of the Cuban insurgents, during the Spanish-American War. Rowan's feat was immortalized in Elbert Hubbard's *A Message to Garcia*.

GASSAWAY

Gassaway was founded in 1904 by the Baltimore & Ohio Railroad and named for Senator Henry Gassaway Davis. (See Davis.)

GAULEY BRIDGE

Located on the Gauley River, and taking its name from the span that crossed it, this village is located in Fayette County. The first bridge was built in the face of strong opposition from local ferrymen. The covered bridge, costing $18,000, was built in 1822 during construction of the James River and Kanawha Turnpike.

The irony of the town's name is that the bridges over the Gauley have burned down three times. It was first destroyed by fire in 1826, by "persons interested in the ferry at that point." The bridge was replaced two years later and, to protect it, the ferrymen were paid a third of all tolls collected on the bridge. In 1861, the bridge was destroyed by retreating Confederate troops.

GENOA

Forget about Italy. Forget about Columbus. This Wayne County village has nothing to do with either of them.

The town was named for Genoa Reed, Postmaster E. P. Reed's daughter.

GHENT

W. O. McGinnis, who helped get the post office opened in this Raleigh County village, said the town was named for the 1814 Treaty of Ghent, the treaty that ended the War of 1812.

GIATTO

The first postmaster in this Mercer County village, C. W. J. Walker, suggested the name Giotto, for the famous Italian painter (ca. 1267–1337). Postal authorities did not read his application carefully, and substituted an "a" where an "o" should be.

GILBERT

Gilbert was named for the creek on which it is located. Gilbert Creek was named for Joseph Gilbert, "an early traveler" or hunter in the area who was ambushed and murdered by Indians.

GLADE FARMS

Glade Farms, Preston County, was sometimes called Twin Churches. Two churches were built in the town within a year or two of each other in the 1860–1870s.

The current name comes from the definition of "glade." A glade in those pioneering days was a marshy piece of land that needed to be drained in order to be farmed.

GLADY

The town of Glady, Randolph County, takes its name from the Glady Fork, on which it is located.

Glady Fork was named for the "glades" on its banks. Before 1900, the town was called Glady Fork.

GLASGOW

In 1913, Harold P. Tompkins and four of his friends organized three companies here: Monarch Carbon Company, the Kanawha Glass Company, and the Glasgow Development Company.

A year later, when the men had to decide on a name for the post office, the men took a secret ballot, or so Tompkins said. The result was Glasgow. Three of the men were Scottish.

GLEN DALE

When this village was first settled in 1798, it was called Upper Flats—it was located on the northern flats of Grave Creek. From 1825 until 1861 it was Gravel Bottom. Until 1876, for the Secessionists who lived there, it became Hell's Half Acre. When the town was laid out in 1876, it was once again called Gravel Bottom.

It became Glen Dale in 1890, for Glendale, the farm of postmaster S. A. Cockayne's mother.

GLEN FERRIS

Until 1895, this village was named Stockton, for Colonel Aaron Stockton of New Jersey, who settled here in 1812. Stockton moved here from Burning Springs and operated a popular stagecoach stop, which later became the Glen Ferris Inn. A patron described the colonel as "a good-natured chunk of a man who cast a shadow of almost the same altitude when lying down as when standing up."

The name source, probably a surname such as found in Glen Easton, cannot be determined.

GLENHAYES

In 1853, due to the popularity of cannel coal, Rutherford B. Hayes bought up 3,000–4,500 acres of coal lands in this area. When he was thinking about running for the presidency, he sold off a large acreage to a friend, James K. Glenn, from Cincinnati.

When the Norfolk & Western Railroad was being built along the Tug River (1903–05), the heirs of both Hayes and Glenn donated land for the railroad station and laid out the town. The name is obviously a merger of the two men's names.

GLENVILLE

The earlier names for Glenville include: The Ford (the state road crossed the Little Kanawha River at this spot); Stewart's Creek (Stewart's Creek flows into the Little Kanawha about a mile east of here); in 1845, Hartford (having something to do with a deer crossing); and, finally, Glenville in 1856.

Colonel Currence B. Conrad suggested the name to postal authorities because of the glen in which the town is nestled.

GORDON

Because a coal company, the Detroit Mining Company, was the major industry in this community, it was popularly called Detroit.

When the post office was established in 1883–84, the first postmaster, Asa White, named it for his nephew, Gordon Mason.

GORMANIA

When first settled, this Grant County village was known as North Branch, since it was situated on the North Branch of the Potomac River. It was still North Branch when Jacob Schaeffer moved here in 1840. When the post office was established, Schaeffer became postmaster, and the town became Schaeffersville.

The name Gormania comes from U.S. Senator Arthur Pue Gorman, a friend of Henry Gassaway Davis and a director of the West Virginia Central & Pittsburgh Railway Company (later the Western Maryland).

GRAFTON

First known as Three Forks Creek, because of its location on that stream, this town grew on land set aside for cultivation by William Robinson in 1773. No farming ever took place, however, and in 1852, when Irish construction workers arrived to help build the Baltimore & Ohio terminus, the land was a tangle of grape vines and wild berry briars.

After the railroad was constructed, the village sprang up. It was incorporated in 1856.

The most reasonable explanation for the naming of the seat of Taylor County is that it was named for John Grafton, a civil engineer who worked for Colonel Benjamin Latrobe, who laid out the Baltimore & Ohio Railroad through here in 1852. Another suggestion, somewhat whimsical, is that the name came from the railroad workers, who referred to the town as a "graftin' on" point of the railroad.

Grafton was strategically important in the Civil War, since several branch lines of the railroad converged into the main line here. The remains of T. Bailey Brown, the first Union soldier to be killed by Confederate troops—during the Battle of Philippi—are buried in Grafton National Cemetery, 431 Walnut Street.

GRAHAM STATION

Graham Station was one of the first post offices in Mason County, in existence as early as 1817.

The community was named for the Reverend William Graham who, in 1798, designed this settlement as a Presbyterian colony. For twenty-one years, Graham served as president of the first academy west of the Blue Ridge. He persevered in his dream, but after his death his followers disbanded and left this community.

GRANTSVILLE

The town of Grantsville was laid out in 1866 by Simon P. Stump and named for Ulysses S. Grant.

Grantsville became the seat of Calhoun County in 1869, at the end of a fiery battle with the town of Arnoldsburg for the honor.

GRANVILLE

Captain Felix Scott laid out this town and, in 1814, the legislature established it under the name of Grandville. When the post office was opened about 1830, the name was modified to Granville to avoid confusion with another Grandville in the state.

GRASSY MEADOWS

Grassy Meadows is located near the Meadow River in Greenbrier County. A post office was established here in the 1870s. It is possible that, like Grass Run, a tributary of the Hughes River, the "grassy" portion of the name came from grass that grew near the mouth of the Meadow River.

GREEN BANK

Green Bank was named during the Civil War for a small green bank on J. Pierce Woodell's land beside the North Fork of Deer Creek. Earlier listings (Green Banks) suggest there was more than one bank.

The Mountain Rifles, a unique Confederate unit, was mustered here in 1861. The more than 100 recruits were all over six feet tall. The majority of them died in the "Bloody Angle" at Spotsylvania, Virginia.

GREEN SULPHUR SPRINGS

There is a sulphur spring located near this village.

536

GREENVILLE

The former name of this community was Centreville. Why and when it was changed to Greenville remain a mystery.

Across Indian Creek is the site of Cook's Fort, built in 1770 by Captain John Cook. Boasting four blockhouses on more than an acre of ground, Cook's Fort was one of the largest of the frontier forts.

GREER

This village was created by the Greer Limestone Company. As a company town, it assumed the corporate name.

GUYAN

This village is a few miles distant from the Guyandot River, and probably took part of the waterway's name for its own. The river was probably named for Henry Guyan, a Frenchman who operated a trading post at the mouth of the river in 1750.

GYPSY

Gypsies once camped in this Harrison County locale.

HALLTOWN

As early as 1795, Davis Harris ran an inn at the site of this village. The Hall family had a large farm nearby called Rion Hall.

Not far from the town is Beall Air, named for Thomas Beall, the grandfather of Colonel Lewis Washington, who was the great-grandnephew of the first president. John Brown kidnapped the colonel and held him hostage 16 October 1859, the night of the raid on Harper's Ferry. Brown demanded that Washington surrender to him a sword that Frederick the Great of Prussia had given George Washington. Brown was wearing the sword, which bears the inscription: "The oldest general in the world to the greatest," when he was captured.

HAMBLETON

Senator Henry Gassaway Davis interested a number of movers and shakers in investing in the West Virginia Central & Pittsburgh Railway Company (later the Western Maryland). For their contributions, many of them had their names placed on new stops along the railroad.

Hambleton, in Tucker County, was no exception. When this town was established in 1889, Senator Stephen B. Elkins named it for John A. Hambleton, the head of a Baltimore bank.

HAMLIN
The Virginia legislature established this Lincoln County village in 1852–53 as Hamline Church. Hamline Church was named for Bishop Leonidas Hamline, a prominent clergyman in the Methodist Episcopal Church. The "e" was dropped from the name by the local postmaster. Ironically, it was the same "e" that the Reverend Hamline had added to his own family name.

HANGING ROCK
The city of Hanging Rock, originally just a post office in Hampshire County, takes its name from Hanging Rocks, a natural feature of perpendicular cliffs above the South Branch of the Potomac.

Hanging Rocks was the scene of fierce fighting, both in 1736 between the Delaware and Catawba Indians and in 1861 between Union and Confederate soldiers.

HARDING
Harding was the name given to this town in 1892 when the Western Maryland Railroad connected between Belington and Elkins. Harding, established as a coal town the next year, was named for Major French Harding of Beverly, West Virginia, a Confederate officer.

The area contributed a large block of coal from a seam of lower Kittatinny coal to the Centennial Exposition in Philadelphia in 1876. Senator Henry Gassaway Davis noticed it and used his great influence to have the Coal & Coke Railroad built into this district.

HARMONY
W. E. Ryan, the postmaster at Ryan, Roane County, established the post office at this site and "named it after a church house there."

HARPERS FERRY
Sometime in the 1730s, Robert Harper came to this area and settled it. At that time, the area was called The Hole.

Within a few years of his arrival, Harper set up his ferries. Harpers Ferry was legally established in the late eighteenth century, and incorporated in the mid-nineteenth.

Harpers Ferry was the site of a federal arsenal and armory, built in 1796 at the suggestion of George Washington.

In the summer of 1859, a stranger arrived in Harpers Ferry. Isaac Smith, as he called himself, moved into the Kennedy Farm on the Maryland side of the Potomac, and there he plotted an attack on the slavery system.

On 16 October 1859, Isaac Smith, really John Brown, and his party raided the federal arsenal. He selected Harper's Ferry because the town was "the safest natural entrance to the Great Black Way . . . Here, amid the mighty protection of overwhelming numbers, lay a path from slavery to freedom. . . ." The self-proclaimed "instrument of God sent to liberate all slaves," was captured by Brevet Colonel Robert E. Lee and Lieutenant J. E. B. Stuart.

The first fatality in Brown's raid was the death of Heywood Shepherd, a railroad porter. Shepherd, a free black, was shot by Brown's men when he failed to obey their order to halt. John Brown was indicted and tried for treason. Found guilty, the man was hanged at Charles Town.

With the outbreak of hostilities between North and South, Harper's Ferry became a strategic location. Stonewall Jackson captured it in September 1862, but retreating Union troops torched the buildings before surrendering the town.

Following the surrender at Appomattox, the government decided to not reopen the arsenal. The town then turned its attention to other pursuits. For example, the bridge across the Potomac became a favorite spot for eloping couples. The tollgate keeper was a retired minister who conducted weddings there.

HARRISVILLE

The seat of Ritchie County, Harrisville began its existence as Harrisville, only to have its name changed to Solus in 1830. Ten years later, it was Ritchie Court House. In 1890, the original name returned to both the post office and the town "by petition of the citizens."

But what about the name? In 1803, Lawrence Maley, a Scotch-Irish Presbyterian, settled the Maley Settlement about a mile from the present-day Harrisville. He died five years later, just as the Harrises and other families moved into the area. The Harrisville name, it appears, comes from John Maley Harris, whose parents were among those early settlers. His brother was General Thomas M. Harris, a distinguished officer in the Civil War, who served on the military commission that tried the men accused of plotting Lincoln's assassination.

HEBRON

Before 1850, this village in Pleasants County was known as Giter, for Mose Williamson, a pioneer nicknamed "Giter."

When the post office was established, a Bible student suggested Hebron, the name of the ancient city in Palestine.

HEDGESVILLE

The 1806 act of establishment for this village lists Josiah Hedges, indicating that the Hedges family was one of the founding families.

Josiah Hedges was more than just "one of the original" settlers. The Mount Zion Episcopal Church at Hedgesville was built in 1817, on ground he donated. But the settlement goes back further than the early nineteenth century, because Foose's Lawn, an old tavern, was built by Robert Snodgrass about 1740. In 1769, while on the way to Warm Springs, George Washington and his stepdaughter Patsy stayed at the Lawn.

At an earlier point in its life, Hedgesville was called Skinner's Gap, and then Hedges Villa.

HELVETIA

In 1869, a New York real estate promoter persuaded a group of Swiss immigrants to settle here. When the townsfolk gathered after the first year to discuss a name for their community, the name Helvetia, Latin for Switzerland, was suggested. Since the majority of the townspeople were Swiss, other names did not have a chance.

HENDERSON

This town was incorporated in 1893 and named for Samuel Bruce Henderson, who owned all the land that made up the town.

The home of the Henderson family, Henderson House, was built in 1831 and called Pohick Hall, for Pohick, Fairfax County, Virginia. The house was ideal for people with a strong interest in the river traffic. Atop the roof is a "widow's walk" and a glassed-in cupola, resembling the pilot house on a river packet. The cupola provided a commanding view of the river.

HENDRICKS

Senator Henry Gassaway Davis named more towns in West Virginia than anyone else. Hendricks is one of them.

Incorporated in 1894, this location was named for Thomas A. Hendricks, vice president of the United States in 1885.

HERNSHAW

Robert Herndon and his partner, a Mr. Renshaw, opened a coal mine off Lens Creek. They built a railroad to the mine and began big-time coal mining. A town grew up at the mine site, and merged the names of the two partners.

HIAWATHA

The coal mines in the Pocahontas Coal Fields all had Indian names. Hiawatha was the name given to the mine in Mercer County.

HICO

When this Fayette County village was established, it was called Beets, after landowner John Beets. This community received its current name in 1895, when postmaster J. A. Sandige moved the post office from his home to a nearby store. One source hints that "hico" was the name of the tobacco he was raising. Another explains that Sandige bought tobacco from Hyco, Virginia, and so used that name, eliminating the "y" to avoid any confusion. There is no Hyco in present-day Virginia.

HILLSBORO

Following a particularly bloody boxing match in 1765, John McNeil ran off into the wilderness, thinking he had killed his opponent. Charles and Jacob Kinnison found him and told him that the supposed victim had recovered. McNeil did not believe them, and asked them to stay with him and help build a settlement. At least, that is what one legend would have us believe.

On the other hand, Hillsboro, Pocahontas County, was established in 1834 and named for John Hill, who "was instrumental in having the town laid out."

HINTON

There is some confusion as to which towns made up Hinton, and how the name came to be. Suffice it to say that the seat of Summers County was once made up of Avis, Bellepoint, and (Upper) Hinton. By 1871, Avis and Hinton existed with a minimal population—there was one house in each community! When the railroad arrived a year later, the towns took off.

In 1927, Avis and Bellepoint became part of Hinton. The origin of the names rests with the former town name. Of course Hinton was named for a Hinton family, but which one? Some say Evan

Hinton, the "father of Summers County." Perhaps. The most likely choice, however, is John "Jack" Hinton, husband of Avis Gwinn Hinton, who owned the land in the town and settled it in 1831. We're confident his wife was honored by the town of Avis.

HOMINY FALLS

Hominy Falls is a village on the Hominy Creek. It was so named for the fifteen-to-twenty-foot waterfall nearby. The word "hominy," from the Algonquian, means a dish of pounded corn.

HUFF JUNCTION

Huff Junction, Logan County, is located on the Huff Creek, a tributary of the Guyandot River.

Huff The creek was named for Peter Huff, a pioneer who was killed by Indians.

HUGHESTON

Hugheston is located on the Hughes Creek.

Both the creek and the village were named for Robert Hughes. Hughes was the area's first settler, and was also held prisoner by Indians for two years.

HUNDRED

Henry Church, an early settler who lived in this Wetzel County community, and died here in 1860 at the age of 109, was known as "Old Hundred." Church first settled the area in 1782, after serving as a British soldier under Cornwallis. He had been captured by Lafayette's troops and remained in this country. His wife, it is said, died when she was 106. Church's second daughter died at age 63, and he consoled himself by saying, "She allus was a puny child, and we know'd we'd never raise her." The community carried on his—and his wife's—name(s).

HUNTERSVILLE

Huntersville, established in 1821, is located in Greenbrier County. When a name was needed, John Bradshaw insisted that the name be Huntersville "as a special compliment to the hunters that swarmed there during the trading season." The locals listened to Bradshaw because, after all, the town grew up around his cabin.

HUNTINGTON

This town was founded in 1871 by Collis P. Huntington, then president of the Chesapeake & Ohio Railroad. But even before the railroad magnate arrived, Huntington gobbled up a number of small towns. These included Holderby's Landing, Guyandot, South Landing, and Brownsville. The earliest settlement was about 1796, when Thomas and Jonathan Buffington established homes on the Guyandot River.

The first white people on the site of Huntington were Captain Celeron de Bienville and a group of explorers, who arrived in 1749. They were sent to reaffirm claims to the Ohio region first made by La Salle in 1669.

HURRICANE

This village is named after nearby Hurricane Creek. Hurricane Creek received its name in 1774 when surveyors witnessed a tornado wreak destruction on the forest. But there is a big difference between a tornado and a hurricane. So why the name?

Old-time residents thought the name came from the cry to the local blacksmith: "Hurry, Cain."

IAGER

Iager may be another typographical error.

The town was incorporated in 1917, and named for Colonel William G. W. Jaeger (Iager) from Philadelphia who, between 1880 and 1890, owned about 45,000 acres in this McDowell County locale. His son William R. platted the town in 1885.

Prior to Jaeger/Iager, the town was known as The Forks, for its location at the junctions of the Dry and Tug Forks, then Williamsburg, apparently for the founder, and finally the current name, in 1890.

INDORE

Indore, Clay County, is an example of an error in spoken language being perpetuated in a written name.

Indore, formerly called Serena, was renamed in 1915. The residents selected the Biblical name of Endor, the Palestinian town where Saul consulted the sorceress before the battle of Gilboa.

INSTITUTE

Institute took its name from the West Virginia State College, established in 1891 as a black school.

INWOOD

Inwood Park, a well-known summer resort, was located here. The Berkeley County village that settled around it took on its name.

ITMANN

When a coal mine was opened at this Wyoming County location, the name commemorated I. T. Mann, head of one of the largest coal operations along the Norfolk & Western route.

J

JACKSON'S MILL

The mill for which this Lewis County village was named was built in about 1808 by Colonel Edward Jackson, grandfather of Confederate General Stonewall Jackson. Stonewall moved to his grandfather's farm from Clarksburg after his mother remarried in 1830. He stayed there until 1842, when he was admitted to the U.S. Military Academy at West Point.

JANE LEW

Town founder Lewis Maxwell, a native of Philadelphia but a three-time congressman from Virginia, named this Lewis County town in 1835 for his mother, Jane Lewis.

Prior to Jane Lew, the town was known as West's Fort, Hackersville, and McWhorter's Mills. Edmund West and his sons built a stockade here in 1770 and called it West's Fort. Indians burned him out nine years later, and the settlers escaped to Buckhannon. Some returned in 1790 and built Fort Beech. Three years later, Henry McWhorter built a gristmill and a log house. The house remained there until 1927, when it was moved to Jackson's Mill and set up on the site of the Jackson House.

JESSE

Postmaster Ott Sanders named this Wyoming County village when it was established in the late nineteenth century. The name honored a local, Jesse Shumate.

JODIE

In the late nineteenth century, this town was called Imboden, for Colonel G.W. Imboden. The name was changed in the 1910s to Jodie, for the nickname of Joseph H. Gaines, a local congressman.

JUMPING BRANCH

Jumping Branch was named for the stream on which it is located. In the early days of this settlement, there was no bridge across the stream, so riders had to "jump" from one bank to the other.

JUNIOR

This village was named by that prime West Virginia namer, Senator Henry Gassaway Davis, for his son John Davis.

KASSON

The first name for this Barbour County village was Danville, for the first settler, Daniel Highly. That name lasted only until 1880. In that year, the name was changed to Kasson, for the first acting postmaster, a Mr. Cassen. Again, a possible typographical-error town.

KEENAN

One of the first settlers to arrive in this area in the 1780s was Edward Keenan. Keenan donated the land on which Rehoboth Church was built, the first church west of the Allegheny Mountains.

KENNA

The name for this Jackson County community was given in 1883, for U.S. Senator John E. Kenna.

KENOVA

Kenova was settled in 1889 close to the borders of three states, from which it takes its name: Kentucky, Ohio, and Virginia.

KENTUCK

The location of this Jackson County community reminded settlers in 1875 of their old Kentucky home, and so they named it New Kentucky. Postal authorities modified the name slightly.

KERMIT

Lower Burning Creek and East Warfield were the earlier names for this Mingo County village. The name was changed in 1906 to honor Kermit, Theodore Roosevelt's son.

KESLERS CROSS ROADS

KESLERS CROSS ROADS
Keslers Cross Roads was once known as Keslers Cross Lanes, a more distinctive title and one rarely found in American place names. The town was named by John R. Cutcheon for his father-in-law, Frederick Kessler, who lived on a hill above the village.

KEYSER
Keyser, the seat of Mineral County, was earlier named Paddy Town and New Creek.

Paddy Town (or Paddytown) was the original name under which a post office was opened in 1811. The name came from an Irishman named Patrick. Sources suggest Patrick Black, a pioneer who lived in the mountain gap, or Patrick McCarthy, operator of an iron furnace below the town. No one is sure which, but it would make sense to choose McCarthy, because he owned the land. It had been granted to him in 1802 by Abraham Inskeep.

The New Creek name remained until 1874, when the town was incorporated as Keyser, for William Keyser, the vice president of the Baltimore & Ohio Railroad at the time of incorporation.

During the Civil War, Keyser was captured and recaptured a total of fourteen times!

KEYSTONE
Formerly known as Cassville, this McDowell County community took its name from its prime industry. The Keystone Coal & Coke Company operated Mine No. 1 at Keystone.

KIAHSVILLE
Early residents of this Wayne County community were the Adkins and Fry families. Both families favored the name Hezekiah, shortened to Kiah, for their male children.

KINGSTON
The earliest name for this Fayette County settlement was Milburn Creek, obviously because of the town's location on the stream. The creek was named for the first person to wander the Kingston Hills, a man named Milburn who dug ginseng by the waterway.

The current name was provided in 1910, when the Pocahontas Coal Company began mining in the area. Probably the name came from the hills.

KINGWOOD

Kingwood, seat of Preston County, was once "a wooded camping site on crown land," called The King's Woods. By 1807, houses were built there, and the town, named Kingwood, was established four years later. A few settlers had cabins here before the turn of the nineteenth century.

The King's Woods, or Kingwood, took its name from a grove of tall, stately trees that were called the "forest kings."

KLINE

Cline's Cross Roads was the earlier name for this Pendelton County location. The name was changed to Kline in about 1875. Both names seem to come from the first postmaster, Samuel Cline or Kline. So much for accurate spellings!

KNOB FORK

Knob Fork, Wetzel County, is located on the Fork of Fish Creek. Previously known as Geaneytown, for a local family, then Uniontown, it may also have been known as Jolliffe or Jolliffe's Store, for a general store established there in 1874.

KOPPERSTON

Kopperston was a model coal community, built by the Koppers Coal Company, and completed in 1938.

LEAD MINE

This Tucker County village takes its name from the nearby stream. The stream, legend has it, received its name after an Indian built a fire beneath a nearby cliff and discovered lead. He molded some bullets and . . . that is where the legend ends.

LEATHERBARK

Leatherbark, Calhoun County, takes its name, given in 1897, from the nearby stream. The stream took its name from the large growths of "leatherbark," a woody plant.

LEETOWN

This Jefferson County village, laid out on land owned by Joist Hite, is named for its most famous resident: General Charles Lee.

General Horatio Gates lived a few miles out of town in his one-and-a-half-story house, Prato Rio.

Following a strong reprimand from George Washington for his premature retreat at the Battle of Monmouth in 1778, Lee vented his temper and was suspended from command. He disappeared to Prato Rio with his Italian bodyguard, his slaves, and a pack of hounds. He gained a reputation for eccentricity while living here.

Lee had few friends, except for generals Horatio Gates and Adam Stephen. Both men suffered the same disciplinary fate as did Lee. When in their cups, they would offer toasts: "to Major General Charles Lee, who was cashiered from the Continental Army because, when he should have advanced, he retreated"; "to Major General Horatio Gates, who was cashiered because, when he should have retreated, he advanced"; and "to Major General Adam Stephen, who was cashiered because, when he might have advanced or retreated, he did neither."

LEFT HAND

This Roane County town could have been "Right Hand."

Taking its current name from a waterway, the town was formerly known as Knights. The Left Hand Creek could have been on the opposite side, depending on where the namer stood.

LEOPOLD

The post office in this Doddridge County village was established in 1883 and called Saint Clara. Three years later, the name was changed by the postmaster, Leopold Hinter.

LESAGE

This village was named for Jules F. M. LeSage, a bandbox manufacturer from Paris, France, who arrived at this site in 1851.

LeSage had left New York after a brief stay and anticipated traveling to Nauvoo, Illinois, where he intended to join a colony founded on the communistic principles of Etienne Cabet. Angry with all the delays in his Ohio River trip, LeSage got off the boat, bought two acres of land, and built a house.

LETART

Letart takes its name from nearby Letart Island, in the Ohio River.

The island was named for James LeTort, son of a French Huguenot and "one of the first white men to enter the wilderness beyond the mountains."

548

LEWISBURG. The General Lewis Inn, Lewisburg, West Virginia, is a fine country inn that was once the home of General Andrew Lewis. The general, whose home was built in 1834, donated his name to the town.

LEWISBURG

Originally named either The Savannah, or Big Levels in the 1750s, Lewisburg is the seat of Greenbrier County.

In 1774, it was Camp Union, the gathering point for the army of General Andrew Lewis preparatory to the Battle of Point Pleasant. The town was established in 1782, and named for the general.

Following the Civil War, Lewisburg lost a great deal of its political clout because of its wartime sympathy for the South.

LICK CREEK

This community was named in 1910 for the nearby stream. Lick Creek took its name from the number of "licks," spots where animals gathered to lick salt, near the mouth of the stream.

LIGHTBURN

This Lewis County village was not named during a blackout. Rather, it was named for General Joseph A. J. Lightburn, a Union officer who became a Baptist minister after the Civil War.

The reverend-general's remains are buried in the graveyard of the Broad Run Baptist Church, organized in 1804.

LILLYBROOK

According to local tradition, Lillybrook was named for the two men, Lilly and Hornbrook, who established it as a mining town.

LIMESTONE

The settling of this village began in 1770, when it was known as Maizeville for the abundant corn crop. When Jonathan Zane and his cohorts created a road here from Wheeling, they changed the name to Limestone, because of the abundance of the mineral.

LINDEN

Linden, Roane County, has nothing to do with trees. The village was named for Confederate Captain Charles Linden Broadus.

LINDSIDE

While Linden had nothing to do with trees, Lindside does.

This Monroe County community was named by James Sweeney, an early settler. The linden tree found in this area is mentioned in George Washington's diary as the "Lynn" tree. "White Lynn Honey" is still available in this area of West Virginia.

LIZEMORES

Lizemores is the result of a postal typographical error. The name submitted was Sizemore, for a local family. The postal people mistook the "S" for an "L" and the result is Lizemores.

LOBELIA

This community takes its name from the lobelia, a plant that thrives in this area. The post office was established in 1878.

LOCKWOOD

As was Belva, Lockwood was named for Belva Lockwood, twice presidential candidate on the Equal Suffrage ticket.

A double grave at Lockwood, at the mouth of Otter Creek, contains the remains of Betsy and Peggy Morris, two little girls who were killed and scalped by Indians in 1792.

LOGAN

The seat of Logan County was laid out before 1830 and named Lawnsville. In 1844, the name was changed to Aracoma, and the state assembly chartered the town in that name.

Aracoma was the daughter of Chief Cornstalk, son of Chief Wingohocking of the Cayugas and a major participant in the Battle of Point Pleasant. Aracoma came here in 1765 to live with her white husband, Bolling Baker. She was fatally wounded in a 1780 battle with settlers from the Greenbrier Valley. Her dying wish was to be buried in town.

LOGAN. At "Stenton," his home in Philadelphia, James Logan entertained Chief Wingohocking and the two decided to swap their names. Wingohocking became Chief Logan, but James Logan copped out and named the stream that ran through his property "Wingohocking." Both men are remembered in Loganville, Pennsylvania, and Logan, West Virginia. [CREDIT: Print and Picture Department, Free Library of Philadelphia]

Though the name Logan Court House and Logan were used earlier, Logan became the official name in 1907. The name comes from Chief Wingohocking paying tribute to an old Indian tradition of transferring one's name to someone an Indian truly respected and loved. Wingohocking held James Logan, William Penn's secretary, in high esteem. One day, he suggested that he and Logan swap names. Logan, not wanting to go down in history as "James Wingohocking," talked the chief into giving his name to a stream at Stenton, Logan's Philadelphia mansion. The chief bought it. He took Logan's name and the stream took his. The waterway is gone now, but a Philadelphia street still carries Wingohocking's name.

Logan is the burial site of Devil Anse Hatfield, leader of the famous Hatfield and McCoy feud. His grave, surmounted by a life-size statue of him, lies south of Logan toward Tug Valley.

LOOKOUT

Lookout, Fayette County, was once known as De Kalb, Pleasant Hill, and, before the Civil War, Locust Lane.

The name comes from the town's proximity to Spy Rock, where white settlers and Indians alike could keep an eye on Big Sewell Mountain and other nearby areas. During the Civil War, Spy Rock was called "the eyes of the Union Army."

LOONEYVILLE

There is nothing crazy about the naming of this Roane County town. It honors the memory of Robert Looney, the first English-speaking settler, who came to the area from Virginia in the 1840s.

LORADO

Located in Logan County, Lorado was named in 1914 by a coal company. The name is drawn from syllables in the company's title: Lorain Coal & Dock Company.

LORENTZ

Financier Jacob Lorentz, a native of Lancaster, Pennsylvania, lived in this town from 1800 until his death, at the age of ninety, in 1866.

In 1783, Dutch settlers founded the town, and Lorentz opened the first store in 1800. All the materials in his store were brought from Richmond by pack train. Lorentz paid for the supplies with cattle and hogs, and the livestock was then driven eastward to market.

LOST CITY

To be quite frank, this community has never been "lost." Previously known as Cover, the name was given by the first postmaster in 1893 for a local landowner. Two years later, the name was changed to Lost City, for the creek on which the town is situated.

LOST CREEK

Lost Creek like Lost City, takes its name from the Lost Creek.

The creek was named by early explorers who found the initials "T.G." carved into several trees. They assumed that the person who did it was lost, and that is what they called the waterway. A post office operated in the town as early as 1779.

LOST RIVER

Lost River was named for the river, on which it is located. The town was settled before 1750, and the 1756 Battle of Lost River, between Captain Jeremiah Smith's company of Virginia militia and a band of fifty or so French and Indians, was fought here.

According to George Washington's diary, the river was named because it "disappears" under Sandy Ridge and, three miles later, is "found" on the other side.

LUMBERPORT

Lumberport, Harrison County, was established by the legislature in 1838 and incorporated in 1901. At one time, employees dressed lumber by hand and floated it on rafts to Pittsburgh.

LYNN CAMP

Lynn Camp, Marshall County, is nowhere near Lynn Camp Run, a tributary of the North Fork of the Hughes River. That waterway was named for a camp of lynn wood (see Linden) constructed by a group of hunters in 1776.

MABEN

Maben, located in Wyoming County, was laid out in 1904 and named for John D. Maben, of Staunton, Virginia.

Maben, along with Colonel Jed Hotchkiss, acquired 64,000 acres of the Welch Tract, in Raleigh and Wyoming counties, in the late nineteenth century. When the Virginian Railroad came through in 1904, Maben became the site of the band-saw and planing mills of the W. M. Ritter Lumber Company.

MACFARLAN

Macfarlan, Richie County, is located on the McFarlan Creek, which was named for an Englishman named Macfarlen who was wounded by Indians here in 1769. (No reason can be found for the switch from "Mac" to "Mc" in the creek's name.)

In 1852, Frederick Lemon discovered a vein of a glossy, black substance that melted when heated. Lemon thought he had discovered coal, but what he actually found was soldified petroleum. His find was the only one of its kind known in the U.S.

A mine explosion in 1874 that killed several miners caused the demise of the enterprise. Superstitious miners thought the shaft was haunted. It was abandoned in 1909, not because of ghosts, but because the owners found that it was less expensive to produce oil than "grahamite," as the substance was known.

MACKSVILLE

This Pendleton County community was named in the 1860s for its first postmaster, Peter McDonald.

MADISON

The seat of Boone County, Madison was first known as Boone Court House. The town was torched by Union troops in 1861, but came back to life by 1906, when it was incorporated.

Some sources presume the town was named for President James Madison, but there is more credence to the name originating with Madison Peyton. Peyton was heavily involved in the coal industry. He opened mines, made cannel-coal oil, and constructed the Coal River lock and dam system. Two towns in the county carry his name, Madison and Peytona.

MAIDSVILLE

A post office was opened in this Monongalia County village in 1845, though it was discontinued in the early twentieth century.

No one is quite sure why the town was called Maidsville, except that, at one time, it had a larger than average percentage of "old maids."

MALDEN

In the earliest days, settlers called this Kanawha County site Saltbro or Terra Salias or the Kanawha Salines. When it came time to select a post office name, the townspeople rejected all previous names and selected Malden. Though there is no definitive proof, it seems probable that the name came from Malden, Massachusetts, home to many of the early settlers.

Near the center of Malden is the site of Booker T. Washington's boyhood home. Washington was born in a slave cabin at Hales Ford, Virginia. His stepfather escaped to West Virginia and, after emancipation, called the family to join him. Washington and his stepfather both worked at the salt furnaces, and Booker T. also worked in the coal mines. After a year in the pits, he became a servant in the home of General Lewis Ruffner. He assumed the surname Washington about that time, because he had never been given one. After attending school at Hampton Normal and Agricultural Institute, Hampton, Virginia, and at Wayland Seminary, Washington, D.C., he moved south and became principal of a black normal school in Tuskegee, Alabama. His school grew from a single frame building and church to an internationally recognized institution.

MALLORY

Mallory was named in 1917, when the Mallory Coal Company began operations in this Logan County area.

MAN

The most frequently mentioned source for the name of this Logan County village is Ulysses Hinchman, a member of the House of Delegates following the Civil War.

MANNINGTON

In about 1845, Samuel Koon built a store and tavern in this Marion County location. Within a short time, Koontown was a bustling mercantile center.

When the railroad arrived in 1852, the town was renamed for James or Charles Manning, a railroad construction engineer. Mannington was established by the legislature in 1856.

MAPLEWOOD

Previously known as Rocky Hill, in 1850, and Mount Ida, this Fayette County village became Maplewood in 1894. The name comes from a large sugar-maple tree near the original post office.

MARFRANCE

The name of this Greenbrier County town was given in about 1912, and represents a combination of the names of the two coal companies that operated here: Margaret and Frances.

MARIE

This Summers County village was named in about 1904, for Gladys Marie Berger, who lived at Hinton.

MARLINTON

Marlinton was settled in 1749 and, until 1887, was known as Marlin's Bottom. The name originated with Jacob Marlin, who, along with Stephen Sewell, made the first recorded settlement west of the Alleghenies in 1749. Sewell and Marlin lived together in a log cabin until they had an awful argument over infant baptism. Sewell moved from the cabin to a hollow tree.

In 1890, Colonel John T. McGraw, of Grafton, visited this site and purchased the farms there for a town. The town was then called Marlin's Bottom. In 1887, when the town became the seat of Pocahontas County, the name was altered to eliminate "Bottom."

Marlinton was known as "the birthplace of rivers," because five major waterways have their sources in the area; the Elk, Tygart, Shaver's Fork, Greenbrier, and the Gauley and its tributaries.

MARMET

The first post office in this Kanawha County community was called Lens Creek, for the stream on which the town is located. Later, it was named Brownstone, for Charles Brown, a resident from 1808 until 1849 who owned a local salt furnace.

The change to Marmet took place in 1900, and was drawn from the Marmet Coal Company, owned by William and Edward Marmet.

MARTINSBURG

First called Martin's Town or Martinsville, Martinsburg, the seat of Berkeley County, was established by the legislature in 1778.

The name came from Colonel Bryan Martin, a wealthy land-owner and nephew of Lord Halifax.

Martinsburg became a major shipping center in 1850 with the construction of the Baltimore & Ohio Railroad. It was also the home of Belle Boyd, Confederate spy.

During the Civil War, some townspeople could not decide which side to take. As Porte Crayon, in his *Personal Recollections of the War*, wrote, "They kept their headquarters at the court-house, sat up nights, arrested each other and everybody else they found prowling about. It was shrewdly suggested," he added, "that the peace of the lonely village might have been better preserved if everybody went quietly to bed and minded their own business."

MASON

Mason was once called Waggener's Bottom, and then Mason City, ostensibly for the county in which it resides. Mason County was named for George W. Mason, author of the Virginia constitution.

The town of Mason was laid out in 1852 by coal mine operators, and incorporated in 1856.

MATEWAN

Incorporated in 1895, Matewan was named after Matteawan, New York, home to the engineer who surveyed the town.

MATOAKA

Matoaka, it is said, was the secret name for Pocahontas, daughter of Chief Powhatan. The name translates to "she amuses herself playing with something."

MAXWELTON

The post office at this location was established in 1894. For several months, it was called Hattie. Unfortunately, that name brought it into conflict with a town in Virginia, so they changed it to Maxwelton because, the story goes, "Maxwelton braes are bonny."

MAYSEL
Originally named Frog Pond, this Clay County village obtained its post office in about 1917. When it came time to decide on a name, Mark C. Kyle, who was in business in the county, suggested naming it for his infant daughter, Maysel. His offer was accepted.

McDOWELL
Though the McDowell Coal and Coke Company was located here, it seems likely that the town's name came from McDowell County.

MEADOR
Agatha Hatfield, principal of the local public school, explained the name of this Mingo County village in 1937: "simply Meadow provincially pronounced." The post office was established in 1901.

MEADOW BLUFF
The name for this Greenbrier County town was given before 1859. The surrounding area had been known for years as Walker's Meadows, but the present name is derived from its geographic location: meadow land and a steep hill.

MEADOW BRIDGE
The first settler arrived in this location in 1846. For a brief period, it was called Clute, for Theodore Clute, the first postmaster.

The present name came about with the construction of a bridge across Meadow Creek.

MERRIMAC
The post office was established in this Mingo County location in 1904. It is possible the town was named for the Civil War engagement between the *Monitor* and the *Merrimac*.

MIAMI
The name of Miami, Kanawha County, seems to be lost. Should it not be in a warmer clime?

The name Miami comes from the Chippewa *omaumeg*, "people who live on the peninsula." The Miami tribe took part in every Indian war in the Ohio Valley until the end of the War of 1812.

MIDDLEBOURNE

Middlebourne, located on Middle Island Creek, is the seat of Tyler County and was established by the legislature in 1813.

Two possibilites for the source of this name are: it was so named because it was midway between Pennsylvania and the salt wells above Charleston, or because it is the middle point between the source and mouth of Middle Island Creek.

MIDKIFF

This village was named for a local family. The family name may have been Midkiff, Midcap, or Metcalf(e).

MILETUS

The namers of Miletus, Doddridge County, may have had Biblical references in mind. Paul the Apostle visited Miletus, in Asia Minor, on his way to Jerusalem to keep Pentecost. In the earlier days of this nation, Miletus was also used as a masculine personal name.

MILL CREEK

The town of Mill Creek, Randolph County, is located on Mill Creek. The waterway received its name from James White's mill, built just below the mouth of the stream.

The town has had several names, including Dog Town, Crickard (1784–94), (for first postmaster Patrick Crickard), Fort Currence, and Currence's Mill Creek. William Currence built a large gristmill at this location on the site of his 1774 fort.

MILL POINT

Mill Point, Pocahontas County, was named for a number of water-driven mills built by pioneers here on the banks of Stamping Creek. Apparently, in the late 1860s, there were two gristmills operating in the town. The north end of town once was called Cackleytown—Valentine Cackley built his mill there in 1778.

MILTON

Milton, Cabell County, was laid out as a town in 1872 and named for Milton Reece, who owned the land on which the town stands. Some locals refer to the town as Milton-on-the-Mud, a reference to the river on which it is located.

MINERALWELLS
Mineralwells, originally two words until the post office got hold of it, was once a fashionable summer resort. A grandiose hotel was built in 1855, only to be abandoned in 1900.

MINGO
This Randolph County town takes its name from the Mingo Run, on which it is located.

The name commemorates the Mingo Indians, who lived and hunted in the surrounding countryside, and had a village where the town of Mingo grew. Depending on what source you believe, the Indian name translates to "spring people" or "stealthy, treacherous."

MINNEHAHA SPRINGS
The first post office located in this community (1890–1906) was called Driscol, for Colonel John Driscol, a lumbering entrepreneur.

The current name comes from a large mineral spring located on the old Lockridge Farm. Minnehaha Springs was once a summer resort, complete with a swimming pool fed by sulphur springs.

MINNORA
The name for this Calhoun County village was given in the 1890s, at the suggestion of Captain Absalom Knotts. Minnora was his youngest daughter's name.

MISSOURI BRANCH
Located in Wayne County, this village was formerly named Preston and Wells Branch. The current name, tradition has it, comes from the Missouri Creek in Wood County—nowhere near this site. The town, however, is not far from the West Fork of Twelvepole Creek.

MOHAWK
This McDowell County community is named for the Mohawk Branch of the Sandy River, on which it is located.

The Mohawk Branch, of course, was named for the Indian tribe.

MONOGAH

This Marion County village was incorporated in 1891, and takes its name from the Monongahela River, on which it is located. To differentiate between the two, the community dropped the last two syllables. Monongahela translates from the Indian to "place of curling waters" or "place of caving or falling banks."

A mining town in its heyday, the town was founded in 1768 by Captain James Booth, who described his settlement as in the "lonely wilds of West Augusts." Booth called his settlement Briartown, and it drew a number of settlers, enough for Booth to organize a company of rangers. He led his unit for thirteen months during the Revolution. He was killed in an Indian ambush in 1778.

A devastating mine disaster in 1907 at Monongah prompted the creation of the federal Bureau of Mines.

MONTERVILLE

The first post office in this Randolph County neighborhood was called Middlebrook in the 1880s. It was not named because it was in the middle of some brook, but for a Mr. Middlebrook. Mr. Middlebrook, we learn, moved back to Connecticut.

In about 1889, the post office moved closer to town and the new postmaster, John Ernest Monterville Bing, changed the name. Mr. Bing thought his name was too long, so he gave Monterville to the post office and thereafter was known as John Ernest Bing.

MONTGOMERY

What utter confusion must have reigned in this Kanawha County town. There was a time before the turn of the twentieth century that it existed under three names . . . simultaneously.

In 1860, the village was called Montgomery's Landing. From 1871 until 1890, the Chesapeake & Ohio Railroad station was named Cannelton. The town (it changed its name from Montgomery's Landing) and the post office became Coal Valley or Coal Valley Post Office (1876–90). In 1890, when the town was incorporated, everything became Montgomery!

The Coal Valley name came from the Coal Valley Coal company, which platted the town and operated a mine there. Montgomery is for James Montgomery, an early settler and farmer.

MONTROSE

Montrose, Randolph County, was incorporated in 1895. Its name came from the proliferation of wild roses growing in the area before the Western Maryland Railroad came to town.

MORGANTOWN

The first settlement on the Monongahela River, in Monongalia County, was made in 1758 by Thomas Decker. He was killed by Indians. Ten years later, Colonel Zackquill Morgan, son of West Virginia's first settler—Morgan Morgan—resettled the area.

The settlement was beseiged by Indian attacks, but the presence of forts Kern and Morgan acted as a major deterrent, and the settlement continued. In 1781, a 400-acre tract belonging to Morgan was laid out in town lots. By 1785, the General Assembly established Morganstown. In 1901, Morgantown absorbed the local communities of Seneca, Greenmont, and South Morgantown.

During the Civil War, Morgantown was spared . . . except for one Confederate incursion. In the spring of 1863, Brigadier General William Ezra Jones bivouacked 2,000 troops here for two days. When they left, they had confiscated all the horses, hats, boots, drugs, and whiskey they could find. One southern gentleman told a Morgantown lady that the local alcoholic beverages were far superior to brands found in the South.

Morgantown is the home of West Virginia University, founded in 1867.

MOUNDSVILLE

A cabin built by Joseph, Samuel, and James Tomlinson in 1770–71 was the beginning of this town. The settlement was then known as Grave Creek. The Tomlinson cabin was about 300 yards from the Grave Creek Burial Mound, the largest prehistoric Indian burial mound of its kind in the world.

In 1798, Joseph T., Jr., divided the land into lots and named it Elizabethtown, for his wife. Simon Purdy established a rival community on the banks of the Ohio River in 1831 and called it Mound City. The two towns were consolidated in 1865 and incorporated as Moundsville. It is the seat of Marshall County.

The town takes its name from the Grave Creek Burial Mound. The mound, eighty feet high and fifty feet long, marks where the Indians buried their dead. It is located in the center of town.

MOUNT CLARE

The present name of this Harrison County community replaced the name of Browns Creek, on which it is located, in 1872. The name Mount Clare was suggested by John P. Lynch for a suburb of Baltimore where the main repair shops of the Baltimore & Ohio were located and where Lynch had friends.

MOUNT HOPE

Mount Hope, Fayette County, was named for its school.

When they were planning the school, a judge noticed that pea vines thrived during the spring snows and provided the farmers with fodder. When the town was incorporated in 1897, that sign of renewed life was selected as the name.

Mount Hope's hopes and dreams came to quick fruition with the rapid opening of coal mines after the arrival of a railroad spur. Mt. Hope was dashed, however, in 1910, when the town succumbed to an almost-fatal fire. Forty businesses and 150 homes were destroyed.

MOUNT NEBO

Mount Nebo, Nicholas County, was settled in the 1890s and named for a Biblical mountain.

MOUNT STORM

The village of Mount Storm, Grant County, is located on the Allegheny Front Mountain. The mountain is subjected to frequent storms, and thus the name of the town.

MULLENS

The name for this Wyoming County village remembers A.J. Mullins, who settled here in the 1890s. When the Virginian Railroad came through, he deeded land to them for a station—with the proviso that the town be named for him.

Unfortunately, when Mullins signed his name, he forgot to dot the "i" and the railroad translated the name as Mullens.

NALLEN

One might nickname this Fayette County village "nepotism."

The Wilderness Lumber Company moved into the area in 1916, and built the world's largest hardwood mill. The next year, a post office opened. The name came from John I. Nallen, secretary-treasurer of the lumber company and son-in-law of Peter Carroll, Wilderness' president.

NAOMA

Once known as Flats, this town was named for Naoma Pettry.

NAUGATUCK

The first name for this Mingo County spot was Mouth of Pigeon, so named because it is situated at the mouth of the Pigeon Creek. Later, a town was settled on the west side of the creek and called Naugatuck, laid out in 1896. The one on the east was named Fairfax. When the Norfolk & Western established a depot here, the railroad called it Naugatuck. Fairfax quickly conformed.

Naugatuck in Algonquian means "one tree."

NEOLA

Neola is the result of a word-jumble. The community was originally called Lowry's Mill, for the mill owner. In 1869, when Lowry sold his mill, the post office moved—but kept its name. Several years later, it became Shyrock, for Thomas Shyrock.

In 1907, a lumber company moved into the area. The next year, a post office was established in the name of Neola. The name, suggested by an official of the lumber company, was a jumble created from the letters of Olean, as in New York—the hometown of the official.

NEWBURG

In 1852, this locale was called 88 or Stop 88, because it is 88 miles west of Cumberland, Maryland. A year later, it became Simpson's Water Station. In 1854, the town became Newburg.

The patron of Newburg was the Baltimore & Ohio, and officials apparently used up most of the good names before trying to name this town. Some wag decided this was a "new" "burg."

NEW CUMBERLAND

The seat of Hancock County was first laid out in 1839 on the site of the 1784 Fort Chapman by John Cuppy. For a brief period of time, it was called Cuppy Town, then Vernon. As Cuppy sold more and more town lots, he was forced by public opinion to change the name to New Cumberland.

New Cumberland, at some time in its past, was called Brick Town, because of the numerous brickyards and pottery works within the town limits.

NEW MARTINSVILLE

Edward Doolin was the original settler in this location. He arrived in 1780, but two years later was killed by Indians "at the door of his cabin." The Indians promised Doolin's widow, a beautiful woman who had just delivered a child, that they would return for her when she was able to travel, and make her the wife of their chief.

Mrs. Doolin did not wait for the wedding bells. She rushed to a fort upstream. In 1810, she sold the title to the land to Presley Martin, who settled it. He named his settlement Martinsville.

The legislature established the town as "Martinsville, now New Martinsville."

NEWTOWN

This Roane County community was formerly called Three Forks of Sandy or Three Forks. But Newton was first established at the mouth of Dog Creek in 1857, named for Isaac Newton Ross, the infant son of postmaster Davidson W. Ross.

Ross moved to Three Forks and received permission to move his post office—including the name.

NITRO

This village was named appropriately in 1918, "because explosives were to be manufactured here." After the war, the plant, Explosives Plant C, closed down and the population almost disappeared.

NORTHFORK

Northfork, McDowell County, was incorporated in 1901 and named for its location at the mouth of the North Fork of the Elkhorn Creek.

NORTH MOUNTAIN

This Berkeley County community takes its name from North Mountain, the ridge "next beyond the Blue Ridge . . . named by the Indians the Endless Mountains."

NUTTER (— FORT, — FARM)

Located on Nutter Run, Nutter Fort takes its name from the waterway. Nutter Run was named for Captain Thomas Nutter, who settled in the area in 1770 and two years later built a fort that bears his name as "a refuge for the early settlers. . . ."

OAK HILL

This Fayette County town was settled as early as 1820, when William Blake arrived. Peter Bowyers opened his mill on the headwaters of the Arbuckle Creek shortly afterward. Between 1848 and 1850, the population soared, as scores of settlers arrived.

The town was named for a gigantic white oak tree in front of an earlier post office at a place called Hill Top. The name is a combination of the oak tree and its location on a hill.

Between 1850 and 1860, the Hill Top post office moved to this location, but the name remained Oak Hill.

OCEANA

This Wyoming County town is not near an ocean. Originally settled in 1850, it was called Cassville. The name was changed to Sumpterville. The final name-change came in 1855, when it became Oceana, for the daughter of Chief Cornstalk. Or was it?

Another source suggests that the town was known as Ginseng before 1853, and that Oceana was established by the legislature in 1853. Some seem to think the name comes from an Indian word which translates to "big bottoms" or "level lands." Others indicate the name was given for Ocie Anna Cooke, the daughter of "Old" William Cooke who was kidnapped by the Indians.

Oceana was established in 1853 by the legislature as the seat of Wyoming County. Thomas Dunn English, author of *Ben Bolt*, persuaded the county court to change the name to honor the daughter of Chief Cornstalk.

ODD

When it came time for the townspeople to decide on a name to grace their new post office, someone came up with the idea that they name their town something different, something unusual. The name "Odd" was suggested by Mrs. M.J. Brown, and immediately accepted.

OLD FIELDS

Established in the mid-eighteenth century, this Hardy County town was named for the corn fields settlers found when they arrived. It seems the Shawnee Indians had plowed and planted the field with corn. Early settlers referred to it as Indian Old Fields.

ONEGO

At the end of the nineteenth century, H.V. Cunningham, a local merchant in this Pendleton County locale, opened a post office and named the town Onego. But why?

One source indicates that Onego was a tribe of the Oneida

Indians, while another states that Oneka was a Mohegan chief of Connecticut, eldest son and heir to the illustrious Chief Uncas.

ORGAN CAVE

Shortly before the Civil War, this Greenbrier County village was called Price's Shop, because Abraham Price had a blacksmith shop here. His brother, J.M. Price, opened the first post office in his store and maintained the name.

The name honors the local cave, where there is a huge stalagmite formation that resembles a pipe organ. In fact, if the "pipes" are struck with sticks or stones, they emit different ranges of tone.

Before 1853, saltpeter was manufactured in the cave. One source indicates that during the Civil War, the cavern was known as General Lee's Underground Powder Works.

ORMA

The Rilla post office was located in this Calhoun County community in 1896, but during the 1903–04 period, it was known as Fez.

The present name was given in 1905 in honor of Orma Stalnaker.

ORTON

When the townspeople submitted a list of possible names for this Gilmer County village, the post office selected Orton from the second list. The name honors Orton Mollohan, who lived near the post office at the time.

PADEN CITY

Obediah Paden, who was among the first settlers of the Ohio Valley, patented land in this Wetzel County location in 1790. Paden fathered ten children and, as a Federal Works Project writer put it, they "fathered the town."

PALESTINE

Though this Wirt County community has always been known as Palestine, its post office was called Reedy Ripple until 1905, because postal authorities believed there would be confusion between Palestine and Palatine, Marion County. The name Reedy Ripple was inspired by a long ripple, caused by an accumulation of gravel, in the Little Kanawha River near the mouth of Reedy Creek.

The name Palestine, we are told, reflects the strong religious leanings of the townspeople.

PANTHER

This McDowell County town was named for the creek on which it is located. Panther Creek was named before the Civil War for a frightening experience: Tommie Lester's rifle failed to fire when he met up with a panther here. He bested the beast with the aid of his dogs and his trusty bowie knife.

PARKERSBURG

Named the seat of Wood County on 1801, Parkersburg was earlier known as The Point or Stokelyville. John Stokley, who received a patent for the land in 1800, laid out a town here on both sides of the Ohio River and, until 1809, called it Newport.

Adjoining Stokley's lands were those of the Parker family. Alexander Parker laid legal claim to his land in 1809, and his daughter donated land for the courthouse and county building; it appears he donated the current name.

After Parker died, Stokley successfully contested the daughter's claim. The town that grew around Stokley's cabin became known as Stokleyville. But the Parkers did not let matters rest.

The year after the Parker family regained control of their land, the state legislature provided for a new town, Parkersburg, that included the older town of Newport.

PARSONS

Reports say that Captain John Parson was "probably" the first white man in Tucker County. He once owned the land on which the village is located.

The Civil War battle of Corrick's Ford was fought here when Union troops caught up with Confederates retreating from Laurel Hill. Confederate General Robert S. Garnett was mortally wounded, and died after the battle . . . in the arms of Union General Thomas A. Morris. They had been classmates at West Point.

PAW PAW

Incorporated in 1891, Paw Paw, Morgan County, was possibly named for the pawpaw tree, *Asimina triloba.*

Union forces used Paw Paw as a staging area during the war. At one point, more than 16,000 troops were encamped here in barracks and a blockhouse.

PAX

This Fayette County village is located on the Packs Branch of the Paint Creek. It is probable that the name is a phonetic spelling of the branch—and not Latin for "peace."

Packs Branch was named for Samuel Pack, an early settler.

PENTRESS

Before Emmanuel Brown laid out the town in 1847–48, and Andrew Brown built the first house, this village was called Statlersville, for Jacob Statler. The town actually has roots dating back to 1766, when Bruce Worley built a cabin here on Dunkard Creek.

In 1906, New Brownsville town lots were sold and the site became Pentress, named by William Prince for a Welsh surname.

PETERSTOWN

The Woods family settled in this Monroe County area in 1769, about four miles east of the present-day town. By 1784, Christian Peters, a Revolutionary War veteran of Lafayette's command at Yorktown, was a well-known homesteader.

PETROLEUM

This Ritchie County village was laid out in 1854 to eagerly await the coming of the Baltimore & Ohio Railroad. It was named for a "nearby petroleum spring."

PEYTONA

One of the greatest boons to the economy of this Boone County locale was the opening of the Peytonia Cannel Coal Company which, in 1856, built locks and dams in the Coal River and erected a mining plant at Peytona.

The name for the company and the town honor Colonel Madison Peyton, an official of the Canneltown Coal Company. When the "i" was dropped is a mystery.

PHILIPPI

Philippi, the seat of Barbour County, was previously known as "the old Booth's Ferry of Randolph," Anglin's Ford, and Booth's Ferry.

These early names commemorate William Anglin, the original landowner who was there by 1783. The earliest settlers, however, were Richard Cottrill and Charity Talbott, who arrived in 1780. By 1810, the name reflected on Daniel Booth, who operated the ferry.

The current name comes from the county, which was named for Phillip Pendleton Barbour, a Supreme Court justice. Barbour seems the logical choice for the name source, even though some would like to hint that the town was named for Philippi, the ruined town in Macedonia.

The first land battle of the Civil War took place here on 3 June 1861. Known as the "Philippi Races," an attack was launched by the Union to retain control of the Baltimore & Ohio Railroad. The nickname for the battle came from the speed at which the Confederate troops, under Colonel George A. Porterfield, retreated.

PICKAWAY

Some sources indicate that Pickaway, Monroe County, commemorates the Pickaway Plains of Ohio, where the government made a treaty with the Shawnees after the Battle of Point Pleasant.

Others suggest that Piqua was the original spelling of the name. Either or both could be right. Piqua (or Pequa) was a sub-tribe of the Shawnees and gave its name to Pickaway County, Ohio.

PIEDMONT

Piedmont was an open field in Hampshire (now Mineral) County when the Baltimore & Ohio Railroad arrived in 1851. The town was laid out in 1855 and established by the legislature a year later. It was built on land owned by the hotel's owner, a Mrs. Burns, who sold out just before the railroad came through.

The name, apparently, comes from the Italian *piedmont*, "lying or forming at the base of mountains."

PIKE

Pike was so named in 1898 because the Northwestern Turnpike and the road to St. Mary's (Routes 16 and 31) met there.

PINCH

This Kanawha County village was first named Pinch Gut for the Pinch Gut, the stream at the site. Both the stream and the village later became Pinch, then Dial, Pinchton, and finally Pinch again.

The phrase "pinch gut" is, perhaps, a play on words. The word "gut" has been used as an occasional name for small streams. During pioneer days, settlers on this stream were often beset by Indians who tried to starve them out, and therefore the "pinch" in the "gut." Sounds great, but is it true?

Dial was named for a Methodist preacher. The post office changed Dial to Pinchton to avoid confusion with Dale; then Pinchton was changed back to Pinch, to avoid conflict with Princeton.

PIPESTEM

Pipestem, a village in Summers County, is located on the Pipestem Creek, and was named for the stream. About 1848, the village was known as Jordan's Chapel from the name of the local church. In 1858, it became known as Pipestem.

Pipestem Creek received its name from "a small bush" that grew on its banks. Elderly smokers used the hollow stem of the bush to make pipe stems.

PLINY

Pliny, Putnam County, does not have a classical background. The place was named in the mid-nineteenth century for M. Pliny Brown, who "first started the ferry between Pliny and Buffalo by tying a wire to the top of a tree on each side of the Kanawha River and letting the current drift the boat across."

POCA

The post office was established at this Putnam County location in 1879. The name appears to be a short version of Pocatalico, the name of the political district (or subdivision) in which it is located.

POCATALICO

This community, located in Putnam County, takes its name from the Pocatalico River, which runs through Kanawha and Roane counties in addition to Putnam. The Indian translation of the river's name comes out to "plenty of fat doe" or "river of the fat doe."

POE

W. T. Burdette, a great admirer of Edgar Allan Poe, was very helpful in getting the post office established in this location.

POINT PLEASANT

When surveying the area in the 1740s, George Washington decided that he liked what he saw, and called the site Point Pleasant. The town was established by the legislature in 1794.

Point Pleasant was where Chief Cornstalk and his son were

ambushed. General Andrew Lewis and his Virginia militiamen were headquartered here, probably at a place called Fort Blair. Fort Randolph replaced that fortification in 1776. There is a monument erected at Point Pleasant to memorialize Chief Cornstalk.

The community around Port Pleasant grew slowly. In 1825, Henry Clay described it as "a beautiful woman clad in rags." When the town was incorporated in 1833, men could still race horses along Main Street.

POINTS

The first postmaster and town founder, I.T. Johnson, recommended that the name for this Hampshire County village be Four Points, for the four "points" of land made by the crossroads. The post office dropped the modifier.

POND GAP

The name of this Kanawha County location was given in the 1890s by L.D. Hill, the town's first postmaster. The name came about from the "gap" formed by the Blue and Bell Creeks. On the Blue Creek side, there is a pond.

POWHATAN

This community was named for Powhatan Coal, located here. The company took its name from Chief Powhatan, one of the most famous names in Virginia history and the father of Pocahontas.

PRATT

From 1781 to 1870, this Kanawha County town was called Clifton. From 1870 to 1899, it became Dego, from a town in northern Italy. The present name source was Charles K. Pratt, whose Charles Pratt Company bought timber and coal lands here.

Near the mouth of nearby Paint Creek, archeologists uncovered an extensive burying ground. Judging by the skeletons, extremely tall people were buried there—one skeleton measured over seven feet.

PREMIER

The location of this McDowell County town was also the base for the Premier Pocahontas Coal Company and the Premier Pocahontas Collieries Company. The name of the town followed suit in 1907.

PRINCETON

Princeton, settled in 1826, was organized as a village eleven years later. In 1839, when it became the seat of Mercer County (named for General Hugh Mercer, who perished at the Revolutionary War battle of Princeton), it took on the name of the New Jersey town.

A local legend centers on a bank organized in 1874 by H.W. Straley. The banking facilities were quite primitive—documents and paper money were stored in a hair-covered trunk, and coins were kept in a large beaver hat. One day, a stranger came to the bank and introduced himself to the bank vice president as a businessman. The banker offered the man a cigar and invited him home to dinner.

The guest, Frank James, brother of Jesse, returned to his gang and told them they would ruin their reputation by robbing such an insignificant institution.

PULLMAN

This Ritchie County village was laid out in 1883. Postal authorities selected the name Pullman in honor of George M. Pullman, who created the famous Pullman railroad car.

QUINNIMONT

The first settlers to this location arrived in 1827. The name appears to refer to the five mountain peaks in the area. Quinnimont is probably a modification of the Latin *quinque,* "five," and *mont,* "mountain."

QUINWOOD

This Greenbrier County village was established in 1919 by Quin Morton and W. S. Wood, both from Charleston, West Virginia.

RACINE

In 1877, this Boone County locality was called Mouth of Short Creek, because it is located on the Coal River at the mouth of Short Creek.

The name, tradition has it, comes from "an old resident whose parents came here from Racine, Ohio . . ."

RADNOR

Some sources suggest that this Wayne County name may be a modification of a common West Virginia surname, Ridenour.

RAINELLE

An earlier name for this Greenbrier County village was Sewell Creek, based on its location. Later, it was Sewell Valley, for the pioneer Stephen Sewell, who tried to settle the area single-handedly. The current name derives from the 1909 owners of the Meadow River Lumber Company, Thomas W. and John Raine.

Postal officials refused the Raines request to name the town Raine, and so Thomas' daughter added the feminine ending.

RAVEN ROCK

The earliest name for this Pleasants County village was Land's End. The name, given in 1810, described the fact that the town was located at the end of the bottom land of the Ohio River. Basil Riggs settled the area around that time, and erected a gristmill.

The current name, and village, grew up in 1877. A post office was established the next year as Raven Rock. Sources differ as to the reason. Some say it was because of a raven's nest high in the mountain rocks above the town; others claim flocks of ravens nested in the rocks. Because of the singular form of "raven," it would seem that the former reason might be more to the point.

RAVENSWOOD

Ravenswood, Jackson County, was laid out in 1835 and established by the legislature in 1852. It may have existed earlier as Ravens-worth, a name suggested by the grandnieces of George Washington, who inherited the land and named it for an English town where relatives lived. The change from "-worth" to "-wood," is supposed to be due to frequent misspellings on maps.

READER

This Wetzel County community was not named in the wake of a literacy movement.

Reader, located at the mouth of Reader Creek, takes its name from the waterway. The creek was named in 1800 for Benjamin Reader, who first settled in the area in 1788. Reader purchased the land from James Troy in return for a bay mare and a ten-gallon copper kettle. He later sold the acreage to Morgan Morgan, grandson of West Virginia's first settler, for a flintlock rifle.

The current town maintained the original name when the Baltimore & Ohio Railroad built here in 1901.

RED CREEK

Previously known as Flanagan Hill, this Tucker County village took the name of the Red Creek, a waterway on which it was originally located. When the post office moved from the banks of the Red Creek, it kept that name! The creek was so named because an abundance of laurel blooms made the creek look red.

RED HOUSE

Red House was first settled in 1806 and named Red House Shoals. Popular sentiment says that both Red House and Red House Shoals, on the Kanawha River, were named for a perpendicular red rock that rises 465 feet from the rear of the village.

The name actually originated when Joseph Ruffner built the "Red House" in 1825, on land granted to George Washington in 1773.

RED JACKET

Red Jacket was named for Chief Red Jacket of the Seneca tribe. He has no historical connection to the area or to West Virginia.

RED SULPHUR SPRINGS

Red Sulphur Springs was once a popular health and social resort. A large hotel was built in 1832, but tax records show that it did not do too well.

During the Civil War, the hotel was used as a Confederate hospital, then it was closed until purchased by Levi P. Morton, Benjamin Harrison's vice president. Morton offered the property to the state as a site for a tuberculosis sanatorium. The offer was declined.

REEDY

This village is situated at the junction of the Middle and Right Forks of Reedy Creek, and thus takes its name from the stream.

Earlier known as Three Forks of Reedy, it became Reedy in 1853 when the post office was established. The creek was named by William Beauchamp, the first settler, for the large number of reeds that grew in the water.

REEDYVILLE

The post office was established at this Roane County town in 1854.

Since the town is located on the Reedy Creek, it is obvious the name, like that of Reedy, came from the stream.

RICHWOOD

Richwood was originally called Cherry Tree Bottom (Bottoms) when the post office was established in this Nicholas County community in 1879. The name was shortened at a later date to Cherry Bottom but both versions of the names were appropriate because the town is situated on the Cherry Creek.

The creek's name came from the abundance of wild cherry trees on its banks.

Cherry Bottom became Richwood in 1900, when the Richwood post office was transferred from Hinkle Mountain, and the settlement was chartered in 1901. The name was selected because of the fine forest timber available in the area.

RIDGE

Located on Warm Spring Ridge, in Morgan County, this town was first called Birch Grove. While the original name described the town's setting, the current name describes its location.

RIDGEVILLE

Ridgeville was named for its proximity to the mountain ridges.

RINGGOLD

See Ringgold, Pennsylvania.

RIO

Located on the North River, this village appears to have taken as its name the Spanish name for river. Before it became Rio, it was known as Smith's Gap, then North River.

RIPLEY

Ripley, the seat of Jackson County, was settled in 1768 by William John and Lewis Rogers. The village was established by the legislature in 1832, then laid out by Jacob Starcher.

Starcher named it for the Reverend Harry Ripley, a minister who met an unfortunate end in 1830 near Big Mill Creek, north of the town. Depending on the source, Ripley died either from exposure to the elements—or by drowning.

RIVESVILLE

This community was established and laid out in 1837 on the land of Elisha Snodgrass. At that time it was known as Milford because the first gristmill in the region was located at a ford in the river.

Rivesville was named for a member of the Rives family: either Henry C. or William Cabell Rives. Both men were noted citizens.

In the center of Rivesville there is a monument to David Morgan. Morgan is said to have risen from his sickbed in the spring of 1774 only to find two Indians stalking his children. Grabbing his flintlock, Morgan fired one shot, killing one Indian in the act of raising his tomahawk above one child's head. Unable to reload, Morgan's first shot drew the second Indian's fire. That shot missed Morgan, but he still had to dodge that man's tomahawk. He lost one finger and fractured another defending himself.

Morgan wrestled with the Indian and, just like in the movies, plunged the Indian's knife into his own side. The legend has a grisly end, with Morgan skinning both Indians and making shot pouches and belts from their skin.

ROCK

Near Sandlick Creek, in Mercer County, stands a 100-foot-high rock that is split near the top. This geological protuberance was the source of the name for this town.

ROCK CAMP

Rock Camp, Monroe County, is located on Rock Camp Creek. The village, settled in the late eighteenth century, takes its name from the stream, which was named for a spot where a band of Indians once camped. Another source suggests the stream was named for a flat rock, located at the waterway's head, that was so large "a team of horses and a wagon can be turned."

ROCK CASTLE

When first settled in the 1830s, this Jackson County town was located about a mile "down the [Thirteenmile] Creek." At that spot, there were "spruce pine trees" and a "cliff of rock." The cliff apparently reminded early settlers of a castle.

ROCK CAVE

Rumor has it that this Upshur County village was once known as Bob Town and Centerville. The post office here was called Rude's Mill (1848–59), for Edwin D. Rude, the first postmaster.

The name Rock Cave was a post office mistake. The name submitted for the post office was Rock Lava—because townspeople had uncovered volcanic stones in the area—but postal authorities did not read the form correctly.

In 1863, members of the Upshur County Militia were drilling under the command of Captain Daniel Gould when they were surprised by a force of Confederates. The group surrendered without a shot being fired. Of the seventy men captured, seven escaped and twenty-five were paroled. The majority died in Confederate prisons.

ROCK OAK

A post office was opened in this Hardy County village in 1888. The name came from the type of timber, called rock oak, cut here.

ROCK VIEW

The first post office of this Wyoming County village was located within 100 yards of Castle Rock, and had a very good view of the rock formation. To underscore that as the source of the name, the town was originally called Castlerock Creek.

RODERFIELD

Roderfield, McDowell County, was named for Roderfield Iaeger, the principal landowner.

ROMANCE

As Tina Turner might ask, "What's love got to do with it?" The answer is nothing.

Romance, Jackson County, established as a post office in 1907, was named for Romance Parsons.

ROMNEY

Established by the legislature in 1762, the seat of Hampshire County was named by Lord Fairfax, for Romney, one of the Cinque Ports of southern England.

In 1738, Job and John Pearsall built houses in this area and called the settlement Pearsall's Flats. Within ten years, 200 settlers arrived. Made aware of this success and hoping to regain some of his fortune, Lord Fairfax sent a surveying team into the region. One of the team's members was a sixteen-year-old George Washington.

The Shawnee and other tribes also noticed the settlement's

success. In 1753, the Indians declared a "death claim" on every inch of ground between the Blue Ridge Mountains and the Ohio. George Washington, now commander of the armies protecting the frontier, worried to Governor Dinwiddie in 1756 that "the inhabitants are removing daily, and in a short time will leave this country as desolate as Hampshire where scarce a family lives."

The Indians, led by Chief Killbuck, abandoned their threat by 1761, so Lord Fairfax proceeded to have town lots laid out on a ten-acre piece of ground, which he named Romney. After the Revolution, Lord Fairfax's fortune dwindled even further. His lands were confiscated for his Tory sympathies.

RONCEVERTE

This community, established about 1800, takes its name from the Ronceverte River, where the village is located. Ronceverte is French for "greenbrier," flora that covers the river area.

About 1800, Thomas Edgar built a gristmill here. The area was renamed Ronceverte in the 1870s when Colonel Cecil Clay, the guiding spirit of the St. Lawrence Boom & Manufacturing Company, bought 800 acres of what was called Edgar's Mill. Despite opposition to a foreign name by townsfolk, Ronceverte was the official name when the town was incorporated in 1882.

ROXALANA

The wife of Colonel Benjamin Smith, of Charleston, who owned land near this Roane County village, was named Roxalana. The post office was the first established in its political district in 1857.

ST. ALBANS

Laid out in 1816, this village had several previous names: Philippi in 1816, for Philip Thomas, an early settler; Coalsmouth, because of its location on the Coal and Kanawha Rivers; Kanawha City in 1871, for its location; and, finally, in 1871, St. Albans, for St. Albans, Vermont.

The land in this area was explored by Thomas Teays in 1774, but he did not settle here. Thirteen years later, Lewis and John Tackett built Fort Tackett. In 1791, the fort was attacked by Indians and almost all the residents were murdered. The next attempt at a local settlement was made by Stephen Teays, son of Thomas, on land he had received from his father. In 1799, he began operating a ferry across Coal River to the lands owned by George Washington.

ST. GEORGE

St. George is a village in Tucker County. The county was named for St. George Tucker, and the political district in which the town resides is also St. George. We feel safe in assuming that the village derived its name from its district, and the district from the county.

ST. MARYS

Alexander Creel is supposed to have had a vision during a night trip on the Ohio River, apparently as he passed this site.

Tradition has it that Creel repurchased land his father had sold and named it for the Blessed Virgin.

Isaac and Jacob La Rue settled here in 1790 on land granted them for service during the Revolution. The town was established by legislative action in 1851, and named in 1849.

SALT ROCK

Salt Rock, Cabell County, is reputed to have taken its name from a business venture of Thomas Ward's who made salt here as early as 1817. Other theories are that in the summer, in earlier times, farmers would put salt on rocks by dried-up streams to entice the animals into range. Another possibility is that salt was produced from the salt rock underlying this area of the state.

SALT SULPHUR SPRINGS

A resort hotel in this vicinity opened in 1823. It boasted three springs—the Salt Sulphur, the Sweet, and the Iodine. Along a popular spot with wealthy Southerners, the hotel was used as a headquarters by Confederate officers during campaigns in this valley.

After the war, the resort's popularity waned. The hotel closed in 1900, but reopened twenty-seven years later.

SAND FORK

This Gilmer County village is located on Sand Fork, near the Little Kanawha River. It takes its name from the waterway. Sand Creek was named for the sandbars found along its course as early as 1814.

The site was established in 1903 as Layopolis, for William R. Lay, of the Eureka Pipe Line Company. At the time, Eureka was active in the county's oil fields.

The post office was always called Sand Fork; it just took a little while to get the two names together.

SANDSTONE

The first settlers in this Summers County area were members of the Richmond family. They named their settlement at New River Falls, New Richmond Depot.

Other names for the same area include: New River Falls about 1860, for its location on New River; New Richmond in 1870; and, finally, about 1880, it was called Sandstone, for a nearby quarry that produced stone for the railroad.

SANDYVILLE

This Tyler County community's name describes the location of the town, or "ville" near Big Sandy Creek.

SCARBORO

Located in Fayette County, Scarboro was named by Samuel Dixon, a Fayette County coal-mine operator who noticed that the family name of Scarbrough was prevalent in the area of his mining town on White Oak Creek. This, tradition has it, reminded him of a town in his native England, Scarborough. No one can explain why there is a difference in the spelling of all three names.

SCHERR

The post office for this Grant County village was established in about 1900. It was named for Arnold C. Scherr, the state's auditor, who took a personal interest in getting a post office here.

SEEBERT

The source of the name of Seebert, Pocahontas County, is the Seybert family. It might be another example of phonetic spelling.

SENECA ROCKS

Seneca Rocks, Pendleton County, takes its name from a geological formation near Seneca Creek.

The translation of *sinnike*, "stony," comes from the Delaware tongue.

SETH

Until 1890, this village was called Coon's Mills. The name was changed to honor Seth Foster, who helped establish a post office here.

SHEPHERDSTOWN. The Thomas Shepherd Inn, located at the corner of German and Duke streets in Shepherdstown, West Virginia, was the early home of Thomas Shepherd who gave his name to the town he founded. [CREDIT: Thomas Shepherd Inn, Shepherdstown, West Virginia]

SHANGHAI

The name of this Berkeley County village is not an example of early global awareness. It was named for the Shanghai Manufacturing Association, which operated here. The association ground sumac and tan bark, and manufactured lumber.

SHEPHERDSTOWN

Established before 1730 by English and German farmers, Shepherdstown is one of the earliest settlements of West Virginia. The legal grant to the land was purchased by Thomas Shepherd in 1732. The original name for the established town was Mecklenberg, from around 1762. Prior to that, it was known as Pack Horse Ford, the place where packhorses crossed over the Potomac River.

James Rumsey demonstrated the first successful steamboat here in 1787. In 1790, George Washington considered moving the nation's capital here.

During the Civil War, Shepherdstown was spared. Though only seven miles from Antietam, it escaped the angry fire.

The name was changed to Shepherdstown in 1798 to honor the founding father.

SHOCK

Don't expect to run into Frankenstein's monster at this Gilmer

County locale. The family that owned the land on which the first post office was located were surnamed Shock, or Schacke, Schack, Schaake, or Schache.

SIAS

The post office at this Lincoln County village was established as Sias in 1908, but was earlier known as Jenks. The current name, which is pronounced like "ice," was the surname of a helper employed by G.B. Adkins, the first postmaster.

SIMON

The name of this Wyoming County village was Junction City, until it was sold out in town lots.

The new—and current—name came from "Uncle Si," assistant postmistress Gladys Hatfield's relative.

SIMPSON

Simpson, Taylor County, is located on the Right Fork of Simpson Creek, and takes its name from the stream.

Simpson Creek was named for John Simpson, a trapper who stopped near here in 1763.

SINKS GROVE

The earliest name for this community was Rocky Point.

The current name was taken from the Sinks Grove Baptist Church, organized in 1845. The land for the church was donated by Matthew Scott, who named the site as soon as he saw it, allegedly for a beautiful grove of trees. Did he also see the "sinks"?

Sinks are funnel-shaped depressions with ugly holes at the bottom and are scattered around this limestone plateau area.

SISTERSVILLE

Charles Wells settled this town in 1802. First named Wells' Landing, then Ziggleton, the town was established in 1815, but not incorporated until 1839. The town was named for his daughters Sarah and Deliah, the eighteenth and nineteenth of his twenty-two children! He named his twentieth child Twenty, the twenty-first Plenty, and the twenty-second Betsey. There must have been something about the waters of the Ohio by Sistersville. A tenant by the name of Scott had twenty-two children, and a neighbor named Gordon had twenty-eight.

SIX

The name of this McDowell county village comes from Six, the number of the Carter Coal Company's mine that was located here.

SMOOT

Smoot, Greenbrier County, is located on the Smoot Branch of Otter Creek, and takes its name from the waterway. The stream, it is said, was named in the early twentieth century for E.D. Smoot, who helped get the post office located here.

SOD

When this village was originally settled, it was called Scioto. In 1904, when the post office was organized, the name became Sod, for the initials of the first postmaster's name: Samuel Odell Dunlap.

SOPHIA

The donor of the name of this Raleigh County village was Sophia McGinnis, who lived here. She was a relative of the Judge McGinnis who named Mount Hope.

SOUTH CHARLESTON

South Charleston, Kanawha County, is on the south bank of the Kanawha River, diagonally opposite of West Charleston.

SPANISHBURG

The first settlers to this Mercer County location in the 1870s were led by James Calahan. He named his settlement for Spanish Brown, one of his relatives. Brown, however, wandered off, and settled on Miller Farm.

SPENCER

Spencer, the seat of Roane County, may once have been called Tanner's Cross Roads, probably in 1812. The source for the name supposedly was Samuel Tanner, a settler who lived nearby in a cave. Other sources contend the town began as Cassville, then changed to New California around 1850–56.

The Tanner's name makes some sense, because Spencer is located on Tanner Run, which was named for storekeeper Samuel Tanner. Though there are no records for the name Cassville, there is a cute story about New California. It seems that Raleigh Butcher left his home on Reedy Creek, and brazenly announced he was moving to California. The loudmouth never got farther than the crossroads, which were christened New California and incorporated under that name in 1858.

There is some disagreement on the source of the name Spencer. On one hand, it is suggested it was named for Judge Spencer Roane, the Virginia jurist who gave his name to the county. Others choose Captain John W. Spencer as the donor. It seems more to the point to name the town after the judge, the donor of the county's name.

SPICE
The name of this Pocahontas County village was derived from the abundant spicewood shrub, or spicebush (*Lindera benzoin*).

SPRING DALE
The only reasonable explanation for the naming of this Fayette County town is the abundance of good springs nearby.

SQUIRE
Board Camp was the earliest name for this McDowell County locale. The name came from an early shelter for cattle rangers, made of white oak timber.

The present name came from A.C. Christian, who lived here in 1901. Because he was a justice of the peace, he was referred to by the community as "Squire." He was also instrumental in getting the post office established here.

STATTS MILLS
Statts Mills, located on the Tug Fork, was settled in the 1850s by Abraham Staats, from New Jersey. The name was selected, tradition has it, for Isaac Staats, who killed the last deer on Tug Fork.

The reason the Staats name was not used by the post office was to avoid confusion with Stout's Mill. Postal officials respelled the name in its current fashion.

STONY BOTTOM
The earlier name for this Pocahontas County village was Seldom Seen. The name was given by A.K. Dysard, the first postmaster, who contended that few people had ever seen the place.

The second postmaster, James A. Barnett, changed the name to Driftwood. That name came from the fact that logs floated down the nearby Greenbrier River would naturally drift ashore at a curve in the river and pile up. This name remained until 1903.

W. R. Moore, when he became postmaster in 1902, decided to change the name again to a description of the area: the land was level and there were numerous rocks "in the ground."

STOTESBURY

E. E. White, president of the E. E. White Coal Company, named this community for his wife. Her maiden name was Stotesbury.

STRANGE CREEK

This Braxton County community is named for the Strange Creek, which was once called Turkey Run.

The current name for the creek honors the memory of William Strange. Strange was a surveyor who lost his way near the headwaters of the Elk River in 1795. Years later, his bones, his rifle, and his dog's bones were found forty miles away from the river, together with his epithet carved in a tree: "Strange is my name, and I'm on strange ground. And strange it is I can't be found."

The village was once named Savage Town, for Jesse S. and William A. Savage, Ohioans who discovered iron ore in the area in 1874.

SUGAR GROVE

The name of this Pendleton County village was given in the 1830s for the many "fine sugar orchards" in the area.

SUMMERS

See Summersville.

SUMMERSVILLE

Summersville, the seat of Nicholas County, was established by law in the 1820s. The name is derived from Judge Lewis Summers, who introduced the bill in the Virginia Assembly to establish the county.

Nancy Hart, a Confederate spy, led an attack on Summersville in 1861. The Union force was captured and the town burned. Hart herself was captured and charged with espionage. Once in the Summersville jail, she posed a problem to her jailers, who were torn between duty and lust. Union forces had control of the area around Summersville, so escape was out of the question and her execution certain. One evening, a guard allowed her to wander about the courtyard. She asked to see his pistol. He complied, and it was the last thing he ever did. Nancy Hart shot him dead and escaped to Confederate lines. After Lee's surrender, she returned to Nicholas County and married Joshua Douglas. She was never prosecuted for the murder of the guard.

SUPERIOR

About 1913, the post office in this location was called Dixopois, a supposed arrangement of Dixie or Dixie Post Office.

The present name came from the Lake Superior Coal Company, which operated its Number 1 mine in this locale.

SWEETLAND

This Lincoln County village was named in 1884 for Van Sweetland, a prominent businessman from Hamlin, West Virginia.

SWEET SPRINGS

This village is located on Sweet Spring Creek, and takes its name from the stream. It was settled by the Lewis family in the 1780s.

Sweet Spring Creek received its name because its waters were considered "mildly . . . cathartic." Sweet Springs was once a fashionable spa, known as "Old Sweet," one of the oldest in the South. The resort was closed in 1930.

Revolutionary War Major William Royall's home was near Old Sweet. In 1786, the major, a widower, hired a scrub woman, a Mrs. Newport. Mrs. Newport was aided by her two daughters. Eleven years later, the major married one of the daughters, Ann Newport Royall (1769–1854). She ruled the house where she once was a servant until the major's death in 1813. In his will, he left the bulk of his estate to his wife. His relatives contested the will . . . and won! Ann Royall, while the suit was in court, traveled the countryside and took notes for a book, *Sketches of History, Life and Manners in the United States*, which brought her minor fame.

She searched for a job, and landed one in 1831, writing little pieces for *Paul Pry*, a small newspaper. That paper was succeeded five years later by *The Huntress*. As a pioneering woman journalist in the nation's capital, Ann Royall was the first woman to force a president into an interview. John Quincy Adams refused her request, but Royall found out where he went for private swims. Seated upon Adams' clothes, she asked questions and the president trod water as he answered.

SWISS

Swiss was settled in 1795, but the farming pioneers found the rugged terrain too difficult to till. Almost a century later, in 1870, five families of Swiss immigrants settled here. What distressed the earlier arrivals reminded the Swiss of their home country. They used farming techniques perfected over centuries in Switzerland.

SWITCHBACK

This McDowell County village received its name from the Norfolk & Western Railroad. A "switchback" is a zigzag arrangement of railroad tracks to enable a train to reach the top of a steep grade.

TAD

The son of the first postmaster in this village was Talmadge Dunlap, whose nickname was Tad. The post office was established in 1917.

TANNER

Tanner, in Gilmer County, is located on the Tanner Creek, and derives its name from the stream.

Tanner Creek was named for a Mr. Tanner, local legend has it, who came from Pennsylvania in the nineteenth century and operated a tannery here. More likely, a tannery or a tanner's shop was located near the waterway.

TERRA ALTA

Terra Alta sits 2,500 feet above sea level, reason enough in 1885 for the townspeople to call it "high ground," from the Latin. The town was once called Green Glades, but when the Baltimore & Ohio arrived, the railroad named its station Cranberry Summit, for the cranberry bogs located here.

The first post office, named Salt Lick, was soon changed to Cranberry to conform to the railroad. In about 1858, the post office name was changed to Portland, by some lumbermen from Maine.

Cranberry was restored as the name by the legislature in 1882, but a few years later, it became Terra Alta.

THACKER

Thacker, Mingo County, is located on the Thacker Creek, and borrows its name from the stream.

Reuben Thacker, from the James River Valley, settled in this area for a few years before moving west. He gave his name to Thacker Creek.

THOMAS

Thomas was incorporated in 1892, and named for Colonel Tom Davis, brother of Senator Henry Gassaway Davis. The town was founded in 1884 by Senators Stephen B. Elkins and Davis as a coal town.

THURMOND

At one time, Thurmond, Fayette County, was the only town in the United States without a main street!

The main thoroughfare of the town was the Chesapeake & Potomac Railroad. In the late nineteenth century, Thurmond was a major rail center. In the early twentieth century, it became known as "Little Monte Carlo" or "Little New York" because of gambling at the Dunglen Hotel. Thurmond's popularity as a casino town declined in 1930, when the Dunglen burned down.

Most sources suspect the town was named for Captain W. D. Thurmond (1820–1910), president of the national bank there. The captain, a Confederate officer who served under General Echols, arrived in the county in 1844.

TOLL GATE

This Ritchie County locale opened its first post office in 1868. Its name came from an old tollgate on the Northwestern Turnpike, one of George Washington's pet projects, that opened in 1838. The tollgates were abandoned during the Civil War.

TORNADO

This village was once named the Upper Falls of Coal River. It obtained its name in a similar way to the town of Hurricane.

TRIDELPHIA

Tridelphia means literally "three brothers" in the Greek language. The town was settled in 1800 by three close friends, Colonel Josias Thompson, Amasa Brown, and John D. Foster.

TROY

Back in the early days of this village, settlers cleared away the forest and built a home. One of these settlers was John Troy.

Soon after a road was completed, the stagecoach began making two weekly trips, bringing mail from Parkersburg and Weston. The mail was usually left in care of John Troy. When the stage travel became irregular, townsfolk had to go to Weston to get their mail. Troy interceded and petitioned for a post office. His petition was granted, and he became the first postmaster of Troy.

TUNNELTON

Cassady's Summit was the first name for this Preston County village located on Tunnel Hill. Later, the town became Greigsville.

In 1897, at the time of incorporation, the name became Tunnelton for the obvious: it was the town at the tunnel.

TWILIGHT

Because of its location in a valley amid towering mountains, twilight is a beautiful time here. The original name was Robin Hood, but the name was changed when the post office opened.

UNEEDA

The name of this site was given in 1898, for the Uneeda Biscuit.

UNION

The seat of Monroe County is located in Union District, and takes its name from that political subdivision. It was legally established in 1800 as Union, but a reference or two calls it Union Town.

The town was settled in 1774 by James Alexander. When the town was named county seat, Alexander donated land for the courthouse.

UPPER TRACT

Upper Tract was once the location of an old fort of the same name, established in 1756 during the French and Indian War. It received its name because of its location at an altitude of about 1,500 feet.

VADIS

Vadis, Lewis County, is an anagram. Unjumbled, the letters spell "Davis," the original name for the post office. The name was changed to avoid confusion. Davis was the first postmaster, and we cannot help but wonder if the namer was any relation to Henry Gassaway Davis.

VALLEY BEND

Valley Bend is located in Valley Bend District, from which it takes its name. The town is located on a bend in the Tygart River Valley.

VALLEY GROVE

The name for this Ohio County village was brought into existence at the turn of the twentieth century from a picnic grove on the farm of Thomas Maxwell.

VAN

This Boone County village was named for Van Linville, the first postmaster. Before operating the post office, Linville had been a Boone County sheriff and a member of the state legislature.

VANDALIA

When the pioneers settled in this Lewis County location, they called it Big Skin Creek. By the 1880s, the name had been toned down a bit to Austin, for Austin Reger, a popular young resident.

About 1890, postmistress Mrs. George Simpson submitted Austin as the town's name for its post office. The submission was rejected because of another Austin in the state, so she tried Vandalia. The townsfolk were not enthusiastic about that name, since it was the nickname of a fierce Teutonic tribe, but Vandalia stuck, and Austin disappeared.

VOLCANO

This Wood County village, once known as White Oak, was one of the oldest and most profitable oil fields in the nation. During the 1870s, both the Volcanic Oil & Coal Company and the Vulcan Oil & Mining Company operated here.

It was renamed Volcano because during the night, flares and fires made the community resemble the crater of an active volcano.

VOLGA

Until 1900, this Barbour County town was known as Burnersville, for Jacob Burner, the first postmaster. In that year, the Century Coal Company changed the name to avoid post office confusion with Burnsville, Braxton County.

The name comes from the Volga River, a Sarmatian word for "the great river." That could be an allusion to the Big Run, on which the town is located.

WALKERSVILLE

The first settlement (1798) in this Lewis County location was called The Forks. In the 1830s, it became known as Bennett's Mill, for William Bennett, owner of the gristmill and the first postmaster.

The change from Bennett's Mill to Walkersville took place in about 1868. Suggested sources include William Walker, who tried to add Nicaragua to the United States; Joe Barnett, who, when delivering the mail was called "some walker" by a passerby, replied: "I'm a walker from walkersville"; and, the most likely, Samuel T. Walker, a close friend of Bennett's son.

WALTON

No one is quite sure why Walton, Roane County, is so named.

In one story, we hear that Charles Droddy, the first settler, thought the town should be called Droddyville, and would not sell or rent the post office space unless his demand was met. Another story says the town was named for John M. Jones' second wife, Amanda Waldon. Unfortunately, the Jones-Waldon marriage did not take place until 1864; the town was named in 1856.

WAR

Bruce Springsteen had nothing to do with the naming of this McDowell County town. The community takes its name from the nearby War Creek, which was the site of a major battle between white settlers and Chief Logan. The chief threatened to kill ten white men for every Indian killed. He almost lived up to his threat.

The town was first called War Creek, but then changed to Miner's City, because of the major local industry. When the post office was organized, the name became War.

WARD

Ward, Kanawha County, was named for Ward Hudnall.

WARDENSVILLE

The village of Wardensville, Hardy County, was established in 1832. The earlier town in this location was named Trout Run.

The Warden name, it is said, came from the French and Indian War fortification of Fort Warden, built by Jacob Warden, one of the original settlers. One credible account indicates that George Washington "laid off land here for William Wallace Warden, November

11, 1749." The account continues that Warden and members of his family were killed by Indians and the fort burned in 1758.

WAR EAGLE
War Eagle, Mingo County, was named in 1901. It is possible the town received its name from the War Eagle Coal Company, which in 1921 operated the War Eagle and Papoose mines here.

WASHBURN
In the late 1890s, the post office of village was located further down the Chevaux de Frise Run, and called Sinnett's Mills.

The name was changed to Washburn for Cyrus Washburn, who promoted moving the post office here.

WASHINGTON
The land of this Wood County locale was once granted to George Washington. In fact, Washington's 1787 map of his Ohio River lands show that he owned three tracts, the first of which is near present-day Washington.

WAYNE
The seat of Wayne County, this town takes its name from its county.

In 1842, it was known as Trout's Hill, for Abraham Trout, first settler and owner of the land on which the town was built. All sources agree that the site was named in honor of General "Mad" Anthony Wayne, of Revolutionary War fame.

Wayne is located above Twelvepole Creek, which got its name from the fact it is ninety-nine miles and twelve poles long.

WEBSTER SPRINGS
The seat of Webster County, Webster was earlier known as Fork Lick, a name used until 1933, when the legislature changed it to Addison.

A struggle occurred between the name of the town and the name of its post office. The town was called Addison, for Addison McLaughlin, who owned the land on which the town was built; the post office, Webster Springs, for the springs located in Webster County. The post office won again.

The springs were discovered by Abraham Meirs in 1785, but the first permanent resident of the site was Polly Arthur, in 1860. The medicinal quality of the springs drew health-seekers, and

Senator Johnson N. Camden built a 300-room hotel to take advantage of their popularity. The hotel was destroyed by fire in 1926, and was not rebuilt.

WEIRTON

This Hancock County area was just farmland in 1909 when the Phillips Sheet & Tin Place Company was founded here. The company later became Weirton Steel Company, and gave its name to the community that developed around it.

The owners were Ernest T. Weir and J. R. Phillips. Weirton Steel merged with the Great Lakes Steel Company in 1930, and became the National Steel Corporation, with Weir as its president.

WELCH

Welch, the seat of McDowell County, was established in the 1890s and named for Confederate Captain Isaiah J. (or A.) Welch, who was instrumental in the founding of this city.

The town was settled in 1885, on John Henry Hunt's land. Together with J. H. Bramwell and J. H. Juring, Welch purchased the land for forty dollars. The town was laid out in 1893, two years after the Norfolk & Western opened up the area.

WELLSBURG

Wellsburg was established by the legislature in 1791 as Charles Town. The name honored Charles Prather, the town's founder. When Brooke County was formed, Wellsburg became its seat. It was named for Alexander Wells, Prather's son-in-law.

The first settlers, Jonathan, Israel, and Friend Cox, built a cabin on the river bank in 1772. Sixteen years later, they sold off 500 acres to Prather. As he sold town lots, he added a proviso that no one could operate a ferry from that location in competition with him or his family. For a time, Wellsburg was known as a West Virginian Gretna Green, a place where "gin weddings" and "marrying parsons" were common.

WEST LIBERTY

About the time of the American Revolution, the townspeople in Black's Cabin, Ohio County, changed the name of their village. The name West Liberty was to connote to others that the town was located in the far west . . . and wholeheartedly supported liberty.

WESTON

Located on the West Fork River, Weston was earlier known as Preston and Fleshersville. In 1818, the town of Fleshersville was incorporated under the name of Preston. The name was returned to Fleshersville, and then changed to Weston in 1819.

There are those who believe the current name came from the town's position on the West Fork River, which was once known as the West River. Others contend the town was named for the West family. The Wests, a farming family, owned the land on which the town was built as late as 1794.

During the Civil War, Union troops took over the local newspaper and named it for their unit, the *Ohio Seventh*.

WESTOVER

This village, established in 1911, was named for its location west of Morgantown. It is a "satellite" of Morgantown.

WEST UNION

West Union was originally named Lewisport in 1816, for Lewis Maxwell, owner of the land on which part of the town was built. Lewisport changed its name to Union in about 1845. About two miles west of this village was another town, developed by Nathan Davis on land he owned. That community, where businesses began to grow, took on the name of West Union. Later, the two villages merged, maintaining the name of the more successful half.

WHEELING

The last battle of the American Revolution took place here 11–13 September 1782, when Fort Henry was attacked by a force of 40 British troops and 260 Indians—news of the surrender had not reached them! Fort Henry was defended by Ebenezer and Silas Zane, who had founded the town in 1769 and called it Zanesburg. The name was changed to Wheeling in 1795, when it was established by the legislature. It is located in Ohio County.

When Virginia seceded from the Union, the western counties met and set up the "Restored Government of Virginia," with Wheeling as the capital. West Virginia was formally admitted to the Union in 1863.

Wheeling remained the state capital until 1870, and took the honor again in 1875–85.

The city's name goes back to before it was settled. In a map published in London in 1755, the names of Weeling Island and Weeling Creek appear. John Brittle, a Pennsylvania pioneer captured by the Delaware Indians in 1791 near the town site, related this tale. Brittle said Chief Hainguypooshies (Big Cat) told him that the first white settlers coming down the Ohio River were captured and beheaded. Their heads were placed on poles near the mouth of the stream to warn off other settlers. The place became known to the Indians as *weeling*, "the place of the skulls." Pioneers mispronounced the name and, since the Indians did not have a written language, added the "h."

WHITE SULPHUR SPRINGS

White Sulphur Springs, Greenbrier County, greeted its first white settler about 1750, when Nathaniel Carpenter established "corn rights" to almost a thousand acres—by planting them. He and most of his family were killed by Indians.

White Sulphur Springs attracted attention as a health spa in 1772. The invalid wife of a settler was carried to the springs, suffering from rheumatism. She regularly bathed in the waters and "drank freely of the fountain," and within a few weeks, was "perfectly restored,"—at least, that is how the story goes. Word traveled fast, and by 1808 James Caldwell, Carpenter's grandson-in-law, opened a tavern on the "corn rights" land and purchased additional acreage. By the 1830s, White Sulphur Springs was a fashionable health and pleasure resort. Just outside the resort was the town of Dry Creek, settled about 1774 and named after its location on the Dry Creek.

Ultimately, the town assumed the name of its resort's major attraction: the "sulphur springs of clear transparency." The site of the original spring is on the grounds of the Greenbrier Hotel. The President's Cottage, erected in 1816 by the hotel, was used as the summer White House by Presidents Van Buren, Tyler, and Fillmore. Tyler even spent his honeymoon here in 1844.

WILEY FORD

James Stickley sold his land in Mineral County in 1913 to the Homestead Development Company. The company, related to the Dixie Realty Company, sold off town lots and named the place Dixie. The post office, when established in 1923, was called Wiley Ford, for a family by that name that owned the land "years back." Besides, Dixie had already been used for a West Virginia post office.

WILLIAMSPORT

Local legend suggests that this Grant County village was named for Colonel Vincent Williams, who was murdered by Killbuck at this location in 1756. The less-dramatic truth of the matter is the town was named for Joseph V. Williams, the first postmaster.

WILLIAMSTOWN

Though there are many suggestions for the source of this town's name, it was probably named after Williams Creek.

The town, it seems, was opened up in 1770, when Samuel and Joseph Tomlinson made a "tomahawk entry." The first settlement was made seventeen years later by Isaac Williams, who served as a ranger and spy under Braddock. He called it Williamston. Prior to 1822, the name was Williamsport. In that year the community was chartered as Williamstown.

WILSON

At one point, this Grant County community had two names: the post office was named Wilson's Mills, for George W. Wilson, a teacher, lumberman, and the first postmaster. The town, on the other hand, was called Camden, for Senator Henry Gassaway Davis' friend, Johnson Newlon Camden. Camden shared the senator's interest in the Western Maryland Railroad, then called the West Virginia Central.

In 1887, the locations merged and Wilson survived.

WINFIELD

The seat of Putnam County, Winfield was platted in 1848 and named for General Winfield Scott.

WOLFCREEK

Wolfcreek, Summers County, takes its name from Wolf Creek, a tributary of the Greenbrier River.

The creek was named for the many wolves that roamed the area and were trapped and destroyed by hunters.

WOLF PEN

Early settlers caught wolves in traps or pens at the mouth of a stream that ultimately took on the name for the practice: Wolf Pen Creek. When it came time to organize a post office, the townspeople took the name of the creek as their own.

WORTHINGTON

Worthington, Marion County, was incorporated in 1893 and named for Colonel George Worthington, an early settler.

The town, however, began its settlement in 1830, when William Cochran, son of Indian fighter Nathaniel Cochran, built a brick house here. The area began to grow in 1852, when Cochran's sons Nathaniel and Charles built a watermill at the location.

YAWKEY

The Yawkey & Freeman Coal Company was the source of the name for this Lincoln County village.

ZENITH

This village was named by the Reverend A.B. Beamer. The post office name, given in the 1880s, is drawn from the Bible.

Bibliography

Alotta, Robert I. *Mermaids, Monasteries, Cherokees and Custer*. Chicago: Bonus Books, 1990.

_____. *Old Names & New Places*. Philadelphia: The Westminster Press, 1979.

Ambler, Charles Henry. *A History of West Virginia*. New York: Prentice-Hall, Inc., 1933.

Andrews, Matthew Page. *Virginia, the Old Dominion*. Garden City, N.Y.: Doubleday, Doran & Co., 1937.

Barber, John W. *Historical Collection of New Jersey: Past and Present*. New Haven: by subscription, 1868.

Barbour, Philip L., "Chickahominy Place Names in Capt. John Smith's True Relations." *Names* 15 (September 1967)3:60–71.

Bartlett, John. *Familiar Quotations*. Christopher Morely and Louella D. Everett, eds. Boston: Little, Brown & Company, 1938.

Beck, Henry Charlton. *Jersey Genesis: The Story of the Mullica River*. New Brunswick, New Jersey: Rutgers University Press, 1945.

_____. *The Roads of Home*. New Brunswick, New Jersey: Rutgers University Press, 1956.

_____. *More Forgotten Towns of Southern New Jersey*. New Brunswick, New Jersey: Rutgers University Press, 1963.

Becker, Donald William. *Indian Place Names in New Jersey*. Cedar Grove, New Jersey: Phillps-Campbell Publishing Company, 1964.

Beyers, Dan. "Gaithers Gather in . . . You Guessed It." *The Washington Post,* 9 June 1991, B1, B5.

Boatner, Mark M., III. *The Civil War Dictionary*. New York: David McKay Company, Inc., 1959.

_____. *Encylopedia of the American Revolution*. New York: David McKay Company, Inc., 1966.

_____. *Landmarks of the American Revolution*. Harrisburg, Pennsylvania: Stackpole Books, 1992.

Bolles, Albert Sydney. *Pennsylvania, Provice and State, 1609–1790*. 2 vols. Philadelphia: John Wanamaker, 1899.

Boyer, Charles S. *Early Forges and Furnaces in New Jersey*. Philadelphia: University of Pennsylvania Press, 1931.

Bozman, John Leeds. *The History of Maryland From Its First Settlement in 1633 to the Restoration in 1660*. Baltimore: James Lucas & E. K. Draver, 1837.

Brey, Jane W. T. *A Quaker Saga*. Philadelphia: Dorrance & Company, 1967.

Brinton, Daniel G., and Albert Anthony: *A Lenape-English Dictionary*. Philadelphia: The Historical Society of Pennsylvania, 1888.

Brodhead, L. H. *The Delaware Water Gap.* Philadelphia: Sherman & Co., 1870.

Buck, Solon J., and Elizabeth H. *The Planting of Civilization in Western Pennsylvania.* Pittsburgh: University of Pittsburgh Press, 1939.

Burgess, George H., and Miles C. Kennedy. *Centennial History of the Pennsylvania Railroad.* Philadelphia: The Pennsylvania Railroad Company, 1949.

Cartmell, T.K. *Shenandoah Valley Pioneers and Their Descendants.* Winchester, Va.: Eddy Press Co., 1909.

Cawley, James and Margaret. *Along the Old York Road.* New Brunswick, New Jersey: Rutgers University Press, 1965.

_____. *Exploring the Little Rivers of New Jersey.* New Brunswick, New Jersey: Rutgers University Press, 1971.

Center of Military History, Norman Miller Cary, Jr., comp. *Guide to U. S. Army Museums and Historical Sites.* Washington, D.C.: U.S. Government Printing Office, 1975.

Chapin, Brenda Boelts. *Recommended Country Inns: Mid-Atlantic and Chesapeake Region.* 4th ed. Chester, Connecticut: The Globe Pequot Press, 1991.

Chase, Stacey. "Bath: no traffic lights, but forests and tourists." *Richmond Times-Dispatch,* 21 July 1991, E1–2.

_____. "Style runs generations deep." *Richmond Times-Dispatch,* 21 July 1991, E1–2.

Dictionary of American Biography. 20 vols., index, and 4 supp. vols. New York: Charles Scribner's Sons, 1928–1974.

Donehoo, Dr. George P. *A History of the Indian Villages and Place Names in Pennsylvania.* Harrisburg: Telegraph Press, 1928.

Duckson, Don W., Jr. "Toponymic Generics in Maryland." *Names* 28(September 1980)3:163–69.

Dunlap, A. R., and C. A. Weslager. "Two Delaware Valley Indian Place Names." *Names* 15(September 1967)3:41–46.

East Jersey Under the Proprietary Governments. Newark: Martin R. Dennis, 1875.

Eckman, Jeannette. *Delaware: A Guide to the First State.* Compiled and written by the Federal Writers' Project of the Works Progress Administration for the State of Delaware, Henry G. Alsberg, ed. New York: Hastings House, 1955.

Espenshade, A. Howry. *Pennsylvania Place Names.* State College, Pennsylvania: The Pennsylvania State University, 1925. Reprint. Detroit: Gale Research Company, 1969.

Fargo, Clarence B. *History of Frenchtown.* New York: privately published, 1933.

Federal Writers' Project of the Works Progress Administration, State of New Jersey. *The Swedes and Finns in New Jersey.* Bayonne, New Jersey: Jersey Printing Co., 1938.

Ferris, Benjamin. *A History of the Original Settlements on the Delaware.* Wilmington: Wilson and Heald, 1846.

Fisher, Sydney George. *The Making of Pennsylvania.* Philadelphia: J.B. Lippincott, 1932.

Flexner, Stuart Berg. *I Hear America Talking.* New York: Touchstone/Simon & Schuster, 1976.

_____. *Listening to America.* New York: Simon & Schuster, 1982.

Folsom, Merrill. *Great American Mansions and Their Stories.* New York: Hastings House, 1963.

_____. *More Great American Mansions and Their Stories.* New York: Hastings House, 1967.

Gannett, Henry. *American Names.* Washington, D.C.: Public Affairs Press, 1947.

Goodwin, Rutherford. *A Brief & True Report Concerning Williamsburg in Virginia: Being an Account of the most important Occurrences in that Place from its first Beginning to the present Time.* Williamsburg: Colonial Williamsburg, 1959.

Griscom, Lloyd E. *The Down-Jerseymen: Spirited Adventurers.* Privately published, 1963.

Groff, Sibyl McC. *New Jersey's Historic Houses.* Cranbury, New Jersey: A. S. Barnes & Co., 1971.

Hanson, Raus McDill. *Virginia Place Names: Derivations, Historical Uses.* Verona, Virginia: McClure Press, 1969.

Harrington, Mark Raymond. *The Indians of New Jersey.* New Brunswick, N.J.: Rutgers University Press, 1963.

Heckenwelder, John. *History, Manners, and Customs of the Indian Nations Who Once Inhabited Pennsylvania and the Neighboring States.* 1819. Reprint. New York: Arno Press, 1971.

Heitman, Francis Bernard. *Historical Register and Dictionary of the United States Army, From Its Organization, Sept. 29, 1789, to March 2, 1903.* 2 vols. Reprint. Urbana: University of Illinois, 1965.

Hendrickson, Robert. *Encyclopedia of Word and Phrase Origins.* New York: Facts on File Publications, 1987.

Hess, William M. E. *On History's Trail.* Point Pleasant Beach, New Jersey: Barnegat Products, 1973.

Heusser, Albert H. *George Washington's Map Maker.* New Brunswick, New Jersey: Rutgers University Press, 1966.

Horle, Craig W., Marianne S. Wokeck, Jeffrey L. Scheib, Joseph S. Foster, David Haugaard, Rosalind J. Beiler, and Joy Wiltenburg. *Lawmaking and Legislators in Pennsylvania: A Biographical Dictionary.* Vol. 1, 1682–1709. Philadelphia: University of Pennsylvania, 1991.

Hunter, Robert F., and Edwin L. Dooley, Jr. *Claudius Crozet: French Engineer in America, 1790–1861.* Charlottesville, Virginia: The University Press of Virginia, 1989.

Jameson, W. C. *Buried Treasures of the Appalachians.* Little Rock: August House Publishers, Inc., 1991.

Johnson, Otto, exec. ed. *Information Please Almanac, 1992.* Boston: Houghton Mifflin Company, 1991.

Johnson, Robert Underwood, and Clarence Clough Buel, eds. *Battles and Leaders of the Civil War.* Vol. 4. New York: The Century Co., 1888.

Jones, Carleton. *Streetwise Baltimore: The Stories Behind Baltimore Street Names.* Chicago: Bonus Books, Inc., 1990.

Jordan, John W. *Colonial and Revolutionary Families of Pennsylvania.* 3 vols. New York: The Lewis Publishing Company, 1911.

Kane, Hana Umlaug, ed. *The World Almanac Book of Who.* New York: World Almanac Publications, 1980.

Katz, Ephraim. *The Film Encyclopedia.* New York: G. P. Putnam's Sons, 1979.

Keatley, J. K. *Place Names of the Eastern Shore of Maryland.* Queenstown, Maryland: Queen Anne Press, 1987.

Kemmerer, Donald L. *Path to Freedom.* Cos Cob, Connecticut: John E. Edwards, 1968.

Kenny, Hamill. *The Placenames of Maryland, Their Origin and Meaning.* Baltimore: Museum and Library of Maryland History/Maryland Historical Society, 1984.

———. *The Origin and Meaning of the Indian Place Names of Maryland.* Baltimore: Waverly Press, 1961.

———. *West Virginia Place Names.* Piedmont, West Virginia: The Place Name Press, 1945.

Latane, Lawrence, III. "Gift of freedom: Tale handed down." *Richmond Times-Dispatch,* 21 July 1991, E1, E3.

Leach, Douglas Edward. *The Northern Colonial Frontier.* New York: Holt, Rinehart and Winston, 1966.

Lee, Francis Bayley. *New Jersey as a Colony and as a State.* 4 vols. New York: The Publishing Society of New Jersey, 1902.

_____. *History of New Jersey.* Newark, New Jersey: Newark Book Publishing and Engraving Co., 1905.

Long, E. B., and Barbara Long. *The Civil War Day by Day: An Almanac, 1861–1865.* New York: Doubleday & Co., 1971.

Malcolm, Andrew H. *U.S. 1: America's Original Main Street.* New York: St. Martin's Press, 1991.

Mathewson, Craig C., Jr. *Post Offices and Postmasters of Cape May County, New Jersey 1802–1970.* Egg Harbor City, New Jersey: 1970.

Maryland: A Guide to the Old Line State. Compiled by workers of the Writers' Program of the Work Projects Administration in the State of Maryland. New York: Oxford University Press, 1940.

McCasky, Andrew. "Ever wonder why they call it Keezletown." *Rockingham Magazine,* April 1991, 5, 21.

McMahon, William. *South Jersey Towns: History and Legend.* New Brunswick, New Jersey: Rutgers University Press, 1973.

Mellick, Andrew D., Jr. *The Old Farm.* Edited by Hubert G. Schmidt. New Brunswick, New Jersey: Rutgers University Press, 1965.

Meyer, Eugene L. *Maryland Lost and Found: People and Places From Chesapeake to Appalachia.* Baltimore: Johns Hopkins University Press, 1986.

Miller, Mary R. "Place-Names of the Northern Neck of Virginia: A Proposal for a Theory of Place-Naming." *Names* 24(March1976)1:9–23.

Miller, Thomas Condit, and Hu Maxwell. *West Virginia and Its People.* 3 vols. New York: Lewis Historical Publishing Co., 1913.

Morris, Clay. *You Take the High Road: A Guide to the Place Names of Colonial Eastern Shore of Maryland.* Easton, Maryland: Easton Publishing Company, 1970.

Morris, Richard B., ed. *Encyclopedia of American History.* New York: Harper & Row, 1976.

Moyer, Armond and Winfred Moyer. *The Origins of Unusual Place- Names.* Harrisburg: Keystone Publishing Associates, 1958.

Nagel, Paul C. *The Lees of Virginia—Seven Generations of an American Family.* New York: Oxford University Press, 1990.

National Archives. *RG 28: Record of Appointment of Postmasters 1832-September 30, 1971: New Jersey State Library Commission.*

New Jersey State Library Commission. *New Jersey: A Guide to Its Present and Past.* New York: Hastings House, 1959.

The Origin of New Jersey Place Names. Compiled by the Works Progress Administration in the State of New Jersey. Trenton, New Jersey: 1939. Reprint. New Jersey Public Library Commission, 1945.

"Our Valley." Supplement to the Harrisonburg (Va.) *Daily News-Record,* 24 May 1991.

Outline History of New Jersey. New Brunswick, New Jersey: Rutgers Union Press, 1950.

Papenfuse, Edward C., Gregory A. Stiverson, Susan A. Collins, and Lois Green Carr, comps. and eds. *Maryland: A New Guide to the Old Line State.* Baltimore: The Johns Hopkins University Press, 1984. [ANG]

Partridge, Eric. *A Dictionary of Slang and Unconventional English.* 6th ed. New York: The Macmillan Company, 1967.

Pepper, Adeline. *Tours of Historic New Jersey.* New Brunswick, New Jersey: Rutgers University Press, 1973.

Pierce, Arthur B. *Iron in the Pines.* New Brunswick, New Jersey: Rutgers University Press, 1957.

Pitzer, Sara. *Pennsylvania: Off the Beaten Path.* 2nd ed. Chester, Connecticut: The Globe Pequot Press, 1991.

Prowell, George R. *The History of Camden County, New Jersey.* Philadelphia, L. J. Richards & Co., 1886.

Quimby, Myron J. *Scratch Ankle, U.S.A.* New York: A. S. Barnes and Company, 1969.

Ringle, Ken, "The Day Slavery Bowed To Conscience," *The Washington Post.* 21 July 1991, F1, F4.

Rucker, Mrs. Maude A., comp. *West Virginia, Her Land, Her People, Her Traditions, Her Resources.* New York: W. Neale, 1930.

Santelli, Robert. *Guide to the Jersey Shore: From Sandy Hook to Cape May.* 2nd ed. Chester, Connecticut: The Globe Pequot Press, 1991.

Sawin, Nancy C., and Esther R. Perkins. *Backroading Through Cecil County, Maryland.* Hockessin, Delaware: The Holly Press, 1977.

Scharf, J. Thomas. *History of Delaware.* 2 vols. Philadelphia: L. J. Reynolds, 1888.

────── and Thompson Westcott. *History of Philadelphia, 1609–1884.* 3 vols. Philadelphia: L. H. Evarts & Co., 1884.

Scheller, William G. *New Jersey: Off the Beaten Path.* 2nd ed. Chester, Connecticut: The Globe Pequot Press, 1991.

Schermerhorn, William E. *The History of Burlington, New Jersey.* Burlington, New Jersey: Enterprise Publishing Co., 1927.

Schonbach, Morris. *Radicals and Visionaries: A History of Dissent in New Jersey.* Princeton, New Jersey: D. Van Nostrand Co., Inc., 1964.

Scott, John Anthony. *Settlers on the Eastern Shore 1607–1750.* New York: Alfred A. Knopf, 1967.

Shaw, William H. *History of Essex and Hudson Counties, New Jersey.* Philadelphia: Everts & Peck, 1884.

Sheppard, Cora June. "How It Got That Name: Places in Cumberland County." *The Vineland Historical Magazine.* 23 (1938).

Shourds, Thomas. *History and Genealogy of Fenwick's Colony.* Bridgeton, New Jersey: George F. Nixon, 1876.

Stevens, Lewis Townsend. *The History of Cape May County.* Cape May City, New Jersey: Lewis T. Stevens, 1897.

Stewart, George R. *American Place Names.* New York: Oxford University Press, 1970.

────── . *Names on the Land: A Historical Account of Place-Naming in the United States.* New York: Random House, 1945.

Tour Book: Mid-Atlantic, Delaware, District of Columbia, Maryland, Virginia, West Virginia. Heathrow, Florida: American Automobile Association, 1990.

Tour Book: New Jersey, Pennsylvania. Heathrow, Florida: American Automobile Association, 1990.

Van Doren, Charles, ed. *Webster's American Biographies.* Springfield, Massachusetts: G. & C. Merriam Company, 1975.

Vecoli, Rudolph J. *The People of New Jersey.* Princeton, New Jersey: D. Van Nostrand Co., Inc., 1965.

Wallechinsky, David, and Irving Wallace. *The People's Almanac.* New York: Doubleday & Company, 1975.

────── . *The People's Almanac #2.* New York: Bantam Books, 1978.

Weigley, Russell F., ed. *Philadelphia: A 300-Year History.* New York: W. W. Norton & Co., 1982.

Weiss, Harry B. *Life in Early New Jersey.* Princeton, New Jersey: D. Van Nostrand Co., Inc., 1964.

────── , and Grace M. Weiss. *The Early Sawmills of New Jersey.* Trenton: New Jersey Agricultural Society, 1968.

Weslager, C. A. *The English on the Delaware: 1610–1682.* New Brunswick: Rutgers University Press, 1967.

_____. "Christina, Christeen, Christiana: A Delaware Connection." *Names* 39(September 1991)3:269–276.

_____. "New Castle, Delaware—and its Former Names." *Names* 24(June 1976)2:101–105.

Whitehead, William A. *East Jersey Under the Proprietary Governments*. Newark: Martin R. Dennis, 1875.

Wildes, Harry Emerson. *The Delaware*. Rivers of America series. New York: Farrar & Rinehart, 1940.

_____. *Twin Rivers: The Raritan and the Passaic*. New York: Farrar & Rinehart, Inc., 1943.

Winiecki, Susan. "Saltville's ice age lure; Tourists, researchers seek relics of ancient life." *Richmond Times-Dispatch*, 7 July 1991, C1–2.

_____. " 'Salt Capital of the Confederacy' welcomes visitors; Fossil from area sent to President Jefferson." *Richmond Times-Dispatch*, 7 July 1991, C2.

Woodward, Ajor E. M., and John F. Hageman. *History of Burlington and Mercer Counties, New Jersey*. Philadelphia: Everts & Peck, 1883.

Worton, Stanley N., Wilbur E. Apgar, Daniel Jacobson, and Abraham Resnick. *New Jersey: Past and Present*. New York: Hayden Book Company, Inc., 1964.

Writers' Program of the Works Projects Administration in the State of Pennsylvania. *Pennsylvania: A Guide to the Keystone State*. New York: Oxford University Press, 1940.

_____. *Virginia: A Guide to the Old Dominion*. New York: Oxford University Press, 1940.

_____. *West Virginia: A Guide to the Mountain State*. New York: Oxford University Press, 1941.

Zinkin, Vivian. "The Specifying Component in West Jersey Place Names." *Names* 34(March 1986)1:62–82.

_____. "The Generic Component in West Jersey Place Names." *Names* 32(September 1984)3:252–266.

_____. "Surviving Indian Town Names in West Jersey." *Names* 26(September 1978)3:209–219.

_____. "Names of Estates in the Province of West Jersey," *Names* 24(December 1976)4:237–247.

Appendix

In some cases, little was known about the reason for the choice of name for a town. These towns have been grouped in the following ways:

Borrowed Names—These place names were borrowed from other cities either in the United States or other countries.

Family Names—These place names were borrowed from family names of early settlers, first postmasters, shopkeepers, railroad officials or some other inhabitants of the towns.

Descriptive Names—These place names describe the area in which the towns are located. In some cases the name was chosen just because it sounded pleasant.

Geograhic Names—These place names were borrowed from the name of a river, mountain or other geographic landmark in the area.

Tree Names—These place names were borrowed from trees or other plant life that was prominent in the area when the town was settled.

Borrowed Names

New Jersey: Annandale (Scot.), Barrington (Eng.), Blenheim (Ger.), Brighton Beach (Eng.), Cambridge (MA), Cardiff (Wales), Chesterfield (Eng.), Clermont (FL), Cologne (Ger.), Cranbury (Eng.), Cumberland (Eng.), Deal (Eng.), Dorchester (Eng.), Erskine (Scot.), Hamburg (Ger.), Haworth (Eng.), Keswick Grove (Eng.), Melrose (Scot.), Miami Beach (FL), Middlesex (Eng.), Monmouth Beach (Eng.), Monmouth Junction (Eng.), Mount Hermon (Palestine), New Milford (PA), Palermo (Sicily), Saint Cloud (France), Somerset (Eng.), Stockholm (Sweden), Woodstock (CT).

Pennsylvania: Abington (Eng.), Andover (Eng.), Arcadia (Greece), Arcola (Ita.), Baden (Ger.), Bala Cynwyd (Wales), Bath (Eng.), Bedminster (Eng.), Belsano (Ita.), Bohemia (Austria), Brockton (MA), Brooklyn (NY), Cheltanham (Eng.), Corsica, Croydon (Eng.), Dalmatia (Austria), Damascus (Syria), Derry (Ire.), Devon (Eng.), Donegal (Ire.), Dublin (Ire.), Duncannon (Ire.), Dundoff (Wales), Edinboro (Scot.), Fannettsburg (Ire.), Galillee (Palestine), Geneva (Switz.), Ghent (Belg.), Glasgow (Scot.), Goshenville (Egypt), Greencastle (Ire.), Hadley (Eng.), Hamburg (Ger.), Hampton (Eng.), Hatfield (Eng.), Hebron (Palestine), Heidelburg (Ger.), Hellam (Eng.), Hereford (Eng.), Jedo (Tokyo), Joliet (IL), Juneau (AK), Kent (Eng.), Lampeter (Wales), Lanark (Scot.), Limerick (Ire.), Lisbon (Portugal), Litchfield (Eng.), Liverpool (Eng.), Livonia (Rus.), Malta, Malvern (Eng.), Manchester (Eng.), Milan (Ita.), Moscow (Rus.), Narberth (Wales), Newburg (Scot.), New Oxford (Eng.), Northhampton (Eng.), Norwood (Eng.), Nottingham (Eng.), Nuremburg (Ger.), Oklahoma, Orangeville (NY), Oxford (Eng.), Paisley (Scot.), Paris (France), Pavia (Ita.), Radnor (Wales), Richmond (Eng.), Ridley Park (Eng.), Sardis (Asia Minor), Scotland, Selkirk (Scot.), Sheffield (Eng.), Shrewsbury (Eng.), Southhampton (Eng.), Swedenland (Sweden), Sweden, Ulster (Ire.), Valencia (Spain), Venetia (Ita.), Venice (Ita.), Wakefield (Eng.), Warminster (Eng.), Warsaw (Poland), Windsor (Eng.).

Delaware: Dublin Hill (Ire.), Warwick (Eng.).

Maryland: Aberdeen (Scot.), Bristol (eng.), Cardiff (Wales), Cheltenham (Eng.), Damascus (Syria), Dover (Eng.), Dublin (Ire.), Ellerslie (Scot.), Essex (Eng.), Hampton (Eng.), Largo (Scot.), Lisbon (Portugal), Little Orleans (France), Long Green (Ire.), Manchester (Eng.), Marlow Heights (Eng.), Melrose (Scot.), Midlothian (Scot.), Mount Carmel (Palestine), New Germany, New London (Eng.), Scotland, Scotland Beach.

Virginia: Alton (Eng.), Amsterdam (Netherlands), Berea (Macedonia), Boston (MA), Cobham (Eng.), Crewe (Eng.), Damascus (Syria), Dublin (Ire.), Ettrick (Scot.), Farnham (Eng.), Guilford (Eng.), Kilmarnock (Scot.), Kinsale (Ire.), Lahore (India), Morven (Scot.), Ontario (Can.), St. Paul (MN), Salem (NJ), Sparta (Greece), Suffolk (Eng.), Vienna (NY), Waterford (Ire.).

Appendix

West Virginia: Berlin (Ger.), Cairo (Egypt), Carlisle (Eng.), Hartford (CT), Ireland, Manila (Phillipines), New Haven (CT), Palermo (Sicily), Plymouth (PA), Salem (NJ), Skelton (Eng.), Springfield (MA), Tioga (PA), Tralee (Ire.), Vienna (VA).

Family Names

New Jersey: Adamston, Anderson, Avenel, Barber, Barbertown, Beesley Point, Bennetts Mill, Bernards, Blawenburg, Bonhamtown, Bradevelt, Brant Beach, Brielle, Browntown, Butler, Buttzville, Carlis Corner, Carlton Hill, Chadwick, Chambers Corner, Clark, Clarksboro, Blarksburg, Clarksville, Clayton, Closter, Colesville, Conovertown, Corbin City, Coytesville, Darlington, Dayton, Deans, Demarest, Denville, Dorothy, Elwood, Elwood Park, Everett, Ewingville, Finesville, Folsom, Fords, Fortescue, Fries Mill, Gibbsboro, Gifford Park, Grasselli, Griggstown, Haleyville Harding, Hardistonville, Harrington Park, Hasbrouck Heights, Haskell, Hazlet, Heislerville, Higbeetown, Hightstown, Hillsborough, Holmeson, Hornestown, Hurffville, Hutchinson, Imlaystown, Iona, Iselin, Jamesburg, Kendall Park, Kirbys Mills, Laurence Harbor, Layton, Leeds Point, Leektown, Leesburg, Lewisville, Lincroft, Linvale, Littletown, Lyons, Manville, Marcella, Marshalls Corner, Marshallville, Martinsville, McAfee, Merchantville, Mickleton, Montague, Morganville, Murray Hill, Nixon, Nortonville, Ogdensburg, Osbornsville, Parkertown, Pattenburg, Pecks Corner, Pedricktown, Pellettown, Perrineville, Pierces Point, Pittstown, Pottersville, Quinton, Randolph, Reaville, Reeds Beach, Ridgeway, Riegelsville, Robinsville, Robertsville, Ross Corner, Sayreville, Schooleys Mountain, Scullville, Sewell, Sicklerville, Smithburg, Smiths Mills, Stephensburg, Stevens, Stewartsville, Swartswood, Taylortown, Titusville, Townsbury, Townsends Islet, Turnersville, Tuttles Corner, Vail, Vanderburg, Van Hiseville, Wall, Warners, Weekstown, Westville, Whitesville, Whiting, Woodruff, Woodruffs Gap.

Pennsylvania: Abbottstown, Ackermanville, Albrightsville, Aldan, Alden, Aldenville, Allis Hollow, Allison Park, Alverton, Amberson, Amesville, Andersonburg, Andrews Settlement, Annisville Ansonville, Arbuckle, Ardenheim, Arendtsville, Arnold, Aultman, Bairdsford, Bakers Summit, Bakerstown, Bakersville, Balls Mills, Bannerville, Bareyville, Barlow, Barnards, Barners, Barrville, Bartonsville, Baxter, Beallsville, Bechtelsville, Bells Landing, Belltown, Bendersville, Bentleyville, Berrysburg, Beyer, Biglerville, Birchardville, Blackwell, Blain, Blakeslee, Blanchard, Bloserville, Bough, Blandburg, Bowmansdale, Bowmanstown, Bowmansville, Brandt, Brentwood, Bressler, Callensburg, Castanas, Chadds Ford, Chaneysville, Chapman, Clarington, Coatesville, Cobbs, Cochranton, Collomsville, Conway, Cooksburg, Coopersburg, Coyleville, Cranesville, Daggett, Darlington, Darlington Corners, Dayton, Dillsburg, Dilltown, Draper, Dravosburg, Elderton, Eldred, Erdman, Everson, Farrandsville, Feasterville, Flemington, Frackville, Freeman, Freemansburg, Germansville, Greens Landing, Greensboro, Greentown, Greenvillage, Harlansburg, Hawley, Hellertown, Hinkeltown, Hookstown, Hopwood, Houtzdale, Hudsondale, Hughestown, Hughesville, Jenkintown, Karns City, Kulpsmont, Kunkle, Kutztown, Landisburg, Landisville, Laughlintown, Leeper, Leesport, Leetsdale, Lewisberry, Lowville, Mansfield, Markelsville, Martinsburg, Masontown, Mausdale, McConnellstown, McCure, McGees Mill, McSherrystown, McVerytown, Meyersdale, Mount Morris, Mundys Corner, Myerstown, New Bedford, Orbisonia, Osterburg, Osterhout, Parkesburg, Porter, Porters Lake, Prescottville, Preston Center, Preston Park, Reedsville, Roberts, Robesonia, Salladasvurg, Schellsburg, Schnecksville Schoenersville, Sharpsville, Shillington, Shimerville, Shimpstown, Shippenville, Stevensville, Stockertown, Sykesville, Tafton, Tarrs, Terrytown, Thompsontown, Townville, Trainer, Tullytown, Uhlerstown, Upton, Vandling, Van Ormer, Vosburg, Wagner, Warnertown, Watsontwon, Weatherly, Wernersville, Wilcox, Yardley, Yarnell, Yeagertown, Yoe, Youngwood, Zehner, Zieglersville, Zullinger.

Delaware: Armstrong, Bennetts Pier, Biddles Corner, Bishops Corner, Blades, Bowers Beach, Bryans Store, Cannon, Clarksville, Coverdales, Cowgills Corner, Davis Corner, Everetts Corner, Fieldsboro, Flemings Landing, Fords Corner, Fowler Beach, Ginns Corner, Hamilton Park, Harmons School, Holloway Terrace, Houston, Johnson, Jones Crossroads, Laffertys Corner, Lowes Crossroads, Lynch Heights, Marvels Crossroads, Masseys Landing, Mathews Corners, Oakley, Owens, Pearsons Corner, Pepper, Pickering Beach, Port Mahon, Postles Corner, Scotts Corners, Sedgely Farms, Stockley, Taylors Bridge, Thomas Corners, Tybouts Corner, Underwood Corner, Verrnon, Whaleys Crossroads, Whitelysburg, Whitesville, Wrights Crossroads.

Maryland: Ady, Andersontown, Arnold, Asher Glade, Bachman Mills, Baldwin, Barnesville, Beantown, Benfield, Birdsville, Bishop, Bishopville, Bittinger, Bowens, Bryantown, Burkittsville, Cearfoss, Chewsville, Clarksburg, Colesville, Collington, Coltons Point, Conaways, Cooksville, Corriganville, Coster, Coxs Corner, Creagerstown, Crumpton, Dares Beach, Davidsonville, Dawson, Dawsonville, Day, Dayton, Dorrs Corner, Dorsey, Doubs, Drury, Dudley Corners, Ewell, Freeland, Funkstown, Gaither, Galestown, Galesville, Gamber, Glenn Dale, Golts, Gortner, Grayton, Hanesville, Harmans, Harwood, Henderson, Henrys Crossroad, Hobbs, Hudson, Hudsons Corner, Huyett, Hyattstown, Hyattsville, Jacobsville, James, Kolbos Corner, Lantz, Lawsonia, Laytonsville, Lloyds, Loveville, Lusby, Maddox, Marston, Massey, Matthews, McDaniel, Millers, Millersville, Morgantown, Motters, Naylor, Neavitt, Norbeck, Owings, Parsonburg, Perryman, Potters Landing, Powellville, Price, Pylesville, Randallstown, Rhodesdale, Roe, Rush, Shepperd, Simpsonville, Slacks Corner, Smithsburg, Sparks, Spencerville, Templeville, Thayerville, Toddville, Tompkinsville, Tracys Landing, Tunis Mills, Wallville, Warfieldsburg, Whites Ferry, Wingate, Wolfsville, Woodensburg, Wynne.

Virginia: Achilles, Adams Grove, Allisonia, Allmondsville, Amissville, Andersonville, Arrington, Atkins, Atlee, Austinville, Aylett, Barhamsville, Bassett, Bastian, Basye, Batesville, Bells Valley, Bishop, Bloxom, Boones Mill, Bosewells Tavern, Boyce, Boykins, Bracey, Branchville, Broadnax, Browntown, Burgess, Burkeville, Burnsville, Callaghan, Capron, Carrsville, Castlewood, Catlett, Chancellorsville, Clary, Claudville, Coles Point, Craigsville, Criglersville, Critz, Cullen, Danieltown, Dante, Davenport, Delaplane, DeWitt, Dranesville, Drewryville, Driver, Dryden, Duffielf, Dunnsville, Earlysville, Eggleston, Estes, Ewing, Fife, Figsboro, Fisherville, Fort Chiswell, Foxwells, Fries, Gainesville, Georges Tavern, Glenn, Golansville, Gore, Gray, Greys Point, Hadensville, Hague, Hamilton, Heathsville, Hillsville, Hiltons, Honaker, Howardsville, Hudgins, Hume, Hurt, Ingram, Irvington, Jamesville, Jetersville, Jewell Ridge, Jonesville, Jordan Mines, Joyner, Kelling, Keene, Kents Store, Keysville, Ladysmith, Lambsburg, Lanesville, Lightfoot, Lottsburg, Lovettsville, Lovingston, Lowesville, Lucketts, Lynch Station, Mappsville, Massies Mill, Mauzy, Mavertown, Merrifield, Miller Tavern, Montross, Morrisville, Moseley, Mustoe, Nasons, Nelson, Nelsonia, Nickelsville, Oldhams, Ottobine, Owens, Painter, Palmer, Palmer Springs, Partlow, Pearisburg, Pennington, Pipers Gap, Proffit, Purcellville, Purdy, Quicksburg, Randolph, Raven, Reedville, Rileyville, Riner, Rixeyville, Rollins Fork, Ruckersville, Ryan, Sandston, Sanford, Savedge, Schuyler, Shacklefords, Shipman, Snell, Spencer, Sperryville, Sprouses Corner, Staffordsville, Stanardsville, Stephens City, Stephenson, Stevensville, Stewartsville, Stuarts Draft, Sutherland, Tabb, Tabscott, Templeman, Thaxton, Townsend, Trevillians, Troutville, Tunstall, Turbeville, Valentines, Walkerton, Wares Wharf, Warfield, Wattsboro, Whaleyville, Whitehall, Williamsville, Willis, Wilson, Wyliesburg.

West Virginia: Adolph, Adrian, Albright, Alexander, Allingdale, Alvy, Amherstdale, Arbuckle, Arnett, Arnettsville, Baileysville, Baker, Ballard, Barker, Barracksville, Beard, Beckwith, Bellton, Bemis, Blundon, Boggs, Bowden, Bowles, Boyer, Brandonville, Brooks, Browns Mill, Caldwell, Cass, Chapmanville, Clinton, Clothier, Colcord, Copen, Copley, Core, Cowen, Craigsville, Cranesville, Crumpler, Davin, Dawson, Delbarton, Dickson, Drennan, Duffy, Earling, Eccles, Elmore, Eskdale, Evans, Evansville, Fellowsville, Forman, Frame, Frametown, Fraziers Bottom, Freeman, Gandeeville, Gary, Gerrardstown, Glen Easton, Glen White, Goffs, Grimms Landing, Hacker Valley, Harman, Hartland, Hartmansville, Heaters, Herndon, Higginsville, Hines, Hodgesville, Holcomb, Horner, Hubball, Hubbardstown, Hurst, Huttonsville, Jarvisville, Jenkinjones, Jenks, Johnstown, Jones Springs, Justice, Kerens, Kimball, Kimberley, Kincaid, Kirby, Kyle, Lahmansville, Lake, Lakin, Landes, Landgraff, Landisburg, Leivasy, Lester, Linn, Littleton, Mabie, Mace, Mahan, Masontown, Mathias, Maysville, McGraws, McKeefrey, McMechen, McNeil, Medley, Milan, Moorefield, Munday, Napier, Neal, Nellis, Nelson, Newell, Nolan, Normantown, Olcott, Omar, Omps, Page, Pageton, Parsley, Peck Run, Pence Springs, Pennsboro, Petersburg, Pettry, Pettus, Pickens, Pierce, Portersville, Powellton, Pruntytown, Purgitsville, Quick, Ramage, Rand, Ranson, Reedsville, Renick, Ridgeley, Ridgeway, Robertsburg, Robson, Romeys Point, Rowlesburg, Russellville, Sam Black Church, Sanderson, Saulsville, Shanks, Sherman, Sherrard, Shinnston, Silverton, Sissonville, Slanesville, Smithburg, Smithfield, Smithville, Sprague, Stephenson, Stumpton, Sutton, Switzer, Unger, Ury, Vallscreek, Varney, Wadeville, Waiteville, Wallace, Wallback, Wharncliffe, Whitesville, Wick, Wileyville, Wilkinson, Williamsburg, Williamson, Wolf Summit, Woodruff, Woosley, Wyatt.

Descriptive Names

New Jersey: Bay Head, Bay Shore, Bayside, Bayville, Bridgeport, Bridgeville, Bridgewater, Brookdale, Brooklawn, Brookside, Brookville, Cliffside Park, Cliffwood, Cold Spring, Crestwood Village, Delmont, Edgewater, Edgewater Park, Englewood Cliffs, Glendale, Glenwood, Green Creek, Harbourtown, Hillsdale, Hillside, Hudson Heights, Lakeside, Lakeview, Landing, Ledgewood, Little Falls, Longport, Montvalle, Mountainside, Mountain View, Park Ridge, Plainsboro, Prospect Plains, Red Bank, Richfield, Richwood, Ridgefield, Riverdale, River Edge, River Vale, Sea Breeze, Sea Bright, Seabrook, Seaside Heights, Shore Acres, Short Hills, Springville, Stillwater, Thorofare, Tranquility, Westfield, Woddcliff Lake, Woodport, Wood Ridge.

Pennsylvania: Bareville, Beach Haven, Beach Lake, Bellegrove, Belleville, Blooming Glen, Blooming Grove, Bloomington, Blooming Valley, Bridgeport, Bridgetown, Bridgeville, Brookhaven, Brookside, Brookville, Center Valley, Centerville, Cokesburg, Cold Spring, Creekside, Crystal Spring, East Brady, Edgemere, Edgemont, Edgewood, Fairview, Fawn Grove, Gap, Garden View, Gardenville, Glenhazel, Glen Rock, Glen Iron, Glen Lyon, Glenmore, Glen Richey, Glen Riddle, Glen Mawr, Glen Summit, Glen Hope, Glenville, Grand Valley, Grassflat, Greenbrier, Greenburr, Greefield, Green Lane, Green Lane Farms, Greenmount, Green Park, Green Point, Green Tree, Harborcreek, Highland, Hillsdale, Hillsgrove, Hillside, Hillsville, Landingville, Lofty, Lumber City, Lumberville, Meadowlands, Nettle Hill, Parkside, Parkwood, Plainfield, Plain Grove, Point Pleasant, Pond Bank, Pond Eddy, Ravine, Ridgebury, Ridgeville, Ridgewood, Riverside, Roadside, Safe Harbor, Shady Grove, Shady Plain, Spring City, Springdale, Springdell, Springfield, Spring Glen, Spring Meadow, Springtown, Springville, State Line, Summit Hill, Vale, Waterfall, White Deer, Wind Gap, Woodbine, Woodbury, Wooddale, Woodland, Woodyn, Woodside.

Delaware: Bay View Beach, Bayville, Cool Spring, Deerhurst, Fairmont, Farmhurst, Forest, Gravel Hill, Green Spring, Milltown, Millville, Overbrook, Rockland, Sandtown, Southwood, Summit Bridge, Woodside.

Maryland: Arundel on the Bay, Bay Ridge, Bayside Beach, Big Spring, Camp Springs, Clear Spring, Deer Park, Edgemere, Edgewater, Fair Hill, Forest Heights, Glenwood, Hill Top, Pleasant Hill, Public Landing, Ridge, Riverside, Rocky Ridge, Tall Timbers, Waterview.

Virginia: Bayview, Clear Brook, Edgehill, Fairfield, Fairview Beach, Ferncliff, Forestville, Greenfield, Lakeside, Meadows of Dan, Meadowview, Meadowville, Norwood, Ocean View, Rockville, Rocky Gap, Sandy Level, Troutdale, Water View, Wilderness.

West Virginia: Clifton, Coal Mountain, East Bank, Fairplain, Falling Waters, Levels, Pleasant Dale, Pleasant Valley, Riverside, Riverton, Valley Head, Valley Point.

Geographic Names

New Jersey: Beaver Lake, Branchville, Budd Lake, Cohansey, Dividing Creek, English Creek, Forked River, Gravelly Run, Lake Hiawatha, Lake Hopatcong.

Pennsylvania: Bear Creek, Bentley Creek, Big Run, Black Lick, Bowman Creek, Briar Creek, Broad Top City, Chillisquaque, Conemaugh, Crooked Creek, Delaware Water Gap, Driftwood, Hunlock Creek, Lewis Run, Maiden Creek, Marshalls Creek, Mount Pocono, Roaring Branch, Sandy Hollow, Sandy Lake, Sandy Ridge, Shade Gap, Slate Run, Spruce Creek, Stony Creek Mills Three Springs, Trout Run.

Delaware: Broad Creek, Concord, Silver Brook.

Maryland: Beaver Creek, Chester, Elk Mills, Elk Neck, Middle River.

Virginia: Ararat, Back Bay, Blue Ridge, Chesapeake Creek, Clover, Clover Creek, Drakes Branch, Elkrun, Falling Spring, Fulks Run, Holston, Lake Jackson, Laurel Fork, Mine Run, Mint Spring, Morattico, Pedlar Mills, Piney River, Rich Creek, Spout Spring, Stone Creek, Sturgeonville, Swift Run.

West Virginia: Alum Creek, Big Creek, Big Run, Big Sandy, Birch River, Blue Creek, Boomer, Bradshaw, Cedarville, Clear Creek, Clover, Curtin, Deer Run, Flatwoods, Great Cacapon, Green Spring, Greenwood, Kanawha Falls, Kanawha Head, Little Birch, Little Otter, Meadow Creek, Milburn, New Creek, Patterson Creek, Peach Creek, Peeltree, Persinger, Queen Shoals, Ranger, Rough Run, Shady Spring, Short Creek, Slab Fork, Sleepy Creek, Smithers, Spring Creek, Surveyor, Tague.

Tree Names

New Jersey: Cedar Grove, Cedar Knolb, Cedarwood Park, Cherry Hill, Hickory, Holly Park, Linden, Lindenwold, Locust, Mount Laurel, Rosemont, Walnut Valley.

Pennsylvania: Buttonwood, Cherry Tree, Cherry Grove, Cherry Flats, Cherry Hill, Cherry Springs, Cherryville, Crabtree, Hemlock, Lone Pine, Maple Glen, Maple Grove Park, Maple Shade, Mapleton, Maplewood, Myrtle, North Oakland, Oakdale, Oak Forest, Oak Grove Oak Hall, Oakhurst, Oakland, Oakland Mills, Oakmont, Oaks, Oakville, Pecan, Pine Bank, Pine City, Pinecroft, Pine Flats, Pine Glen, Pine Grove, Pine Grove Furnace, Pine Grove Mills, Pine Station, Pine Valley, Pineville.

Delaware: Hollyville, Laurel, Oak Grove, Oak Orchard, Pine Tree Corners, Seven Hickories, Willow Grove.

Maryland: Arbutus, Aspen Hill, Aspen Run, Cedar Grove, Cedar Lawn, Cedartown, Cedarville, Cherry Hill, Holly, Linwood, Magnolia, Pinehurst, Pine Orchard, Piney Grove, Piney Point, Willows, Woodbine.

Virgina: Barley, Catalpa, Cedar Bluff, Cedar Springs, Cedarville, Evergreen, Hollybrook, Laurel Mills, Linden, Locust Dale, Locust Grove, Locust Hill, Locustville, Magnolia, Oak Grove, Oakville, Oakwood, Orchid, Red Oak, Rose Hill.

West Virginia: Beech Glen, Cherry Grove, Crab Orchard, Hollywood, Oakvale, Pine Grove, Pineville, Rosedale.

Index

Note: Main entries for places are not listed in the index. Place entries have been conveniently arranged alphabetically within each state within the body of the book.

A

Abbeville [see Wytheville, Va.]
Abbott, John, 430
Abbottstown, Pa., 605
Aberdeen, Md., 605
Aberdeen (Scotland), University of, 67
Abingdon, Berkshire, England, 317, 408
Abingdon, Lord, 408
Abington, Pa., 605
Abraham Roe's Landing [see Chews Landing, N.J.]
Absecon Island, 4
Acadians, 132, 271, 336, 365
Accident Tract, 317
Accokeek, Md., 317
Achilles, Va., 605
Ackerman, Pa., 605
Ackerson Estate, [see Fair Lawn, N.J.]
Acquackanonk Bridge [see Passaic, N.J.]
Acquackanonk Patent, 81
Adam Link House, 523
Adam's Mill [see Adamstown, Pa.]
Adams, Alvin, 500
Adams, Bud, 511
Adams, John, 362, 504
Adams, John Quincy, 254, 586
Adams Express Company, 500
Adams Grove, Va., 605
Adamston, N.J., 605
Adamstown Junction [see Adamstown, Md.]
Adamsville [see Adamstown, Md.]
Addison, Joseph, 119
Addison [see Webster Springs, W.Va.]
Adkins, G. B., 582
Admiralty [see Eccles, W.Va.]
Adolphi, W.Va., 605
Adrian, W.Va., 605
Advance [see Seat Pleasant, Md.]
Adventure Estate, The Perry Hall [see Perry Hall, Md.]
Aiken, Matthew, 301
Aikenstown [see Aiken, Md.]
Aikentown [see Glasgow, Del.]
Airey family, 318
Alaska [see Fort Ashby, W.Va.]
Albany, New York, 119
Albany Treaty of 1754, 194

Alberts [see Ashley, Pa.]
Albertson, Ephraim, 72
Albright, W.Va., 605
Albrightsville, Pa., 605
Aldan, Pa., 605
Alden, Pa., 605
Aldenville, Pa., 605
Alderson, John, 499
Aldie Castle, Scotland, 410
Alexander, Freidrich Wilhelm Heinrich, Freiherr von Humboldt, 193
Alexander, James, 93, 589
Alexander, John, 409
Alexander, W.Va., 605
Alexander, William, 42, 93
Alexandria [see Frenchtown, N.J.]
"Alfarata, the Maid of Juniata," 119
Aliquippa, Queen, 119–20
Allegewi [Alligewi] Tribe, 136
Allegheny Mountains, 111, 119, 510, 519, 555
Allegheny River, 180, 202, 239, 248, 251
Allen, Job, 8
Allen, John, 319
Allen, Joseph S. C., 318
Allen, Nathaniel, 277
Allen, Robert, 76
Allen, William, 2, 111
Allen, William C., 2
Allen's Mill [see Allens Fresh, Md.]
Allentown [see New Gretna, N.J.]
Alliance [see Carmel, N.J.]
Allingdale, W.Va., 605
Allis Hollow, Pa., 605
Allison Park, Pa., 605
Allisonia, Va., 605
Allmondsville, Va., 605
Alloway, Chief, 2
Alloway, N.J., 2, 37
Allsworth, Robert Warner, 492
Allsworth, William, 166
Alma River, battle of the, 410
Almstead [see Maitland, W.Va.]
Alonzo [see Justice, W.Va.]
Alpha Portland Cement Works, 2
Alpine [see Alpena, W.Va.]
Alton, Derbyshire, England, 306
Alton, Illinois, 306
Alton, Va., 605
Altona, Schleswig-Holstein, 111
Alum Bridge, W.Va., 605
Alumine [see Henry, Va.]

Aluminum Company of America [ALCOA], 119
Alverton, Pa., 605
Alvin Adams, 500
Alvy, W.Va., 605
Amberson, Pa., 605
Ambler, Joseph, 111
Ambo Point [see Perth Amboy, N.J.]
Amelia Sophia, Princess, 410
American Bridge Company, 121
American Iron Company, 80
"American Liberty," 156, 324, 429
American Magazine, 114
American Moravian Church, 158
American Pharmaceutical Association, 440
American Revolution, xii, 6, 55, 80, 88–89, 105, 108, 148, 161, 194, 203, 258, 280, 291, 292, 297–98, 301, 351, 353, 428, 451, 497, 549
Amesville, Pa., 605
Amherst, Lord Jeffrey, 410
Amherstdale, W.Va., 605
Amie [see Amma, W.Va.]
Amissville, Va., 605
Amity Hall, 122
Amity Homestead [see Homestead, Pa.]
Amity Presbyterian Church, 121
Amsterdam, Netherlands, 309
Amsterdam, Va., 605
Anaconda Plan, 107
Ancocas [see Rancocas, N.J.]
Ancocas Ferry [see Bridgeboro, N.J.]
Ancocus [Tribe], 88
Anderson, Etta, 215
Anderson, James, 173
Anderson, N.J., 605
Anderson's Ferry [see Waterford]
Andersonburg, Pa., 605
Andersontown, Md., 605
Andersonville, Va., 605
Andover, Pa., 605
Andover Furnace and Forge, 3
Andrew's Mill Creek [see Tuckerton Creek]
Andrews, Charles R., 319
Andrews family, 107
Andrews, Frank, 439
Andrews, Frank D., 19
Andrews Air Force Base, 393
Andrews Settlement, Pa., 605
Anglesea [see North Wildwood, N.J.]